THE
CHRONICLES
OF
NARNIA

NARNIA®

Although *The Magician's Nephew* was written several years after C.S. Lewis first began THE CHRONICLES OF NARNIA®, he wanted it to be read as the first book in the series. HarperCollins is happy to present these books in the order in which Professor Lewis preferred.

Published in the United States of America in 2005 by HarperEntertainment™. HarperEntertainment is a trademark of HarperCollins Publishers, 1350 Avenue of the Americas, New York, NY10019.

This edition published in Great Britain in 2008 by HarperCollins Publishers,
77-85 Fulham Palace Road, Hammersmith, London W6 8JB.

www.narnia.com

The Chronicles of
NARNIA

C. S. LEWIS

With illustrations by Pauline Baynes

HarperCollins*Publishers*

Contents

THE MAGICIAN'S
NEPHEW

THE MAGICIAN'S NEPHEW

CONTENTS

TO THE KILMER FAMILY

CHAPTER ONE

THE WRONG DOOR

This is a story about something that happened long ago when your grandfather was a child. It is a very important story because it shows how all the comings and goings between our own world and the land of Narnia first began.

In those days Mr Sherlock Holmes was still living in Baker Street and the Bastables were looking for treasure in the Lewisham Road. In those days, if you were a boy you had to wear a stiff Eton collar every day, and schools were usually nastier than now. But meals were nicer; and as for sweets, I won't tell you how cheap and good they were, because it would only make your mouth water in vain. And in those days there lived in London a girl called Polly Plummer.

She lived in one of a long row of houses which were all joined together. One morning she was out in the back garden when a boy scrambled up from the garden next door and put his face over the wall. Polly was very surprised because up till now there had never been any children in that house, but only Mr Ketterley and Miss Ketterley, a brother and sister, old bachelor and old maid, living together. So she looked up, full of curiosity. The face of the strange boy was very grubby. It could hardly have been grubbier if he had first rubbed his hands in the earth, and then had a good cry, and then dried his face with his hands. As a matter of fact, this was very nearly what he had been doing.

"Hullo," said Polly.

"Hullo," said the boy. "What's your name?"

"Polly," said Polly. "What's yours?"

"Digory," said the boy.

"I say, what a funny name!" said Polly.

"It isn't half so funny as Polly," said Digory.

"Yes it is," said Polly.

"No, it isn't," said Digory.

"At any rate I *do* wash my face," said Polly. "Which is what you need to do; especially after—" and then she stopped. She had been going to say "After you've been blubbing," but she thought that wouldn't be polite.

"All right, I have then," said Digory in a much louder voice, like a boy who was so miserable that he didn't care who knew he had been crying. "And so would you," he went on, "if you'd lived all your life in the country and had a pony, and a river at the bottom of the garden, and then been brought to live in a beastly Hole like this."

"London isn't a Hole," said Polly indignantly. But the boy was too wound up to take any notice of her, and he went on –

"And if your father was away in India – and you had to come and live with an Aunt and an Uncle who's mad (who would like that?) – and if the reason was that they were looking after your Mother – and if your Mother was ill and was going to – going to – die." Then his face went the wrong sort of shape as it does if you're trying to keep back your tears.

"I didn't know. I'm sorry," said Polly humbly. And then, because she hardly knew what to say, and also to turn Digory's mind to cheerful subjects, she asked:

"Is Mr Ketterley really mad?"

"Well, either he's mad," said Digory, "or there's some other mystery. He has a study on the top floor and Aunt Letty says I must never go up there. Well, that looks fishy to begin with. And then there's another thing. Whenever he tries to say anything to me at meal times – he never even tries to talk to *her* – she always shuts him up. She says, 'Don't worry the boy, Andrew', or, 'I'm sure Digory doesn't want to hear about *that*', or else, 'Now, Digory, wouldn't you like to go out and play in the garden?' "

"What sort of things does he try to say?"

"I don't know. He never gets far enough. But there's more than that. One night – it was last night in fact – as I was going past the foot of the attic stairs on my way to bed (and I don't much care for going past them either) I'm sure I heard a yell."

"Perhaps he keeps a mad wife shut up there."

"Yes, I've thought of that."

"Or perhaps he's a coiner."

"Or he might have been a pirate, like the man at the beginning of *Treasure Island*, and be always hiding from his old shipmates."

"How exciting!" said Polly, "I never knew your house was so interesting."

"*You* may think it interesting," said Digory. "But you wouldn't like it if you had to sleep there. How would you like to lie awake listening for Uncle Andrew's step to come creeping along the passage to your room? And he has such awful eyes."

That was how Polly and Digory got to know one another: and as it was just the beginning of the summer holidays and neither of them was going to the sea that year, they met nearly every day.

Their adventures began chiefly because it was one of the wettest and coldest summers there had been for years. That drove them to do indoor things: you might say, indoor exploration. It is wonderful how much exploring you can do with a stump of candle in a big house, or in a row of houses. Polly had discovered long ago that if you opened a certain little door in the box-room attic of her house you would find the cistern and a dark place behind it which you could get into by a little careful climbing. The dark place was like a long tunnel with brick wall on one side and sloping roof on the other. In the roof there were little chunks of light between the slates. There was no floor in this tunnel: you had to step from rafter to rafter, and between them there was only plaster. If you stepped on this you would find yourself falling through the ceiling of the room below. Polly had used the bit of the tunnel just beside the cistern as a smugglers' cave. She had brought up bits of old packing cases and the seats of broken kitchen chairs, and things of that sort, and spread them across from rafter to rafter so as to make a bit of floor. Here she kept a cash-box containing various treasures, and a story she was writing and usually a few apples. She had often drunk a quiet bottle of ginger-beer in there: the old bottles made it look more like a smugglers' cave.

Digory quite liked the cave (she wouldn't let him see the story) but he was more interested in exploring.

"Look here," he said. "How long does this tunnel go on for? I mean, does it stop where your house ends?"

"No," said Polly. "The walls don't go out to the roof. It goes on. I don't know how far."

"Then we could get the length of the whole row of houses."

"So we could," said Polly. "And oh, I say!"

"What?"

"We could get *into* the other houses."

"Yes, and get taken up for burglars! No thanks."

"Don't be so jolly clever. I was thinking of the house beyond yours."

"What about it?"

"Why, it's the empty one. Daddy says it's always been empty since we came here."

"I suppose we ought to have a look at it then," said Digory. He was a good deal more excited than you'd have thought from the way he spoke. For of course he was thinking, just as you would have been, of all the reasons why the house might have been empty so long. So was Polly. Neither of them said the word "haunted". And both felt that once the thing had been suggested, it would be feeble not to do it.

"Shall we go and try it now?" said Digory.

"All right," said Polly.

"Don't if you'd rather not," said Digory.

"I'm game if you are," said she.

"How are we to know we're in the next house but one?"

They decided they would have to go out into the box-room and walk across it taking steps as long as the steps from one rafter to the next. That would give them an idea of how many rafters went to a room. Then they would allow about four more for the passage between the two attics in Polly's house, and then the same number for the maid's bedroom as for the box-room. That would give them the length of the house. When they had done that distance twice they would be at the end of Digory's house; any door they came to after that would let them into an attic of the empty house.

"But I don't expect it's really empty at all," said Digory.

"What *do* you expect?"

"I expect someone lives there in secret, only coming in and out at night, with a dark lantern. We shall probably discover a gang of desperate criminals and get a reward. It's all rot to say a house would be empty all those years unless there was some mystery."

"Daddy thought it must be the drains," said Polly.

"Pooh! Grown-ups are always thinking of uninteresting explanations," said Digory. Now that they were talking by daylight in the attic instead of by candlelight in the Smugglers' Cave it seemed much less likely that the empty house would be haunted.

When they had measured the attic they had to get a pencil and do a sum. They both got different answers to it at first, and even when they agreed I am not sure they got it right. They were in a hurry to start on the exploration.

"We mustn't make a sound," said Polly as they climbed in again behind the cistern. Because it was such an important occasion they took a candle each (Polly had a good store of them in her cave).

It was very dark and dusty and draughty and they stepped from rafter to rafter without a word except when they whispered to one another, "We're opposite *your* attic now", or "This must be halfway through *our* house". And neither of them stumbled and the candles didn't go out, and at last they came to where they could see a little door in the brick wall on their right. There was no bolt or handle on this side of it, of course, for the door had been made for getting in, not for getting out; but there was a catch (as there often is on the inside of a cupboard door) which they felt sure they would be able to turn.

"Shall I?" said Digory.

"I'm game if you are," said Polly, just as she had said before. Both felt that it was becoming very serious, but neither would draw back. Digory pushed round the catch with some difficulty. The door swung open and the sudden daylight made them blink. Then, with a great shock, they saw that they were looking, not into a deserted attic, but into a furnished room. But it seemed empty enough. It was dead silent. Polly's curiosity got the better of her. She blew out her candle and stepped out into the strange room, making no more noise than a mouse.

It was shaped, of course, like an attic, but furnished as a sitting-room. Every bit of the walls was lined with shelves and every bit of the shelves was full of books. A fire was burning in the grate (you remember that it was a very cold wet summer that year) and in front of the fireplace with its back towards them was a high-backed armchair. Between the chair and Polly, and filling most of the middle of the room, was a big table piled with all sorts of things – printed books, and books of the sort you write in, and ink bottles and pens and sealing-wax and a microscope. But what she noticed first was a bright red wooden tray with a number of rings on it. They were in pairs – a yellow one and a green one together, then a little space, and then another yellow one and another green one. They were no bigger than ordinary rings, and no one could help noticing them because they were so bright. They were the most beautiful shiny little things you can imagine. If Polly had been a very little younger she would have wanted to put one in her mouth.

The room was so quiet that you noticed the ticking of the clock at once. And yet, as she now found, it was not absolutely quiet either. There was a faint – a very, very faint – humming sound. If Hoovers had been invented in those days Polly would have thought it was the sound of a Hoover being worked a long way off – several rooms away and several floors below. But it was a nicer sound than that, a more musical tone: only so faint that you could hardly hear it.

"It's all right; there's no one here," said Polly over her shoulder to Digory. She was speaking above a whisper now. And Digory came out, blinking and looking extremely dirty – as indeed Polly was too.

"This is no good," he said. "It's not an empty house at all. We'd better bunk before anyone comes."

"What do you think those are?" said Polly, pointing at the coloured rings.

"Oh, come *on*," said Digory. "The sooner——"

He never finished what he was going to say for at that moment something happened. The high-backed chair in front of the fire moved suddenly and there rose up out of it – like a pantomime demon coming up out of a trapdoor – the alarming form of Uncle Andrew. They were not in the empty house at all; they were in Digory's house and in the forbidden study! Both children said "O-o-oh" and realized their terrible mistake. They felt they ought to have known all along that they hadn't gone nearly far enough.

Uncle Andrew was tall and very thin. He had a long clean-shaven face with a sharply pointed nose and extremely bright eyes and a great tousled mop of grey hair.

Digory was quite speechless, for Uncle Andrew looked a thousand times more alarming than he had ever looked before. Polly was not so frightened yet; but she soon was. For the very first thing Uncle Andrew did was to walk across to the door of the room, shut it, and turn the key in the lock. Then he turned round, fixed the children with his bright eyes, and smiled, showing all his teeth.

"There!" he said. "Now my fool of a sister can't get at you!"

It was dreadfully unlike anything a grown-up would be expected to do. Polly's heart came into her mouth, and she and Digory started backing towards the little door they had come in by. Uncle Andrew was too quick for them. He got behind them and shut that door too and stood in front of it. Then he rubbed his hands and made his knuckles crack. He had very long, beautifully white, fingers.

"I am delighted to see you," he said. "Two children are just what I wanted."

"Please, Mr Ketterley," said Polly. "It's nearly my dinner time and I've got to go home. Will you let us out, please?"

"Not just yet," said Uncle Andrew. "This is too good an opportunity to miss. I wanted two children. You see, I'm in the middle of a great experiment. I've tried it on a guinea-pig and it seemed to work. But then a guinea-pig can't tell you anything. And you can't explain to it how to come back."

"Look here, Uncle Andrew," said Digory, "it really is dinner time and they'll be looking for us in a moment. You must let us out."

"Must?" said Uncle Andrew.

Digory and Polly glanced at one another. They dared not say anything, but the glances meant "Isn't this dreadful?" and "We must humour him."

"If you let us go for our dinner now," said Polly, "we could come back after dinner."

"Ah, but how do I know that you would?" said Uncle Andrew with a cunning smile. Then he seemed to change his mind.

"Well, well," he said, "if you really must go, I suppose you must. I can't expect two youngsters like you to find it much fun talking to an old buffer like me." He sighed and went on. "You've no idea how lonely I sometimes am. But no matter. Go to your dinner. But I must give you a present before you go. It's not every day that I see a little girl in my dingy old study; especially, if I may say so, such a very attractive young lady as yourself."

Polly began to think he might not really be mad after all.

"Wouldn't you like a ring, my dear?" said Uncle Andrew to Polly.

"Do you mean one of those yellow or green ones?" said Polly. "How lovely!"

"Not a green one," said Uncle Andrew. "I'm afraid I can't give the green ones away. But I'd be delighted to give you any of the yellow ones, with my love: come and try one on."

Polly had now quite got over her fright and felt sure that the old gentleman was not mad; and there was certainly something strangely attractive about those bright rings. She moved over to the tray.

"Why! I declare," she said. "That humming noise gets louder here. It's almost as if the rings were making it."

"What a funny fancy, my dear," said Uncle Andrew with a laugh. It sounded a very natural laugh, but Digory had seen an eager, almost a greedy, look on his face.

"Polly! Don't be a fool!" he shouted. "Don't touch them."

It was too late. Exactly as he spoke, Polly's hand went out to touch one of the rings. And immediately, without a flash or a noise or a warning of any sort, there was no Polly. Digory and his Uncle were alone in the room.

CHAPTER TWO

DIGORY AND HIS UNCLE

It was so sudden, and so horribly unlike anything that had ever happened to Digory even in a nightmare, that he let out a scream. Instantly Uncle Andrew's hand was over his mouth. "None of that!" he hissed in Digory's ear. "If you start making a noise your Mother'll hear it. And you know what a fright might do to her."

As Digory said afterwards, the horrible meanness of getting at a chap in *that* way almost made him sick. But of course he didn't scream again.

"That's better," said Uncle Andrew. "Perhaps you couldn't help it. It *is* a shock when you first see someone vanish. Why, it gave even me a turn when the guinea-pig did it the other night."

"Was that when you yelled?" asked Digory.

"Oh, you heard *that*, did you? I hope you haven't been spying on me?"

"No, I haven't," said Digory indignantly. "But what's happened to Polly?"

"Congratulate me, my dear boy," said Uncle Andrew, rubbing his hands. "My experiment has succeeded. The little girl's gone – vanished – right out of the world."

"What have you done to her?"

"Sent her to – well – to another place."

"What *do* you mean?" asked Digory.

Uncle Andrew sat down and said, "Well, I'll tell you all about it. Have you ever heard of old Mrs Lefay?"

"Wasn't she a great-aunt or something?" said Digory.

"Not exactly," said Uncle Andrew. "She was my godmother. That's her, there, on the wall."

Digory looked and saw a faded photograph: it showed the face of an old woman in a bonnet. And he could now remember that he had once seen a photo of the same face in an old drawer, at home, in the country. He had asked his Mother who it was and Mother had not seemed to want to talk about the subject much. It was not at all a nice face, Digory thought, though of course with those early photographs one could never really tell.

"Was there — wasn't there — something wrong about her, Uncle Andrew?" he asked.

"Well," said Uncle Andrew with a chuckle, "it depends what you call *wrong*. People are so narrow-minded. She certainly got very queer in later life. Did very unwise things. That was why they shut her up."

"In an asylum, do you mean?"

"Oh no, no, no," said Uncle Andrew in a shocked voice. "Nothing of that sort. Only in prison."

"I say!" said Digory. "What had she done?"

"Ah, poor woman," said Uncle Andrew. "She had been very unwise. There were a good many different things. We needn't go into all that. She was always very kind to me."

"But look here, what has all this got to do with Polly? I do wish you'd—"

"All in good time, my boy," said Uncle Andrew. "They let old Mrs Lefay out before she died and I was one of the very few people whom she would allow to see her in her last illness. She had got to dislike ordinary, ignorant people, you understand. I do myself. But she and I were interested in the same sort of things. It was only a few days before her death that she told me to go to an old bureau in her house and open a secret drawer and bring her a little box that I would find there. The moment I picked up that box I could tell by the pricking in my fingers that I held some great secret in my hands. She gave it to me and made me promise that as soon as she was dead I would burn it, unopened, with certain ceremonies. That promise I did not keep."

"Well, then, it was jolly rotten of you," said Digory.

"Rotten?" said Uncle Andrew with a puzzled look. "Oh, I see. You mean that little boys ought to keep their promises. Very true: most right and proper, I'm sure, and I'm very glad you have been taught to do it. But of course you must understand that rules of that sort, however excellent they may be for little boys — and servants — and women — and even people in general, can't possibly be expected to apply to profound students and great thinkers and sages. No, Digory. Men like me, who possess hidden wisdom, are freed from common rules just as we are cut off from common pleasures. Ours, my boy, is a high and lonely destiny."

As he said this he sighed and looked so grave and noble and mysterious that for a second Digory really thought he was saying something rather fine. But then he remembered the ugly look he had seen on his Uncle's face the moment before Polly had vanished: and all at once he saw through Uncle Andrew's grand words. "All it means," he said to himself, "is that he thinks he can do anything he likes to get anything he wants."

"Of course," said Uncle Andrew, "I didn't dare to open the box for a long time, for I knew it might contain something highly dangerous. For my godmother was a *very* remarkable woman. The truth is, she was one of the last mortals in this country who had fairy blood in her. (She said there had been two others in her time. One was a duchess and the other a charwoman.) In fact, Digory, you are now talking to the last man (possibly) who really had a fairy godmother. There! That'll be something for you to remember when you are an old man yourself."

"I bet she was a bad fairy," thought Digory; and added out loud, "But what about Polly?"

"How you do harp on that!" said Uncle Andrew. "As if that was what mattered! My first task was of course to study the box itself. It was very ancient. And I knew enough even then to know that it wasn't Greek, or Old Egyptian, or Babylonian, or Hittite, or Chinese. It was older than any of those nations. Ah – that was a great day when I at last found out the truth. The box was Atlantean; it came from the lost island of Atlantis. That meant it was centuries older than any of the stone-age things they dig up in Europe. And it wasn't a rough, crude thing like them either. For in the very dawn of time Atlantis was already a great city with palaces and temples and learned men."

He paused for a moment as if he expected Digory to say something. But Digory was disliking his Uncle more every minute, so he said nothing.

"Meanwhile," continued Uncle Andrew, "I was learning a good deal in other ways (it wouldn't be proper to explain them to a child) about Magic in general. That meant that I came to have a fair idea what sort of things might be in the box. By various tests I narrowed down the possibilities. I had to get to know some – well, some devilish queer people, and go through some very disagreeable experiences. That was what turned my head grey. One doesn't become a magician for nothing. My health broke down in the end. But I got better. And at last I actually *knew*."

Although there was not really the least chance of anyone overhearing them, he leaned forward and almost whispered as he said:

"The Atlantean box contained something that had been brought from another world when our world was only just beginning."

"What?" asked Digory, who was now interested in spite of himself.

"Only dust," said Uncle Andrew. "Fine, dry dust. Nothing much to look at. Not much to show for a lifetime of toil, you might say. Ah, but when I looked at that dust (I took jolly good care not to touch it) and thought that every grain had once been in another world – I don't mean another planet, you know; they're part of our world and you could get to them if you went far enough – but a really Other World – another Nature – another universe – somewhere you would never reach even if you travelled through the space of this universe for ever and ever – a world that could be reached only by Magic – well!" Here Uncle Andrew rubbed his hands till his knuckles cracked like fireworks.

"I knew," he went on, "that if only you could get it into the right form, that dust would draw you back to the place it had come from. But the difficulty was to get it into the right form. My earlier experiments were all failures. I tried them on guinea-pigs. Some of them only died. Some exploded like little bombs—"

"It was a jolly cruel thing to do," said Digory, who had once had a guinea-pig of his own.

"How you do keep getting off the point!" said Uncle Andrew. "That's what the creatures were for. I'd bought them myself. Let me see – where was I? Ah yes. At last I succeeded in making the rings: the yellow rings. But now a new difficulty arose. I was pretty sure, now, that a yellow ring would send any creature that touched it into the Other Place. But what would be the good of that if I couldn't get them back to tell me what they had found there?"

"And what about *them*?" said Digory. "A nice mess they'd be in if they couldn't get back!"

"You will keep on looking at everything from the wrong point of view," said Uncle Andrew with a look of impatience. "Can't you understand that the thing is a great experiment? The whole point of sending anyone into the Other Place is that I want to find out what it's like."

"Well, why didn't you go yourself then?"

Digory had hardly ever seen anyone look so surprised and offended as his Uncle did at this simple question. "Me? Me?" he exclaimed. "The boy must be mad! A man at my time of life, and in my state of health, to risk the shock and the dangers of being flung suddenly into a different universe? I never heard anything so preposterous in my life! Do you realize what you're saying? Think what Another World means – you might meet anything – anything."

"And I suppose you've sent Polly into it then," said Digory. His cheeks were flaming with anger now. "And all I can say," he added, "even if you are my Uncle – is that you've behaved like a coward, sending a girl to a place you're afraid to go to yourself."

"Silence, sir!" said Uncle Andrew, bringing his hand down on the table. "I will not be talked to like that by a little, dirty, schoolboy. You don't understand. I am the great scholar, the magician, the adept, who is *doing* the experiment. Of course I need subjects to do it *on*. Bless my soul, you'll be telling me next that I ought to have asked the guinea-pigs' permission before I used *them*! No great wisdom can be reached without sacrifice. But the idea of my going myself is ridiculous. It's like asking a general to fight as a common soldier. Supposing I got killed, what would become of my life's work?"

"Oh, do stop jawing," said Digory. "Are you going to bring Polly back?"

"I was going to tell you, when you so rudely interrupted me," said Uncle Andrew, "that I did at last find out a way of doing the return journey. The green rings draw you back."

"But Polly hasn't got a green ring."

"No," said Uncle Andrew with a cruel smile.

"Then she can't get back," shouted Digory. "And it's exactly the same as if you'd murdered her."

"She can get back," said Uncle Andrew, "if someone else will go after her, wearing a yellow ring himself and taking two green rings, one to bring himself back and one to bring her back."

And now of course Digory saw the trap in which he was caught: and he stared at Uncle Andrew, saying nothing, with his mouth wide open. His cheeks had gone very pale.

"I hope," said Uncle Andrew presently in a very high and mighty voice, just as if he were a perfect Uncle who had given one a handsome tip and some good advice, "I *hope*, Digory, you are not given to showing the white feather. I should be very sorry to think that anyone of our family had not enough honour and chivalry to go to the aid of – er – a lady in distress."

"Oh shut up!" said Digory. "If you had any honour and all that, you'd be going yourself. But I know you won't. All right. I see I've got to go. But you *are* a beast. I suppose you planned the whole thing, so that she'd go without knowing it and then I'd have to go after her."

"Of course," said Uncle Andrew, with his hateful smile.

"Very well. I'll go. But there's one thing I jolly well mean to say first. I didn't believe in Magic till today. I see now it's real. Well, if it is, I suppose all the old fairy tales are more or less true. And you're simply a wicked, cruel magician like the ones in the stories. Well, I've never read a story in which people of that sort weren't paid out in the end, and I bet you will be. And serve you right."

Of all the things Digory had said this was the first that really went home. Uncle Andrew started and there came over his face a look of such horror that, beast though he was, you could almost feel sorry for him. But a second later he smoothed it all away and said with a rather forced laugh, "Well, well, I suppose that is a natural thing for a child to think – brought up among women, as you have been. Old wives' tales, eh? I don't think you need worry about *my* danger, Digory. Wouldn't it be better to worry about the danger of your little friend? She's been gone some time. If there are any dangers Over There – well, it would be a pity to arrive a moment too late."

"A lot *you* care," said Digory fiercely. "But I'm sick of this jaw. What have I got to do?"

"You really must learn to control that temper of yours, my boy," said Uncle Andrew coolly. "Otherwise you'll grow up like your Aunt Letty. Now. Attend to me."

He got up, put on a pair of gloves, and walked over to the tray that contained the rings.

"They only work," he said, "if they're actually touching your skin. Wearing gloves, I can pick them up – like this – and nothing happens. If you carried one in your pocket nothing would happen: but of course you'd have to be careful not to put your hand in your pocket and touch it by accident. The moment you touch a yellow ring, you vanish out of this world. When you are in the Other Place I expect – of course this hasn't been tested yet, but I *expect* – that the moment you touch a green ring you vanish out of that world and – I expect – reappear in this. Now. I take these two greens and drop them into your right-hand pocket. Remember very carefully which pocket the greens are in. G for green and R for right. G.R. you see: which are the first two letters of green. One for you and one for the little girl. And now you pick up a yellow one for yourself. I should put it on – on your finger – if I were you. There'll be less chance of dropping it."

Digory had almost picked up the yellow ring when he suddenly checked himself.

"Look here," he said. "What about Mother? Supposing she asks where I am?"

"The sooner you go, the sooner you'll be back," said Uncle Andrew cheerfully.

"But you don't really know whether I can get back."

Uncle Andrew shrugged his shoulders, walked across to the door, unlocked it, threw it open, and said:

"Oh, very well then. Just as you please. Go down and have your dinner. Leave the little girl to be eaten by wild animals or drowned or starved in Otherworld or lost there for good, if that's what you prefer. It's all one to me. Perhaps before tea time you'd better drop in on Mrs Plummer and explain that she'll never see her daughter again; because you were afraid to put on a ring."

"By gum," said Digory, "don't I just wish I was big enough to punch your head!"

Then he buttoned up his coat, took a deep breath, and picked up the ring. And he thought then, as he always thought afterwards too, that he could not decently have done anything else.

CHAPTER THREE

THE WOOD BETWEEN THE WORLDS

Uncle Andrew and his study vanished instantly. Then, for a moment, everything became muddled. The next thing Digory knew was that there was a soft green light coming down on him from above, and darkness below. He didn't seem to be standing on anything, or sitting, or lying. Nothing appeared to be touching him. "I believe I'm in water," said Digory. "Or *under* water." This frightened him for a second, but almost at once he could feel that he was rushing upwards. Then his head suddenly came out into the air and he found himself scrambling ashore, out on to smooth grassy ground at the edge of a pool.

As he rose to his feet he noticed that he was neither dripping nor panting for breath as anyone would expect after being under water. His clothes were perfectly dry. He was standing by the edge of a small pool — not more than ten feet from side to side — in a wood. The trees grew close together and were so leafy that he could get no glimpse of the sky. All the light was green light that came through the leaves: but there must have been a very strong sun overhead, for this green daylight was bright and warm. It was the quietest wood you could possibly imagine. There were no birds, no insects, no animals, and no wind. You could almost feel the trees growing. The pool he had just got out of was not the only pool. There were dozens of others — a pool every few yards as far as his eyes could reach. You could almost feel the trees drinking the water up with their roots. This wood was very much alive. When he tried to describe it afterwards Digory always said, "It was a *rich* place: as rich as plum cake."

The strangest thing was that, almost before he had looked about him, Digory had half forgotten how he had come there. At any rate, he was certainly not thinking about Polly, or Uncle Andrew, or even his Mother. He was not in the least frightened, or excited, or curious. If anyone had asked him "Where did you come from?" he would probably have said, "I've always been here." That was what it felt like — as if one had always been in that place and never been bored although nothing had ever happened. As he said long afterwards, "It's not the sort of place where things happen. The trees go on growing, that's all."

After Digory had looked at the wood for a long time he noticed that there was a girl lying on her back at the foot of a tree a few yards away. Her eyes were nearly shut but not quite, as if she were just between sleeping and waking. So he looked at her for a long time and said nothing. And at last she opened her eyes and looked at him for a long time and she also said nothing. Then she spoke, in a dreamy, contented sort of voice.

"I think I've seen you before," she said.

"I rather think so too," said Digory. "Have you been here long?"

"Oh, always," said the girl. "At least — I don't know — a very long time."

"So have I," said Digory.

"No, you haven't," said she. "I've just seen you come up out of that pool."

"Yes, I suppose I did," said Digory with a puzzled air. "I'd forgotten."

Then for quite a long time neither said any more.

"Look here," said the girl presently, "I wonder, did we ever really meet before? I had a sort of idea — a sort of picture in my head — of a boy and a girl, like us — living somewhere quite different — and doing all sorts of things. Perhaps it was only a dream."

"I've had that same dream, I think," said Digory. "About a boy and a girl, living next door — and something about crawling among rafters. I remember the girl had a dirty face."

"Aren't you getting it mixed? In my dream it was the boy who had the dirty face."

"I can't remember the boy's face," said Digory and then added, "Hullo! What's that?"

"Why! It's a guinea-pig," said the girl. And it was — a fat guinea-pig, nosing about in the grass.

But round the middle of the guinea-pig there ran a tape and, tied on to it by the tape, was a bright yellow ring.

"Look! Look," cried Digory. "The ring! And look! You've got one on your finger. And so have I."

The girl now sat up, really interested at last. They stared very hard at one another, trying to remember. And then, at exactly the same moment, she shouted out, "Mr Ketterley", and he shouted out, "Uncle Andrew", and they knew who they were and began to remember the whole story. After a few minutes' hard talking they had got it straight. Digory explained how beastly Uncle Andrew had been.

"What do we do now?" said Polly. "Take the guinea-pig and go home?"

"There's no hurry," said Digory, with a huge yawn.

"I think there is," said Polly. "This place is too quiet. It's so – so dreamy. You're almost asleep. If we once give in to it we shall just lie down and drowse for ever and ever."

"It's very nice here," said Digory.

"Yes, it is," said Polly. "But we've got to get back." She stood up and began to go cautiously towards the guinea-pig. But then she changed her mind.

"We might as well leave the guinea-pig," she said. "It's perfectly happy here, and your uncle will only do something horrid to it if we take it home."

"I bet he would," answered Digory. "Look at the way he's treated *us*. By the way, how *do* we get home?"

"Go back into the pool, I expect."

They came and stood together at the edge, looking down into the smooth water. It was full of the reflection of the green, leafy branches; they made it look very deep.

"We haven't any bathing things," said Polly.

"We shan't need them, silly," said Digory. "We're going in with our clothes on. Don't you remember it didn't wet us on the way up?"

"Can you swim?"

"A bit. Can you?"

"Well – not much."

"I don't think we shall need to swim," said Digory. "We want to go *down*, don't we?"

Neither of them much liked the idea of jumping into that pool, but neither said so to the other. They took hands and said "One – Two – Three – Go" and jumped. There was a great splash and of course they closed their eyes. But when they opened them again they found they were still standing, hand in hand, in the green wood, and hardly up to their ankles in water. The pool was apparently only a couple of inches deep. They splashed back on to the dry ground.

"What on earth's gone wrong?" said Polly in a frightened voice; but not quite so frightened as you might expect, because it is hard to feel really frightened in that wood. The place is too peaceful.

"Oh! I know," said Digory. "Of course it won't work. We're still wearing our yellow rings. They're for the outward journey, you know. The green ones take you home. We must change rings. Have you got pockets? Good.

Put your yellow ring in your left. I've got two greens. Here's one for you."

They put on their green rings and came back to the pool. But before they tried another jump Digory gave a long "O-o-oh!"

"What's the matter?" said Polly.

"I've just had a really wonderful idea," said Digory. "What are all the other pools?"

"How do you mean?"

"Why, if we can get back to our own world by jumping into *this* pool, mightn't we get somewhere else by jumping into one of the others? Supposing there was a world at the bottom of every pool."

"But I thought we were already in your Uncle Andrew's Other World or Other Place or whatever he called it. Didn't you say—"

"Oh, bother Uncle Andrew," interrupted Digory. "I don't believe he knows anything about it. He never had the pluck to come here himself. He only talked of *one* Other World. But suppose there were dozens?"

"You mean, this wood might be only one of them?"

"No, I don't believe this wood is a world at all. I think it's just a sort of in-between place."

Polly looked puzzled.

"Don't you see?" said Digory. "No, do listen. Think of our tunnel under the slates at home. It isn't a room in any of the houses. In a way, it isn't really part of any of the houses. But once you're in the tunnel you can go along it and come into any of the houses in the row. Mightn't this wood be the same? – a place that isn't in any of the worlds, but once you've found that place you can get into them all."

"Well, even if you can—" began Polly, but Digory went on as if he hadn't heard her.

"And of course that explains everything," he said. "That's why it is so quiet and sleepy here. Nothing ever happens here. Like at home. It's in the houses that people talk, and do things, and have meals. Nothing goes on in the in-between places, behind the walls and above the ceilings and under the floor, or in our own tunnel. But when you come out of our tunnel you may find yourself in *any* house. I think we can get out of this place into jolly well anywhere! We don't need to jump back into the same pool we came up by. Or not just yet."

"The Wood between the Worlds," said Polly dreamily. "It sounds rather nice."

"Come on," said Digory. "Which pool shall we try?"

"Look here," said Polly, "I'm not going to try any new pool till we've made sure that we *can* get back by the old one. We're not even sure if it'll work yet."

"Yes," said Digory. "And get caught by Uncle Andrew and have our rings taken away before we've had any fun. No thanks."

"Couldn't we just go part of the way down into our own pool?" said Polly. "Just to see if it works. Then if it does, we'll change rings and come up again before we're really back in Mr Ketterley's study."

"Can we go *part* of the way down?"

"Well, it took time coming up. I suppose it'll take a little time going back."

Digory made rather a fuss about agreeing to this, but he had to in the end because Polly absolutely refused to do any exploring in new worlds until she had made sure about getting back to the old one. She was quite as brave as he about some dangers (wasps, for instance) but she was not so interested in finding out things nobody had ever heard of before; for Digory was the sort of person who wants to know everything, and when he grew up he became the famous Professor Kirke who comes into other books.

After a good deal of arguing they agreed to put on their green rings ("Green for safety," said Digory, "so you can't help remembering which is which") and hold hands and jump. But as soon as they seemed to be getting back to Uncle Andrew's study, or even to their own world, Polly was to shout, "Change", and they would slip off their greens and put on their yellows. Digory wanted to be the one who shouted, "Change", but Polly wouldn't agree.

They put on the green rings, took hands, and once more shouted "One – Two – Three – Go". This time it worked. It is very hard to tell you what it felt like, for everything happened so quickly. At first there were bright lights moving about in a black sky; Digory always thinks these were stars and even swears that he saw Jupiter quite close – close enough to see its moon. But almost at once there were rows and rows of roofs and chimney pots about them, and they could see St Paul's and knew they were looking at London. But you could see through the walls of all the houses. Then they could see Uncle Andrew, very vague and shadowy, but getting clearer and more solid-looking all the time, just as if he were coming into focus. But before he became quite real Polly shouted "Change", and they did change, and our world faded away like a dream, and the green light above grew stronger and stronger, till their heads came out of the pool and they scrambled ashore. And there was the wood all about them, as green and bright and still as ever. The whole thing had taken less than a minute.

"There!" said Digory. "That's all right. Now for the adventure. Any pool will do. Come on. Let's try that one."

"Stop!" said Polly. "Aren't we going to mark *this* pool?"

They stared at each other and turned quite white as they realized the dreadful thing that Digory had just been going to do. For there were any number of pools in the wood, and the pools were all alike and the trees were all alike, so that if they had once left behind the pool that led to our own world without making some sort of landmark, the chances would have been a hundred to one against their ever finding it again.

Digory's hand was shaking as he opened his penknife and cut out a long strip of turf on the bank of the pool. The soil (which smelled nice) was of a rich reddish brown and showed up well against the green. "It's a good thing *one* of us has some sense," said Polly.

"Well, don't keep on gassing about it," said Digory. "Come along, I want to see what's in one of the other pools." And Polly gave him a pretty sharp answer and he said something even nastier in reply. The quarrel lasted for several minutes but it would be dull to write it all down. Let us skip on to the moment at which they stood with beating hearts and rather scared faces on the edge of the unknown pool with their yellow rings on and held hands and once more said "One – Two – Three – Go!"

Splash! Once again it hadn't worked. This pool, too, appeared to be only a puddle. Instead of reaching a new world they only got their feet wet and splashed their legs for the second time that morning (if it was a morning: it seems to be always the same time in the Wood between the Worlds).

"Blast and botheration!" exclaimed Digory. "What's gone wrong now? We've put our yellow rings on all right. He said yellow for the outward journey."

Now the truth was that Uncle Andrew, who knew nothing about the Wood between the Worlds, had quite a wrong idea about the rings. The yellow ones weren't "outward" rings and the green ones weren't "homeward" rings; at least, not in the way he thought. The stuff of which both were made had all come from the wood. The stuff in the yellow rings had the power of drawing you into the wood; it was stuff that wanted to get back to its own place, the in-between place. But the stuff in the green rings is stuff that is trying to get out of its own place; so that a green ring would take you out of the wood into a world. Uncle Andrew, you see, was working with things he did not really understand; most magicians are. Of course Digory did not realize the truth quite clearly either, or not till later. But when they had talked it over, they decided to try their green rings on the new pool, just to see what happened.

"I'm game if you are," said Polly. But she really said this because, in her heart of hearts, she now felt sure that neither kind of ring was going to work at all in the new pool, and so there was nothing worse to be afraid of than another splash. I am not quite sure that Digory had not the same feeling. At any rate, when they had both put on their greens and come back to the edge of the water, and taken hands again, they were certainly a good deal more cheerful and less solemn than they had been the first time.

"One – Two – Three – Go!" said Digory. And they jumped.

Chapter Four

The Bell and the Hammer

There was no doubt about the Magic this time. Down and down they rushed, first through darkness and then through a mass of vague and whirling shapes which might have been almost anything. It grew lighter. Then suddenly they felt that they were standing on something solid. A moment later everything came into focus and they were able to look about them.

"What a queer place!" said Digory.

"I don't like it," said Polly, with something like a shudder.

What they noticed first was the light. It wasn't like sunlight, and it wasn't like electric light, or lamps, or candles, or any other light they had ever seen. It was a dull, rather red light, not at all cheerful. It was steady and did not flicker. They were standing on a flat paved surface and buildings rose all around them. There was no roof overhead; they were in a sort of courtyard. The sky was extraordinarily dark – a blue that was almost black. When you had seen that sky you wondered that there should be any light at all.

"It's very funny weather here," said Digory. "I wonder if we've arrived just in time for a thunderstorm; or an eclipse."

"I don't like it," said Polly.

Both of them, without quite knowing why, were talking in whispers. And though there was no reason why they should still go on holding hands after their jump, they didn't let go.

The walls rose very high all round that courtyard. They had many great windows in them, windows without glass, through which you saw nothing but black darkness. Lower down there were great pillared arches, yawning

31

blackly like the mouths of railway tunnels. It was rather cold.

The stone of which everything was built seemed to be red, but that might only be because of the curious light. It was obviously very old. Many of the flat stones that paved the courtyard had cracks across them. None of them fitted closely together and the sharp corners were all worn off. One of the arched doorways was half filled up with rubble. The two children kept on turning round and round to look at the different sides of the courtyard. One reason was that they were afraid of somebody – or something – looking out of those windows at them when their backs were turned.

"Do you think anyone lives here?" said Digory at last, still in a whisper.

"No," said Polly. "It's all in ruins. We haven't heard a sound since we came."

"Let's stand still and listen for a bit," suggested Digory.

They stood still and listened, but all they could hear was the thump-thump of their own hearts. This place was at least as quiet as the Wood between the Worlds. But it was a different kind of quietness. The silence of the wood had been rich and warm (you could almost hear the trees growing) and full of life: this was a dead, cold, empty silence. You couldn't imagine anything growing in it.

"Let's go home," said Polly.

"But we haven't seen anything yet," said Digory. "Now we're here, we simply must have a look round."

"I'm sure there's nothing at all interesting here."

"There's not much point in finding a magic ring that lets you into other worlds if you're afraid to look at them when you've got there."

"Who's talking about being afraid?" said Polly, letting go of Digory's hand.

"I only thought you didn't seem very keen on exploring this place."

"I'll go anywhere you go."

"We can get away the moment we want to," said Digory. "Let's take off our green rings and put them in our right-hand pockets. All we've got to do is to remember that our yellows are in our left-hand pockets. You can keep your hand as near your pocket as you like, but don't put it in or you'll touch your yellow and vanish."

They did this and went quietly up to one of the big arched doorways which led into the inside of the building. And when they stood on the threshold and could look in, they saw it was not so dark inside as they had thought at first. It led into a vast, shadowy hall which appeared to be empty; but on the far side there was a row of pillars with arches between them and through those arches there streamed in some more of the same tired-looking light. They crossed the hall, walking very carefully for fear of holes in the floor or of anything lying about that they might trip over. It seemed a long walk. When they had reached the other side they came out through the arches and found themselves in another and larger courtyard.

"That doesn't look very safe," said Polly, pointing at a place where the wall bulged outward and looked as if it were ready to fall over into the courtyard. In one place a pillar was missing between two arches and the bit that came down to where the top of the pillar ought to have been hung there with nothing to support it. Clearly, the place had been deserted for hundreds, perhaps thousands, of years.

"If it's lasted till now, I suppose it'll last a bit longer," said Digory. "But we must be very quiet. You know a noise sometimes brings things down – like an avalanche in the Alps."

They went on out of that courtyard into another doorway, and up a great flight of steps and through vast rooms that opened out of one another till you were dizzy with the mere size of the place. Every now and then they thought they were going to get out into the open and see what sort of country lay around the enormous palace. But each time they only got into another courtyard. They must have been magnificent places when people were still living there. In one there had once been a fountain. A great stone monster with widespread wings stood with its mouth open and you could still see a bit of piping at the back of its mouth, out of which the water used to pour. Under it was a wide stone basin to hold the water; but it was as dry as a bone. In other places there were the dry sticks of some sort of climbing plant which had wound itself round the pillars and helped to pull some of them down. But it had died long ago. And there were no ants or spiders or any of the other living things you expect to see in a ruin; and where the dry earth showed between the broken flagstones there was no grass or moss.

It was all so dreary and all so much the same that even Digory was thinking they had better put on their yellow rings and get back to the warm, green, living forest of the In-between place, when they came to two huge doors of some metal that might possibly be gold. One stood a little ajar. So of course they went to look in. Both started back and drew a long breath: for here at last was something worth seeing.

For a second they thought the room was full of people – hundreds of people, all seated, and all perfectly still. Polly and Digory, as you may guess, stood perfectly still themselves for a good long time, looking in. But presently they decided that what they were looking at could not be real people. There was not a movement nor the sound of a breath among them all. They were like the most wonderful waxworks you ever saw.

This time Polly took the lead. There was something in this room which interested her more than it interested Digory: all the figures were wearing magnificent clothes. If you were interested in clothes at all, you could hardly help going in to see them closer. And the blaze of their colours made this room look, not exactly cheerful, but at any rate rich and majestic after all the dust and emptiness of the others. It had more windows, too, and was a good deal lighter.

I can hardly describe the clothes. The figures were all robed and had crowns on their heads. Their robes were of crimson and silvery grey and deep purple and vivid green: and there were patterns, and pictures of flowers and strange beasts, in needlework all over them. Precious stones of astonishing size and brightness stared from their crowns and hung in chains round their necks and peeped out from all the places where anything was fastened.

"Why haven't these clothes all rotted away long ago?" asked Polly.

"Magic," whispered Digory. "Can't you feel it? I bet this whole room is just stiff with enchantments. I could feel it the moment we came in."

"Any one of these dresses would cost hundreds of pounds," said Polly.

But Digory was more interested in the faces, and indeed these were well worth looking at. The people sat in their stone chairs on each side of the room and the floor was left free down the middle. You could walk down and look at the faces in turn.

"They were *nice* people, I think," said Digory.

Polly nodded. All the faces they could see were certainly nice. Both the men and women looked kind and wise, and they seemed to come of a handsome race. But after the children had gone a few steps down the room they came to faces that looked a little different. These were very solemn faces. You felt you would have to mind your P's and Q's, if you ever met living people who looked like that. When they had gone a little further, they found themselves among faces they didn't like: this was about the middle of the room. The faces here looked very strong and proud and happy, but they looked cruel. A little further on they looked crueller. Further on again, they were still cruel but they no longer looked happy. They were even despairing faces: as if the people they belonged to had done dreadful things and also suffered dreadful things. The last figure of all was the most interesting – a woman even more richly dressed than the others, very tall (but every figure in that room was taller than the people of our world), with a look of such fierceness and pride that it took your breath away. Yet she was beautiful too. Years afterwards when he was an old man, Digory said he had never in all his life known a woman so beautiful. It is only fair to add that Polly always said she couldn't see anything specially beautiful about her.

This woman, as I said, was the last: but there were plenty of empty chairs beyond her, as if the room had been intended for a much larger collection of images.

"I do wish we knew the story that's behind all this," said Digory. "Let's go back and look at that table sort of thing in the middle of the room."

The thing in the middle of the room was not exactly a table. It was a square pillar about four feet high and on it there rose a little golden arch from which there hung a little golden bell; and beside this there lay a little golden hammer to hit the bell with.

"I wonder... I wonder... I wonder..." said Digory.

"There seems to be something written here," said Polly, stooping down and looking at the side of the pillar.

"By gum, so there is," said Digory. "But of course we shan't be able to read it."

"Shan't we? I'm not so sure," said Polly.

They both looked at it hard and, as you might have expected, the letters cut in the stone were strange. But now a great wonder happened: for, as they looked, though the shape of the strange letters never altered, they found that they could understand them. If only Digory had remembered what he himself had said a few minutes ago, that this was an enchanted room, he might have guessed that the enchantment was beginning to work. But he was too wild with curiosity to think about that. He was longing more and more to know what was written on the pillar. And very soon they both knew. What it said was something like this – at least this is the sense of it though the poetry, when you read it there, was better:

> *Make your choice, adventurous Stranger;*
> *Strike the bell and bide the danger,*
> *Or wonder, till it drives you mad,*
> *What would have followed if you had.*

"No fear!" said Polly. "We don't want any danger."

"Oh, but don't you see it's no good?" said Digory. "We can't get out of it now. We shall always be wondering what else would have happened if we had struck the bell. I'm not going home to be driven mad by always thinking of that. No fear!"

"Don't be so silly," said Polly. "As if anyone would! What does it matter what would have happened?"

"I expect anyone who's come as far as this is bound to go on wondering till it sends him dotty. That's the Magic of it, you see. I can feel it beginning to work on me already."

"Well, I don't," said Polly crossly. "And I don't believe you do either. You're just putting it on."

"That's all *you* know," said Digory. "It's because you're a girl. Girls never want to know anything but gossip and rot about people getting engaged."

"You looked exactly like your Uncle when you said that," said Polly.

"Why can't you keep to the point?" said Digory. "What we're talking about is—"

"How exactly like a man!" said Polly in a very grown-up voice; but she added hastily, in her real voice, "And don't say I'm just like a woman, or you'll be a beastly copy-cat."

"I should never dream of calling a kid like you a woman," said Digory loftily.

"Oh, I'm a kid, am I?" said Polly, who was now in a real rage. "Well, you needn't be bothered by having a kid with you any longer then. I'm off. I've had enough of this place. And I've had enough of you too – you beastly, stuck-up, obstinate pig!"

"None of that!" said Digory in a voice even nastier than he meant it to be; for he saw Polly's hand moving to her pocket to get hold of her yellow ring. I can't excuse what he did next except by saying that he was very sorry for it afterwards (and so were a good many other people). Before Polly's hand reached her pocket, he grabbed her wrist, leaning across with his back against her chest. Then, keeping her other arm out of the way with his other elbow, he leaned forward, picked up the hammer, and struck the golden bell a light, smart tap. Then he let her go and they fell apart staring at each other and breathing hard. Polly was just beginning to cry, not with fear, and not even because he had hurt her wrist quite badly, but with furious anger. Within two seconds, however, they had something to think about that drove their own quarrels quite out of their minds.

As soon as the bell was struck it gave out a note, a sweet note such as you might have expected, and not very loud. But instead of dying away again, it went on; and as it went on it grew louder. Before a minute had passed it was twice as loud as it had been to begin with. It was soon so loud that if the children had tried to speak (but they weren't thinking of speaking now – they were just standing with their mouths open) they would not have heard one another. Very soon it was so loud that they could not have heard one another even by shouting. And still it grew: all on one note, a continuous sweet sound, though the sweetness had something horrible about it, till all the air in that great room was throbbing with it and they could feel the stone floor trembling under their feet. Then at last it began to be mixed with another sound, a vague, disastrous noise which sounded first like the roar of a distant train, and then like the crash of a falling tree. They heard something like great weights falling. Finally, with a sudden rush and thunder, and a shake that nearly flung them off their feet, about a quarter of the roof at one end of the room fell in, great blocks of masonry fell all round them, and the walls rocked. The noise of the bell stopped. The clouds of dust cleared away. Everything became quiet again.

It was never found out whether the fall of the roof was due to Magic or whether that unbearably loud sound from the bell just happened to strike the note which was more than those crumbling walls could stand.

"There! I hope you're satisfied now," panted Polly.

"Well, it's all over, anyway," said Digory.

And both thought it was; but they had never been more mistaken in their lives.

CHAPTER FIVE

THE DEPLORABLE WORD

The children were facing one another across the pillar where the bell hung, still trembling, though it no longer gave out any note. Suddenly they heard a soft noise from the end of the room which was still undamaged. They turned as quick as lightning to see what it was. One of the robed figures, the furthest-off one of all, the woman whom Digory thought so beautiful, was rising from its chair. When she stood up they realized that she was even taller than they had thought. And you could see at once, not only from her crown and robes, but from the flash of her eyes and the curve of her lips, that she was a great queen. She looked round the room and saw the damage and saw the children, but you could not guess from her face what she thought of either or whether she was surprised. She came forward with long, swift strides.

"Who has awaked me? Who has broken the spell?" she asked.

"I think it must have been me," said Digory.

"You!" said the Queen, laying her hand on his shoulder – a white, beautiful hand, but Digory could feel that it was strong as steel pincers. "You? But you are only a child, a common child. Anyone can see at a glance that you have no drop of royal or noble blood in your veins. How did such as you dare to enter this house?"

"We've come from another world; by Magic," said Polly, who thought it was high time the Queen took some notice of her as well as of Digory.

"Is this true?" said the Queen, still looking at Digory and not giving Polly even a glance.

"Yes, it is," said he.

The Queen put her other hand under his chin and forced it up so that she could see his face better. Digory tried to stare back but he soon had to let his eyes drop. There was something about hers that overpowered him. After she had studied him for well over a minute, she let go of his chin and said:

"You are no magician. The mark of it is not on you. You must be only the servant of a magician. It is on another's Magic that you have travelled here."

"It was my Uncle Andrew," said Digory.

At that moment, not in the room itself but from somewhere very close, there came, first a rumbling, then a creaking, and then a roar of falling masonry, and the floor shook.

"There is great peril here," said the Queen. "The whole palace is breaking up. If we are not out of it in a few minutes we shall be buried under the ruin." She spoke as calmly as if she had been merely mentioning the time of day. "Come," she added, and held out a hand to each of the children. Polly, who was disliking the Queen and feeling rather sulky, would not have let her hand be taken if she could have helped it. But though the Queen spoke so calmly, her movements were as quick as thought. Before Polly knew what was happening her left hand had been caught in a hand so much larger and stronger than her own that she could do nothing about it.

"This is a terrible woman," thought Polly. "She's strong enough to break my arm with one twist. And now that she's got my left hand I can't get at my yellow ring. If I tried to stretch across and get my right hand into my left pocket I mightn't be able to reach it before she asked me what I was doing. Whatever happens we mustn't let her know about the rings. I do hope Digory has the sense to keep his mouth shut. I wish I could get a word with him alone."

The Queen led them out of the Hall of Images into a long corridor and then through a whole maze of halls and stairs and courtyards. Again and again they heard parts of the great palace collapsing, sometimes quite close to them. Once a huge arch came thundering down only a moment after they had passed through it. The Queen was walking quickly — the children had to trot to keep up with her — but she showed no sign of fear. Digory thought, "She's wonderfully brave. And strong. She's what I call a Queen! I do hope she's going to tell us the story of this place."

She did tell them certain things as they went along:

"That is the door to the dungeons," she would say, or "That passage leads to the principal torture chambers," or "This was the old banqueting hall where my great-grandfather bade seven hundred nobles to a feast and killed them all before they had drunk their fill. They had had rebellious thoughts."

They came at last into a hall larger and loftier than any they had yet seen. From its size and from the great doors at the far end, Digory thought that now at last they must be coming to the main entrance. In this he was quite right. The doors were dead black, either ebony or some black metal which is not found in our world. They were fastened with great bars, most of them too high to reach and all too heavy to lift. He wondered how they would get out.

The Queen let go of his hand and raised her arm. She drew herself up to her full height and stood rigid. Then she said something which they couldn't understand (but it sounded horrid) and made an action as if she were throwing something towards the doors. And those high and heavy doors trembled for a second as if they were made of silk and then crumbled away till there was nothing left of them but a heap of dust on the threshold.

"Whew!" whistled Digory.

"Has your master magician, your uncle, power like mine?" asked the Queen, firmly seizing Digory's hand again. "But I shall know later. In the meantime, remember what you have seen. This is what happens to things, and to people, who stand in my way."

Much more light than they had yet seen in that country was pouring in through the now empty doorway, and when the Queen led them out through it they were not surprised to find themselves in the open air. The wind that blew in their faces was cold, yet somehow stale. They were looking from a high terrace and there was a great landscape out below them.

Low down and near the horizon hung a great, red sun, far bigger than our sun. Digory felt at once that it was also older than ours: a sun near the end of its life, weary of looking down upon that world. To the left of the sun, and higher up, there was a single star, big and bright. Those were the only two things to be seen in the dark sky; they made a dismal group. And on the earth, in every direction, as far as the eye could reach, there spread a vast city in which there was no living thing to be seen. And all the temples, towers, palaces, pyramids and bridges cast long, disastrous-looking shadows in the light of that withered sun. Once a great river had flowed through the city, but the water had long since vanished, and there was now only a wide ditch of grey dust.

"Look well on that which no eyes will ever see again," said the Queen. "Such was Charn, that great city, the city of the King of Kings, the wonder of the world, perhaps of all worlds. Does your uncle rule any city as great as this, boy?"

"No," said Digory. He was going to explain that Uncle Andrew didn't rule any cities, but the Queen went on:

"It is silent now. But I have stood here when the whole air was full of the noises of Charn; the trampling of feet, the creaking of wheels, the cracking of the whips and the groaning of slaves, the thunder of chariots, and the sacrificial drums beating in the temples. I have stood here (but that was near the end) when the roar of battle went up from every street and the river of Charn ran red." She paused and added, "All in one moment one woman blotted it out for ever."

"Who?" said Digory in a faint voice; but he had already guessed the answer.

"I," said the Queen. "I, Jadis the last Queen, but the Queen of the World."

The two children stood silent, shivering in the cold wind.

"It was my sister's fault," said the Queen. "She drove me to it. May the curse of all the Powers rest upon her for ever! At any moment I was ready to make peace — yes, and to spare her life too, if only she would yield me the throne. But she would not. Her pride has destroyed the whole world. Even after the war had begun, there was a solemn promise that neither side would use Magic. But when she broke her promise, what could I do? Fool! As if she did not know that I had more Magic than she! She even knew that I had the secret of the Deplorable Word. Did she think — she was always a weakling — that I would not use it?"

"What was it?" said Digory.

"That was the secret of secrets," said the Queen Jadis. "It had long been known to the great kings of our race that there was a word which, if spoken with the proper ceremonies, would destroy all living things except the one who spoke it. But the ancient kings were weak and soft-hearted and bound themselves and all who should come after them with great oaths never even to seek after the knowledge of that word. But I learned it in a secret place and paid a terrible price to learn it. I did not use it until she forced me to it. I fought to overcome her by every other means. I poured out the blood of my armies like water—"

"Beast!" muttered Polly.

"The last great battle," said the Queen, "raged for three days here in Charn itself. For three days I looked down upon it from this very spot. I did not use my power till the last of my soldiers had fallen, and the accursed woman, my sister, at the head of her rebels was halfway up those great stairs that lead up from the city to the terrace. Then I waited till we were so close that we could see one another's faces. She flashed her horrible, wicked eyes upon me and said, 'Victory'. 'Yes,' said I, 'Victory, but not yours.' Then I spoke the Deplorable Word. A moment later I was the only living thing beneath the sun."

"But the people?" gasped Digory.

"What people, boy?" asked the Queen.

"All the ordinary people," said Polly, "who'd never done you any harm. And the women, and the children, and the animals."

"Don't you understand?" said the Queen (still speaking to Digory). "I was the Queen. They were all *my* people. What else were they there for but to do my will?"

"It was rather hard luck on them, all the same," said he.

"I had forgotten that you are only a common boy. How should you understand reasons of State? You must learn, child, that what would be wrong for you or for any of the common people is not wrong in a great Queen such as I. The weight of the world is on our shoulders. We must be freed from all rules. Ours is a high and lonely destiny."

Digory suddenly remembered that Uncle Andrew had used exactly the same words. But they sounded much grander when Queen Jadis said them; perhaps because Uncle Andrew was not seven feet tall and dazzlingly beautiful.

"And what did you do then?" said Digory.

"I had already cast strong spells on the hall where the images of my ancestors sit. And the force of those spells was that I should sleep among them, like an image myself, and need neither food nor fire, though it were a thousand years, till one came and struck the bell and awoke me."

"Was it the Deplorable Word that made the sun like that?" asked Digory.

"Like what?" said Jadis.

"So big, so red, and so cold."

"It has always been so," said Jadis. "At least, for hundreds of thousands of years. Have you a different sort of sun in your world?"

"Yes, it's smaller and yellower. And it gives a good deal more heat."

The Queen gave a long drawn "A-a-ah!" And Digory saw on her face that same hungry and greedy look which he had lately seen on Uncle Andrew's. "So," she said, "yours is a younger world."

She paused for a moment to look once more at the deserted city – and if she was sorry for all the evil she had done there, she certainly didn't show it – and then said:

"Now, let us be going. It is cold here at the end of all the ages."

"Going where?" asked both the children.

"Where?" repeated Jadis in surprise. "To your world, of course."

Polly and Digory looked at each other, aghast. Polly had disliked the Queen from the first; and even Digory, now that he had heard the story, felt that he had seen quite as much of her as he wanted. Certainly, she was not at all the sort of person one would like to take home. And if they did like, they didn't know how they could. What they wanted was to get away themselves: but Polly couldn't get at her ring and of course Digory couldn't go without her. Digory got very red in the face and stammered.

"Oh – oh – our world. I d-didn't know you wanted to go there."

"What else were you sent here for if not to fetch me?" asked Jadis.

"I'm sure you wouldn't like our world at all," said Digory. "It's not her sort of place, is it, Polly? It's very dull; not worth seeing, really."

"It will soon be worth seeing when I rule it," answered the Queen.

"Oh, but you can't," said Digory. "It's not like that. They wouldn't let you, you know."

The Queen gave a contemptuous smile. "Many great kings," she said, "thought they could stand against the House of Charn. But they all fell, and their very names are forgotten. Foolish boy! Do you think that I, with my beauty and my Magic, will not have your whole world at my feet before a year has passed? Prepare your incantations and take me there at once."

"This is perfectly frightful," said Digory to Polly.

"Perhaps you fear for this Uncle of yours," said Jadis. "But if he honours me duly, he shall keep his life and his throne. I am not coming to fight against *him*. He must be a very great Magician, if he has found how to send you here. Is he King of your whole world or only of part?"

"He isn't King of anywhere," said Digory.

"You are lying," said the Queen. "Does not Magic always go with the royal blood? Who ever heard of common people being Magicians? I can see the truth whether you speak it or not. Your Uncle is the great King and the great Enchanter of your world. And by his art he has seen the shadow of my face, in some magic mirror or some enchanted pool; and for the love of my beauty he has made a potent spell which shook your world to its foundations and sent you across the vast gulf between world and world to ask my favour and to bring me to him. Answer me: is that not how it was?"

"Well, not *exactly*," said Digory.

"Not exactly," shouted Polly. "Why, it's absolute bosh from beginning to end."

"Minions!" cried the Queen, turning in rage upon Polly and seizing her hair, at the very top of her head where it hurts most. But in so doing she let go of both the children's hands. "Now," shouted Digory; and "Quick!" shouted Polly. They plunged their left hands into their pockets. They did not even need to put the rings on. The moment they touched them, the whole of that dreary world vanished from their eyes. They were rushing upward and a warm green light was growing nearer overhead.

CHAPTER SIX

THE BEGINNING OF UNCLE ANDREW'S TROUBLES

"Let go! Let go!" screamed Polly.

"I'm not touching you!" said Digory.

Then their heads came out of the pool and, once more, the sunny quietness of the Wood between the Worlds was all about them, and it seemed richer and warmer and more peaceful than ever after the staleness and ruin of the place they had just left. I think that, if they had been given the chance, they would again have forgotten who they were and where they came from and would have lain down and enjoyed themselves, half asleep, listening to the growing of the trees. But this time there was something that kept them as wide-awake as possible: for as soon as they had got out on to the grass, they found that they were not alone. The Queen, or the Witch (whichever you like to call her) had come up with them, holding on fast by Polly's hair. That was why Polly had been shouting out "Let go!"

This proved, by the way, another thing about the rings which Uncle Andrew hadn't told Digory because he didn't know it himself. In order to jump from world to world by one of those rings you don't need to be wearing or touching it yourself; it is enough if you are touching someone who is touching it. In that way they work like a magnet; and everyone knows that if you pick up a pin with a magnet, any other pin which is touching the first pin will come too.

Now that you saw her in the wood, Queen Jadis looked different. She was much paler than she had been; so pale that hardly any of her beauty was left. And she was stooped and seemed to be finding it hard to breathe, as if the air of that place stifled her. Neither of the children felt in the least afraid of her now.

"Let go! Let go of my hair," said Polly. "What do you mean by it?"

"Here! Let go of her hair. At once," said Digory.

They both turned and struggled with her. They were stronger than she and in a few seconds they had forced her to let go. She reeled back, panting, and there was a look of terror in her eyes.

"Quick, Digory!" said Polly. "Change rings and into the home pool."

"Help! Help! Mercy!" cried the Witch in a faint voice, staggering after them. "Take me with you. You cannot mean to leave me in this horrible place. It is killing me."

"It's a reason of State," said Polly spitefully. "Like when you killed all those people in your own world. Do be quick, Digory." They had put on their green rings, but Digory said:

"Oh, bother! What *are* we to do?" He couldn't help feeling a little sorry for the Queen.

"Oh, don't be such an ass," said Polly. "Ten to one she's only shamming. Do come *on*." And then both children plunged into the home pool. "It's a good thing we made that mark," thought Polly. But as they jumped Digory felt that a large cold finger and thumb had caught him by the ear. And as they sank down and the confused shapes of our own world began to appear, the grip of that finger and thumb grew stronger. The Witch was apparently recovering her strength. Digory struggled and kicked, but it was not of the least use. In a moment they found themselves in Uncle Andrew's study; and there was Uncle Andrew himself, staring at the wonderful creature that Digory had brought back from beyond the world.

And well he might stare. Digory and Polly stared too. There was no doubt that the Witch had got over her faintness; and now that one saw her in our own world, with ordinary things around her, she fairly took one's breath away. In Charn she had been alarming enough: in London, she was terrifying. For one thing, they had not realized till now how very big she was. "Hardly human" was what Digory thought when he looked at her; and he may have been right, for some say there is giantish blood in the royal family of Charn. But even her height was nothing compared with her beauty, her fierceness, and her wildness. She looked ten times more alive than most of the people one meets in London. Uncle Andrew was bowing and rubbing his hands and looking, to tell the truth, extremely frightened. He seemed a little shrimp of a creature beside the Witch. And yet, as Polly said afterwards, there was a sort of likeness between her face and his, something in the expression. It was the look that all wicked Magicians have, the "Mark" which Jadis had said she could not find in Digory's face. One good thing about seeing the two together was that you would never again be afraid of Uncle Andrew, any more than you'd be afraid of a worm after you had met a rattlesnake or afraid of a cow after you had met a mad bull.

"Pooh!" thought Digory to himself. "*Him* a Magician! Not much. Now *she's* the real thing."

Uncle Andrew kept on rubbing his hands and bowing. He was trying to say something very polite, but his mouth had gone all dry so that he could not speak. His "experiment" with the rings, as he called it, was turning out more successful than he liked: for though he had dabbled in Magic for years he had always left all the dangers (as far as one can) to other people. Nothing at all like this had ever happened to him before.

Then Jadis spoke; not very loud, but there was something in her voice that made the whole room quiver.

"Where is the Magician who has called me into this world?"

"Ah – ah – Madam," gasped Uncle Andrew, "I am most honoured – highly gratified – a most unexpected pleasure – if only I had had the opportunity of making any preparations – I – I—"

"Where is the Magician, Fool?" said Jadis.

"I – I am, Madam. I hope you will excuse any – er – liberty these naughty children may have taken. I assure you there was no intention—"

"You?" said the Queen in a still more terrible voice. Then, in one stride, she crossed the room, seized a great handful of Uncle Andrew's grey hair and pulled his head back so that his face looked up into hers. Then she studied his face just as she had studied Digory's face in the palace of Charn. He blinked and licked his lips nervously all the time. At last she let him go: so suddenly that he reeled back against the wall.

"I see," she said scornfully, "you are a Magician – of a sort. Stand up, dog, and don't sprawl there as if you were speaking to your equals. How do you come to know Magic? *You* are not of royal blood, I'll swear."

"Well – ah – not perhaps in the strict sense," stammered Uncle Andrew. "Not exactly royal, Ma'am. The Ketterleys are, however, a very old family. An old Dorsetshire family, Ma'am."

"Peace," said the Witch. "I see what you are. You are a little, peddling Magician who works by rules and books. There is no real Magic in your blood and heart. Your kind was made an end of in my world a thousand years ago. But here I shall allow you to be my servant."

"I should be most happy – delighted to be of any service – a p-pleasure, I assure you."

"Peace! You talk far too much. Listen to your first task. I see we are in a large city. Procure for me at once a chariot or a flying carpet or a well-trained dragon, or whatever is usual for royal and noble persons in your land. Then bring me to places where I can get clothes and jewels and slaves fit for my rank. Tomorrow I will begin the conquest of the world."

"I – I – I'll go and order a cab at once," gasped Uncle Andrew.

"Stop," said the Witch, just as he reached the door. "Do not dream of treachery. My eyes can see through walls and into the minds of men. They will be on you wherever you go. At the first sign of disobedience I will lay such spells on you that anything you sit down on will feel like red hot iron and whenever you lie in a bed there will be invisible blocks of ice at your feet. Now go."

The old man went out, looking like a dog with its tail between its legs. The children were now afraid that Jadis would have something to say to them about what had happened in the wood. As it turned out, however, she never mentioned it either then or afterwards. I think (and Digory thinks too) that her mind was of a sort which cannot remember that quiet place at all, and however often you took her there and however long you left her there, she would still know nothing about it. Now that she was left alone with the children, she took no notice of either of them. And that was like her too. In Charn she had taken no notice of Polly (till the very end) because Digory was the one she wanted to make use of. Now that she had Uncle Andrew, she took no notice of Digory. I expect most witches are like that. They are not interested in things or people unless they can use them; they are terribly practical. So there was silence in the room for a minute or two. But you could tell by the way Jadis tapped her foot on the floor that she was growing impatient.

Presently she said, as if to herself, "What is the old fool doing? I should have brought a whip." She stalked out of the room in pursuit of Uncle Andrew without one glance at the children.

"Whew!" said Polly, letting out a long breath of relief. "And now I must get home. It's frightfully late. I shall catch it."

"Well do, do come back as soon as you can," said Digory. "This is simply ghastly, having her here. We must make some sort of plan."

"That's up to your Uncle now," said Polly. "It was he who started all this messing about with Magic."

"All the same, you will come back, won't you? Hang it all, you can't leave me alone in a scrape like this."

"I shall go home by the tunnel," said Polly rather coldly. "That'll be the quickest way. And if you want me to come back, hadn't you better say you're sorry?"

"Sorry?" exclaimed Digory. "Well now, if that isn't just like a girl! What have *I* done?"

"Oh, nothing of course," said Polly sarcastically. "Only nearly screwed my wrist off in that room with all the waxworks, like a cowardly bully.

Only struck the bell with the hammer, like a silly idiot. Only turned back in the wood so that she had time to catch hold of you before we jumped into our own pool. That's all."

"Oh," said Digory, very surprised. "Well, all right, I'll say I'm sorry. And I really am sorry about what happened in the waxworks room. There: I've said I'm sorry. And now, do be decent and come back. I shall be in a frightful hole if you don't."

"I don't see what's going to happen to you. It's Mr Ketterley who's going to sit on red hot chairs and have ice in his bed, isn't it?"

"It isn't that sort of thing," said Digory. "What I'm bothered about is Mother. Suppose that creature went into her room? She might frighten her to death."

"Oh, I see," said Polly, in rather a different voice. "All right. We'll call it Pax. I'll come back – if I can. But I must go now." And she crawled through the little door into the tunnel; and that dark place among the rafters which had seemed so exciting and adventurous a few hours ago seemed quite tame and homely now.

We must now go back to Uncle Andrew. His poor old heart went pit-a-pat as he staggered down the attic stairs and he kept on dabbing at his forehead with a handkerchief. When he reached his bedroom, which was the floor below, he locked himself in. And the very first thing he did was to grope in his wardrobe for a bottle and a wine-glass which he always kept hidden there where Aunt Letty could not find them. He poured himself out a glassful of some nasty, grown-up drink and drank it off at one gulp. Then he drew a deep breath.

"Upon my word," he said to himself. "I'm dreadfully shaken. Most upsetting! And at my time of life!"

He poured out a second glass and drank it too; then he began to change his clothes. You have never seen such clothes, but I can remember them. He put on a very high, shiny, stiff collar of the sort that made you hold your chin up all the time. He put on a white waistcoat with a pattern on it and arranged his gold watch chain across the front. He put on his best frock-coat, the one he kept for weddings and funerals. He got out his best tall hat and polished it up. There was a vase of flowers (put there by Aunt Letty) on his dressing table; he took one and put it in his button-hole. He took a clean handkerchief (a lovely one such as you couldn't buy today) out of the little left-hand drawer and put a few drops of scent on it. He took his eye-glass, with the thick black ribbon, and screwed it into his eye; then he looked at himself in the mirror.

Children have one kind of silliness, as you know, and grown-ups have another kind. At this moment Uncle Andrew was beginning to be silly in a very grown-up way. Now that the Witch was no longer in the same room with him he was quickly forgetting how she had frightened him and thinking more and more of her wonderful beauty. He kept on saying to himself, "A dem fine woman, sir, a dem fine woman. A superb creature." He had also somehow managed to forget that it was the children who had got hold of this "superb creature": he felt as if he himself by his Magic had called her out of unknown worlds.

"Andrew, my boy," he said to himself as he looked in the glass, "you're a devilish well-preserved fellow for your age. A distinguished-looking man, sir."

You see, the foolish old man was actually beginning to imagine the Witch would fall in love with him. The two drinks probably had something to do with it, and so had his best clothes. But he was, in any case, as vain as a peacock; that was why he had become a Magician.

He unlocked the door, went downstairs, sent the housemaid out to fetch a hansom (everyone had lots of servants in those days) and looked into the drawing-room. There, as he expected, he found Aunt Letty. She was busily mending a mattress. It lay on the floor near the window and she was kneeling on it.

"Ah, Letitia my dear," said Uncle Andrew, "I – ah – have to go out. Just lend me five pounds or so, there's a good gel." ("Gel" was the way he pronounced girl.)

"No, Andrew dear," said Aunt Letty in her firm, quiet voice, without looking up from her work. "I've told you times without number that I *will not* lend you money."

"Now pray don't be troublesome, my dear gel," said Uncle Andrew. "It's most important. You will put me in a deucedly awkward position if you don't."

"Andrew," said Aunt Letty, looking him straight in the face, "I wonder *you* are not ashamed to ask *me* for money."

There was a long, dull story of a grown-up kind behind these words. All you need to know about it is that Uncle Andrew, what with "managing dear Letty's business matters for her", and never doing any work, and running up large bills for brandy and cigars (which Aunt Letty had paid again and again) had made her a good deal poorer than she had been thirty years ago.

"My dear gel," said Uncle Andrew, "you don't understand. I shall have some quite unexpected expenses today. I have to do a little entertaining. Come now, don't be tiresome."

"And who, pray, are *you* going to entertain, Andrew?" asked Aunt Letty.

"A – a most distinguished visitor has just arrived."

"Distinguished fiddlestick!" said Aunt Letty. "There hasn't been a ring at the bell for the last hour."

At that moment the door was suddenly flung open. Aunt Letty looked round and saw with amazement that an enormous woman, splendidly dressed, with bare arms and flashing eyes, stood in the doorway. It was the Witch.

Chapter Seven

What Happened at the Front Door

"Now, slave, how long am I to wait for my chariot?" thundered the Witch. Uncle Andrew cowered away from her. Now that she was really present, all the silly thoughts he had had while looking at himself in the glass were oozing out of him. But Aunt Letty at once got up from her knees and came over to the centre of the room.

"And who is this young person, Andrew, may I ask?" said Aunt Letty in icy tones.

"Distinguished foreigner – v-very important p-person," he stammered.

"Rubbish!" said Aunt Letty, and then, turning to the Witch, "Get out of my house this moment, you shameless hussy, or I'll send for the police." She thought the Witch must be someone out of a circus and she did not approve of bare arms.

"What woman is this?" said Jadis. "Down on your knees, minion, before I blast you."

"No strong language in this house *if* you please, young woman," said Aunt Letty.

Instantly, as it seemed to Uncle Andrew, the Queen towered up to an even greater height. Fire flashed from her eyes: she flung out her arm with the same gesture and the same horrible-sounding words that had lately turned the palace-gates of Charn to dust. But nothing happened except that Aunt Letty, thinking that those horrible words were meant to be ordinary English, said:

"I thought as much. The woman is drunk. Drunk! She can't even speak clearly."

It must have been a terrible moment for the Witch when she suddenly realized that her power of turning people into dust, which had been quite real in her own world, was not going to work in ours. But she did not lose her nerve even for a second. Without wasting a thought on her disappointment, she lunged forward, caught Aunt Letty round the neck and the knees, raised her high above her head as if she had been no heavier than a doll, and threw her across the room. While Aunt Letty was still hurtling through the air, the housemaid (who was having a beautifully exciting morning) put her head in at the door and said, "If you please, sir, the 'ansom's come."

"Lead on, Slave," said the Witch to Uncle Andrew. He began muttering something about "regrettable violence — must really protest", but at a single glance from Jadis he became speechless. She drove him out of the room and out of the house; and Digory came running down the stairs just in time to see the front door close behind them.

"Jiminy!" he said. "She's loose in London. And with Uncle Andrew. I wonder what on earth is going to happen now."

"Oh, Master Digory," said the housemaid (who was really having a wonderful day), "I think Miss Ketterley's hurt herself somehow." So they both rushed into the drawing-room to find out what had happened.

If Aunt Letty had fallen on bare boards or even on the carpet, I suppose all her bones would have been broken: but by great good luck she had fallen on the mattress. Aunt Letty was a very tough old lady: aunts often were in those days. After she had had some *sal volatile* and sat still for a few minutes, she said there was nothing the matter with her except a few bruises. Very soon she was taking charge of the situation.

"Sarah," she said to the housemaid (who had never had such a day before), "go around to the police station at once and tell them there is a dangerous lunatic at large. I will take Mrs Kirke's lunch up myself." Mrs Kirke was, of course, Digory's mother.

When Mother's lunch had been seen to, Digory and Aunt Letty had their own. After that he did some hard thinking.

The problem was how to get the Witch back to her own world, or at any rate out of ours, as soon as possible. Whatever happened, she must not be allowed to go rampaging about the house. Mother must not see her. And, if possible, she must not be allowed to go rampaging about London either. Digory had not been in the drawing-room when she tried to "blast" Aunt Letty, but he had seen her "blast" the gates at Charn: so he knew her terrible powers and did not know that she had lost any of them by coming into our world. And he knew she meant to conquer our world. At the present moment, as far as he could see, she might be blasting Buckingham Palace or the Houses of Parliament: and it was almost certain that quite a number of policemen had by now been reduced to little heaps of dust.

And there didn't seem to be anything he could do about that. "But the rings seem to work like magnets," thought Digory. "If I can only touch her and then slip on my yellow, we shall both go into the Wood between the Worlds. I wonder, will she go all faint again there? Was that something the place does to her, or was it only the shock of being pulled out of her own world? But I suppose I'll have to risk that. And how am I to find the beast? I don't suppose Aunt Letty would let me go out, not unless I said where I was going. And I haven't got more than twopence. I'd need any amount of money for buses and trams if I went looking all over London. Anyway, I haven't the faintest idea where to look. I wonder if Uncle Andrew is still with her."

It seemed in the end that the only thing he could do was to wait and hope that Uncle Andrew and the Witch would come back. If they did, he must rush out and get hold of the Witch and put on his yellow Ring before she had a chance to get into the house. This meant that he must watch the front door like a cat watching a mouse's hole; he dared not leave his post for a moment. So he went into the dining-room and "glued his face" as they say, to the window. It was a bow-window from which you could see the steps up to the front door and see up and down the street, so that no one could reach the front door without your knowing. "I wonder what Polly's doing?" thought Digory.

He wondered about this a good deal as the first slow half-hour ticked on. But you need not wonder, for I am going to tell you. She had got home late for her dinner, with her shoes and stockings very wet. And when they asked her where she had been and what on earth she had been doing, she said she had been out with Digory Kirke. Under further questioning she said she had got her feet wet in a pool of water, and that the pool was in a wood. Asked where the wood was, she said she didn't know. Asked if it was in one of the parks, she said truthfully enough that she supposed it might be a sort of park. From all of this Polly's mother got the idea that Polly had gone off, without telling anyone, to some part of London she didn't know, and gone into a strange park and amused herself jumping into puddles. As a result she was told that she had been very naughty indeed and that she wouldn't be allowed to play with "that Kirke boy" any more if anything of the sort ever happened again. Then she was given dinner with all the nice parts left out and sent to bed for two solid hours. It was a thing that happened to one quite often in those days.

So while Digory was staring out of the dining-room window, Polly was lying in bed, and both were thinking how terribly slowly the time could go. I think, myself, I would rather have been in Polly's position. She had only to wait for the end of her two hours: but every few minutes Digory would hear a cab or a baker's van or a butcher's boy coming round the corner and think "Here she comes", and then find it wasn't. And in between these false alarms, for what seemed hours and hours, the clock ticked on and one big fly — high up and far out of reach — buzzed against the window. It was one of those houses that get very quiet and dull in the afternoon and always seem to smell of mutton.

During his long watching and waiting one small thing happened which I shall have to mention because something important came of it later on. A lady called with some grapes for Digory's Mother; and as the dining-room door was open, Digory couldn't help overhearing Aunt Letty and the lady as they talked in the hall.

"What lovely grapes!" came Aunt Letty's voice. "I'm sure if anything could do her good these would. But poor, dear little Mabel! I'm afraid it would need fruit from the land of youth to help her now. Nothing in *this* world will do much." Then they both lowered their voices and said a lot more that he could not hear.

If he had heard that bit about the land of youth a few days ago he would have thought Aunt Letty was just talking without meaning anything in particular, the way grown-ups do, and it wouldn't have interested him. He almost thought so now. But suddenly it flashed upon his mind that he now knew (even if Aunt Letty didn't) that there really were other worlds and that he himself had been in one of them. At that rate there might be a real Land of Youth somewhere. There might be almost anything. There might be fruit in some other world that would really cure his mother! And oh, oh— Well, you know how it feels if you begin hoping for something that you want desperately badly; you almost fight against the hope because it is too good to be true; you've been disappointed so often before. That was how Digory felt. But it was no good trying to throttle this hope. It might — really, really, it just might be true. So many odd things had happened already. And he had the magic rings. There must be worlds you could get to through every pool in the wood. He could hunt through them all. And then — *Mother well again.* Everything right again. He forgot all about watching for the Witch. His hand was already going into the pocket where he kept the yellow ring, when all at once he heard a sound of galloping.

"Hullo! What's that?" thought Digory. "Fire engine? I wonder what house is on fire. Great Scott, it's coming here. Why, it's Her."

I needn't tell you who he meant by *Her.*

First came the hansom. There was no one in the driver's seat. On the roof — not sitting, but standing on the roof — swaying with superb balance as it came at full speed round the corner with one wheel in the air — was Jadis the Queen of Queens and the Terror of Charn. Her teeth were bared, her eyes shone like fire, and her long hair streamed out behind her like a comet's tail. She was flogging the horse without mercy. Its nostrils were wide and red and its sides were spotted with foam. It galloped madly up to the front door, missing the lamp-post by an inch, and then reared up on its hind legs. The hansom crashed into the lamp-post and shattered into several pieces. The Witch, with a magnificent jump, had sprung clear just in time and landed on the horse's back. She settled herself astride and leaned forward, whispering things in its ear. They must have been things meant not to quiet it but to madden it. It was on its hind legs again in a moment, and his neigh was like a scream; it was all hoofs and teeth and eyes and tossing mane. Only a splendid rider could have stayed on its back.

Before Digory had recovered his breath a good many other things began to happen. A second hansom dashed up close behind the first: out of it there jumped a fat man in a frock-coat and a policeman. Then came a third hansom with two more policemen in it. After it came about twenty people (mostly errand boys) on bicycles, all ringing their bells and letting out cheers and cat-calls. Last of all came a crowd of people on foot: all very hot with running, but obviously enjoying themselves. Windows shot up in all the houses of that street and a housemaid or a butler appeared at every front door. They wanted to see the fun.

Meanwhile an old gentleman had begun to struggle shakily out of the ruins of the first hansom. Several people rushed forward to help him; but as one pulled him one way and another another, perhaps he would have got out quite as quickly on his own. Digory guessed that the old gentleman must be Uncle Andrew but you couldn't see his face; his tall hat had been bashed down over it.

Digory rushed out and joined the crowd.

"That's the woman, that's the woman," cried the fat man, pointing at Jadis. "Do your duty, Constable. Hundreds and thousands of pounds' worth she's taken out of my shop. Look at that rope of pearls round her neck. That's mine. And she's given me a black eye too, what's more."

"That she 'as, guv'nor," said one of the crowd. "And as lovely a black eye as I'd wish to see. Beautiful bit of work that must 'ave been. Gor! Ain't she strong then!"

"You ought to put a nice raw beefsteak on it, Mister, that's what it wants," said a butcher's boy.

"Now then," said the most important of the policemen, "what's all this 'ere?"

"I tell you she——" began the fat man, when someone else called out:

"Don't let the old cove in the cab get away. 'E put 'er up to it."

The old gentleman, who was certainly Uncle Andrew, had just succeeded in standing up and was rubbing his bruises. "Now then," said the policeman, turning to him. "What's all this?"

"Womfle – pomy – shomf," came Uncle Andrew's voice from inside the hat.

"None of that now," said the policeman sternly. "You'll find this is no laughing matter. Take that 'at off, see?"

This was more easily said than done. But after Uncle Andrew had struggled in vain with the hat for some time, two other policemen seized it by the brim and forced it off.

"Thank you, thank you," said Uncle Andrew in a faint voice. "Thank you. Dear me, I'm terribly shaken. If someone could give me a small glass of brandy——"

"Now you attend to me, if you please," said the policeman, taking out a very large note-book and a very small pencil. "Are you in charge of that there young woman?"

"Look out!" called several voices, and the policeman jumped a step backwards just in time. The horse had aimed a kick at him which would probably have killed him. Then the Witch wheeled the horse round so that she faced the crowd and its hind-legs were on the footpath. She had a long, bright knife in her hand and had been busily cutting the horse free from the wreck of the hansom.

All this time Digory had been trying to get into a position from which he could touch the Witch. This wasn't at all easy because, on the side nearest to him, there were too many people. And in order to get round to the other side he had to pass between the horse's hoofs and the railings of the "area" that surrounded the house; for the Ketterleys' house had a basement. If you know anything about horses, and especially if you had seen what a state that horse was in at the moment, you will realize that this was a ticklish thing to do. Digory knew lots about horses, but he set his teeth and got ready to make a dash for it as soon as he saw a favourable moment.

A red-faced man in a bowler hat had now shouldered his way to the front of the crowd.

"Hi! P'leeceman," he said, "that's my 'orse what she's sitting on, same as it's my cab what she's made matchwood of."

"One at a time, please, one at a time," said the policeman.

"But there ain't no time," said the Cabby. "I know that 'orse better'n you do. 'Tain't an ordinary 'orse. 'Is father was a hofficer's charger in the cavalry, 'e was. And if the young woman goes on hexcitin' 'im, there'll be murder done. 'Ere, let me get at him."

The policeman was only too glad to have a good reason for standing further away from the horse. The Cabby took a step nearer, looked up at Jadis, and said in a not unkindly voice:

"Now, Missie, let me get at 'is 'ead, and just you get off. You're a Lidy, and you don't want all these roughs going for you, do you? You want to go 'ome and 'ave a nice cup of tea and a lay-down quiet like; then you'll feel ever so much better." At the same time he stretched out his hand towards the horse's head with the words, "Steady, Strawberry, old boy. Steady now."

Then for the first time the Witch spoke.

"Dog!" came her cold, clear voice, ringing loud above all the other noises. "Dog, unhand our royal charger. We are the Empress Jadis."

Chapter Eight

The Fight at the Lamp-post

"Ho! Hempress, are you? We'll see about that," said a voice. Then another voice said, "Three cheers for the Hempress of Colney 'Atch" and quite a number joined in. A flush of colour came into the Witch's face and she bowed ever so slightly. But the cheers died away into roars of laughter and she saw that they had only been making fun of her. A change came over her expression and she changed the knife to her left hand. Then, without warning, she did a thing that was dreadful to see. Lightly, easily, as if it were the most ordinary thing in the world, she stretched up her right arm and wrenched off one of the cross-bars of the lamp-post. If she had lost some magical powers in our world, she had not lost her strength; she could break an iron bar as if it were a stick of barley-sugar. She tossed her new weapon up in the air, caught it again, brandished it, and urged the horse forward.

"Now's my chance," thought Digory. He darted between the horse and the railings and began going forward. If only the brute would stay still for a moment he might catch the Witch's heel. As he rushed, he heard a sickening crash and a thud. The Witch had brought the bar down on the chief policeman's helmet: the man fell like a ninepin.

"Quick, Digory. This *must* be stopped," said a voice beside him. It was Polly, who had rushed down the moment she was allowed out of bed.

"You *are* a brick," said Digory. "Hold on to me tight. You'll have to manage the ring. Yellow, remember. And don't put it on till I shout."

There was a second crash and another policeman crumpled up. There came an angry roar from the crowd: "Pull her down. Get a few paving-stones. Call out the Military." But most of them were getting as far away as they could. The Cabby, however, obviously the bravest as well as the kindest person present, was keeping close to the horse, dodging this way and that to avoid the bar, but still trying to catch Strawberry's head.

The crowd booed and bellowed again. A stone whistled over Digory's head. Then came the voice of the Witch, clear like a great bell, and sounding as if, for once, she were almost happy.

"Scum! You shall pay dearly for this when I have conquered your world. Not one stone of your city will be left. I will make it as Charn, as Felinda, as Sorlis, as Bramandin."

Digory at last caught her ankle. She kicked back with her heel and hit him in the mouth. In his pain he lost hold. His lip was cut and his mouth full of blood. From somewhere very close by came the voice of Uncle Andrew in a sort of trembling scream. "Madam — my dear young lady — for heaven's sake — compose yourself." Digory made a second grab at her heel, and was again shaken off. More men were knocked down by the iron bar. He made a third grab: caught the heel: held on like grim death, shouting to Polly "Go!" then — oh, thank goodness. The angry, frightened faces had vanished. The angry, frightened voices were silenced. All except Uncle Andrew's. Close beside Digory in the darkness, it was wailing on: "Oh, oh, is this delirium? Is it the end? I can't bear it. It's not fair. I never meant to be a Magician. It's all a misunderstanding. It's all my godmother's fault; I must protest against this. In my state of health too. A very old Dorsetshire family."

"Bother!" thought Digory. "We didn't want to bring *him* along. My hat, what a picnic. Are you there, Polly?"

"Yes, I'm here. Don't keep on shoving."

"I'm not," began Digory, but before he could say anything more, their heads came out into the warm, green sunshine of the wood. And as they stepped out of the pool Polly cried out:

"Oh, look! We've brought the old horse with us too. *And* Mr Ketterley. *And* the Cabby. This is a pretty kettle of fish!"

As soon as the Witch saw that she was once more in the wood she turned pale and bent down till her face touched the mane of the horse. You could see she felt deadly sick. Uncle Andrew was shivering. But Strawberry, the horse, shook his head, gave a cheerful whinny, and seemed to feel better. He became quiet for the first time since Digory had seen him. His ears, which had been laid flat back on his skull, came into their proper position, and the fire went out of his eyes.

"That's right, old boy," said the Cabby, slapping Strawberry's neck. "That's better. Take it easy."

Strawberry did the most natural thing in the world. Being very thirsty (and no wonder) he walked slowly across to the nearest pool and stepped into it to have a drink. Digory was still holding the Witch's heel and Polly was holding Digory's hand. One of the Cabby's hands was on Strawberry; and Uncle Andrew, still very shaky, had just grabbed the Cabby's other hand.

"Quick," said Polly, with a look at Digory. "Greens!"

So the horse never got his drink. Instead, the whole party found themselves sinking into darkness. Strawberry neighed; Uncle Andrew whimpered. Digory said, "That was a bit of luck."

There was a short pause. Then Polly said, "Oughtn't we to be nearly there now?"

"We do seem to be somewhere," said Digory. "At least I'm standing on something solid."

"Why, so am I, now that I come to think of it," said Polly. "But why's it so dark? I say, do you think we got into the wrong pool?"

"Perhaps this *is* Charn," said Digory. "Only we've got back in the middle of the night."

"This is not Charn," came the Witch's voice. "This is an empty world. This is Nothing."

And really it was uncommonly like Nothing. There were no stars. It was so dark that they couldn't see one another at all and it made no difference whether you kept your eyes shut or open. Under their feet there was a cool, flat something which might have been earth, and was certainly not grass or wood. The air was cold and dry and there was no wind.

"My doom has come upon me," said the Witch in a voice of horrible calmness.

"Oh don't say that," babbled Uncle Andrew. "My dear young lady, pray don't say such things. It can't be as bad as that. Ah – Cabman – my good man – you don't happen to have a flask about you? A drop of spirits is just what I need."

"Now then, now then," came the Cabby's voice, a good firm, hardy voice. "Keep cool, everyone, that's what I say. No bones broken, anyone? Good. Well, there's something to be thankful for straight away, and more than anyone could expect after falling all that way. Now, if we've fallen down some diggings – as it might be for a new station on the Underground – someone will come and get us out presently, see! And if we're dead – which I don't deny it might be – well, you got to remember that worse things 'appen at sea and a chap's got to die sometime. And there ain't nothing to be afraid of if a chap's led a decent life. And if you ask me, I think the best thing we could do to pass the time would be sing a 'ymn."

And he did. He struck up at once a harvest thanksgiving hymn, all about crops being "safely gathered in". It was not very suitable to a place which felt as if nothing had ever grown there since the beginning of time, but it was the one he could remember best. He had a fine voice and the children joined in; it was very cheering. Uncle Andrew and the Witch did not join in.

Towards the end of the hymn Digory felt someone plucking at his elbow and from a general smell of brandy and cigars and good clothes he decided that it must be Uncle Andrew. Uncle Andrew was cautiously pulling him away from the others. When they had gone a little distance, the old man put his mouth so close to Digory's ear that it tickled, and whispered:

"Now, my boy. Slip on your ring. Let's be off."

But the Witch had very good ears. "Fool!" came her voice and she leapt off the horse. "Have you forgotten that I can hear men's thoughts? Let go the boy. If you attempt treachery I will take such vengeance upon you as never was heard of in all worlds from the beginning."

"And," added Digory, "if you think I'm such a mean pig as to go off and leave Polly – and the Cabby – and the horse – in a place like this, you're well mistaken."

"You are a very naughty and impertinent little boy," said Uncle Andrew.

"Hush!" said the Cabby. They all listened.

In the darkness something was happening at last. A voice had begun to sing. It was very far away and Digory found it hard to decide from what direction it was coming. Sometimes it seemed to come from all directions at once. Sometimes he almost thought it was coming out of the earth beneath them. Its lower notes were deep enough to be the voice of the earth herself. There were no words. There was hardly even a tune. But it was, beyond comparison, the most beautiful noise he had ever heard. It was so beautiful he could hardly bear it. The horse seemed to like it too; he gave the sort of whinny a horse would give if, after years of being a cab-horse, it found itself back in the old field where it had played as a foal, and saw someone whom it remembered and loved coming across the field to bring it a lump of sugar.

"Gawd!" said the Cabby. "Ain't it lovely?"

Then two wonders happened at the same moment. One was that the voice was suddenly joined by the other voices; more voices than you could possibly count. They were in harmony with it, but far higher up the scale: cold, tingling, silvery voices. The second wonder was that the blackness overhead, all at once, was blazing with stars. They didn't come out gently one by one, as they do on a summer evening. One moment there had been nothing but darkness; next moment a thousand, thousand points of light leapt out – single stars, constellations, and planets, brighter and bigger than any in our world. There were no clouds. The new stars and the new voices began at exactly the same time. If you had seen and heard it, as Digory did, you would have felt quite certain that it was the stars themselves which were singing, and that it was the First Voice, the deep one, which had made them appear and made them sing.

"Glory be!" said the Cabby. "I'd ha' been a better man all my life if I'd known there were things like this."

The Voice on the earth was now louder and more triumphant; but the voices in the sky, after singing loudly with it for a time, began to get fainter. And now something else was happening.

Far away, and down near the horizon, the sky began to turn grey. A light wind, very fresh, began to stir. The sky, in that one place, grew slowly and steadily paler. You could see shapes of hills standing up dark against it. All the time the Voice went on singing.

There was soon light enough for them to see one another's faces. The Cabby and the two children had open mouths and shining eyes; they were drinking in the sound, and they looked as if it reminded them of something. Uncle Andrew's mouth was open too, but not open with joy. He looked more as if his chin had simply dropped away from the rest of his face. His shoulders were stooped and his knees shook. He was not liking the Voice. If he could have got away from it by creeping into a rat's hole, he would have done so. But the Witch looked as if, in a way, she understood the music better than any of them. Her mouth was shut, her lips were pressed together, and her fists were clenched. Ever since the song began she had felt that this whole world was filled with a Magic different from hers and stronger. She hated it. She would have smashed that whole world, or all worlds, to pieces, if it would only stop the singing. The horse stood with its ears well forward, and twitching. Every now and then it snorted and stamped the ground. It no longer looked like a tired old cab-horse; you could now well believe that its father had been in battles.

The eastern sky changed from white to pink and from pink to gold. The Voice rose and rose, till all the air was shaking with it. And just as it swelled to the mightiest and most glorious sound it had yet produced, the sun arose.

Digory had never seen such a sun. The sun above the ruins of Charn had looked older than ours: this looked younger. You could imagine that it laughed for joy as it came up. And as its beams shot across the land the travellers could see for the first time what sort of place they were in. It was a valley through which a broad, swift river wound its way, flowing eastward towards the sun. Southward there were mountains, northward there were lower hills. But it was a valley of mere earth, rock and water; there was not a tree, not a bush, not a blade of grass to be seen. The earth was of many colours: they were fresh, hot and vivid. They made you feel excited; until you saw the Singer himself, and then you forgot everything else.

It was a Lion. Huge, shaggy, and bright, it stood facing the risen sun. Its mouth was wide open in song and it was about three hundred yards away.

"This is a terrible world," said the Witch. "We must fly at once. Prepare the Magic."

"I quite agree with you, Madam," said Uncle Andrew. "A most disagreeable place. Completely uncivilized. If only I were a younger man and had a gun——"

"Garn!" said the Cabby. "You don't think you could shoot 'im, do you?"

"And who *would*?" said Polly.

"Prepare the Magic, old fool," said Jadis.

"Certainly, Madam," said Uncle Andrew cunningly. "I must have both the children touching me. Put on your homeward ring at once, Digory." He wanted to get away without the Witch.

"Oh, it's *rings*, is it?" cried Jadis. She would have had her hands in Digory's pocket before you could say knife, but Digory grabbed Polly and shouted out:

"Take care. If either of you come half an inch nearer, we two will vanish and you'll be left here for good. Yes: I have a ring in my pocket that will take Polly and me home. And look! My hand is just ready. So keep your distance. I'm sorry about you" (he looked at the Cabby) "and about the horse, but I can't help that. As for you two" (he looked at Uncle Andrew and the Queen), "you're both magicians, so you ought to enjoy living together."

" 'Old your noise, everyone," said the Cabby. "I want to listen to the moosic."

For the song had now changed.

CHAPTER NINE

THE FOUNDING OF NARNIA

The Lion was pacing to and fro about that empty land and singing his new song. It was softer and more lilting than the song by which he had called up the stars and the sun; a gentle, rippling music. And as he walked and sang, the valley grew green with grass. It spread out from the Lion like a pool. It ran up the sides of the little hills like a wave. In a few minutes it was creeping up the lower slopes of the distant mountains, making that young world every moment softer. The light wind could now be heard ruffling the grass. Soon there were other things besides grass. The higher slopes grew dark with heather. Patches of rougher and more bristling green appeared in the valley. Digory did not know what they were until one began coming up quite close to him. It was a little, spiky thing that threw out dozens of arms and covered these arms with green and grew larger at the rate of about an inch every two seconds. There were dozens of these things all round him now. When they were nearly as tall as himself he saw what they were. "Trees!" he exclaimed.

The nuisance of it, as Polly said afterwards, was that you weren't left in peace to watch it all. Just as Digory said "Trees!" he had to jump because Uncle Andrew had sidled up to him again and was going to pick his pocket. It wouldn't have done Uncle Andrew much good if he had succeeded, for he was aiming at the right-hand pocket because he still thought the green rings were "homeward" rings. But of course Digory didn't want to lose either.

"Stop!" cried the Witch. "Stand back. No, further back. If anyone goes within ten paces of either of the children, I will knock out his brains." She was poising in her hand the iron bar that she had torn off the lamp-post, ready to throw it. Somehow no one doubted that she would be a very good shot.

"So!" she said. "You would steal back to your own world with the boy and leave me here."

Uncle Andrew's temper at last got the better of his fears. "Yes, Ma'am, I would," he said. "Most undoubtedly I would. I should be perfectly in my rights. I have been most shamefully, most abominably treated. I have done my best to show you such civilities as were in my power. And what has been my reward? You have robbed – I must repeat the word – *robbed* a highly respectable jeweller. You have insisted on my entertaining you to an exceedingly expensive, not to say ostentatious, lunch, though I was obliged to pawn my watch and chain in order to do so (and let me tell you, Ma'am, that none of our family have been in the habit of frequenting pawnshops, except my cousin Edward, and he was in the Yeomanry). During that indigestible meal – I'm feeling the worse for it at this very moment – your behaviour and conversation attracted the unfavourable attention of everyone present. I feel I have been publicly disgraced. I shall never be able to show my face in that restaurant again. You have assaulted the police. You have stolen——"

"Oh stow it, Guv'nor, do stow it," said the Cabby. "Watchin' and listenin's the thing at present; not talking."

There was certainly plenty to watch and to listen to. The tree which Digory had noticed was now a full-grown beech whose branches swayed gently above his head. They stood on cool, green grass, sprinkled with daisies and buttercups. A little way off, along the river bank, willows were growing. On the other side tangles of flowering currant, lilac, wild rose, and rhododendron closed them in. The horse was tearing up delicious mouthfuls of new grass.

All this time the Lion's song, and his stately prowl, to and fro, backwards and forwards, was going on. What was rather alarming was that at each turn he came a little nearer. Polly was finding the song more and more interesting because she thought she was beginning to see the connection between the music and the things that were happening. When a line of dark firs sprang up on a ridge about a hundred yards away she felt that they were connected with a series of deep, prolonged notes which the Lion had sung a second before. And when he burst into a rapid series of lighter notes she was not surprised to see primroses suddenly appearing in every direction. Thus, with an unspeakable thrill, she felt quite certain that all the things were coming (as she said) "out of the Lion's head". When you listened to his song you heard the things he was making up: when you looked around you, you saw them. This was so exciting that she had no time to be afraid. But Digory and the Cabby could not help feeling a bit nervous as each turn of the Lion's walk brought him nearer. As for Uncle Andrew, his teeth were chattering, but his knees were shaking so that he could not run away.

Suddenly the Witch stepped boldly out towards the Lion. It was coming on, always singing, with a slow, heavy pace. It was only twelve yards away. She raised her arm and flung the iron bar straight at its head.

Nobody, least of all Jadis, could have missed at that range. The bar struck the Lion fair between the eyes. It glanced off and fell with a thud in the grass. The Lion came on. Its walk was neither slower nor faster than before; you could not tell whether it even knew it had been hit. Though its soft pads made no noise, you could feel the earth shake beneath their weight.

The Witch shrieked and ran; in a few moments she was out of sight among the trees. Uncle Andrew turned to do likewise, tripped over a root, and fell flat on his face in a little brook that ran down to join the river. The children could not move. They were not even quite sure that they wanted to. The Lion paid no attention to them. Its huge red mouth was open, but open in song not in a snarl. It passed by them so close that they could have touched its mane. They were terribly afraid it would turn and look at them, yet in some queer way they wished it would. But for all the notice it took of them they might just as well have been invisible and unsmellable. When it had passed them and gone a few paces further it turned, passed them again, and continued its march eastward.

Uncle Andrew, coughing and spluttering, picked himself up.

"Now, Digory," he said, "we've got rid of that woman, and the brute of a lion is gone. Give me your hand and put on your ring at once."

"Keep off," said Digory, backing away from him. "Keep clear of him, Polly. Come over here beside me. Now I warn you, Uncle Andrew, don't come one step nearer, we'll just vanish."

"Do what you're told this minute, sir," said Uncle Andrew. "You're an extremely disobedient, ill-behaved little boy."

"No fear," said Digory. "We want to stay and see what happens. I thought you wanted to know about other worlds. Don't you like it now you're here?"

"Like it!" exclaimed Uncle Andrew. "Just look at the state I'm in. And it was my best coat and waistcoat, too." He certainly was a dreadful sight by now: for of course, the more dressed up you were to begin with, the worse you look after you've crawled out of a smashed hansom-cab and fallen into a muddy brook. "I'm not saying," he added, "that this is not a most interesting place. If I were a younger man, now – perhaps I could get some lively young fellow to come here first. One of those big-game hunters. Something might be made of this country. The climate is delightful. I never felt such air. I believe it would have done me good if — if circumstances had been more favourable. If only we'd had a gun."

"Guns be blowed," said the Cabby. "I think I'll go and see if I can give Strawberry a rub down. That horse 'as more sense than some 'umans as I could mention." He walked back to Strawberry and began making the hissing noises that grooms make.

"Do you still think *that* Lion could be killed by a gun?" asked Digory. "He didn't mind the iron bar much."

"With all her faults," said Uncle Andrew, "that's a plucky gel, my boy. It was a spirited thing to do." He rubbed his hands and cracked his knuckles, as if he were once more forgetting how the Witch frightened him whenever she was really there.

"It was a wicked thing to do," said Polly. "What harm had he done her?"

"Hullo! What's that?" said Digory. He had darted forward to examine something only a few yards away. "I say, Polly," he called back. "Do come and look."

Uncle Andrew came with her; not because he wanted to see but because he wanted to keep close to the children — there might be a chance of stealing their rings. But when he saw what Digory was looking at, even he began to take an interest. It was a perfect little model of a lamp-post, about three feet high but lengthening, and thickening in proportion, as they watched it; in fact growing just as the trees had grown.

"It's alive too — I mean, it's lit," said Digory. And so it was; though of course the brightness of the sun made the little flame in the lantern hard to see unless your shadow fell on it.

"Remarkable, most remarkable," muttered Uncle Andrew. "Even I never dreamt of Magic like this. We're in a world where everything, even a lamp-post, comes to life and grows. Now I wonder what sort of seed a lamp-post grows from?"

"Don't you see?" said Digory. "This is where the bar fell — the bar she tore off the lamp-post at home. It sank into the ground and now it's coming up as a young lamp-post." (But not so very young now; it was as tall as Digory while he said this.)

"That's it! Stupendous, stupendous," said Uncle Andrew, rubbing his hands harder than ever. "Ho, ho! They laughed at my Magic. That fool of a sister of mine thinks I'm a lunatic. I wonder what they'll say now? I have discovered a world where everything is bursting with life and growth. Columbus, now, they talk about Columbus. But what was America to this? The commercial possibilities of this country are unbounded. Bring a few old bits of scrap iron here, bury 'em, and up they come as brand new railway engines, battleships, anything you please. They'll cost nothing, and I can sell 'em at full prices in England. I shall be a millionaire. And then the climate! I feel years younger already. I can run it as a health resort. A good sanatorium here might be worth twenty thousand a year. Of course I shall have to let a few people into the secret. The first thing is to get that brute shot."

"You're just like the Witch," said Polly. "All you think of is killing things."

"And then as regards oneself," Uncle Andrew continued in a happy dream, "there's no knowing how long I might live if I settled here. And that's a big consideration when a fellow has turned sixty. I shouldn't be surprised if I never grew a day older in this country! Stupendous! The land of youth!"

"Oh!" cried Digory. "The land of youth! Do you think it really is?" For of course he remembered what Aunt Letty had said to the lady who brought the grapes, and that sweet hope rushed back upon him. "Uncle Andrew," he said, "do you think there's anything here that would cure Mother?"

"What are you talking about?" said Uncle Andrew. "This isn't a chemist's shop. But as I was saying—"

"You don't care twopence about her," said Digory savagely. "I thought you might; after all, she's your sister as well as my Mother. Well, no matter. I'm jolly well going to ask the Lion himself if he can help me." And he turned and walked briskly away. Polly waited for a moment and then went after him.

"Here! Stop! Come back! The boy's gone mad," said Uncle Andrew. He followed the children at a cautious distance behind; for he didn't want to get too far away from the green rings or too near the Lion.

In a few minutes Digory came to the edge of the wood and there he stopped. The Lion was singing still. But now the song had once more changed. It was more like what we should call a tune, but it was also far wilder. It made you want to run and jump and climb. It made you want to shout. It made you want to rush at other people and either hug them or fight them. It made Digory hot and red in the face. It had some effect on Uncle Andrew, for Digory could hear him saying, "A spirited gel, sir. It's a pity about her temper, but a dem fine woman all the same, a dem fine woman." But what the song did to the two humans was nothing compared with what it was doing to the country.

Can you imagine a stretch of grassy land bubbling like water in a pot? For that is really the best description of what was happening. In all directions it was swelling into humps. They were of very different sizes, some no bigger than molehills, some as big as wheelbarrows, two the size of cottages. And the humps moved and swelled till they burst, and the crumbled earth poured out of them, and from each hump there came out an animal. The moles came out just as you might see a mole come out in England. The dogs came out, barking the moment their heads were free, and struggling as you've seen them do when they are getting through a narrow hole in a hedge. The stags were the queerest to watch, for of course the antlers came up a long time before the rest of them, so at first Digory thought they were trees. The frogs, who all came up near the river, went straight into it with a plop-plop and a loud croaking. The panthers, leopards and things of that sort, sat down at once to wash the loose earth off their hind quarters and then stood up against the trees to sharpen their front claws. Showers of birds came out of the trees. Butterflies fluttered. Bees got to work on the flowers as if they hadn't a second to lose. But the greatest moment of all was when the biggest hump broke like a small earthquake and out came the sloping back, the large, wise head, and the four baggy-trousered legs of an elephant. And now you could hardly hear the song of the Lion; there was so much cawing, cooing, crowing, braying, neighing, baying, barking, lowing, bleating, and trumpeting.

But though Digory could no longer hear the Lion, he could see it. It was so big and so bright that he could not take his eyes off it. The other animals did not appear to be afraid of it. Indeed, at that very moment, Digory heard the sound of hooves from behind; a second later the old cab-horse trotted past him and joined the other beasts. (The air had apparently suited him as well as it had suited Uncle Andrew. He no longer looked like the poor old slave he had been in London; he was picking up his feet and holding his head erect.) And now, for the first time, the Lion was quite silent. He was going to and fro among the animals. And every now and then he would go up to two of them (always two at a time) and touch their noses with his. He would touch two beavers among all the beavers, two leopards among all the leopards, one stag and one deer among all the deer, and leave the rest. Some sorts of animal he passed over altogether. But the pairs which he had touched instantly left their own kinds and followed him. At last he stood still and all the creatures whom he had touched came and stood in a wide circle around him. The others whom he had not touched began to wander away. Their noises faded gradually into the distance. The chosen beasts who remained were now utterly silent, all with their eyes fixed intently upon the Lion. The cat-like ones gave an occasional twitch of the tail but otherwise all were still. For the first time that day there was complete silence, except for the noise of running water. Digory's heart beat wildly; he knew something very solemn was going to be done. He had not forgotten about his Mother, but he knew jolly well that, even for her, he couldn't interrupt a thing like this.

The Lion, whose eyes never blinked, stared at the animals as hard as if he was going to burn them up with his mere stare. And gradually a change came over them. The smaller ones – the rabbits, moles and such-like – grew a good deal larger. The very big ones – you noticed it most with the elephants – grew a little smaller. Many animals sat up on their hind legs. Most put their heads on one side as if they were trying very hard to understand. The Lion opened his mouth, but no sound came from it; he was breathing out, a long, warm breath; it seemed to sway all the beasts as the wind sways a line of trees. Far overhead from beyond the veil of blue sky which hid them the stars sang again; a pure, cold, difficult music. Then there came a swift flash like fire (but it burnt nobody) either from the sky or from the Lion itself, and every drop of blood tingled in the children's bodies, and the deepest, wildest voice they had ever heard was saying:

"Narnia, Narnia, Narnia, awake. Love. Think. Speak. Be walking trees. Be talking beasts. Be divine waters."

CHAPTER TEN

THE FIRST JOKE AND OTHER MATTERS

It was of course the Lion's voice. The children had long felt sure that he could speak: yet it was a lovely and terrible shock when he did.

Out of the trees wild people stepped forth, gods Fauns and Satyrs and Dwarfs. Out of the river rose the river god with his Naiad daughters. And all these and all the beasts and birds in their different voices, low or high or thick or clear, replied:

"Hail, Aslan. We hear and obey. We are awake. We love. We think. We speak. We know."

"But please, we don't know very much yet," said a nosey and snorty kind of voice. And that really did make the children jump, for it was the cab-horse who had spoken.

"Good old Strawberry," said Polly. "I *am* glad he was one of the ones picked out to be a Talking Beast." And the Cabby, who was now standing beside the children, said, "Strike me pink. I always did say that 'oss 'ad a lot of sense, though."

"Creatures, I give you yourselves," said the strong, happy voice of Aslan. "I give to you for ever this land of Narnia. I give you the woods, the fruits, the rivers. I give you the stars and I give you myself. The Dumb Beasts whom I have not chosen are yours also. Treat them gently and cherish them but do not go back to their ways lest you cease to be Talking Beasts. For out of them you were taken and into them you can return. Do not so."

"No, Aslan, we won't, we won't," said everyone. But one perky jackdaw added in a loud voice, "No fear!" and everyone else had finished just before he said it so that his words came out quite clear in a dead silence; and

perhaps you have found out how awful that can be – say, at a party.
The Jackdaw became so embarrassed that it hid its head under its wings as if it was going to sleep. And all the other animals began making various queer noises which are their ways of laughing and which, of course, no one has ever heard in our world. They tried at first to repress it, but Aslan said:

"Laugh and fear not, creatures. Now that you are no longer dumb and witless, you need not always be grave. For jokes as well as justice come in with speech."

So they all let themselves go. And there was such merriment that the Jackdaw himself plucked up courage again and perched on the cab-horse's head, between its ears, clapping its wings, and said:

"Aslan! Aslan! Have I made the first joke? Will everybody always be told how I made the first joke?"

"No, little friend," said the Lion. "You have not *made* the first joke, you have only *been* the first joke." Then everyone laughed more than ever; but the Jackdaw didn't mind and laughed just as loud till the horse shook its head and the Jackdaw lost its balance and fell off, but remembered its wings (they were still new to it) before it reached the ground.

"And now," said Aslan, "Narnia is established. We must next take thought for keeping it safe. I will call some of you to my council. Come hither to me, you the chief Dwarf, and you the River-god, and you Oak and the He-Owl, and both the Ravens and the Bull-Elephant. We must talk together. For though the world is not five hours old an evil has already entered it."

The creatures he had named came forward and he turned away eastward with them. The others all began talking, saying things like "*What did he say had entered the world? – A Neevil – What's a Neevil? – No, he didn't say a Neevil, he said a weevil – Well, what's that?*"

"Look here," said Digory to Polly, "I've got to go after him – Aslan, I mean, the Lion. I must speak to him."

"Do you think we can?" said Polly. "I wouldn't dare."

"I've got to," said Digory. "It's about Mother. If anyone could give me something that would do her good, it would be him."

"I'll come along with you," said the Cabby. "I liked the looks of 'im. And I don't reckon these other beasts will go for us. And I want a word with old Strawberry."

So all three of them stepped out boldly – or as boldly as they could – towards the assembly of animals. The creatures were so busy talking to one another and making friends that they didn't notice the three humans until they were very close; nor did they hear Uncle Andrew, who was standing trembling in his buttoned boots a good way off and shouting (but by no means at the top of his voice):

"Digory! Come back! Come back at once when you're told. I forbid you to go a step further."

When at last they were right in among the animals, the animals all stopped talking and stared at them.

"Well?" said the He-Beaver at last. "What, in the name of Aslan, are these?"

"Please," began Digory in rather a breathless voice, when a Rabbit said, "They're a kind of large lettuce, that's my belief."

"No, we're not, honestly we're not," said Polly hastily. "We're not at all nice to eat."

"There!" said the Mole. "They can talk. Who ever heard of a talking lettuce?"

"Perhaps they're the Second Joke," suggested the Jackdaw.

A Panther, which had been washing its face, stopped for a moment to say, "Well, if they are, they're nothing like so good as the first one. At least, *I* don't see anything very funny about them." It yawned and went on with its wash.

"Oh, please," said Digory. "I'm in such a hurry. I want to see the Lion."

All this time the Cabby had been trying to catch Strawberry's eye. Now he did. "Now, Strawberry, old boy," he said. "You know me. You ain't going to stand there and say as you don't know me."

"What's the thing talking about, Horse?" said several voices.

"Well," said Strawberry very slowly, "I don't exactly know. I think most of us don't know much about anything yet. But I've a sort of idea I've seen a thing like this before. I've a feeling I lived somewhere else – or was something else – before Aslan woke us all up a few minutes ago. It's all very muddled. Like a dream. But there were things like these three in the dream."

"What?" said the Cabby. "Not know me? Me what used to bring you a hot mash of an evening when you was out of sorts? Me what rubbed you down proper? Me what never forgot to put your cloth on you if you was standing in the cold? I wouldn't 'ave thought it of you, Strawberry."

"It *does* begin to come back," said the Horse thoughtfully. "Yes. Let me think now, let me think. Yes, you used to tie a horrid black thing behind me and then hit me to make me run, and however far I ran this black thing would always be coming rattle-rattle behind me."

"We 'ad our living to earn, see," said the Cabby. "Yours the same as mine. And if there 'adn't been no work and no whip there'd 'ave been no stable, no hay, no mash, and no oats. For you did get a taste of oats when I could afford 'em, which no one can deny."

"Oats?" said the Horse, pricking up his ears. "Yes, I remember something about that. Yes, I remember more and more. You were always sitting up somewhere behind, and I was always running in front, pulling you and the black thing. I know I did all the work."

"Summer, I grant you," said the Cabby. " 'Ot work for you and a cool seat for me. But what about winter, old boy, when you was keeping yourself warm and I was sitting up there with my feet like ice and my nose fair pinched off me with the wind, and my 'ands that numb I couldn't 'ardly 'old the reins?"

"It was a hard, cruel country," said Strawberry. "There was no grass. All hard stones."

"Too true, mate, too true!" said the Cabby. "A 'ard world it was. I always did say those paving-stones weren't fair on any 'oss. That's Lunn'on, that is. I didn't like it no more than what you did. You were a country 'oss, and I was a country man. Used to sing in the choir, I did, down at 'ome. But there wasn't a living for me there."

"Oh please, please," said Digory. "Could we get on? The Lion's getting further and further away. And I do want to speak to him so dreadfully badly."

"Look 'ere, Strawberry," said the Cabby. "This young gen'leman 'as something on his mind that he wants to talk to the Lion about; 'im you call Aslan. Suppose you was to let 'im ride on your back (which 'e'd take it very kindly) and trot 'im over to where the Lion is. And me and the little girl will be following along."

"Ride?" said Strawberry. "Oh, I remember now. That means sitting on my back. I remember there used to be a little one of you two-leggers who used to do that long ago. He used to have little hard, square lumps of some white stuff that he gave me. They tasted – oh, wonderful, sweeter than grass."

"Ah, that'd be sugar," said the Cabby.

"Please, Strawberry," begged Digory, "do, do let me get up and take me to Aslan."

"Well, I don't mind," said the Horse. "Not for once in a way. Up you get."

"Good old Strawberry," said the Cabby. "'Ere, young 'un, I'll give you a lift." Digory was soon on Strawberry's back, and quite comfortable, for he had ridden bare-back before on his own pony.

"Now, do gee up, Strawberry," he said.

"You don't happen to have a bit of that white stuff about you, I suppose?" said the Horse.

"No. I'm afraid I haven't," said Digory.

"Well, it can't be helped," said Strawberry, and off they went.

At that moment a large Bulldog, who had been sniffing and staring very hard, said:

"Look! Isn't there another of these queer creatures – over there, beside the river, under the trees?"

Then all the animals looked and saw Uncle Andrew, standing very still among the rhododendrons and hoping he wouldn't be noticed.

"Come on!" said several voices. "Let's go and find out." So, while Strawberry was briskly trotting away with Digory in one direction (and Polly and the Cabby were following on foot) most of the creatures rushed towards Uncle Andrew with roars, barks, grunts, and various noises of cheerful interest.

We must now go back a bit and explain what the whole scene had looked like from Uncle Andrew's point of view. It had not made at all the same impression on him as on the Cabby and the children. For what you see and hear depends a good deal on where you are standing: it also depends on what sort of person you are.

Ever since the animals had first appeared, Uncle Andrew had been shrinking further and further back into the thicket. He watched them very hard of course; but he wasn't really interested in seeing what they were doing, only in seeing whether they were going to make a rush at him. Like the Witch, he was dreadfully practical. He simply didn't notice that Aslan was choosing one pair out of every kind of beasts. All he saw, or thought he saw, was a lot of dangerous wild animals walking vaguely about. And he kept on wondering why the other animals didn't run away from the big Lion.

When the great moment came and the Beasts spoke, he missed the whole point; for a rather interesting reason. When the Lion had first begun singing, long ago when it was still quite dark, he had realized that the noise was a song. And he had disliked the song very much. It made him think and feel things he did not want to think and feel. Then, when the sun rose and he saw that the singer was a lion (*"only* a lion," as he said to himself) he tried his hardest to make believe that it wasn't singing and never had been singing – only roaring as any lion might in a zoo in our own world. "Of course it can't really have been singing," he thought, "I must have imagined it. I've been letting my nerves get out of order. Who ever heard of a lion singing?" And the longer and more beautifully the Lion sang, the harder Uncle Andrew tried to make himself believe that he could hear nothing but roaring. Now the trouble about trying to make yourself stupider than you really are is that you very often succeed. Uncle Andrew did. He soon did hear nothing but roaring in Aslan's song. Soon he couldn't have heard anything else even if he had wanted to. And when at last the Lion spoke and said, "Narnia, awake," he didn't hear any words: he heard only a snarl. And when the Beasts spoke in answer, he heard only barkings, growlings, baying, and howlings. And when they laughed – well, you can imagine. That was worse for Uncle Andrew than anything that had happened yet. Such a horrid, bloodthirsty din of hungry and angry brutes he had never heard in his life. Then, to his utter rage and horror, he saw the other three humans actually walking out into the open to meet the animals.

"The fools!" he said to himself. "Now those brutes will eat the rings along with the children and I'll never be able to get home again. What a selfish little boy that Digory is! And the others are just as bad. If they want to throw away their own lives, that's their business. But what about *me*? They don't seem to think of that. No one thinks of *me*."

Finally, when a whole crowd of animals came rushing towards him, he turned and ran for his life. And now anyone could see that the air of that young world was really doing the old gentleman good. In London he had been far too old to run: now, he ran at a speed which would have made him certain to win the hundred yards' race at any Prep school in England. His coat-tails flying out behind him were a fine sight. But of course it was no use. Many of the animals behind him were swift ones; it was the first run they had ever taken in their lives and they were all longing to use their new muscles. "After him! After him!" they shouted. "Perhaps he's that Neevil! Tally-ho! Tantivy! Cut him off! Round him up! Keep it up! Hurray!"

In a very few minutes some of them got ahead of him. They lined up in a row and barred his way. Others hemmed him in from behind. Wherever he looked he saw terrors. Antlers of great elks and the huge face of an elephant towered over him. Heavy, serious-minded bears and boars grunted behind him. Cool-looking leopards and panthers with sarcastic faces (as he thought) stared at him and waved their tails. What struck him most of all was the number of open mouths. The animals had really opened their mouths to pant; he thought they had opened their mouths to eat him.

Uncle Andrew stood trembling and swaying this way and that. He had never liked animals at the best of times, being usually rather afraid of them; and of course years of doing cruel experiments on animals had made him hate and fear them far more.

"Now, sir," said the Bulldog in his business-like way, "are you animal, vegetable, or mineral?" That was what it really said; but all Uncle Andrew heard was "Gr-r-r-arrh-ow!"

Chapter Eleven

Digory and his Uncle are Both in Trouble

You may think the animals were very stupid not to see at once that Uncle Andrew was the same kind of creature as the two children and the Cabby. But you must remember that the animals knew nothing about clothes. They thought that Polly's frock and Digory's Norfolk suit and the Cabby's bowler hat were as much parts of them as their own fur and feathers. They wouldn't have known even that those three were all of the same kind if they hadn't spoken to them and if Strawberry had not seemed to think so. And Uncle Andrew was a great deal taller than the children and a good deal thinner than the Cabby. He was all in black except for his white waistcoat (not very white by now), and the great grey mop of his hair (now very wild indeed) didn't look to them like anything they had seen in the three other humans. So it was only natural that they should be puzzled. Worst of all, he didn't seem to be able to talk.

He had tried to. When the Bulldog spoke to him (or, as he thought, first snarled and then growled at him) he held out his shaking hand and gasped "Good Doggie, then, poor old fellow." But the beasts could not understand him any more than he could understand them. They didn't hear any words: only a vague sizzling noise. Perhaps it was just as well they didn't, for no dog that I ever knew, least of all a Talking Dog of Narnia, likes being called a "Good Doggie then"; any more than you would like being called "My Little Man".

Then Uncle Andrew dropped down in a dead faint.

"There!" said a Warthog. "It's only a tree. I always thought so." (Remember, they had never yet seen a faint or even a fall.)

The Bulldog, who had been sniffing Uncle Andrew all over, raised its head and said, "It's an animal. Certainly an animal. And probably the same kind as those other ones."

"I don't see that," said one of the Bears. "An animal wouldn't just roll over like that. We're animals and we don't roll over. We stand up. Like this." He rose to his hind legs, took a step backwards, tripped over a low branch and fell flat on his back.

"The Third Joke, the Third Joke, the Third Joke!" said the Jackdaw in great excitement.

"I still think it's a sort of tree," said the Warthog.

"If it's a tree," said the Other Bear, "there might be a bees' nest in it."

"I'm sure it's not a tree," said the Badger. "I had a sort of idea it was trying to speak before it toppled over."

"That was only the wind in its branches," said the Warthog.

"You surely don't mean," said the Jackdaw to the Badger, "that you think it's a *talking* animal! It didn't say any words."

"And yet, you know," said the Elephant (the She-Elephant, of course; her husband, as you remember, had been called away by Aslan), "and yet, you know, it might be an animal of some kind. Mightn't the whitish lump at this end be a sort of face? And couldn't those holes be eyes and a mouth? No nose, of course. But then — ahem — one mustn't be narrow-minded. Very few of us have what could exactly be called a Nose." She squinted down the length of her own trunk with pardonable pride.

"I object to that remark very strongly," said the Bulldog.

"The Elephant is quite right," said the Tapir.

"I tell you what!" said the Donkey brightly. "Perhaps it's an animal that can't talk but thinks it can."

"Can it be made to stand up?" said the Elephant thoughtfully. She took the limp form of Uncle Andrew gently in her trunk and set him up on end: upside down, unfortunately, so that two half-sovereigns, three half-crowns, and a sixpence fell out of his pocket. But it was no use. Uncle Andrew merely collapsed again.

"There!" said several voices. "It isn't an animal at all. It's not alive."

"I tell you, it *is* an animal," said the Bulldog. "Smell it for yourself."

"Smelling isn't everything," said the Elephant.

"Why," said the Bulldog, "if a fellow can't trust his nose, what is he to trust?"

"Well, his brains perhaps," she replied mildly.

"I object to that remark very strongly," said the Bulldog.

"Well, we must do something about it," said the Elephant. "Because it may be the Neevil, and it must be shown to Aslan. What do most of us think? Is it an animal or something of the tree kind?"

"Tree! Tree!" said a dozen voices.

"Very well," said the Elephant. "Then, if it's a tree it wants to be planted. We must dig a hole."

The two Moles settled that part of the business pretty quickly. There was some dispute as to which way up Uncle Andrew ought to be put into the hole, and he had a very narrow escape from being put in head foremost. Several animals said his legs must be his branches and therefore the grey, fluffy thing (they meant his head) must be his root. But then others said that the forked end of him was the muddier and that it spread out more, as roots ought to do. So finally he was planted right way up. When they had patted down the earth it came up above his knees.

"It looks dreadfully withered," said the Donkey.

"Of course it wants some watering," said the Elephant. "I think I *might* say (meaning no offence to anyone present) that, perhaps, for *that* sort of work, my kind of nose—"

"I object to that remark very strongly," said the Bulldog. But the Elephant walked quietly to the river, filled her trunk with water, and came back to attend to Uncle Andrew. The sagacious animal went on doing this till gallons of water had been squirted over him, and water was running out of the skirts of his frock-coat as if he had been for a bath with all his clothes on. In the end it revived him. He awoke from his faint. What a wakening it was! But we must leave him to think over his wicked deeds (if he was likely to do anything so sensible) and turn to more important things.

Strawberry trotted on with Digory on his back till the noise of the other animals died away, and now the little group of Aslan and his chosen councillors was quite close. Digory knew that he couldn't possibly break in on so solemn a meeting, but there was no need to do so. At a word from Aslan, the He-Elephant, the Ravens, and all the rest of them drew aside. Digory slipped off the horse and found himself face to face with Aslan. And Aslan was bigger and more beautiful and more brightly golden and more terrible than he had thought. He dared not look into the great eyes.

"Please – Mr Lion – Aslan – Sir," said Digory, "could you – may I – please, will you give me some magic fruit of this country to make Mother well?"

He had been desperately hoping that the Lion would say "Yes"; he had been horribly afraid it might say "No". But he was taken aback when it did neither.

"This is the Boy," said Aslan, looking, not at Digory, but at his councillors. "This is the Boy who did it."

"Oh dear," thought Digory, "what have I done now?"

"Son of Adam," said the Lion. "There is an evil Witch abroad in my new land of Narnia. Tell these good Beasts how she came here."

A dozen different things that he might say flashed through Digory's mind, but he had the sense to say nothing except the exact truth.

"I brought her, Aslan," he answered in a low voice.

"For what purpose?"

"I wanted to get her out of my own world back into her own. I thought I was taking her back to her own place."

"How came she to be in your world, Son of Adam?"

"By — by Magic."

The Lion said nothing and Digory knew that he had not told enough.

"It was my Uncle, Aslan," he said. "He sent us out of our own world by magic rings, at least I had to go because he sent Polly first, and then we met the Witch in a place called Charn and she just held on to us when—"

"You *met* the Witch?" said Aslan in a low voice which had the threat of a growl in it.

"She woke up," said Digory wretchedly. And then, turning very white, "I mean, I woke her. Because I wanted to know what would happen if I struck a bell. Polly didn't want to. It wasn't her fault. I — I fought her. I know I shouldn't have. I think I was a bit enchanted by the writing under the bell."

"Do you?" asked Aslan; still speaking very low and deep.

"No," said Digory. "I see now I wasn't. I was only pretending."

There was a long pause. And Digory was thinking all the time, "I've spoiled everything. There's no chance of getting anything for Mother now."

When the Lion spoke again, it was not to Digory.

"You see, friends," he said, "that before the new, clean world I gave you is seven hours old, a force of evil has already entered it; waked and brought hither by this son of Adam." The Beasts, even Strawberry, all turned their eyes on Digory till he felt that he wished the ground would swallow him up. "But do not be cast down," said Aslan, still speaking to the Beasts. "Evil will come of that evil, but it is still a long way off, and I will see to it that the worst falls upon myself. In the meantime, let us take such order that for many hundred years yet this shall be a merry land in a merry world. And as Adam's race has done the harm, Adam's race shall help to heal it. Draw near, you other two."

The last words were spoken to Polly and the Cabby who had now arrived. Polly, all eyes and mouth, was staring at Aslan and holding the Cabby's hand rather tightly. The Cabby gave one glance at the Lion, and took off his bowler hat: no one had yet seen him without it. When it was off, he looked younger and nicer, and more like a countryman and less like a London cabman.

"Son," said Aslan to the Cabby. "I have known you long. Do you know me?"

"Well, no, sir," said the Cabby. "Leastways, not in an ordinary manner of speaking. Yet I feel somehow, if I may make so free, as 'ow we've met before."

"It is well," said the Lion. "You know better than you think you know, and you shall live to know me better yet. How does this land please you?"

"It's a fair treat, sir," said the Cabby.

"Would you like to live here always?"

"Well, you see, sir, I'm a married man," said the Cabby. "If my wife was here neither of us would ever want to go back to London, I reckon. We're both country folks really."

Aslan threw up his shaggy head, opened his mouth, and uttered a long, single note; not very loud, but full of power. Polly's heart jumped in her body when she heard it. She felt sure that it was a call, and that anyone who heard that call would want to obey it and (what's more) would be able to obey it, however many worlds and ages lay between. And so, though she was filled with wonder, she was not really astonished or shocked when all of a sudden a young woman, with a kind, honest face stepped out of nowhere and stood beside her. Polly knew at once that it was the Cabby's wife, fetched out of our world not by any tiresome magic rings, but quickly, simply and sweetly as a bird flies to its nest. The young woman had apparently been in the middle of a washing day, for she wore an apron, her sleeves were rolled up to the elbow, and there were soapsuds on her hands. If she had had time to put on her good clothes (her best hat had imitation cherries on it) she would have looked dreadful; as it was, she looked rather nice.

Of course she thought she was dreaming. That was why she didn't rush across to her husband and ask him what on earth had happened to them both. But when she looked at the Lion she didn't feel quite so sure it was a dream, yet for some reason she did not appear to be very frightened. Then she dropped a little half curtsey, as some country girls still knew how to do in those days. After that, she went and put her hand in the Cabby's and stood there looking round her a little shyly.

"My children," said Aslan, fixing his eyes on both of them, "you are to be the first King and Queen of Narnia."

The Cabby opened his mouth in astonishment, and his wife turned very red.

"You shall rule and name all these creatures, and do justice among them, and protect them from their enemies when enemies arise. And enemies will arise, for there is an evil Witch in this world."

The Cabby swallowed hard two or three times and cleared his throat.

"Begging your pardon, sir," he said, "and thanking you very much I'm sure (which my Missus does the same) but I ain't no sort of a chap for a job like that. I never 'ad much eddycation, you see."

"Well," said Aslan, "can you use a spade and a plough and raise food out of the earth?"

"Yes, sir, I could do a bit of that sort of work: being brought up to it, like."

"Can you rule these creatures kindly and fairly, remembering that they are not slaves like the dumb beasts of the world you were born in, but Talking Beasts and free subjects?"

"I see that, sir," replied the Cabby. "I'd try to do the square thing by them all."

"And would you bring up your children and grandchildren to do the same?"

"It'd be up to me to try, sir. I'd do my best: wouldn't we, Nellie?"

"And you wouldn't have favourites either among your own children or among the other creatures, or let any hold another under or use it hardly?"

"I never could abide such goings on, sir, and that's the truth. I'd give 'em what for if I caught 'em at it," said the Cabby. (All through this conversation his voice was growing slower and richer. More like the country voice he must have had as a boy and less like the sharp, quick voice of a cockney.)

"And if enemies came against the land (for enemies will arise) and there was war, would you be the first in the charge and the last in the retreat?"

"Well, sir," said the Cabby very slowly, "a chap don't exactly know till he's been tried. I dare say I might turn out ever such a soft 'un. Never did no fighting except with my fists. I'd try – that is, I 'ope I'd try – to do my bit."

"Then," said Aslan, "you will have done all that a King should do. Your coronation will be held presently. And you and your children and grandchildren shall be blessed, and some will be Kings of Narnia, and others will be Kings of Archenland which lies yonder over the Southern Mountains. And you, little Daughter (here he turned to Polly) are welcome. Have you forgiven the Boy for the violence he did you in the hall of images in the desolate palace of accursed Charn?"

"Yes, Aslan, we've made it up," said Polly.

"That is well," said Aslan. "And now for the Boy himself."

CHAPTER TWELVE

STRAWBERRY'S ADVENTURE

Digory kept his mouth very tight shut. He had been growing more and more uncomfortable. He hoped that, whatever happened, he wouldn't blub or do anything ridiculous.

"Son of Adam," said Aslan. "Are you ready to undo the wrong that you have done to my sweet country of Narnia on the very day of its birth?"

"Well, I don't see what I can do," said Digory. "You see, the Queen ran away and—"

"I asked, are you ready?" said the Lion.

"Yes," said Digory. He had had for a second some wild idea of saying, "I'll try to help you if you'll promise to help my Mother," but he realized in time that the Lion was not at all the sort of person one could try to make bargains with. But when he had said "Yes", he thought of his Mother, and he thought of the great hopes he had had, and how they were all dying away, and a lump came in his throat and tears in his eyes, and he blurted out:

"But please, please – won't you – can't you give me something that will cure Mother?" Up till then he had been looking at the Lion's great feet and the huge claws on them; now, in his despair, he looked up at its face. What he saw surprised him as much as anything in his whole life. For the tawny face was bent down near his own and (wonder of wonders) great shining tears stood in the Lion's eyes. They were such big, bright tears compared with Digory's own that for a moment he felt as if the Lion must really be sorrier about his Mother than he was himself.

"My son, my son," said Aslan. "I know. Grief is great. Only you and I in this land know that yet. Let us be good to one another. But I have to think of hundreds of years in the life of Narnia. The Witch whom you have brought into this world will come back to Narnia again. But it need not be yet. It is my wish to plant in Narnia a tree that she will not dare to approach, and that tree will protect Narnia from her for many years. So this land shall have a long, bright morning before any clouds come over the sun. You must get me the seed from which that tree is to grow."

"Yes, sir," said Digory. He didn't know how it was to be done but he felt quite sure now that he would be able to do it. The Lion drew a deep breath, stooped its head even lower and gave him a Lion's kiss. And at once Digory felt that new strength and courage had gone into him.

"Dear son," said Aslan, "I will tell you what you must do. Turn and look to the West and tell me what do you see?"

"I see terribly big mountains, Aslan," said Digory. "I see this river coming down cliffs in a waterfall. And beyond the cliff there are high green hills with forests. And beyond those there are higher ranges that look almost black. And then, far away, there are big snowy mountains all heaped up together – like pictures of the Alps. And behind those there's nothing but the sky."

"You see well," said the Lion. "Now the land of Narnia ends where the waterfall comes down, and once you have reached the top of the cliffs you will be out of Narnia and into the Western Wild. You must journey through those mountains till you find a green valley with a blue lake in it, walled round by mountains of ice. At the end of the lake there is a steep, green hill. On the top of that hill there is a garden. In the centre of that garden is a tree. Pluck an apple from that tree and bring it back to me."

"Yes, sir," said Digory again. He hadn't the least idea of how he was to climb the cliff and find his way among all the mountains, but he didn't like to say that for fear it would sound like making excuses. But he did say, "I hope, Aslan, you're not in a hurry. I shan't be able to get there and back very quickly."

"Little son of Adam, you shall have help," said Aslan. He then turned to the Horse who had been standing quietly beside them all this time, swishing his tail to keep the flies off, and listening with his head on one side as if the conversation were a little difficult to understand.

"My dear," said Aslan to the Horse, "would you like to be a winged horse?"

You should have seen how the Horse shook its mane and how its nostrils widened, and the little tap it gave the ground with one back hoof. Clearly it would very much like to be a winged horse. But it only said:

"If you wish, Aslan – if you really mean – I don't know why it should be me – I'm not a very clever horse."

"Be winged. Be the father of all flying horses," roared Aslan in a voice that shook the ground. "Your name is Fledge."

The horse shied, just as it might have shied in the old, miserable days when it pulled a hansom. Then it roared. It strained its neck back as if there were a fly biting its shoulders and it wanted to scratch them. And then, just as the beasts had burst out of the earth, there burst out from the shoulders of Fledge wings that spread and grew, larger than eagles', larger than swans', larger than angels' wings in church windows. The feathers shone chestnut colour and copper colour. He gave a great sweep with them and leapt into the air. Twenty feet above Aslan and Digory he snorted, neighed, and curvetted. Then, after circling once round them, he dropped to the earth, all four hoofs together, looking awkward and surprised, but extremely pleased.

"Is it good, Fledge?" said Aslan.

"It is very good, Aslan," said Fledge.

"Will you carry this little son of Adam on your back to the mountain valley I spoke of?"

"What? Now? At once?" said Strawberry — or Fledge, as we must now call him — "Hurray! Come on, little one, I've had things like you on my back before. Long, long ago. When there were green fields; and sugar."

"What are the two daughters of Eve whispering about?" said Aslan, turning very suddenly on Polly and the Cabby's wife, who had in fact been making friends.

"If you please, sir," said Queen Helen (for that is what Nellie the cabman's wife now was), "I think the little girl would love to go too, if it weren't no trouble."

"What does Fledge say about that?" asked the Lion.

"Oh, I don't mind two, not when they're little ones," said Fledge. "But I hope the Elephant doesn't want to come as well."

The Elephant had no such wish, and the new King of Narnia helped both the children up: that is, he gave Digory a rough heave and set Polly as gently and daintily on the horse's back as if she were made of china and might break. "There they are, Strawberry — Fledge, I should say. This is a rum go."

"Do not fly too high," said Aslan. "Do not try to go over the tops of the great ice-mountains. Look out for the valleys, the green places, and fly through them. There will always be a way through. And now, be gone with my blessing."

"Oh, Fledge!" said Digory, leaning forward to pat the Horse's glossy neck. "This *is* fun. Hold on to me tight, Polly."

Next moment the country dropped away beneath them, and whirled round as Fledge, like a huge pigeon, circled once or twice before setting off on his long westward flight. Looking down, Polly could hardly see the King and the Queen, and even Aslan himself was only a bright yellow spot on the green grass. Soon the wind was in their faces and Fledge's wings settled down to a steady beat.

All Narnia, many-coloured with lawns and rocks and heather and different sorts of trees, lay spread out below them, the river winding through it like a ribbon of quicksilver. They could already see over the tops of the low hills which lay northward on their right; beyond those hills a great moorland sloped gently up and up to the horizon. On their left the mountains were much higher, but every now and then there was a gap when you could see, between steep pine woods, a glimpse of the southern lands that lay beyond them, looking blue and far away.

"That'll be where Archenland is," said Polly.

"Yes, but look ahead!" said Digory.

For now a great barrier of cliffs rose before them and they were almost dazzled by the sunlight dancing on the great waterfall by which the river roars and sparkles down into Narnia itself from the high western lands in which it rises. They were flying so high already that the thunder of those falls could only just be heard as a small, thin sound, but they were not yet high enough to fly over the top of the cliffs.

"We'll have to do a bit of zigzagging here," said Fledge. "Hold on tight."

He began flying to and fro, getting higher at each turn. The air grew colder, and they heard the call of eagles far below them.

"I say, look back! Look behind," said Polly.

There they could see the whole valley of Narnia stretched out to where, just before the eastern horizon, there was a gleam of the sea. And now they were so high that they could see tiny-looking jagged mountains appearing beyond the northwest moors, and plains of what looked like sand far in the south.

"I wish we had someone to tell us what all those places are," said Digory.

"I don't suppose they're anywhere yet," said Polly. "I mean, there's no one there, and nothing happening. The world only began today."

"No, but people *will* get there," said Digory. "And then they'll have histories, you know."

"Well, it's a jolly good thing they haven't now," said Polly. "Because nobody can be made to learn it. Battles and dates and all that rot."

Now they were over the top of the cliffs and in a few minutes the valley land of Narnia had sunk out of sight behind them. They were flying over a wild country of steep hills and dark forests, still following the course of the river. The really big mountains loomed ahead. But the sun was now in the travellers' eyes and they couldn't see things very clearly in that direction. For the sun sank lower and lower till the western sky was all like one great furnace full of melted gold; and it set at last behind a jagged peak which stood up against the brightness as sharp and flat as if it were cut out of cardboard.

"It's none too warm up here," said Polly.

"And my wings are beginning to ache," said Fledge. "There's no sign of the valley with a Lake in it, like what Aslan said. What about coming down and looking out for a decent spot to spend the night in? We shan't reach that place tonight."

"Yes, and surely it's about time for supper?" said Digory.

So Fledge came lower and lower. As they came down nearer to the earth and among the hills, the air grew warmer and after travelling so many hours with nothing to listen to but the beat of Fledge's wings, it was nice to hear the homely and earthy noises again – the chatter of the river on its stony bed and the creaking of trees in the light wind. A warm, good smell of sun-baked earth and grass and flowers came up to them. At last Fledge alighted. Digory rolled off and helped Polly to dismount. Both were glad to stretch their stiff legs.

The valley in which they had come down was in the heart of the mountains; snowy heights, one of them looking rose-red in the reflections of the sunset, towered above them.

"I *am* hungry," said Digory.

"Well, tuck in," said Fledge, taking a big mouthful of grass. Then he raised his head, still chewing and with bits of grass sticking out on each side of his mouth like whiskers, and said, "Come on, you two. Don't be shy. There's plenty for us all."

"But we can't eat grass," said Digory.

"H'm, h'm," said Fledge, speaking with his mouth full. "Well – h'm – don't know quite what you'll do then. Very good grass too."

Polly and Digory stared at one another in dismay.

"Well, I *do* think someone might have arranged about our meals," said Digory.

"I'm sure Aslan would have, if you'd asked him," said Fledge.

"Wouldn't he know without being asked?" said Polly.

"I've no doubt he would," said the Horse (still with his mouth full). "But I've a sort of idea he likes to be asked."

"But what on earth are we to do?" asked Digory.

"I'm sure I don't know," said Fledge. "Unless you try the grass. You might like it better than you think."

"Oh, don't be silly," said Polly, stamping her foot. "Of course humans can't eat grass, any more than you could eat a mutton chop."

"For goodness' sake don't talk about chops and things," said Digory. "It only makes it worse."

Digory said that Polly had better take herself home by ring and get something to eat there; he couldn't himself because he had promised to go straight on his message for Aslan and, if once he showed up again at home, anything might happen to prevent his getting back. But Polly said she wouldn't leave him, and Digory said it was jolly decent of her.

"I say," said Polly, "I've still got the remains of that bag of toffees in my jacket. It'll be better than nothing."

"A lot better," said Digory. "But be careful to get your hand into your pocket without touching your ring."

This was a difficult and delicate job but they managed it in the end. The little paper bag was very squashy and sticky when they finally got it out, so that it was more a question of tearing the bag off the toffees than of getting the toffees out of the bag. Some grown-ups (you know how fussy they can be about that sort of thing) would rather have gone without supper altogether than eaten those toffees. There were nine of them all told. It was Digory who had the bright idea of eating four each and planting the ninth; for, as he said, "if the bar off the lamp-post turned into a little light-tree, why shouldn't this turn into a toffee-tree?" So they dibbled a small hole in the turf and buried the piece of toffee. Then they ate the other pieces, making them last as long as they could. It was a poor meal, even with all the paper they couldn't help eating as well.

When Fledge had quite finished his own excellent supper he lay down. The children came and sat one on each side of him leaning against his warm body, and when he had spread a wing over each they were really quite snug. As the bright young stars of that new world came out they talked over everything: how Digory had hoped to get something for his Mother and how, instead of that, he had been sent on this message. And they repeated to one another all the signs by which they would know the places they were looking for – the blue lake and the hill with a garden on top of it. The talk was just beginning to slow down as they got sleepy, when suddenly Polly sat up wide awake and said, "Hush!"

Everyone listened as hard as they could.

"Perhaps it was only the wind in the trees," said Digory presently.

"I'm not so sure," said Fledge. "Anyway – wait! There it goes again. By Aslan, it *is* something."

The horse scrambled to its feet with a great noise and a great upheaval; the children were already on theirs. Fledge trotted to and fro, sniffing and whinnying. The children tiptoed this way and that, looking behind every bush and tree. They kept on thinking they saw things, and there was one time when Polly was perfectly certain she had seen a tall, dark figure gliding quickly away in a westerly direction. But they caught nothing and in the end Fledge lay down again and the children re-snuggled (if that is the right word) under his wings. They went to sleep at once. Fledge stayed awake much longer, moving his ears to and fro in the darkness and sometimes giving a little shiver with his skin as if a fly had lighted on him: but in the end he too slept.

CHAPTER THIRTEEN

AN UNEXPECTED MEETING

"Wake up, Digory, wake up, Fledge," came the voice of Polly. "It *has* turned into a toffee-tree. And it's the loveliest morning."

The low early sunshine was streaming through the wood and the grass was grey with dew and the cobwebs were like silver. Just beside them was a little, very dark-wooded tree, about the size of an apple tree. The leaves were whitish and rather papery, like the herb called honesty, and it was loaded with little brown fruits that looked rather like dates.

"Hurray!" said Digory. "But I'm going to have a dip first." He rushed through a flowering thicket or two down to the river's edge. Have you ever bathed in a mountain river that is running in shallow cataracts over red and blue and yellow stones with the sun on it? It is as good as the sea: in some ways almost better. Of course, he had to dress again without drying but it was well worth it. When he came back, Polly went down and had her bathe; at least she said that was what she'd been doing, but we know she was not much of a swimmer and perhaps it is best not to ask too many questions. Fledge visited the river too but he only stood in midstream, stooping down for a long drink of water and then shaking his mane and neighing several times.

Polly and Digory got to work on the toffee-tree. The fruit was delicious; not exactly like toffee — softer for one thing, and juicy — but like fruit which reminded one of toffee. Fledge also made an excellent breakfast; he tried one of the toffee fruits and liked it but said he felt more like grass at that hour in the morning. Then with some difficulty the children got on his back and the second journey began.

It was even better than yesterday, partly because everyone was feeling so fresh, and partly because the newly risen sun was at their backs and, of course, everything looks nicer when the light is behind you. It was a wonderful ride. The big snowy mountains rose above them in every direction. The valleys, far beneath them, were so green, and all the streams which tumbled down from the glaciers into the main river were so blue, that it was like flying over gigantic pieces of jewellery. They would have liked this part of the adventure to go on longer than it did. But quite soon they were all sniffing the air and saying "What is it?" and "Did you smell something?" and "Where's it coming from?" For a heavenly smell, warm and golden, as if from all the most delicious fruits and flowers of the world, was coming up to them from somewhere ahead.

"It's coming from that valley with the lake in it," said Fledge.

"So it is," said Digory. "And look! There's a green hill at the far end of the lake. And look how blue the water is."

"It must be the Place," said all three.

Fledge came lower and lower in wide circles. The icy peaks rose up higher and higher above. The air came up warmer and sweeter every moment, so sweet that it almost brought the tears to your eyes. Fledge was now gliding with his wings spread out motionless on each side, and his hoofs pawing for the ground. The steep green hill was rushing towards them. A moment later he alighted on its slope, a little awkwardly. The children rolled off, fell without hurting themselves on the warm, fine grass, and stood up, panting a little.

They were three-quarters of the way up the hill, and set out at once to climb to the top. (I don't think Fledge could have managed this without his wings to balance him and to give him the help of a flutter now and then.) All round the very top of the hill ran a high wall of green turf. Inside the wall, trees were growing. Their branches hung out over the wall; their leaves showed not only green but also blue and silver when the wind stirred them. When the travellers reached the top they walked nearly all the way round it outside the green wall before they found the gates: high gates of gold, fast shut, facing due east.

Up till now I think Fledge and Polly had had the idea that they would go in with Digory. But they thought so no longer. You never saw a place which was so obviously private. You could see at a glance that it belonged to someone else. Only a fool would dream of going in unless he had been sent there on very special business. Digory himself understood at once that the others wouldn't and couldn't come in with him. He went forward to the gates alone.

When he had come close up to them he saw words written on the gold with silver letters; something like this:

Come in by the gold gates or not at all,
Take of my fruit for others or forbear,
For those who steal or those who climb my wall
Shall find their heart's desire and find despair.

"*Take of my fruit for others,*" said Digory to himself. "Well, that's what I'm going to do. It means I mustn't eat any myself, I suppose. I don't know what all that jaw in the last line is about. *Come in by the gold gates.* Well, who'd want to climb a wall if he could get in by a gate! But how do the gates open?" He laid his hand on them and instantly they swung apart, opening inwards, turning on their hinges without the least noise.

Now that he could see into the place it looked more private than ever. He went in very solemnly, looking about him. Everything was very quiet inside. Even the fountain which rose near the middle of the garden made only the faintest sound. The lovely smell was all round him: it was a happy place but very serious.

He knew which was the right tree at once, partly because it stood in the very centre and partly because the great silver apples with which it was loaded shone so and cast a light of their own down on the shadowy places where the sunlight did not reach. He walked straight across to it, picked an apple, and put it in the breast pocket of his Norfolk jacket. But he couldn't help looking at it and smelling it before he put it away.

It would have been better if he had not. A terrible thirst and hunger came over him and a longing to taste that fruit. He put it hastily into his pocket; but there were plenty of others. Could it be wrong to taste one? After all, he thought, the notice on the gate might not have been exactly an order; it might have been only a piece of advice – and who cares about advice? Or even if it were an order, would he be disobeying it by eating an apple? He had already obeyed the part about taking one "for others".

While he was thinking of all this he happened to look up through the branches towards the top of the tree. There, on a branch above his head, a wonderful bird was roosting. I say "roosting" because it seemed almost asleep; perhaps not quite. The tiniest slit of one eye was open. It was larger than an eagle, its breast saffron, its head crested with scarlet, and its tail purple.

"And it just shows," said Digory afterwards when he was telling the story to others, "that you can't be too careful in these magical places. You never know what may be watching you." But I think Digory would not have taken an apple for himself in any case. Things like Do Not Steal were, I think, hammered into boys' heads a good deal harder in those days than they are now. Still, we can never be certain.

Digory was just turning to go back to the gates when he stopped to have one last look around. He got a terrible shock. He was not alone. There, only a few yards away from him, stood the Witch. She was just throwing away the core of an apple which she had eaten. The juice was darker than you would expect and had made a horrid stain round her mouth. Digory guessed at once that she must have climbed in over the wall. And he began to see that there might be some sense in that last line about getting your heart's desire and getting despair along with it. For the Witch looked stronger and prouder than ever, and even, in a way, triumphant; but her face was deadly white, white as salt.

All this flashed through Digory's mind in a second; then he took to his heels and ran for the gates as hard as he could pelt; the Witch after him. As soon as he was out, the gates closed behind him of their own accord. That gave him the lead but not for long. By the time he had reached the others and was shouting out "Quick, get on, Polly! Get up, Fledge", the Witch had climbed the wall, or vaulted over it, and was close behind him again.

"Stay where you are," cried Digory, turning round to face her, "or we'll all vanish. Don't come an inch nearer."

"Foolish boy," said the Witch. "Why do you run from me? I mean you no harm. If you do not stop and listen to me now, you will miss some knowledge that would have made you happy all your life."

"Well, I don't want to hear it, thanks," said Digory. But he did.

"I know what errand you have come on," continued the Witch. "For it was I who was close beside you in the woods last night and heard all your counsels. You have plucked fruit in the garden yonder. You have it in your pocket now. And you are going to carry it back, untasted, to the Lion; for *him* to eat, for *him* to use. You simpleton! Do you know what that fruit is? I will tell you. It is the apple of youth, the apple of life. I know, for I have tasted it; and I feel already such changes in myself that I know I shall never grow old or die. Eat it, Boy, eat it; and you and I will both live for ever and be king and queen of this whole world – or of your world, if we decide to go back there."

"No thanks," said Digory, "I don't know that I care much about living on and on after everyone I know is dead. I'd rather live an ordinary time and die and go to Heaven."

"But what about this Mother of yours whom you pretend to love so?"

"What's she got to do with it?" said Digory.

"Do you not see, Fool, that one bite of that apple would heal her? You have it in your pocket. We are here by ourselves and the Lion is far away. Use your Magic and go back to your own world. A minute later you can be at your Mother's bedside, giving her the fruit. Five minutes later you will see the colour coming back to her face. She will tell you the pain is gone. Soon she will tell you she feels stronger. Then she will fall asleep – think of that; hours of sweet natural sleep, without pain, without drugs. Next day everyone will be saying how wonderfully she has recovered. Soon she will be quite well again. All will be well again. Your home will be happy again. You will be like other boys."

"Oh!" gasped Digory as if he had been hurt, and put his hand to his head. For he now knew that the most terrible choice lay before him.

"What has the Lion ever done for you that you should be his slave?" said the Witch. "What can he do to you once you are back in your own world? And what would your Mother think if she knew that you *could* have taken her pain away and given her back her life and saved your Father's heart from being broken, and that you *wouldn't* – that you'd rather run messages for a wild animal in a strange world that is no business of yours?"

"I – I don't think he is a wild animal," said Digory in a dried-up sort of voice. "He is – I don't know—"

"Then he is something worse," said the Witch. "Look what he has done to you already; look how heartless he has made you. That is what he does to everyone who listens to him. Cruel, pitiless boy! You would let your own Mother die rather than—"

"Oh, shut up," said the miserable Digory, still in the same voice. "Do you think I don't see? But I – I promised."

"Ah, but you didn't know what you were promising. And no one here can prevent you."

"Mother herself," said Digory, getting the words out with difficulty, "wouldn't like it – awfully strict about keeping promises – and not stealing – and all that sort of thing. *She'd* tell me not to do it – quick as anything – if she was here."

"But she need never know," said the Witch, speaking more sweetly than you would have thought anyone with so fierce a face could speak. "You wouldn't tell her how you'd got the apple. Your Father need never know. No one in your world need know anything about this whole story. You needn't take the little girl back with you, you know."

That was where the Witch made her fatal mistake. Of course Digory knew that Polly could get away by her own ring as easily as he could get away by his. But apparently the Witch didn't know this. And the meanness of the suggestion that he should leave Polly behind suddenly made all the other things the Witch had been saying to him sound false and hollow. And even in the midst of all his misery, his head suddenly cleared, and he said (in a different and much louder voice):

"Look here; where do *you* come into all this? Why are *you* so precious fond of *my* Mother all of a sudden? What's it got to do with you? What's your game?"

"Good for you, Digs," whispered Polly in his ear. "Quick! Get away *now*."

She hadn't dared to say anything all through the argument because, you see, it wasn't *her* Mother who was dying.

"Up then," said Digory, heaving her on to Fledge's back and then scrambling up as quickly as he could. The horse spread its wings.

"Go then, Fools," called the Witch. "Think of me, Boy, when you lie old and weak and dying, and remember how you threw away the chance of endless youth! It won't be offered you again."

They were already so high that they could only just hear her. Nor did the Witch waste any time gazing up at them; they saw her set off northward down the slope of the hill.

They had started early that morning and what happened in the garden had not taken very long, so that Fledge and Polly both said they would easily get back to Narnia before nightfall. Digory never spoke on the way back, and the others were shy of speaking to him. He was very sad and he wasn't even sure all the time that he had done the right thing; but whenever he remembered the shining tears in Aslan's eyes he became sure.

All day Fledge flew steadily with untiring wings; eastward with the river to guide him, through the mountains and over the wild wooded hills, and then over the great waterfall and down, and down, to where the woods of Narnia were darkened by the shadow of the mighty cliff, till at last, when the sky was growing red with sunset behind them, he saw a place where many creatures were gathered together by the riverside. And soon he could see Aslan himself in the midst of them. Fledge glided down, spread out his four legs, closed his wings, and landed cantering. Then he pulled up. The children dismounted. Digory saw all the animals, dwarfs, satyrs, nymphs, and other things drawing back to the left and right to make way for him. He walked up to Aslan, handed him the apple and said:

"I've brought you the apple you wanted, sir."

The Planting of the Tree

"Well done," said Aslan in a voice that made the earth shake. Then Digory knew that all the Narnians had heard those words and that the story of them would be handed down from father to son in that new world for hundreds of years and perhaps for ever. But he was in no danger of feeling conceited for he didn't think about it at all now that he was face to face with Aslan. This time he found he could look straight into the Lion's eyes. He had forgotten his troubles and felt absolutely content.

"Well done, son of Adam," said the Lion again. "For this fruit you have hungered and thirsted and wept. No hand but yours shall sow the seed of the Tree that is to be the protection of Narnia. Throw the apple towards the river bank where the ground is soft."

Digory did as he was told. Everyone had grown so quiet that you could hear the soft thump where it fell into the mud.

"It is well thrown," said Aslan. "Let us now proceed to the Coronation of King Frank of Narnia and Helen his Queen."

The children now noticed these two for the first time. They were dressed in strange and beautiful clothes, and from their shoulders rich robes flowed out behind them to where four dwarfs held up the King's train and four river-nymphs the Queen's. Their heads were bare; but Helen had let her hair down and it made a great improvement in her appearance. But it was neither hair nor clothes that made them look so different from their old selves. Their faces had a new expression, especially the King's. All the sharpness and cunning and quarrelsomeness which he had picked up as a London cabby seemed to have been washed away, and the courage and kindness which he had always had were easier to see.

Perhaps it was the air of the young world that had done it, or talking with Aslan, or both.

"Upon my word," whispered Fledge to Polly. "My old master's been changed nearly as much as I have! Why, he's a real master now."

"Yes, but don't buzz in my ear like that," said Polly. "It tickles so."

"Now," said Aslan, "some of you undo that tangle you have made with those trees and let us see what we shall find there."

Digory now saw that where four trees grew close together their branches had all been laced together or tied together with switches so as to make a sort of cage. The two Elephants with their trunks and a few dwarfs with their little axes soon got it all undone. There were three things inside. One was a young tree that seemed to be made of gold; the second was a young tree that seemed to be made of silver; but the third was a miserable object in muddy clothes, sitting hunched up
between them.

"Gosh!" whispered Digory. "Uncle Andrew!"

To explain all this we must go back a bit. The Beasts, you remember, had tried planting and watering him. When the watering brought him to his senses, he found himself soaking wet, buried up to his thighs in earth (which was quickly turning into mud) and surrounded by more wild animals than he had ever dreamed of in his life before. It is perhaps not surprising that he began to scream and howl. This was in a way a good thing, for it at last persuaded everyone (even the Warthog) that he was alive. So they dug him up again (his trousers were in a really shocking state by now). As soon as his legs were free he tried to bolt, but one swift curl of the Elephant's trunk round his waist soon put an end to that. Everyone now thought he must be safely kept somewhere till Aslan had time to come and see him and say what should be done about him. So they made a sort of cage or coop all round him. They then offered him everything they could think of to eat.

The Donkey collected great piles of thistles and threw them in, but Uncle Andrew didn't seem to care about them. The Squirrels bombarded him with volleys of nuts, but he only covered his head with his hands and tried to keep out of the way. Several birds flew to and fro diligently dropping worms on him. The Bear was especially kind. During the afternoon he found a wild bees' nest and instead of eating it himself (which he would very much like to have done) this worthy creature brought it back to Uncle Andrew. But this was in fact the worst failure of all. The Bear lobbed the whole sticky mass over the top of the enclosure and unfortunately it hit Uncle Andrew slap in the face (not all the bees were dead). The Bear, who would not at all have minded being hit in the face by a honeycomb himself, could not understand why Uncle Andrew staggered back, slipped, and sat down. And it was sheer bad luck that he sat down on the pile of thistles. "And anyway," as the Warthog said, "quite a lot of honey has got into the creature's mouth and that's bound to have done it some good." They were really getting quite fond of their strange pet and hoped that Aslan would allow them to keep it. The cleverer ones were quite sure by now that at least some of the noises which came out of his mouth had a meaning. They christened him Brandy because he made that noise so often.

In the end, however, they had to leave him there for the night. Aslan was busy all that day instructing the new King and Queen and doing other important things, and could not attend to "poor old Brandy". What with the nuts, pears, apples, and bananas that had been thrown in to him, he did fairly well for supper; but it wouldn't be true to say that he passed an agreeable night.

"Bring out that creature," said Aslan. One of the Elephants lifted Uncle Andrew in its trunk and laid him at the Lion's feet. He was too frightened to move.

"Please, Aslan," said Polly, "could you say something to – to unfrighten him? And then could you say something to prevent him from ever coming back here again?"

"Do you think he *wants* to?" said Aslan.

"Well, Aslan," said Polly, "he might send someone else. He's so excited about the bar off the lamp-post growing into a lamp-post tree and he thinks—"

"He thinks great folly, child," said Aslan. "This world is bursting with life for these few days because the song with which I called it into life still hangs in the air and rumbles in the ground. It will not be so for long. But I cannot tell that to this old sinner, and I cannot comfort him either; he has made himself unable to hear my voice. If I spoke to him, he would hear only growlings and roarings. Oh, Adam's sons, how cleverly you defend yourselves against all that might do you good! But I will give him the only gift he is still able to receive."

He bowed his great head rather sadly, and breathed into the Magician's terrified face. "Sleep," he said. "Sleep and be separated for some few hours from all the torments you have devised for yourself." Uncle Andrew immediately rolled over with closed eyes and began breathing peacefully.

"Carry him aside and lay him down," said Aslan. "Now, dwarfs! Show your smith-craft. Let me see you make two crowns for your King and Queen."

More Dwarfs than you could dream of rushed forward to the Golden Tree. They had all its leaves stripped off, and some of its branches torn off too, before you could say Jack Robinson. And now the children could see that it did not merely look golden but was of real, soft gold. It had of course sprung up from the half-sovereigns which had fallen out of Uncle Andrew's pocket when he was turned upside down; just as the silver tree had grown up from the half-crowns. From nowhere, as it seemed, piles of dry brushwood for fuel, a little anvil, hammers, tongs, and bellows were produced. Next moment (how those dwarfs loved their work!) the fire was blazing, the bellows were roaring, the gold was melting, the hammers were clinking. Two Moles, whom Aslan had set to dig (which was what they liked best) earlier in the day, poured out a pile of precious stones at the dwarfs' feet. Under the clever fingers of the little smiths two crowns took shape – not ugly, heavy things like modern European crowns, but light, delicate, beautifully shaped circles that you could really wear and look nicer by wearing. The King's was set with rubies and the Queen's with emeralds.

When the crowns had been cooled in the river, Aslan made Frank and Helen kneel before him and he placed the crowns on their heads. Then he said, "Rise up, King and Queen of Narnia, father and mother of many kings that shall be in Narnia and the Isles and Archenland. Be just and merciful and brave. The blessing is upon you."

Then everyone cheered or bayed or neighed or trumpeted or clapped its wings and the royal pair stood looking solemn and a little shy, but all the nobler for their shyness. And while Digory was still cheering he heard the deep voice of Aslan beside him, saying:

"Look!"

Everyone in that crowd turned its head, and then everyone drew a long breath of wonder and delight. A little way off, towering over their heads, they saw a tree which had certainly not been there before. It must have grown up silently, yet swiftly as a flag rises when you pull it up on a flagstaff, while they were all busied about the coronation. Its spreading branches seemed to cast a light rather than a shade, and silver apples peeped out like stars from under every leaf. But it was the smell which came from it, even more than the sight, that had made everyone draw in their breath. For a moment one could hardly think about anything else.

"Son of Adam," said Aslan, "you have sown well. And you, Narnians, let it be your first care to guard this Tree, for it is your Shield. The Witch of whom I told you has fled far away into the North of the world; she will live on there, growing stronger in dark Magic. But while that Tree flourishes she will never come down into Narnia. She dare not come within a hundred miles of the Tree, for its smell, which is joy and life and health to you, is death and horror and despair to her."

Everyone was staring solemnly at the Tree when Aslan suddenly swung round his head (scattering golden gleams of light from his mane as he did so) and fixed his large eyes on the children. "What is it, children?" he said, for he caught them in the very act of whispering and nudging one another.

"Oh – Aslan, sir," said Digory, turning red, "I forgot to tell you. The Witch has already eaten one of those apples, one of the same kind that Tree grew from." He hadn't really said all he was thinking, but Polly at once said it for him. (Digory was always much more afraid than she of looking a fool.)

"So we thought, Aslan," she said, "that there must be some mistake, and she can't really mind the smell of those apples."

"Why do you think that, Daughter of Eve?" asked the Lion.

"Well, she ate one."

"Child," he replied, "that is why all the rest are now a horror to her. That is what happens to those who pluck and eat fruits at the wrong time and in the wrong way. The fruit is good, but they loathe it ever after."

"Oh, I see," said Polly. "And I suppose because she took it in the wrong way it won't work for her. I mean it won't make her always young and all that?"

"Alas," said Aslan, shaking his head. "It will. Things always work according to their nature. She has won her heart's desire; she has unwearying strength and endless days like a goddess. But length of days with an evil heart is only length of misery and already she begins to know it. All get what they want; they do not always like it."

"I – I nearly ate one myself, Aslan," said Digory. "Would I—"

"You would, child," said Aslan. "For the fruit always works – it must work – but it does not work happily for any who pluck it at their own will. If any Narnian, unbidden, had stolen an apple and planted it here to protect Narnia, it would have protected Narnia. But it would have done so by making Narnia into another strong and cruel empire like Charn, not the kindly land I mean it to be. And the Witch tempted you to do another thing, my son, did she not?"

"Yes, Aslan. She wanted me to take an apple home to Mother."

"Understand, then, that it would have healed her; but not to your joy or hers. The day would have come when both you and she would have looked back and said it would have been better to die in that illness."

And Digory could say nothing, for tears choked him and he gave up all hopes of saving his Mother's life; but at the same time he knew that the Lion knew what would have happened, and that there might be things more terrible even than losing someone you love by death. But now Aslan was speaking again, almost in a whisper:

"That is what *would* have happened, child, with a stolen apple. It is not what will happen now. What I give you now will bring joy. It will not, in your world, give endless life, but it will heal. Go. Pluck her an apple from the Tree."

For a second Digory could hardly understand. It was as if the whole world had turned inside out and upside down. And then, like someone in a dream, he was walking across to the Tree, and the King and Queen were cheering him and all the creatures were cheering too. He plucked the apple and put it in his pocket. Then he came back to Aslan.

"Please," he said, "may we go home now?" He had forgotten to say "Thank you", but he meant it, and Aslan understood.

Chapter Fifteen

The End of this Story and the Beginning of all the Others

"You need no rings when I am with you," said the voice of Aslan. The children blinked and looked about them. They were once more in the Wood between the Worlds; Uncle Andrew lay on the grass, still asleep; Aslan stood beside them.

"Come," said Aslan, "it is time that you went back. But there are two things to see first; a warning, and a command. Look here, children."

They looked and saw a little hollow in the grass, with a grassy bottom, warm and dry.

"When you were last here," said Aslan, "that hollow was a pool, and when you jumped into it you came to the world where a dying sun shone over the ruins of Charn. There is no pool now. That world is ended, as if it had never been. Let the race of Adam and Eve take warning."

"Yes, Aslan," said both the children. But Polly added, "But we're not quite as bad as that world, are we, Aslan?"

"Not yet, Daughter of Eve," he said. "Not yet. But you are growing more like it. It is not certain that some wicked one of your race will not find out a secret as evil as the Deplorable Word and use it to destroy all living things. And soon, very soon, before you are an old man and an old woman, great nations in your world will be ruled by tyrants who care no more for joy and justice and mercy than the Empress Jadis. Let your world beware. That is the warning. Now for the command. As soon as you can, take from this Uncle of yours his magic rings and bury them so that no one can use them again."

Both the children were looking up into the Lion's face as he spoke these words. And all at once (they never knew exactly how it happened) the face seemed to be a sea of tossing gold in which they were floating, and such a sweetness and power rolled about them and over them and entered into them that they felt they had never really been happy or wise or good, or even alive and awake, before. And the memory of that moment stayed with them always, so that as long as they both lived, if ever they were sad or afraid or angry, the thought of all that golden goodness, and the feeling that it was still there, quite close, just round some corner or just behind some door, would come back and make them sure, deep down inside, that all was well. Next minute all three of them (Uncle Andrew now awake) came tumbling into the noise, heat, and hot smells of London.

They were on the pavement outside the Ketterleys' front door, and except that the Witch, the Horse, and the Cabby were gone, everything was exactly as they had left it. There was the lamp-post, with one arm missing; there was the wreck of the hansom cab; and there was the crowd. Everyone was still talking and people were kneeling beside the damaged policeman, saying things like, "He's coming round" or "How do you feel now, old chap?" or "The ambulance will be here in a jiffy."

"Great Scott!" thought Digory. "I believe the whole adventure's taken no time at all."

Most people were wildly looking round for Jadis and the horse. No one took any notice of the children for no one had seen them go or noticed them coming back. As for Uncle Andrew, between the state of his clothes and the honey on his face, he could not have been recognized by anyone. Fortunately the front door of the house was open and the housemaid was standing in the doorway staring at the fun (what a day that girl was having!) so the children had no difficulty in bustling Uncle Andrew indoors before anyone asked any questions.

He raced up the stairs before them and at first they were very afraid he was heading for his attic and meant to hide his remaining magic rings. But they needn't have bothered. What he was thinking about was the bottle in his wardrobe, and he disappeared at once into his bedroom and locked the door. When he came out again (which was not for a long time) he was in his dressing-gown and made straight for the bathroom.

"Can you get the other rings, Poll?" said Digory. "I want to go to Mother."

"Right. See you later," said Polly and clattered up the attic stairs.

Then Digory took a minute to get his breath, and then went softly into his Mother's room. And there she lay, as he had seen her lie so many other times, propped up on the pillows, with a thin, pale face that would make you cry to look at it. Digory took the Apple of Life out of his pocket.

And just as the Witch Jadis had looked different when you saw her in our world instead of in her own, so the fruit of that mountain garden looked different too. There were of course all sorts of coloured things in the bedroom; the coloured counterpane on the bed, the wallpaper, the sunlight from the window, and Mother's pretty, pale blue dressing jacket. But the moment Digory took the Apple out of his pocket, all those things seemed to have scarcely any colour at all. Everyone of them, even the sunlight, looked faded and dingy. The brightness of the Apple threw strange lights on the ceiling. Nothing else was worth looking at: you couldn't look at anything else. And the smell of the Apple of Youth was as if there was a window in the room that opened on Heaven.

"Oh, darling, how lovely," said Digory's Mother.

"You will eat it, won't you? Please," said Digory.

"I don't know what the Doctor would say," she answered. "But really – I almost feel as if I could."

He peeled it and cut it up and gave it to her piece by piece. And no sooner had she finished it than she smiled and her head sank back on the pillow and she was asleep: a real, natural, gentle sleep, without any of those nasty drugs, which was, as Digory knew, the thing in the whole world that she wanted most. And he was sure now that her face looked a little different. He bent down and kissed her very softly and stole out of the room with a beating heart, taking the core of the apple with him. For the rest of that day, whenever he looked at the things about him, and saw how ordinary and unmagical they were, he hardly dared to hope; but when he remembered the face of Aslan he did hope.

That evening he buried the core of the Apple in the back garden.

Next morning when the Doctor made his usual visit, Digory leant over the banisters to listen. He heard the Doctor come out with Aunt Letty and say:

"Miss Ketterley, this is the most extraordinary case I have known in my whole medical career. It is – it is like a miracle. I wouldn't tell the little boy anything at present; we don't want to raise any false hopes. But in my opinion—" Then his voice became too low to hear.

That afternoon he went down the garden and whistled their agreed secret signal for Polly (she hadn't been able to get back the day before).

"What luck?" said Polly, looking over the wall. "I mean, about your Mother?"

"I think – I *think* it is going to be all right," said Digory. "But if you don't mind I'd really rather not talk about it yet. What about the rings?"

"I've got them all," said Polly. "Look, it's all right, I'm wearing gloves. Let's bury them."

"Yes, let's. I've marked the place where I buried the core of the Apple yesterday."

Then Polly came over the wall and they went together to the place. But, as it turned out, Digory need not have marked the place. Something was already coming up. It was not growing so that you could see it grow as the new trees had done in Narnia; but it was already well above ground. They got a trowel and buried all the magic rings, including their own ones, in a circle round it.

About a week after this it was quite certain that Digory's Mother was getting better. About a fortnight later she was able to sit out in the garden. And a month later that whole house had become a different place. Aunt Letty did everything that Mother liked; windows were opened, frowsy curtains were drawn back to brighten up the rooms, there were new flowers everywhere, and nicer things to eat, and the old piano was tuned and Mother took up her singing again, and had such games with Digory and Polly that Aunt Letty would say "I declare, Mabel, you're the biggest baby of the three."

When things go wrong, you'll find they usually go on getting worse for some time; but when things once start going right they often go on getting better and better. After about six weeks of this lovely life there came a long letter from Father in India, which had wonderful news in it. Old Great-Uncle Kirke had died and this meant, apparently, that Father was now very rich. He was going to retire and come home from India for ever and ever. And the great big house in the country, which Digory had heard of all his life and never seen, would now be their home; the big house with the suits of armour, the stables, the kennels, the river, the park, the hot-houses, the vineries, the woods, and the mountains behind it. So that Digory felt just as sure as you that they were all going to live happily ever after. But perhaps you would like to know just one or two things more.

Polly and Digory were always great friends and she came nearly every holidays to stay with them at their beautiful house in the country; and that was where she learned to ride and swim and milk and bake and climb.

In Narnia the Beasts lived in great peace and joy and neither the Witch nor any other enemy came to trouble that pleasant land for many hundred years. King Frank and Queen Helen and their children lived happily in Narnia and their second son became King of Archenland. The boys married nymphs and the girls married wood-gods and river-gods. The lamp-post which the Witch had planted (without knowing it) shone day and night in the Narnian forest, so that the place where it grew came to be called Lantern Waste; and when, many years later, another child from our world got into Narnia, on a snowy night, she found the light still burning. And that adventure was, in a way, connected with the ones I have just been telling you.

It was like this. The tree which sprang from the core of the Apple that

Digory planted in the back garden, lived and grew into a fine tree. Growing in the soil of our world, far out of the sound of Aslan's voice and far from the young air of Narnia, it did not bear apples that would revive a dying woman as Digory's Mother had been revived, though it did bear apples more beautiful than any others in England, and they were extremely good for you, though not fully magical. But inside itself, in the very sap of it, the tree (so to speak) never forgot that other tree in Narnia to which it belonged. Sometimes it would move mysteriously when there was no wind blowing: I think that when this happened there were high winds in Narnia and the English tree quivered because, at that moment, the Narnia tree was rocking and swaying in a strong south-western gale. However that might be, it was proved later that there was still magic in its wood. For when Digory was quite middle-aged (and he was a famous learned man, a Professor, and a great traveller by that time) and the Ketterleys' old house belonged to him, there was a great storm all over the south of England which blew the tree down. He couldn't bear to have it simply chopped up for firewood, so he had part of the timber made into a wardrobe, which he put in his big house in the country. And though he himself did not discover the magic properties of that wardrobe, someone else did. That was the beginning of all the comings and goings between Narnia and our world, which you can read of in other books.

When Digory and his people went to live in the big country house, they took Uncle Andrew to live with them; for Digory's father said, "We must try to keep the old fellow out of mischief, and it isn't fair that poor Letty should have him always on her hands." Uncle Andrew never tried any magic again as long as he lived. He had learned his lesson, and in his old age he became a nicer and less selfish old man than he had ever been before. But he always liked to get visitors alone in the billiard-room and tell them stories about a mysterious lady, a foreign royalty, with whom he had driven about London. "A devilish temper she had," he would say. "But she was a dem fine woman, sir, a dem fine woman."

THE LION, THE WITCH
AND THE WARDROBE

THE LION, THE WITCH AND THE WARDROBE

CONTENTS

TO LUCY BARFIELD

My Dear Lucy,

I wrote this story for you, but when I began it I had not realized that girls grow quicker than books. As a result you are already too old for fairy tales, and by the time it is printed and bound you will be older still. But some day you will be old enough to start reading fairy tales again. You can then take it down from some upper shelf, dust it, and tell me what you think of it. I shall probably be too deaf to hear, and too old to understand, a word you say, but I shall still be

your affectionate Godfather,

C. S. Lewis

CHAPTER ONE

LUCY LOOKS INTO A WARDROBE

Once there were four children whose names were Peter, Susan, Edmund and Lucy. This story is about something that happened to them when they were sent away from London during the war because of the air-raids. They were sent to the house of an old Professor who lived in the heart of the country, ten miles from the nearest railway station and two miles from the nearest post office. He had no wife and he lived in a very large house with a housekeeper called Mrs Macready and three servants. (Their names were Ivy, Margaret and Betty, but they do not come into the story much.) He himself was a very old man with shaggy white hair which grew over most of his face as well as on his head, and they liked him almost at once; but on the first evening when he came out to meet them at the front door he was so odd-looking that Lucy (who was the youngest) was a little afraid of him, and Edmund (who was the next youngest) wanted to laugh and had to keep on pretending he was blowing his nose to hide it.

As soon as they had said goodnight to the Professor and gone upstairs on the first night, the boys came into the girls' room and they all talked it over.

"We've fallen on our feet and no mistake," said Peter. "This is going to be perfectly splendid. That old chap will let us do anything we like."

"I think he's an old dear," said Susan.

"Oh, come off it!" said Edmund, who was tired and pretending not to be tired, which always made him bad-tempered. "Don't go on talking like that."

"Like what?" said Susan; "and anyway, it's time you were in bed."

"Trying to talk like Mother," said Edmund. "And who are you to say when I'm to go to bed? Go to bed yourself."

"Hadn't we all better go to bed?" said Lucy. "There's sure to be a row if we're heard talking here."

"No there won't," said Peter. "I tell you this is the sort of house where no one's going to mind what we do. Anyway, they won't hear us. It's about ten minutes' walk from here down to that dining-room, and any amount of stairs and passages in between."

"What's that noise?" said Lucy suddenly. It was a far larger house than she had ever been in before and the thought of all those long passages and rows of doors leading into empty rooms was beginning to make her feel a little creepy.

"It's only a bird, silly," said Edmund.

"It's an owl," said Peter. "This is going to be a wonderful place for birds. I shall go to bed now. I say, let's go and explore tomorrow. You might find anything in a place like this. Did you see those mountains as we came along? And the woods? There might be eagles. There might be stags. There'll be hawks."

"Badgers!" said Lucy.

"Foxes!" said Edmund.

"Rabbits!" said Susan.

But when the next morning came there was a steady rain falling, so thick that when you looked out of the window you could see neither the mountains nor the woods nor even the stream in the garden.

"Of course it would be raining!" said Edmund. They had just finished their breakfast with the Professor and were upstairs in the room he had set apart for them — a long, low room with two windows looking out in one direction and two in another.

"Do stop grumbling, Ed," said Susan. "Ten to one it'll clear up in an hour or so. And in the meantime we're pretty well off. There's a wireless and lots of books."

"Not for me," said Peter; "I'm going to explore in the house."

Everyone agreed to this and that was how the adventures began. It was the sort of house that you never seem to come to the end of, and it was full of unexpected places. The first few doors they tried led only into spare bedrooms, as everyone had expected that they would; but soon they came to a very long room full of pictures, and there they found a suit of armour; and after that was a room all hung with green, with a harp in one corner; and then came three steps down and five steps up, and then a kind of little upstairs hall and a door that led out on to a balcony, and then a whole series of rooms that led into each other and were lined with books — most of them very old books and some bigger than a Bible in a church. And shortly after that they looked into a room that was quite empty except for one big wardrobe; the sort that has a looking-glass in the door. There was nothing else in the room at all except a dead bluebottle on the window-sill.

"Nothing there!" said Peter, and they all trooped out again – all except Lucy. She stayed behind because she thought it would be worthwhile trying the door of the wardrobe, even though she felt almost sure that it would be locked. To her surprise it opened quite easily, and two mothballs dropped out.

Looking into the inside, she saw several coats hanging up – mostly long fur coats. There was nothing Lucy liked so much as the smell and feel of fur. She immediately stepped into the wardrobe and got in among the coats and rubbed her face against them, leaving the door open, of course, because she knew that it is very foolish to shut oneself into any wardrobe. Soon she went further in and found that there was a second row of coats hanging up behind the first one. It was almost quite dark in there and she kept her arms stretched out in front of her so as not to bump her face into the back of the wardrobe. She took a step further in – then two or three steps – always expecting to feel woodwork against the tips of her fingers. But she could not feel it.

"This must be a simply enormous wardrobe!" thought Lucy, going still further in and pushing the soft folds of the coats aside to make room for her. Then she noticed that there was something crunching under her feet. "I wonder is that more mothballs?" she thought, stooping down to feel it with her hand. But instead of feeling the hard, smooth wood of the floor of the wardrobe, she felt something soft and powdery and extremely cold. "This is very queer," she said, and went on a step or two further.

Next moment she found that what was rubbing against her face and hands was no longer soft fur but something hard and rough and even prickly. "Why, it is just like branches of trees!" exclaimed Lucy. And then she saw that there was a light ahead of her; not a few inches away where the back of the wardrobe ought to have been, but a long way off. Something cold and soft was falling on her. A moment later she found that she was standing in the middle of a wood at night-time with snow under her feet and snowflakes falling through the air.

Lucy felt a little frightened, but she felt very inquisitive and excited as well. She looked back over her shoulder and there, between the dark tree-trunks, she could still see the open doorway of the wardrobe and even catch a glimpse of the empty room from which she had set out. (She had, of course, left the door open, for she knew that it is a very silly thing to shut oneself into a wardrobe.) It seemed to be still daylight there. "I can always get back if anything goes wrong," thought Lucy. She began to walk forward, *crunch-crunch* over the snow and through the wood towards the other light. In about ten minutes she reached it and found it was a lamp-post. As she stood looking at it, wondering why there was a lamp-post in the middle of a wood and wondering what to do next, she heard a pitter patter of feet coming towards her. And soon after that a very strange person stepped out from among the trees into the light of the lamp-post.

He was only a little taller than Lucy herself and he carried over his head an umbrella, white with snow. From the waist upwards he was like a man, but his legs were shaped like a goat's (the hair on them was glossy black) and instead of feet he had goat's hoofs. He also had a tail, but Lucy did not notice this at first because it was neatly caught up over the arm that held the umbrella so as to keep it from trailing in the snow. He had a red woollen muffler round his neck, and his skin was rather reddish too. He had a strange, but pleasant little face, with a short pointed beard and curly hair, and out of the hair there stuck two horns, one on each side of his forehead. One of his hands, as I have said, held the umbrella; in the other arm he carried several brown-paper parcels. What with the parcels and the snow it looked just as if he had been doing his Christmas shopping. He was a Faun. And when he saw Lucy he gave such a start of surprise that he dropped all his parcels.

"Goodness gracious me!" exclaimed the Faun.

CHAPTER TWO

WHAT LUCY FOUND THERE

"Good evening," said Lucy. But the Faun was so busy picking up its parcels that at first it did not reply. When it had finished, it made her a little bow.

"Good evening, good evening," said the Faun. "Excuse me – I don't want to be inquisitive – but should I be right in thinking that you are a Daughter of Eve?"

"My name's Lucy," said she, not quite understanding him.

"But you are – forgive me – you are what they call a girl?" said the Faun.

"Of course I'm a girl," said Lucy.

"You are in fact Human?"

"Of course I'm human," said Lucy, still a little puzzled.

"To be sure, to be sure," said the Faun. "How stupid of me! But I've never seen a Son of Adam or a Daughter of Eve before. I am delighted. That is to say—" and then it stopped as if it had been going to say something it had not intended but had remembered in time. "Delighted, delighted," it went on. "Allow me to introduce myself. My name is Tumnus."

"I am very pleased to meet you, Mr Tumnus," said Lucy.

"And may I ask, O Lucy Daughter of Eve," said Mr Tumnus, "how you have come into Narnia?"

"Narnia? What's that?" said Lucy.

"This is the land of Narnia," said the Faun, "where we are now; all that lies between the lamp-post and the great castle of Cair Paravel on the eastern sea. And you – you have come from the Wild Woods of the West?"

"I – I got in through the wardrobe in the spare room," said Lucy.

"Ah!" said Mr Tumnus in a rather melancholy voice, "if only I had worked harder at geography when I was a little Faun, I should no doubt know all about those strange countries. It is too late now."

"But they aren't countries at all," said Lucy, almost laughing. "It's only just back there – at least – I'm not sure. It is summer there."

"Meanwhile," said Mr Tumnus, "it is winter in Narnia, and has been for ever so long, and we shall both catch cold if we stand here talking in the snow. Daughter of Eve from the far land of Spare Oom where eternal summer reigns around the bright city of War Drobe, how would it be if you came and had tea with me?"

"Thank you very much, Mr Tumnus," said Lucy. "But I was wondering whether I ought to be getting back."

"It's only just round the corner," said the Faun, "and there'll be a roaring fire – and toast – and sardines – and cake."

"Well, it's very kind of you," said Lucy. "But I shan't be able to stay long."

"If you will take my arm, Daughter of Eve," said Mr Tumnus, "I shall be able to hold the umbrella over both of us. That's the way. Now – off we go."

And so Lucy found herself walking through the wood arm in arm with this strange creature as if they had known one another all their lives.

They had not gone far before they came to a place where the ground became rough and there were rocks all about and little hills up and little hills down. At the bottom of one small valley Mr Tumnus turned suddenly aside as if he were going to walk straight into an unusually large rock, but at the last moment Lucy found he was leading her into the entrance of a cave. As soon as they were inside she found herself blinking in the light of a wood fire. Then Mr Tumnus stooped and took a flaming piece of wood out of the fire with a neat little pair of tongs, and lit a lamp. "Now we shan't be long," he said, and immediately put a kettle on.

Lucy thought she had never been in a nicer place. It was a little, dry, clean cave of reddish stone with a carpet on the floor and two little chairs ("One for me and one for a friend," said Mr Tumnus) and a table and a dresser and a mantelpiece over the fire and above that a picture of an old Faun with a grey beard. In one corner there was a door which Lucy thought must lead to Mr Tumnus's bedroom, and on one wall was a shelf full of books. Lucy looked at these while he was setting out the tea things. They had titles like *The Life and Letters of Silenus* or *Nymphs and Their Ways* or *Men, Monks and Gamekeepers; A Study in Popular Legend* or *Is Man a Myth?*

"Now, Daughter of Eve!" said the Faun.

And really it was a wonderful tea. There was a nice brown egg, lightly boiled, for each of them, and then sardines on toast, and then buttered toast, and then toast with honey, and then a sugar-topped cake. And when Lucy was tired of eating, the Faun began to talk. He had wonderful tales to tell of life in the forest. He told about the midnight dances and how the

Nymphs who lived in the wells and the Dryads who lived in the trees came out to dance with the Fauns; about long hunting parties after the milk-white stag who could give you wishes if you caught him; about feasting and treasure-seeking with the wild Red Dwarfs in deep mines and caverns far beneath the forest floor; and then about summer when the woods were green and old Silenus on his fat donkey would come to visit them, and sometimes Bacchus himself, and then the streams would run with wine instead of water and the whole forest would give itself up to jollification for weeks on end. "Not that it isn't always winter now," he added gloomily. Then to cheer himself up he took out from its case on the dresser a strange little flute that looked as if it were made of straw, and began to play. And the tune he played made Lucy want to cry and laugh and dance and go to sleep all at the same time. It must have been hours later when she shook herself and said:

"Oh, Mr Tumnus – I'm so sorry to stop you, and I do love that tune – but really, I must go home. I only meant to stay for a few minutes."

"It's no good *now*, you know," said the Faun, laying down its flute and shaking its head at her very sorrowfully.

"No good?" said Lucy, jumping up and feeling rather frightened. "What do you mean? I've got to go home at once. The others will be wondering what has happened to me." But a moment later she asked, "Mr Tumnus! Whatever is the matter?" for the Faun's brown eyes had filled with tears and then the tears began trickling down its cheeks, and soon they were running off the end of its nose; and at last it covered its face with its hands and began to howl.

"Mr Tumnus! Mr Tumnus!" said Lucy in great distress. "Don't! Don't! What is the matter? Aren't you well? Dear Mr Tumnus, do tell me what is wrong."

But the Faun continued sobbing as if his heart would break. And even when Lucy went over and put her arms round him and lent him her handkerchief, he did not stop. He merely took the handkerchief and kept on using it, wringing it out with both hands whenever it got too wet to be any more use, so that presently Lucy was standing in a damp patch.

"Mr Tumnus!" bawled Lucy in his ear, shaking him. "Do stop. Stop it at once! You ought to be ashamed of yourself, a great big Faun like you. What on earth are you crying about?"

"Oh – oh – oh!" sobbed Mr Tumnus. "I'm crying because I'm such a bad Faun."

"I don't think you're a bad Faun at all," said Lucy. "I think you are a very good Faun. You are the nicest Faun I've ever met."

"Oh – oh – you wouldn't say that if you knew," replied Mr Tumnus between his sobs. "No, I'm a bad Faun. I don't suppose there ever was a worse Faun since the beginning of the world."

"But what have you done?" asked Lucy.

"My old father, now," said Mr Tumnus; "that's his picture over the mantelpiece. He would never have done a thing like this."

"A thing like what?" said Lucy.

"Like what I've done," said the Faun. "Taken service under the White Witch. That's what I am. I'm in the pay of the White Witch."

"The White Witch? Who is she?"

"Why, it is she who has got all Narnia under her thumb. It's she who makes it always winter. Always winter and never Christmas; think of that!"

"How awful!" said Lucy. "But what does she pay *you* for?"

"That's the worst of it," said Mr Tumnus with a deep groan. "I'm a kidnapper for her, that's what I am. Look at me, Daughter of Eve. Would you believe that I'm the sort of Faun to meet a poor innocent child in the wood, one that had never done me any harm, and pretend to be friendly with it, and invite it home to my cave, all for the sake of lulling it asleep and then handing it over to the White Witch?"

"No," said Lucy. "I'm sure you wouldn't do anything of the sort."

"But I have," said the Faun.

"Well," said Lucy rather slowly (for she wanted to be truthful and yet not be too hard on him), "well, that was pretty bad. But you're so sorry for it that I'm sure you will never do it again."

"Daughter of Eve, don't you understand?" said the Faun. "It isn't something I *have* done. I'm doing it now, this very moment."

"What do you mean?" cried Lucy, turning very white.

"You are the child," said Tumnus. "I had orders from the White Witch that if ever I saw a Son of Adam or a Daughter of Eve in the wood, I was to catch them and hand them over to her. And you are the first I have ever met. And I've pretended to be your friend and asked you to tea, and all the time I've been meaning to wait till you were asleep and then go and tell *Her*."

"Oh, but you won't, Mr Tumnus," said Lucy. "You won't, will you? Indeed, indeed you really mustn't."

"And if I don't," said he, beginning to cry again, "she's sure to find out. And she'll have my tail cut off, and my horns sawn off, and my beard plucked out, and she'll wave her wand over my beautiful cloven hoofs and turn them into horrid solid hoofs like a wretched horse's. And if she is extra and specially angry she'll turn me into stone and I shall be only a statue of a Faun in her horrible house until the four thrones at Cair Paravel are filled – and goodness knows when that will happen, or whether it will ever happen at all."

"I'm very sorry, Mr Tumnus," said Lucy. "But please let me go home."

"Of course I will," said the Faun. "Of course I've got to. I see that now. I hadn't known what Humans were like before I met you. Of course I can't give you up to the Witch, not now that I know you. But we must be off at once. I'll see you back to the lamp-post. I suppose you can find your own way from there back to Spare Oom and War Drobe?"

"I'm sure I can," said Lucy.

"We must go as quietly as we can," said Mr Tumnus. "The whole wood is full of *her* spies. Even some of the trees are on her side."

They both got up and left the tea things on the table, and Mr Tumnus once more put up his umbrella and gave Lucy his arm, and they went out into the snow. The journey back was not at all like the journey to the Faun's cave; they stole along as quickly as they could, without speaking a word, and Mr Tumnus kept to the darkest places. Lucy was relieved when they reached the lamp-post again.

"Do you know your way from here, Daughter of Eve?" said Mr Tumnus.

Lucy looked very hard between the trees and could just see in the distance a patch of light that looked like daylight. "Yes," she said, "I can see the wardrobe door."

"Then be off home as quick as you can," said the Faun, "and — c-can you ever forgive me for what I meant to do?"

"Why, of course I can," said Lucy, shaking him heartily by the hand. "And I do hope you won't get into dreadful trouble on my account."

"Farewell, Daughter of Eve," said he. "Perhaps I may keep the handkerchief?"

"Rather!" said Lucy, and then ran towards the far-off patch of daylight as quickly as her legs would carry her. And presently instead of rough branches brushing past her she felt coats, and instead of crunching snow under her feet she felt wooden boards, and all at once she found herself jumping out of the wardrobe into the same empty room from which the whole adventure had started. She shut the wardrobe door tightly behind her and looked around, panting for breath. It was still raining and she could hear the voices of the others in the passage.

"I'm here," she shouted. "I'm here. I've come back, I'm all right."

CHAPTER THREE

EDMUND AND THE WARDROBE

Lucy ran out of the empty room into the passage and found the other three.

"It's all right," she repeated, "I've come back."

"What on earth are you talking about, Lucy?" asked Susan.

"Why," said Lucy in amazement, "haven't you all been wondering where I was?"

"So you've been hiding, have you?" said Peter. "Poor old Lu, hiding and nobody noticed! You'll have to hide longer than that if you want people to start looking for you."

"But I've been away for hours and hours," said Lucy.

The others all stared at one another.

"Batty!" said Edmund, tapping his head. "Quite batty."

"What do you mean, Lu?" asked Peter.

"What I said," answered Lucy. "It was just after breakfast when I went into the wardrobe, and I've been away for hours and hours, and had tea, and all sorts of things have happened."

"Don't be silly, Lucy," said Susan. "We've only just come out of that room a moment ago, and you were there then."

"She's not being silly at all," said Peter, "she's just making up a story for fun, aren't you, Lu? And why shouldn't she?"

"No, Peter, I'm not," she said. "It's – it's a magic wardrobe. There's a wood inside it, and it's snowing, and there's a Faun and a Witch and it's called Narnia; come and see."

The others did not know what to think, but Lucy was so excited that they all went back with her into the room. She rushed ahead of them, flung open the door of the wardrobe and cried, "Now! Go in and see for yourselves."

"Why, you goose," said Susan, putting her head inside and pulling the fur coats apart, "it's just an ordinary wardrobe; look! There's the back of it."

Then everyone looked in and pulled the coats apart; and they all saw – Lucy herself saw – a perfectly ordinary wardrobe. There was no wood and no snow, only the back of the wardrobe, with hooks on it. Peter went in and rapped his knuckles on it to make sure that it was solid.

"A jolly good hoax, Lu," he said as he came out again; "you have really taken us in, I must admit. We half believed you."

"But it wasn't a hoax at all," said Lucy, "really and truly. It was all different a moment ago. Honestly it was. I promise."

"Come, Lu," said Peter, "that's going a bit far. You've had your joke. Hadn't you better drop it now?"

Lucy grew very red in the face and tried to say something, though she hardly knew what she was trying to say, and burst into tears.

For the next few days she was very miserable. She could have made it up with the others quite easily at any moment if she could have brought herself to say that the whole thing was only a story made up for fun. But Lucy was a very truthful girl and she knew that she was really in the right; and she could not bring herself to say this. The others who thought she was telling a lie, and a silly lie too, made her very unhappy. The two elder ones did this without meaning to do it, but Edmund could be spiteful, and on this occasion he *was* spiteful. He sneered and jeered at Lucy and kept on asking her if she'd found any other new countries in other cupboards all over the house. What made it worse was that these days ought to have been delightful. The weather was fine and they were out of doors from morning to night, bathing, fishing, climbing trees, and lying in the heather. But Lucy could not properly enjoy any of it. And so things went on until the next wet day.

That day, when it came to the afternoon and there was still no sign of a break in the weather, they decided to play hide-and-seek. Susan was "It" and as soon as the others scattered to hide, Lucy went to the room where the wardrobe was. She did not mean to hide in the wardrobe, because she knew that would only set the others talking again about the whole wretched business. But she did want to have one more look inside it; for by this time she was beginning to wonder herself whether Narnia and the Faun had not been a dream. The house was so large and complicated and full of hiding-places that she thought she would have time to have one look into the wardrobe and then hide somewhere else. But as soon as she reached it she heard steps in the passage outside, and then there was nothing for it but to jump into the wardrobe and hold the door closed behind her. She did not shut it properly because she knew that it is very silly to shut oneself into a wardrobe, even if it is not a magic one.

Now the steps she had heard were those of Edmund; and he came into the room just in time to see Lucy vanishing into the wardrobe. He at once decided to get into it himself – not because he thought it a particularly good place to hide but because he wanted to go on teasing her about her imaginary country. He opened the door. There were the coats hanging up as usual, and a smell of mothballs, and darkness and silence, and no sign of Lucy. "She thinks I'm Susan come to catch her," said Edmund to himself, "and so she's keeping very quiet at the back." He jumped in and shut the door, forgetting what a very foolish thing this is to do. Then he began feeling about for Lucy in the dark. He had expected to find her in a few seconds and was very surprised when he did not. He decided to open the door again and let in some light. But he could not find the door either. He didn't like this at all and began groping wildly in every direction; he even shouted out, "Lucy! Lu! Where are you? I know you're here."

There was no answer and Edmund noticed that his own voice had a curious sound – not the sound you expect in a cupboard, but a kind of open-air sound. He also noticed that he was unexpectedly cold; and then he saw a light.

"Thank goodness," said Edmund, "the door must have swung open of its own accord." He forgot all about Lucy and went towards the light, which he thought was the open door of the wardrobe. But instead of finding himself stepping out into the spare room he found himself stepping out from the shadow of some thick dark fir trees into an open place in the middle of a wood.

There was crisp, dry snow under his feet and more snow lying on the branches of the trees. Overhead there was pale blue sky, the sort of sky one sees on a fine winter day in the morning. Straight ahead of him he saw between the tree-trunks the sun, just rising, very red and clear. Everything was perfectly still, as if he were the only living creature in that country. There was not even a robin or a squirrel among the trees, and the wood stretched as far as he could see in every direction. He shivered.

He now remembered that he had been looking for Lucy: and also how unpleasant he had been to her about her "imaginary country" which now turned out not to have been imaginary at all. He thought that she must be somewhere quite close and so he shouted, "Lucy! Lucy! I'm here too – Edmund."

There was no answer.

"She's angry about all the things I've been saying lately," thought Edmund. And though he did not like to admit that he had been wrong, he also did not much like being alone in this strange, cold, quiet place; so he shouted again:

"I say, Lu! I'm sorry I didn't believe you. I see now you were right all along. Do come out. Make it Pax."

Still there was no answer.

"Just like a girl," said Edmund to himself, "sulking somewhere, and won't accept an apology." He looked round him again and decided he did not much like this place, and had almost made up his mind to go home, when he heard, very far off in the wood, a sound of bells. He listened and the sound came nearer and nearer and at last there swept into sight a sledge drawn by two reindeer.

The reindeer were about the size of Shetland ponies and their hair was so white that even the snow hardly looked white compared with them; their branching horns were gilded and shone like something on fire when the sunrise caught them. Their harness was of scarlet leather and covered with bells. On the sledge, driving the reindeer, sat a fat dwarf who would have been about three feet high if he had been standing. He was dressed in polar bear's fur and on his head he wore a red hood with a long gold tassel hanging down from its point; his huge beard covered his knees and served him instead of a rug. But behind him, on a much higher seat in the middle of the sledge sat a very different person – a great lady, taller than any woman that Edmund had ever seen. She also was covered in white fur up to her throat and held a long straight golden wand in her right hand and wore a golden crown on her head. Her face was white – not merely pale, but white like snow or paper or icing-sugar, except for her very red mouth. It was a beautiful face in other respects, but proud and cold and stern.

The sledge was a fine sight as it came sweeping towards Edmund with the bells jingling and the dwarf cracking his whip and the snow flying up on each side of it.

"Stop!" said the Lady, and the dwarf pulled the reindeer up so sharply that they almost sat down. Then they recovered themselves and stood champing their bits and blowing. In the frosty air the breath coming out of their nostrils looked like smoke.

"And what, pray, are you?" said the Lady, looking hard at Edmund.

"I'm – I'm – my name's Edmund," said Edmund rather awkwardly. He did not like the way she looked at him.

The Lady frowned. "Is that how you address a Queen?" she asked, looking sterner than ever.

"I beg your pardon, your Majesty, I didn't know," said Edmund.

"Not know the Queen of Narnia?" cried she. "Ha! You shall know us better hereafter. But I repeat – what are you?"

"Please, your Majesty," said Edmund, "I don't know what you mean. I'm at school – at least I was – it's the holidays now."

CHAPTER FOUR

TURKISH DELIGHT

"But what *are* you?" said the Queen again. "Are you a great overgrown dwarf that has cut off its beard?"

"No, your Majesty," said Edmund. "I never had a beard. I'm a boy."

"A boy!" said she. "Do you mean you are a Son of Adam?"

Edmund stood still, saying nothing. He was too confused by this time to understand what the question meant.

"I see you are an idiot, whatever else you may be," said the Queen. "Answer me, once and for all, or I shall lose my patience. Are you human?"

"Yes, your Majesty," said Edmund.

"And how, pray, did you come to enter my dominions?"

"Please, your Majesty, I came in through a wardrobe."

"A wardrobe? What do you mean?"

"I – I opened a door and just found myself here, your Majesty," said Edmund.

"Ha!" said the Queen, speaking more to herself than to him. "A door. A door from the world of men! I have heard of such things. This may wreck all. But he is only one, and he is easily dealt with." As she spoke these words she rose from her seat and looked Edmund full in the face, her eyes flaming; at the same moment she raised her wand. Edmund felt sure that she was going to do something dreadful but he seemed unable to move. Then, just as he gave himself up for lost, she appeared to change her mind.

"My poor child," she said in quite a different voice, "how cold you look! Come and sit with me here on the sledge and I will put my mantle round you and we will talk."

Edmund did not like this arrangement at all but he dared not disobey;

he stepped on to the sledge and sat at her feet, and she put a fold of her fur mantle round him and tucked it well in.

"Perhaps something hot to drink?" said the Queen. "Should you like that?"

"Yes, please, your Majesty," said Edmund, whose teeth were chattering.

The Queen took from somewhere among her wrappings a very small bottle which looked as if it were made of copper. Then, holding out her arm, she let one drop fall from it on the snow beside the sledge. Edmund saw the drop for a second in mid-air, shining like a diamond. But the moment it touched the snow there was a hissing sound and there stood a jewelled cup full of something that steamed. The dwarf immediately took this and handed it to Edmund with a bow and a smile; not a very nice smile. Edmund felt much better as he began to sip the hot drink. It was something he had never tasted before, very sweet and foamy and creamy, and it warmed him right down to his toes.

"It is dull, Son of Adam, to drink without eating," said the Queen presently. "What would you like best to eat?"

"Turkish Delight, please, your Majesty," said Edmund.

The Queen let another drop fall from her bottle on to the snow, and instantly there appeared a round box, tied with green silk ribbon, which, when opened, turned out to contain several pounds of the best Turkish Delight. Each piece was sweet and light to the very centre and Edmund had never tasted anything more delicious. He was quite warm now, and very comfortable.

While he was eating, the Queen kept asking him questions. At first Edmund tried to remember that it is rude to speak with one's mouth full, but soon he forgot about this and thought only of trying to shovel down as much Turkish Delight as he could, and the more he ate the more he wanted to eat, and he never asked himself why the Queen should be so inquisitive. She got him to tell her that he had one brother and two sisters, and that one of his sisters had already been in Narnia and had met a Faun there, and that no one except himself and his brother and his sisters knew anything about Narnia. She seemed especially interested in the fact that there were four of them, and kept on coming back to it. "You are sure there are just four of you?" she asked. "Two Sons of Adam and two Daughters of Eve, neither more nor less?" and Edmund, with his mouth full of Turkish Delight, kept on saying, "Yes, I told you that before," and forgetting to call her "Your Majesty", but she didn't seem to mind now.

At last the Turkish Delight was all finished and Edmund was looking very hard at the empty box and wishing that she would ask him whether he would like some more. Probably the Queen knew quite well what he was thinking; for she knew, though Edmund did not, that this was enchanted Turkish Delight and that anyone who had once tasted it would want more and more of it, and would even, if they were allowed, go on eating it till they killed themselves. But she did not offer him any more. Instead, she said to him,

"Son of Adam, I should so much like to see your brother and your two sisters. Will you bring them to see me?"

"I'll try," said Edmund, still looking at the empty box.

"Because, if you did come again – bringing them with you of course – I'd be able to give you some more Turkish Delight. I can't do it now, the magic will only work once. In my own house it would be another matter."

"Why can't we go to your house now?" said Edmund. When he had first got on to the sledge he had been afraid that she might drive away with him to some unknown place from which he would not be able to get back; but he had forgotten about that fear now.

"It is a lovely place, my house," said the Queen. "I am sure you would like it. There are whole rooms full of Turkish Delight, and what's more, I have no children of my own. I want a nice boy whom I could bring up as a Prince and who would be King of Narnia when I am gone. While he was Prince he would wear a gold crown and eat Turkish Delight all day long; and you are much the cleverest and handsomest young man I've ever met. I think I would like to make you the Prince – some day, when you bring the others to visit me."

"Why not now?" said Edmund. His face had become very red and his mouth and fingers were sticky. He did not look either clever or handsome, whatever the Queen might say.

"Oh, but if I took you there now," said she, "I shouldn't see your brother and your sisters. I very much want to know your charming relations. You are to be the Prince and – later on – the King; that is understood. But you must have courtiers and nobles. I will make your brother a Duke and your sisters Duchesses."

"There's nothing special about *them*," said Edmund, "and anyway, I could always bring them some other time."

"Ah, but once you were in my house," said the Queen, "you might forget all about them. You would be enjoying yourself so much that you wouldn't want the bother of going to fetch them. No. You must go back to your own country now and come to me another day, *with them*, you understand. It is no good coming without them."

"But I don't even know the way back to my own country," pleaded Edmund.

"That's easy," answered the Queen. "Do you see that lamp?" She pointed with her wand and Edmund turned and saw the same lamp-post under which Lucy had met the Faun. "Straight on, beyond that, is the way to the World of Men. And now look the other way" — here she pointed in the opposite direction — "and tell me if you can see two little hills rising above the trees."

"I think I can," said Edmund.

"Well, my house is between those two hills. So next time you come you have only to find the lamp-post and look for those two hills and walk through the wood till you reach my house. But remember — you must bring the others with you. I might have to be very angry with you if you came alone."

"I'll do my best," said Edmund.

"And, by the way," said the Queen, "you needn't tell them about me. It would be fun to keep it a secret between us two, wouldn't it? Make it a surprise for them. Just bring them along to the two hills — a clever boy like you will easily think of some excuse for doing that — and when you come to my house you could just say, 'Let's see who lives here', or something like that. I am sure that would be best. If your sister has met one of the Fauns, she may have heard strange stories about me — nasty stories that might make her afraid to come to me. Fauns will say anything, you know, and now——"

"Please, please," said Edmund suddenly, "please couldn't I have just one piece of Turkish Delight to eat on the way home?"

"No, no," said the Queen with a laugh, "you must wait till next time." While she spoke, she signalled to the dwarf to drive on, but as the sledge swept away out of sight, the Queen waved to Edmund, calling out, "Next time! Next time! Don't forget. Come soon."

Edmund was still staring after the sledge when he heard someone calling his own name, and looking round he saw Lucy coming towards him from another part of the wood.

"Oh, Edmund!" she cried. "So you've got in too! Isn't it wonderful, and now——"

"All right," said Edmund, "I see you were right and it is a magic wardrobe after all. I'll say I'm sorry if you like. But where on earth have you been all this time? I've been looking for you everywhere."

"If I'd known you had got in I'd have waited for you," said Lucy, who was too happy and excited to notice how snappishly Edmund spoke or how flushed and strange his face was. "I've been having lunch with dear Mr Tumnus, the Faun, and he's very well and the White Witch has done nothing to him for letting me go, so he thinks she can't have found out and perhaps everything is going to be all right after all."

"The White Witch?" said Edmund; "who's she?"

"She is a perfectly terrible person," said Lucy. "She calls herself the Queen of Narnia though she has no right to be queen at all, and all the

Fauns and Dryads and Naiads and Dwarfs and Animals – at least all the good ones – simply hate her. And she can turn people into stone and do all kinds of horrible things. And she has made a magic so that it is always winter in Narnia – always winter, but it never gets to Christmas. And she drives about on a sledge, drawn by reindeer, with her wand in her hand and a crown on her head."

Edmund was already feeling uncomfortable from having eaten too many sweets, and when he heard that the Lady he had made friends with was a dangerous witch he felt even more uncomfortable. But he still wanted to taste that Turkish Delight again more than he wanted anything else.

"Who told you all that stuff about the White Witch?" he asked.

"Mr Tumnus, the Faun," said Lucy.

"You can't always believe what Fauns say," said Edmund, trying to sound as if he knew far more about them than Lucy.

"Who said so?" asked Lucy.

"Everyone knows it," said Edmund; "ask anybody you like. But it's pretty poor sport standing here in the snow. Let's go home."

"Yes, let's," said Lucy. "Oh, Edmund, I am glad you've got in too. The others will have to believe in Narnia now that both of us have been there. What fun it will be!"

But Edmund secretly thought that it would not be as good fun for him as for her. He would have to admit that Lucy had been right, before all the others, and he felt sure the others would all be on the side of the Fauns and the animals; but he was already more than half on the side of the Witch. He did not know what he would say, or how he would keep his secret once they were all talking about Narnia.

By this time they had walked a good way. Then suddenly they felt coats around them instead of branches and the next moment they were both standing outside the wardrobe in the empty room.

"I say," said Lucy, "you do look awful, Edmund. Don't you feel well?"

"I'm all right," said Edmund, but this was not true. He was feeling very sick.

"Come on, then," said Lucy, "let's find the others. What a lot of adventures we shall have now that we're all in it together."

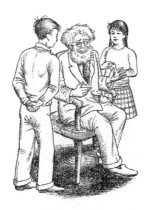

Chapter Five

BACK ON THIS SIDE OF THE DOOR

Because the game of hide-and-seek was still going on, it took Edmund and Lucy some time to find the others. But when at last they were all together (which happened in the long room, where the suit of armour was) Lucy burst out:

"Peter! Susan! It's all true. Edmund has seen it too. There *is* a country you can get to through the wardrobe. Edmund and I both got in. We met one another in there, in the wood. Go on, Edmund; tell them all about it."

"What's all this about, Ed?" said Peter.

And now we come to one of the nastiest things in this story. Up to that moment Edmund had been feeling sick, and sulky, and annoyed with Lucy for being right, but he hadn't made up his mind what to do. When Peter suddenly asked him the question he decided all at once to do the meanest and most spiteful thing he could think of. He decided to let Lucy down.

"Tell us, Ed," said Susan.

And Edmund gave a very superior look as if he were far older than Lucy (there was really only a year's difference) and then a little snigger and said, "Oh, yes, Lucy and I have been playing – pretending that all her story about a country in the wardrobe is true. Just for fun, of course. There's nothing there really."

Poor Lucy gave Edmund one look and rushed out of the room.

Edmund, who was becoming a nastier person every minute, thought that he had scored a great success, and went on at once to say, "There she goes again. What's the matter with her? That's the worst of young kids, they always—"

"Look here," said Peter, turning on him savagely, "shut up! You've been

129

perfectly beastly to Lu ever since she started this nonsense about the wardrobe, and now you go playing games with her about it and setting her off again. I believe you did it simply out of spite."

"But it's all nonsense," said Edmund, very taken aback.

"Of course it's all nonsense," said Peter, "that's just the point. Lu was perfectly all right when we left home, but since we've been down here she seems to be either going queer in the head or else turning into a most frightful liar. But whichever it is, what good do you think you'll do by jeering and nagging at her one day and encouraging her the next?"

"I thought – I thought—" said Edmund; but he couldn't think of anything to say.

"You didn't think anything at all," said Peter; "it's just spite. You've always liked being beastly to anyone smaller than yourself; we've seen that at school before now."

"Do stop it," said Susan; "it won't make things any better having a row between you two. Let's go and find Lucy."

It was not surprising that when they found Lucy, a good deal later, everyone could see that she had been crying. Nothing they could say to her made any difference. She stuck to her story and said:

"I don't care what you think, and I don't care what you say. You can tell the Professor or you can write to Mother or you can do anything you like. I know I've met a Faun in there and – I wish I'd stayed there and you are all beasts, beasts."

It was an unpleasant evening. Lucy was miserable and Edmund was beginning to feel that his plan wasn't working as well as he had expected. The two older ones were really beginning to think that Lucy was out of her mind. They stood in the passage talking about it in whispers long after she had gone to bed.

The result was the next morning they decided that they really would go and tell the whole thing to the Professor. "He'll write to Father if he thinks there is really something wrong with Lu," said Peter; "it's getting beyond us." So they went and knocked at the study door, and the Professor said, "Come in," and got up and found chairs for them and said he was quite at their disposal. Then he sat listening to them with the tips of his fingers pressed together and never interrupting, till they had finished the whole story. After that he said nothing for quite a long time. Then he cleared his throat and said the last thing either of them expected:

"How do you know," he asked, "that your sister's story is not true?"

"Oh, but—" began Susan, and then stopped. Anyone could see from the old man's face that he was perfectly serious. Then Susan pulled herself together and said, "But Edmund said they had only been pretending."

"That is a point," said the Professor, "which certainly deserves consideration; very careful consideration. For instance – if you will excuse me for asking the question – does your experience lead you to regard your brother or your sister as the more reliable? I mean, which is the more truthful?"

"That's just the funny thing about it, sir," said Peter. "Up till now, I'd have said Lucy every time."

"And what do you think, my dear?" said the Professor, turning to Susan.

"Well," said Susan, "in general, I'd say the same as Peter, but this couldn't be true – all this about the wood and the faun."

"That is more than I know," said the Professor, "and a charge of lying against someone whom you have always found truthful is a very serious thing; a very serious thing indeed."

"We were afraid it mightn't even be lying," said Susan; "we thought there might be something wrong with Lucy."

"Madness, you mean?" said the Professor quite coolly. "Oh, you can make your minds easy about that. One has only to look at her and talk to her to see that she is not mad."

"But then," said Susan, and stopped. She had never dreamed that a grown-up would talk like the professor and didn't know what to think.

"Logic!" said the Professor half to himself. "Why don't they teach logic at these schools? There are only three possibilities. Either your sister is telling lies, or she is mad, or she is telling the truth. You know she doesn't tell lies and it is obvious that she is not mad. For the moment then and unless any further evidence turns up, we must assume that she is telling the truth."

Susan looked at him very hard and was quite sure from the expression on his face that he was not making fun of them.

"But how could it be true, sir?" said Peter.

"Why do you say that?" asked the Professor.

"Well, for one thing," said Peter, "if it was real why doesn't everyone find this country every time they go to the wardrobe? I mean, there was nothing there when we looked; even Lucy didn't pretend there was."

"What has that to do with it?" said the Professor.

"Well, sir, if things are real, they're there all the time."

"Are they?" said the Professor; and Peter did not know quite what to say.

"But there was no time," said Susan. "Lucy had had no time to have gone anywhere, even if there was such a place. She came running after us the very moment we were out of the room. It was less than a minute, and she pretended to have been away for hours."

"That is the very thing that makes her story so likely to be true," said the Professor. "If there really is a door in this house that leads to some other world (and I should warn you that this is a very strange house, and even I know very little about it) – if, I say, she had got into another world, I should not be at all surprised to find that the other world had a separate time of its own; so that however long you stayed there it would never take up any of our time. On the other hand, I don't think many girls of her age would invent that idea for themselves. If she had been pretending, she would have hidden for a reasonable time before coming out and telling her story."

"But do you really mean, sir," said Peter, "that there could be other worlds – all over the place, just round the corner – like that?"

"Nothing is more probable," said the Professor, taking off his spectacles and beginning to polish them, while he muttered to himself, "I wonder what they *do* teach them at these schools."

"But what are we to do?" said Susan. She felt that the conversation was beginning to get off the point.

"My dear young lady," said the Professor, suddenly looking up with a very sharp expression at both of them, "there is one plan which no one has yet suggested and which is well worth trying."

"What's that?" said Susan.

"We might all try minding our own business," said he. And that was the end of that conversation.

After this, things were a good deal better for Lucy. Peter saw to it that Edmund stopped jeering at her, and neither she nor anyone else felt inclined to talk about the wardrobe at all. It had become a rather alarming subject. And so for a time it looked as if all the adventures were coming to an end; but that was not to be.

This house of the Professor's – which even he knew so little about – was so old and famous that people from all over England used to come and ask permission to see over it. It was the sort of house that is mentioned in guide books and even in histories; and well it might be, for all manner of stories were told about it, some of them even stranger than the one I am telling you now. And when parties of sightseers arrived and asked to see the house, the Professor always gave them permission, and Mrs Macready, the housekeeper, showed them round, telling them about the pictures and the armour, and the rare books in the library. Mrs Macready was not fond of children, and did not like to be interrupted when she was telling visitors all the things she knew. She had said to Susan and Peter almost on the first morning (along with a good many other instructions), "And please remember you're to keep out of the way whenever I'm taking a party over the house."

"Just as if any of us would *want* to waste half the morning trailing round with a crowd of strange grown-ups!" said Edmund, and the other three thought the same. That was how the adventures began for the third time.

A few mornings later Peter and Edmund were looking at the suit of armour and wondering if they could take it to bits when the two girls rushed into the room and said, "Look out! Here comes the Macready and a whole gang with her."

"Sharp's the word," and Peter, and all four made off through the door at the far end of the room. But when they had got out into the Green Room and beyond it, into the Library, they suddenly heard voices ahead of them, and realized that Mrs Macready must be bringing her party of sightseers up the back stairs — instead of up the front stairs as they had expected. And after that — whether it was that they lost their heads, or that Mrs Macready was trying to catch them, or that some magic in the house had come to life and was chasing them into Narnia — they seemed to find themselves being followed everywhere, until at last Susan said, "Oh, bother those trippers! Here — let's get into the Wardrobe Room till they've passed. No one will follow us in there." But the moment they were inside they heard the voices in the passage — and then someone fumbling at the door — and then they saw the handle turning.

"Quick!" said Peter, "there's nowhere else," and flung open the wardrobe. All four of them bundled inside it and sat there, panting, in the dark. Peter held the door closed but did not shut it; for, of course, he remembered, as every sensible person does, that you should never, never shut yourself in a wardrobe.

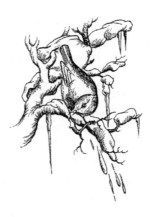

CHAPTER SIX

INTO THE FOREST

"I wish the Macready would hurry up and take all these people away," said Susan presently, "I'm getting horribly cramped."

"And what a filthy smell of camphor!" said Edmund.

"I expect the pockets of these coats are full of it," said Susan, "to keep away the moths."

"There's something sticking into my back," said Peter.

"And isn't it cold?" said Susan.

"Now that you mention it, it is cold," said Peter, "and hang it all, it's wet too. What's the matter with this place? I'm sitting on something wet. It's getting wetter every minute." He struggled to his feet.

"Let's get out," said Edmund, "they've gone."

"O-o-oh!" said Susan suddenly, and everyone asked her what was the matter.

"I'm sitting against a tree," said Susan, "and look! It's getting light – over there."

"By jove, you're right," said Peter, "and look there – and there. It's trees all round. And this wet stuff is snow. Why, I do believe we've got into Lucy's wood after all."

And now there was no mistaking it and all four children stood blinking in the daylight of a winter day. Behind them were coats hanging on pegs, in front of them were snow-covered trees.

Peter turned at once to Lucy.

"I apologize for not believing you," he said, "I'm sorry. Will you shake hands?"

"Of course," said Lucy, and did.

"And now," said Susan, "what do we do next?"

"Do?" said Peter, "why, go and explore the wood, of course."

"Ugh!" said Susan, stamping her feet, "it's pretty cold. What about putting on some of these coats?"

"They're not ours," said Peter doubtfully.

"I am sure nobody would mind," said Susan; "it isn't as if we wanted to take them out of the house; we shan't take them even out of the wardrobe."

"I never thought of that, Su," said Peter. "Of course, now you put it that way, I see. No one could say you had bagged a coat as long as you leave it in the wardrobe where you found it. And I suppose this whole country is in the wardrobe."

They immediately carried out Susan's very sensible plan. The coats were rather too big for them so that they came down to their heels and looked more like royal robes than coats when they had put them on. But they all felt a good deal warmer and each thought the others looked better in their new get-up and more suitable to the landscape.

"We can pretend we are Arctic explorers," said Lucy.

"This is going to be exciting enough without pretending," said Peter, as he began leading the way forward into the forest. There were heavy, darkish clouds overhead and it looked as if there might be more snow before night.

"I say," began Edmund presently, "oughtn't we to be bearing a bit more to the left, that is, if we are aiming for the lamp-post?" He had forgotten for the moment that he must pretend never to have been in the wood before. The moment the words were out of his mouth he realized that he had given himself away. Everyone stopped; everyone stared at him. Peter whistled.

"So you really were here," he said, "that time Lu said she'd met you in here – and you made out she was telling lies."

There was a dead silence. "Well, of all the poisonous little beasts——" said Peter, and shrugged his shoulders and said no more. There seemed, indeed, no more to say, and presently the four resumed their journey; but Edmund was saying to himself, "I'll pay you all out for this, you pack of stuck-up, self-satisfied prigs."

"Where *are* we going anyway?" said Susan, chiefly for the sake of changing the subject.

"I think Lu ought to be the leader," said Peter; "Goodness knows she deserves it. Where will you take us, Lu?"

"What about going to see Mr Tumnus?" said Lucy. "He's the nice Faun I told you about."

Everyone agreed to this and off they went, walking briskly and stamping their feet. Lucy proved a good leader. At first she wondered whether she would be able to find the way, but she recognized an odd-looking tree in one place and a stump in another and brought them on to where the ground became uneven and into the little valley and at last to the very door of Mr Tumnus's cave. But there a terrible surprise awaited them.

The door had been wrenched off its hinges and broken to bits. Inside, the cave was dark and cold and had the damp feel and smell of a place that had not been lived in for several days. Snow had drifted in from the doorway and was heaped on the floor, mixed with something black, which turned out to be the charred sticks and ashes from the fire. Someone had apparently flung it about the room and then stamped it out. The crockery lay smashed on the floor and the picture of the Faun's father had been slashed into shreds with a knife.

"This is a pretty good wash-out," said Edmund; "not much good coming here."

"What is this?" said Peter, stooping down. He had just noticed a piece of paper which had been nailed through the carpet to the floor.

"Is there anything written on it?" asked Susan.

"Yes, I think there is," answered Peter, "but I can't read it in this light. Let's get out into the open air."

They all went out in the daylight and crowded round Peter as he read out the following words:

> *The former occupant of these premises, the Faun Tumnus, is under arrest and awaiting his trial on a charge of High Treason against her Imperial Majesty Jadis, Queen of Narnia, Chatelaine of Cair Paravel, Empress of the Lone Islands, etc., also of comforting her said Majesty's enemies, harbouring spies and fraternizing with humans.*
>
> *signed MAUGRIM, Captain of the Secret Police,*
> *LONG LIVE THE QUEEN!*

The children stared at each other.

"I don't know that I'm going to like this place after all," said Susan.

"Who is this Queen, Lu?" said Peter. "Do you know anything about her?"

"She isn't a real queen at all," answered Lucy; "she's a horrible witch, the White Witch. Everyone – all the wood people – hate her. She has made an enchantment over the whole country so that it is always winter here and never Christmas."

"I – I wonder if there's any point in going on," said Susan. "I mean, it doesn't seem particularly safe here and it looks as if it won't be much fun either. And it's getting colder every minute, and we've brought nothing to eat. What about just going home?"

"Oh, but we can't, we can't," said Lucy suddenly; "don't you see? We can't just go home, not after this. It is all on my account that the poor Faun has got into this trouble. He hid me from the Witch and showed me the way back. That's what it means by comforting the Queen's enemies and fraternizing with Humans. We simply must try to rescue him."

"A lot *we* could do!" said Edmund, "when we haven't even got anything to eat!"

"Shut up – you!" said Peter, who was still very angry with Edmund. "What do you think, Susan?"

"I've a horrid feeling that Lu is right," said Susan. "I don't want to go a step further and I wish we'd never come. But I think we must try to do something for Mr Whatever-his-name is – I mean the Faun."

"That's what I feel too," said Peter. "I'm worried about having no food with us. I'd vote for going back and getting something from the larder, only there doesn't seem to be any certainty of getting into this country again when once you've got out of it. I think we'll have to go on."

"So do I," said both the girls.

"If only we knew where the poor chap was imprisoned!" said Peter.

They were all still wondering what to do next, when Lucy said, "Look! There's a robin, with such a red breast. It's the first bird I've seen here. I say! – I wonder, can birds talk in Narnia? It almost looks as if it wanted to say something to us." Then she turned to the Robin and said, "Please, can you tell us where Tumnus the Faun has been taken to?" As she said this she took a step towards the bird. It at once flew away but only as far as to the next tree. There it perched and looked at them very hard as if it understood all they had been saying. Almost without noticing that they had done so, the four children went a step or two nearer to it. At this the Robin flew away again to the next tree and once more looked at them very hard. (You couldn't have found a robin with a redder chest or a brighter eye.)

"Do you know," said Lucy, "I really believe he means us to follow him."

"I've an idea he does," said Susan. "What do you think, Peter?"

"Well, we might as well try it," answered Peter.

The Robin appeared to understand the matter thoroughly. It kept going from tree to tree, always a few yards ahead of them, but always so near that they could easily follow it. In this way it led them on, slightly downhill. Wherever the Robin alighted a little shower of snow would fall off the branch. Presently the clouds parted overhead and the winter sun came out and the snow all around them grew dazzlingly bright. They had been travelling in this way for about half an hour, with the two girls in front, when Edmund said to Peter, "If you're not still too high and mighty to talk to me, I've something to say which you'd better listen to."

"What is it?" asked Peter.

"Hush! Not so loud," said Edmund; "there's no good frightening the girls. But have you realized what we're doing?"

"What?" said Peter, lowering his voice to a whisper.

"We're following a guide we know nothing about. How do we know which side that bird is on? Why shouldn't it be leading us into a trap?"

"That's a nasty idea. Still — a robin, you know. They're good birds in all the stories I've ever read. I'm sure a robin wouldn't be on the wrong side."

"If it comes to that, which is the right side? How do we know that the fauns are in the right and the Queen (yes, I know we've been *told* she's a witch) is in the wrong? We don't really know anything about either."

"The Faun saved Lucy."

"He *said* he did. But how do we know? And there's another thing too. Has anyone the least idea of the way home from here?"

"Great Scott!" said Peter. "I hadn't thought of that."

"And no chance of dinner either," said Edmund.

A DAY WITH THE BEAVERS

While the two boys were whispering behind, both the girls suddenly cried "Oh!" and stopped.

"The robin!" cried Lucy. "The robin. It's flown away." And so it had – right out of sight.

"And now what are we to do?" said Edmund, giving Peter a look which was as much as to say, "What did I tell you?"

"Sh! Look!" said Susan.

"What?" said Peter.

"There's something moving among the trees over there to the left."

They all stared as hard as they could, and no one felt very comfortable.

"There it goes again," said Susan presently.

"I saw it that time too," said Peter. "It's still there. It's just gone behind that big tree."

"What is it?" asked Lucy, trying very hard not to sound nervous.

"Whatever it is," said Peter, "it's dodging us. It's something that doesn't want to be seen."

"Let's go home," said Susan. And then, though nobody said it out loud, everyone suddenly realized the same fact that Edmund had whispered to Peter at the end of the last chapter. They were lost.

"What's it like?" said Lucy.

"It's – it's a kind of animal," said Susan; and then, "Look! Look! Quick! There it is."

They all saw it this time, a whiskered furry face which had looked out at them from behind a tree. But this time it didn't immediately draw back. Instead, the animal put its paw against its mouth just as humans put their finger on their lips when they are signalling to you to be quiet. Then it disappeared again. The children all stood holding their breath.

A moment later the stranger came out from behind the tree, glanced all round as if it were afraid someone was watching, said, "Hush", made signs to them to join it in the thicker bit of wood where it was standing, and then once more disappeared.

"I know what it is," said Peter; "it's a beaver. I saw the tail."

"It wants us to go to it," said Susan, "and it is warning us not to make a noise."

"I know," said Peter. "The question is, are we to go to it or not? What do you think, Lu?"

"I think it's a nice beaver," said Lucy.

"Yes, but how do we *know*?" said Edmund.

"Shan't we have to risk it?" said Susan. "I mean, it's no good just standing here and I feel I want some dinner."

At this moment the Beaver again popped its head out from behind the tree and beckoned earnestly to them.

"Come on," said Peter, "let's give it a try. All keep close together. We ought to be a match for one beaver if it turns out to be an enemy."

So the children all got close together and walked up to the tree and in behind it, and there, sure enough, they found the Beaver; but it still drew back, saying to them in a hoarse throaty whisper, "Further in, come further in. Right in here. We're not safe in the open!" Only when it had led them into a dark spot where four trees grew so close together that their boughs met and the brown earth and pine needles could be seen underfoot because no snow had been able to fall there, did it begin to talk to them.

"Are you the Sons of Adam and the Daughters of Eve?" it said.

"We're some of them," said Peter.

"S-s-s-sh!" said the Beaver, "not so loud, please. We're not safe even here."

"Why, who are you afraid of?" said Peter. "There's no one here but ourselves."

"There are the trees," said the Beaver. "They're always listening. Most of them are on our side, but there *are* trees that would betray us to *her*; you know who I mean," and it nodded its head several times.

"If it comes to talking about sides," said Edmund, "how do we know you're a friend?"

"Not meaning to be rude, Mr Beaver," added Peter, "but you see, we're strangers."

"Quite right, quite right," said the Beaver. "Here is my token." With these words it held up to them a little white object. They all looked at it in surprise, till suddenly Lucy said, "Oh, of course. It's my handkerchief – the one I gave to poor Mr Tumnus."

"That's right," said the Beaver. "Poor fellow, he got wind of the arrest before it actually happened and handed this over to me. He said that if anything happened to him I must meet you here and take you on to—" Here the Beaver's voice sank into silence and it gave one or two very mysterious nods. Then, signalling to the children to stand as close around it as they possibly could, so that their faces were actually tickled by its whiskers, it added in a low whisper —

"They say Aslan is on the move – perhaps has already landed."

And now a very curious thing happened. None of the children knew who Aslan was any more than you do; but the moment the Beaver had spoken these words everyone felt quite different. Perhaps it has sometimes happened to you in a dream that someone says something which you don't understand but in the dream it feels as if it has some enormous meaning – either a terrifying one which turns the whole dream into a nightmare or else a lovely meaning too lovely to put into words, which makes the dream so beautiful that you remember it all your life and are always wishing you could get into that dream again. It was like that now. At the name of Aslan each one of the children felt something jump in its inside. Edmund felt a sensation of mysterious horror. Peter felt suddenly brave and adventurous. Susan felt as if some delicious smell or some delightful strain of music had just floated by her. And Lucy got the feeling you have when you wake up in the morning and realize that it is the beginning of the holidays or the beginning of summer.

"And what about Mr Tumnus," said Lucy; "where is he?"

"S-s-s-sh," said the Beaver, "not here. I must bring you where we can have a real talk and also dinner."

No one except Edmund felt any difficulty about trusting the Beaver now, and everyone, including Edmund, was very glad to hear the word "dinner". They therefore all hurried along behind their new friend who led them at a surprisingly quick pace, and always in the thickest parts of the forest, for over an hour. Everyone was feeling very tired and very hungry when suddenly the trees began to get thinner in front of them and the ground to fall steeply downhill. A minute later they came out under the open sky (the sun was still shining) and found themselves looking down on a fine sight.

They were standing on the edge of a steep, narrow valley at the bottom of which ran – at least it would have been running if it hadn't been frozen – a fairly large river. Just below them a dam had been built across this river, and when they saw it everyone suddenly remembered that of course beavers are always making dams and felt quite sure that Mr Beaver had made this one. They also noticed that he now had a sort of modest expression on his face – the sort of look people have when you are visiting a garden they've made or reading a story they've written. So it was only common politeness when Susan said, "What a lovely dam!" And Mr Beaver didn't say, "Hush" this time but, "Merely a trifle! Merely a trifle! And it isn't really finished!"

Above the dam there was what ought to have been a deep pool but was now, of course, a level floor of dark green ice. And below the dam, much lower down, was more ice, but instead of being smooth this was all frozen into the foamy and wavy shapes in which the water had been rushing along at the very moment when the frost came. And where the water had been trickling over and spurting through the dam there was now a glittering wall of icicles, as if the side of the dam had been covered all over with flowers and wreaths and festoons of the purest sugar. And out in the middle, and partly on top of the dam was a funny little house shaped rather like an enormous beehive, and from a hole in the roof smoke was going up, so that when you saw it (especially if you were hungry) you at once thought of cooking and became hungrier than you were before.

That was what the others chiefly noticed, but Edmund noticed something else. A little lower down the river there was another small river which came down another small valley to join it. And looking up that valley, Edmund could see two small hills, and he was almost sure they were the two hills which the White Witch had pointed out to him when he parted from her at the lamp-post that other day. And then between them, he thought, must be her palace, only a mile off or less. And he thought about Turkish Delight and about being a King ("And I wonder how Peter will like that?" he asked himself) and horrible ideas came into his head.

"Here we are," said Mr Beaver, "and it looks as if Mrs Beaver is expecting us. I'll lead the way. But be careful and don't slip."

The top of the dam was wide enough to walk on, though not (for humans) a very nice place to walk because it was covered with ice, and though the frozen pool was level with it on one side, there was a nasty drop to the lower river on the other. Along this route Mr Beaver led them in single file right out to the middle where they could look a long way up the river and a long way down it. And when they had reached the middle they were at the door of the house.

"Here we are, Mrs Beaver," said Mr Beaver, "I've found them. Here are the Sons and Daughters of Adam and Eve" – and they all went in.

The first thing Lucy noticed as she went in was a burring sound, and the first thing she saw was a kind-looking old she-beaver sitting in the corner with a thread in her mouth working busily at her sewing machine, and it was from it that the sound came. She stopped her work and got up as soon as the children came in.

"So you've come at last!" she said, holding out both her wrinkled old paws. "At last! To think that ever I should live to see this day! The potatoes are boiling and the kettle's singing and I daresay, Mr Beaver, you'll get us some fish."

"That I will," said Mr Beaver, and he went out of the house (Peter went with him), and across the ice of the deep pool to where he had a little hole in the ice which he kept open every day with his hatchet. They took a pail with them. Mr Beaver sat down quietly at the edge of the hole (he didn't seem to mind it being so chilly), looked hard into it, then suddenly shot in his paw, and before you could say Jack Robinson had whisked out a beautiful trout. Then he did it all over again until they had a fine catch of fish.

Meanwhile the girls were helping Mrs Beaver to fill the kettle and lay the table and cut the bread and put the plates in the oven to heat and draw a huge jug of beer for Mr Beaver from a barrel which stood in one corner of the house, and to put on the frying-pan and get the dripping hot. Lucy thought the Beavers had a very snug little home though it was not at all like Mr Tumnus's cave. There were no books or pictures, and instead of beds there were bunks, like on board ship, built into the wall. And there were hams and strings of onions hanging from the roof, and against the walls were gumboots and oilskins and hatchets and pairs of shears and spades and trowels and things for carrying mortar in and fishing-rods and fishing-nets and sacks. And the cloth on the table, though very clean, was very rough.

Just as the frying-pan was nicely hissing, Peter and Mr Beaver came in with the fish which Mr Beaver had already opened with his knife and cleaned out in the open air. You can think how good the new-caught fish smelled while they were frying and how the hungry children longed for them to be done and how very much hungrier still they had become before Mr Beaver said, "Now we're nearly ready." Susan drained the potatoes and then put them all back in the empty pot to dry on the side of the range while Lucy was helping Mrs Beaver to dish up the trout, so that in a very few minutes everyone was drawing up their stools (it was all three-legged stools in the Beavers' house except for Mrs Beaver's own special rocking-chair beside the fire) and preparing to enjoy themselves. There was a jug of creamy milk for the children (Mr Beaver stuck to beer) and a great big lump of deep yellow butter in the middle of the table from which everyone took as much as he wanted to go with his potatoes, and all the children thought — and I agree with them — that there's nothing to beat good freshwater fish if you eat it when it has been alive half an hour ago and has come out of the pan half a minute ago. And when they had finished the fish Mrs Beaver brought unexpectedly out of the oven a great and gloriously sticky marmalade roll, steaming hot, and at the same time moved the kettle onto the fire, so that when they had finished the marmalade roll the tea was made and ready to be poured out. And when each person had got his (or her) cup of tea, each person shoved back his (or her) stool so as to be able to lean against the wall, and gave a long sigh of contentment.

"And now," said Mr Beaver, pushing away his empty beer mug and pulling his cup of tea towards him, "if you'll just wait till I've got my pipe lit up and going nicely – why, now we can get to business. It's snowing again," he added, cocking his eye at the window. "That's all the better, because it means we shan't have any visitors; and if anyone should have been trying to follow you, why he won't find any tracks."

CHAPTER EIGHT

WHAT HAPPENED AFTER DINNER

"And now," said Lucy, "do please tell us what's happened to Mr Tumnus."

"Ah, that's bad," said Mr Beaver, shaking his head. "That's a very, very bad business. There's no doubt he was taken off by the police. I got that from a bird who saw it done."

"But where's he been taken to?" asked Lucy.

"Well, they were heading northwards when they were last seen, and we all know what that means."

"No, *we* don't," said Susan. Mr Beaver shook his head in a very gloomy fashion.

"I'm afraid it means they were taking him to her House," he said.

"But what'll they do to him, Mr Beaver?" gasped Lucy.

"Well," said Mr Beaver, "you can't exactly say for sure. But there's not many taken in there that ever comes out again. Statues. All full of statues they say it is – in the courtyard and up the stairs and in the hall. People she's turned" – he paused and shuddered – "turned into stone."

"But, Mr Beaver," said Lucy, "can't we – I mean, we *must* do something to save him. It's too dreadful and it's all on my account."

"I don't doubt you'd save him if you could, dearie," said Mrs Beaver, "but you've no chance of getting into that House against her will and ever coming out alive."

"Couldn't we have some stratagem?" said Peter. "I mean, couldn't we dress up as something, or pretend to be – oh, pedlars or anything – or watch till she was gone out – or – oh, hang it all, there must be *some* way. This Faun saved my sister at his own risk, Mr Beaver. We can't just leave him to be – to be – to have that done to him."

"It's no good, Son of Adam," said Mr Beaver, "no good *your* trying, of all people. But now that Aslan is on the move——"

"Oh, yes! Tell us about Aslan!" said several voices at once, for once again that strange feeling – like the first signs of spring, like good news – had come over them.

"Who is Aslan?" asked Susan.

"Aslan?" said Mr Beaver. "Why, don't you know? He's the King. He's the Lord of the whole wood, but not often here, you understand. Never in my time or my father's time. But the word has reached us that he has come back. He is in Narnia at this moment. He'll settle the White Queen all right. It is he, not you, who will save Mr Tumnus."

"She won't turn him into stone too?" said Edmund.

"Lord love you, Son of Adam, what a simple thing to say!" answered Mr Beaver with a great laugh. "Turn *him* into stone? If she can stand on her two feet and look him in the face it'll be the most she can do and more than I expect of her. No, no. He'll put all to rights as it says in an old rhyme in these parts:

Wrong will be right, when Aslan comes in sight,
At the sound of his roar, sorrows will be no more,
When he bares his teeth, winter meets its death,
And when he shakes his mane, we shall have spring again.

You'll understand when you see him."

"But shall we see him?" asked Susan.

"Why, Daughter of Eve, that's what I brought you here for. I'm to lead you where you shall meet him," said Mr Beaver.

"Is – is he a man?" asked Lucy.

"Aslan a man!" said Mr Beaver sternly. "Certainly not. I tell you he is the King of the wood and the son of the great Emperor-beyond-the-Sea. Don't you know who is the King of Beasts? Aslan is a lion – *the* Lion, the great Lion."

"Ooh!" said Susan. "I'd thought he was a man. Is he – quite safe? I shall feel rather nervous about meeting a lion."

"That you will, dearie, and no mistake," said Mrs Beaver; "if there's anyone who can appear before Aslan without their knees knocking, they're either braver than most or else just silly."

"Then he isn't safe?" said Lucy.

"Safe?" said Mr Beaver; "don't you hear what Mrs Beaver tells you? Who said anything about safe? 'Course he isn't safe. But he's good. He's the King, I tell you."

"I'm longing to see him," said Peter, "even if I do feel frightened when it comes to the point."

"That's right, Son of Adam," said Mr Beaver, bringing his paw down on the table with a crash that made all the cups and saucers rattle. "And so you shall. Word has been sent that you *are* to meet him, tomorrow if you can, at the Stone Table."

"Where's that?" said Lucy.

"I'll show you," said Mr Beaver. "It's down the river, a good step from here. I'll take you to it!"

"But meanwhile what about poor Mr Tumnus?" said Lucy.

"The quickest way you can help him is by going to meet Aslan," said Mr Beaver. "Once he's with us, then we can begin doing things. Not that we don't need you too. For that's another of the old rhymes:

> *When Adam's flesh and Adam's bone*
> *Sits at Cair Paravel in throne,*
> *The evil time will be over and done.*

So things must be drawing near their end now he's come and you've come. We've heard of Aslan coming into these parts before — long ago, nobody can say when. But there's never been any of your race here before."

"That's what I don't understand, Mr Beaver," said Peter. "I mean isn't the Witch herself human?"

"She'd like us to believe it," said Mr Beaver, "and it's on that that she bases her claim to be Queen. But she's no Daughter of Eve. She comes of your father Adam's" — here Mr Beaver bowed — "your father Adam's first wife, her they called Lilith. And she was one of the Jinn. That's what she comes from on one side. And on the other she comes of the giants. No, no, there isn't a drop of real human blood in the Witch."

"That's why she's bad all through, Mr Beaver," said Mrs Beaver.

"True enough, Mrs Beaver," replied he. "There may be two views about humans (meaning no offence to the present company), but there's no two views about things that look like humans and aren't."

"I've known good Dwarfs," said Mrs Beaver.

"So've I, now you come to speak of it," said her husband, "but precious few, and they were the ones least like men. But in general, take my advice, when you meet anything that's going to be human and isn't yet, or used to be human once and isn't now, or ought to be human and isn't, you keep your eyes on it and feel for your hatchet. And that's why the Witch is always on the lookout for any humans in Narnia. She's been watching for you this many a year, and if she knew there were four of you she'd be more dangerous still."

"What's that to do with it?" asked Peter.

"Because of another prophecy," said Mr Beaver. "Down at Cair Paravel – that's the castle on the sea coast down at the mouth of this river which ought to be the capital of the whole country if all was as it should be – down at Cair Paravel there are four thrones and it's a saying in Narnia time out of mind that when two Sons of Adam and two Daughters of Eve sit on those four thrones, then it will be the end not only of the White Witch's reign but of her life, and that is why we had to be so cautious as we came along, for if she knew about you four, your lives wouldn't be worth a shake of my whiskers!"

All the children had been attending so hard to what Mr Beaver was telling them that they had noticed nothing else for a long time. Then during the moment of silence that followed his last remark, Lucy suddenly said:

"I say – where's Edmund?"

There was a dreadful pause, and then everyone began asking, "Who saw him last? How long has he been missing? Is he outside?" and then all rushed to the door and looked out. The snow was falling thickly and steadily, the green ice of the pool had vanished under a thick white blanket, and from where the little house stood in the centre of the dam you could hardly see either bank. Out they went, plunging well over their ankles into the soft new snow, and went round the house in every direction. "Edmund! Edmund!" they called till they were hoarse. But the silently falling snow seemed to muffle their voices and there was not even an echo in answer.

"How perfectly dreadful!" said Susan as they at last came back in despair. "Oh, how I wish we'd never come."

"What on earth are we to do, Mr Beaver?" said Peter.

"Do?" said Mr Beaver, who was already putting on his snow-boots. "Do? We must be off at once. We haven't a moment to spare!"

"We'd better divide into four search parties," said Peter, "and all go in different directions. Whoever finds him must come back here at once and—"

"Search parties, Son of Adam?" said Mr Beaver; "what for?"

"Why, to look for Edmund, of course!"

"There's no point in looking for him," said Mr Beaver.

"What do you mean?" said Susan. "He can't be far away yet. And we've got to find him. What do you mean when you say there's no use looking for him?"

"The reason there's no use looking," said Mr Beaver, "is that we know already where he's gone!" Everyone stared in amazement. "Don't you understand?" said Mr Beaver. "He's gone to *her*, to the White Witch. He has betrayed us all."

"Oh, surely — oh, really!" said Susan. "He can't have done that."

"Can't he?" said Mr Beaver, looking very hard at the three children, and everything they wanted to say died on their lips, for each felt suddenly quite certain inside that this was exactly what Edmund had done.

"But will he know the way?" said Peter.

"Has he been in this country before?" asked Mr Beaver. "Has he ever been here alone?"

"Yes," said Lucy, almost in a whisper. "I'm afraid he has."

"And did he tell you what he'd done or who he'd met?"

"Well, no, he didn't," said Lucy.

"Then mark my words," said Mr Beaver, "he has already met the White Witch and joined her side, and been told where she lives. I didn't like to mention it before (he being your brother and all) but the moment I set eyes on that brother of yours I said to myself 'Treacherous'. He had the look of one who has been with the Witch and eaten her food. You can always tell them if you've lived long in Narnia; something about their eyes."

"All the same," said Peter in a rather choking sort of voice, "we'll still have to go and look for him. He is our brother after all, even if he is rather a little beast. And he's only a kid."

"Go to the Witch's House?" said Mrs Beaver. "Don't you see that the only chance of saving either him or yourselves is to keep away from her?"

"How do you mean?" said Lucy.

"Why, all she wants is to get all four of you (she's thinking all the time of those four thrones at Cair Paravel). Once you were all four inside her House her job would be done — and there'd be four new statues in her collection before you'd had time to speak. But she'll keep him alive as long as he's the only one she's got, because she'll want to use him as a decoy; as bait to catch the rest of you with."

"Oh, can *no* one help us?" wailed Lucy.

"Only Aslan," said Mr Beaver. "We must go on and meet him. That's our only chance now."

"It seems to me, my dears," said Mrs Beaver, "that it is very important to know just *when* he slipped away. How much he can tell her depends on how much he heard. For instance, had we started talking of Aslan before he left? If not, then we may do very well, for she won't know that Aslan has come to Narnia, or that we are meeting him, and will be quite off her guard as far as *that* is concerned."

"I don't remember his being here when we were talking about Aslan—" began Peter, but Lucy interrupted him.

"Oh yes, he was," she said miserably; "don't you remember, it was he who asked whether the Witch couldn't turn Aslan into stone too?"

"So he did, by Jove," said Peter; "just the sort of thing he would say, too!"

"Worse and worse," said Mr Beaver, "and the next thing is this. Was he still here when I told you that the place for meeting Aslan was the Stone Table?"

And of course no one knew the answer to this question.

"Because, if he was," continued Mr Beaver, "then she'll simply sledge down in that direction and get between us and the Stone Table and catch us on our way down. In fact we shall be cut off from Aslan."

"But that isn't what she'll do first," said Mrs Beaver, "not if I know her. The moment that Edmund tells her that we're all here she'll set out to catch us this very night, and if he's been gone about half an hour, she'll be here in about another twenty minutes."

"You're right, Mrs Beaver," said her husband, "we must all get away from here. There's not a moment to lose."

CHAPTER NINE

IN THE WITCH'S HOUSE

And now of course you want to know what had happened to Edmund. He had eaten his share of the dinner, but he hadn't really enjoyed it because he was thinking all the time about Turkish Delight – and there's nothing that spoils the taste of good ordinary food half so much as the memory of bad magic food. And he had heard the conversation, and hadn't enjoyed it much either, because he kept on thinking that the others were taking no notice of him and trying to give him the cold shoulder. They weren't, but he imagined it. And then he had listened until Mr Beaver told them about Aslan and until he had heard the whole arrangement for meeting Aslan at the Stone Table. It was then that he began very quietly to edge himself under the curtain which hung over the door. For the mention of Aslan gave him a mysterious and horrible feeling just as it gave the others a mysterious and lovely feeling.

Just as Mr Beaver had been repeating the rhyme about *Adam's flesh and Adam's bone* Edmund had been very quietly turning the door-handle; and just before Mr Beaver had begun telling them that the White Witch wasn't really human at all but half a Jinn and half a giantess, Edmund had got outside into the snow and cautiously closed the door behind him.

You mustn't think that even now Edmund was quite so bad that he actually wanted his brother and sisters to be turned into stone. He did want Turkish Delight and to be a Prince (and later a King) and to pay Peter back for calling him a beast. As for what the Witch would do with the others, he didn't want her to be particularly nice to them – certainly not to put them on the same level as himself; but he managed to believe, or to pretend he believed, that she wouldn't do anything very bad to them. "Because," he said to himself, "all these people who say nasty things about her are her enemies and probably half of it isn't true. She was jolly nice to me, anyway, much nicer than they are. I expect she is the rightful Queen really. Anyway, she'll be better than that awful Aslan!" At least, that was the excuse he made in his own mind for what he was doing. It wasn't a very good excuse, however, for deep down inside him he really knew that the White Witch was bad and cruel.

The first thing he realized, when he got outside and found the snow falling all round him, was that he had left his coat behind in the Beavers' house. And of course there was no chance of going back to get it now. The next thing he realized was that the daylight was almost gone, for it had been nearly three o'clock when they sat down to dinner and the winter days were short. He hadn't reckoned on this; but he had to make the best of it. So he turned up his collar and shuffled across the top of the dam (luckily it wasn't so slippery since the snow had fallen) to the far side of the river.

It was pretty bad when he reached the far side. It was growing darker every minute and what with that and the snowflakes swirling all round him he could hardly see three feet ahead. And then too there was no road. He kept slipping into deep drifts of snow, and skidding on frozen puddles, and tripping over fallen tree-trunks, and sliding down steep banks, and barking his shins against rocks, till he was wet and cold and bruised all over. The silence and the loneliness were dreadful. In fact I really think he might have given up the whole plan and gone back and owned up and made friends with the others, if he hadn't happened to say to himself, "When I'm King of Narnia the first thing I shall do will be to make some decent roads." And of course that set him off thinking about being a King and all the other things he would do and this cheered him up a good deal. He had just settled in his mind what sort of palace he would have and how many cars and all about his private cinema and where the principal railways would run and what laws he would make against beavers and dams and was putting the finishing touches to some schemes for keeping Peter in his place, when the weather changed. First the snow stopped. Then a wind sprang up and it became freezing cold. Finally, the clouds rolled away and the moon came out. It was a full moon and, shining on all that snow, it made everything almost as bright as day – only the shadows were rather confusing.

He would never have found his way if the moon hadn't come out by the time he got to the other river – you remember he had seen (when they first arrived at the Beavers') a smaller river flowing into the great one lower down. He now reached this and turned to follow it up. But the little valley down which it came was much steeper and rockier than the one he had just left and much overgrown with bushes, so that he could not have managed it at all in the dark. Even as it was, he got wet through for he had to stoop under branches, and great loads of snow came sliding off on to his back. And every time this happened he thought more and more how he hated Peter – just as if all this had been Peter's fault.

But at last he came to a part where it was more level and the valley opened out. And there, on the other side of the river, quite close to him, in the middle of a little plain between two hills, he saw what must be the White Witch's House. And the moon was shining brighter than ever. The House was really a small castle. It seemed to be all towers; little towers with long pointed spires on them, sharp as needles. They looked like huge dunces' caps or sorcerers' caps. And they shone in the moonlight and their long shadows looked strange on the snow. Edmund began to be afraid of the House.

But it was too late to think of turning back now. He crossed the river on the ice and walked up to the House. There was nothing stirring; not the slightest sound anywhere. Even his own feet made no noise on the deep newly-fallen snow. He walked on and on, past corner after corner of the House, and past turret after turret to find the door. He had to go right round to the far side before he found it. It was a huge arch but the great iron gates stood wide open.

Edmund crept up to the arch and looked inside into the courtyard, and there he saw a sight that nearly made his heart stop beating. Just inside the gate, with the moonlight shining on it, stood an enormous lion crouched as if it was ready to spring. And Edmund stood in the shadow of the arch, afraid to go on and afraid to go back, with his knees knocking together. He stood there so long that his teeth would have been chattering with cold even if they had not been chattering with fear. How long this really lasted I don't know, but it seemed to Edmund to last for hours.

Then at last he began to wonder why the lion was standing so still – for it hadn't moved one inch since he first set eyes on it. Edmund now ventured a little nearer, still keeping in the shadow of the arch as much as he could. He now saw from the way the lion was standing that it couldn't have been looking at him at all. ("But supposing it turns its head?" thought Edmund.) In fact it was staring at something else – namely a little dwarf who stood with his back to it about four feet away. "Aha!" thought Edmund. "When it springs at the dwarf then will be my chance to escape." But still the lion never moved, nor did the dwarf. And now at last Edmund remembered what the others had said about the White Witch turning people into stone. Perhaps this was only a stone lion. And as soon as he had thought of that he noticed that the lion's back and the top of its head were covered with snow. Of course it must be only a statue! No living animal would have let itself get covered with snow. Then very slowly and with his heart beating as if it would burst, Edmund ventured to go up to the lion. Even now he hardly dared touch it, but at last he put out his hand, very quickly, and did. It was cold stone. He had been frightened of a mere statue!

The relief which Edmund felt was so great that in spite of the cold he suddenly got warm all over right down to his toes, and at the same time there came into his head what seemed a perfectly lovely idea. "Probably," he thought, "this is the great Lion Aslan that they were all talking about. She's caught him already and turned him into stone. So *that's* the end of all their fine ideas about him! Pooh! Who's afraid of Aslan?"

And he stood there gloating over the stone lion, and presently he did something very silly and childish. He took a stump of lead pencil out of his pocket and scribbled a moustache on the lion's upper lip and then a pair of spectacles on its eyes. Then he said, "Yah! Silly old Aslan! How do you like being a stone? You thought yourself mighty fine, didn't you?" But in spite of the scribbles on it the face of the great stone beast still looked so terrible, and sad, and noble, staring up in the moonlight, that Edmund didn't really get any fun out of jeering at it. He turned away and began to cross the courtyard.

As he got into the middle of it he saw that there were dozens of statues all about – standing here and there rather as the pieces stand on a chessboard when it is halfway through the game. There were stone satyrs, and stone wolves, and bears and foxes and cat-a-mountains of stone. There were lovely stone shapes that looked like women but who were really the spirits of trees. There was the great shape of a centaur and a winged horse and a long lithe creature that Edmund took to be a dragon. They all looked so strange standing there perfectly life-like and also perfectly still, in the bright cold moonlight, that it was eerie work crossing the courtyard. Right in the very middle stood a huge shape like a man, but as tall as a tree, with a fierce face and a shaggy beard and a great club in its right hand. Even though he knew that it was only a stone giant and not a live one, Edmund did not like going past it.

He now saw that there was a dim light showing from a doorway on the far side of the courtyard. He went to it; there was a flight of stone steps going up to an open door. Edmund went up them. Across the threshold lay a great wolf.

"It's all right, it's all right," he kept saying to himself; "it's only a stone wolf. It can't hurt me," and he raised his leg to step over it. Instantly the huge creature rose, with all the hair bristling along its back, opened a great, red mouth and said in a growling voice:

"Who's there? Who's there? Stand still, stranger, and tell me who you are."

"If you please, sir," said Edmund, trembling so that he could hardly speak, "my name is Edmund, and I'm the Son of Adam that Her Majesty met in the wood the other day, and I've come to bring her the news that my brother and sisters are now in Narnia – quite close, in the Beavers' house. She – she wanted to see them."

"I will tell Her Majesty," said the Wolf. "Meanwhile, stand still on the threshold, as you value your life." Then it vanished into the house.

Edmund stood and waited, his fingers aching with cold and his heart pounding in his chest, and presently the great wolf, Maugrim, the Chief of the Witch's Secret Police, came bounding back and said, "Come in! Come in! Fortunate favourite of the Queen – or else not so fortunate."

And Edmund went in, taking great care not to tread on the Wolf's paws.

He found himself in a long gloomy hall with many pillars, full, as the courtyard had been, of statues. The one nearest the door was a little Faun with a very sad expression on its face, and Edmund couldn't help wondering if this might be Lucy's friend. The only light came from a single lamp and close beside this sat the White Witch.

"I'm come, your Majesty," said Edmund, rushing eagerly forward.

"How dare you come alone?" said the Witch in a terrible voice. "Did I not tell you to bring the others with you?"

"Please, your Majesty," said Edmund, "I've done the best I can. I've brought them quite close. They're in the little house on top of the dam just up the river – with Mr and Mrs Beaver."

A slow cruel smile came over the Witch's face.

"Is this all your news?" she asked.

"No, your Majesty," said Edmund, and proceeded to tell her all he had heard before leaving the Beavers' house.

"What! Aslan?" cried the Queen. "Aslan! Is this true? If I find you have lied to me—"

"Please, I'm only repeating what they said," stammered Edmund.

But the Queen, who was no longer attending to him, clapped her hands. Instantly the same dwarf whom Edmund had seen with her before appeared.

"Make ready our sledge," ordered the Witch, "and use the harness without bells."

Chapter Ten

The Spell Begins to Break

Now we must go back to Mr and Mrs Beaver and the three other children. As soon as Mr Beaver said, "There's no time to lose," everyone began bundling themselves into coats, except Mrs Beaver, who started picking up sacks and laying them on the table and said: "Now, Mr Beaver, just reach down that ham. And here's a packet of tea, and there's sugar, and some matches. And if someone will get two or three loaves out of the crock over there in the corner."

"What *are* you doing, Mrs Beaver?" exclaimed Susan.

"Packing a load for each of us, dearie," said Mrs Beaver very coolly. "You didn't think we'd set out on a journey with nothing to eat, did you?"

"But we haven't time!" said Susan, buttoning the collar of her coat. "She may be here any minute."

"That's what I say," chimed in Mr Beaver.

"Get along with you all," said his wife. "Think it over, Mr Beaver. She can't be here for quarter of an hour at least."

"But don't we want as big a start as we can possibly get," said Peter, "if we're to reach the Stone Table before her?"

"You've got to remember *that*, Mrs Beaver," said Susan. "As soon as she has looked in here and finds we're gone she'll be off at top speed."

"That she will," said Mrs Beaver. "But we can't get there before her whatever we do, for she'll be on a sledge and we'll be walking."

"Then – have we no hope?" said Susan.

"Now don't you get fussing, there's a dear," said Mrs Beaver, "but just get half a dozen clean handkerchiefs out of the drawer. 'Course we've got a hope. We can't get there *before* her but we can keep under cover and go by ways she won't expect and perhaps we'll get through."

"That's true enough, Mrs Beaver," said her husband. "But it's time we were out of this."

"And don't *you* start fussing either, Mr Beaver," said his wife. "There. That's better. There's five loads and the smallest for the smallest of us: that's you, my dear," she added, looking at Lucy.

"Well, I'm nearly ready now," answered Mrs Beaver at last, allowing her husband to help her into her snow-boots. "I suppose the sewing machine's too heavy to bring?"

"Yes. It *is*," said Mr Beaver. "A great deal too heavy. And you don't think you'll be able to use it while we're on the run, I suppose?"

"I can't abide the thought of that Witch fiddling with it," said Mrs Beaver, "and breaking it or stealing it, as likely as not."

"Oh, please, please, please, do hurry!" said the three children. And so at last they all got outside and Mr Beaver locked the door ("It'll delay her a bit," he said) and they set off, all carrying their loads over their shoulders.

The snow had stopped and the moon had come out when they began their journey. They went in single file – first Mr Beaver, then Lucy, then Peter, then Susan, and Mrs Beaver last of all. Mr Beaver led them across the dam and on to the right bank of the river and then along a very rough sort of path among the trees right down by the river-bank. The sides of the valley, shining in the moonlight, towered up far above them on either side. "Best keep down here as much as possible," he said. "She'll have to keep to the top, for you couldn't bring a sledge down here."

It would have been a pretty enough scene to look at it through a window from a comfortable armchair; and even as things were, Lucy enjoyed it at first. But as they went on walking and walking – and walking – and as the sack she was carrying felt heavier and heavier, she began to wonder how she was going to keep up at all. And she stopped looking at the dazzling brightness of the frozen river with all its waterfalls of ice and at the white masses of the tree-tops and the great glaring moon and the countless stars and could only watch the little short legs of Mr Beaver going pad-pad-pad-pad through the snow in front of her as if they were never going to stop. Then the moon disappeared and the snow began to fall once more. And at last Lucy was so tired that she was almost asleep and walking at the same time when suddenly she found that Mr Beaver had turned away from the river-bank to the right and was leading them steeply uphill into the very thickest bushes. And then as she came fully awake she found that Mr Beaver was just vanishing into a little hole in the bank which had been almost hidden under the bushes until you were quite on top of it. In fact, by the time she realized what was happening, only his short flat tail was showing.

Lucy immediately stooped down and crawled in after him. Then she heard noises of scrambling and puffing and panting behind her and in a moment all five of them were inside.

"Wherever is this?" said Peter's voice, sounding tired and pale in the darkness. (I hope you know what I mean by a voice sounding pale.)

"It's an old hiding-place for beavers in bad times," said Mr Beaver, "and a great secret. It's not much of a place but we must get a few hours' sleep."

"If you hadn't all been in such a plaguey fuss when we were starting, I'd have brought some pillows," said Mrs Beaver.

It wasn't nearly such a nice cave as Mr Tumnus's, Lucy thought – just a hole in the ground but dry and earthy. It was very small so that when they all lay down they were all a bundle of clothes together, and what with that and being warmed up by their long walk they were really rather snug. If only the floor of the cave had been a little smoother! Then Mrs Beaver handed round in the dark a little flask out of which everyone drank something – it made one cough and splutter a little and stung the throat, but it also made you feel deliciously warm after you'd swallowed – and everyone went straight to sleep.

It seemed to Lucy only the next minute (though really it was hours and hours later) when she woke up feeling a little cold and dreadfully stiff and thinking how she would like a hot bath. Then she felt a set of long whiskers tickling her cheek and saw the cold daylight coming in through the mouth of the cave. But immediately after that she was very wide awake indeed, and so was everyone else. In fact they were all sitting up with their mouths and eyes wide open listening to a sound which was the very sound they'd all been thinking of (and sometimes imagining they heard) during their walk last night. It was a sound of jingling bells.

Mr Beaver was out of the cave like a flash the moment he heard it. Perhaps you think, as Lucy thought for a moment, that this was a very silly thing to do? But it was really a very sensible one. He knew he could scramble to the top of the bank among bushes and brambles without being seen; and he wanted above all things to see which way the Witch's sledge went. The others all sat in the cave waiting and wondering. They waited nearly five minutes. Then they heard something that frightened them very much. They heard voices. "Oh," thought Lucy, "he's been seen. She's caught him!" Great was their surprise when a little later, they heard Mr Beaver's voice calling to them from just outside the cave.

"It's all right," he was shouting. "Come out, Mrs Beaver. Come out, Sons and Daughters of Adam. It's all right! It isn't *Her*!" This was bad grammar of course, but that is how beavers talk when they are excited; I mean, in Narnia – in our world they usually don't talk at all.

So Mrs Beaver and the children came bundling out of the cave, all blinking in the daylight, and with earth all over them, and looking very frowsty and unbrushed and uncombed and with the sleep in their eyes.

"Come on!" cried Mr Beaver, who was almost dancing with delight. "Come and see! This is a nasty knock for the Witch! It looks as if her power is already crumbling."

"What *do* you mean, Mr Beaver?" panted Peter as they all scrambled up the steep bank of the valley together.

"Didn't I tell you," answered Mr Beaver, "that she'd made it always winter and never Christmas? Didn't I tell you? Well, just come and see!"

And then they were all at the top and did see.

It *was* a sledge, and it *was* reindeer with bells on their harness. But they were far bigger than the Witch's reindeer, and they were not white but brown. And on the sledge sat a person whom everyone knew the moment they set eyes on him. He was a huge man in a bright red robe (bright as hollyberries) with a hood that had fur inside it and a great white beard that fell like a foamy waterfall over his chest. Everyone knew him because, though you see people of his sort only in Narnia, you see pictures of them and hear them talked about even in our world – the world on this side of the wardrobe door. But when you really see them in Narnia it is rather different. Some of the pictures of Father Christmas in our world make him look only funny and jolly. But now that the children actually stood looking at him they didn't find it quite like that. He was so big, and so glad, and so real, that they all became quite still. They felt very glad, but also solemn.

"I've come at last," said he. "She has kept me out for a long time, but I have got in at last. Aslan is on the move. The Witch's magic is weakening."

And Lucy felt running through her that deep shiver of gladness which you only get if you are being solemn and still.

"And now," said Father Christmas, "for your presents. There is a new and better sewing machine for you, Mrs Beaver. I will drop it in your house as I pass."

"If you please, sir," said Mrs Beaver, making a curtsey. "It's locked up."

"Locks and bolts make no difference to me," said Father Christmas. "And as for you, Mr Beaver, when you get home you will find your dam finished and mended and all the leaks stopped and a new sluice-gate fitted."

Mr Beaver was so pleased that he opened his mouth very wide and then found he couldn't say anything at all.

"Peter, Adam's Son," said Father Christmas.

"Here, sir," said Peter.

"These are your presents," was the answer, "and they are tools, not toys. The time to use them is perhaps near at hand. Bear them well." With these words he handed to Peter a shield and a sword. The shield was the colour of silver and across it there ramped a red lion, as bright as a ripe strawberry at the moment when you pick it. The hilt of the sword was of gold and it had a sheath and a sword belt and everything it needed, and it was just the right size and weight for Peter to use. Peter was silent and solemn as he received these gifts, for he felt they were a very serious kind of present.

"Susan, Eve's Daughter," said Father Christmas. "These are for you," and he handed her a bow and a quiver full of arrows and a little ivory horn. "You must use the bow only in great need," he said, "for I do not mean you to fight in the battle. It does not easily miss. And when you put this horn to your lips and blow it, then, wherever you are, I think help of some kind will come to you."

Last of all he said, "Lucy, Eve's Daughter," and Lucy came forward. He gave her a little bottle of what looked like glass (but people said afterwards that it was made of diamond) and a small dagger. "In this bottle," he said, "there is a cordial made of the juice of one of the fire-flowers that grow in the mountains of the sun. If you or any of your friends is hurt, a few drops of this will restore them. And the dagger is to defend yourself at great need. For you also are not to be in the battle."

"Why, sir?" said Lucy. "I think – I don't know – but I think I could be brave enough."

"That is not the point," he said. "But battles are ugly when women fight. And now" – here he suddenly looked less grave – "here is something for the moment for you all!" and he brought out (I suppose from the big bag at his back, but nobody quite saw him do it) a large tray containing five cups and saucers, a bowl of lump sugar, a jug of cream, and a great big teapot all sizzling and piping hot. Then he cried out, "Merry Christmas! Long live the true King!" and cracked his whip, and he and the reindeer and the sledge and all were out of sight before anyone realized that they had started.

Peter had just drawn his sword out of its sheath and was showing it to Mr Beaver, when Mrs Beaver said:

"Now then, now then! Don't stand talking there till the tea's got cold. Just like men. Come and help to carry the tray down and we'll have breakfast. What a mercy I thought of bringing the bread-knife."

So down the steep bank they went and back to the cave, and Mr Beaver cut some of the bread and ham into sandwiches and Mrs Beaver poured out the tea and everyone enjoyed themselves. But long before they had finished enjoying themselves Mr Beaver said, "Time to be moving on now."

Chapter Eleven

Aslan is Nearer

Edmund meanwhile had been having a most disappointing time. When the dwarf had gone to get the sledge ready he expected that the Witch would start being nice to him, as she had been at their last meeting. But she said nothing at all. And when at last Edmund plucked up his courage to say, "Please, your Majesty, could I have some Turkish Delight? You – you – said—" she answered, "Silence, fool!" Then she appeared to change her mind and said, as if to herself, "And yet it will not do to have the brat fainting on the way," and once more clapped her hands. Another dwarf appeared.

"Bring the human creature food and drink," she said.

The dwarf went away and presently returned bringing an iron bowl with some water in it and an iron plate with a hunk of dry bread on it. He grinned in a repulsive manner as he set them down on the floor beside Edmund and said:

"Turkish Delight for the little Prince. Ha! Ha! Ha!"

"Take it away," said Edmund sulkily. "I don't want dry bread." But the Witch suddenly turned on him with such a terrible expression on her face that he apologized and began to nibble at the bread, though it was so stale he could hardly get it down.

"You may be glad enough of it before you taste bread again," said the Witch.

While he was still chewing away, the first dwarf came back and announced that the sledge was ready. The White Witch rose and went out, ordering Edmund to go with her. The snow was again falling as they came into the courtyard, but she took no notice of that and made Edmund sit beside her on the sledge. But before they drove off she called Maugrim and he came bounding like an enormous dog to the side of the sledge.

"Take with you the swiftest of your wolves and go at once to the house of the Beavers," said the Witch, "and kill whatever you find there. If they are already gone, then make all speed to the Stone Table, but do not be seen. Wait for me there in hiding. I meanwhile must go many miles to the West before I find a place where I can drive across the river. You may overtake these humans before they reach the Stone Table. You will know what to do if you find them!"

"I hear and obey, O Queen," growled the Wolf, and immediately he shot away into the snow and darkness, as quickly as a horse can gallop. In a few minutes he had called another wolf and was with him down on the dam sniffing at the Beavers' house. But of course they found it empty. It would have been a dreadful thing for the Beavers and the children if the night had remained fine, for the wolves would then have been able to follow their trail – and ten to one would have overtaken them before they had got to the cave. But now that the snow had begun again the scent was cold and even the footprints were covered up.

Meanwhile the dwarf whipped up the reindeer, and the Witch and Edmund drove out under the archway and on and away into the darkness and the cold. This was a terrible journey for Edmund, who had no coat. Before they had been going quarter of an hour all the front of him was covered with snow – he soon stopped trying to shake it off because, as quickly as he did that, a new lot gathered, and he was so tired. Soon he was wet to the skin. And oh, how miserable he was! It didn't look now as if the Witch intended to make him a King. All the things he had said to make himself believe that she was good and kind and that her side was really the right side sounded to him silly now. He would have given anything to meet the others at this moment – even Peter! The only way to comfort himself now was to try to believe that the whole thing was a dream and that he might wake up any moment. And as they went on, hour after hour, it did come to seem like a dream.

This lasted longer than I could describe even if I wrote pages and pages about it. But I will skip on to the time when the snow had stopped and the morning had come and they were racing along in the daylight. And still they went on and on, with no sound but the everlasting swish of the snow and the creaking of the reindeer's harness. And then at last the Witch said, "What have we here? Stop!" and they did.

How Edmund hoped she was going to say something about breakfast! But she had stopped for quite a different reason. A little way off at the foot of a tree sat a merry party, a squirrel and his wife with their children and two satyrs and a dwarf and an old dog-fox, all on stools round a table.

Edmund couldn't quite see what they were eating, but it smelled lovely and there seemed to be decorations of holly and he wasn't at all sure that he didn't see something like a plum pudding. At the moment when the sledge stopped, the Fox, who was obviously the oldest person present, had just risen to its feet, holding a glass in its right paw as if it was going to say something. But when the whole party saw the sledge stopping and who was in it, all the gaiety went out of their faces. The father squirrel stopped eating with his fork halfway to his mouth and one of the satyrs stopped with its fork actually in its mouth, and the baby squirrels squeaked with terror.

"What is the meaning of this?" asked the Witch Queen. Nobody answered.

"Speak, vermin!" she said again. "Or do you want my dwarf to find you a tongue with his whip? What is the meaning of all this gluttony, this waste, this self-indulgence? Where did you get all these things?"

"Please, your Majesty," said the Fox, "we were given them. And if I might make so bold as to drink your Majesty's very good health—"

"Who gave them to you?" said the Witch.

"F-F-F-Father Christmas," stammered the Fox.

"What?" roared the Witch, springing from the sledge and taking a few strides nearer to the terrified animals. "He has not been here! He cannot have been here! How dare you – but no. Say you have been lying and you shall even now be forgiven."

At that moment one of the young squirrels lost its head completely.

"He has – he has – he has!" it squeaked, beating its little spoon on the table.

Edmund saw the Witch bite her lips so that a drop of blood appeared on her white cheek. Then she raised her wand.

"Oh, don't, don't, please don't," shouted Edmund, but even while he was shouting she had waved her wand and instantly where the merry party had been there were only statues of creatures (one with its stone fork fixed for ever halfway to its stone mouth) seated around a stone table on which there were stone plates and a stone plum pudding.

"As for you," said the Witch, giving Edmund a stunning blow on the face as she re-mounted the sledge, "let that teach you to ask favour for spies and traitors. Drive on!" And Edmund, for the first time in this story, felt sorry for someone besides himself. It seemed so pitiful to think of those little stone figures sitting there all the silent days and all the dark nights, year after year, till the moss grew on them and at last even their faces crumbled away.

Now they were steadily racing on again. And soon Edmund noticed that the snow which splashed against them as they rushed through it was much wetter than it had been all last night. At the same time he noticed that he was feeling much less cold. It was also becoming foggy. In fact every minute it grew foggier and warmer. And the sledge was not running nearly as well as it had been running up till now. At first he thought this was because the reindeer were tired, but soon he saw that that couldn't be the real reason. The sledge jerked, and skidded and kept on jolting as if it had struck against stones. And however the dwarf whipped the poor reindeer the sledge went slower and slower. There also seemed to be a curious noise all round them, but the noise of their driving and jolting and the dwarf's shouting at the reindeer prevented Edmund from hearing what it was, until suddenly the sledge stuck so fast that it wouldn't go on at all. When that happened there was a moment's silence. And in that silence Edmund could at last listen to the other noise properly. A strange, sweet, rustling, chattering noise – and yet not so strange, for he'd heard it before – if only he could remember where! Then all at once he did remember. It was the noise of running water. All round them though out of sight, there were streams, chattering, murmuring, bubbling, splashing and even (in the distance) roaring. And his heart gave a great leap (though he hardly knew why) when he realized that the frost was over. And much nearer there was a drip-drip-drip from the branches of all the trees. And then, as he looked at one tree he saw a great load of snow slide off it and for the first time since he had entered Narnia he saw the dark green of a fir tree. But he hadn't time to listen or watch any longer, for the Witch said:

"Don't sit staring, fool! Get out and help."

And of course Edmund had to obey. He stepped out into the snow – but it was really only slush by now – and began helping the dwarf to get the sledge out of the muddy hole it had got into. They got it out in the end, and by being very cruel to the reindeer the dwarf managed to get it on the move again, and they drove a little further. And now the snow was really melting in earnest and patches of green grass were beginning to appear in every direction. Unless you have looked at a world of snow as long as Edmund had been looking at it, you will hardly be able to imagine what a relief those green patches were after the endless white. Then the sledge stopped again.

"It's no good, your Majesty," said the dwarf. "We can't sledge in this thaw."

"Then we must walk," said the Witch.

"We shall never overtake them walking," growled the dwarf. "Not with the start they've got."

"Are you my councillor or my slave?" said the Witch. "Do as you're told. Tie the hands of the human creature behind it and keep hold of the end of the rope. And take your whip. And cut the harness of the reindeer; they'll find their own way home."

The dwarf obeyed, and in a few minutes Edmund found himself being forced to walk as fast as he could with his hands tied behind him. He kept on slipping in the slush and mud and wet grass, and every time he slipped, the dwarf gave him a curse and sometimes a flick with the whip. The Witch walked behind the dwarf and kept on saying, "Faster! Faster!"

Every moment the patches of green grew bigger and the patches of snow grew smaller. Every moment more and more of the trees shook off their robes of snow. Soon, wherever you looked, instead of white shapes you saw the dark green of firs or the black prickly branches of bare oaks and beeches and elms. Then the mist turned from white to gold and presently cleared away altogether. Shafts of delicious sunlight struck down on to the forest floor and overhead you could see a blue sky between the tree tops.

Soon there were more wonderful things happening. Coming suddenly round a corner into a glade of silver birch trees Edmund saw the ground covered in all directions with little yellow flowers – celandines. The noise of water grew louder. Presently they actually crossed a stream. Beyond it they found snowdrops growing.

"Mind your own business!" said the dwarf when he saw that Edmund had turned his head to look at them; and he gave the rope a vicious jerk.

But of course this didn't prevent Edmund from seeing. Only five minutes later he noticed a dozen crocuses growing round the foot of an old tree – gold and purple and white. Then came a sound even more delicious than the sound of the water. Close beside the path they were following, a bird suddenly chirped from the branch of a tree. It was answered by the chuckle of another bird a little further off. And then, as if that had been a signal, there was chattering and chirruping in every direction, and then a moment of full song, and within five minutes the whole wood was ringing with birds' music, and wherever Edmund's eyes turned he saw birds alighting on branches, or sailing overhead or chasing one another or having their little quarrels or tidying up their feathers with their beaks.

"Faster! Faster!" said the Witch.

There was no trace of the fog now. The sky became bluer and bluer, and now there were white clouds hurrying across it from time to time. In the wide glades there were primroses. A light breeze sprang up which scattered drops of moisture from the swaying branches and carried cool, delicious scents against the faces of the travellers. The trees began to come fully alive. The larches and birches were covered with green, the laburnums with gold. Soon the beech trees had put forth their delicate, transparent leaves. As the travellers walked under them the light also became green. A bee buzzed across their path.

"This is no thaw," said the dwarf, suddenly stopping. "This is Spring. What are we to do? Your winter has been destroyed, I tell you! This is Aslan's doing."

"If either of you mention that name again," said the Witch, "he shall instantly be killed."

Chapter Twelve

Peter's First Battle

While the dwarf and the White Witch were saying this, miles away the Beavers and the children were walking on hour after hour into what seemed a delicious dream. Long ago they had left the coats behind them. And by now they had even stopped saying to one another, "Look! There's a kingfisher," or, "I say, bluebells!" or, "What was that lovely smell?" or, "Just listen to that thrush!" They walked on in silence drinking it all in, passing through patches of warm sunlight into cool, green thickets and out again into wide mossy glades where tall elms raised the leafy roof far overhead, and then into dense masses of flowering currant and among hawthorn bushes where the sweet smell was almost overpowering.

They had been just as surprised as Edmund when they saw the winter vanishing and the whole wood passing in a few hours or so from January to May. They hadn't even known for certain (as the Witch did) that this was what would happen when Aslan came to Narnia. But they all knew that it was her spells which had produced the endless winter; and therefore they all knew when this magic spring began that something had gone wrong, and badly wrong, with the Witch's schemes. And after the thaw had been going on for some time they all realized that the Witch would no longer be able to use her sledge. After that they didn't hurry so much and they allowed themselves more rests and longer ones. They were pretty tired by now of course; but not what I'd call bitterly tired — only slow and feeling very dreamy and quiet inside as one does when one is coming to the end of a long day in the open. Susan had a slight blister on one heel.

They had left the course of the big river some time ago; for one had to turn a little to the right (that meant a little to the south) to reach the place of the Stone Table. Even if this had not been their way they couldn't have kept to the river valley once the thaw began, for with all that melting snow the river was soon in flood – a wonderful, roaring, thundering yellow flood – and their path would have been under water.

And now the sun got low and the light got redder and the shadows got longer and the flowers began to think about closing.

"Not long now," said Mr Beaver, and began leading them uphill across some very deep, springy moss (it felt nice under their tired feet) in a place where only tall trees grew, very wide apart. The climb, coming at the end of the long day, made them all pant and blow. And just as Lucy was wondering whether she could really get to the top without another long rest, suddenly they *were* at the top. And this is what they saw.

They were on a green open space from which you could look down on the forest spreading as far as one could see in every direction – except right ahead. There, far to the East, was something twinkling and moving. "By gum!" whispered Peter to Susan. "The sea!" In the very middle of this open hill-top was the Stone Table. It was a great grim slab of grey stone supported on four upright stones. It looked very old; and it was cut all over with strange lines and figures that might be the letters of an unknown language. They gave you a curious feeling when you looked at them. The next thing they saw was a pavilion pitched on one side of the open place. A wonderful pavilion it was – and especially now when the light of the setting sun fell upon it – with sides of what looked like yellow silk and cords of crimson and tent-pegs of ivory; and high above it on a pole a banner which bore a red rampant lion fluttering in the breeze which was blowing in their faces from the far-off sea. While they were looking at this they heard a sound of music on their right; and turning in that direction they saw what they had come to see.

Aslan stood in the centre of a crowd of creatures who had grouped themselves round him in the shape of a half-moon. There were Tree-Women there and Well-Women (Dryads and Naiads as they used to be called in our world) who had stringed instruments; it was they who had made the music. There were four great centaurs. The horse part of them was like huge English farm horses, and the man part was like stern but beautiful giants. There was also a unicorn, and a bull with the head of a man, and a pelican, and an eagle, and a great Dog. And next to Aslan stood two leopards of whom one carried his crown and the other his standard.

But as for Aslan himself, the Beavers and the children didn't know what to do or say when they saw him. People who have not been in Narnia sometimes think that a thing cannot be good and terrible at the same time. If the children had ever thought so, they were cured of it now. For when they tried to look at Aslan's face they just caught a glimpse of the golden mane and the great, royal, solemn, overwhelming eyes; and then they found they couldn't look at him and went all trembly.

"Go on," whispered Mr Beaver.

"No," whispered Peter, "you first."

"No, Sons of Adam before animals," whispered Mr Beaver back again.

"Susan," whispered Peter. "What about you? Ladies first."

"No, you're the eldest," whispered Susan. And of course the longer they went on doing this the more awkward they felt. Then at last Peter realized that it was up to him. He drew his sword and raised it to the salute and, hastily saying to the others, "Come on. Pull yourselves together," he advanced to the Lion and said:

"We have come – Aslan."

"Welcome, Peter, Son of Adam," said Aslan. "Welcome, Susan and Lucy, Daughters of Eve. Welcome, He-Beaver and She-Beaver."

His voice was deep and rich and somehow took the fidgets out of them. They now felt glad and quiet and it didn't seem awkward to them to stand and say nothing.

"But where is the fourth?" asked Aslan.

"He has tried to betray them and joined the White Witch, O Aslan," said Mr Beaver. And then something made Peter say,

"That was partly my fault, Aslan. I was angry with him and I think that helped him to go wrong."

And Aslan said nothing either to excuse Peter or to blame him but merely stood looking at him with his great unchanging eyes. And it seemed to all of them that there was nothing to be said.

"Please – Aslan," said Lucy, "can anything be done to save Edmund?"

"All shall be done," said Aslan. "But it may be harder than you think." And then he was silent again for some time. Up to that moment Lucy had been thinking how royal and strong and peaceful his face looked; now it suddenly came into her head that he looked sad as well. But in the next minute that expression was quite gone. The Lion shook his mane and clapped his paws together ("Terrible paws," thought Lucy, "if he didn't know how to velvet them!") and said,

"Meanwhile, let the feast be prepared. Ladies, take these Daughters of Eve to the pavilion and minister to them."

When the girls had gone Aslan laid his paw – and though it was velveted it was very heavy – on Peter's shoulder and said, "Come, Son of Adam, and I will show you a far-off sight of the castle where you are to be King."

And Peter with his sword still drawn in his hand went with the Lion to the eastern edge of the hilltop. There a beautiful sight met their eyes. The sun was setting behind their backs. That meant that the whole country below them lay in the evening light – forest and hills and valleys and, winding away like a silver snake, the lower part of the great river. And beyond all this, miles away, was the sea, and beyond the sea the sky, full of clouds which were just turning rose colour with the reflection of the sunset. But just where the land of Narnia met the sea – in fact, at the mouth of the great river – there was something on a little hill, shining. It was shining because it was a castle and of course the sunlight was reflected from all the windows which looked towards Peter and the sunset; but to Peter it looked like a great star resting on the seashore.

"That, O Man," said Aslan, "is Cair Paravel of the four thrones, in one of which you must sit as King. I show it to you because you are the first-born and you will be High King over all the rest."

And once more Peter said nothing, for at that moment a strange noise woke the silence suddenly. It was like a bugle, but richer.

"It is your sister's horn," said Aslan to Peter in a low voice; so low as to be almost a purr, if it is not disrespectful to think of a lion purring.

For a moment Peter did not understand. Then, when he saw all the other creatures start forward and heard Aslan say with a wave of his paw, "Back! Let the Prince win his spurs," he did understand, and set off running as hard as he could to the pavilion. And there he saw a dreadful sight.

The Naiads and Dryads were scattering in every direction. Lucy was running towards him as fast as her short legs would carry her and her face was as white as paper. Then he saw Susan make a dash for a tree, and swing herself up, followed by a huge grey beast. At first Peter thought it was a bear. Then he saw that it looked like an Alsatian, though it was far too big to be a dog. Then he realized that it was a wolf – a wolf standing on its hind legs, with its front paws against the tree-trunk, snapping and snarling. All the hair on its back stood up on end. Susan had not been able to get higher than the second big branch. One of her legs hung down so that her foot was only an inch or two above the snapping teeth. Peter wondered why she did not get higher or at least take a better grip; then he realized that she was just going to faint and that if she fainted she would fall off.

Peter did not feel very brave; indeed, he felt he was going to be sick. But that made no difference to what he had to do. He rushed straight up to the monster and aimed a slash of his sword at its side. That stroke never reached the Wolf. Quick as lightning it turned round, its eyes flaming, and its mouth wide open in a howl of anger. If it had not been so angry that it simply had to howl it would have got him by the throat at once. As it was – though all this happened too quickly for Peter to think at all – he had just time to duck down and plunge his sword, as hard as he could, between the brute's forelegs into its heart. Then came a horrible, confused moment like something in a nightmare. He was tugging and pulling and the Wolf seemed neither alive nor dead, and its bared teeth knocked against his forehead, and everything was blood and heat and hair. A moment later he found that the monster lay dead and he had drawn his sword out of it and was straightening his back and rubbing the sweat off his face and out of his eyes. He felt tired all over.

Then, after a bit, Susan came down the tree. She and Peter felt pretty shaky when they met and I won't say there wasn't kissing and crying on both sides. But in Narnia no one thinks any the worse of you for that.

"Quick! Quick!" shouted the voice of Aslan. "Centaurs! Eagles! I see another wolf in the thickets. There — behind you. He has just darted away. After him, all of you. He will be going to his mistress. Now is your chance to find the Witch and rescue the fourth Son of Adam." And instantly with a thunder of hoofs and beating of wings a dozen or so of the swiftest creatures disappeared into the gathering darkness.

Peter, still out of breath, turned and saw Aslan close at hand.

"You have forgotten to clean your sword," said Aslan.

It was true. Peter blushed when he looked at the bright blade and saw it all smeared with the Wolf's hair and blood. He stooped down and wiped it quite clean on the grass, and then wiped it quite dry on his coat.

"Hand it to me and kneel, Son of Adam," said Aslan. And when Peter had done so he struck him with the flat of the blade and said, "Rise up, Sir Peter Wolf's-Bane. And, whatever happens, never forget to wipe your sword."

CHAPTER THIRTEEN

DEEP MAGIC FROM THE DAWN OF TIME

Now we must get back to Edmund. When he had been made to walk far further than he had ever known that anybody *could* walk, the Witch at last halted in a dark valley all overshadowed with fir trees and yew trees. Edmund simply sank down and lay on his face doing nothing at all and not even caring what was going to happen next provided they would let him lie still. He was too tired even to notice how hungry and thirsty he was. The Witch and the dwarf were talking close beside him in low tones.

"No," said the dwarf, "it is no use now, O Queen. They must have reached the Stone Table by now."

"Perhaps the Wolf will smell us out and bring us news," said the Witch.

"It cannot be good news if he does," said the dwarf.

"Four thrones in Cair Paravel," said the Witch. "How if only three were filled? That would not fulfil the prophecy."

"What difference would that make now that *He* is here?" said the dwarf. He did not dare, even now, to mention the name of Aslan to his mistress.

"He may not stay long. And then – we would fall upon the three at Cair."

"Yet it might be better," said the dwarf, "to keep this one" (here he kicked Edmund) "for bargaining with."

"Yes! And have him rescued," said the Witch scornfully.

"Then," said the dwarf, "we had better do what we have to do at once."

"I would like to have it done on the Stone Table itself," said the Witch. "That is the proper place. That is where it has always been done before."

"It will be a long time now before the Stone Table can again be put to its proper use," said the dwarf.

"True," said the Witch; and then, "Well, I will begin."

At that moment with a rush and a snarl a Wolf rushed up to them.

"I have seen them. They are all at the Stone Table, with Him. They have killed my captain, Maugrim. I was hidden in the thickets and saw it all. One of the Sons of Adam killed him. Fly! Fly!"

"No," said the Witch. "There need be no flying. Go quickly. Summon all our people to meet me here as speedily as they can. Call out the giants and the werewolves and the spirits of those trees who are on our side. Call the Ghouls, and the Boggles, the Ogres and the Minotaurs. Call the Cruels, the Hags, the Spectres, and the people of the Toadstools. We will fight. What? Have I not still my wand? Will not their ranks turn into stone even as they come on? Be off quickly, I have a little thing to finish here while you are away."

The great brute bowed its head, turned, and galloped away.

"Now!" she said. "We have no table – let me see. We had better put it against the trunk of a tree."

Edmund found himself being roughly forced to his feet. Then the dwarf set him with his back against a tree and bound him fast. He saw the Witch take off her outer mantle. Her arms were bare underneath it and terribly white. Because they were so very white he could see them, but he could not see much else, it was so dark in this valley under the dark trees.

"Prepare the victim," said the Witch. And the Dwarf undid Edmund's collar and folded back his shirt at the neck. Then he took Edmund's hair and pulled his head back so that he had to raise his chin. After that Edmund heard a strange noise – whizz – whizz – whizz. For a moment he couldn't think what it was. Then he realized. It was the sound of a knife being sharpened.

At that very moment he heard loud shouts from every direction – a drumming of hoofs and a beating of wings – a scream from the Witch – confusion all round him. And then he found he was being untied. Strong arms were round him and he heard big, kind voices saying things like –

"Let him lie down – give him some wine – drink this – steady now – you'll be all right in a minute."

Then he heard the voices of people who were not talking to him but to one another. And they were saying things like, "Who's got the Witch?"– "I thought you had her." "I didn't see her after I knocked the knife out of her hand – I was after the dwarf – do you mean to say she's escaped?" "A chap can't mind everything at once – what's that? Oh, sorry, it's only an old stump!" But just at this point Edmund went off in a dead faint.

Presently the centaurs and unicorns and deer and birds (they were of course the rescue party which Aslan had sent in the last chapter) all set off to go back to the Stone Table, carrying Edmund with them. But if they could have seen what happened in that valley after they had gone, I think they might have been surprised.

It was perfectly still and presently the moon grew bright; if you had been there you would have seen the moonlight shining on an old tree-stump and on a fair-sized boulder. But if you had gone on looking you would gradually have begun to think there was something odd about both the stump and the boulder. And next you would have thought that the stump did look really remarkably like a little fat man crouching on the ground. And if you had watched long enough you would have seen the stump walk across to the boulder and the boulder sit up and begin talking to the stump; for in reality the stump and the boulder were simply the Witch and the dwarf. For it was part of her magic that she could make things look like what they aren't, and she had the presence of mind to do so at the very moment when the knife was knocked out of her hand. She had kept hold of her wand, so it had been kept safe, too.

When the other children woke up the next morning (they had been sleeping on piles of cushions in the pavilion) the first thing they heard — from Mrs Beaver — was that their brother had been rescued and brought into camp late last night; and was at that moment with Aslan. As soon as they had breakfasted they all went out, and there they saw Aslan and Edmund walking together in the dewy grass, apart from the rest of the court. There is no need to tell you (and no one ever heard) what Aslan was saying, but it was a conversation which Edmund never forgot. As the others drew nearer Aslan turned to meet them, bringing Edmund with him.

"Here is your brother," he said, "and — there is no need to talk to him about what is past."

Edmund shook hands with each of the others and said to each of them in turn, "I'm sorry," and everyone said, "That's all right." And then everyone wanted very hard to say something which would make it quite clear that they were all friends with him again — something ordinary and natural — and of course no one could think of anything in the world to say. But before they had time to feel really awkward one of the leopards approached Aslan and said,

"Sire, there is a messenger from the enemy who craves audience."

"Let him approach," said Aslan.

The leopard went away and soon returned leading the Witch's dwarf.

"What is your message, Son of Earth?" asked Aslan.

"The Queen of Narnia and Empress of the Lone Islands desires a safe conduct to come and speak with you," said the dwarf, "on a matter which is as much to your advantage as to hers."

"Queen of Narnia, indeed!" said Mr Beaver. "Of all the cheek——"

"Peace, Beaver," said Aslan. "All names will soon be restored to their proper owners. In the meantime we will not dispute about them. Tell your mistress, Son of Earth, that I grant her safe conduct on condition that she leaves her wand behind her at that great oak."

This was agreed to and two leopards went back with the dwarf to see that the conditions were properly carried out. "But supposing she turns the two leopards into stone?" whispered Lucy to Peter. I think the same idea had occurred to the leopards themselves; at any rate, as they walked off their fur was all standing up on their backs and their tails were bristling – like a cat's when it sees a strange dog.

"It'll be all right," whispered Peter in reply. "He wouldn't send them if it weren't."

A few minutes later the Witch herself walked out on to the top of the hill and came straight across and stood before Aslan. The three children who had not seen her before felt shudders running down their backs at the sight of her face; and there were low growls among all the animals present. Though it was bright sunshine everyone felt suddenly cold. The only two people present who seemed to be quite at their ease were Aslan and the Witch herself. It was the oddest thing to see those two faces – the golden face and the dead-white face – so close together. Not that the Witch looked Aslan exactly in his eyes; Mrs Beaver particularly noticed this.

"You have a traitor there, Aslan," said the Witch. Of course everyone present knew that she meant Edmund. But Edmund had got past thinking about himself after all he'd been through and after the talk he'd had that morning. He just went on looking at Aslan. It didn't seem to matter what the Witch said.

"Well," said Aslan. "His offence was not against you."

"Have you forgotten the Deep Magic?" asked the Witch.

"Let us say I have forgotten it," answered Aslan gravely. "Tell us of this Deep Magic."

"Tell you?" said the Witch, her voice growing suddenly shriller. "Tell you what is written on the very Table of Stone which stands beside us? Tell you what is written in letters deep as a spear is long on the fire-stones on the Secret Hill? Tell you what is engraved on the sceptre of the Emperor-beyond-the-Sea? You at least know the Magic which the Emperor put into Narnia at the very beginning. You know that every traitor belongs to me as my lawful prey and that for every treachery I have a right to a kill."

"Oh," said Mr Beaver. "So *that's* how you came to imagine yourself a queen – because you were the Emperor's hangman. I see."

"Peace, Beaver," said Aslan, with a very low growl.

"And so," continued the Witch, "that human creature is mine. His life is forfeit to me. His blood is my property."

"Come and take it then," said the Bull with the man's head, in a great bellowing voice.

"Fool," said the Witch with a savage smile that was almost a snarl, "do you really think your master can rob me of my rights by mere force? He knows the Deep Magic better than that. He knows that unless I have blood as the Law says, all Narnia will be overturned and perish in fire and water."

"It is very true," said Aslan. "I do not deny it."

"Oh, Aslan!" whispered Susan in the Lion's ear. "Can't we – I mean, you won't, will you? Can't we do something about the Deep Magic? Isn't there something you can work against it?"

"Work against the Emperor's Magic?" said Aslan, turning to her with something like a frown on his face. And nobody ever made that suggestion to him again.

Edmund was on the other side of Aslan, looking all the time at Aslan's face. He felt a choking feeling and wondered if he ought to say something; but a moment later he felt that he was not expected to do anything except to wait, and do what he was told.

"Fall back, all of you," said Aslan, "and I will talk to the Witch alone."

They all obeyed. It was a terrible time this – waiting and wondering while the Lion and the Witch talked earnestly together in low voices. Lucy said, "Oh, Edmund!" and began to cry. Peter stood with his back to the others looking out at the distant sea. The Beavers stood holding each other's paws with their heads bowed. The centaurs stamped uneasily with their hoofs. But everyone became perfectly still in the end, so that you noticed even small sounds like a bumble-bee flying past, or the birds in the forest down below them, or the wind rustling the leaves. And still the talk between Aslan and the White Witch went on.

At last they heard Aslan's voice. "You can all come back," he said. "I have settled the matter. She has renounced the claim on your brother's blood." And all over the hill there was a noise as if everyone had been holding their breath and had now begun breathing again, and then a murmur of talk.

The Witch was just turning away with a look of fierce joy on her face when she stopped and said,

"But how do I know this promise will be kept?"

"Haa-a-arrh!" roared Aslan, half rising from his throne; and his great mouth opened wider and wider and the roar grew louder and louder, and the Witch, after staring for a moment with her lips wide apart, picked up her skirts and fairly ran for her life.

CHAPTER FOURTEEN

THE TRIUMPH OF THE WITCH

As soon as the Witch had gone Aslan said, "We must move from this place at once, it will be wanted for other purposes. We shall encamp tonight at the Fords of Beruna."

Of course everyone was dying to ask him how he had arranged matters with the Witch; but his face was stern and everyone's ears were still ringing with the sound of his roar and so nobody dared.

After a meal, which was taken in the open air on the hill-top (for the sun had got strong by now and dried the grass), they were busy for a while taking the pavilion down and packing things up. Before two o'clock they were on the march and set off in a north-easterly direction, walking at an easy pace, for they had not far to go.

During the first part of the journey Aslan explained to Peter his plan of campaign. "As soon as she has finished her business in these parts," he said, "the Witch and her crew will almost certainly fall back to her House and prepare for a siege. You may or may not be able to cut her off and prevent her from reaching it." He then went on to outline two plans of battle – one for fighting the Witch and her people in the wood and another for assaulting her castle. And all the time he was advising Peter how to conduct the operations, saying things like, "You must put your Centaurs in such and such a place" or "You must post scouts to see that she doesn't do so-and-so," till at last Peter said,

"But you will be there yourself, Aslan."

"I can give you no promise of that," answered the Lion. And he continued giving Peter his instructions.

For the last part of the journey it was Susan and Lucy who saw most of him. He did not talk very much and seemed to them to be sad.

It was still afternoon when they came down to a place where the river valley had widened out and the river was broad and shallow. This was the Fords of Beruna and Aslan gave orders to halt on this side of the water. But Peter said,

"Wouldn't it be better to camp on the far side — for fear she should try a night attack or anything?"

Aslan, who seemed to have been thinking about something else, roused himself with a shake of his magnificent mane and said, "Eh? What's that?" Peter said it all over again.

"No," said Aslan in a dull voice, as if it didn't matter. "No. She will not make an attack tonight." And then he sighed deeply. But presently he added, "All the same it was well thought of. That is how a soldier ought to think. But it doesn't really matter." So they proceeded to pitch their camp.

Aslan's mood affected everyone that evening. Peter was feeling uncomfortable too at the idea of fighting the battle on his own; the news that Aslan might not be there had come as a great shock to him. Supper that evening was a quiet meal. Everyone felt how different it had been the previous night or even that morning. It was as if the good times, having just begun, were already drawing to their end.

This feeling affected Susan so much that she couldn't get to sleep when she went to bed. And after she had lain counting sheep and turning over and over she heard Lucy give a long sigh and turn over just beside her in the darkness.

"Can't you get to sleep either?" said Susan.

"No," said Lucy. "I thought you were asleep. I say, Susan!"

"What?"

"I've a most horrible feeling — as if something were hanging over us."

"Have you? Because, as a matter of fact, so have I."

"Something about Aslan," said Lucy. "Either some dreadful thing is going to happen to him, or something dreadful that he's going to do."

"There's been something wrong with him all afternoon," said Susan. "Lucy! What was that he said about not being with us at the battle? You don't think he could be stealing away and leaving us tonight, do you?"

"Where is he now?" said Lucy. "Is he here in the pavilion?"

"I don't think so."

"Susan! Let's go outside and have a look round. We might see him."

"All right. Let's," said Susan; "we might just as well be doing that as lying awake here."

Very quietly the two girls groped their way among the other sleepers and crept out of the tent. The moonlight was bright and everything was quite still except for the noise of the river chattering over the stones. Then

Susan suddenly caught Lucy's arm and said, "Look!" On the far side of the camping ground, just where the trees began, they saw the Lion slowly walking away from them into the wood. Without a word they both followed him.

He led them up the steep slope out of the river valley and then slightly to the right – apparently by the very same route which they had used that afternoon in coming from the Hill of the Stone Table. On and on he led them, into dark shadows and out into pale moonlight, getting their feet wet with the heavy dew. He looked somehow different from the Aslan they knew. His tail and his head hung low and he walked slowly as if he were very, very tired. Then, when they were crossing a wide open place where there were no shadows for them to hide in, he stopped and looked round. It was no good trying to run away so they came towards him. When they were closer he said,

"Oh, children, children, why are you following me?"

"We couldn't sleep," said Lucy – and then felt sure that she need say no more and that Aslan knew all they had been thinking.

"Please, may we come with you – wherever you're going?" asked Susan.

"Well – " said Aslan, and seemed to be thinking. Then he said, "I should be glad of company tonight. Yes, you may come, if you will promise to stop when I tell you, and after that leave me to go on alone."

"Oh, thank you, thank you. And we will," said the two girls.

Forward they went again and one of the girls walked on each side of the Lion. But how slowly he walked! And his great, royal head drooped so that his nose nearly touched the grass. Presently he stumbled and gave a low moan.

"Aslan! Dear Aslan!" said Lucy, "what is wrong? Can't you tell us?"

"Are you ill, dear Aslan?" asked Susan.

"No," said Aslan. "I am sad and lonely. Lay your hands on my mane so that I can feel you are there and let us walk like that."

And so the girls did what they would never have dared to do without his permission, what they had longed to do ever since they first saw him – buried their cold hands in the beautiful sea of fur and stroked it and, so doing, walked with him. And presently they saw that they were going with him up the slope of the hill on which the Stone Table stood. They went up at the side where the trees came furthest up, and when they got to the last tree (it was one that had some bushes about it) Aslan stopped and said,

"Oh, children, children. Here you must stop. And whatever happens, do not let yourselves be seen. Farewell."

And both the girls cried bitterly (though they hardly knew why) and clung to the Lion and kissed his mane and his nose and his paws and his great, sad eyes. Then he turned from them and walked out on to the top of the hill. And Lucy and Susan, crouching in the bushes, looked after him, and this is what they saw.

A great crowd of people were standing all round the Stone Table and though the moon was shining many of them carried torches which burned with evil-looking red flames and black smoke. But such people! Ogres with monstrous teeth, and wolves, and bull-headed men; spirits of evil trees and poisonous plants; and other creatures whom I won't describe because if I did the grown-ups would probably not let you read this book – Cruels and Hags and Incubuses, Wraiths, Horrors, Efreets, Sprites, Orknies, Wooses, and Ettins. In fact here were all those who were on the Witch's side and whom the Wolf had summoned at her command. And right in the middle, standing by the Table, was the Witch herself.

A howl and a gibber of dismay went up from the creatures when they first saw the great Lion pacing towards them, and for a moment even the Witch seemed to be struck with fear. Then she recovered herself and gave a wild fierce laugh.

"The fool!" she cried. "The fool has come. Bind him fast."

Lucy and Susan held their breaths waiting for Aslan's roar and his spring upon his enemies. But it never came. Four Hags, grinning and leering, yet also (at first) hanging back and half afraid of what they had to do, had approached him. "Bind him, I say!" repeated the White Witch. The Hags made a dart at him and shrieked with triumph when they found that he made no resistance at all. Then others – evil dwarfs and apes – rushed in to help them, and between them they rolled the huge Lion over on his back and tied all his four paws together, shouting and cheering as if they had done something brave, though, had the Lion chosen, one of those paws could have been the death of them all. But he made no noise, even when the enemies, straining and tugging, pulled the cords so tight that they cut into his flesh. Then they began to drag him towards the Stone Table.

"Stop!" said the Witch. "Let him first be shaved."

Another roar of mean laughter went up from her followers as an ogre with a pair of shears came forward and squatted down by Aslan's head. Snip-snip-snip went the shears and masses of curling gold began to fall to the ground. Then the ogre stood back and the children, watching from their hiding-place, could see the face of Aslan looking all small and different without its mane. The enemies also saw the difference.

"Why, he's only a great cat after all!" cried one.

"Is *that* what we were afraid of?" said another.

And they surged round Aslan, jeering at him, saying things like, "Puss, Puss! Poor Pussy," and, "How many mice have you caught today, Cat?" and, "Would you like a saucer of milk, Pussums?"

"Oh, how *can* they?" said Lucy, tears streaming down h.
brutes, the brutes!" For now that the first shock was over, th
Aslan looked to her braver, and more beautiful, and more
ever.

"Muzzle him!" said the Witch. And even now, as they worke
face putting on the muzzle, one bite from his jaws would have c   .wo or
three of them their hands. But he never moved. And this seemed to enrage
all that rabble. Everyone was at him now. Those who had been afraid to
come near him even after he was bound began to find their courage, and
for a few minutes the two girls could not even see him — so thickly was he
surrounded by the whole crowd of creatures kicking him, hitting him,
spitting on him, jeering at him.

At last the rabble had had enough of this. They began to drag the bound
and muzzled Lion to the Stone Table, some pulling and some pushing. He
was so huge that even when they got him there it took all their efforts to
hoist him on to the surface of it. Then there was more tying and tightening
of cords.

"The cowards! The cowards!" sobbed Susan. "Are they *still* afraid of him,
even now?"

When once Aslan had been tied (and tied so that he was really a mass of
cords) on the flat stone, a hush fell on the crowd. Four Hags, holding four
torches, stood at the corners of the Table. The Witch bared her arms as she
had bared them the previous night when it had been Edmund instead of
Aslan. Then she began to whet her knife. It looked to the children, when
the gleam of the torchlight fell on it, as if the knife were made of stone, not
of steel, and it was of a strange and evil shape.

At last she drew near. She stood by Aslan's head. Her face was working
and twitching with passion, but his looked up at the sky, still quiet, neither
angry nor afraid, but a little sad. Then, just before she gave the blow, she
stooped down and said in a quivering voice,

"And now, who has won? Fool, did you think that by all this you would
save the human traitor? Now I will kill you instead of him as our pact was
and so the Deep Magic will be appeased. But when you are dead what will
prevent me from killing him as well? And who will take him out of my
hand *then*? Understand that you have given me Narnia for ever, you have
lost your own life and you have not saved his. In that knowledge, despair
and die."

The children did not see the actual moment of the killing. They
couldn't bear to look and had covered their eyes.

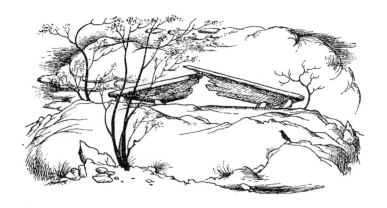

Chapter Fifteen

Deeper Magic from Before the Dawn of Time

While the two girls still crouched in the bushes with their hands over their faces, they heard the voice of the Witch calling out,

"Now! Follow me all and we will set about what remains of this war! It will not take us long to crush the human vermin and the traitors now that the great Fool, the great Cat, lies dead."

At this moment the children were for a few seconds in very great danger. For with wild cries and a noise of skirling pipes and shrill horns blowing, the whole of that vile rabble came sweeping off the hill-top and down the slope right past their hiding-place. They felt the Spectres go by them like a cold wind and they felt the ground shake beneath them under the galloping feet of the Minotaurs; and overhead there went a flurry of foul wings and a blackness of vultures and giant bats. At any other time they would have trembled with fear; but now the sadness and shame and horror of Aslan's death so filled their minds that they hardly thought of it.

As soon as the wood was silent again Susan and Lucy crept out onto the open hill-top. The moon was getting low and thin clouds were passing across her, but still they could see the shape of the Lion lying dead in his bonds. And down they both knelt in the wet grass and kissed his cold face and stroked his beautiful fur – what was left of it – and cried till they could cry no more. And then they looked at each other and held each other's hands for mere loneliness and cried again; and then again were silent. At last Lucy said,

"I can't bear to look at that horrible muzzle. I wonder, could we take it off?"

So they tried. And after a lot of working at it (for their fingers were cold and it was now the darkest part of the night) they succeeded. And when they saw his face without it they burst out crying again and kissed it and fondled it and wiped away the blood and the foam as well as they could. And it was all more lonely and hopeless and horrid than I know how to describe.

"I wonder, could we untie him as well?" said Susan presently. But the enemies, out of pure spitefulness, had drawn the cords so tight that the girls could make nothing of the knots.

I hope no one who reads this book has been quite as miserable as Susan and Lucy were that night; but if you have been – if you've been up all night and cried till you have no more tears left in you – you will know that there comes in the end a sort of quietness. You feel as if nothing is ever going to happen again. At any rate that was how it felt to these two. Hours and hours seemed to go by in this dead calm, and they hardly noticed that they were getting colder and colder. But at last Lucy noticed two other things. One was that the sky on the east side of the hill was a little less dark than it had been an hour ago. The other was some tiny movement going on in the grass at her feet. At first she took no interest in this. What did it matter? Nothing mattered now! But at last she saw that whatever-it-was had begun to move up the upright stones of the Stone Table. And now whatever-they-were were moving about on Aslan's body. She peered closer. They were little grey things.

"Ugh!" said Susan from the other side of the Table. "How beastly! There are horrid little mice crawling over him. Go away, you little beasts." And she raised her hand to frighten them away.

"Wait!" said Lucy, who had been looking at them more closely still. "Can you see what they're doing?"

Both girls bent down and stared.

"I do believe——" said Susan. "But how queer! They're nibbling away at the cords!"

"That's what I thought," said Lucy. "I think they're friendly mice. Poor little things – they don't realize he's dead. They think it'll do some good untying him."

It was quite definitely lighter by now. Each of the girls noticed for the first time the white face of the other. They could see the mice nibbling away; dozens and dozens, even hundreds, of little field mice. And at last, one by one, the ropes were all gnawed through.

The sky in the east was whitish by now and the stars were getting fainter – all except one very big one low down on the eastern horizon. They felt colder than they had been all night. The mice crept away again.

The girls cleared away the remains of the gnawed ropes. Aslan looked more like himself without them. Every moment his dead face looked nobler, as the light grew and they could see it better.

In the wood behind them a bird gave a chuckling sound. It had been so still for hours and hours that it startled them. Then another bird answered it. Soon there were birds singing all over the place.

It was quite definitely early morning now, not late night.

"I'm so cold," said Lucy.

"So am I," said Susan. "Let's walk about a bit."

They walked to the eastern edge of the hill and looked down. The one big star had almost disappeared. The country all looked dark grey, but beyond, at the very end of the world, the sea showed pale. The sky began to turn red. They walked to and fro more times than they could count between the dead Aslan and the eastern ridge, trying to keep warm; and oh, how tired their legs felt. Then at last, as they stood for a moment looking out towards the sea and Cair Paravel (which they could now just make out) the red turned to gold along the line where the sea and the sky met and very slowly up came the edge of the sun. At that moment they heard from behind them a loud noise – a great cracking, deafening noise as if a giant had broken a giant's plate.

"What's that?" said Lucy, clutching Susan's arm.

"I – I feel afraid to turn round," said Susan; "something awful is happening."

"They're doing something worse to *Him*," said Lucy. "Come on!" And she turned, pulling Susan round with her.

The rising of the sun had made everything look so different – all colours and shadows were changed – that for a moment they didn't see the important thing. Then they did. The Stone Table was broken into two pieces by a great crack that ran down it from end to end; and there was no Aslan.

"Oh, oh, oh!" cried the two girls, rushing back to the Table.

"Oh, it's *too* bad," sobbed Lucy; "they might have left the body alone."

"Who's done it?" cried Susan. "What does it mean? Is it magic?"

"Yes!" said a great voice behind their backs. "It is more magic." They looked round. There, shining in the sunrise, larger than they had seen him before, shaking his mane (for it had apparently grown again) stood Aslan himself.

"Oh, Aslan!" cried both the children, staring up at him, almost as much frightened as they were glad.

"Aren't you dead then, dear Aslan?" said Lucy.

"Not now," said Aslan.

"You're not – not a——?" asked Susan in a shaky voice. She couldn't bring herself to say the word *ghost*. Aslan stooped his golden head and licked her forehead. The warmth of his breath and a rich sort of smell that seemed to hang about his hair came all over her.

"Do I look it?" he said.

"Oh, you're real, you're real! Oh, Aslan!" cried Lucy, and both girls flung themselves upon him and covered him with kisses.

"But what does it all mean?" asked Susan when they were somewhat calmer.

"It means," said Aslan, "that though the Witch knew the Deep Magic, there is a magic deeper still which she did not know. Her knowledge goes back only to the dawn of time. But if she could have looked a little further back, into the stillness and the darkness before Time dawned, she would have read there a different incantation. She would have known that when a willing victim who had committed no treachery was killed in a traitor's stead, the Table would crack and Death itself would start working backwards. And now——"

"Oh yes. Now?" said Lucy, jumping up and clapping her hands.

"Oh, children," said the Lion, "I feel my strength coming back to me. Oh, children, catch me if you can!" He stood for a second, his eyes very bright, his limbs quivering, lashing himself with his tail. Then he made a leap high over their heads and landed on the other side of the Table. Laughing, though she didn't know why, Lucy scrambled over it to reach him. Aslan leaped again. A mad chase began. Round and round the hill-top he led them, now hopelessly out of their reach, now letting them almost catch his tail, now diving between them, now tossing them in the air with his huge and beautifully velveted paws and catching them again, and now stopping unexpectedly so that all three of them rolled over together in a happy laughing heap of fur and arms and legs. It was such a romp as no one has ever had except in Narnia; and whether it was more like playing with a thunderstorm or playing with a kitten Lucy could never make up her mind. And the funny thing was that when all three finally lay together panting in the sun, the girls no longer felt in the least tired or hungry or thirsty.

"And now," said Aslan presently, "to business. I feel I am going to roar. You had better put your fingers in your ears."

And they did. And Aslan stood up and when he opened his mouth to roar his face became so terrible that they did not dare to look at it. And they saw all the trees in front of him bend before the blast of his roaring as grass bends in a meadow before the wind. Then he said,

"We have a long journey to go. You must ride on me." And he crouched down and the children climbed on to his warm, golden back, and Susan sat first, holding on tightly to his mane and Lucy sat behind holding on tightly to Susan. And with a great heave he rose underneath them and then shot off, faster than any horse could go, downhill and into the thick of the forest.

That ride was perhaps the most wonderful thing that happened to them in Narnia. Have you ever had a gallop on a horse? Think of that; and then take away the heavy noise of the hoofs and the jingle of the bit and imagine instead the almost noiseless padding of the great paws. Then imagine instead of the black or grey or chestnut back of the horse the soft roughness of golden fur, and the mane flying back in the wind. And then imagine you are going about twice as fast as the fastest racehorse. But this is a mount that doesn't need to be guided and never grows tired. He rushes on and on, never missing his footing, never hesitating, threading his way with perfect skill between tree trunks, jumping over bush and briar and the smaller streams, wading the larger, swimming the largest of all. And you are riding not on a road nor in a park nor even on the downs, but right across Narnia, in spring, down solemn avenues of beech and across sunny glades of oak, through wild orchards of snow-white cherry trees, past roaring waterfalls and mossy rocks and echoing caverns, up windy slopes alight with gorse bushes, and across the shoulders of heathery mountains and along giddy ridges and down, down, down again into wild valleys and out into acres of blue flowers.

It was nearly midday when they found themselves looking down a steep hillside at a castle — a little toy castle it looked from where they stood — which seemed to be all pointed towers. But the Lion was rushing down at such a speed that it grew larger every moment and before they had time even to ask themselves what it was they were already on a level with it. And now it no longer looked like a toy castle but rose frowning in front of them. No face looked over the battlements and the gates were fast shut. And Aslan, not at all slacking his pace, rushed straight as a bullet towards it.

"The Witch's home!" he cried. "Now, children, hold tight."

Next moment the whole world seemed to turn upside down, and the children felt as if they had left their insides behind them; for the Lion had gathered himself together for a greater leap than any he had yet made and jumped — or you may call it flying rather than jumping — right over the castle wall. The two girls, breathless but unhurt, found themselves tumbling off his back in the middle of a wide stone courtyard full of statues.

CHAPTER SIXTEEN

WHAT HAPPENED ABOUT THE STATUES

"What an extraordinary place!" cried Lucy. "All those stone animals – and people too! It's – like a museum."

"Hush," said Susan, "Aslan's doing something."

He was indeed. He had bounded up to the stone lion and breathed on him. Then without waiting a moment he whisked round – almost as if he had been a cat chasing its tail – and breathed also on the stone dwarf, which (as you remember) was standing a few feet from the lion with his back to it. Then he pounced on a tall stone dryad which stood beyond the dwarf, turned rapidly aside to deal with a stone rabbit on his right, and rushed on to two centaurs. But at that moment Lucy said,

"Oh, Susan! Look! Look at the lion."

I expect you've seen someone put a lighted match to a bit of newspaper which is propped up in a grate against an unlit fire. And for a second nothing seems to have happened; and then you notice a tiny streak of flame creeping along the edge of the newspaper. It was like that now. For a second after Aslan had breathed upon him the stone lion looked just the same. Then a tiny streak of gold began to run along his white marble back – then it spread – then the colour seemed to lick all over him as the flame licks all over a bit of paper – then, while his hindquarters were still obviously stone, the lion shook his mane and all the heavy, stone folds rippled into living hair. Then he opened a great red mouth, warm and living, and gave a prodigious yawn. And now his hind legs had come to life. He lifted one of them and scratched himself. Then, having caught sight of Aslan, he went bounding after him and frisked around him, whimpering with delight and jumping up to lick his face.

Of course the children's eyes turned to follow the lion; but the sight they saw was so wonderful that they soon forgot about *him*. Everywhere the statues were coming to life. The courtyard looked no longer like a museum; it looked more like a zoo. Creatures were running after Aslan and dancing round him till he was almost hidden in the crowd. Instead of all that deadly white the courtyard was now a blaze of colours; glossy chestnut sides of centaurs, indigo horns of unicorns, dazzling plumage of birds, reddy-brown of foxes, dogs and satyrs, yellow stockings and crimson hoods of dwarfs; and the birch-girls in silver, and the beech-girls in fresh, transparent green, and the larch-girls in green so bright that it was almost yellow. And instead of the deadly silence the whole place rang with the sound of happy roarings, brayings, yelpings, barkings, squealings, cooings, neighings, stampings, shouts, hurrahs, songs and laughter.

"Oh!" said Susan in a different tone. "Look! I wonder — I mean, is it safe?"

Lucy looked and saw that Aslan had just breathed on the feet of the stone giant.

"It's all right!" shouted Aslan joyously. "Once the feet are put right, all the rest of him will follow."

"That wasn't exactly what I meant," whispered Susan to Lucy. But it was too late to do anything about it now even if Aslan would have listened to her. The change was already creeping up the Giant's legs. Now he was moving his feet. A moment later he lifted his club off his shoulder, rubbed his eyes and said,

"Bless me! I must have been asleep. Now! Where's that dratted little Witch that was running about on the ground? Somewhere just by my feet it was." But when everyone had shouted up to him to explain what had really happened, and when the Giant had put his hand to his ear and got them to repeat it all again so that at last he understood, then he bowed down till his head was no further off than the top of a haystack and touched his cap repeatedly to Aslan, beaming all over his honest ugly face. (Giants of any sort are now so rare in England and so few giants are good-tempered that ten to one you have never seen a giant when his face is beaming. It's a sight well worth looking at.)

"Now for the inside of this house!" said Aslan. "Look alive, everyone. Up stairs and down stairs and in my lady's chamber! Leave no corner unsearched. You never know where some poor prisoner may be concealed."

And into the interior they all rushed and for several minutes the whole of that dark, horrible, fusty old castle echoed with the opening of windows and with everyone's voices crying out at once, "Don't forget the dungeons – Give us a hand with this door! – Here's another little winding stair – Oh! I say. Here's a poor kangaroo. Call Aslan – Phew! How it smells in here –

Look out for trap-doors — Up here! There are a whole lot more on the landing!" But the best of all was when Lucy came rushing upstairs shouting out,

"Aslan! Aslan! I've found Mr Tumnus. Oh, do come quick."

A moment later Lucy and the little Faun were holding each other by both hands and dancing round and round for joy. The little chap was none the worse for having been a statue and was of course very interested in all she had to tell him.

But at last the ransacking of the Witch's fortress was ended. The whole castle stood empty with every door and window open and the light and the sweet spring air flooding into all the dark and evil places which needed them so badly. The whole crowd of liberated statues surged back into the courtyard. And it was then that someone (Tumnus, I think) first said,

"But how are we going to get out?" for Aslan had got in by a jump and the gates were still locked.

"That'll be all right," said Aslan; and then, rising on his hind legs, he bawled up at the Giant. "Hi! You up there," he roared. "What's your name?"

"Giant Rumblebuffin, if it please your honour," said the Giant, once more touching his cap.

"Well then, Giant Rumblebuffin," said Aslan, "just let us out of this, will you?"

"Certainly, your honour. It will be a pleasure," said Giant Rumblebuffin. "Stand well away from the gates, all you little 'uns." Then he strode to the gate himself and bang — bang — bang — went his huge club. The gates creaked at the first blow, cracked at the second, and shivered at the third. Then he tackled the towers on each side of them and after a few minutes of crashing and thudding both the towers and a good bit of the wall on each side went thundering down in a mass of hopeless rubble; and when the dust cleared it was odd, standing in that dry, grim, stony yard, to see through the gap all the grass and waving trees and sparkling streams of the forest, and the blue hills beyond that and beyond them the sky.

"Blowed if I ain't all in a muck sweat," said the Giant, puffing like the largest railway engine. "Comes of being out of condition. I suppose neither of you young ladies has such a thing as a pocket-handkerchee about you?"

"Yes, I have," said Lucy, standing on tiptoe and holding her handkerchief up as far as she could reach.

"Thank you, Missie," said Giant Rumblebuffin, stooping down. Next moment Lucy got rather a fright for she found herself caught up in mid-air between the Giant's finger and thumb. But just as she was getting near his face he suddenly started and then put her gently back on the ground muttering, "Bless me! I've picked up the little girl instead. I beg your pardon, Missie, I thought you *was* the handkerchee!"

"No, no," said Lucy, laughing, "here it is!" This time he managed to get it but it was only about the same size to him that a saccharine tablet would be to you, so that when she saw him solemnly rubbing it to and fro across his great red face, she said, "I'm afraid it's not much use to you, Mr Rumblebuffin."

"Not at all. Not at all," said the giant politely. "Never met a nicer handkerchee. So fine, so handy. So − I don't know how to describe it."

"What a nice giant he is!" said Lucy to Mr Tumnus.

"Oh, yes," replied the Faun. "All the buffins always were. One of the most respected of all the giant families in Narnia. Not very clever, perhaps (I never knew a giant that was), but an old family. With traditions, you know. If he'd been the other sort she'd never have turned him into stone."

At this point Aslan clapped his paws together and called for silence.

"Our day's work is not yet over," he said, "and if the Witch is to be finally defeated before bedtime we must find the battle at once."

"And join in, I hope, sir!" added the largest of the Centaurs.

"Of course," said Aslan. "And now! Those who can't keep up − that is, children, dwarfs, and small animals − must ride on the backs of those who can − that is, lions, centaurs, unicorns, horses, giants and eagles. Those who are good with their noses must come in front with us lions to smell out where the battle is. Look lively and sort yourselves."

And with a great deal of bustle and cheering they did. The most pleased of the lot was the other Lion who kept running about everywhere pretending to be very busy but really in order to say to everyone he met. "Did you hear what he said? *Us Lions.* That means him and me. *Us Lions.* That's what I like about Aslan. No side, no stand-off-ishness. *Us Lions.* That meant him and me." At least he went on saying this till Aslan had loaded him up with three dwarfs, one dryad, two rabbits, and a hedgehog. That steadied him a bit.

When all were ready (it was a big sheep-dog who actually helped Aslan most in getting them sorted into their proper order) they set out through the gap in the castle wall. At first the lions and dogs went nosing about in all directions. But then suddenly one great hound picked up the scent and gave a bay. There was no time lost after that. Soon all the dogs and lions and wolves and other hunting animals were going at full speed with their noses to the ground, and all the others, streaked out for about half a mile behind them, were following as fast as they could. The noise was like an English fox-hunt only better because every now and then with the music of the hounds was mixed the roar of the other lion and sometimes the far deeper and more awful roar of Aslan himself. Faster and faster they went as the scent became easier and easier to follow. And then, just as they came to the last curve in a narrow, winding valley, Lucy heard above all these noises another noise – a different one, which gave her a queer feeling inside. It was a noise of shouts and shrieks and of the clashing of metal against metal.

Then they came out of the narrow valley and at once she saw the reason. There stood Peter and Edmund and all the rest of Aslan's army fighting desperately against the crowd of horrible creatures whom she had seen last night; only now, in the daylight, they looked even stranger and more evil and more deformed. There also seemed to be far more of them. Peter's army – which had their backs to her – looked terribly few. And there were statues dotted all over the battlefield, so apparently the Witch had been using her wand. But she did not seem to be using it now. She was fighting with her stone knife. It was Peter she was fighting – both of them going at it so hard that Lucy could hardly make out what was happening; she only saw the stone knife and Peter's sword flashing so quickly that they looked like three knives and three swords. That pair were in the centre. On each side the line stretched out. Horrible things were happening wherever she looked.

"Off my back, children," shouted Aslan. And they both tumbled off. Then with a roar that shook all Narnia from the western lamp-post to the shores of the eastern sea the great beast flung himself upon the White Witch. Lucy saw her face lifted towards him for one second with an expression of terror and amazement. Then Lion and Witch had rolled over together but with the Witch underneath; and at the same moment all war-like creatures whom Aslan had led from the Witch's house rushed madly on the enemy lines, dwarfs with their battleaxes, dogs with teeth, the Giant with his club (and his feet also crushed dozens of the foe), unicorns with their horns, centaurs with swords and hoofs. And Peter's tired army cheered, and the newcomers roared, and the enemy squealed and gibbered till the wood re-echoed with the din of that onset.

CHAPTER SEVENTEEN

THE HUNTING OF THE WHITE STAG

The battle was all over a few minutes after their arrival. Most of the enemy had been killed in the first charge of Aslan and his companions; and when those who were still living saw that the Witch was dead they either gave themselves up or took flight. The next thing that Lucy knew was that Peter and Aslan were shaking hands. It was strange to her to see Peter looking as he looked now – his face was so pale and stern and he seemed so much older.

"It was all Edmund's doing, Aslan," Peter was saying. "We'd have been beaten if it hadn't been for him. The Witch was turning our troops into stone right and left. But nothing would stop him. He fought his way through three ogres to where she was just turning one of your leopards into a statue. And when he reached her he had the sense to bring his sword smashing down on her wand instead of trying to go for her directly and simply getting made a statue himself for his pains. That was the mistake all the rest were making. Once her wand was broken we began to have some chance – if we hadn't lost so many already. He was terribly wounded. We must go and see him."

They found Edmund in charge of Mrs Beaver a little way back from the fighting line. He was covered with blood, his mouth was open, and his face a nasty green colour.

"Quick, Lucy," said Aslan.

And then, almost for the first time, Lucy remembered the precious cordial that had been given her for a Christmas present. Her hands trembled so much that she could hardly undo the stopper, but she managed it in the end and poured a few drops into her brother's mouth.

"There are other people wounded," said Aslan while she was still looking eagerly into Edmund's pale face and wondering if the cordial would have any result.

"Yes, I know," said Lucy crossly. "Wait a minute."

"Daughter of Eve," said Aslan in a graver voice, "others also are at the point of death. Must *more* people die for Edmund?"

"I'm sorry, Aslan," said Lucy, getting up and going with him. And for the next half-hour they were busy – she attending to the wounded while he restored those who had been turned into stone. When at last she was free to come back to Edmund she found him standing on his feet and not only healed of his wounds but looking better than she had seen him look – oh, for ages; in fact ever since his first term at that horrid school which was where he had begun to go wrong. He had become his real old self again and could look you in the face. And there on the field of battle Aslan made him a knight.

"Does he know," whispered Lucy to Susan, "what Aslan did for him? Does he know what the arrangement with the Witch really was?"

"Hush! No, of course not," said Susan.

"Oughtn't he to be told?" said Lucy.

"Oh, surely not," said Susan. "It would be too awful for him. Think how you'd feel if you were he."

"All the same I think he ought to know," said Lucy. But at that moment they were interrupted.

That night they slept where they were. How Aslan provided food for them all I don't know; but somehow or other they found themselves all sitting down on the grass to a fine high tea at about eight o'clock. The next day they began marching eastward down the side of the great river. And the next day after that, at about teatime, they actually reached the mouth. The castle of Cair Paravel on its little hill towered up above them; before them were the sands, with rocks and little pools of salt water, and seaweed, and the smell of the sea and long miles of bluish-green waves breaking for ever and ever on the beach. And oh, the cry of the seagulls! Have you heard it? Can you remember?

That evening after tea the four children all managed to get down to the beach again and get their shoes and stockings off and feel the sand between their toes. But the next day was more solemn. For then, in the Great Hall of Cair Paravel – that wonderful hall with the ivory roof and the west wall hung with peacocks' feathers and the eastern door which looks towards the sea, in the presence of all their friends and to the sound of trumpets, Aslan solemnly crowned them and led them to the four thrones amid deafening shouts of, "Long Live King Peter! Long Live Queen Susan! Long Live King Edmund! Long Live Queen Lucy!"

"Once a king or queen in Narnia, always a king or queen. Bear it well, Sons of Adam! Bear it well, Daughters of Eve!" said Aslan.

And through the eastern door, which was wide open, came the voices of the mermen and the mermaids swimming close to the shore and singing in honour of their new Kings and Queens.

So the children sat on their thrones, and sceptres were put into their hands and they gave rewards and honours to all their friends, to Tumnus the Faun, and to the Beavers, and Giant Rumblebuffin, to the leopards, and the good centaurs, and the good dwarfs, and to the Lion. And that night there was a great feast in Cair Paravel, and revelry and dancing, and gold flashed and wine flowed, and answering to the music inside, but stranger, sweeter, and more piercing, came the music of the sea people.

But amidst all these rejoicings Aslan himself quietly slipped away. And when the Kings and Queens noticed that he wasn't there they said nothing about it. For Mr Beaver had warned them. "He'll be coming and going," he had said. "One day you'll see him and another you won't. He doesn't like being tied down – and of course he has other countries to attend to. It's quite all right. He'll often drop in. Only you mustn't press him. He's wild, you know. Not like a *tame* lion."

And now, as you see, this story is nearly (but not quite) at an end. These two Kings and two Queens governed Narnia well, and long and happy was their reign. At first much of their time was spent in seeking out the remnants of the White Witch's army and destroying them, and indeed for a long time there would be news of evil things lurking in the wilder parts of the forest – a haunting here and a killing there, a glimpse of a werewolf one month and a rumour of a hag the next. But in the end all that foul brood was stamped out. And they made good laws and kept the peace and saved good trees from being unnecessarily cut down, and liberated young dwarfs and young satyrs from being sent to school, and generally stopped busybodies and interferers and encouraged ordinary people who wanted to live and let live. And they drove back the fierce giants (quite a different sort from Giant Rumblebuffin) in the north of Narnia when these ventured across the frontier. And they entered into friendship and alliance with countries beyond the sea and paid them visits of state and received visits of state from them. And they themselves grew and changed as the years passed over them. And Peter became a tall and deep-chested man and a great warrior, and he was called King Peter the Magnificent. And Susan grew into a tall and gracious woman with black hair that fell almost to her feet and the kings of the countries beyond the sea began to send ambassadors asking for her hand in marriage. And she was called Queen Susan the Gentle. Edmund was a graver and quieter man than Peter, and great in council and judgement. He was called King Edmund the Just. But as for Lucy, she was always gay and golden-haired, and all princes in those parts desired her to be their Queen, and her own people called her Queen Lucy the Valiant.

So they lived in great joy and if ever they remembered their life in this world it was only as one remembers a dream. And one year it fell out that Tumnus (who was a middle-aged Faun by now and beginning to be stout) came down river and brought them news that the White Stag had once more appeared in his parts – the White Stag who would give you wishes if you caught him. So these two Kings and two Queens with the principal members of their court, rode a-hunting with horns and hounds in the Western Woods to follow the White Stag. And they had not hunted long before they had a sight of him. And he led them a great pace over rough and smooth and through thick and thin, till the horses of all the courtiers were tired out and these four were still following. And they saw the stag enter into a thicket where their horses could not follow. Then said King Peter (for they talked in quite a different style now, having been Kings and Queens for so long), "Fair Consorts, let us now alight from our horses and follow this beast into the thicket; for in all my days I never hunted a nobler quarry."

"Sir," said the others, "even so let us do."

So they alighted and tied their horses to trees and went on into the thick wood on foot. And as soon as they had entered it Queen Susan said,

"Fair friends, here is a great marvel, for I seem to see a tree of iron."

"Madam," said King Edmund, "if you look well upon it you shall see it is a pillar of iron with a lantern set on the top thereof."

"By the Lion's Mane, a strange device," said King Peter, "to set a lantern here where the trees cluster so thick about it and so high above it that if it were lit it should give light to no man!"

"Sir," said Queen Lucy. "By likelihood when this post and this lamp were set here there were smaller trees in the place, or fewer, or none. For this is a young wood and the iron post is old." And they stood looking upon it.

Then said King Edmund, "I know not how it is, but this lamp on the post worketh upon me strangely. It runs in my mind that I have seen the like before; as it were in a dream, or in the dream of a dream."

"Sir," answered they all, "it is even so with us also."

"And more," said Queen Lucy, "for it will not go out of my mind that if we pass this post and lantern either we shall find strange adventures or else some great change of our fortunes."

"Madam," said King Edmund, "the like foreboding stirreth in my heart also."

"And in mine, fair brother," said King Peter.

"And in mine too," said Queen Susan. "Wherefore by my counsel we shall lightly return to our horses and follow this White Stag no further."

"Madam," said King Peter, "therein I pray thee to have me excused. For never since we four were Kings and Queens in Narnia have we set our hands to any high matter, as battles, quests, feats of arms, acts of justice, and the like, and then given over; but always what we have taken in hand, the same we have achieved."

"Sister," said Queen Lucy, "my royal brother speaks rightly. And it seems to me we should be shamed if for any fearing or foreboding we turned back from following so noble a beast as now we have in chase."

"And so say I," said King Edmund. "And I have such desire to find the signification of this thing that I would not by my good will turn back for the richest jewel in all Narnia and all the islands."

"Then in the name of Aslan," said Queen Susan, "if ye will all have it so, let us go on and take the adventure that shall fall to us."

So these Kings and Queens entered the thicket, and before they had gone a score of paces they all remembered that the thing they had seen was called a lamp-post, and before they had gone twenty more they noticed that they were making their way not through branches but through coats. And the next moment they all came tumbling out of a wardrobe door into the empty room, and they were no longer Kings and Queens in their hunting array but just Peter, Susan, Edmund and Lucy in their old clothes. It was the same day and the same hour of the day on which they had all gone into the wardrobe to hide. Mrs Macready and the visitors were still talking in the passage; but luckily they never came into the empty room and so the children weren't caught.

And that would have been the very end of the story if it hadn't been that they felt they really must explain to the Professor why four of the coats out of his wardrobe were missing. And the Professor, who was a very remarkable man, didn't tell them not to be silly or not to tell lies, but believed the whole story. "No," he said, "I don't think it will be any good trying to go back through the wardrobe door to get the coats. You won't get into Narnia again by *that* route. Nor would the coats be much use by now if you did! Eh? What's that? Yes, of course you'll get back to Narnia again some day. Once a King in Narnia, always a King in Narnia. But don't go trying to use the same route twice. Indeed, don't *try* to get there at all. It'll happen when you're not looking for it. And don't talk too much about it even among yourselves. And don't mention it to anyone else unless you find that they've had adventures of the same sort themselves. What's that? How will you know? Oh, you'll *know* all right. Odd things they say – even their looks – will let the secret out. Keep your eyes open. Bless me, what *do* they teach them at these schools?"

And that is the very end of the adventure of the wardrobe. But if the Professor was right, it was only the beginning of the adventures of Narnia.

THE HORSE AND

HIS BOY

Mt. Pire

Anvard

narrow gorge

DESERT

Rock

N
W E
S

Stormness Head

ass into Narnia

ARCHENLAND

R. Winding Arrow

Oasis

DESERT

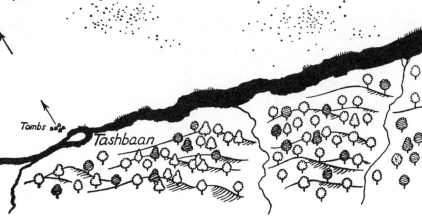

Tombs

Tashbaan

The Horse and his Boy

Contents

To David and Douglas Gresham

CHAPTER ONE

How Shasta Set Out on his Travels

This is the story of an adventure that happened in Narnia and Calormen and the lands between, in the Golden Age when Peter was High King in Narnia and his brother and his two sisters were King and Queens under him.

In those days, far south in Calormen on a little creek of the sea, there lived a poor fisherman called Arsheesh, and with him there lived a boy who called him Father. The boy's name was Shasta. On most days Arsheesh went out in his boat to fish in the morning, and in the afternoon he harnessed his donkey to a cart and loaded the cart with fish and went a mile or so southward to the village to sell it. If it had sold well he would come home in a moderately good temper and say nothing to Shasta, but if it had sold badly he would find fault with him and perhaps beat him. There was always something to find fault with for Shasta had plenty of work to do, mending and washing the nets, cooking the supper, and cleaning the cottage in which they both lived.

Shasta was not at all interested in anything that lay south of his home because he had once or twice been to the village with Arsheesh and he knew that there was nothing very interesting there. In the village he only met other men who were just like his father – men with long, dirty robes, and wooden shoes turned up at the toe, and turbans on their heads, and beards, talking to one another very slowly about things that sounded dull. But he was very interested in everything that lay to the North because no one ever went that way and he was never allowed to go there himself. When he was sitting out of doors mending the nets, and all alone, he would often look eagerly to the North. One could see nothing but a grassy slope running up to a level ridge and beyond that the sky with perhaps a few birds in it.

Sometimes if Arsheesh was there Shasta would say, "O my Father, what is there beyond the hill?" And then if the fisherman was in a bad temper he would box Shasta's ears and tell him to attend to his work. Or if he was in a peaceable mood he would say, "O my son, do not allow your mind to be distracted by idle questions. For one of the poets has said, 'Application to business is the root of prosperity, but those who ask questions that do not concern them are steering the ship of folly towards the rock of indigence'."

Shasta thought that beyond the hill there must be some delightful secret which his father wished to hide from him. In reality, however, the fisherman talked like this because he didn't know what lay to the North. Neither did he care. He had a very practical mind.

One day there came from the south a stranger who was unlike any man that Shasta had seen before. He rode upon a strong dappled horse with flowing mane and tail, and his stirrups and bridle were inlaid with silver. The spike of a helmet projected from the middle of his silken turban and he wore a shirt of chain mail. By his side hung a curving scimitar; a round shield studded with bosses of brass hung at his back, and his right hand grasped a lance. His face was dark, but this did not surprise Shasta because all the people of Calormen are like that; what did surprise him was the man's beard which was dyed crimson, and curled and gleaming with scented oil. But Arsheesh knew by the gold on the stranger's bare arm that he was a Tarkaan or great lord, and he bowed kneeling before him till his beard touched the earth, and made signs to Shasta to kneel also.

The stranger demanded hospitality for the night which of course the fisherman dared not refuse. All the best they had was set before the Tarkaan for supper (and he didn't think much of it) and Shasta, as always happened when the fisherman had company, was given a hunk of bread and turned out of the cottage. On these occasions he usually slept with the donkey in its little thatched stable. But it was much too early to go to sleep yet, and Shasta, who had never learned that it is wrong to listen behind doors, sat down with his ear to a crack in the wooden wall of the cottage to hear what the grown-ups were talking about. And this is what he heard:

"And now, O my host," said the Tarkaan, "I have a mind to buy that boy of yours."

"O my master," replied the fisherman (and Shasta knew by the wheedling tone the greedy look that was probably coming into his face as he said it), "what price could induce your servant, poor though he is, to sell into slavery his only child and his own flesh? Has not one of the poets said, 'Natural affection is stronger than soup and offspring more precious than carbuncles'?"

"It is even so," replied the guest dryly. "But another poet has likewise said, 'He who attempts to deceive the judicious is already baring his own back for the scourge'. Do not load your aged mouth with falsehoods. This boy is manifestly no son of yours, for your cheek is as black as mine but the boy is fair and white like the accursed but beautiful barbarians who inhabit the remote North."

"How well it was said," answered the fisherman, "that swords can be kept off with shields but the Eye of Wisdom pierces through every defence! Know then, O my formidable guest, that because of my extreme poverty I have never married and have no child. But in that same year in which the Tisroc (may he live for ever) began his august and beneficent reign, on a night when the moon was at her full, it pleased the gods to deprive me of my sleep. Therefore I arose from my bed in this hovel and went forth to the beach to refresh myself with looking upon the water and the moon and breathing the cool air. And presently I heard a noise as of oars coming to me across the water and then, as it were, a weak cry. And shortly after, the tide brought to the land a little boat in which there was nothing but a man lean with extreme hunger and thirst who seemed to have died but a few moments before (for he was still warm), and an empty water-skin, and a child, still living. 'Doubtless,' said I, 'these unfortunates have escaped from the wreck of a great ship, but by the admirable designs of the gods, the elder has starved himself to keep the child alive and has perished in sight of land.' Accordingly, remembering how the gods never fail to reward those who befriend the destitute, and being moved by compassion (for your servant is a man of tender heart)—"

"Leave out all these idle words in your own praise," interrupted the Tarkaan. "It is enough to know that you took the child – and have had ten times the worth of his daily bread out of him in labour, as anyone can see. And now tell me at once what price you put on him, for I am wearied with your loquacity."

"You yourself have wisely said," answered Arsheesh, "that the boy's labour has been to me of inestimable value. This must be taken into account in fixing the price. For if I sell the boy I must undoubtedly either buy or hire another to do his work."

"I'll give you fifteen crescents for him," said the Tarkaan.

"Fifteen!" cried Arsheesh in a voice that was something between a whine and a scream. "Fifteen! For the prop of my old age and the delight of my eyes! Do not mock my grey beard, Tarkaan though you be. My price is seventy."

At this point Shasta got up and tiptoed away. He had heard all he wanted, for he had often listened when men were bargaining in the village and knew how it was done. He was quite certain that Arsheesh would sell him in the end for something much more than fifteen crescents and much less than seventy, but that he and the Tarkaan would take hours in getting to an agreement.

You must not imagine that Shasta felt at all as you and I would feel if we had just overheard our parents talking about selling us for slaves. For one thing, his life was already little better than slavery; for all he knew, the lordly stranger on the great horse might be kinder to him than Arsheesh. For another, the story about his own discovery in the boat had filled him with excitement and with a sense of relief. He had often been uneasy because, try as he might, he had never been able to love the fisherman, and he knew that a boy ought to love his father. And now, apparently, he was no relation to Arsheesh at all. That took a great weight off his mind. "Why, I might be anyone!" he thought. "I might be the son of a Tarkaan myself – or the son of the Tisroc (may he live for ever) – or of a god!"

He was standing out in the grassy place before the cottage while he thought these things. Twilight was coming on apace and a star or two was already out, but the remains of the sunset could still be seen in the west. Not far away the stranger's horse, loosely tied to an iron ring in the wall of the donkey's stable, was grazing. Shasta strolled over to it and patted its neck. It went on tearing up the grass and took no notice of him.

Then another thought came into Shasta's mind. "I wonder what sort of a man that Tarkaan is," he said out loud. "It would be splendid if he was kind. Some of the slaves in a great lord's house have next to nothing to do. They wear lovely clothes and eat meat every day. Perhaps he'd take me to the wars and I'd save his life in a battle and then he'd set me free and adopt me as his son and give me a palace and a chariot and a suit of armour. But then he might be a horrid cruel man. He might send me to work on the fields in chains. I wish I knew. How can I know? I bet this horse knows, if only he could tell me."

The Horse had lifted its head. Shasta stroked its smooth-as-satin nose and said, "I wish *you* could talk, old fellow."

And then for a second he thought he was dreaming, for quite distinctly, though in a low voice, the Horse said, "But I can."

Shasta stared into its great eyes and his own grew almost as big, with astonishment.

"How ever did *you* learn to talk?"

"Hush! Not so loud," replied the Horse. "Where I come from, nearly all the animals talk."

"Wherever is that?" asked Shasta.

"Narnia," answered the Horse. "The happy land of Narnia – Narnia of the heathery mountains and the thymy downs, Narnia of the many rivers, the plashing glens, the mossy caverns and the deep forests ringing with the hammers of the Dwarfs. Oh, the sweet air of Narnia! An hour's life there is better than a thousand years in Calormen." It ended with a whinny that sounded very like a sigh.

"How did you get here?" said Shasta.

"Kidnapped," said the Horse. "Or stolen, or captured – whichever you like to call it. I was only a foal at the time. My mother warned me not to range the Southern slopes, into Archenland and beyond, but I wouldn't heed her. And by the Lion's Mane I have paid for my folly. All these years I have been a slave to humans, hiding my true nature and pretending to be dumb and witless like their horses."

"Why didn't you tell them who you were?"

"Not such a fool, that's why. If they'd once found out I could talk they would have made a show of me at fairs and guarded me more carefully than ever. My last chance of escape would have been gone."

"And why—" began Shasta, but the Horse interrupted him.

"Now look," it said, "we mustn't waste time on idle questions. You want to know about my master the Tarkaan Anradin. Well, he's bad. Not too bad to me, for a war-horse costs too much to be treated very badly. But you'd be better lying dead tonight than go to be a human slave in his house tomorrow."

"Then I'd better run away," said Shasta, turning very pale.

"Yes, you had," said the Horse. "But why not run away with me?"

"Are you going to run away too?" said Shasta.

"Yes, if you'll come with me," answered the Horse. "This is the chance for both of us. You see, if I run away without a rider, everyone who sees me will say 'Stray horse' and be after me as quick as he can. With a rider I've a chance to get through. That's where you can help me. On the other hand, you can't get very far on those two silly legs of yours (what absurd legs humans have!) without being overtaken. But on me you can outdistance any other horse in this country. That's where I can help you. By the way, I suppose you know how to ride?"

"Oh yes, of course," said Shasta. "At least, I've ridden the donkey."

"Ridden the *what*?" retorted the Horse with extreme contempt. (At least, that is what he meant. Actually it came out in a sort of neigh – "Ridden the wha-ha-ha-ha-ha?" Talking horses always become more horsy in accent when they are angry.)

"In other words," he continued, "you *can't* ride. That's a drawback. I'll have to teach you as we go along. If you can't ride, can you fall?"

"I suppose anyone can fall," said Shasta.

"I mean can you fall and get up again without crying and mount again and fall again and yet not be afraid of falling?"

"I – I'll try," said Shasta.

"Poor little beast," said the Horse in a gentler tone. "I forget you're only a foal. We'll make a fine rider of you in time. And now – we mustn't start until those two in the hut are asleep. Meantime we can make our plans. My Tarkaan is on his way North to the great city, to Tashbaan itself and the court of the Tisroc—"

"I say," put in Shasta in rather a shocked voice, "oughtn't you to say 'May he live for ever'?"

"Why?" asked the Horse. "I'm a free Narnian. And why should I talk slaves' and fools' talk? I don't want him to live for ever, and I know that he's not going to live for ever whether I want him to or not. And I can see you're from the free North too. No more of this Southern jargon between you and me! And now, back to our plans. As I said, my human was on his way North to Tashbaan."

"Does that mean we'd better go to the South?"

"I think not," said the Horse. "You see, he thinks I'm dumb and witless like his other horses. Now if I really were, the moment I got loose I'd go back home to my stable and paddock; back to his palace which is two days' journey South. That's where he'll look for me. He'd never dream of my going on North on my own. And anyway he will probably think that someone in the last village who saw him ride through has followed us to here and stolen me."

"Oh, hurray!" said Shasta. "Then we'll go North. I've been longing to go to the North all my life."

"Of course you have," said the Horse. "That's because of the blood that's in you. I'm sure you're true Northern stock. But not too loud. I should think they'd be asleep soon now."

"I'd better creep back and see," suggested Shasta.

"That's a good idea," said the Horse. "But take care you're not caught."

It was a good deal darker now and very silent except for the sound of the waves on the beach, which Shasta hardly noticed because he had been hearing it day and night as long as he could remember. The cottage, as he approached it, showed no light. When he listened at the front there was no noise. When he went round to the only window, he could hear, after a second or two, the familiar noise of the old fisherman's squeaky snore. It was funny to think that if all went well he would never hear it again. Holding his breath and feeling a little bit sorry, but much less sorry than he was glad, Shasta glided away over the grass and went to the donkey's stable, groped along to a place he knew where the key was hidden, opened the door and found the Horse's saddle and bridle which had been locked up there for the night. He bent forward and kissed the donkey's nose. "I'm sorry we can't take *you*," he said.

"There you are at last," said the Horse when he got back to it. "I was beginning to wonder what had become of you."

"I was getting your things out of the stable," replied Shasta. "And now, can you tell me how to put them on?"

For the next few minutes Shasta was at work, very cautiously to avoid jingling, while the Horse said things like, "Get that girth a bit tighter" or, "You'll find a buckle lower down" or, "You'll need to shorten those stirrups a good bit." When all was finished he said:

"Now; we've got to have reins for the look of the thing, but you won't be using them. Tie them to the saddle-bow: very slack so that I can do what I like with my head. And, remember – you are not to touch them."

"What are they for, then?" asked Shasta.

"Ordinarily they are for directing me," replied the Horse. "But as I intend to do all the directing on this journey, you'll please keep your hands to yourself. And there's another thing. I'm not going to have you grabbing my mane."

"But I say," pleaded Shasta. "If I'm not to hold on by the reins or by your mane, what *am* I to hold on by?"

"You hold on with your knees," said the Horse. "That's the secret of good riding. Grip my body between your knees as hard as you like; sit straight up, straight as a poker; keep your elbows in. And by the way, what did you do with the spurs?"

"Put them on my heels, of course," said Shasta. "I do know that much."

"Then you can take them off and put them in the saddle-bag. We may be able to sell them when we get to Tashbaan. Ready? And now I think you can get up."

"Ooh! You're a dreadful height," gasped Shasta after his first, and unsuccessful, attempt.

"I'm a horse, that's all," was the reply. "Anyone would think I was a haystack from the way you're trying to climb up me! There, that's better. Now sit *up* and remember what I told you about your knees. Funny to think of me who has led cavalry charges and won races having a potato-sack like you in the saddle! However, off we go." He chuckled, not unkindly.

And he certainly began their night journey with great caution. First of all he went just south of the fisherman's cottage to the little river which there ran into the sea, and took care to leave in the mud some very plain hoof-marks pointing South. But as soon as they were in the middle of the ford he turned upstream and waded till they were about a hundred yards further inland than the cottage. Then he selected a nice gravelly bit of bank which would take no footprints and came out on the Northern side. Then, still at a walking pace, he went Northward till the cottage, the one tree, the donkey's stable, and the creek – everything, in fact, that Shasta had ever known – had sunk out of sight in the grey summer-night darkness. They had been going uphill and now were at the top of the ridge – that ridge which had always been the boundary of Shasta's known world. He could not see what was ahead except that it was all open and grassy. It looked endless: wild and lonely and free.

"I say!" observed the Horse. "What a place for a gallop, eh?"

"Oh, don't let's," said Shasta. "Not yet. I don't know how to – please, Horse. I don't know your name."

"Breehy-hinny-brinny-hoohy-hah," said the Horse.

"I'll never be able to say that," said Shasta. "Can I call you Bree?"

"Well, if it's the best you can do, I suppose you must," said the Horse. "And what shall I call you?"

"I'm called Shasta."

"H'm," said Bree. "Well, now, there's a name that's *really* hard to pronounce. But now about this gallop. It's a good deal easier than trotting if you only knew, because you don't have to rise and fall. Grip with your knees and keep your eyes straight ahead between my ears. Don't look at the ground. If you think you're going to fall just grip harder and sit up straighter. Ready? Now: for Narnia and the North."

Chapter Two

A Wayside Adventure

It was nearly noon on the following day when Shasta was wakened by something warm and soft moving over his face. He opened his eyes and found himself staring into the long face of a horse; its nose and lips were almost touching his. He remembered the exciting events of the previous night and sat up. But as he did so he groaned.

"Ow, Bree," he gasped. "I'm so sore. All over. I can hardly move."

"Good morning, small one," said Bree. "I was afraid you might feel a bit stiff. It can't be the falls. You didn't have more than a dozen or so, and it was all lovely, soft, springy turf that must have been almost a pleasure to fall on. And the only one that might have been nasty was broken by that gorse bush. No: it's the riding itself that comes hard at first. What about breakfast? I've had mine."

"Oh, bother breakfast. Bother everything," said Shasta. "I tell you I can't move." But the Horse nuzzled at him with his nose and pawed him gently with a hoof till he had to get up. And then he looked about him and saw where they were. Behind them lay a little copse. Before them the turf, dotted with white flowers, sloped down to the brow of a cliff. Far below them, so that the sound of the breaking waves was very faint, lay the sea. Shasta had never seen it from such a height and never seen so much of it before, nor dreamed how many colours it had. On either hand the coast stretched away, headland after headland, and at the points you could see the white foam running up the rocks but making no noise because it was so far off. There were gulls flying overhead and the heat shivered on the ground; it was a blazing day. But what Shasta chiefly noticed was the air. He couldn't think what was missing, until at last he realized that there was no smell of fish in it. For of course, neither in the cottage nor among the nets, had he ever been away from that smell in his life. And this new air was so delicious, and all his old life seemed so far away, that he forgot for a moment about his bruises and his aching muscles and said:

"I say, Bree, didn't you say something about breakfast?"

"Yes, I did," answered Bree. "I think you'll find something in the saddle-bags. They're over there on that tree where you hung them up last night – or early this morning, rather."

They investigated the saddle-bags and the results were cheering – a meat pasty, only slightly stale, a lump of dried figs and another lump of green cheese, a little flask of wine, and some money; about forty crescents in all, which was more than Shasta had ever seen.

While Shasta sat down – painfully and cautiously – with his back against a tree and started on the pasty, Bree had a few more mouthfuls of grass to keep him company.

"Won't it be stealing to use the money?" asked Shasta.

"Oh," said the Horse, looking up with his mouth full of grass, "I never thought of that. A free horse and a talking horse mustn't steal, of course. But I think it's all right. We're prisoners and captives in enemy country. That money is booty, spoil. Besides, how are we to get any food for you without it? I suppose, like all humans, you won't eat natural food like grass and oats."

"I can't."

"Ever tried?"

"Yes, I have. I can't get it down at all. You couldn't either if you were me."

"You're rum little creatures, you humans," remarked Bree.

When Shasta had finished his breakfast (which was by far the nicest he had ever eaten), Bree said, "I think I'll have a nice roll before we put on that saddle again." And he proceeded to do so. "That's good. That's very good," he said, rubbing his back on the turf and waving all four legs in the air. "You ought to have one too, Shasta," he snorted. "It's most refreshing."

But Shasta burst out laughing and said, "You do look funny when you're on your back!"

"I look nothing of the sort," said Bree. But then suddenly he rolled round on his side, raised his head and looked hard at Shasta, blowing a little.

"Does it really look funny?" he asked in an anxious voice.

"Yes, it does," replied Shasta. "But what does it matter?"

"You don't think, do you," said Bree, "that it might be a thing *talking* horses never do – a silly, clownish trick I've learned from the dumb ones?

It would be dreadful to find, when I get back to Narnia, that I've picked up a lot of low, bad habits. What do you think, Shasta? Honestly, now. Don't spare my feelings. Do you think the real, free horses – the talking kind – roll?"

"How should I know? Anyway, I don't think I should bother about it if I were you. We've got to get there first. Do you know the way?"

"I know my way to Tashbaan. After that comes the desert. Oh, we'll manage the desert somehow, never fear. Why, we'll be in sight of the Northern mountains then. Think of it! To Narnia and the North! Nothing will stop us then. But I'd be glad to be past Tashbaan. You and I are safer away from cities."

"Can't we avoid it?"

"Not without going a long way inland, and that would take us into cultivated land and main roads; and I wouldn't know the way. No, we'll just have to creep along the coast. Up here on the downs we'll meet nothing but sheep and rabbits and gulls and a few shepherds. And by the way, what about starting?"

Shasta's legs ached terribly as he saddled Bree and climbed into the saddle, but the Horse was kindly to him and went at a soft pace all afternoon. When evening twilight came they dropped by steep tracks into a valley and found a village. Before they got into it Shasta dismounted and entered it on foot to buy a loaf and some onions and radishes. The Horse trotted round by the fields in the dusk and met Shasta at the far side. This became their regular plan every second night.

These were great days for Shasta, and every day better than the last as his muscles hardened and he fell less often. Even at the end of his training Bree still said he sat like a bag of flour in the saddle. "And even if it was safe, young 'un, I'd be ashamed to be seen with you on the main road." But in spite of his rude words Bree was a patient teacher. No one can teach riding so well as a horse. Shasta learned to trot, to canter, to jump, and to keep his seat even when Bree pulled up suddenly or swung unexpectedly to the left or the right – which, as Bree told him, was a thing you might have to do at any moment in a battle. And then of course Shasta begged to be told of the battles and wars in which Bree had carried the Tarkaan. And Bree would tell of forced marches and the fording of swift rivers, of charges and of fierce fights between cavalry and cavalry when the war horses fought as well as the men, being all fierce stallions, trained to bite and kick, and to rear at the right moment so that the horse's weight as well as the rider's would come down on an enemy's crest in the stroke of a sword or battleaxe. But Bree did not want to talk about the wars as often as Shasta wanted to hear about them. "Don't speak of them, youngster," he would say. "They were only the Tisroc's wars and I fought in them as a slave and a dumb beast. Give me the Narnian wars where I shall fight as a free Horse among my own people! Those will be wars worth talking about. Narnia and the North! Bra-ha-ha! Broo hoo!"

Shasta soon learned, when he heard Bree talking like that, to prepare for a gallop.

After they had travelled on for weeks and weeks, past more bays and headlands and rivers and villages than Shasta could remember, there came a moonlit night when they started their journey at evening, having slept during the day. They had left the downs behind them and were crossing a wide plain with a forest about half a mile away on their left. The sea, hidden by low sandhills, was about the same distance on their right. They had jogged along for about an hour, sometimes trotting and sometimes walking, when Bree suddenly stopped.

"What's up?" said Shasta.

"S-s-ssh!" said Bree, craning his neck round and twitching his ears. "Did you hear something? Listen."

"It sounds like another horse – between us and the wood," said Shasta after he had listened for about a minute.

"It *is* another horse," said Bree. "And that's what I don't like."

"Isn't it probably just a farmer riding home late?" said Shasta with a yawn.

"Don't tell me!" said Bree. "*That's* not a farmer's riding. Nor a farmer's horse either. Can't you tell by the sound? That's quality, that horse is. And it's being ridden by a real horseman. I tell you what it is, Shasta. There's a Tarkaan under the edge of that wood. Not on his war horse – it's too light for that. On a fine blood mare, I should say."

"Well, it's stopped now, whatever it is," said Shasta.

"You're right," said Bree. "And why should he stop just when we do? Shasta, my boy, I do believe there's someone shadowing us at last."

"What shall we do?" said Shasta in a lower whisper than before. "Do you think he can see us as well as hear us?"

"Not in this light so long as we stay quite still," answered Bree. "But look! There's a cloud coming up. I'll wait till that gets over the moon. Then we'll get off to our right as quietly as we can, down to the shore. We can hide among the sandhills if the worst comes to the worst."

They waited till the cloud covered the moon and then, first at a walking pace and afterwards at a gentle trot, made for the shore.

The cloud was bigger and thicker than it had looked at first and soon the night grew very dark. Just as Shasta was saying to himself, "We must be nearly at those sandhills by now," his heart leaped into his mouth because an appalling noise had suddenly risen up out of the darkness ahead; a long snarling roar, melancholy and utterly savage. Instantly Bree swerved round and began galloping inland again as fast as he could gallop.

"What is it?" gasped Shasta.

"Lions!" said Bree, without checking his pace or turning his head.

After that there was nothing but sheer galloping for some time. At last they splashed across a wide, shallow stream and Bree came to a stop on the far side. Shasta noticed that he was trembling and sweating all over.

"That water may have thrown the brute off our scent," panted Bree when he had partly got his breath again. "We can walk for a bit now."

As they walked Bree said, "Shasta, I'm ashamed of myself. I'm just as frightened as a common, dumb Calormene horse. I am really. I don't feel like a Talking Horse at all. I don't mind swords and lances and arrows but I can't bear — those creatures. I think I'll trot for a bit."

About a minute later, however, he broke into a gallop again, and no wonder. For the roar broke out again, this time on their left from the direction of the forest.

"Two of them," moaned Bree.

When they had galloped for several minutes without any further noise from the lions Shasta said, "I say! That other horse is galloping beside us now. Only a stone's throw away."

"All the b-better," panted Bree. "Tarkaan on it — will have a sword — protect us all."

"But, Bree!" said Shasta. "We might just as well be killed by lions as caught. Or I might. They'll hang me for horse-stealing." He was feeling less frightened of lions than Bree because he had never met a lion; Bree had.

Bree only snorted in answer but he did sheer away to his right. Oddly enough the other horse seemed also to be sheering away to the left, so that in a few seconds the space between them had widened a good deal. But as soon as it did so there came two more lions' roars, immediately after one another, one on the right and the other on the left, and the horses began drawing nearer together. So, apparently, did the lions. The roaring of the brutes on each side was horribly close and they seemed to be keeping up with the galloping horses quite easily. Then the cloud rolled away. The moonlight, astonishingly bright, showed up everything almost as if it were broad day. The two horses and two riders were galloping almost neck to neck and knee to knee just as if they were in a race. Indeed Bree said (afterwards) that a finer race had never been seen in Calormen.

Shasta now gave himself up for lost and began to wonder whether lions killed you quickly or played with you as a cat plays with a mouse and how much it would hurt. At the same time (one sometimes does this at the most frightful moments) he noticed everything. He saw that the other rider was a very small, slender person, mail-clad (the moon shone on the mail) and riding magnificently. He had no beard.

Something flat and shining was spread out before them. Before Shasta had time even to guess what it was there was a great splash and he found his mouth half full of salt water. The shining thing had been a long inlet of the sea. Both horses were swimming and the water was up to Shasta's knees. There was an angry roaring behind them and, looking back, Shasta saw a great, shaggy and terrible shape crouched on the water's edge; but only one. "We must have shaken off the other lion," he thought.

The lion apparently did not think its prey worth a wetting; at any rate it made no attempt to take to the water in pursuit. The two horses, side by side, were now well out into the middle of the creek and the opposite shore could be clearly seen. The Tarkaan had not yet spoken a word. "But he will," thought Shasta. "As soon as we have landed. What am I to say? I must begin thinking out a story."

Then, suddenly, two voices spoke at his side.

"Oh, I *am* so tired," said the one.

"Hold your tongue, Hwin, and don't be a fool," said the other.

"I'm dreaming," thought Shasta. "I could have sworn that other horse spoke."

Soon the horses were no longer swimming but walking and soon, with a great sound of water running off their sides and tails and with a great crunching of pebbles under eight hoofs, they came out on the farther beach of the inlet. The Tarkaan, to Shasta's surprise, showed no wish to ask questions. He did not even look at Shasta but seemed anxious to urge his horse straight on. Bree, however, at once shouldered himself in the other horse's way.

"Broo-hoo-hah!" he snorted. "Steady there! I *heard* you, I did. There's no good pretending, Ma'am. *I* heard you. You're a Talking Horse, a Narnian horse just like me."

"What's it got to do with you if she is?" said the strange rider fiercely, laying hand on sword-hilt. But the voice in which the words were spoken had already told Shasta something.

"Why, it's only a girl!" he exclaimed.

"And what business is it of yours if I am *only* a girl?" snapped the stranger. "You're only a boy: a rude, common little boy — a slave probably, who's stolen his master's horse."

"That's all *you* know," said Shasta.

"He's not a thief, little Tarkheena," said Bree. "At least, if there's been any stealing, you might just as well say I stole *him*. And as for its not being my business, you wouldn't expect me to pass a lady of my own race in this strange country without speaking to her? It's only natural I should."

"I think it's very natural too," said the mare.

"I wish you'd held your tongue, Hwin," said the girl. "Look at the trouble you've got us into."

"I don't know about trouble," said Shasta. "You can clear off as soon as you like. We shan't keep you."

"No, you shan't," said the girl.

"What quarrelsome creatures these humans are," said Bree to the mare. "They're as bad as mules. Let's try to talk a little sense. I take it, Ma'am, your story is the same as mine? Captured in early youth – years of slavery among the Calormenes?"

"Too true, sir," said the mare, with a melancholy whinny.

"And now, perhaps – escape?"

"Tell him to mind his own business, Hwin," said the girl.

"No, I won't, Aravis," said the mare, putting her ears back. "This is my escape just as much as yours. And I'm sure a noble war-horse like this is not going to betray us. We are trying to escape, to get to Narnia."

"And so, of course, are we," said Bree. "Of course you guessed that at once. A little boy in rags riding (or trying to ride) a war-horse at dead of night couldn't mean anything but an escape of some sort. And, if I may say so, a high-born Tarkheena riding alone at night – dressed up in her brother's armour – and very anxious for everyone to mind their own business and ask her no questions – well, if that's not fishy, call me a cob!"

"All right then," said Aravis. "You've guessed it. Hwin and I are running away. We are trying to get to Narnia. And now, what about it?"

"Why, in that case, what is to prevent us all going together?" said Bree. "I trust, Madam Hwin, you will accept such assistance and protection as I may be able to give you on the journey?"

"Why do you keep talking to my horse instead of to me?" asked the girl.

"Excuse me, Tarkheena," said Bree (with just the slightest backward tilt of his ears), "but that's Calormene talk. We're free Narnians, Hwin and I, and I suppose, if you're running away to Narnia, you want to be one too. In that case Hwin isn't *your* horse any longer. One might just as well say you're *her* human."

The girl opened her mouth to speak and then stopped. Obviously she had not quite seen it in that light before.

"Still," she said after a moment's pause, "I don't know that there's so much point in all going together. Aren't we more likely to be noticed?"

"Less," said Bree; and the mare said, "Oh, do let's. I should feel much more comfortable. We're not even certain of the way. I'm sure a great charger like this knows far more than we do."

"Oh, come on, Bree," said Shasta, "and let them go their own way. Can't you see they don't want us?"

"We do," said Hwin.

"Look here," said the girl. "I don't mind going with *you*, Mr War-Horse, but what about this boy? How do I know he's not a spy?"

"Why don't you say at once that you think I'm not good enough for you?" said Shasta.

"Be quiet, Shasta," said Bree. "The Tarkheena's question is quite reasonable. I'll vouch for the boy, Tarkheena. He's been true to me and a good friend. And he's certainly either a Narnian or an Archenlander."

"All right, then. Let's go together." But she didn't say anything to Shasta and it was obvious that she wanted Bree, not him.

"Splendid!" said Bree. "And now that we've got the water between us and those dreadful animals, what about you two humans taking off our saddles and our all having a rest and hearing one another's stories."

Both the children unsaddled their Horses and the Horses had a little grass and Aravis produced rather nice things to eat from her saddle-bag. But Shasta sulked and said, No thanks, and that he wasn't hungry. And he tried to put on what he thought very grand and stiff manners, but as a fisherman's hut is not usually a good place for learning grand manners, the result was dreadful. And he half knew that it wasn't a success and then became sulkier and more awkward than ever. Meanwhile the two Horses were getting on splendidly. They remembered the very same places in Narnia – "the grasslands up above Beaversdam" – and found that they were some sort of second cousins once removed. This made things more and more uncomfortable for the humans until at last Bree said, "And now, Tarkheena, tell us your story. And don't hurry it – I'm feeling comfortable now."

Aravis immediately began, sitting quite still and using a rather different tone and style from her usual one. For in Calormen, story-telling (whether the stories are true or made up) is a thing you're taught, just as English boys and girls are taught essay-writing. The difference is that people want to hear the stories, whereas I never heard of anyone who wanted to read the essays.

CHAPTER THREE

AT THE GATES OF TASHBAAN

"My name," said the girl at once, "is Aravis Tarkheena and I am the only daughter of Kidrash Tarkaan, the son of Rishti Tarkaan, the son of Kidrash Tarkaan, the son of Ilsombreh Tisroc, the son of Ardeeb Tisroc who was descended in a right line from the god Tash. My father is the lord of the province of Calavar and is one who has the right of standing on his feet in his shoes before the face of Tisroc himself (may he live for ever). My mother (on whom be the peace of the gods) is dead and my father has married another wife. One of my brothers has fallen in battle against the rebels in the far west and the other is a child. Now it came to pass that my father's wife, my stepmother, hated me, and the sun appeared dark in her eyes as long as I lived in my father's house. And so she persuaded my father to promise me in marriage to Ahoshta Tarkaan. Now this Ahoshta is of base birth, though in these latter years he has won the favour of the Tisroc (may he live for ever) by flattery and evil counsels, and is now made a Tarkaan and the lord of many cities and is likely to be chosen as the Grand Vizier when the present Grand Vizier dies. Moreover he is at least sixty years old and has a hump on his back and his face resembles that of an ape. Nevertheless my father, because of the wealth and power of this Ahoshta, and being persuaded by his wife, sent messengers offering me in marriage, and the offer was favourably accepted and Ahoshta sent word that he would marry me this very year at the time of high summer.

"When this news was brought to me the sun appeared dark in my eyes and I laid myself on my bed and wept for a day. But on the second day I rose up and washed my face and caused my mare Hwin to be saddled and took with me a sharp dagger which my brother had carried in the western wars

221

and rode out alone. And when my father's house was out of sight and I was come to a green open place in a certain wood where there were no dwellings of men, I dismounted from Hwin my mare and took out the dagger. Then I parted my clothes where I thought the readiest way lay to my heart and I prayed to all the gods that as soon as I was dead I might find myself with my brother. After that I shut my eyes and my teeth and prepared to drive the dagger into my heart. But before I had done so, this mare spoke with the voice of one of the daughters of men and said, 'O my mistress, do not by any means destroy yourself, for if you live you may yet have good fortune but all the dead are dead alike'."

"I didn't say it half so well as that," muttered the mare.

"Hush, Ma'am, hush," said Bree, who was thoroughly enjoying the story. "She's telling it in the grand Calormene manner and no story-teller in a Tisroc's court could do it better. Pray go on, Tarkheena."

"When I heard the language of men uttered by my mare," continued Aravis, "I said to myself, the fear of death has disordered my reason and subjected me to delusions. And I became full of shame for none of my lineage ought to fear death more than the biting of a gnat. Therefore I addressed myself a second time to the stabbing, but Hwin came near to me and put her head in between me and the dagger and discoursed to me most excellent reasons and rebuked me as a mother rebukes her daughter. And now my wonder was so great that I forgot about killing myself and about Ahoshta and said, 'O my mare, how have you learned to speak like one of the daughters of men?' And Hwin told me what is known to all this company, that in Narnia there are beasts that talk, and how she herself was stolen from thence when she was a little foal. She told me also of the woods and waters of Narnia and the castles and the great ships, till I said, 'In the name of Tash and Azaroth and Zardeenah, Lady of the Night, I have a great wish to be in that country of Narnia.' 'O my mistress,' answered the mare, 'if you were in Narnia you would be happy, for in that land no maiden is forced to marry against her will.'

"And when we had talked together for a great time hope returned to me and I rejoiced that I had not killed myself. Moreover it was agreed between Hwin and me that we should steal ourselves away together and we planned it in this fashion. We returned to my father's house and I put on my gayest clothes and sang and danced before my father and pretended to be delighted with the marriage which he had prepared for me. Also I said to him, 'O my father and O the delight of my eyes, give me your licence and permission to go with one of my maidens alone for three days into the woods to do secret sacrifices to Zardeenah, Lady of the Night and of Maidens, as is proper and customary for damsels when they must bid farewell to the service of Zardeenah and prepare themselves for marriage.'

And he answered, 'O my daughter and O the delight of my eyes, so shall it be.'

"But when I came out from the presence of my father I went immediately to the oldest of his slaves, his secretary, who had dandled me on his knees when I was a baby and loved me more than the air and the light. And I swore him to be secret and begged him to write a certain letter for me. And he wept and implored me to change my resolution but in the end he said, 'To hear is to obey,' and did all my will. And I sealed the letter and hid it in my bosom."

"But what was in the letter?" asked Shasta.

"Be quiet, youngster," said Bree. "You're spoiling the story. She'll tell us all about the letter in the right place. Go on, Tarkheena."

"Then I called the maid who was to go with me to the woods and perform the rites of Zardeenah and told her to wake me very early in the morning. And I became merry with her and gave her wine to drink; but I had mixed such things in her cup that I knew she must sleep for a night and a day. As soon as the household of my father had committed themselves to sleep I arose and put on an armour of my brother's which I always kept in my chamber in his memory. I put into my girdle all the money I had and certain choice jewels and provided myself also with food, and saddled the mare with my own hands and rode away in the second watch of the night. I directed my course not to the woods where my father supposed that I would go but north and east to Tashbaan.

"Now for three days and more I knew that my father would not seek me, being deceived by the words I had said to him. And on the fourth day we arrived at the city of Azim Balda. Now Azim Balda stands at the meeting of many roads and from it the posts of the Tisroc (may he live for ever) ride on swift horses to every part of the empire: and it is one of the rights and privileges of the greater Tarkaans to send messages by them. I therefore went to the Chief of the Messengers in the House of Imperial Posts in Azim Balda and said, 'O dispatcher of messages, here is a letter from my uncle Ahoshta Tarkaan to Kidrash Tarkaan, lord of Calavar. Take now these five crescents and cause it to be sent to him.' And the Chief of the Messengers said, 'To hear is to obey.'

"This letter was feigned to be written by Ahoshta and this was the signification of the writing: 'Ahoshta Tarkaan to Kidrash Tarkaan, salutation and peace. In the name of Tash the irresistible, the inexorable. Be it known to you that as I made my journey towards your house to perform the contract of marriage between me and your daughter Aravis Tarkheena, it pleased fortune and the gods that I fell in with her in the forest when she had ended the rites and sacrifices of Zardeenah according to the custom of maidens. And when I learned who she was, being delighted with her beauty and discretion, I became inflamed with love and it appeared to me that the sun would be dark to me if I did not marry her at once. Accordingly I prepared the necessary sacrifices and married your daughter the same hour that I met her and have returned with her to my own house. And we both pray and charge you to come hither as speedily as you may that we may be delighted with your face and speech; and also that you may bring with you the dowry of my wife, which, by reason of my great charges and expenses, I require without delay. And because thou and I are brothers I assure myself that you will not be angered by the haste of my marriage which is wholly occasioned by the great love I bear your daughter. And I commit you to the care of all the gods.'

"As soon as I had done this I rode on in all haste from Azim Balda, fearing no pursuit and expecting that my father, having received such a letter, would send messages to Ahoshta or go to him himself, and that before the matter was discovered I should be beyond Tashbaan. And that is the pith of my story until this very night when I was chased by lions and met you at the swimming of the salt water."

"And what happened to the girl – the one you drugged?" asked Shasta.

"Doubtless she was beaten for sleeping late," said Aravis coolly. "But she was a tool and spy of my stepmother's. I am very glad they should beat her."

"I say, that was hardly fair," said Shasta.

"I did not do any of these things for the sake of pleasing *you*," said Aravis.

"And there's another thing I don't understand about that story," said Shasta. "You're not grown up, I don't believe you're any older than I am. I don't believe you're as old. How could you be getting married at your age?"

Aravis said nothing, but Bree at once said, "Shasta, don't display your ignorance. They're always married at that age in the great Tarkaan families."

Shasta turned very red (though it was hardly light enough for the others to see this) and felt snubbed. Aravis asked Bree for his story. Bree told it, and Shasta thought that he put in a great deal more than he needed about the falls and the bad riding. Bree obviously thought it very funny, but Aravis did not laugh. When Bree had finished they all went to sleep.

The next day all four of them, two horses and two humans, continued their journey together. Shasta thought it had been much pleasanter when he and Bree were on their own. For now it was Bree and Aravis who did nearly all the talking. Bree had lived a long time in Calormen and had always been among Tarkaans and Tarkaans' horses, and so of course he knew a great many of the same people and places that Aravis knew. She would always be saying things like, "But if you were at the fight of

Zulindreh you would have seen my cousin Alimash," and Bree would answer, "Oh, yes, Alimash, he was only captain of the chariots, you know. I don't quite hold with chariots or the kind of horses who draw chariots. That's not real cavalry. But he is a worthy nobleman. He filled my nosebag with sugar after the taking of Teebeth." Or else Bree would say, "I was down at the lake of Mezreel that summer," and Aravis would say, "Oh, Mezreel! I had a friend there, Lasaraleen Tarkheena. What a delightful place it is. Those gardens, and the Valley of the Thousand Perfumes!" Bree was not in the least trying to leave Shasta out of things, though Shasta sometimes nearly thought he was. People who know a lot of the same things can hardly help talking about them, and if you're there you can hardly help feeling that you're out of it.

Hwin the mare was rather shy before a great war-horse like Bree and said very little. And Aravis never spoke to Shasta at all if she could help it.

Soon, however, they had more important things to think of. They were getting near Tashbaan. There were more, and larger, villages, and more people on the roads. They now did nearly all their travelling by night and hid as best they could during the day. And at every halt they argued and argued about what they were to do when they reached Tashbaan. Everyone had been putting off this difficulty, but now it could be put off no longer. During these discussions Aravis became a little, a very little, less unfriendly to Shasta; one usually gets on better with people when one is making plans than when one is talking about nothing in particular.

Bree said the first thing now to do was to fix a place where they would all promise to meet on the far side of Tashbaan even if, by any ill luck, they got separated in passing the city. He said the best place would be the Tombs of the Ancient Kings on the very edge of the desert. "Things like great stone beehives," he said. "You can't possibly miss them. And the best of it is that none of the Calormenes will go near them because they think the place is haunted by ghouls and are afraid of it." Aravis asked if it wasn't really haunted by ghouls. But Bree said he was a free Narnian horse and didn't believe in these Calormene tales. And then Shasta said he wasn't a Calormene either and didn't care a straw about these old stories of ghouls. This wasn't quite true. But it rather impressed Aravis (though at the moment it annoyed her too) and of course she said she didn't mind any number of ghouls either. So it was settled that the Tombs should be their assembly place on the other side of Tashbaan, and everyone felt they were getting on very well till Hwin humbly pointed out that the real problem was not where they should go when they had got through Tashbaan but how they were to get through it.

"We'll settle that tomorrow, Ma'am," said Bree. "Time for a little sleep now."

But it wasn't easy to settle. Aravis's first suggestion was that they should swim across the river below the city during the night and not go into Tashbaan at all. But Bree had two reasons against this. One was that the river-mouth was very wide and it would be far too long a swim for Hwin to do, especially with a rider on her back. (He thought it would be too long for himself too, but he said much less about that.) The other was that it would be full of shipping and of course anyone on the deck of a ship who saw two horses swimming past would be almost certain to be inquisitive.

Shasta thought they should go up the river above Tashbaan and cross it where it was narrower. But Bree explained that there were gardens and pleasure houses on both banks of the river for miles and that there would be Tarkaans and Tarkheenas living in them and riding about the roads and having water parties on the river. In fact it would be the most likely place in the world for meeting someone who would recognize Aravis or even himself.

"We'll have to have a disguise," said Shasta.

Hwin said it looked to her as if the safest thing was to go right through the city itself from gate to gate because one was less likely to be noticed in the crowd. But she approved of the idea of disguise as well. She said, "Both the humans will have to dress in rags and look like peasants or slaves. And all Aravis's armour and our saddles and things must be made into bundles and put on our backs, and the children just pretend to drive us and people will think we're only pack-horses."

"My dear Hwin!" said Aravis rather scornfully. "As if anyone could mistake Bree for anything but a war-horse however you disguised him!"

"I should think not, indeed," said Bree, snorting and letting his ears go ever so slightly back.

"I know it's not a *very* good plan," said Hwin. "But I think it's our only chance. And we haven't been groomed for ages and we're not looking quite ourselves (at least, I'm sure I'm not). I do think if we get well plastered with mud and go along with our heads down as if we're tired and lazy – and don't lift our hooves hardly at all – we might not be noticed. And our tails ought to be cut shorter: not neatly, you know, but all ragged."

"My dear Madam," said Bree. "Have you pictured to yourself how very disagreeable it would be to arrive in Narnia in *that* condition?"

"Well," said Hwin humbly (she was a very sensible mare), "the main thing is to get there."

Though nobody much liked it, it was Hwin's plan which had to be adopted in the end. It was a troublesome one and involved a certain amount of what Shasta called stealing, and Bree called "raiding". One farm lost a few sacks that evening and another lost a coil of rope the next: but some tattered old boy's clothes for Aravis to wear had to be fairly bought and paid for in a village. Shasta returned with them in triumph just as evening was closing in. The others were waiting for him among the trees at the foot of a low range of wooded hills which lay right across their path. Everyone was feeling excited because this was the last hill; when they reached the ridge at the top they would be looking down on Tashbaan.

"I do wish we were safely past it," muttered Shasta to Hwin.

"Oh, I do, I do," said Hwin fervently.

That night they wound their way through the woods up to the ridge by a woodcutter's track. And when they came out of the woods at the top they could see thousands of lights in the valley below them. Shasta had had no notion of what a great city would be like and it frightened him. They had their supper and the children got some sleep. But the Horses woke them very early in the morning.

The stars were still out and the grass was terribly cold and wet, but daybreak was just beginning, far to their right across the sea. Aravis went a few steps away into the wood and came back looking odd in her new, ragged clothes and carrying her real ones in a bundle. These, and her armour and shield and scimitar and the two saddles and the rest of the horses' fine furnishings were put into the sacks. Bree and Hwin had already got themselves as dirty and bedraggled as they could and it remained to shorten their tails. As the only tool for doing this was Aravis's scimitar, one of the packs had to be undone again in order to get it out. It was a longish job and rather hurt the Horses.

"My word!" said Bree, "if I wasn't a Talking Horse, what a lovely kick in the face I could give you! I thought you were going to cut it, not pull it out. That's what it feels like."

But in spite of semi-darkness and cold fingers, all was done in the end: the big packs bound on the Horses, the rope halters (which they were now wearing instead of bridles and reins) in the children's hands, and the journey began.

"Remember," said Bree. "Keep together if we possibly can. If not, meet at the Tombs of the Ancient Kings, and whoever gets there first must wait for the others."

"And remember," said Shasta. "Don't you two Horses forget yourselves and start *talking*, whatever happens."

CHAPTER FOUR

SHASTA FALLS IN WITH THE NARNIANS

At first Shasta could see nothing in the valley below him but a sea of mist with a few domes and pinnacles rising from it; but as the light increased and the mist cleared away he saw more and more. A broad river divided itself into two streams and on the island between them stood the city of Tashbaan, one of the wonders of the world. Round the very edge of the island, so that the water lapped against the stone, ran high walls strengthened with so many towers that he soon gave up trying to count them. Inside the walls the island rose in a hill and every bit of that hill, up to the Tisroc's palace and the great temple of Tash at the top, was completely covered with buildings – terrace above terrace, street above street, zigzag roads or huge flights of steps bordered with orange trees and lemon trees, roof-gardens, balconies, deep archways, pillared colonnades, spires, battlements, minarets, pinnacles. And when at last the sun rose out of the sea and the great silver-plated dome of the temple flashed back its light, he was almost dazzled.

"Get on, Shasta," Bree kept saying.

The river banks on each side of the valley were such a mass of gardens that they looked at first like forest, until you got closer and saw the white walls of innumerable houses peeping out from beneath the trees. Soon after that, Shasta noticed a delicious smell of flowers and fruit. About fifteen minutes later they were down among them, plodding on a level road with white walls on each side and trees bending over the walls.

"I say," said Shasta in an awed voice. "This is a wonderful place!"

"I dare say," said Bree. "But I wish we were safely through it and out on the other side. Narnia and the North!"

At that moment a low, throbbing noise began which gradually swelled louder and louder till the whole valley seemed to be swaying with it. It was a musical noise, but so strong and solemn as to be a little frightening.

"That's the horns blowing for the city gates to be open," said Bree. "We shall be there in a minute. Now, Aravis, do droop your shoulders a bit and step heavier and try to look less like a princess. Try to imagine you've been kicked and cuffed and called names all your life."

"If it comes to that," said Aravis, "what about you drooping your head a bit more and arching your neck a bit less and trying to look less like a war-horse?"

"Hush," said Bree. "Here we are."

And they were. They had come to the river's edge and the road ahead of them ran along a many-arched bridge. The water danced brightly in the early sunlight; away to their right nearer the river's mouth, they caught a glimpse of ships' masts. Several other travellers were before them on the bridge, mostly peasants driving laden donkeys and mules, or carrying baskets on their heads. The children and horses joined the crowd.

"Is anything wrong?" whispered Shasta to Aravis, who had an odd look on her face.

"Oh, it's all very well for *you*," whispered Aravis rather savagely. "What would *you* care about Tashbaan? But I ought to be riding in on a litter with soldiers before me and slaves behind, and perhaps going to a feast in the Tisroc's palace (may he live for ever) – not sneaking in like this. It's different for you."

Shasta thought all this very silly.

At the far end of the bridge the walls of the city towered high above them and the brazen gates stood open in the gateway which was really wide but looked narrow because it was so very high. Half a dozen soldiers, leaning on their spears, stood on each side. Aravis couldn't help thinking, "They'd all jump to attention and salute me if they knew whose daughter I am." But the others were only thinking of how they'd get through, and hoping the soldiers would not ask any questions. Fortunately they did not. But one of them picked a carrot out of a peasant's basket and threw it at Shasta with a rough laugh, saying:

"Hey! Horse-boy! You'll catch it if your master finds you've been using his saddle-horse for pack work."

This frightened him badly for of course it showed that no one who knew anything about horses would mistake Bree for anything but a charger.

"It's my master's orders, so there!" said Shasta. But it would have been better if he had held his tongue for the soldier gave him a box on the side of his face that nearly knocked him down and said, "Take that, you young filth, to teach you how to talk to freemen." But they all slunk into the city without being stopped. Shasta cried only a very little; he was used to hard knocks.

Inside the gates Tashbaan did not at first seem so splendid as it had looked from a distance. The first street was narrow and there were hardly any windows in the walls on each side. It was much more crowded than Shasta had expected: crowded partly by the peasants (on their way to market) who had come in with them, but also with watersellers, sweetmeat sellers, porters, soldiers, beggars, ragged children, hens, stray dogs, and bare-footed slaves. What you would chiefly have noticed if you had been there were the smells, which came from unwashed people, unwashed dogs, scent, garlic, onions, and the piles of refuse which lay everywhere.

Shasta was pretending to lead but it was really Bree, who knew the way and kept guiding him by little nudges with his nose. They soon turned to the left and began going up a steep hill. It was much fresher and pleasanter, for the road was bordered by trees and there were houses only on the right side; on the other they looked out over the roofs of houses in the lower town and could see some way up the river. Then they went round a hairpin bend to their right and continued rising. They were zigzagging up to the centre of Tashbaan. Soon they came to finer streets. Great statues of the gods and heroes of Calormen – who are mostly impressive rather than agreeable to look at – rose on shining pedestals. Palm trees and pillared arcades cast shadows over the burning pavements. And through the arched gateways of many a palace Shasta caught sight of green branches, cool fountains, and smooth lawns. It must be nice inside, he thought.

At every turn Shasta hoped they were getting out of the crowd, but they never did. This made their progress very slow, and every now and then they had to stop altogether. This usually happened because a loud voice shouted out, "Way, way, way, for the Tarkaan" or, "for the Tarkheena" or, "for the fifteenth Vizier" or, "for the Ambassador", and everyone in the crowd would crush back against the walls; and above their heads Shasta would sometimes see the great lord or lady for whom all the fuss was being made, lolling upon a litter which four or even six gigantic slaves carried on their bare shoulders. For in Tashbaan there is only one traffic regulation, which is that everyone who is less important has to get out of the way for everyone who is more important; unless you want a cut from a whip or a punch from the butt end of a spear.

It was in a splendid street very near the top of the city (the Tisroc's palace was the only thing above it) that the most disastrous of these stoppages occurred.

"Way! Way! Way!" came the voice. "Way for the White Barbarian King, the guest of the Tisroc (may he live for ever)! Way for the Narnian lords."

Shasta tried to get out of the way and to make Bree go back. But no horse, not even a talking Horse from Narnia, backs easily. And a woman with a very edgy basket in her hands, who was just behind Shasta, pushed the basket hard against his shoulders, and said, "Now then! Who are you shoving?" And then someone else jostled him from the side and in the confusion of the moment he lost hold of Bree. And then the whole crowd behind him became so stiffened and packed tight that he couldn't move at all. So he found himself, unintentionally, in the first row and had a fine sight of the party that was coming down the street.

It was quite unlike any other party they had seen that day. The crier who went before it shouting, "Way, way!" was the only Calormene in it. And there was no litter; everyone was on foot. There were about half a dozen men and Shasta had never seen anyone like them before. For one thing, they were all as fair-skinned as himself, and most of them had fair hair. And they were not dressed like men of Calormen. Most of them had legs bare to the knee. Their tunics were of fine, bright, hardy colours — woodland green, or gay yellow, or fresh blue. Instead of turbans they wore steel or silver caps, some of them set with jewels, and one with little wings on each side of it. A few were bare-headed. The swords at their sides were long and straight, not curved like Calormene scimitars. And instead of being grave and mysterious like most Calormenes, they walked with a swing and let their arms and shoulders go free, and chatted and laughed. One was whistling. You could see that they were ready to be friends with anyone who was friendly, and didn't give a fig for anyone who wasn't. Shasta thought he had never seen anything so lovely in his life.

But there was no time to enjoy it for at once a really dreadful thing happened. The leader of the fair-haired men suddenly pointed at Shasta, cried out, "There he is! There's our runaway!" and seized him by the shoulder. Next moment he gave Shasta a smack — not a cruel one to make you cry but a sharp one to let you know you are in disgrace and added, shaking:

"Shame on you, my lord! Fie for shame! Queen Susan's eyes are red with weeping because of you. What! Truant for a whole night! Where have you been?"

Shasta would have darted under Bree's body and tried to make himself scarce in the crowd if he had had the least chance; but the fair-haired men were all round him by now and he was held firm.

Of course his first impulse was to say that he was only poor Arsheesh the fisherman's son and that the foreign lord must have mistaken him for someone else. But then, the very last thing he wanted to do in that crowded place was to start explaining who he was and what he was doing. If he started on that, he would soon be asked where he had got his horse from, and who Aravis was – and then, goodbye to any chance of getting through Tashbaan. His next impulse was to look at Bree for help. But Bree had no intention of letting all the crowd know that he could talk, and stood looking just as stupid as a horse can. As for Aravis, Shasta did not even dare to look at her for fear of drawing attention. And there was no time to think, for the leader of the Narnians said at once:

"Take one of his little lordship's hands, Peridan, of your courtesy, and I'll take the other. And now, on. Our royal sister's mind will be greatly eased when she sees our young scapegrace safe in our lodging."

And so, before they were halfway through Tashbaan, all their plans were ruined, and without even a chance to say goodbye to the others Shasta found himself being marched off among strangers and quite unable to guess what might be going to happen next. The Narnian King – for Shasta began to see by the way the rest spoke to him that he must be a king – kept on asking him questions: where he had been, how he had got out, what he had done with his clothes, and didn't he know that he had been very naughty. Only the king called it "naught" instead of naughty.

And Shasta said nothing in answer, because he couldn't think of anything to say that would not be dangerous.

"What! All mum?" asked the king. "I must plainly tell you, prince, that this hangdog silence becomes one of your blood even less than the scape itself. To run away might pass for a boy's frolic with some spirit in it. But the king's son of Archenland should avouch his deed; not hang his head like a Calormene slave."

This was very unpleasant, for Shasta felt all the time that this young king was the very nicest kind of grown-up and would have liked to make a good impression on him.

The strangers led him – held tightly by both hands – along a narrow street and down a flight of shallow stairs and then up another to a wide doorway in a white wall with two tall, dark cypress trees, one on each side of it. Once through the arch, Shasta found himself in a courtyard which was also a garden. A marble basin of clear water in the centre was kept continually rippling by the fountain that fell into it. Orange trees grew round it out of smooth grass, and the four white walls which surrounded the lawn were covered with climbing roses. The noise and dust and crowding of the streets seemed suddenly far away. He was led rapidly across the garden and then into a dark doorway. The crier remained outside. After that they took him along a corridor, where the stone floor felt beautifully cool to his hot feet, and up some stairs. A moment later he found himself blinking in the light of a big, airy room with wide open windows, all looking North so that no sun came in. There was a carpet on the floor more wonderfully coloured than anything he had ever seen and his feet sank down into it as if he were treading in thick moss. All round the walls there were low sofas with rich cushions on them, and the room seemed to be full of people; very queer people some of them, thought Shasta. But he had no time to think of that before the most beautiful lady he had ever seen rose from her place and threw her arms round him and kissed him, saying:

"Oh Corin, Corin, how could you? And thou and I such close friends ever since thy mother died. And what should I have said to thy royal father if I came home without thee? Would have been a cause almost of war between Archenland and Narnia which are friends time out of mind. It was naught, playmate, very naught of thee to use us so."

"Apparently," thought Shasta to himself, "I'm being mistaken for a prince of Archenland, wherever that is. And these must be the Narnians. I wonder where the real Corin is?" But these thoughts did not help him say anything out loud.

"Where hast been, Corin?" said the lady, her hands still on Shasta's shoulders.

"I — I don't know," stammered Shasta.

"There it is, Susan," said the King. "I could get no tale out of him, true or false."

"Your Majesties! Queen Susan! King Edmund!" said a voice: and when Shasta turned to look at the speaker he nearly jumped out of his skin with surprise. For this was one of these queer people whom he had noticed out of the corner of his eye when he first came into the room. He was about the same height as Shasta himself. From the waist upwards he was like a man, but his legs were hairy like a goat's, and shaped like a goat's and he had goat's hooves and a tail. His skin was rather red and he had curly hair and a short pointed beard and two little horns. He was in fact a Faun, which is a creature Shasta had never seen a picture of or even heard of. And if you've read a book called *The Lion, the Witch and the Wardrobe* you may like to know that this was the very same Faun, Tumnus by name, whom Queen Susan's sister Lucy had met on the very first day when she found her way into Narnia. But he was a good deal older now for by this time Peter and Susan and Edmund and Lucy had been Kings and Queens of Narnia for several years.

"Your Majesties," he was saying, "His little Highness has had a touch of the sun. Look at him! He is dazed. He does not know where he is."

Then of course everyone stopped scolding Shasta and asking him questions and he was made much of and laid on a sofa and cushions were put under his head and he was given iced sherbet in a golden cup to drink, and told to keep very quiet.

Nothing like this had ever happened to Shasta in his life before. He had never even imagined lying on anything so comfortable as that sofa or drinking anything so delicious as that sherbet. He was still wondering what had happened to the others and how on earth he was going to escape and meet them at the Tombs, and what would happen when the real Corin turned up again. But none of these worries seemed so pressing now that he was comfortable. And perhaps, later on, there would be nice things to eat!

Meanwhile the people in that cool airy room were very interesting. Besides the Faun there were two Dwarfs (a kind of creature he had never seen before) and a very large Raven. The rest were all humans; grown-ups, but young, and all of them, both men and women, had nicer faces and voices than most Calormenes. And soon Shasta found himself taking an interest in the conversation. "Now, Madam," the King was saying to Queen Susan (the lady who had kissed Shasta). "What think you? We have been in this city fully three weeks. Have you yet settled in your mind whether you will marry this dark-faced lover of yours, this Prince Rabadash, or no?"

The lady shook her head. "No, brother," she said, "not for all the jewels in Tashbaan." ("Hullo!" thought Shasta. "Although they're king and queen, they're brother and sister, not married to one another.")

"Truly, sister," said the King, "I should have loved you the less if you had taken him. And I tell you that at the first coming of the Tisroc's ambassadors into Narnia to treat of this marriage, and later when the Prince was our guest at Cair Paravel, it was a wonder to me that ever you could find it in your heart to show him so much favour."

"That was my folly, Edmund," said Queen Susan, "of which I cry you mercy. Yet when he was with us in Narnia, truly this Prince bore himself in another fashion than he does now in Tashbaan. For I take you all to witness what marvellous feats he did in that great tournament and hastilude which our brother the High King made for him, and how meekly and courteously he consorted with us the space of seven days. But here, in his own city, he has shown another face."

"Ah!" croaked the Raven. "It is an old saying: see the bear in his own den before you judge of his conditions."

"That's very true, Sallowpad," said one of the dwarfs. "And another is, Come, live with me and you'll know me."

"Yes," said the King. "We have now seen him for what he is: that is, a most proud, bloody, luxurious, cruel, and self-pleasing tyrant."

"Then in the name of Aslan," said Susan, "let us leave Tashbaan this very day."

"There's the rub, sister," said Edmund. "For now I must open to you all that has been growing in my mind these last two days and more. Peridan, of your courtesy, look to the door and see that there is no spy upon us. All well? So. For now we must be secret."

Everyone had begun to look very serious. Queen Susan jumped up and ran to her brother. "Oh, Edmund," she cried. "What is it? There is something dreadful in your face."

CHAPTER FIVE

PRINCE CORIN

"My dear sister and very good Lady," said King Edmund, "you must now show your courage. For I tell you plainly we are in no small danger."

"What is it, Edmund?" asked the Queen.

"It is this," said Edmund. "I do not think we shall find it easy to leave Tashbaan. While the Prince had hope that you would take him, we were honoured guests. But by the Lion's Mane, I think that as soon as he has your flat denial we shall be no better than prisoners."

One of the Dwarfs gave a low whistle.

"I warned your Majesties, I warned you," said Sallowpad the Raven. "Easily in but not easily out, as the lobster said in the lobster pot!"

"I have been with the Prince this morning," continued Edmund. "He is little used (more's the pity) to having his will crossed. And he is very chafed at your long delays and doubtful answers. This morning he pressed very hard to know your mind. I put it aside – meaning at the same time to diminish his hopes – with some light common jests about women's fancies, and hinted that his suit was likely to be cold. He grew angry and dangerous. There was a sort of threatening, though still veiled under a show of courtesy, in every word he spoke."

"Yes," said Tumnus. "And when I supped with the Grand Vizier last night, it was the same. He asked me how I liked Tashbaan. And I (for I could not tell him I hated every stone of it and I would not lie) told him that now, when high summer was coming on, my heart turned to the cool woods and dewy slopes of Narnia. He gave a smile that meant no good and said, 'There is nothing to hinder you from dancing there again, little goatfoot, *always provided you leave us in exchange a bride for our prince.*'"

"Do you mean he would make me his wife by force?" exclaimed Susan.

"That's my fear, Susan," said Edmund. "Wife: or slave, which is worse."

"But how can he? Does the Tisroc think our brother the High King would suffer such an outrage?"

"Sire," said Peridan to the King. "They would not be so mad. Do they think there are no swords and spears in Narnia?"

"Alas," said Edmund. "My guess is that the Tisroc has very small fear of Narnia. We are a little land. And little lands on the borders of a great empire were always hateful to the lords of the great empire. He longs to blot them out, gobble them up. When first he suffered the Prince to come to Cair Paravel as your lover, sister, it may be that he was only seeking an occasion against us. Most likely he hopes to make one mouthful of Narnia and Archenland both."

"Let him try," said the second Dwarf. "At sea we are as big as he is. And if he assaults us by land, he has the desert to cross."

"True, friend," said Edmund. "But is the desert a sure defence? What does Sallowpad say?"

"I know that desert well," said the Raven. "For I have flown above it far and wide in my younger days," (you may be sure that Shasta pricked up his ears at this point). "And this is certain; that if the Tisroc goes by the great oasis he can never lead a great army across it into Archenland. For though they could reach the oasis by the end of their first day's march, yet the springs there would be too little for the thirst of all those soldiers and their beasts. But there is another way."

Shasta listened more attentively still.

"He that would find that way," said the Raven, "must start from the Tombs of the Ancient Kings and ride northwest so that the double peak of Mount Pire is always straight ahead of him. And so, in a day's riding or a little more, he shall come to the head of a stony valley, which is so narrow that a man might be within a furlong of it a thousand times and never know that it was there. And looking down this valley he will see neither grass nor water nor anything else good. But if he rides on down it he will come to a river and can ride by the water all the way into Archenland."

"And do the Calormenes know of this Western way?" asked the Queen.

"Friends, friends," said Edmund, "what is the use of all this discourse? We are not asking whether Narnia or Calormen would win if war arose between them. We are asking how to save the honour of the Queen and our own lives out of this devilish city. For though my brother, Peter the High King, defeated the Tisroc a dozen times over, yet long before that day our throats would be cut and the Queen's grace would be the wife, or more likely, the slave, of this prince."

"We have our weapons, King," said the first Dwarf. "And this is a reasonably defensible house."

"As to that," said the King, "I do not doubt that every one of us would sell our lives dearly at the gate and they would not come at the Queen but over our dead bodies. Yet we should be merely rats fighting in a trap when all's said."

"Very true," croaked the Raven. "These last stands in a house make good stories, but nothing ever came of them. After their first few repulses the enemy always set the house on fire."

"I am the cause of all this," said Susan, bursting into tears. "Oh, if only I had never left Cair Paravel. Our last happy day was before those ambassadors came from Calormen. The Moles were planting an orchard for us ... oh ... oh." And she buried her face in her hands and sobbed.

"Courage, Su, courage," said Edmund. "Remember – but what is the matter with *you*, Mister Tumnus?" For the Faun was holding both his horns with his hands as if he were trying to keep his head on by them and writhing to and fro as if he had a pain in his inside.

"Don't speak to me, don't speak to me," said Tumnus. "I'm thinking. I'm thinking so that I can hardly breathe. Wait, wait, do wait."

There was a moment's puzzled silence and then the Faun looked up, drew a long breath, mopped his forehead and said:

"The only difficulty is how to get down to our ship – with some stores, too – without being seen and stopped."

"Yes," said a Dwarf dryly. "Just as the beggar's only difficulty about riding is that he has no horse."

"Wait, wait," said Mr Tumnus impatiently. "All we need is some pretext for going down to our ship today and taking stuff on board."

"Yes," said King Edmund doubtfully.

"Well, then," said the Faun, "how would it be if your Majesties bade the Prince to a great banquet to be held on board our own galleon, the *Splendour Hyaline*, tomorrow night? And let the message be worded as graciously as the Queen can contrive without pledging her honour: so as to give the Prince a hope that she is weakening."

"This is very good counsel, sire," croaked the Raven.

"And then," continued Tumnus excitedly, "everyone will expect us to be going down to the ship all day, making preparations for our guests. And let some of us go to the bazaars and spend every minim we have at the fruiterers and the sweetmeat sellers and the wine merchants, just as we would if we were really giving a feast. And let us order magicians and jugglers and dancing girls and flute players, all to be on board tomorrow night."

"I see, I see," said King Edmund, rubbing his hands.

"And then," said Tumnus, "we'll all be on board tonight. And as soon as it is quite dark—"

"Up sails and out oars—!" said the King.

"And so to sea," cried Tumnus, leaping up and beginning to dance.

"And our nose Northward," said the first Dwarf.

"Running for home! Hurrah for Narnia and the North!" said the other.

"And the Prince waking the next morning and finding his birds flown!" said Peridan, clapping his hands.

"Oh, Master Tumnus, dear Master Tumnus," said the Queen, catching his hands and swinging with him as he danced. "You have saved us all."

"The Prince will chase us," said another lord, whose name Shasta had not heard.

"That's the least of my fears," said Edmund. "I have seen all the shipping in the river and there's no tall ship of war nor swift galley there. I wish he may chase us! For the *Splendour Hyaline* could sink anything he has to send after her – if we were overtaken at all."

"Sire," said the Raven. "You shall hear no better plot than the Faun's though we sat in council for seven days. And now, as we birds say, nests before eggs. Which is as much as to say, let us all take our food and then at once be about our business."

Everyone arose at this and the doors were opened and the lords and the creatures stood aside for the King and Queen to go out first. Shasta wondered what he ought to do, but Mr Tumnus said, "Lie there, your Highness, and I will bring you up a little feast to yourself in a few moments. There is no need for you to move until we are all ready to embark." Shasta laid his head down again on the pillows and soon he was alone in the room.

"This is perfectly dreadful," thought Shasta. It never came into his head to tell these Narnians the whole truth and ask for their help. Having been brought up by a hard, close-fisted man like Arsheesh, he had a fixed habit of never telling grown-ups anything if he could help it: he thought they would always spoil or stop whatever you were trying to do. And he thought that even if the Narnian King might be friendly to the two horses, because they were Talking Beasts of Narnia, he would hate Aravis, because she was a Calormene, and either sell her for a slave or send her back to her father. As for himself, "I simply daren't tell them I'm not Prince Corin *now*," thought Shasta. "I've heard all their plans. If they knew I wasn't one of themselves, they'd never let me out of this house alive. They'd be afraid I'd betray them to the Tisroc. They'd kill me. And if the real Corin turns up, it'll all come out, and they *will*!" He had, you see, no idea of how noble and free-born people behave.

"What am I to do? What am I to do?" he kept saying to himself. "What – hullo, here comes that goaty little creature again."

The Faun trotted in, half dancing, with a tray in his hands which was nearly as large as himself. This he set on an inlaid table beside Shasta's sofa, and sat down himself on the carpeted floor with his goaty legs crossed.

"Now, princeling," he said. "Make a good dinner. It will be your last meal in Tashbaan."

It was a fine meal after the Calormene fashion. I don't know whether you would have liked it or not, but Shasta did. There were lobsters, and salad, and snipe stuffed with almonds and truffles, and a complicated dish made of chicken-livers and rice and raisins and nuts, and there were cool melons and gooseberry fools and mulberry fools, and every kind of nice thing that can be made with ice. There was also a little flagon of the sort of wine that is called "white" though it is really yellow.

While Shasta was eating, the good little Faun, who thought he was still dazed with sunstroke, kept talking to him about the fine times he would have when they all got home; about his good old father King Lune of Archenland and the little castle where he lived on the southern slopes of the pass. "And don't forget," said Mr Tumnus, "that you are promised your first suit of armour and your first war-horse on your next birthday. And then your Highness will begin to learn how to tilt and joust. And in a few years, if all goes well, King Peter has promised your royal father that he himself will make you Knight at Cair Paravel. And in the meantime there will be plenty of comings and goings between Narnia and Archenland across the neck of the mountains. And of course you remember you have promised to come for a whole week to stay with me for the summer Festival, and there'll be bonfires and all-night dances of Fauns and Dryads in the heart of the woods and, who knows? – we might see Aslan himself!"

When the meal was over the Faun told Shasta to stay quietly where he was. "And it wouldn't do you any harm to have a little sleep," he added. "I'll call you in plenty of time to get on board. And then, Home. Narnia and the North!"

Shasta had so enjoyed his dinner and all the things Tumnus had been telling him that when he was left alone his thoughts took a different turn. He only hoped now that the real Prince Corin would not turn up until it was too late and that he would be taken away to Narnia by ship. I am afraid he did not think at all of what might happen to the real Corin when he was left behind in Tashbaan. He was a little worried about Aravis and Bree waiting for him at the Tombs. But then he said to himself, "Well, how can I help it?" and, "Anyway, that Aravis thinks she's too good to go about with me, so she can jolly well go alone," and at the same time he couldn't help feeling that it would be much nicer going to Narnia by sea than toiling across the desert.

When he had thought all this, he did what I expect you would have done if you had been up very early and had a long walk and a great deal of excitement and then a very good meal, and were lying on a sofa in a cool room with no noise in it except when a bee came buzzing in through the wide open windows. He fell asleep.

What woke him was a loud crash. He jumped up off the sofa, staring. He saw at once from the mere look of the room – the lights and shadows all looked different – that he must have slept for several hours. He saw also what had made the crash: a costly porcelain vase which had been standing on the window-sill lay on the floor broken into about thirty pieces. But he hardly noticed all these things. What he did notice was two hands gripping the window-sill from outside. They gripped harder and harder (getting white at the knuckles) and then up came a head and a pair of shoulders. A moment later there was a boy of Shasta's own age sitting astride the sill with one leg hanging down inside the room.

Shasta had never seen his own face in a looking-glass. Even if he had, he might not have realized that the other boy was (at ordinary times) almost exactly like himself. At the moment this boy was not particularly like anyone for he had the finest black eye you ever saw, and a tooth missing, and his clothes (which must have been splendid ones when he put them on) were torn and dirty, and there was both blood and mud on his face.

"Who are you?" said the boy in a whisper.

"Are you Prince Corin?" said Shasta.

"Yes, of course," said the other. "But who are you?"

"I'm nobody, nobody in particular, I mean," said Shasta. "King Edmund caught me in the street and mistook me for you. I suppose we must look like one another. Can I get out the way you've got in?"

"Yes, if you're any good at climbing," said Corin. "But why are you in such a hurry? I say: we ought to be able to get some fun out of this being mistaken for one another."

"No, no," said Shasta. "We must change places at once. It'll be simply frightful if Mr Tumnus comes back and finds us both here. I've had to pretend to be you. And you're starting tonight – secretly. And where were you all this time?"

"A boy in the street made a beastly joke about Queen Susan," said Prince Corin, "so I knocked him down. He ran howling into a house and his big brother came out. So I knocked the big brother down. Then they all followed me until we ran into three old men with spears who are called the Watch. So I fought the Watch and they knocked me down. It was getting dark by now. Then the Watch took me along to lock me up somewhere. So I asked them if they'd like a stoup of wine and they said they didn't mind if they did. Then I took them to a wine shop and got them some and they all sat down and drank till they fell asleep. I thought it was time for me to be off so I came out quietly and then I found the first boy –

the one who had started all the trouble — still hanging about. So I knocked him down again. After that I climbed up a pipe onto the roof of a house and lay quiet till it began to get light this morning. Ever since that I've been finding my way back. I say, is there anything to drink?"

"No, I drank it," said Shasta. "And now, show me how you got in. There's not a minute to lose. You'd better lie down on the sofa and pretend — but I forgot. It'll be no good with all those bruises and black eye. You'll just have to tell them the truth, once I'm safely away."

"What else did you think I'd be telling them?" asked the Prince with a rather angry look. "And who are *you?*"

"There's no time," said Shasta in a frantic whisper. "I'm a Narnian, I believe; something Northern anyway. But I've been brought up all my life in Calormen. And I'm escaping: across the desert; with a talking Horse called Bree. And now, quick! How do I get away?"

"Look," said Corin. "Drop from this window onto the roof of the verandah. But you must do it lightly, on your toes, or someone will hear you. Then along to your left and you can get up to the top of that wall if you're any good at all as a climber. Then along the wall to the corner. Drop onto the rubbish heap you will find outside, and there you are."

"Thanks," said Shasta, who was already sitting on the sill. The two boys were looking into each other's faces and suddenly found that they were friends.

"Goodbye," said Corin. "And *good* luck. I do hope you get safe away."

"Goodbye," said Shasta. "I say, you have been having some adventures!"

"Nothing to yours," said the Prince. "Now drop; lightly — I say," he added as Shasta dropped, "I hope we meet in Archenland. Go to my father King Lune and tell him you're a friend of mine. Look out! I hear someone coming."

Chapter Six

Shasta among the Tombs

Shasta ran lightly along the roof on tiptoe. It felt hot to his bare feet. He was only a few seconds scrambling up the wall at the far end, and when he got to the corner he found himself looking down into a narrow, smelly street, and there was a rubbish heap against the outside of the wall just as Corin had told him. Before jumping down he took a rapid glance round him to get his bearings. Apparently he had now come over the crown of the island-hill on which Tashbaan is built. Everything sloped away before him, flat roofs below flat roofs, down to the towers and battlements of the city's Northern wall. Beyond that was the river and beyond the river a short slope covered with gardens. But beyond that again there was something he had never seen the like of – a great yellowish-grey thing, flat as a calm sea, and stretching for miles. On the far side of it were huge blue things, lumpy but with jagged edges, and some of them with white tops. "The desert! the mountains!" thought Shasta.

He jumped down onto the rubbish and began trotting along downhill as fast as he could in the narrow lane, which soon brought him into a wider street where there were more people. No one bothered to look at a little ragged boy running along on bare feet. Still, he was anxious and uneasy till he turned a corner and there saw the city gate in front of him. Here he was pressed and jostled a bit, for a good many other people were also going out; and on the bridge beyond the gate the crowd became quite a slow procession, more like a queue than a crowd. Out there, with clear running water on each side it was deliciously fresh after the smell and heat and noise of Tashbaan.

When once Shasta had reached the far end of the bridge he found the crowd melting away; everyone seemed to be going either to the left or right along the river bank. He went straight ahead up a road that did not appear to be much used, between gardens. In a few paces he was alone, and a few more brought him to the top of the slope. There he stood and stared. It was like coming to the end of the world for all the grass stopped quite suddenly a few feet before him and the sand began: endless level sand like on a sea shore but a bit rougher because it was never wet. The mountains, which now looked further off than before, loomed ahead. Greatly to his relief he saw, about five minutes' walk away on his left, what must certainly be the Tombs, just as Bree had described them; great masses of mouldering stone shaped like gigantic beehives, but a little narrower. They looked very black and grim, for the sun was now setting right behind them.

He turned his face West and trotted towards the Tombs. He could not help looking out very hard for any sign of his friends, though the setting sun shone in his face so that he could see hardly anything. "And anyway," he thought, "of course they'll be round on the far side of the farthest Tomb, not this side where anyone might see them from the city."

There were about twelve Tombs, each with a low arched doorway that opened into absolute blackness. They were dotted about in no kind of order, so that it took a long time, going round this one and going round that one, before you could be sure that you had looked round every side of every tomb. This was what Shasta had to do. There was nobody there.

It was very quiet here out on the edge of the desert; and now the sun had really set.

Suddenly from somewhere behind him there came a terrible sound. Shasta's heart gave a great jump and he had to bite his tongue to keep himself from screaming. Next moment he realized what it was: the horns of Tashbaan blowing for the closing of the gates. "Don't be a silly little coward," said Shasta to himself. "Why, it's only the same noise you heard this morning." But there is a great difference between a noise heard letting you in with your friends in the morning, and a noise heard alone at nightfall, shutting you out. And now that the gates were shut he knew there was no chance of the others joining him that evening. "Either they're shut up in Tashbaan for the night," thought Shasta, "or else they've gone on without me. It's just the sort of thing that Aravis would do. But Bree wouldn't. Oh, he wouldn't – now, would he?"

In this idea about Aravis Shasta was once more quite wrong. She was proud and could be hard enough but she was as true as steel and would never have deserted a companion, whether she liked him or not.

Now that Shasta knew he would have to spend the night alone (it was getting darker every minute) he began to like the look of the place less and less. There was something very uncomfortable about those great, silent shapes of stone. He had been trying his hardest for a long time not to think of ghouls: but he couldn't keep it up any longer.

"Ow! Ow! Help!" he shouted suddenly, for at that very moment he felt something touch his leg. I don't think anyone can be blamed for shouting if something comes up from behind and touches him; not in such a place and at such a time, when he is frightened already. Shasta at any rate was too frightened to run. Anything would be better than being chased round and round the burial places of the Ancient Kings with something he dared not look at behind him. Instead, he did what was really the most sensible thing he could do. He looked round; and his heart almost burst with relief. What had touched him was only a cat.

The light was too bad now for Shasta to see much of the cat except that it was big and very solemn. It looked as if it might have lived for long, long years among the Tombs, alone. Its eyes made you think it knew secrets it would not tell.

"Puss, puss," said Shasta. "I suppose you're not a *talking* cat."

The cat stared at him harder than ever. Then it started walking away, and of course Shasta followed it. It led him right through the Tombs and out on the desert side of them. There it sat bolt upright with its tail curled round its feet and its face set towards the desert and towards Narnia and the North, as still as if it were watching for some enemy. Shasta lay down beside it with his back against the cat and his face towards the Tombs, because if one is nervous there's nothing like having your face towards the danger and having something warm and solid at your back. The sand wouldn't have seemed very comfortable to you, but Shasta had been sleeping on the ground for weeks and hardly noticed it. Very soon he fell asleep, though even in his dreams he went on wondering what had happened to Bree and Aravis and Hwin.

He was wakened suddenly by a noise he had never heard before. "Perhaps it was only a nightmare," said Shasta to himself. At the same moment he noticed that the cat had gone from his back, and he wished it hadn't. But he lay quite still without even opening his eyes because he felt sure he would be more frightened if he sat up and looked round at the Tombs and the loneliness: just as you or I might lie still with the clothes over our heads. But then the noise came again — a harsh, piercing cry from behind him out of the desert. Then of course he had to open his eyes and sit up.

The moon was shining brightly. The Tombs — far bigger and nearer than he had thought they would be — looked grey in the moonlight. In fact, they looked horribly like huge people, draped in grey robes that covered their heads and faces. They were not at all nice things to have near you when spending a night alone in a strange place. But the noise had come from the opposite side, from the desert. Shasta had to turn his back on the Tombs (he didn't like that much) and stare out across the level sand. The wild cry rang out again.

"I hope it's not more lions," thought Shasta. It was in fact not very like the lion's roars he had heard on the night when they met Hwin and Aravis, and was really the cry of a jackal. But of course Shasta did not know this. Even if he had known, he would not have wanted very much to meet a jackal.

The cries rang out again and again. "There's more than one of them, whatever they are," thought Shasta. "And they're coming nearer."

I suppose that if he had been an entirely sensible boy he would have gone back through the Tombs nearer to the river where there were houses, and wild beasts would be less likely to come. But then there were (or he thought there were) the ghouls. To go back through the Tombs would mean going past those dark openings in the Tombs; and what might come out of them? It may have been silly, but Shasta felt he would rather risk the wild beasts. Then, as the cries came nearer and nearer, he began to change his mind.

He was just going to run for it when suddenly, between him and the desert, a huge animal bounded into view. As the moon was behind it, it looked quite black, and Shasta did not know what it was, except that it had a very big, shaggy head and went on four legs. It did not seem to have noticed Shasta, for it suddenly stopped, turned its head towards the desert and let out a roar which re-echoed through the Tombs and seemed to shake the sand under Shasta's feet. The cries of the other creatures suddenly stopped and he thought he could hear feet scampering away. Then the great beast turned to examine Shasta.

"It's a lion, I know it's a lion," thought Shasta. "I'm done. I wonder, will it hurt much? I wish it was over. I wonder, does anything happen to people after they're dead? O-o-oh! Here it comes!" And he shut his eyes and his teeth tight.

But instead of teeth and claws he only felt something warm lying down at his feet. And when he opened his eyes he said, "Why, it's not nearly as big as I thought! It's only half the size. No, it isn't even quarter the size. I do declare it's only the cat!! I must have dreamed all that about its being as big as a horse."

And whether he really had been dreaming or not, what was now lying at his feet, and staring him out of countenance with its big, green, unwinking eyes, was the cat; though certainly one of the largest cats he had ever seen.

"Oh, Puss," gasped Shasta. "I *am* so glad to see you again. I've been having such horrible dreams." And he at once lay down again, back to back with the cat as they had been at the beginning of the night. The warmth from it spread all over him.

"I'll never do anything nasty to a cat again as long as I live," said Shasta, half to the cat and half to himself. "I did once, you know. I threw stones at a half-starved mangy old stray. Hey! Stop that." For the cat had turned round and given him a scratch. "None of that," said Shasta. "It isn't as if you could understand what I'm saying." Then he dozed off.

Next morning when he woke, the cat was gone, the sun was already up, and the sand hot. Shasta, very thirsty, sat up and rubbed his eyes. The desert was blindingly white and, though there was a murmur of noises from the city behind him, where he sat everything was perfectly still. When he looked a little left and west, so that the sun was not in his eyes, he could see the mountains on the far side of the desert, so sharp and clear that they looked only a stone's throw away. He particularly noticed one blue height that divided into two peaks at the top and decided that it must be Mount Pire. "That's our direction, judging by what the Raven said," he thought, "so I'll just make sure of it, so as not to waste any time when the others turn up." So he made a good, deep straight furrow with his foot pointing exactly to Mount Pire.

The next job, clearly, was to get something to eat and drink. Shasta trotted back through the Tombs – they looked quite ordinary now and he wondered how he could ever have been afraid of them – and down into the cultivated land by the river's side. There were a few people about but not very many, for the city gates had been open several hours and the early morning crowds had already gone in. So he had no difficulty in doing a little "raiding" (as Bree called it). It involved a climb over a garden wall and the results were three oranges, a melon, a fig or two, and a pomegranate. After that, he went down to the river bank, but not too near the bridge, and had a drink. The water was so nice that he took off his hot, dirty clothes and had a dip; for of course Shasta, having lived on the shore all his life, had learned to swim almost as soon as he had learned to walk. When he came out he lay on the grass looking across the water at Tashbaan – all the splendour and strength and glory of it. But that made him remember the dangers of it too. He suddenly realized that the others might have reached the Tombs while he was bathing ("and gone on without me, as likely as not"), so he dressed in a fright and tore back at such a speed that he was all hot and thirsty when he arrived and so the good of his bathe was gone.

Like most days when you are alone and waiting for something, this day seemed about a hundred hours long. He had plenty to think of, of course, but sitting alone, just thinking, is pretty slow. He thought a good deal about the Narnians and especially about Corin. He wondered what had happened when they discovered that the boy who had been lying on the sofa and hearing all their secret plans wasn't really Corin at all. It was very unpleasant to think of all those nice people imagining him a traitor.

But as the sun slowly, slowly climbed up to the top of the sky and then slowly, slowly began going downwards to the West, and no one came and nothing at all happened, he began to get more and more anxious. And of course he now realized that when they arranged to wait for one another at the Tombs no one had said anything about how long. He couldn't wait here for the rest of his life! And soon it would be dark again, and he would have another night just like last night. A dozen different plans went through his head, all wretched ones, and at last he fixed on the worst plan of all. He decided to wait till it was dark and then go back to the river and steal as many melons as he could carry and set out for Mount Pire alone, trusting for his direction to the line he had drawn that morning in the sand. It was a crazy idea and if he had read as many books as you have about journeys over deserts he would never have dreamed of it. But Shasta had read no books at all.

Before the sun set something did happen. Shasta was sitting in the shadow of one of the Tombs when he looked up and saw two horses coming towards him. Then his heart gave a great leap, for he recognized them as Bree and Hwin. But the next moment his heart went down into his toes again. There was no sign of Aravis. The Horses were being led by a strange man, an armed man pretty handsomely dressed like an upper slave in a great family. Bree and Hwin were no longer got up like pack-horses, but saddled and bridled. And what could it all mean? "It's a trap," thought Shasta. "Somebody has caught Aravis and perhaps they've tortured her and she's given the whole thing away. They want me to jump out and run up and speak to Bree and then I'll be caught too! And yet if I don't, I may be losing my only chance to meet the others. Oh, I do wish I knew what had happened." And he skulked behind the Tomb, looking out every few minutes, and wondering which was the least dangerous thing to do.

CHAPTER SEVEN

ARAVIS IN TASHBAAN

What had really happened was this. When Aravis saw Shasta hurried away by the Narnians and found herself alone with two horses who (very wisely) wouldn't say a word, she never lost her head even for a moment. She grabbed Bree's halter and stood still, holding both the horses; and though her heart was beating as hard as a hammer, she did nothing to show it. As soon as the Narnian lords had passed she tried to move on again. But before she could take a step, another crier ("Bother all these people," thought Aravis) was heard shouting out, "Way, way, way! Way for the Tarkheena Lasaraleen!" and immediately, following the crier, came four armed slaves and then four bearers carrying a litter which was all a-flutter with silken curtains and all a-jingle with silver bells and which scented the whole street with perfumes and flowers. After the litter, female slaves in beautiful clothes, and then a few grooms, runners, pages, and the like. And now Aravis made her first mistake.

She knew Lasaraleen quite well — almost as if they had been at school together — because they had often stayed in the same houses and been to the same parties. And Aravis couldn't help looking up to see what Lasaraleen looked like now that she was married and a very great person indeed.

It was fatal. The eyes of the two girls met. And immediately Lasaraleen sat up in the litter and burst out at the top of her voice.

"Aravis! What on earth are you doing here? Your father—"

There was not a moment to lose. Without a second's delay Aravis let go the Horses, caught the edge of the litter, swung herself up beside Lasaraleen and whispered furiously in her ear.

"Shut up! Do you hear? Shut up. You must hide me. Tell your people——"

"But darling——" began Lasaraleen in the same loud voice. (She didn't in the least mind making people stare; in fact she rather liked it.)

"Do what I tell you or I'll never speak to you again," hissed Aravis. "Please, please be quick, Las. It's frightfully important. Tell your people to bring those two horses along. Pull all the curtains of the litter and get away somewhere where I can't be found. And do *hurry*."

"All right, darling," said Lasaraleen in her lazy voice. "Here. Two of you take the Tarkheena's horses." (This was to the slaves.) "And now home. I say, darling, do you think we really want the curtains drawn on a day like this? I mean to say——"

But Aravis had already drawn the curtains, enclosing Lasaraleen and herself in a rich and scented, but rather stuffy, kind of tent.

"I mustn't be seen," she said. "My father doesn't know I'm here. I'm running away."

"My dear, how perfectly thrilling," said Lasaraleen. "I'm dying to hear all about it. Darling, you're sitting on my dress. Do you mind? That's better. It is a new one. Do you like it? I got it at——"

"Oh, Las, do be serious," said Aravis. "Where is my father?"

"Didn't you know?" said Lasaraleen. "He's here, of course. He came to town yesterday and is asking about you everywhere. And to think of you and me being here together and his not knowing anything about it! It's the funniest thing I ever heard." And she went off into giggles. She always had been a terrible giggler, as Aravis now remembered.

"It isn't funny at all," she said. "It's dreadfully serious. Where can you hide me?"

"No difficulty at all, my dear girl," said Lasaraleen. "I'll take you home. My husband's away and no one will see you. Phew! It's not much fun with the curtains drawn. I want to see people. There's no point in having a new dress on if one's to go about shut up like this."

"I hope no one heard you when you shouted out to me like that," said Aravis.

"No, no, of course, darling," said Lasaraleen absentmindedly. "But you haven't even told me yet what you think of the dress."

"Another thing," said Aravis. "You must tell your people to treat those two horses very respectfully. That's part of the secret. They're really Talking Horses from Narnia."

"Fancy!" said Lasaraleen. "How exciting! And oh, darling, have you seen the barbarian queen from Narnia? She's staying in Tashbaan at present. They say Prince Rabadash is madly in love with her. There have been the most wonderful parties and hunts and things all this last fortnight. I can't see that she's so very pretty myself. But some of the Narnian *men* are lovely.

I was taken out on a river party the day before yesterday, and I was wearing my—"

"How shall we prevent your people telling everyone that you've got a visitor – dressed like a beggar's brat – in your house? It might so easily get round to my father."

"Now don't keep on fussing, there's a dear," said Lasaraleen. "We'll get you some proper clothes in a moment. And here we are!"

The bearers had stopped and the litter was being lowered. When the curtains had been drawn Aravis found that she was in a courtyard-garden very like the one that Shasta had been taken to a few minutes earlier in another part of the city. Lasaraleen would have gone indoors at once but Aravis reminded her in a frantic whisper to say something to the slaves about not telling anyone of their mistress's strange visitor.

"Sorry, darling, it had gone right out of my head," said Lasaraleen. "Here. All of you. And you, doorkeeper. No one is to be let out of the house today. And anyone I catch talking about this young lady will be first beaten to death and then burned alive and after that be kept on bread and water for six weeks. There."

Although Lasaraleen had said she was dying to hear Aravis's story, she showed no sign of really wanting to hear it at all. She was, in fact, much better at talking than at listening. She insisted on Aravis having a long and luxurious bath (Calormene baths are famous) and then dressing her up in the finest clothes before she would let her explain anything. The fuss she made about choosing the dresses nearly drove Aravis mad. She remembered now that Lasaraleen had always been like that, interested in clothes and parties and gossip. Aravis had always been more interested in bows and arrows and horses and dogs and swimming. You will guess that each thought the other silly. But when at last they were both seated after a meal (it was chiefly of the whipped cream and jelly and fruit and ice sort) in a beautiful pillared room (which Aravis would have liked better if Lasaraleen's spoiled pet monkey hadn't been climbing about it all the time) Lasaraleen at last asked her why she was running away from home.

When Aravis had finished telling her story, Lasaraleen said, "But, darling, why *don't* you marry Ahoshta Tarkaan? Everyone's crazy about him. My husband says he is beginning to be one of the greatest men in Calormen. He has just been made Grand Vizier now old Axartha has died. Didn't you know?"

"I don't care. I can't stand the sight of him," said Aravis.

"But, darling, only think! Three palaces, and one of them that beautiful one down on the lake at Ilkeen. Positively ropes of pearls, I'm told. Baths of asses' milk. And you'd see such a lot of *me*."

"He can keep his pearls and palaces as far as I'm concerned," said Aravis.

"You always *were* a queer girl, Aravis," said Lasaraleen. "What more *do* you want?"

In the end, however, Aravis managed to make her friend believe that she was in earnest, and even to discuss plans. There would be no difficulty now about getting the two horses out of the North gate and then on to the Tombs. No one would stop or question a groom in fine clothes leading a war-horse and a lady's saddle-horse down to the river, and Lasaraleen had plenty of grooms to send. It wasn't so easy to decide what to do about Aravis herself. She suggested that she could be carried out in the litter with the curtains drawn. But Lasaraleen told her that litters were only used in the city and the sight of one going out through the gate would be certain to lead to questions.

When they had talked for a long time – and it was all the longer because Aravis found it hard to keep her friend to the point – at last Lasaraleen clapped her hands and said, "Oh, I have an idea. There is one way of getting out of the city without using the gates. The Tisroc's garden (may he live for ever!) runs right down to the water and there is a little water-door. Only for the palace people of course – but then you know, dear," (here she tittered a little) "we almost *are* palace people. I say, it is lucky for you that you came to *me*. The dear Tisroc (may he live for ever!) is *so* kind. We're asked to the palace almost every day and it is like a second home. I love all the dear princes and princesses and I positively *adore* Prince Rabadash. I might run in and see any of the palace ladies at any hour of the day or night. Why shouldn't I slip in with you, after dark, and let you out by the water-door? There are always a few punts and things tied up outside it. And even if we were caught—"

"All would be lost," said Aravis.

"Oh, darling, don't get so excited," said Lasaraleen. "I was going to say, even if we were caught everyone would only say it was one of my mad jokes. I'm getting quite well known for them. Only the other day – do listen, dear, this is frightfully funny—"

"I meant, all would be lost *for me*," said Aravis a little sharply.

"Oh – ah – yes – I *do* see what you mean, darling. Well, can you think of any better plan?"

Aravis couldn't, and answered, "No. We'll have to risk it. When can we start?"

"Oh, not tonight," said Lasaraleen. "Of course not tonight. There's a great feast on tonight (I must start getting my hair done for it in a few minutes) and the whole place will be a blaze of lights. And such a crowd too! It would have to be tomorrow night."

This was bad news for Aravis, but she had to make the best of it. The afternoon passed very slowly and it was a relief when Lasaraleen went out to the banquet, for Aravis was very tired of her giggling and her talk about dresses and parties, weddings and engagements and scandals. She went to bed early and that part she did enjoy: it was so nice to have pillows and sheets again.

But the next day passed very slowly. Lasaraleen wanted to go back on the whole arrangement and kept on telling Aravis that Narnia was a country of perpetual snow and ice inhabited by demons and sorcerers, and she was mad to think of going there. "And with a peasant boy, too!" said Lasaraleen. "Darling, think of it! It's not Nice." Aravis had thought of it a good deal, but she was so tired of Lasaraleen's silliness by now that, for the first time, she began to think that travelling with Shasta was really rather more fun than fashionable life in Tashbaan. So she only replied, "You forget that I'll be nobody, just like him, when we get to Narnia. And anyway, I promised."

"And to think," said Lasaraleen, almost crying, "that if only you had sense you could be the wife of a Grand Vizier!" Aravis went away to have a private word with the Horses.

"You must go with a groom a little before sunset down to the Tombs," she said. "No more of those packs. You'll be saddled and bridled again. But there'll have to be food in Hwin's saddle-bags and a full water-skin behind yours, Bree. The man has orders to let you both have a good long drink at the far side of the bridge."

"And then, Narnia and the North!" whispered Bree. "But what if Shasta is not at the Tombs?"

"Wait for him, of course," said Aravis. "I hope you've been quite comfortable."

"Never better stabled in my life," said Bree. "But if the husband of that tittering Tarkheena friend of yours is paying his head groom to get the best oats, then I think the head groom is cheating him."

Aravis and Lasaraleen had supper in the pillared room.

About two hours later they were ready to start. Aravis was dressed to look like a superior slave-girl in a great house and wore a veil over her face. They had agreed that if any questions were asked, Lasaraleen would pretend that Aravis was a slave she was taking as a present to one of the princesses.

The two girls went out on foot. A very few minutes brought them to the palace gates. Here there were of course soldiers on guard but the officer knew Lasaraleen quite well and called his men to attention and saluted. They passed at once into the Hall of Black Marble. A fair number of courtiers, slaves and others were still moving about here but this only made the two girls less conspicuous. They passed on into the Hall of Pillars and then into the Hall of Statues and down the colonnade, passing the great beaten-copper doors of the throne room. It was all magnificent beyond description; what they could see of it in the dim light of the lamps.

Presently they came out into the garden-court which sloped downhill in a number of terraces. On the far side of that they came to the Old Palace. It had already grown almost dark and they now found themselves in a maze of corridors lit only by occasional torches fixed in brackets to the walls. Lasaraleen halted at a place where you had to go either left or right.

"Go on, do go on," whispered Aravis, whose heart was beating terribly and who still felt that her father might run into them at any corner.

"I'm just wondering..." said Lasaraleen. "I'm not absolutely sure which way we go from here. I *think* it's the left. Yes, I'm almost sure it's the left. What fun this is!"

They took the left hand way and found themselves in a passage that was hardly lit at all and which soon began going down steps.

"It's all right," said Lasaraleen. "I'm sure we're right now. I remember these steps." But at that moment a moving light appeared ahead. A second later there appeared from round a distant corner the dark shapes of two men walking backwards and carrying tall candles. And of course it is only before royalties that people walk backwards. Aravis felt Lasaraleen grip her arm — that sort of sudden grip which is almost a pinch and which means that the person who is gripping you is very frightened indeed. Aravis thought it odd that Lasaraleen should be so afraid of the Tisroc if he were really such a friend of hers, but there was no time to go on thinking. Lasaraleen was hurrying her back to the top of the steps, on tiptoe, and groping wildly along the wall.

"Here's a door," she whispered. "Quick."

They went in, drew the door very softly behind them, and found themselves in pitch darkness. Aravis could hear by Lasaraleen's breathing that she was terrified.

"Tash preserve us!" whispered Lasaraleen. "What *shall* we do if he comes in here? Can we hide?"

There was a soft carpet under their feet. They groped forward into the room and blundered onto a sofa.

"Let's lie down behind it," whimpered Lasaraleen. "Oh, I do wish we hadn't come."

There was just room between the sofa and the curtained wall and the two girls got down. Lasaraleen managed to get the better position and was completely covered. The upper part of Aravis's face stuck out beyond the sofa, so that if anyone came into that room with a light and happened to look in exactly the right place they would see her. But of course, because she was wearing a veil, what they saw would not at once look like a forehead and a pair of eyes. Aravis shoved desperately to try to make

Lasaraleen give her a little more room. But Lasaraleen, now quite selfish in her panic, fought back and pinched her feet. They gave it up and lay still, panting a little. Their own breath seemed dreadfully noisy, but there was no other noise.

"Is it safe?" said Aravis at last in the tiniest possible whisper.

"I – I – *think* so," began Lasaraleen. "But my poor nerves—" and then came the most terrible noise they could have heard at that moment: the noise of the door opening. And then came light. And because Aravis couldn't get her head any further in behind the sofa, she saw everything.

First came the two slaves (deaf and dumb, as Aravis rightly guessed, and therefore used at the most secret councils) walking backwards and carrying the candles. They took up their stand one at each end of the sofa. This was a good thing, for of course it was now harder for anyone to see Aravis once a slave was in front of her and she was looking between his heels. Then came an old man, very fat, wearing a curious pointed cap by which she immediately knew that he was the Tisroc. The least of the jewels with which he was covered was worth more than all the clothes and weapons of the Narnian lords put together: but he was so fat and such a mass of frills and pleats and bobbles and buttons and tassels and talismans that Aravis couldn't help thinking the Narnian fashions (at any rate for men) looked nicer. After him came a tall young man with a feathered and jewelled turban on his head and an ivory-sheathed scimitar at his side. He seemed very excited and his eyes and teeth flashed fiercely in the candlelight. Last of all came a little hump-backed, wizened old man in whom she recognized with a shudder the new Grand Vizier and her own betrothed husband, Ahoshta Tarkaan himself.

As soon as all three had entered the room and the door was shut, the Tisroc seated himself on the divan with a sigh of contentment, the young man took his place, standing, before him, and the Grand Vizier got down on his knees and elbows and laid his face flat on the carpet.

CHAPTER EIGHT

IN THE HOUSE OF THE TISROC

"Oh-my-father-and-oh-the-delight-of-my-eyes," began the young man, muttering the words very quickly and sulkily and not at all as if the Tisroc *were* the delight of his eyes. "May you live for ever, but you have utterly destroyed me. If you had given me the swiftest of the galleys at sunrise when I first saw that the ship of the accursed barbarians was gone from her place I would perhaps have overtaken them. But you persuaded me to send first and see if they had not merely moved round the point into better anchorage. And now the whole day has been wasted. And they are gone – gone – out of my reach! The false jade, the—" and here he added a great many descriptions of Queen Susan which would not look at all nice in print. For of course this young man was Prince Rabadash and of course the false jade was Susan of Narnia.

"Compose yourself, O my son," said the Tisroc. "For the departure of guests makes a wound that is easily healed in the heart of a judicious host."

"But I *want* her," cried the Prince. "I must have her. I shall die if I do not get her – false, proud, black-hearted daughter of a dog that she is! I cannot sleep and my food has no savour and my eyes are darkened because of her beauty. I must have the barbarian queen."

"How well it was said by a gifted poet," observed the Vizier, raising his face (in a somewhat dusty condition) from the carpet, "that deep draughts from the fountain of reason are desirable in order to extinguish the fire of youthful love."

This seemed to exasperate the Prince. "Dog," he shouted, directing a series of well-aimed kicks at
the hindquarters of the Vizier, "do not dare to quote the poets to me. I

have had maxims and verses flung at me all day and I can endure them no more." I am afraid Aravis did not feel at all sorry for the Vizier.

The Tisroc was apparently sunk in thought, but when, after a long pause, he noticed what was happening, he said tranquilly:

"My son, by all means desist from kicking the venerable and enlightened Vizier: for as a costly jewel retains its value even if hidden in a dung-hill, so old age and discretion are to be respected even in the vile persons of our subjects. Desist therefore, and tell us what you desire and propose."

"I desire and propose, O my father," said Rabadash, "that you immediately call out your invincible armies and invade the thrice-accursed land of Narnia and waste it with fire and sword and add it to your illimitable empire, killing their High King and all of his blood except the queen Susan. For I must have her as my wife, though she shall learn a sharp lesson first."

"Understand, O my son," said the Tisroc, "that no words you can speak will move me to open war against Narnia."

"If you were not my father, O ever-living Tisroc," said the Prince, grinding his teeth, "I should say that was the word of a coward."

"And if you were not my son, O most inflammable Rabadash," replied his father, "your life would be short and your death slow when you had said it." (The cool, placid voice in which he spoke these words made Aravis's blood run cold.)

"But why, O my father," said the Prince — this time in a much more respectful voice, "why should we think twice about punishing Narnia any more than about hanging an idle slave or sending a worn-out horse to be made into dog's-meat? It is not the fourth size of one of your least provinces. A thousand spears could conquer it in five weeks. It is an unseemly blot on the skirts of your empire."

"Most undoubtedly," said the Tisroc. "These little barbarian countries that call themselves *free* (which is as much as to say, idle, disordered, and unprofitable) are hateful to the gods and to all persons of discernment."

"Then why have we suffered such a land as Narnia to remain thus long unsubdued?"

"Know, O enlightened Prince," said the Grand Vizier, "that until the year in which your exalted father began his salutary and unending reign, the land of Narnia was covered with ice and snow and was moreover ruled by a most powerful enchantress."

"This I know very well, O loquacious Vizier," answered the Prince. "But I know also that the enchantress is dead. And the ice and snow have vanished, so that Narnia is now wholesome, fruitful, and delicious."

"And this change, O most learned Prince, has doubtless been brought to pass by the powerful incantations of those wicked persons who now call themselves kings and queens of Narnia."

"I am rather of the opinion," said Rabadash, "that it has come about by the alteration of the stars and the operation of natural causes."

"All this," said the Tisroc, "is a question for the disputations of learned men. I will never believe that so great an alteration, and the killing of the old enchantress, were effected without the aid of strong magic. And such things are to be expected in that land, which is chiefly inhabited by demons in the shape of beasts that talk like men, and monsters that are half man and half beast. It is commonly reported that the High King of Narnia (whom may the gods utterly reject) is supported by a demon of hideous aspect and irresistible maleficence who appears in the shape of a Lion. Therefore the attacking of Narnia is a dark and doubtful enterprise, and I am determined not to put my hand out farther than I can draw it back."

"How blessed is Calormen," said the Vizier, popping up his face again, "on whose ruler the gods have been pleased to bestow prudence and circumspection! Yet as the irrefutable and sapient Tisroc has said it is very grievous to be constrained to keep our hands off such a dainty dish as Narnia. Gifted was that poet who said—" but at this point Ahoshta noticed an impatient movement of the Prince's toe and became suddenly silent.

"It is very grievous," said the Tisroc in his deep, quiet voice. "Every morning the sun is darkened in my eyes, and every night my sleep is the less refreshing, because I remember that Narnia is still free."

"O my father," said Rabadash. "How if I show you a way by which you can stretch out your arm to take Narnia and yet draw it back unharmed if the attempt prove unfortunate?"

"If you can show me that, O Rabadash," said the Tisroc, "you will be the best of sons."

"Hear then, O father. This very night and in this hour I will take but two hundred horse and ride across the desert. And it shall seem to all men that you know nothing of my going. On the second morning I shall be at the gates of King Lune's castle of Anvard in Archenland. They are at peace with us and unprepared and I shall take Anvard before they have bestirred themselves. Then I will ride through the pass above Anvard and down through Narnia to Cair Paravel. The High King will not be there; when I left them he was already preparing a raid against the giants on his northern border. I shall find Cair Paravel, most likely with open gates, and ride in. I shall exercise prudence and courtesy and spill as little Narnian blood as I can. And what then remains but to sit there till the *Splendour Hyaline* puts in, with Queen Susan on board, catch my strayed bird as she sets foot ashore, swing her into the saddle, and then, ride, ride, ride back to Anvard?"

"But is it not probable, O my son," said the Tisroc, "that at the taking of the woman either King Edmund or you will lose his life?"

"They will be a small company," said Rabadash, "and I will order ten of my men to disarm and bind him: restraining my vehement desire for his blood so that there shall be no deadly cause of war between you and the High King."

"And how if the *Splendour Hyaline* is at Cair Paravel before you?"

"I do not look for that with these winds, O my father."

"And lastly, O my resourceful son," said the Tisroc, "you have made clear how all this might give you the barbarian woman, but not how it helps me to the overthrowing of Narnia."

"O my father, can it have escaped you that though I and my horsemen will come and go through Narnia like an arrow from a bow, yet we shall have Anvard for ever? And when you hold Anvard you sit in the very gate of Narnia, and your garrison in Anvard can be increased by little and little till it is a great host."

"It is spoken with understanding and foresight. But how do I draw back my arm if all this miscarries?"

"You shall say that I did it without your knowledge and against your will, and without your blessing, being constrained by the violence of my love and the impetuosity of youth."

"And how if the High King then demands that we send back the barbarian woman, his sister?"

"O my father, be assured that he will not. For though the fancy of a woman has rejected this marriage, the High King Peter is a man of prudence and understanding who will in no way wish to lose the high honour and advantage of being allied to our House and seeing his nephew and grand nephew on the throne of Calormen."

"He will not see that if I live for ever as is no doubt your wish," said the Tisroc in an even drier voice than usual.

"And also, O my father and O the delight of my eyes," said the Prince, after a moment of awkward silence, "we shall write letters as if from the Queen to say that she loves me and has no desire to return to Narnia. For it is well known that women are as changeable as weathercocks. And even if they do not wholly believe the letters, they will not dare to come to Tashbaan in arms to fetch her."

"O enlightened Vizier," said the Tisroc, "bestow your wisdom upon us concerning this strange proposal."

"O eternal Tisroc," answered Ahoshta, "the strength of paternal affection is not unknown to me and I have often heard that sons are in the eyes of their fathers more precious than carbuncles. How then shall I dare freely to unfold to you my mind in a matter which may imperil the life of this exalted Prince?"

"Undoubtedly you will dare," replied the Tisroc. "Because you will find that the dangers of not doing so are at least equally great."

"To hear is to obey," moaned the wretched man. "Know then, O most reasonable Tisroc, in the first place, that the danger of the Prince is not altogether so great as might appear. For the gods have withheld from the barbarians the light of discretion, as that their poetry is not, like ours, full of choice apophthegms and useful maxims, but is all of love and war. Therefore nothing will appear to them more noble and admirable than such a mad enterprise as this of— ow!" For the Prince, at the word "mad", had kicked him again.

"Desist, O my son," said the Tisroc. "And you, estimable Vizier, whether he desists or not, by no means allow the flow of your eloquence to be interrupted. For nothing is more suitable to persons of gravity and decorum than to endure minor inconveniences with constancy."

"To hear is to obey," said the Vizier, wriggling himself round a little so as to get his hinder parts further away from Rabadash's toe. "Nothing, I say, will seem as pardonable, if not estimable, in their eyes as this – er – hazardous attempt, especially because it is undertaken for the love of a woman. Therefore, if the Prince by misfortune fell into their hands, they would assuredly not kill him. Nay, it may even be, that though he failed to carry off the queen, yet the sight of his great valour and of the extremity of his passion might incline her heart to him."

"That is a good point, old babbler," said Rabadash. "Very good, however it came into your ugly head."

"The praise of my masters is the light of my eyes," said Ahoshta. "And secondly, O Tisroc, whose reign must and shall be interminable, I think that with the aid of the gods it is very likely that Anvard will fall into the Prince's hands. And if so, we have Narnia by the throat."

There was a long pause and the room became so silent that the two girls hardly dared to breathe. At last the Tisroc spoke.

"Go, my son," he said. "And do as you have said. But expect no help nor countenance from me. I will not avenge you if you are killed and I will not deliver you if the barbarians cast you into prison. And if, either in success or failure, you shed a drop more than you need of Narnian noble blood and open war arises from it, my favour shall never fall upon you again and your next brother shall have your place in Calormen. Now go. Be swift, secret, and fortunate. May the strength of Tash the inexorable, the irresistible, be in your sword and lance."

"To hear is to obey," cried Rabadash, and after kneeling for a moment to kiss his father's hands he rushed from the room. Greatly to the disappointment of Aravis, who was now horribly cramped, the Tisroc and Vizier remained.

"O Vizier," said the Tisroc, "is it certain that no living soul knows of this council we three have held here tonight?"

"O my master," said Ahoshta, "it is not possible that any should know. For that very reason I proposed, and you in your wisdom agreed, that we should meet here in the Old Palace where no council is ever held and none of the household has any occasion to come."

"It is well," said the Tisroc. "If any man knew, I would see to it that he died before an hour had passed. And do you also, O prudent Vizier, forget it. I sponge away from my own heart and from yours all knowledge of the Prince's plans. He is gone without my knowledge or my consent, I know not whither, because of his violence and the rash and disobedient disposition of youth. No man will be more astonished than you and I to hear that Anvard is in his hands."

"To hear is to obey," said Ahoshta.

"That is why you will never think even in your secret heart that I am the hardest hearted of fathers who thus sends my first-born son on an errand so likely to be his death; pleasing as it must be to you who do not love the Prince. For I see into the bottom of your mind."

"O impeccable Tisroc," said the Vizier. "In comparison with you I love neither the Prince nor my own life nor bread nor water nor the light of the sun."

"Your sentiments," said the Tisroc, "are elevated and correct. I also love none of these things in comparison with the glory and strength of my throne. If the Prince succeeds, we have Archenland, and perhaps hereafter Narnia. If he fails – I have eighteen other sons and Rabadash, after the manner of the eldest sons of kings, was beginning to be dangerous. More than five Tisrocs in Tashbaan have died before their time because their eldest sons, enlightened princes, grew tired of waiting for their throne. He had better cool his blood abroad than boil it in inaction here. And now, O excellent Vizier, the excess of my paternal anxiety inclines me to sleep. Command the musicians to my chamber. But before you lie down, call back the pardon we wrote for the third cook. I feel within me the manifest prognostics of indigestion."

"To hear is to obey," said the Grand Vizier. He crawled backwards on all fours to the door, rose, bowed, and went out. Even then the Tisroc remained seated in silence on the divan till Aravis almost began to be afraid that he had dropped asleep. But at last with a great creaking and sighing he heaved up his enormous body, signed to the slaves to precede him with the lights, and went out. The door closed behind him, the room was once more totally dark, and the two girls could breathe freely again.

CHAPTER NINE

ACROSS THE DESERT

"How dreadful! How perfectly dreadful!" whimpered Lasaraleen. "Oh, darling, I *am* so frightened. I'm shaking all over. Feel me."

"Come on," said Aravis, who was trembling herself. "They've gone back to the new palace. Once we're out of this room we're safe enough. But it's wasted a terrible time. Get me down to that water-gate as quick as you can."

"Darling, how *can* you?" squeaked Lasaraleen. "I can't do anything – not now. My poor nerves! No: we must just lie still a bit and then go back."

"Why back?" asked Aravis.

"Oh, you don't understand. You're so unsympathetic," said Lasaraleen, beginning to cry. Aravis decided it was no occasion for mercy.

"Look here!" she said, catching Lasaraleen and giving her a good shake. "If you say another word about going back, and if you don't start taking me to that water-gate at once – do you know what I'll do? I'll rush out into that passage and scream. Then we'll both be caught."

"But we shall both be k-k-killed!" said Lasaraleen. "Didn't you hear what the Tisroc (may he live for ever) said?"

"Yes, and I'd sooner be killed than married to Ahoshta. So come *on*."

"Oh, you *are* unkind," said Lasaraleen. "And I in such a state!"

But in the end she had to give in to Aravis. She led the way down the steps they had already descended, and along another corridor and so finally out into the open air. They were now in the palace garden which sloped down in terraces to the city wall. The moon shone brightly. One of the drawbacks about adventures is that when you come to the most beautiful places you are often too anxious and hurried to appreciate them;

so that Aravis (though she remembered them years later) had only a vague impression of grey lawns, quietly bubbling fountains, and the long black shadows of cypress trees.

When they reached the very bottom and the wall rose frowning above them, Lasaraleen was shaking so much that she could not unbolt the gate. Aravis did it. There, at last, was the river, full of reflected moonlight, and a little landing stage and a few pleasure boats.

"Goodbye," said Aravis, "and thank you. I'm sorry if I've been a pig. But think what I'm flying from!"

"Oh, Aravis darling," said Lasaraleen. "Won't you change your mind? Now that you've seen what a very great man Ahoshta is!"

"Great man!" said Aravis. "A hideous grovelling slave who flatters when he's kicked but treasures it all up and hopes to get his own back by egging on that horrible Tisroc to plot his son's death. Faugh! I'd sooner marry my father's scullion than a creature like that."

"Oh, Aravis, Aravis! How can you say such dreadful things; and about the Tisroc (may he live for ever) too. It must be right if *he's* going to do it!"

"Goodbye," said Aravis, "and I thought your dresses were lovely. And I think your house is lovely too. I'm sure you'll have a lovely life – though it wouldn't suit me. Close the door softly behind me."

She tore herself away from her friend's affectionate embraces, stepped into a punt, cast off, and a moment later was out in midstream with a huge real moon overhead and a huge reflected moon down, deep down, in the river. The air was fresh and cool and as she drew near the farther bank she heard the hooting of an owl. "Ah! That's better!" thought Aravis. She had always lived in the country and had hated every minute of her time in Tashbaan.

When she stepped ashore she found herself in darkness, for the rise of the ground, and the trees, cut off the moonlight. But she managed to find the same road that Shasta had found, and came just as he had done to the end of the grass and the beginning of the sand, and looked (like him) to her left and saw the big, black Tombs. And now at last, brave girl though she was, her heart quailed. Supposing the others weren't there! Supposing the ghouls were! But she stuck out her chin (and a little bit of her tongue too) and went straight towards them.

But before she had reached them she saw Bree and Hwin and the groom.

"You can go back to your mistress now," said Aravis (quite forgetting that he couldn't, until the city gates opened next morning). "Here is money for your pains."

"To hear is to obey," said the groom, and at once set off at a remarkable speed in the direction of the city. There was no need to tell him to make haste: he also had been thinking a good deal about ghouls.

For the next few seconds Aravis was busy kissing the noses and patting the necks of Hwin and Bree just as if they were quite ordinary horses.

"And here comes Shasta! Thanks be to the Lion!" said Bree.

Aravis looked round, and there, right enough, was Shasta who had come out of hiding the moment he saw the groom going away.

"And now," said Aravis, "there's not a moment to lose." And in hasty words she told them about Rabadash's expedition.

"Treacherous hounds!" said Bree, shaking his mane and stamping with his hoof. "An attack in time of peace, without defiance sent! But we'll grease his oats for him. We'll be there before he is."

"Can we?" said Aravis, swinging herself into Hwin's saddle. Shasta wished he could mount like that.

"Brooh-hoo!" snorted Bree. "Up you get, Shasta. Can we! And with a good start too!"

"He said he was going to start at once," said Aravis.

"That's how humans talk," said Bree. "But you don't get a company of two hundred horse and horsemen watered and victualled and armed and saddled and started all in a minute. Now: what's our direction? Due North?"

"No," said Shasta. "I know about that. I've drawn a line. I'll explain later. Bear a bit to our left, both you horses. Ah – here it is!"

"Now," said Bree. "All that about galloping for a day and a night, like in stories, can't really be done. It must be walk and trot: but brisk trots and short walks. And whenever we walk you two humans can slip off and walk too. Now. Are you ready, Hwin? Off we go. Narnia and the North!"

At first it was delightful. The night had now been going on for so many hours that the sand had almost finished giving back all the sun-heat it had received during the day, and the air was cool, fresh, and clear. Under the moonlight the sand, in every direction and as far as they could see, gleamed as if it were smooth water or a great silver tray. Except for the noise of Bree's and Hwin's hoofs there was not a sound to be heard. Shasta would nearly have fallen asleep if he had not had to dismount and walk every now and then.

This seemed to last for hours. Then there came a time when there was no longer any moon. They seemed to ride in the dead darkness for hours and hours. And after that there came a moment when Shasta noticed that he could see Bree's neck and head in front of him a little more clearly than before; and slowly, very slowly, he began to notice the vast grey flatness on every side. It looked absolutely dead, like something in a dead world; and Shasta felt quite terribly tired and noticed that he was getting cold and that his lips were dry. And all the time the squeak of the leather, the jingle of the bits, and the noise of the hoofs – not *propputty-propputty* as it would be on a hard road, but *thubbudy-thubbudy* on the dry sand.

At last, after hours of riding, far away on his right there came a single long streak of paler grey, low down on the horizon. Then a streak of red. It was the morning at last, but without a single bird to sing about it. He was glad of the walking bits now, for he was colder than ever.

Then suddenly the sun rose and everything changed in a moment. The grey sand turned yellow and twinkled as if it were strewn with diamonds. On their left the shadows of Shasta and Hwin and Bree and Aravis, enormously long, raced beside them. The double peak of Mount Pire, far ahead, flashed in the sunlight and Shasta saw they were a little out of the course. "A bit left, a bit left," he sang out. Best of all, when you looked back, Tashbaan was already small and remote. The Tombs were quite invisible: swallowed up in that single, jagged-edged hump which was the city of the Tisroc. Everyone felt better.

But not for long. Though Tashbaan looked very far away when they first saw it, it refused to look any further away as they went on. Shasta gave up looking back at it, for it only gave him the feeling that they were not moving at all. Then the light became a nuisance. The glare of the sand made his eyes ache: but he knew he mustn't shut them. He must screw them up and keep on looking ahead at Mount Pire and shouting out directions. Then came the heat. He noticed it for the first time when he had to dismount and walk: as he slipped down to the sand the heat from it struck up into his face as if from the opening of an oven door. Next time it was worse. But the third time, as his bare feet touched the sand he screamed with pain and got one foot back in the stirrup and the other half over Bree's back before you could have said knife.

"Sorry, Bree," he gasped. "I can't walk. It burns my feet."

"Of course!" panted Bree. "Should have thought of that myself. Stay on. Can't be helped."

"It's all right for *you*," said Shasta to Aravis who was walking beside Hwin. "You've got shoes on."

Aravis said nothing and looked prim. Let's hope she didn't mean to, but she did.

On again, trot and walk and trot, jingle-jingle-jingle, squeak-squeak-squeak, smell of hot horse, smell of hot self, blinding glare, headache. And nothing at all different for mile after mile. Tashbaan would never look any further away. The mountains would never look any nearer. You felt this had been going on for always – jingle-jingle-jingle, squeak-squeak-squeak, smell of hot horse, smell of hot self.

Of course one tried all sorts of games with oneself to try to make the time pass: and of course they were all no good. And one tried very hard not to think of drinks – iced sherbet in a palace in Tashbaan; clear spring water tinkling with a dark earthy sound; cold, smooth milk just creamy enough and not too creamy – and the harder you tried not to think, the more you thought.

At last there was something different – a mass of rock sticking up out of the sand about fifty yards long and thirty feet high. It did not cast much shadow, for the sun was now very high, but it cast a little. Into that shade they crowded. There they ate some food and drank a little water. It is not easy giving a horse a drink out of a skin bottle, but Bree and Hwin were clever with their lips. No one had anything like enough. No one spoke. The Horses were flecked with foam and their breathing was noisy. The children were pale.

After a very short rest they went on again. Same noises, same smells, same glare, till at last their shadows began to fall on their right, and then got longer and longer till they seemed to stretch out to the Eastern end of the world. Very slowly the sun drew nearer to the Western horizon. And now at last he was down and, thank goodness, the merciless glare was gone, though the heat coming up from the sand was still as bad as ever. Four pairs of eyes were looking out eagerly for any sign of the valley that Sallowpad the Raven had spoken about. But, mile after mile, there was nothing but level sand. And now the day was quite definitely done, and most of the stars were out, and still the Horses thundered on and the children rose and sank in their saddles, miserable with thirst and weariness. Not till the moon had risen did Shasta – in the strange, barking voice of someone whose mouth is perfectly dry – shout out:

"There it is!"

There was no mistaking it now. Ahead, and a little to their right, there was at last a slope: a slope downward and hummocks of rock on each side. The Horses were far too tired to speak but they swung round towards it and in a minute or two they were entering the gully. At first it was worse in there than it had been out in the open desert, for there was a breathless stuffiness between the rocky walls and less moonlight. The slope continued steeply downwards and the rocks on either hand rose to the height of cliffs. Then they began to meet vegetation – prickly cactus-like plants and coarse grass of the kind that would prick your fingers. Soon the horse-hooves were falling on pebbles and stones instead of sand. Round every bend of the valley – and it had many bends – they looked eagerly for water. The Horses were nearly at the end of their strength now, and Hwin, stumbling and panting, was lagging behind Bree. They were almost in despair before at last they came to a little muddiness and a tiny trickle of water through softer and better grass. And the trickle became a brook, and the brook became a stream with bushes on each side, and the stream became a river and there came (after more disappointments than I could possibly describe) a moment when Shasta, who had been in a kind of doze, suddenly realized that Bree had stopped, and found himself slipping off. Before them a little cataract of water poured into a broad pool: and both the Horses were already in the pool with their heads down, drinking, drinking, drinking. "O-o-oh," said Shasta and plunged in — it was about up to his knees — and stooped his head right into the cataract. It was perhaps the loveliest moment in his life.

It was about ten minutes later when all four of them (the two children wet nearly all over) came out and began to notice their surroundings. The moon was now high enough to peep down into the valley. There was soft grass on both sides of the river and, beyond the grass, trees and bushes sloped up to the bases of the cliffs. There must have been some wonderful flowering shrubs hidden in that shadowy undergrowth for the whole glade was full of the coolest and most delicious smells. And out of the darkest recess among the trees there came a sound Shasta had never heard before — a nightingale.

Everyone was much too tired to speak or to eat. The Horses, without waiting to be unsaddled, lay down at once. So did Aravis and Shasta.

About ten minutes later the careful Hwin said, "But we mustn't go to sleep. We've got to keep ahead of that Rabadash."

"No," said Bree very slowly. "Mustn't go to sleep. Just a little rest."

Shasta knew (for a moment) that they would all go to sleep if he didn't get up and do something about it, and felt that he ought to. In fact he decided that he would get up and persuade them to go on. But presently; not yet; not just yet...

Very soon the moon shone, and the nightingale sang over two horses and two human children, all fast asleep.

It was Aravis who awoke first. The sun was already high in the heavens and the cool morning hours were already wasted. "It's my fault," she said to herself furiously as she jumped up and began rousing the others. "One wouldn't expect Horses to keep awake after a day's work like that, even if they *can* talk. And of course that Boy wouldn't; he's had no decent training. But *I* ought to have known better."

The others were dazed and stupid with the heaviness of their sleep.

"Heigh-ho — broo-hoo," said Bree. "Been sleeping in my saddle, eh? I'll never do that again. Most uncomfortable—"

"Oh, come on, come on," said Aravis. "We've lost half the morning already. There isn't a moment to spare."

"A fellow's got to have a mouthful of grass," said Bree.

"I'm afraid we can't wait," said Aravis.

"What's the terrible hurry?" said Bree. "We've crossed the desert, haven't we?"

"But we're not in Archenland yet," said Aravis. "And we've got to get there before Rabadash."

"Oh, we must be miles ahead of him," said Bree. "Haven't we been coming a shorter way? Didn't that Raven friend of yours say this was a short cut, Shasta?"

"He didn't say anything about *shorter*," answered Shasta. "He only said *better*, because you got to a river this way. If the oasis is due North of Tashbaan, then I'm afraid this may be longer."

"Well, I can't go on without a snack," said Bree. "Take my bridle off, Shasta."

"P-please," said Hwin, very shyly, "I feel just like Bree that I *can't* go on. But when horses have humans (with spurs and things) on their backs, aren't they often made to go on when they're feeling like this? and then they find they can. I m-mean – oughtn't we to be able to do even more, now that we're free? It's all for Narnia."

"I think, Ma'am," said Bree very crushingly, "that I know a little more about campaigns and forced marches and what a horse can stand than you do."

To this, Hwin made no answer, being, like most highly bred mares, a very nervous and gentle person who was easily put down. In reality she was quite right, and if Bree had had a Tarkaan on his back at that moment to make him go on, he would have found that he was good for several hours' hard going. But one of the worst results of being a slave and being forced to do things is that when there is no one to force you any more you find you have almost lost the power of forcing yourself.

So they had to wait while Bree had a snack and a drink, and of course Hwin and the children had a snack and a drink too. It must have been nearly eleven o'clock in the morning before they finally got going again. And even then Bree took things much more gently than yesterday. It was really Hwin, though she was the weaker and more tired of the two, who set the pace.

The valley itself, with its brown, cool river, and grass and moss and wild flowers and rhododendrons, was such a pleasant place that it made you want to ride slowly.

CHAPTER TEN

THE HERMIT OF THE SOUTHERN MARCH

After they had ridden for several hours down the valley, it widened out and they could see what was ahead of them. The river which they had been following here joined a broader river, wide and turbulent, which flowed from their left to their right, towards the east. Beyond this new river a delightful country rose gently in low hills, ridge beyond ridge, to the Northern Mountains themselves. To the right there were rocky pinnacles, one or two of them with snow clinging to the ledges. To the left, pine-clad slopes, frowning cliffs, narrow gorges, and blue peaks stretched away as far as the eye could reach. Shasta could no longer make out Mount Pire. Straight ahead the mountain range sank to a wooded saddle which of course had to be the pass from Archenland into Narnia.

"Broo-hoo-hoo, the North, the green North!" neighed Bree: and certainly the lower hills looked greener and fresher than anything that Aravis and Shasta, with their southern-bred eyes, had ever imagined. Spirits rose as they clattered down to the water's-meet of the two rivers.

The eastern-flowing river, which was pouring from the higher mountains at the western end of the range, was far too swift and too broken with rapids for them to think of swimming it; but after some casting about, up and down the bank, they found a place shallow enough to wade. The roar and clatter of water, the great swirl against the Horses' fetlocks, the cool, stirring air and the darting dragonflies, filled Shasta with a strange excitement.

"Friends, we are in Archenland!" said Bree proudly as he splashed and churned his way out on the Northern bank. "I think that river we've just crossed is called the Winding Arrow."

"I hope we're in time," murmured Hwin.

Then they began going up, slowly and zigzagging a good deal, for the hills were steep. It was all open park-like country with no roads or houses in sight. Scattered trees, never thick enough to be a forest, were everywhere. Shasta, who had lived all his life in an almost tree-less grassland, had never seen so many or so many kinds. If you had been there you would probably have known (he didn't) that he was seeing oaks, beeches, silver birches, rowans, and sweet chestnuts. Rabbits scurried away in every direction as they advanced, and presently they saw a whole herd of fallow deer making off among the trees.

"Isn't it simply glorious!" said Aravis.

At the first ridge Shasta turned in the saddle and looked back. There was no sign of Tashbaan; the desert, unbroken except by the narrow green crack down which they had travelled, spread to the horizon.

"Hullo!" he said suddenly. "What's that?"

"What's what?" said Bree, turning round. Hwin and Aravis did the same.

"That," said Shasta, pointing. "It looks like smoke. Is it a fire?"

"Sand-storm, I should say," said Bree.

"Not much wind to raise it," said Aravis.

"Oh!" exclaimed Hwin. "Look! There are things flashing in it. Look! They're helmets – and armour. And it's moving: moving this way."

"By Tash!" said Aravis. "It's the army. It's Rabadash."

"Of course it is," said Hwin. "Just what I was afraid of. Quick! We must get to Anvard before it." And without another word she whisked round and began galloping North. Bree tossed his head and did the same.

"Come *on*, Bree, come on," yelled Aravis over her shoulder.

The race was very gruelling for the Horses. As they topped each ridge they found another valley and another ridge beyond it; and though they knew they were going in more or less the right direction, no one knew how far it was to Anvard. From the top of the second ridge Shasta looked back again. Instead of a dust-cloud well out in the desert he now saw a black, moving mass, rather like ants, on the far bank of the Winding Arrow. They were doubtless looking for a ford.

"They're on the river!" he yelled wildly.

"Quick! Quick!" shouted Aravis. "We might as well not have come at all if we don't reach Anvard in time. Gallop, Bree, gallop. Remember you're a war-horse."

It was all Shasta could do to prevent himself from shouting out similar instructions; but he thought, "The poor chap's doing all he can already," and held his tongue. And certainly both Horses were doing, if not all they could; all they thought they could, which is not quite the same thing. Bree had caught up with Hwin and they thundered side by side over the turf. It didn't look as if Hwin could possibly keep it up much longer.

At that moment everyone's feelings were completely altered by a sound from behind. It was not the sound they had been expecting to hear – the noise of hooves and jingling armour, mixed, perhaps, with Calormene battle-cries. Yet Shasta knew it at once. It was the same snarling roar he had heard that moonlit night when they first met Aravis and Hwin. Bree knew it too. His eyes gleamed red and his ears lay flat back on his skull. And Bree now discovered that he had not really been going as fast – not quite as fast – as he could. Shasta felt the change at once. Now they were really going all out. In a few seconds they were well ahead of Hwin.

"It's not fair," thought Shasta. "I *did* think we'd be safe from lions here!"

He looked over his shoulder. Everything was only too clear. A huge tawny creature, its body low to the ground, like a cat streaking across the lawn to a tree when a strange dog has got into the garden, was behind them. And it was nearer every second and half second.

He looked forward again and saw something which he did not take in, or even think about. Their way was barred by a smooth green wall about ten feet high. In the middle of that wall there was a gate, open. In the middle of the gateway stood a tall man dressed, down to his bare feet, in a robe coloured like autumn leaves, leaning on a straight staff. His beard fell almost to his knees.

Shasta saw all this in a glance and looked back again. The lion had almost got Hwin now. It was making snaps at her hind legs, and there was no hope now in her foam-flecked, wide-eyed face.

"Stop," bellowed Shasta in Bree's ear. "Must go back. Must help!"

Bree always said afterwards that he never heard, or never understood this; and as he was in general a very truthful horse we must accept his word.

Shasta slipped his feet out of the stirrups, slid both his legs over the left side, hesitated for one hideous hundredth of a second, and jumped. It hurt horribly and nearly winded him; but before he knew how it hurt him he was staggering back to help Aravis. He had never done anything like this in his life before and hardly knew why he was doing it now.

One of the most terrible noises in the world, a horse's scream, broke from Hwin's lips. Aravis was stooping low over Hwin's neck and seemed to be trying to draw her sword. And now all three – Aravis, Hwin, and the lion – were almost on top of Shasta. Before they reached him the lion rose on its hind legs, larger than you would have believed a lion could be, and jabbed at Aravis with its right paw. Shasta could see all the terrible claws extended. Aravis screamed and reeled in the saddle. The lion was tearing her shoulders. Shasta, half mad with horror, managed to lurch towards the brute. He had no weapon, not even a stick or a stone. He shouted out, idiotically, at the lion as one would at a dog, "Go home! Go home!" For a fraction of a second he was staring right into its wide-opened, raging mouth. Then, to his utter astonishment, the lion, still on its hind legs, checked itself suddenly, turned head over heels, picked itself up, and rushed away.

Shasta did not for a moment suppose it had gone for good. He turned and raced for the gate in the green wall which, now for the first time, he remembered seeing. Hwin, stumbling and nearly fainting, was just entering the gate; Aravis still kept her seat but her back was covered with blood.

"Come in, my daughter, come in," the robed and bearded man was saying, and then, "Come in, my son" as Shasta panted up to him. He heard the gate closed behind him; and the bearded stranger was already helping Aravis off her horse.

They were in a wide and perfectly circular enclosure, protected by a high wall of green turf. A pool of perfectly still water, so full that the water was almost exactly level with the ground, lay before him. At one end of the pool, completely overshadowing it with its branches, there grew the hugest and most beautiful tree that Shasta had ever seen. Beyond the pool was a little low house of stone roofed with deep and ancient thatch. There was a sound of bleating and over at the far side of the enclosure there were some goats. The level ground was completely covered with the finest grass.

"Are – are – are you," panted Shasta, "are you King Lune of Archenland?"

The old man shook his head. "No," he replied in a quiet voice, "I am the Hermit of the Southern March. And now, my son, waste no time on questions, but obey. This damsel is wounded. Your horses are spent. Rabadash is at this moment finding a ford over the Winding Arrow. If you run now, without a moment's rest, you will still be in time to warn King Lune."

Shasta's heart fainted at these words for he felt he had no strength left. And he writhed inside at what seemed the cruelty and unfairness of the demand. He had not yet learned that if you do one good deed your reward usually is to be set to do another and harder and better one. But all he said out loud was:

"Where is the King?"

The Hermit turned and pointed with his staff. "Look," he said. "There is another gate, right opposite to the one you entered by. Open it and go straight ahead: always straight ahead, over level or steep, over smooth or rough, over dry or wet. I know by my art that you will find King Lune straight ahead. But run, run: always run."

Shasta nodded his head, ran to the northern gate and disappeared beyond it. Then the Hermit took Aravis, whom he had all this time been supporting with his left arm, and half led, half carried her into the house. After a long time he came out again.

"Now, cousins," he said to the Horses. "It is your turn."

Without waiting for an answer — and indeed they were too exhausted to speak — he took the bridles and saddles off both of them. Then he rubbed them both down, so well that a groom in a King's stable could not have done it better.

"There, cousins," he said, "dismiss it all from your minds and be comforted. Here is water and there is grass. You shall have a hot mash when I have milked my other cousins, the goats."

"Sir," said Hwin, finding her voice at last, "will the Tarkheena live? Has the lion killed her?"

"I who know many present things by my art," replied the Hermit with a smile, "have yet little knowledge of things future. Therefore I do not know whether any man or woman or beast in the whole world will be alive when the sun sets tonight. But be of good hope. The damsel is likely to live as long as any of her age."

When Aravis came to herself she found that she was lying on her face on a low bed of extraordinary softness in a cool, bare room with walls of undressed stone. She couldn't understand why she had been laid on her face; but when she tried to turn and felt the hot, burning pains all over her back, she remembered, and realized why. She couldn't understand what delightfully springy stuff the bed was made of, because it was made of heather (which is the best bedding) and heather was a thing she had never seen or heard of.

The door opened and the Hermit entered, carrying a large wooden bowl in his hand. After carefully setting this down, he came to the bedside, and asked:

"How do you find yourself, my daughter?"

"My back is very sore, father," said Aravis, "but there is nothing else wrong with me."

He knelt beside her, laid his hand on her forehead, and felt her pulse.

"There is no fever," he said. "You will do well. Indeed there is no reason why you should not get up tomorrow. But now, drink this."

He fetched the wooden bowl and held it to her lips. Aravis couldn't help making a face when she tasted it, for goats' milk is rather a shock when you are not used to it. But she was very thirsty and managed to drink it all and felt better when she had finished.

"Now, my daughter, you may sleep when you wish," said the Hermit. "For your wounds are washed and dressed and though they smart they are no more serious than if they had been the cuts of a whip. It must have been a very strange lion; for instead of catching you out of the saddle and getting his teeth into you, he has only drawn his claws across your back. Ten scratches: sore, but not deep or dangerous."

"I say!" said Aravis. "I *have* had luck."

"Daughter," said the Hermit, "I have now lived a hundred and nine winters in this world and have never yet met any such thing as Luck. There is something about all this that I do not understand: but if ever we need to know it, you may be sure that we shall."

"And what about Rabadash and his two hundred horse?" asked Aravis.

"They will not pass this way, I think," said the Hermit. "They must have found a ford by now well to the east of us. From there they will try to ride straight to Anvard."

"Poor Shasta!" said Aravis. "Has he far to go? Will he get there first?"

"There is good hope of it," said the old man.

Aravis lay down again (on her side this time) and said, "Have I been asleep for a long time? It seems to be getting dark."

The Hermit was looking out of the only window, which faced north. "This is not the darkness of night," he said presently. "The clouds are falling down from Stormness Head. Our foul weather always comes from there in these parts. There will be thick fog tonight."

Next day, except for her sore back, Aravis felt so well that after breakfast (which was porridge and cream) the Hermit said she could get up. And of course she at once went out to speak to the Horses. The weather had changed and the whole of that green enclosure was filled, like a great green cup, with sunlight. It was a very peaceful place, lonely and quiet.

Hwin at once trotted across to Aravis and gave her a horse-kiss.

"But where's Bree?" said Aravis when each had asked after the other's health and sleep.

"Over there," said Hwin, pointing with her nose to the far side of the circle. "And I wish you'd come and talk to him. There's something wrong, I can't get a word out of him."

They strolled across and found Bree lying with his face towards the wall, and though he must have heard them coming, he never turned his head or spoke a word.

"Good morning, Bree," said Aravis. "How are you this morning?"

Bree muttered something that no one could hear.

"The Hermit says that Shasta probably got to King Lune in time," continued Aravis, "so it looks as if all our troubles are over. Narnia, at last, Bree!"

"I shall never see Narnia," said Bree in a low voice.

"Aren't you well, Bree dear?" said Aravis.

Bree turned round at last, his face mournful as only a horse's can be.

"I shall go back to Calormen," he said.

"What?" said Aravis. "Back to slavery?"

"Yes," said Bree. "Slavery is all I'm fit for. How can I ever show my face among the free Horses of Narnia? – I who left a mare and a girl and a boy to be eaten by lions while I galloped all I could to save my own wretched skin!"

"We all ran as hard as we could," said Hwin.

"Shasta didn't!" snorted Bree. "At least he ran in the right direction: ran *back*. And that is what shames me most of all. I, who called myself a war-horse and boasted of a hundred fights, to be beaten by a little human boy – a child, a mere foal, who had never held a sword nor had any good nurture or example in his life!"

"I know," said Aravis. "I felt just the same. Shasta was marvellous. I'm just as bad as you, Bree. I've been snubbing him and looking down on him ever since you met us and now he turns out to be the best of us all. But I think it would be better to stay and say we're sorry than to go back to Calormen."

"It's all very well for you," said Bree. "You haven't disgraced yourself. But I've lost everything."

"My good Horse," said the Hermit, who had approached them unnoticed because his bare feet made so little noise on that sweet, dewy grass. "My good Horse, you've lost nothing but your self-conceit. No, no, cousin. Don't put back your ears and shake your mane at me. If you are really so humbled as you sounded a minute ago, you must learn to listen to sense. You're not quite the great Horse you had come to think, from living among poor dumb horses. Of course you were braver and cleverer than *them*. You could hardly help being that. It doesn't follow that you'll be anyone very special in Narnia. But as long as you know you're nobody special, you'll be a very decent sort of Horse, on the whole, and taking one thing with another. And now, if you and my other four-footed cousin will come round to the kitchen door we'll see about the other half of that mash."

Chapter Eleven

The Unwelcome Fellow Traveller

When Shasta went through the gate he found a slope of grass and a little heather running up before him to some trees. He had nothing to think about now and no plans to make: he had only to run, and that was quite enough. His limbs were shaking, a terrible stitch was beginning in his side, and the sweat that kept dropping into his eyes blinded them and made them smart. He was unsteady on his feet too, and more than once he nearly turned his ankle on a loose stone.

The trees were thicker now than they had yet been and in the more open spaces there was bracken. The sun had gone in without making it any cooler. It had become one of those hot, grey days when there seem to be twice as many flies as usual. Shasta's face was covered with them; he didn't even try to shake them off – he had too much else to do.

Suddenly he heard a horn – not a great throbbing horn like the horns of Tashbaan but a merry call, Ti-ro-to-to-ho! Next moment he came out into a wide glade and found himself in a crowd of people.

At least, it looked a crowd to him. In reality there were about fifteen or twenty of them, all gentlemen in green hunting-dress, with their horses; some in the saddle and some standing by their horses' heads. In the centre someone was holding the stirrup for a man to mount. And the man he was holding it for was the jolliest, fattest, most apple-cheeked, twinkling-eyed King you could imagine.

As soon as Shasta came in sight this King forgot all about mounting his horse. He spread out his arms to Shasta, his face lit up, and he cried out in a great, deep voice that seemed to come from the bottom of his chest:

"Corin! My son! And on foot, and in rags! What——"

"No," panted Shasta, shaking his head. "Not Prince Corin. I – I – know I'm like him... saw his Highness in Tashbaan... sent his greetings."

The King was staring at Shasta with an extraordinary expression on his face.

"Are you K-King Lune?" gasped Shasta. And then, without waiting for an answer, "Lord King – fly – Anvard – shut the gates – enemies upon you – Rabadash and two hundred horse."

"Have you assurance of this, boy?" asked one of the other gentlemen.

"My own eyes," said Shasta. "I've seen them. Raced them all the way from Tashbaan."

"On foot?" said the gentleman, raising his eyebrows a little.

"Horses – with the Hermit," said Shasta.

"Question him no more, Darrin," said King Lune. "I see truth in his face. We must ride for it, gentlemen. A spare horse there, for the boy. You can ride fast, friend?"

For answer Shasta put his foot in the stirrup of the horse which had been led towards him and a moment later he was in the saddle. He had done it a hundred times with Bree in the last few weeks, and his mounting was very different now from what it had been on that first night when Bree had said that he climbed up a horse as if he were climbing a haystack.

He was pleased to hear the Lord Darrin say to the King, "The boy has a true horseman's seat, sire. I'll warrant there's noble blood in him."

"His blood, aye, there's the point," said the King. And he stared hard at Shasta again with that curious expression, almost a hungry expression, in his steady grey eyes.

But by now the whole party was moving off at a brisk canter. Shasta's seat was excellent but he was sadly puzzled as to what to do with his reins, for he had never touched the reins while he was on Bree's back. But he looked very carefully out of the corners of his eyes to see what the others were doing (as some of us have done at parties when we weren't quite sure which knife or fork we were meant to use) and tried to get his fingers right. But he didn't dare to try really directing the horse; he trusted it would follow the rest. The horse was of course an ordinary horse, not a Talking Horse; but it had quite wits enough to realize that the strange boy on its back had no whip and no spurs and was not really master of the situation. That was why Shasta soon found himself at the tail end of the procession.

Even so, he was going pretty fast. There were no flies now and the air in his face was delicious. He had got his breath back too. And his errand had succeeded. For the first time since the arrival at Tashbaan (how long ago it seemed!) he was beginning to enjoy himself.

He looked up to see how much nearer the mountain tops had come. To his disappointment he could not see them at all: only a vague greyness, rolling down towards them. He had never been in mountain country before and was surprised. "It's a cloud," he said to himself, "a cloud coming down. I see. Up here in the hills one is really in the sky. I shall see what the inside of a cloud is like. What fun! I've often wondered." Far away on his left and a little behind him, the sun was getting ready to set.

They had come to a rough kind of road by now and were making very good speed. But Shasta's horse was still the last of the lot. Once or twice when the road made a bend (there was now continuous forest on each side of it) he lost sight of the others for a second or two.

Then they plunged into the fog, or else the fog rolled over them. The world became grey. Shasta had not realized how cold and wet the inside of a cloud would be; nor how dark. The grey turned to black with alarming speed.

Someone at the head of the column winded the horn every now and then, and each time the sound came from a little farther off. He couldn't see any of the others now, but of course he'd be able to as soon as he got round the next bend. But when he rounded it he still couldn't see them. In fact he could see nothing at all. His horse was walking now. "Get on, Horse, get on," said Shasta. Then came the horn, very faint. Bree had always told him that he must keep his heels well turned out, and Shasta had got the idea that something very terrible would happen if he dug his heels into a horse's sides. This seemed to him an occasion for trying it. "Look here, horse," he said, "if you don't buck up, do you know what I'll do? I'll dig my heels into you. I really will." The horse, however, took no notice of this threat. So Shasta settled himself firmly in the saddle, gripped with his knees, clenched his teeth, and punched both the horse's sides with his heels as hard as he could.

The only result was that the horse broke into a kind of pretence of a trot for five or six paces and then subsided into a walk again. And now it was quite dark and they seemed to have given up blowing that horn. The only sound was a steady drip-drip from the branches of the trees.

"Well, I suppose even a walk will get us somewhere sometime," said Shasta to himself. "I only hope I shan't run into Rabadash and his people."

He went on for what seemed a long time, always at a walking pace. He began to hate that horse, and he was also beginning to feel very hungry.

Presently he came to a place where the road divided into two. He was just wondering which led to Anvard when he was startled by a noise from behind him. It was the noise of trotting horses. "Rabadash!" thought Shasta. He had no way of guessing which road Rabadash would take. "But if I take one," said Shasta to himself, "he *may* take the other: and if I stay at the crossroads I'm *sure* to be caught." He dismounted and led his horse as quickly as he could along the right-hand road.

The sound of the cavalry grew rapidly nearer and in a minute or two Shasta realized that they were at the crossroads. He held his breath, waiting to see which way they would take.

There came a low word of command – "Halt!" – then a moment of horsey noises – nostrils blowing, hooves pawing, bits being champed, necks being patted. Then a voice spoke:

"Attend, all of you," it said. "We are now within a furlong of the castle. Remember your orders. Once we are in Narnia, as we should be by sunrise, you are to kill as little as possible. On this venture you are to regard every drop of Narnian blood as more precious than a gallon of your own. On *this* venture, I say. The gods will send us a happier hour and then you must leave nothing alive between Cair Paravel and the Western Waste. But we are not yet in Narnia. Here in Archenland it is another thing. In the assault on this castle of King Lune's, nothing matters but speed. Show your mettle. It must be mine within an hour. And if it is, I give it all to you. I reserve no booty for myself. Kill me every barbarian male within its walls, down to the child that was born yesterday, and everything else is yours to divide as you please – the women, the gold, the jewels, the weapons, and the wine. The man that I see hanging back when we come to the gates shall be burned alive. In the name of Tash the irresistible, the inexorable – forward!"

With a great cloppitty-clop the column began to move, and Shasta breathed again. They had taken the other road.

Shasta thought they took a long time going past, for though he had been talking and thinking about "two hundred horse" all day, he had not realized how many they really were. But at last the sound died away and once more he was alone amid the drip-drip from the trees.

He now knew the way to Anvard but of course he could not now go there: that would only mean running into the arms of Rabadash's troopers. "What on earth am I to do?" said Shasta to himself. But he remounted his horse and continued along the road he had chosen, in the faint hope of finding some cottage where he might ask for shelter and a meal. He had thought, of course, of going back to Aravis and Bree and Hwin at the hermitage, but he couldn't because by now he had not the least idea of the direction.

"After all," said Shasta, "this road is bound to get to somewhere."

But that all depends on what you mean by somewhere. The road kept on getting to somewhere in the sense that it got to more and more trees, all dark and dripping, and to colder and colder air. And strange, icy winds kept blowing the mist past him though they never blew it away. If he had been used to mountain country he would have realized that this meant he was now very high up – perhaps right at the top of the pass. But Shasta knew nothing about mountains.

"I *do* think," said Shasta, "that I must be the most unfortunate boy that ever lived in the whole world. Everything goes right for everyone except me. Those Narnian lords and ladies got safe away from Tashbaan; I was left behind. Aravis and Bree and Hwin are all as snug as anything with that old Hermit; of course I was the one who was sent on. King Lune and his people must have got safely into the castle and shut the gates long before Rabadash arrived, but I get left out."

And being very tired and having nothing inside him, he felt so sorry for himself that the tears rolled down his cheeks.

What put a stop to all this was a sudden fright. Shasta discovered that someone or somebody was walking beside him. It was pitch dark and he could see nothing. And the Thing (or Person) was going so quietly that he could hardly hear any footfalls. What he could hear was breathing. His invisible companion seemed to breathe on a very large scale, and Shasta got the impression that it was a very large creature. And he had come to notice this breathing so gradually that he had really no idea how long it had been there. It was a horrible shock.

It darted into his mind that he had heard long ago that there were giants in these Northern countries. He bit his lip in terror. But now that he really had something to cry about, he stopped crying.

The Thing (unless it was a Person) went on beside him so very quietly that Shasta began to hope he had only imagined it. But just as he was becoming quite sure of it, there suddenly came a deep, rich sigh out of the darkness beside him. That couldn't be imagination! Anyway, he had felt the hot breath of that sigh on his chilly left hand.

If the horse had been any good — or if he had known how to get any good out of the horse — he would have risked everything on a break away and a wild gallop. But he knew he couldn't make that horse gallop. So he went on at a walking pace and the unseen companion walked and breathed beside him. At last he could bear it no longer.

"Who are you?" he said, scarcely above a whisper.

"One who has waited long for you to speak," said the Thing. Its voice was not loud, but very large and deep.

"Are you — are you a giant?" asked Shasta.

"You might call me a giant," said the Large Voice. "But I am not like the creatures you call giants."

"I can't see you at all," said Shasta, after staring very hard. Then (for an even more terrible idea had come into his head) he said, almost in a scream, "You're not — not something *dead*, are you? Oh, please — please do go away. What harm have I ever done you? Oh, I am the unluckiest person in the whole world!"

Once more he felt the warm breath of the Thing on his hand and face.

"There," it said, "that is not the breath of a ghost. Tell me your sorrows."

Shasta was a little reassured by the breath: so he told how he had never known his real father or mother and had been brought up sternly by the fisherman. And then he told the story of his escape and how they were chased by lions and forced to swim for their lives; and of all their dangers in Tashbaan and about his night among the tombs and how the beasts howled at him out of the desert. And he told about the heat and thirst of their desert journey and how they were almost at their goal when another lion chased them and wounded Aravis. And also, how very long it was since he had had anything to eat.

"I do not call you unfortunate," said the Large Voice.

"Don't you think it was bad luck to meet so many lions?" said Shasta.

"There was only one lion," said the Voice.

"What on earth do you mean? I've just told you there were at least two the first night, and—"

"There was only one: but he was swift of foot."

"How do you know?"

"I was the lion." And as Shasta gaped with open mouth and said nothing, the Voice continued. "I was the lion who forced you to join with Aravis. I was the cat who comforted you among the houses of the dead. I was the lion who drove the jackals from you while you slept. I was the lion who gave the Horses the new strength of fear for the last mile so that you should reach King Lune in time. And I was the lion you do not remember who pushed the boat in which you lay, a child near death, so that it came to shore where a man sat, wakeful at midnight, to receive you."

"Then it was you who wounded Aravis?"

"It was I."

"But what for?"

"Child," said the Voice, "I am telling you your story, not hers. I tell no one any story but his own."

"Who *are* you?" asked Shasta.

"Myself," said the voice, very deep and low so that the earth shook: and again, "Myself", loud and clear and gay: and then the third time "Myself", whispered so softly you could hardly hear it, and yet it seemed to come from all round you as if the leaves rustled with it.

Shasta was no longer afraid that the Voice belonged to something that would eat him, nor that it was the voice of a ghost. But a new and different sort of trembling came over him. Yet he felt glad too.

The mist was turning from black to grey and from grey to white. This must have begun to happen some time ago, but while he had been talking to the thing he had not been noticing anything else. Now, the whiteness around him became a shining whiteness; his eyes began to blink.

Somewhere ahead he could hear birds singing. He knew the night was over at last. He could see the mane and ears and head of his horse quite easily now. A golden light fell on them from the left. He thought it was the sun.

He turned and saw, pacing beside him, taller than the horse, a Lion. The horse did not seem to be afraid of it or else could not see it. It was from the Lion that the light came. No one ever saw anything more terrible or beautiful.

Luckily Shasta had lived all his life too far south in Calormen to have heard the tales that were whispered in Tashbaan about a dreadful Narnian demon that appeared in the form of a lion. And of course he knew none of the true stories about Aslan, the great Lion, the son of the Emperor-beyond-the-Sea, the High King above all kings in Narnia. But after one glance at the Lion's face he slipped out of the saddle and fell at its feet. He couldn't say anything but then he didn't want to say anything, and he knew he needn't say anything.

The High King above all kings stooped towards him. Its mane, and some strange and solemn perfume that hung about the mane, was all round him. It touched his forehead with its tongue. He lifted his face and their eyes met. Then instantly the pale brightness of the mist and the fiery brightness of the Lion rolled themselves together into a swirling glory and gathered themselves up and disappeared. He was alone with the horse on a grassy hillside under a blue sky. And there were birds singing.

Chapter Twelve

Shasta in Narnia

"Was it all a dream?" wondered Shasta. But it couldn't have been a dream for there in the grass before him he saw the deep, large print of the Lion's front right paw. It took one's breath away to think of the weight that could make a footprint like that. But there was something more remarkable than the size about it. As he looked at it, water had already filled the bottom of it. Soon it was full to the brim, and then overflowing, and a little stream was running downhill, past him, over the grass.

Shasta stooped and drank – a very long drink – and then dipped his face in and splashed his head. It was extremely cold, and clear as glass, and refreshed him very much. After that he stood up, shaking the water out of his ears and flinging the wet hair back from his forehead, and began to take stock of his surroundings.

Apparently it was still very early morning. The sun had only just risen, and it had risen out of the forests which he saw low down and far away on his right. The country which he was looking at was absolutely new to him. It was a green valley-land dotted with trees through which he caught the gleam of a river that wound away roughly to the North-West. On the far side of the valley there were high and even rocky hills, but they were lower than the mountains he had seen yesterday. Then he began to guess where he was. He turned and looked behind him and saw that the slope on which he was standing belonged to a range of far higher mountains.

"I see," said Shasta to himself. "Those are the big mountains between Archenland and Narnia. I was on the other side of them yesterday. I must have come through the pass in the night. What luck that I hit it! – at least it wasn't luck at all really, it was *Him*. And now I'm in Narnia."

He turned and unsaddled his horse and took off its bridle – "Though you *are* a perfectly horrid horse," he said. It took no notice of this remark and immediately began eating grass. That horse had a very low opinion of Shasta.

"I wish I could eat grass!" thought Shasta. "It's no good going back to Anvard, it'll all be besieged. I'd better get lower down into the valley and see if I can get anything to eat."

So he went on downhill (the thick dew was cruelly cold to his bare feet) till he came into a wood. There was a kind of track running through it and he had not followed this for many minutes when he heard a thick and rather wheezy voice saying to him,

"Good morning, neighbour."

Shasta looked round eagerly to find the speaker and presently saw a small, prickly person with a dark face who had just come out from among the trees. At least, it was small for a person but very big indeed for a hedgehog, which was what it was.

"Good morning," said Shasta. "But I'm not a neighbour. In fact I'm a stranger in these parts."

"Ah?" said the Hedgehog inquiringly.

"I've come over the mountains – from Archenland, you know."

"Ah, Archenland," said the Hedgehog. "That's a terrible long way. Never been there myself."

"And I think, perhaps," said Shasta, "someone ought to be told that there's an army of savage Calormenes attacking Anvard at this very moment."

"You don't say so!" answered the Hedgehog. "Well, think of that. And they do say that Calormen is hundreds and thousands of miles away, right at the world's end, across a great sea of sand."

"It's not nearly as far as you think," said Shasta. "And oughtn't something to be done about this attack on Anvard? Oughtn't your High King to be told?"

"Certain sure, something ought to be done about it," said the Hedgehog. "But you see I'm just on my way to bed for a good day's sleep. Hullo, neighbour!"

The last words were addressed to an immense biscuit-coloured rabbit whose head had just popped up from somewhere beside the path. The Hedgehog immediately told the Rabbit what it had just learned from Shasta. The Rabbit agreed that this was very remarkable news and that somebody ought to tell someone about it with a view to doing something.

And so it went on. Every few minutes they were joined by other creatures, some from the branches overhead and some from little underground houses at their feet, till the party consisted of five rabbits, a squirrel, two magpies, a goat-foot faun, and a mouse, who all talked at the same time and all agreed with the Hedgehog. For the truth was that in that golden age when the Witch and the Winter had gone and Peter the High King ruled at Cair Paravel, the smaller woodland people of Narnia were so safe and happy that they were getting a little careless.

Presently, however, two more practical people arrived in the little wood. One was a Red Dwarf whose name appeared to be Duffle. The other was a stag, a beautiful lordly creature with wide liquid eyes, dappled flanks and legs so thin and graceful that they looked as if you could break them with two fingers.

"Lion alive!" roared the Dwarf as soon as he had heard the news. "And if that's so, why are we all standing still, chattering? Enemies at Anvard! News must be sent to Cair Paravel at once. The army must be called out. Narnia must go to the aid of King Lune."

"Ah!" said the Hedgehog. "But you won't find the High King at Cair. He's away to the North trouncing those giants. And talking of giants, neighbours, that puts me in mind—"

"Who'll take our message?" interrupted the Dwarf. "Anyone here got more speed than me?"

"I've got speed," said the Stag. "What's my message? How many Calormenes?"

"Two hundred: under Prince Rabadash. And—" But the Stag was already away — all four legs off the ground at once, and in a moment its white stern had disappeared among the remoter trees.

"Wonder where he's going," said a rabbit. "He won't find the High King at Cair Paravel, you know."

"He'll find Queen Lucy," said Duffle. "And then — hullo! What's wrong with the Human? It looks pretty green. Why, I do believe it's quite faint. Perhaps it's mortal hungry. When did you last have a meal, youngster?"

"Yesterday morning," said Shasta weakly.

"Come on, then, come on," said the Dwarf, at once throwing his thick little arms round Shasta's waist to support him. "Why, neighbours, we all ought to be ashamed of ourselves! You come with me, lad. Breakfast! Better than talking."

With a great deal of bustle, muttering reproaches to itself, the Dwarf half led and half supported Shasta at a great speed further into the wood and a little downhill. It was a longer walk than Shasta wanted at that moment and his legs had begun to feel very shaky before they came out from the trees on to bare hillside. There they found a little house with a smoking chimney and an open door, and as they came to the doorway Duffle called out,

"Hey, brothers! A visitor for breakfast."

And immediately, mixed with a sizzling sound, there came to Shasta a simply delightful smell. It was one he had never smelt in his life before, but I hope you have. It was, in fact, the smell of bacon and eggs and mushrooms all frying in a pan.

"Mind your head, lad," said Duffle a moment too late, for Shasta had already bashed his forehead against the low lintel of the door. "Now," continued the Dwarf, "sit you down. The table's a bit low for you, but then the stool's low too. That's right. And here's porridge – and here's a jug of cream – and here's a spoon."

By the time Shasta had finished his porridge, the Dwarf's two brothers (whose names were Rogin and Bricklethumb) were putting the dish of bacon and eggs and mushrooms, and the coffee pot and the hot milk, and the toast, on the table.

It was all new and wonderful to Shasta for Calormene food is quite different. He didn't even know what the slices of brown stuff were, for he had never seen toast before. He didn't know what the yellow soft thing they smeared on the toast was, because in Calormen you nearly always get oil instead of butter. And the house itself was quite different from the dark, frowsty, fish-smelling hut of Arsheesh and from the pillared and carpeted halls in the palaces of Tashbaan. The roof was very low, and everything was made of wood, and there was a cuckoo-clock and a red-and-white checked tablecloth and a bowl of wild flowers and little curtains on the thick-paned windows. It was also rather troublesome having to use dwarf cups and plates and knives and forks. This meant that helpings were very small, but then there were a great many helpings, so that Shasta's plate or cup was being filled every moment, and every moment the Dwarfs themselves were saying, "Butter please", or, "Another cup of coffee", or, "I'd like a few more mushrooms", or, "What about frying another egg or so?" And when at last they had all eaten as much as they possibly could the three Dwarfs drew lots for who would do the washing-up, and Rogin was the unlucky one. Then Duffle and Bricklethumb took Shasta outside to a bench which ran against the cottage wall, and they all stretched out their legs and gave a great sigh of contentment and the two Dwarfs lit their pipes. The dew was off the grass now and the sun was warm; indeed, if there hadn't been a light breeze, it would have been too hot.

"Now, Stranger," said Duffle, "I'll show you the lie of the land. You can see nearly all South Narnia from here, and we're rather proud of the view. Right away on your left, beyond those near hills, you can just see the Western Mountains. And that round hill away on your right is called the Hill of the Stone Table. Just beyond—"

But at that moment he was interrupted by a snore from Shasta who, what with his night's journey and his excellent breakfast, had fallen fast asleep. The kindly Dwarfs, as soon as they noticed this, began making signs to each other not to wake him, and indeed did so much whispering and nodding and getting up and tiptoeing away that they certainly would have waked him if he had been less tired.

He slept pretty well nearly all day but woke up in time for supper. The beds in that house were all too small for him but they made him a fine bed of heather on the floor, and he never stirred nor dreamed all night. Next morning they had just finished breakfast when they heard a shrill, exciting sound from outside.

"Trumpets!" said all the Dwarfs, as they and Shasta all came running out.

The trumpets sounded again: a new noise to Shasta, not huge and solemn like the horns of Tashbaan nor gay and merry like King Lune's hunting horn, but clear and sharp and valiant. The noise was coming from the woods to the East, and soon there was a noise of horse-hoofs mixed with it. A moment later the head of the column came into sight.

First came the Lord Peridan on a bay horse carrying the great banner of Narnia — a red lion on a green ground. Shasta knew him at once. Then came three people riding abreast, two on great chargers and one on a pony. The two on the chargers were King Edmund and a fair-haired lady with a very merry face who wore a helmet and a mail shirt and carried a bow across her shoulder and a quiver full of arrows at her side. ("The Queen Lucy," whispered Duffle.) But the one on the pony was Corin. After that came the main body of the army: men on ordinary horses, men on Talking Horses (who didn't mind being ridden on proper occasions, as when Narnia went to war), centaurs, stern, hard-bitten bears, great Talking Dogs, and last of all six giants. For there are good giants in Narnia. But though he knew they were on the right side Shasta at first could hardly bear to look at them; there are some things that take a lot of getting used to.

Just as the King and Queen reached the cottage and the Dwarfs began making low bows to them, King Edmund called out,

"Now, friends! Time for a halt and a morsel!" and at once there was a great bustle of people dismounting and haversacks being opened and conversation beginning when Corin came running up to Shasta and seized both his hands and cried,

"What! *You* here! So you got through all right? I *am* glad. Now we shall have some sport. And isn't it luck! We only got into harbour at Cair Paravel yesterday morning and the very first person who met us was Chervy the Stag with all this news of an attack on Anvard. Don't you think—"

"Who is your Highness's friend?" said King Edmund, who had just got off his horse.

"Don't you see, Sire?" said Corin. "It's my double: the boy you mistook me for at Tashbaan."

"Why, so he is your double," exclaimed Queen Lucy. "As like as two twins. This is a marvellous thing."

"Please, your Majesty," said Shasta to King Edmund, "I was no traitor, really I wasn't. And I couldn't help hearing your plans. But I'd never have dreamed of telling them to your enemies."

"I know now that you were no traitor, boy," said King Edmund, laying his hand on Shasta's head. "But if you would not be taken for one, another time try not to hear what's meant for other ears. But all's well."

After that there was so much bustle and talk and coming and going that Shasta for a few minutes lost sight of Corin and Edmund and Lucy. But Corin was the sort of boy whom one is sure to hear of pretty soon and it wasn't very long before Shasta heard King Edmund saying in a loud voice:

"By the Lion's Mane, prince, this is too much! Will your Highness never be better? You are more of a heart's-scald than our whole army together! I'd as lief have a regiment of hornets in my command as you."

Shasta wormed his way through the crowd and there saw Edmund, looking very angry indeed, Corin looking a little ashamed of himself, and a strange Dwarf sitting on the ground making faces. A couple of fauns had apparently just been helping it out of its armour.

"If I had but my cordial with me," Queen Lucy was saying, "I could soon mend this. But the High King has so strictly charged me not to carry it commonly to the wars and to keep it only for great extremities!"

What had happened was this. As soon as Corin had spoken to Shasta, Corin's elbow had been plucked by a Dwarf in the army called Thornbut.

"What is it, Thornbut?" Corin had said.

"Your Royal Highness," said Thornbut, drawing him aside, "our march today will bring us through the pass and right to your royal father's castle. We may be in battle before night."

"I know," said Corin. "Isn't it splendid?"

"Splendid or not," said Thornbut, "I have the strictest orders from King Edmund to see to it that your Highness is not in the fight. You will be allowed to see it, and that's treat enough for your Highness's little years."

"Oh, what nonsense!" Corin burst out. "Of course I'm going to fight. Why, the Queen Lucy's going to be with the archers."

"The Queen's grace will do as she pleases," said Thornbut. "But you are in my charge. Either I must have your solemn and princely word that you'll keep your pony beside mine – not half a neck ahead – till I give your Highness leave to depart: or else – it is his Majesty's word – we must go with our wrists tied together like two prisoners."

"I'll knock you down if you try to bind me," said Corin.

"I'd like to see your Highness do it," said the Dwarf.

That was quite enough for a boy like Corin and in a second he and the Dwarf were at it hammer and tongs. It would have been an even match for, though Corin had longer arms and more height, the Dwarf was older and tougher. But it was never fought out (that's the worst of fights on a rough hillside) for by very bad luck Thornbut trod on a loose stone, came flat down on his nose, and found when he tried to get up that he had sprained his ankle: a really excruciating sprain which would keep him from walking or riding for at least a fortnight.

"See what your Highness has done," said King Edmund. "Deprived us of a proved warrior on the very edge of battle."

"I'll take his place, Sire," said Corin.

"Pshaw," said Edmund. "No one doubts your courage. But a boy in battle is a danger only to his own side."

At that moment the King was called away to attend to something else, and Corin, after apologizing handsomely to the Dwarf, rushed up to Shasta and whispered,

"Quick! There's a spare pony now, and the Dwarf's armour. Put it on before anyone notices."

"What for?" said Shasta.

"Why, so that you and I can fight in the battle of course! Don't you want to?"

"Oh — ah, yes, of course," said Shasta. But he hadn't been thinking of doing so at all, and began to get a most uncomfortable prickly feeling in his spine.

"That's right," said Corin. "Over your head. Now the sword-belt. But we must ride near the tail of the column and keep as quiet as mice. Once the battle begins everyone will be far too busy to notice us."

CHAPTER THIRTEEN

THE FIGHT AT ANVARD

By about eleven o'clock the whole company was once more on the march, riding westward with the mountains on their left. Corin and Shasta rode right at the rear with the Giants immediately in front of them. Lucy and Edmund and Peridan were busy with their plans for the battle and though Lucy once said, "But where is his goosecap Highness?" Edmund only replied, "Not in the front, and that's good news enough. Leave well alone."

Shasta told Corin most of his adventures and explained that he had learned all his riding from a horse and didn't really know how to use the reins. Corin instructed him in this, besides telling him all about their secret sailing from Tashbaan.

"And where is the Queen Susan?"

"At Cair Paravel," said Corin. "She's not like Lucy, you know, who's as good as a man, or at any rate as good as a boy. Queen Susan is more like an ordinary grown-up lady. She doesn't ride to the wars, though she is an excellent archer."

The hillside path which they were following became narrower all the time and the drop on their right hand became steeper. At last they were going in single file along the edge of a precipice and Shasta shuddered to think that he had done the same last night without knowing it. "But of course," he thought, "I was quite safe. That is why the Lion kept on my left. He was between me and the edge all the time."

Then the path went left and south away from the cliff and there were thick woods on both sides of it and they went steeply up and up into the pass. There would have been a splendid view from the top if it were open ground but among all those trees you could see nothing – only, every now and then, some huge pinnacle of rock above the tree-tops, and an eagle or two wheeling high up in the blue air.

"They smell battle," said Corin, pointing at the birds. "They know we're preparing a feed for them."

Shasta didn't like this at all.

When they had crossed the neck of the pass and come a good deal lower they reached more open ground and from here Shasta could see all Archenland, blue and hazy, spread out below him and even (he thought) a hint of the desert beyond it. But the sun, which had perhaps two hours or so to go before it set, was in his eyes and he couldn't make things out distinctly.

Here the army halted and spread out in a line, and there was a great deal of rearranging. A whole detachment of very dangerous-looking Talking Beasts whom Shasta had not noticed before and who were mostly of the cat kind (leopards, panthers, and the like) went padding and growling to take up their positions on the left. The giants were ordered to the right, and before going there they all took off something they had been carrying on their backs and sat down for a moment. Then Shasta saw that what they had been carrying and were now putting on were pairs of boots: horrid, heavy, spiked boots which came up to their knees. Then they sloped their huge clubs over their shoulders and marched to their battle position. The archers, with Queen Lucy, fell to the rear and you could first see them bending their bows and then hear the twang-twang as they tested the strings. And wherever you looked you could see people tightening girths, putting on helmets, drawing swords, and throwing cloaks to the ground. There was hardly any talking now. It was very solemn and very dreadful. "I'm in for it now — I really am in for it now," thought Shasta. Then there came noises far ahead: the sound of many men shouting and a steady thud-thud-thud.

"Battering ram," whispered Corin. "They're battering the gate."

Even Corin looked quite serious now.

"Why doesn't King Edmund get *on*?" he said. "I can't stand this waiting about. Chilly too."

Shasta nodded: hoping he didn't look as frightened as he felt.

The trumpet at last! On the move now — now trotting — the banner streaming out in the wind. They had topped a low ridge now, and below them the whole scene suddenly opened out; a little, many-towered castle with its gate towards them. No moat, unfortunately, but of course the gate shut and the portcullis down. On the walls they could see, like little white dots, the faces of the defenders. Down below, about fifty of the Calormenes, dismounted, were steadily swinging a great tree trunk against the gate. But at once the scene changed. The main bulk of Rabadash's men had been on foot ready to assault the gate. But now he had seen the Narnians sweeping down from the ridge. There is no doubt those Calormenes are wonderfully trained. It seemed to Shasta only a second before a whole line of the enemy were on horseback again, wheeling round to meet them, swinging towards them.

And now a gallop. The ground between the two armies grew less every moment. Faster, faster. All swords out now, all shields up to the nose, all prayers said, all teeth clenched. Shasta was dreadfully frightened. But it suddenly came into his head, "If you funk this, you'll funk every battle all your life. Now or never."

But when at last the two lines met he had really very little idea of what happened. There was a frightful confusion and an appalling noise. His sword was knocked clean out of his hand pretty soon. And he'd got the reins tangled somehow. Then he found himself slipping. Then a spear came straight at him and as he ducked to avoid it he rolled right off his horse, bashed his left knuckles terribly against someone else's armour, and then—

But it is no use trying to describe the battle from Shasta's point of view; he understood too little of the fight in general and even of his own part in it. The best way I can tell you what really happened is to take you some miles away to where the Hermit of the Southern March sat gazing into the smooth pool beneath the spreading tree, with Bree and Hwin and Aravis beside him.

For it was in this pool that the Hermit looked when he wanted to know what was going on in the world outside the green walls of his hermitage. There, as in a mirror, he could see, at certain times, what was going on in the streets of cities far further south than Tashbaan, or what whips were putting into Redhaven in the remote Seven Isles, or what robbers or wild beasts stirred in the great Western forests between Lantern Waste and Telmar. And all this day he had hardly left his pool, even to eat or drink, for he knew that great events were afoot in Archenland. Aravis and the Horses gazed into it too. They could see it was a magic pool: instead of reflecting the tree and the sky it revealed cloudy and coloured shapes moving, always moving, in its depths. But they could see nothing clearly. The Hermit could and from time to time he told them what he saw. A little while before Shasta rode into his first battle, the Hermit had begun speaking like this:

"I see one – two – three eagles wheeling in the gap by Stormness Head. One is the oldest of all the eagles. He would not be out unless battle was at hand. I see him wheel to and fro, peering down sometimes at Anvard and sometimes to the east, behind Stormness. Ah – I see now what Rabadash and his men have been so busy at all day. They have felled and lopped a great tree and they are now coming out of the woods carrying it as a ram. They have learned something from the failure of last night's assault. He would have been wiser if he had set his men to making ladders: but it takes too long and he is impatient. Fool that he is! He ought to have ridden back to Tashbaan as soon as the first attack failed, for his whole plan depended on speed and surprise. Now they are bringing their ram into position. King Lune's men are shooting hard from the walls. Five Calormenes have fallen: but not many will. They have their shields above their heads. Rabadash is giving his orders now. With him are his most trusted lords, fierce Tarkaans from the eastern provinces. I can see their faces. There is Corradin of Castle Tormunt, and Azrooh, and Chlamash, and Ilgamuth of the twisted lip, and a tall Tarkaan with a crimson beard—"

"By the Mane, my old master Anradin!" said Bree.

"S-s-sh," said Aravis.

"Now the ram has started. If I could hear as well as see, what a noise that would make! Stroke after stroke: and no gate can stand it for ever. But wait! Something up by Stormness has scared the birds. They're coming out in masses. And wait again... I can't see yet... ah! Now I can. The whole ridge, up on the east, is black with horsemen. If only the wind would catch that standard and spread it out. They're over the ridge now, whoever they are. Aha! I've seen the banner now. Narnia, Narnia! It's the red lion. They're in full career down the hill now. I can see King Edmund. There's a woman behind among the archers. Oh!—"

"What is it?" asked Hwin breathlessly.

"All his cats are dashing out from the left of the line."

"Cats?" said Aravis.

"Great cats, leopards and such," said the Hermit impatiently. "I see, I see. The Cats are coming round in a circle to get at the horses of the dismounted men. A good stroke. The Calormene horses are mad with terror already. Now the Cats are in among them. But Rabadash has reformed his line and has a hundred men in the saddle. They're riding to meet the Narnians. There's only a hundred yards between the two lines now. Only fifty. I can see King Edmund, I can see the Lord Peridan. There are two mere children in the Narnian line. What can the King be about to let them into battle? Only ten yards – the lines have met. The Giants on the Narnian right are doing wonders... but one's down... shot through the eye, I suppose. The centre's all in a muddle. I can see more on the left. There are the two boys again. Lion alive! One is Prince Corin. The other, like him as two peas. It's your little Shasta. Corin is fighting like a man. He's killed a Calormene. I can see a bit of the centre now. Rabadash and Edmund almost met then, but the press has separated them—"

"What about Shasta?" said Aravis.

"Oh, the fool!" groaned the Hermit. "Poor, brave little fool. He knows nothing about this work. He's making no use at all of his shield. His whole side's exposed. He hasn't the faintest idea what to do with his sword. Oh, he's remembered it now. He's waving it wildly about. . . nearly cut his own pony's head off, and he will in a moment if he's not careful. It's been knocked out of his hand now. It's mere murder sending a child into the battle; he can't live five minutes. Duck, you fool – oh, he's down."

"Killed?" asked three voices breathlessly.

"How can I tell?" said the Hermit. "The Cats have done their work. All the riderless horses are dead or escaped now: no retreat for the Calormenes on *them*. Now the Cats are turning back into the main battle. They're leaping on the rams-men. The ram is down. Oh, good! Good! The gates are opening from the inside: there's going to be a sortie. The first three are out. It's King Lune in the middle: the brothers Dar and Darrin on each side of him. Behind them are Tran and Shar and Cole with his brother Colin. There are ten – twenty – nearly thirty of them out by now. The Calormene line is being forced back upon them. King Edmund is dealing marvellous strokes. He's just slashed Corradin's head off. Lots of Calormenes have thrown down their arms and are running for the woods. Those that remain are hard pressed. The Giants are closing in on the right – Cats on the left – King Lune from their rear. The Calormenes are a little knot now, fighting back to back. Your Tarkaan's down, Bree. Lune and Azrooh are fighting hand to hand; the King looks like winning – the King is keeping it up well – the King has won. Azrooh's down. King Edmund's down – no, he's up again: he's at it with Rabadash. They're fighting in the very gate of the castle. Several Calormenes have surrendered. Darrin has killed Ilgamuth. I can't see what's happened to Rabadash. I think he's dead, leaning against the castle wall, but I don't know. Chlamash and King Edmund are still fighting but the battle is over everywhere else. Chlamash has surrendered. The battle *is* over. The Calormenes are utterly defeated."

When Shasta fell off his horse he gave himself up for lost. But horses, even in battle, tread on human beings very much less than you would suppose. After a very horrible ten minutes or so Shasta realized suddenly that there were no longer any horses stamping about in the immediate neighbourhood and that the noise (for there were still a good many noises going on) was no longer that of a battle. He sat up and stared about him. Even he, little as he knew of battles, could soon see that the Archenlanders and Narnians had won. The only living Calormenes he could see were prisoners, the castle gates were wide open, and King Lune and King Edmund were shaking hands across the battering ram. From the circle of lords and warriors around them there arose a sound of breathless and excited, but obviously cheerful, conversation. And then, suddenly, it all united and swelled into a great roar of laughter.

Shasta picked himself up, feeling uncommonly stiff, and ran towards the sound to see what the joke was. A very curious sight met his eyes. The unfortunate Rabadash appeared to be suspended from the castle walls. His feet, which were about two feet from the ground, were kicking wildly. His chain-shirt was somehow hitched up so that it was horribly tight under the arms and came halfway over his face. In fact he looked just as a man looks if you catch him in the very act of getting into a stiff shirt that is a little too small for him. As far as could be made out afterwards (and you may be sure the story was well talked over for many a day) what happened was something like this. Early in the battle one of the Giants had made an unsuccessful stamp at Rabadash with his spiked boot: unsuccessful because it didn't crush Raba-dash, which was what the Giant had intended, but not quite useless because one of the spikes tore the chain mail, just as you or I might tear an ordinary shirt. So Rabadash, by the time he encountered Edmund at the gate, had a hole in the back of his hauberk. And when Edmund pressed him back nearer and nearer to the wall, he jumped up on a mounting block and stood there raining down blows on Edmund from above. But then, finding that this position, by raising him above the heads of everyone else, made him a mark for every arrow from the Narnian bows, he decided to jump down again. And he meant to look and sound – no doubt for a moment he *did* look and sound – very grand and very dreadful as he jumped, crying, "The bolt of Tash falls from above." But he had to jump sideways because the crowd in front of him left him no landing place in that direction. And then, in the neatest way you could wish, the tear in the back of his hauberk caught on a hook in the wall. (Ages ago this hook had had a ring in it for tying horses to.) And there he found himself, like a piece of washing hung up to dry, with everyone laughing at him.

"Let me down, Edmund," howled Rabadash. "Let me down and fight me like a king and a man; or if you are too great a coward to do that, kill me at once."

"Certainly," began King Edmund, but King Lune interrupted.

"By your Majesty's good leave," said King Lune to Edmund. "Not so." Then turning to Rabadash he said, "Your royal Highness, if you had given that challenge a week ago, I'll answer for it there was no one in King Edmund's dominion, from the High King down to the smallest Talking Mouse, who would have refused it. But by attacking our castle of Anvard in time of peace without defiance sent, you have proved yourself no knight, but a traitor, and one rather to be whipped by the hangman than to be suffered to cross swords with any person of honour. Take him down, bind him, and carry him within till our pleasure is further known."

Strong hands wrenched Rabadash's sword from him and he was carried away into the castle, shouting, threatening, cursing, and even crying. For though he could have faced torture he couldn't bear being made ridiculous. In Tashbaan everyone had always taken him seriously.

At that moment Corin ran up to Shasta, seized his hand and started dragging him towards King Lune. "Here he is, Father, here he is," cried Corin.

"Aye, and here *thou* art, at last," said the King in a very gruff voice. "And hast been in the battle, clean contrary to your obedience. A boy to break a father's heart! At your age a rod to your breech were fitter than a sword in your fist, ha!" But everyone, including Corin, could see that the King was very proud of him.

"Chide him no more, Sire, if it please you," said Lord Darrin. "His Highness would not be your son if he did not inherit your conditions. It would grieve your Majesty more if he had to be reproved for the opposite fault."

"Well, well," grumbled the King. "We'll pass it over for this time. And now——"

What came next surprised Shasta as much as anything that had ever happened to him in his life. He found himself suddenly embraced in a bear-like hug by King Lune and kissed on both cheeks. Then the King set him down again and said, "Stand here together, boys, and let all the court see you. Hold up your heads. Now, gentlemen, look on them both. Has any man any doubts?"

And still Shasta could not understand why everyone stared at him and at Corin, nor what all the cheering was about.

CHAPTER FOURTEEN

HOW BREE BECAME A WISER HORSE

We must now return to Aravis and the Horses. The Hermit, watching his pool, was able to tell them that Shasta was not killed or even seriously wounded, for he saw him get up and saw how affectionately he was greeted by King Lune. But as he could only see, not hear, he did not know what anyone was saying and, once the fighting had stopped and the talking had begun, it was not worthwhile looking in the pool any longer.

Next morning, while the Hermit was indoors, the three of them discussed what they should do next.

"I've had enough of this," said Hwin. "The Hermit has been very good to us and I'm very much obliged to him, I'm sure. But I'm getting as fat as a pet pony, eating all day and getting no exercise. Let's go on to Narnia."

"Oh, not today, Ma'am," said Bree. "I wouldn't hurry things. Some other day, don't you think?"

"We must see Shasta first and say goodbye to him — and — apologize," said Aravis.

"Exactly!" said Bree with great enthusiasm. "Just what I was going to say."

"Oh, of course," said Hwin. "I expect he is in Anvard. Naturally we'd look in on him and say goodbye. But that's on our way. And why shouldn't we start at once? After all, I thought it was Narnia we all wanted to get to?"

"I suppose so," said Aravis. She was beginning to wonder what exactly she would do when she got there, and was feeling a little lonely.

"Of course, of course," said Bree hastily. "But there's no need to rush things, if you know what I mean."

"No, I don't know what you mean," said Hwin. "Why don't you want to go?"

"M-m-m, broo-hoo," muttered Bree. "Well, don't you see, Ma'am – it's an important occasion – returning to one's country – entering society – the best society – it is so essential to make a good impression – not perhaps looking quite ourselves, yet, eh?"

Hwin broke out into a horse-laugh. "It's your tail, Bree! I see it all now. You want to wait till your tail's grown again! And we don't even know if tails are worn long in Narnia. Really, Bree, you're as vain as that Tarkheena in Tashbaan!"

"You *are* silly, Bree," said Aravis.

"By the Lion's Mane, Tarkheena, I'm nothing of the sort," said Bree indignantly. "I have a proper respect for myself and for my fellow horses, that's all."

"Bree," said Aravis, who was not very interested in the cut of his tail, "I've been wanting to ask you something for a long time. Why do you keep on swearing *By the Lion* and *By the Lion's Mane*? I thought you hated lions."

"So I do," answered Bree. "But when I speak of *the* Lion, of course I mean Aslan, the great deliverer of Narnia who drove away the Witch and the Winter. All Narnians swear by *him*."

"But is he a lion?"

"No, no, of course not," said Bree in a rather shocked voice.

"All the stories about him in Tashbaan say he is," replied Aravis. "And if he isn't a lion why do you call him a lion?"

"Well, you'd hardly understand that at your age," said Bree. "And I was only a little foal when I left so I don't quite fully understand it myself."

(Bree was standing with his back to the green wall while he said this, and the other two were facing him. He was talking in rather a superior tone with his eyes half shut; that was why he didn't see the changed expression in the faces of Hwin and Aravis. They had good reason to have open mouths and staring eyes, because while Bree spoke they saw an enormous lion leap up from outside and balance itself on the top of the green wall; only it was a brighter yellow and it was bigger and more beautiful and more alarming than any lion they had ever seen. And at once it jumped down inside the wall and began approaching Bree from behind. It made no noise at all. And Hwin and Aravis couldn't make any noise themselves, no more than if they were frozen.)

"No doubt," continued Bree, "when they speak of him as a Lion, they only mean he's as strong as a lion or (to our enemies, of course) as fierce as a lion. Or something of that kind. Even a little girl like you, Aravis, must see that it would be quite absurd to suppose he is a real lion. Indeed it would be disrespectful. If he was a lion he'd have to be a beast just like the rest of us. Why!" (and here Bree began to laugh) "If he was a lion he'd have four paws, and a tail, and *Whiskers*!. . . Aie, ooh, hoo-hoo! Help!"

For just as he said the word *Whiskers* one of Aslan's had actually tickled his ear. Bree shot away like an arrow to the other side of the enclosure and there turned; the wall was too high for him to jump and he could fly no further. Aravis and Hwin both started back. There was about a second of intense silence.

Then Hwin, though shaking all over, gave a strange little neigh, and trotted across to the Lion.

"Please," she said, "you're so beautiful. You may eat me if you like. I'd sooner be eaten by you than fed by anyone else."

"Dearest daughter," said Aslan, planting a lion's kiss on her twitching, velvet nose, "I knew you would not be long in coming to me. Joy shall be yours."

Then he lifted his head and spoke in a louder voice:

"Now, Bree," he said, "you poor, proud frightened Horse, draw near. Nearer still, my son. Do not dare not to dare. Touch me. Smell me. Here are my paws, here is my tail, these are my whiskers. I am a true Beast."

"Aslan," said Bree in a shaken voice, "I'm afraid I must be rather a fool."

"Happy the Horse who knows that while he is still young. Or the Human either. Draw near, Aravis my daughter. See! My paws are velveted. You will not be torn this time."

"This time, sir?" said Aravis.

"It was I who wounded you," said Aslan. "I am the only lion you met in all your journeyings. Do you know why I tore you?"

"No, sir."

"The scratches on your back, tear for tear, throb for throb, blood for blood, were equal to the stripes laid on the back of your stepmother's slave because of the drugged sleep you cast upon her. You needed to know what it felt like."

"Yes, sir. Please——"

"Ask on, my dear," said Aslan.

"Will any more harm come to her by what I did?"

"Child," said the Lion, "I am telling you your story, not hers. No one is told any story but their own." Then he shook his head and spoke in a lighter voice:

"Be merry, little ones," he said. "We shall meet again soon. But before that you will have another visitor." Then in one bound he reached the top of the wall and vanished from their sight.

Strange to say, they felt no inclination to talk to one another about him after he had gone. They all moved slowly away to different parts of the quiet grass and there paced to and fro, each alone, thinking.

About half an hour later the two Horses were summoned to the back of the house to eat something nice that the Hermit had got ready for them and Aravis, still walking and thinking, was startled by the harsh sound of a trumpet outside the gate.

"Who is there?" asked Aravis.

"His Royal Highness Prince Cor of Archenland," said a voice from outside.

Aravis undid the door and opened it, drawing back a little way to let the strangers in.

Two soldiers with halberds came first and took their stand at each side of the entry. Then followed a herald, and the trumpeter.

"His Royal Highness Prince Cor of Archenland desires an audience of the Lady Aravis," said the Herald. Then he and the trumpeter drew aside and bowed and the soldiers saluted and the Prince himself came in. All his attendants withdrew and closed the gate behind them.

The Prince bowed, and a very clumsy bow for a Prince it was. Aravis curtsied in the Calormene style (which is not at all like ours) and did it very well because, of course, she had been taught how. Then she looked up and saw what sort of person this Prince was.

She saw a mere boy. He was bare-headed and his fair hair was encircled with a very thin band of gold, hardly thicker than a wire. His upper tunic was of white cambric, as fine as a handkerchief, so that the bright red tunic beneath it showed through. His left hand, which rested on his enamelled sword hilt, was bandaged.

Aravis looked twice at his face before she gasped and said, "Why! It's Shasta!"

Shasta all at once turned very red and began speaking very quickly. "Look here, Aravis," he said, "I do hope you won't think I'm got up like this (and the trumpeter and all) to try to impress you or make out that I'm different or any rot of that sort. Because I'd far rather have come in my old clothes, but they're burnt now, and my father said—"

"Your father?" said Aravis.

"Apparently King Lune is my father," said Shasta. "I might really have guessed it, Corin being so like me. We were twins, you see. Oh, and my name isn't Shasta, it's Cor."

"Cor is a nicer name than Shasta," said Aravis.

"Brothers' names run like that in Archenland," said Shasta (or Prince Cor as we must now call him). "Like Dar and Darrin, Cole and Colin and so on."

"Shasta— I mean Cor," said Aravis. "No, shut up. There's something I've got to say at once. I'm sorry I've been such a pig. But I did change before I knew you were a Prince, honestly I did: when you went back, and faced the Lion."

"It wasn't really going to kill you at all, that Lion," said Cor.

"I know," said Aravis, nodding. Both were still and solemn for a moment as each saw that the other knew about Aslan.

Suddenly Aravis remembered Cor's bandaged hand. "I say!" she cried, "I forgot! You've been in a battle. Is that a wound?"

"A mere scratch," said Cor, using for the first time a rather lordly tone. But a moment later he burst out laughing and said, "If you want to know the truth, it isn't a proper wound at all. I only took the skin off my knuckles just as any clumsy fool might do without going near a battle."

"Still, you were in the battle," said Aravis. "It must have been wonderful."

"It wasn't at all like what I thought," said Cor.

"But Sha— Cor, I mean – you haven't told me anything yet about King Lune and how he found out who you were."

"Well, let's sit down," said Cor. "For it's rather a long story. And by the way, Father's an absolute brick. I'd be just as pleased – or very nearly – at finding he was my father even if he weren't a king. Even though Education and all sorts of horrible things are going to happen to me. But you want the story. Well, Corin and I are twins. And about a week after we were both born, apparently, they took us to a wise old Centaur in Narnia to be blessed or something. Now this Centaur was a prophet as a good many Centaurs are. Perhaps you haven't seen any centaurs yet? There were some in the battle yesterday. Most remarkable people, but I can't say I feel quite at home with them yet. I say, Aravis, there are going to be a lot of things to get used to in these northern countries."

"Yes, there are," said Aravis. "But get on with the story."

"Well, as soon as he saw Corin and me, it seems this Centaur looked at me and said, 'A day will come when that boy will save Archenland from the deadliest danger in which ever she lay'. So of course my Father and Mother were very pleased. But there was someone present who wasn't. This was a chap called the Lord Bar who had been Father's Lord Chancellor. And apparently he'd done something wrong – *bezzling* or some word like that – I didn't understand that part very well – and Father had had to dismiss him. But nothing else was done to him and he was allowed to go on living in Archenland. But he must have been as bad as he could be, for it came out afterwards he had been in the pay of the Tisroc and had sent a lot of secret information to Tashbaan. So as soon as he heard I was going to save Archenland from a great danger he decided I must be put out of the way. Well, he succeeded in kidnapping me (I don't exactly know how) and rode away down the Winding Arrow to the coast. He'd had everything prepared and there was a ship manned with his own followers lying ready for him and he put out to sea with me on board. But Father got wind of it, though not quite in time, and was after him as quickly as he could. The Lord Bar was already at sea when Father reached the coast, but not out of sight. And Father was embarked in one of his own warships within twenty minutes.

"It must have been a wonderful chase. They were six days following Bar's galleon and brought her to battle on the seventh. It was a great sea-fight (I heard a lot about it yesterday evening) from ten o'clock in the morning till sunset. Our people took the ship in the end. But I wasn't there. The Lord Bar himself had been killed in the battle. But one of his men said that, early that morning, as soon as he saw he was certain to be overhauled, Bar had given me to one of his knights and sent us both away in the ship's boat. And that boat was never seen again. But of course that was the same boat that Aslan (he seems to be at the back of all the stories) pushed ashore at the right place for Arsheesh to pick me up. I wish I knew that knight's name, for he must have kept me alive and starved himself to do it."

"I suppose Aslan would say that was part of someone else's story," said Aravis.

"I was forgetting that," said Cor.

"And I wonder how the prophecy will work out," said Aravis, "and what the great danger is that you're to save Archenland from."

"Well," said Cor rather awkwardly, "they seem to think I've done it already."

Aravis clapped her hands. "Why, of course!" she said. "How stupid I am. And how wonderful! Archenland can never be in much greater danger than it was when Rabadash had crossed the Arrow with his two hundred horse and you hadn't yet got through with your message. Don't you feel proud?"

"I think I feel a bit scared," said Cor.

"And you'll be living at Anvard now," said Aravis rather wistfully.

"Oh!" said Cor. "I'd nearly forgotten what I came about. Father wants you to come and live with us. He says there's been no lady in the court (they call it the court, I don't know why) since Mother died. Do, Aravis. You'll like Father – and Corin. They're not like me; they've been properly brought up. You needn't be afraid that—"

"Oh, stop it," said Aravis, "or we'll have a real fight. Of course I'll come."

"Now let's go and see the Horses," said Cor.

There was a great and joyous meeting between Bree and Cor, and Bree, who was still in a rather subdued frame of mind, agreed to set out for Anvard at once: he and Hwin would cross into Narnia on the following day. All four bade an affectionate farewell to the Hermit and promised that they would visit him again soon. By about the middle of the morning they were on their way. The Horses had expected that Aravis and Cor would ride, but Cor explained that except in war, where everyone must do what he can do best, no one in Narnia or Archenland ever dreamed of mounting a Talking Horse.

This reminded poor Bree again of how little he knew about Narnian customs and what dreadful mistakes he might make. So while Hwin strolled along in a happy dream, Bree got more nervous and more self-conscious with every step he took.

"Buck up, Bree," said Cor. "It's far worse for me than for you. You aren't going to be *educated*. I shall be learning reading and writing and heraldry and dancing and history and music while you'll be galloping and rolling on the hills of Narnia to your heart's content."

"But that's just the point," groaned Bree. "Do Talking Horses roll? Supposing they don't? I can't bear to give it up. What do you think, Hwin?"

"I'm going to roll anyway," said Hwin. "I don't suppose any of them will care two lumps of sugar whether you roll or not."

"Are we near the castle?" said Bree to Cor.

"Round the next bend," said the Prince.

"Well," said Bree, "I'm going to have a good one now: it may be the last. Wait for me a minute."

It was five minutes before he rose again, blowing hard and covered with bits of bracken.

"Now I'm ready," he said in a voice of profound gloom. "Lead on, Prince Cor. Narnia and the North."

But he looked more like a horse going to a funeral than a long-lost captive returning to home and freedom.

CHAPTER FIFTEEN

RABADASH THE RIDICULOUS

The next turn of the road brought them out from among the trees and there, across green lawns, sheltered from the north wind by the high wooded ridge at its back, they saw the castle of Anvard. It was very old and built of a warm, reddish-brown stone.

Before they had reached the gate King Lune came out to meet them, not looking at all like Aravis's idea of a king and wearing the oldest of old clothes; for he had just come from making a round of the kennels with his Huntsman and had only stopped for a moment to wash his doggy hands. But the bow with which he greeted Aravis as he took her hand would have been stately enough for an Emperor.

"Little lady," he said, "we bid you very heartily welcome. If my dear wife were still alive we could make you better cheer but could not do it with a better will. And I am sorry that you have had misfortunes and been driven from your father's house, which cannot but be a grief to you. My son Cor has told me about your adventures together and all your valour."

"It was he who did all that, Sir," said Aravis. "Why, he rushed at a lion to save me."

"Eh, what's that?" said King Lune, his face brightening. "I haven't heard that part of the story."

Then Aravis told it. And Cor, who had very much wanted the story to be known, though he felt he couldn't tell it himself, didn't enjoy it so much as he had expected, and indeed felt rather foolish. But his father enjoyed it very much indeed and in the course of the next few weeks told it to so many people that Cor wished it had never happened.

Then the King turned to Hwin and Bree and was just as polite to them as to Aravis, and asked them a lot of questions about their families and where they had lived in Narnia before they had been captured. The Horses were rather tongue-tied for they weren't yet used to being talked to as equals by Humans – grown-up Humans, that is. They didn't mind Aravis and Cor.

Presently Queen Lucy came out from the castle and joined them and King Lune said to Aravis, "My dear, here is a loving friend of our house, and she has been seeing that your apartments are put to rights for you better than I could have done it."

"You'd like to come and see them, wouldn't you?" said Lucy, kissing Aravis. They liked each other at once and soon went away together to talk about Aravis's bedroom and Aravis's boudoir and about getting clothes for her, and all the sort of things girls do talk about on such an occasion.

After lunch, which they had on the terrace (it was cold birds and game pie and wine and bread and cheese), King Lune ruffled up his brow and heaved a sigh and said, "Heigh-ho! We have still that sorry creature Rabadash on our hands, my friends, and must needs resolve what to do with him."

Lucy was sitting on the King's right and Aravis on his left. King Edmund sat at one end of the table and the Lord Darrin faced him at the other. Dar and Peridan and Cor and Corin were on the same side as the King.

"Your Majesty would have a perfect right to strike off his head," said Peridan. "Such an assault as he made puts him on a level with assassins."

"It is very true," said Edmund. "But even a traitor may mend. I have known one that did." And he looked very thoughtful.

"To kill this Rabadash would go near to raising war with the Tisroc," said Darrin.

"A fig for the Tisroc," said King Lune. "His strength is in numbers and numbers will never cross the desert. But I have no stomach for killing men (even traitors) in cold blood. To have cut his throat in the battle would have eased my heart mightily: but this is a different thing."

"By my counsel," said Lucy, "your Majesty shall give him another trial. Let him go free on strait promise of fair dealing in the future. It may be that he will keep his word."

"Maybe Apes will grow honest, Sister," said Edmund. "But, by the Lion, if he breaks it again, may it be in such time and place that any of us could swap off his head in clean battle."

"It shall be tried," said the King: and then to one of the attendants, "Send for the prisoner, friend."

Rabadash was brought before them in chains. To look at him anyone would have supposed that he had passed the night in a noisome dungeon without food or water; but in reality he had been shut up in quite a comfortable room and provided with an excellent supper. But as he was sulking far too furiously to touch the supper and had spent the whole night stamping and roaring and cursing, he naturally did not now look his best.

"Your royal Highness needs not to be told," said King Lune, "that by the law of nations as well as by all reasons of prudent policy, we have as good right to your head as ever one mortal man had against another. Nevertheless, in consideration of your youth and the ill nurture, devoid of all *gentilesse* and courtesy, which you have doubtless had in the land of slaves and tyrants, we are disposed to set you free, unharmed, on these conditions: first, that—"

"Curse you for a barbarian dog!" spluttered Rabadash. "Do you think I will even hear your conditions? Faugh! You talk very largely of nurture and I know not what. It's easy, to a man in chains, ha! Take off these vile bonds, give me a sword, and let any of you who dares then debate with me."

Nearly all the lords sprang to their feet, and Corin shouted:

"Father! Can I *box* him? Please."

"Peace! Your Majesties! My Lords!" said King Lune. "Have we no more gravity among us than to be so chafed by the taunt of a pajock? Sit down, Corin, or shalt leave the table. I ask your Highness again, to hear our conditions."

"I hear no conditions from barbarians and sorcerers," said Rabadash. "Not one of you dare touch a hair of my head. Every insult you have heaped on me shall be paid with oceans of Narnian and Archenlandish blood. Terrible shall the vengeance of the Tisroc be: even now. But kill me, and the burnings and torturings in these northern lands shall become a tale to frighten the world a thousand years hence. Beware! Beware! Beware! The bolt of Tash falls from above!"

"Does it ever get caught on a hook halfway?" asked Corin.

"Shame, Corin," said the King. "Never taunt a man save when he is stronger than you: then, as you please."

"Oh, you foolish Rabadash," sighed Lucy.

Next moment Cor wondered why everyone at the table had risen and was standing perfectly still. Of course he did the same himself. And then he saw the reason. Aslan was among them though no one had seen him coming. Rabadash started as the immense shape of the Lion paced softly in between him and his accusers.

"Rabadash," said Aslan. "Take heed. Your doom is very near, but you may still avoid it. Forget your pride (what have you to be proud of?) and your anger (who has done you wrong?) and accept the mercy of these good kings."

Then Rabadash rolled his eyes and spread out his mouth into a horrible, long mirthless grin like a shark, and wagged his ears up and down (anyone can learn how to do this if they take the trouble). He had always found this very effective in Calormen. The bravest had trembled when he made these faces, and ordinary people had fallen to the floor, and sensitive people had often fainted. But what Rabadash hadn't realized is that it is very easy to frighten people who know you can have them boiled alive the moment you give the word. The grimaces didn't look at all alarming in Archenland; indeed Lucy only thought Rabadash was going to be sick.

"Demon! Demon! Demon!" shrieked the Prince. "I know you. You are the foul fiend of Narnia. You are the enemy of the gods. Learn who *I* am, horrible phantasm. I am descended from Tash, the inexorable, the irresistible. The curse of Tash is upon you. Lightning in the shape of scorpions shall be rained on you. The mountains of Narnia shall be ground into dust. The——"

"Have a care, Rabadash," said Aslan quietly. "The doom is nearer now: it is at the door: it has lifted the latch."

"Let the skies fall," shrieked Rabadash. "Let the earth gape! Let blood and fire obliterate the world! But be sure I will never desist till I have dragged to my palace by her hair the barbarian queen, the daughter of dogs, the——"

"The hour has struck," said Aslan: and Rabadash saw, to his supreme horror, that everyone had begun to laugh.

They couldn't help it. Rabadash had been wagging his ears all the time and as soon as Aslan said, "The hour has struck!" the ears began to change. They grew longer and more pointed and soon were covered with grey hair. And while everyone was wondering where they had seen ears like that before, Rabadash's face began to change too. It grew longer, and thicker at the top and larger eyed, and the nose sank back into the face (or else the face swelled out and became all nose) and there was hair all over it. And his arms grew longer and came down in front of him till his hands were resting on the ground: only they weren't hands, now, they were hooves. And he was standing on all fours, and his clothes disappeared, and everyone laughed louder and louder (because they couldn't help it) for now what had been Rabadash was, simply and unmistakably, a donkey. The terrible thing was that his human speech lasted just a moment longer than his human shape, so that when he realized the change that was coming over him, he screamed out:

"Oh, not a Donkey! Mercy! If it were even a horse – e'en – a hor – eeh – auh, eeh-auh." And so the words died away into a donkey's bray.

"Now hear me, Rabadash," said Aslan. "Justice shall be mixed with mercy. You shall not always be an Ass."

At this of course the Donkey twitched its ears forward – and that also was so funny that everybody laughed all the more. They tried not to, but they tried in vain.

"You have appealed to Tash," said Aslan. "And in the temple of Tash you shall be healed. You must stand before the altar of Tash in Tashbaan at the great Autumn Feast this year and there, in the sight of all Tashbaan, your ass's shape will fall from you and all men will know you for Prince Rabadash. But as long as you live, if ever you go more than ten miles away from the great temple in Tashbaan you shall instantly become again as you now are. And from that second change there will be no return."

There was a short silence and then they all stirred and looked at one another as if they were waking from sleep. Aslan was gone. But there was a brightness in the air and on the grass, and a joy in their hearts, which assured them that he had been no dream: and anyway, there was the donkey in front of them.

King Lune was the kindest-hearted of men and on seeing his enemy in this regrettable condition he forgot all his anger.

"Your royal Highness," he said. "I am most truly sorry that things have come to this extremity. Your Highness will bear witness that it was none of our doing. And of course we shall be delighted to provide your Highness with shipping back to Tashbaan for the – er – treatment which Aslan has prescribed. You shall have every comfort which your Highness's situation allows: the best of the cattle-boats – the freshest carrots and thistles—"

But a deafening bray from the Donkey and a well-aimed kick at one of the guards made it clear that these kindly offers were ungratefully received.

And here, to get him out of the way, I'd better finish off the story of Rabadash. He (or it) was duly sent back by boat to Tashbaan and brought into the temple of Tash at the great Autumn Festival, and then he became a man again. But of course four or five thousand people had seen the transformation and the affair could not possibly be hushed up. And after the old Tisroc's death when Rabadash became Tisroc in his place he turned out the most peaceable Tisroc Calormen had ever known. This was because, not daring to go more than ten miles from Tashbaan, he could never go on a war himself: and he didn't want his Tarkaans to win fame in the wars at his expense, for that is the way Tisrocs get overthrown. But though his reasons were selfish, it made things much more comfortable for all the smaller countries round Calormen. His own people never forgot that he had been a donkey. During his reign, and to his face, he was called Rabadash the Peacemaker, but after his death and behind his back he was called Rabadash the Ridiculous, and if you look him up in a good History of Calormen (try the local library) you will find him under that name. And to this day in Calormene schools, if you do anything unusually stupid, you are very likely to be called "a second Rabadash".

Meanwhile at Anvard everyone was very glad that he had been disposed of before the real fun began, which was a grand feast held that evening on the lawn before the castle, with dozens of lanterns to help the moonlight. And the wine flowed and tales were told and jokes were cracked, and then silence was made and the King's poet with two fiddlers stepped out into the middle of the circle. Aravis and Cor prepared themselves to be bored, for the only poetry they knew was the Calormene kind, and you know now what that was like. But at the very first scrape of the fiddles a rocket seemed to go up inside their heads, and the poet sang the great old lay of Fair Olvin and how he fought the Giant Pire and turned him into stone (and that is the origin of Mount Pire — it was a two-headed giant) and won the Lady Liln for his bride; and when it was over they wished it was going to begin again. And though Bree couldn't sing he told the story of the fight at Zulindreh. And Lucy told again (they had all, except Aravis and Cor, heard it many times but they all wanted it again) the Tale of the Wardrobe and how she and King Edmund and Queen Susan and Peter the High King had first come into Narnia.

And presently, as was certain to happen sooner or later, King Lune said it was time for young people to be in bed. "And tomorrow, Cor," he added, "shalt come over all the castle with me and see the estate, and mark all its strength and weakness: for it will be thine to guard when I'm gone."

"But Corin will be the King then, Father," said Cor.

"Nay, lad," said King Lune, "thou art my heir. The crown comes to thee."

"But I don't want it," said Cor. "I'd far rather—"

"'Tis no question what thou wantest, Cor, nor I either. 'Tis in the course of law."

"But if we're twins we must be the same age."

"Nay," said the King with a laugh. "One must come first. Art Corin's elder by full twenty minutes. And his better too, let's hope, though that's no great mastery." And he looked at Corin with a twinkle in his eyes.

"But, Father, couldn't you make whichever you like to be the next King?"

"No. The King's under the law, for it's the law makes him a king. Hast no more power to start away from thy crown than any sentry from his post."

"Oh dear," said Cor. "I don't want to at all. And Corin — I am most dreadfully sorry. I never dreamed my turning up was going to chisel you out of your kingdom."

"Hurray! Hurray!" said Corin. "I shan't have to be King. I shan't have to be King. I'll always be a prince. It's princes have all the fun."

"And that's truer than thy brother knows, Cor," said King Lune. "For this is what it means to be a king: to be first in every desperate attack and last in every desperate retreat, and when there's hunger in the land (as must be now and then in bad years) to wear finer clothes and laugh louder over a scantier meal than any man in your land."

When the two boys were going upstairs to bed Cor again asked Corin if nothing could be done about it. And Corin said:

"If you say another word about it, I'll – I'll knock you down."

It would be nice to end the story by saying that after that the two brothers never disagreed about anything again, but I am afraid it would not be true. In reality they quarrelled and fought just about as often as any other two boys would, and all their fights ended (if they didn't begin) with Cor getting knocked down. For though, when they had both grown up and become swordsmen, Cor was the most dangerous man in battle, neither he nor anyone else in the North Countries could ever equal Corin as a boxer. That was how he got his name of Corin Thunder-Fist; and how he performed his great exploit against the Lapsed Bear of Stormness, which was really a Talking Bear but had gone back to Wild Bear habits. Corin climbed up to its lair on the Narnian side of Stormness one winter day when the snow was on the hills and boxed it without a time-keeper for thirty-three rounds. And at the end it couldn't see out of its eyes and became a reformed character.

Aravis also had many quarrels (and, I'm afraid, even fights) with Cor, but they always made it up again: so that years later, when they were grown up, they were so used to quarrelling and making it up again that they got married so as to go on doing it more conveniently. And after King Lune's death they made a good King and Queen of Archenland, and Ram the Great, the most famous of all the kings of Archenland, was their son. Bree and Hwin lived happily to a great age in Narnia and both got married but not to one another. And there weren't many months in which one or both of them didn't come trotting over the pass to visit their friends at Anvard.

PRINCE CASPIAN

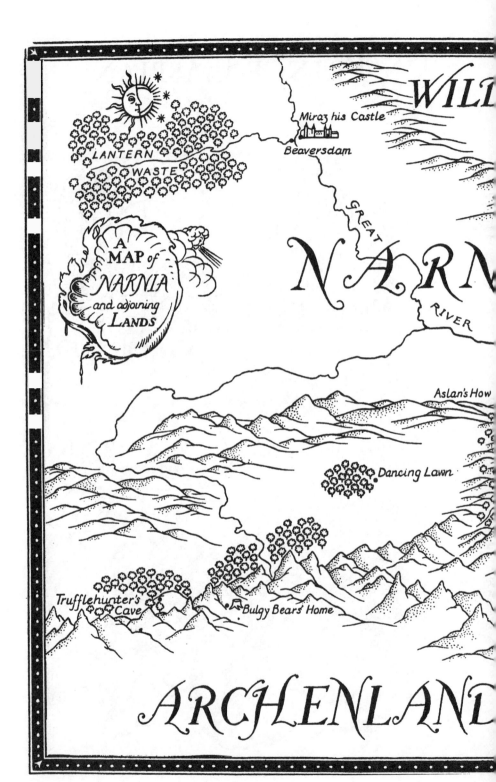

ANDS _of the_ NORTH

BERUNA

RUSH

Cair Paravel

GLASSWATER

Prince Caspian

Contents

CHAPTER ONE

THE ISLAND

Once there were four children whose names were Peter, Susan, Edmund and Lucy, and it has been told in another book called *The Lion, the Witch and the Wardrobe* how they had a remarkable adventure. They had opened the door of a magic wardrobe and found themselves in a quite different world from ours, and in that different world they had become Kings and Queens in a country called Narnia. While they were in Narnia they seemed to reign for years and years; but when they came back through the door and found themselves in England again, it all seemed to have taken no time at all. At any rate, no one noticed that they had ever been away, and they never told anyone except one very wise grown-up.

That had all happened a year ago, and now all four of them were sitting on a seat at a railway station with trunks and playboxes piled up round them. They were, in fact, on their way back to school. They had travelled together as far as this station, which was a junction; and here, in a few minutes, one train would arrive and take the girls away to one school, and in about half an hour another train would arrive and the boys would go off to another school. The first part of the journey, when they were all together, always seemed to be part of the holidays; but now when they would be saying goodbye and going different ways so soon, everyone felt that the holidays were really over and everyone felt their term-time feeling beginning again, and they were all rather gloomy and no one could think of anything to say. Lucy was going to boarding school for the first time.

It was an empty, sleepy, country station and there was hardly anyone on the platform except themselves. Suddenly Lucy gave a sharp little cry, like someone who has been stung by a wasp.

"What's up, Lu?" said Edmund – and then suddenly broke off and made a noise like "Ow!"

"What on earth—" began Peter, and then he too suddenly changed what he had been going to say. Instead, he said, "Susan, let go! What are you doing? Where are you dragging me to?"

"I'm not touching you," said Susan. "Someone is pulling *me*. Oh – oh – oh – stop it!"

Everyone noticed that all the others' faces had gone very white.

"I felt just the same," said Edmund in a breathless voice. "As if I were being dragged along. A most frightful pulling – ugh! It's beginning again."

"Me too," said Lucy. "Oh, I can't bear it."

"Look sharp!" shouted Edmund. "All catch hands and keep together. This is magic – I can tell by the feeling. Quick!"

"Yes," said Susan. "Hold hands. Oh, I do wish it would stop – oh!"

Next moment the luggage, the seat, the platform, and the station had completely vanished. The four children, holding hands and panting, found themselves standing in a woody place – such a woody place that branches were sticking into them and there was hardly room to move. They all rubbed their eyes and took a deep breath.

"Oh, Peter!" exclaimed Lucy. "Do you think we can possibly have got back to Narnia?"

"It might be anywhere," said Peter. "I can't see a yard in all these trees. Let's try to get into the open – if there is any open."

With some difficulty, and with some stings from nettles and pricks from thorns, they struggled out of the thicket. Then they had another surprise. Everything became much brighter, and after a few steps they found themselves at the edge of the wood, looking down on a sandy beach. A few yards away a very calm sea was falling on the sand with such tiny ripples that it made hardly any sound. There was no land in sight and no clouds in the sky. The sun was about where it ought to be at ten o'clock in the morning, and the sea was a dazzling blue. They stood sniffing in the sea-smell.

"By Jove!" said Peter. "This is good enough."

Five minutes later everyone was barefooted and wading in the cool clear water.

"This is better than being in a stuffy train on the way back to Latin and French and Algebra!" said Edmund. And then for quite a long time there was no more talking, only splashing and looking for shrimps and crabs.

"All the same," said Susan presently, "I suppose we'll have to make some plans. We shall want something to eat before long."

"We've got the sandwiches Mother gave us for the journey," said Edmund. "At least I've got mine."

"Not me," said Lucy. "Mine were in my little bag."

"So were mine," said Susan.

"Mine are in my coat pocket, there on the beach," said Peter. "That'll be two lunches among four. This isn't going to be such fun."

"At present," said Lucy, "I want something to drink more than something to eat."

Everyone else now felt thirsty, as one usually is after wading in salt water under a hot sun.

"It's like being shipwrecked," remarked Edmund. "In the books they always find springs of clear, fresh water on the island. We'd better go and look for them."

"Does that mean we have to go back into all that thick wood?" said Susan.

"Not a bit of it," said Peter. "If there are streams they're bound to come down to the sea, and if we walk along the beach we're bound to come to them."

They all now waded back and went first across the smooth, wet sand and then up to the dry, crumbly sand that sticks to one's toes, and began putting on their shoes and socks. Edmund and Lucy wanted to leave them behind and do their exploring with bare feet, but Susan said this would be a mad thing to do. "We might never find them again," she pointed out, "and we shall want them if we're still here when night comes and it begins to be cold."

When they were dressed again they set out along the shore with the sea on their left hand and the wood on their right. Except for an occasional seagull it was a very quiet place. The wood was so thick and tangled that they could hardly see into it at all; and nothing in it moved – not a bird, not even an insect.

Shells and seaweed and anemones, or tiny crabs in rock-pools, are all very well, but you soon get tired of them if you are thirsty. The children's feet, after the change from the cool water, felt hot and heavy. Susan and Lucy had raincoats to carry. Edmund had put down his coat on the station seat just before the magic overtook them, and he and Peter took it in turns to carry Peter's great-coat.

Presently the shore began to curve round to the right. About quarter of an hour later, after they had crossed a rocky ridge which ran out into a point, it made quite a sharp turn. Their backs were now to the part of the sea which had met them when they first came out of the wood, and now, looking ahead, they could see across the water another shore, thickly wooded like the one they were exploring.

"I wonder, is that an island or do we join on to it presently?" said Lucy.

"Don't know," said Peter and they all plodded on in silence.

The shore that they were walking on drew nearer and nearer to the opposite shore, and as they came round each promontory the children expected to find the place where the two joined. But in this they were disappointed. They came to some rocks which they had to climb and from the top they could see a fair way ahead and – "Oh, bother!" said Edmund. "It's no good. We shan't be able to get to those other woods at all. We're on an island!"

It was true. At this point the channel between them and the opposite coast was only about thirty or forty yards wide; but they could now see that this was its narrowest place. After that, their own coast bent round to the right again and they could see open sea between it and the mainland. It was obvious that they had already come much more than halfway round the island.

"Look!" said Lucy suddenly. "What's that?" She pointed to a long, silvery, snake-like thing that lay across the beach.

"A stream! A stream!" shouted the others, and, tired as they were, they lost no time in clattering down the rocks and racing to the fresh water. They knew that the stream would be better to drink farther up, away from the beach, so they went at once to the spot where it came out of the wood. The trees were as thick as ever, but the stream had made itself a deep course between high mossy banks so that by stooping you could follow it up in a sort of tunnel of leaves. They dropped on their knees by the first brown, dimply pool and drank and drank, and dipped their faces in the water, and then dipped their arms in up to the elbow.

"Now," said Edmund, "what about those sandwiches?"

"Oh, hadn't we better save them?" said Susan. "We may need them far worse later on."

"I do wish," said Lucy, "now that we're not thirsty, we could go on feeling as not-hungry as we did when we *were* thirsty."

"But what about those sandwiches?" repeated Edmund. "There's no good saving them till they go bad. You've got to remember it's a good deal hotter here than in England and we've been carrying them about in pockets for hours." So they got out the two packets and divided them into four portions, and nobody had quite enough, but it was a great deal better than nothing. Then they talked about their plans for the next meal. Lucy wanted to go back to the sea and catch shrimps, until someone pointed out that they had no nets. Edmund said they must gather gulls' eggs from the rocks, but when they came to think of it they couldn't remember having seen any gulls' eggs and wouldn't be able to cook them if they found any. Peter thought to himself that unless they had some stroke of luck they would soon be glad to eat eggs raw, but he didn't see any point in saying this out loud. Susan said it was a pity they had eaten the sandwiches so soon. One or two tempers very nearly got lost at this stage. Finally Edmund said:

"Look here. There's only one thing to be done. We must explore the wood. Hermits and knights-errant and people like that always manage to live somehow if they're in a forest. They find roots and berries and things."

"What sort of roots?" asked Susan.

"I always thought it meant roots of trees," said Lucy.

"Come on," said Peter, "Ed is right. And we must try to do something. And it'll be better than going out into the glare and the sun again."

So they all got up and began to follow the stream. It was very hard work. They had to stoop under branches and climb over branches, and they blundered through great masses of stuff like rhododendrons and tore their clothes and got their feet wet in the stream; and still there was no noise at all except the noise of the stream and the noises they were making themselves. They were beginning to get very tired of it when they noticed a delicious smell, and then a flash of bright colour high above them at the top of the right bank.

"I say!" exclaimed Lucy. "I do believe that's an apple tree."

It was. They panted up the steep bank, forced their way through some brambles, and found themselves standing round an old tree that was heavy with large yellowish-golden apples as firm and juicy as you could wish to see.

"And this is not the only tree," said Edmund with his mouth full of apple. "Look there – and there."

"Why, there are dozens of them," said Susan, throwing away the core of her first apple and picking her second. "This must have been an orchard – long, long ago, before the place went wild and the wood grew up."

"Then this was once an inhabited island," said Peter.

"And what's that?" said Lucy, pointing ahead.

"By Jove, it's a wall," said Peter. "An old stone wall."

Pressing their way between the laden branches they reached the wall. It was very old, and broken down in places, with moss and wallflowers growing on it, but it was higher than all but the tallest trees. And when they came quite close to it they found a great arch which must once have had a gate in it but was now almost filled up with the largest of all the apple trees. They had to break some of the branches to get past, and when they had done so they all blinked because the daylight became suddenly much brighter. They found themselves in a wide open place with walls all round it. In here there were no trees, only level grass and daisies, and ivy, and grey walls. It was a bright, secret, quiet place, and rather sad; and all four stepped out into the middle of it, glad to be able to straighten their backs and move their limbs freely.

CHAPTER TWO

THE ANCIENT TREASURE HOUSE

"This wasn't a garden," said Susan presently. "It was a castle and this must have been the courtyard."

"I see what you mean," said Peter. "Yes. That is the remains of a tower. And there is what used to be a flight of steps going up to the top of the walls. And look at those other steps – the broad, shallow ones – going up to that doorway. It must have been the door into the great hall."

"Ages ago, by the look of it," said Edmund.

"Yes, ages ago," said Peter. "I wish we could find out who the people were that lived in this castle; and how long ago."

"It gives me a queer feeling," said Lucy.

"Does it, Lu?" said Peter, turning and looking hard at her. "Because it does the same to me. It is the queerest thing that has happened this queer day. I wonder where we are and what it all means?"

While they were talking they had crossed the courtyard and gone through the other doorway into what had once been the hall. This was now very like the courtyard, for the roof had long since disappeared and it was merely another space of grass and daisies, except that it was shorter and narrower and the walls were higher. Across the far end there was a kind of terrace about three feet higher than the rest.

"I wonder, was it really the hall?" said Susan. "What is that terrace kind of thing?"

"Why, you silly," said Peter (who had become strangely excited), "don't you see? That was the dais where the High Table was, where the King and the great lords sat. Anyone would think you had forgotten that we ourselves were once Kings and Queens and sat on a dais just like that, in our great hall."

"In our castle of Cair Paravel," continued Susan in a dreamy and rather sing-song voice, "at the mouth of the great river of Narnia. How could I forget?"

"How it all comes back!" said Lucy. "We could pretend we were in Cair Paravel now. This hall must have been very like the great hall we feasted in."

"But unfortunately without the feast," said Edmund. "It's getting late, you know. Look how long the shadows are. And have you noticed that it isn't so hot?"

"We shall need a camp-fire if we've got to spend the night here," said Peter. "I've got matches. Let's go and see if we can collect some dry wood."

Everyone saw the sense of this, and for the next half-hour they were busy. The orchard through which they had first come into the ruins turned out not to be a good place for firewood. They tried the other side of the castle, passing out of the hall by a little side door into a maze of stony humps and hollows which must once have been passages and smaller rooms but was now all nettles and wild roses. Beyond this they found a wide gap in the castle wall and stepped through it into a wood of darker and bigger trees where they found dead branches and rotten wood and sticks and dry leaves and fir-cones in plenty. They went to and fro with bundles until they had a good pile on the dais. At the fifth journey they found the well, just outside the hall, hidden in weeds, but clean and fresh and deep when they had cleared these away. The remains of a stone pavement ran halfway round it. Then the girls went out to pick some more apples and the boys built the fire, on the dais and fairly close to the corner between two walls, which they thought would be the snuggest and warmest place. They had great difficulty in lighting it and used a lot of matches, but they succeeded in the end. Finally, all four sat down with their backs to the wall and their faces to the fire. They tried roasting some of the apples on the ends of sticks. But roast apples are not much good without sugar, and they are too hot to eat with your fingers till they are too cold to be worth eating. So they had to content themselves with raw apples, which, as Edmund said, made one realize that school suppers weren't so bad after all – "I shouldn't mind a good thick slice of bread and margarine this minute," he added. But the spirit of adventure was rising in them all, and no one really wanted to be back at school.

Shortly after the last apple had been eaten, Susan went out to the well to get another drink. When she came back she was carrying something in her hand.

"Look," she said in a rather choking kind of voice. "I found it by the well." She handed it to Peter and sat down. The others thought she looked and sounded as if she might be going to cry. Edmund and Lucy eagerly bent forward to see what was in Peter's hand – a little, bright thing that gleamed in the firelight.

"Well, I'm – I'm jiggered," said Peter, and his voice also sounded queer. Then he handed it to the others.

All now saw what it was – a little chess-knight, ordinary in size but extraordinarily heavy because it was made of pure gold; and the eyes in the horse's head were two tiny little rubies – or rather one was, for the other had been knocked out.

"Why!" said Lucy, "it's exactly like one of the golden chessmen we used to play with when we were Kings and Queens at Cair Paravel."

"Cheer up, Su," said Peter to his other sister.

"I can't help it," said Susan. "It brought back – oh, such lovely times. And I remembered playing chess with fauns and good giants, and the mer-people singing in the sea, and my beautiful horse – and – and—"

"Now," said Peter in a quite different voice, "it's about time we four started using our brains."

"What about?" asked Edmund.

"Have none of you guessed where we are?" said Peter.

"Go on, go on," said Lucy. "I've felt for hours that there was some wonderful mystery hanging over this place."

"Fire ahead, Peter," said Edmund. "We're all listening."

"We are in the ruins of Cair Paravel itself," said Peter.

"But, I say," replied Edmund. "I mean, how do you make that out? This place has been ruined for ages. Look at all those big trees growing right up to the gates. Look at the very stones. Anyone can see that nobody has lived here for hundreds of years."

"I know," said Peter. "That is the difficulty. But let's leave that out for the moment. I want to take the points one by one. First point: this hall is exactly the same shape and size as the hall at Cair Paravel. Just picture a roof on this, and a coloured pavement instead of grass, and tapestries on the walls, and you get our royal banqueting hall."

No one said anything.

"Second point," continued Peter. "The castle well is exactly where our well was, a little to the south of the great hall; and it is exactly the same size and shape."

Again there was no reply.

"Third point: Susan has just found one of our old chessmen – or something as like one of them as two peas."

Still nobody answered.

"Fourth point. Don't you remember – it was the very day before the ambassadors came from the King of Calormen – don't you remember planting the orchard outside the north gate of Cair Paravel? The greatest of all the wood-people, Pomona herself, came to put good spells on it. It was those very decent little chaps, the moles, who did the actual digging. Can you have forgotten that funny old Lilygloves, the chief mole, leaning on his spade and saying, 'Believe me, your Majesty, you'll be glad of these fruit trees one day.' And by Jove he was right."

"I do! I do!" said Lucy, and clapped her hands.

"But look here, Peter," said Edmund. "This must be all rot. To begin with, we didn't plant the orchard slap up against the gate. We wouldn't have been such fools."

"No, of course not," said Peter. "But it has grown up to the gate since."

"And for another thing," said Edmund, "Cair Paravel wasn't on an island."

"Yes, I've been wondering about that. But it was a what-do-you-call-it, a peninsula. Jolly nearly an island. Couldn't it have been made an island since our time? Somebody has dug a channel."

"But half a moment!" said Edmund. "You keep on saying *since our time*. But it's only a year ago since we came back from Narnia. And you want to make out that in one year, castles have fallen down, and great forests have grown up, and little trees we saw planted ourselves have turned into a big old orchard, and goodness knows what else. It's all impossible."

"There's one thing," said Lucy. "If this is Cair Paravel there ought to be a door at this end of the dais. In fact we ought to be sitting with our backs against it at this moment. You know – the door that led down to the treasure chamber."

"I suppose there *isn't* a door," said Peter, getting up.

The wall behind them was a mass of ivy.

"We can soon find out," said Edmund, taking up one of the sticks that they had laid ready for putting on the fire. He began beating the ivied wall. Tap-tap went the stick against the stone, and again, tap-tap; and then, all at once, boom-boom, with a quite different sound, a hollow, wooden sound.

"Great Scott!" said Edmund.

"We must clear this ivy away," said Peter.

"Oh, do let's leave it alone," said Susan. "We can try it in the morning. If we've got to spend the night here I don't want an open door at my back and a great big black hole that anything might come out of, besides the draught and the damp. And it'll soon be dark."

"Susan! How can you?" said Lucy with a reproachful glance. But both the boys were too much excited to take any notice of Susan's advice. They worked at the ivy with their hands and with Peter's pocket-knife till the knife broke. After that they used Edmund's. Soon the whole place where they had been sitting was covered with ivy; and at last they had the door cleared.

"Locked, of course," said Peter.

"But the wood's all rotten," said Edmund. "We can pull it to bits in no time, and it will make extra firewood. Come on."

It took them longer than they expected and, before they had done, the great hall had grown dusky and the first star or two had come out overhead. Susan was not the only one who felt a slight shudder as the boys stood above the pile of splintered wood, rubbing the dirt off their hands and staring into the cold, dark opening they had made.

"Now for a torch," said Peter.

"Oh, what *is* the good?" said Susan. "And as Edmund said—"

"I'm not saying it now," Edmund interrupted. "I still don't understand, but we can settle that later. I suppose you're coming down, Peter?"

"We must," said Peter. "Cheer up, Susan. It's no good behaving like kids now that we are back in Narnia. You're a Queen here. And anyway no one could go to sleep with a mystery like this on their minds."

They tried to use long sticks as torches but this was not a success. If you held them with the lighted end up they went out, and if you held them the other way they scorched your hand and the smoke got in your eyes. In the end they had to use Edmund's electric torch; luckily it had been a birthday present less than a week ago and the battery was almost new. He went first, with the light. Then came Lucy, then Susan, and Peter brought up the rear.

"I've come to the top of the steps," said Edmund.

"Count them," said Peter.

"One – two – three," said Edmund, as he went cautiously down, and so up to sixteen. "And this is the bottom," he shouted back.

"Then it really must be Cair Paravel," said Lucy. "There were sixteen." Nothing more was said till all four were standing in a knot together at the foot of the stairway. Then Edmund flashed his torch slowly round.

"O – o – o – oh!!" said all the children at once.

For now all knew that it was indeed the ancient treasure chamber of Cair Paravel where they had once reigned as Kings and Queens of Narnia. There was a kind of path up the middle (as it might be in a greenhouse), and along each side at intervals stood rich suits of armour, like knights guarding the treasures. In between the suits of armour, and on each side of the path, were shelves covered with precious things – necklaces and arm rings and finger rings and golden bowls and dishes and long tusks of ivory, brooches and coronets and chains of gold, and heaps of unset stones lying piled anyhow as if they were marbles or potatoes – diamonds, rubies, carbuncles, emeralds, topazes, and amethysts. Under the shelves stood great chests of oak strengthened with iron bars and heavily padlocked. And it was bitterly cold, and so still that they could hear themselves breathing, and the treasures were so covered with dust that unless they had realized where they were and remembered most of the things, they would hardly have known they were treasures. There was something sad and a little frightening about the place, because it all seemed so forsaken and long ago. That was why nobody said anything for at least a minute.

Then, of course, they began walking about and picking things up to look at. It was like meeting very old friends. If you had been there you would have heard them saying things like, "Oh, look! Our coronation rings – do you remember first wearing this? – Why, this is the little brooch we all thought was lost – I say, isn't that the armour you wore in the great tournament in the Lone Islands? – Do you remember the dwarf making that for me? – Do you remember drinking out of that horn? – Do you remember, do you remember?"

But suddenly Edmund said, "Look here. We mustn't waste the battery: goodness knows how often we shall need it. Hadn't we better take what we want and get out again?"

"We must take the gifts," said Peter. For long ago at a Christmas in Narnia he and Susan and Lucy had been given certain presents which they valued more than their whole kingdom. Edmund had had no gift, because he was not with them at the time. (This was his own fault, and you can read about it in the other book.)

They all agreed with Peter and walked up the path to the wall at the far end of the treasure chamber, and there, sure enough, the gifts were still hanging. Lucy's was the smallest for it was only a little bottle. But the bottle was made of diamond instead of glass, and it was still more than half full of the magical cordial which would heal almost every wound and every illness. Lucy said nothing and looked very solemn as she took her gift down from its place and slung the belt over her shoulder and once more felt the bottle at her side where it used to hang in the old days. Susan's gift had been a bow and arrows and a horn. The bow was still there, and the ivory quiver, full of well-feathered arrows, but – "Oh, Susan," said Lucy. "Where's the horn?"

"Oh, bother, bother, bother," said Susan after she had thought for a moment. "I remember now. I took it with me the last day of all, the day we went hunting the White Stag. It must have got lost when we blundered back into that other place – England, I mean."

Edmund whistled. It was indeed a shattering loss; for this was an enchanted horn and, whenever you blew it, help was certain to come to you, wherever you were.

"Just the sort of thing that might come in handy in a place like this," said Edmund.

"Never mind," said Susan, "I've still got the bow." And she took it.

"Won't the string be perished, Su?" said Peter.

But whether by some magic in the air of the treasure chamber or not, the bow was still in working order. Archery and swimming were the things Susan was good at. In a moment she had bent the bow and then she gave one little pluck to the string. It twanged: a chirruping twang that vibrated through the whole room. And that one small noise brought back the old days to the children's minds more than anything that had happened yet. All the battles and hunts and feasts came rushing into their heads together.

Then she unstrung the bow again and slung the quiver at her side.

Next, Peter took down his gift – the shield with the great red lion on it, and the royal sword. He blew, and rapped them on the floor, to get off the dust. He fitted the shield on his arm and slung the sword by his side. He was afraid at first that it might be rusty and stick to the sheath. But it was not so. With one swift motion he drew it and held it up, shining in the torchlight.

"It is my sword Rhindon," he said; "with it I killed the Wolf." There was a new tone in his voice, and the others all felt that he was really Peter the High King again. Then, after a little pause, everyone remembered that they must save the battery.

They climbed the stairs again and made up a good fire and lay down close together for warmth. The ground was very hard and uncomfortable, but they fell asleep in the end.

CHAPTER THREE

THE DWARF

The worst of sleeping out of doors is that you wake up so dreadfully early. And when you wake you have to get up because the ground is so hard that you are uncomfortable. And it makes matters worse if there is nothing but apples for breakfast and you have had nothing but apples for supper the night before. When Lucy had said – truly enough – that it was a glorious morning, there did not seem to be anything else nice to be said. Edmund said what everyone was feeling, "We've simply got to get off this island."

When they had drunk from the well and splashed their faces they all went down the stream again to the shore and stared at the channel which divided them from the mainland.

"We'll have to swim," said Edmund.

"It would be all right for Su," said Peter (Susan had won prizes for swimming at school). "But I don't know about the rest of us." By "the rest of us" he really meant Edmund who couldn't yet do two lengths at the school baths, and Lucy, who could hardly swim at all.

"Anyway," said Susan, "there may be currents. Father says it's never wise to bathe in a place you don't know."

"But, Peter," said Lucy, "look here. I know I can't swim for nuts at home – in England, I mean. But couldn't we all swim long ago – if it was long ago – when we were Kings and Queens in Narnia? We could ride then too, and do all sorts of things. Don't you think—?"

"Ah, but we were sort of grown-up then," said Peter. "We reigned for years and years and learned to do things. Aren't we just back at our proper ages again now?"

"Oh!" said Edmund in a voice which made everyone stop talking and listen to him.

"I've just seen it all," he said.

"Seen what?" asked Peter.

"Why, the whole thing," said Edmund. "You know what we were puzzling about last night, that it was only a year ago since we left Narnia but everything looks as if no one had lived in Cair Paravel for hundreds of years? Well, don't you see? You know that, however long we seemed to have lived in Narnia, when we got back through the wardrobe it seemed to have taken no time at all?"

"Go on," said Susan. "I think I'm beginning to understand."

"And that means," continued Edmund, "that, once you're out of Narnia, you have no idea how Narnian time is going. Why shouldn't hundreds of years have gone past in Narnia while only one year has passed for us in England?"

"By Jove, Ed," said Peter. "I believe you've got it. In that sense it really was hundreds of years ago that we lived in Cair Paravel. And now we're coming back to Narnia just as if we were Crusaders or Anglo-Saxons or Ancient Britons or someone coming back to modern England!"

"How excited they'll be to see us—" began Lucy, but at the same moment everyone else said, "Hush!" or, "Look!" For now something was happening.

There was a wooded point on the mainland a little to their right, and they all felt sure that just beyond that point must be the mouth of the river. And now, round that point there came into sight a boat. When it had cleared the point, it turned and began coming along the channel towards them. There were two people on board: one rowing, the other sitting in the stern and holding a bundle that twitched and moved as if it were alive. Both these people seemed to be soldiers. They had steel caps on their heads and light shirts of chain-mail. Their faces were bearded and hard. The children drew back from the beach into the wood and watched without moving a finger.

"This'll do," said the soldier in the stern when the boat had come about opposite to them.

"What about tying a stone to his feet, Corporal?" said the other, resting on his oars.

"Garn!" growled the other. "We don't need that, and we haven't brought one. He'll drown sure enough without a stone, as long as we've tied the cords right." With these words he rose and lifted his bundle. Peter now saw that it was really alive and was in fact a Dwarf, bound hand and foot but struggling as hard as he could. Next moment he heard a twang just beside his ear, and all at once the soldier threw up his arms, dropping the Dwarf into the bottom of the boat, and fell over into the water. He floundered away to the far bank and Peter knew that Susan's arrow had struck his helmet. He turned and saw that she was very pale but was already fitting a second arrow to the string. But it was never used. As soon as he saw his companion fall, the other soldier, with a loud cry, jumped out of the boat on the far side, and he also floundered through the water (which was apparently just in his depth) and disappeared into the woods of the mainland.

"Quick! Before she drifts!" shouted Peter. He and Susan, fully dressed as they were, plunged in, and before the water was up to their shoulders, their hands were on the side of the boat. In a few seconds they had hauled her to the bank and lifted the Dwarf out, and Edmund was busily engaged in cutting his bonds with the pocket knife. (Peter's sword would have been sharper, but a sword is very inconvenient for this sort of work because you can't hold it anywhere lower than the hilt.) When at last the Dwarf was free, he sat up, rubbed his arms and legs, and exclaimed:

"Well, whatever they say, you don't *feel* like ghosts."

Like most Dwarfs he was very stocky and deep-chested. He would have been about three feet high if he had been standing up, and an immense beard and whiskers of coarse red hair left little of his face to be seen except a beak-like nose and twinkling black eyes.

"Anyway," he continued, "ghosts or not, you've saved my life and I'm extremely obliged to you."

"But why should we be ghosts?" asked Lucy.

"I've been told all my life," said the Dwarf, "that these woods along the shore were as full of ghosts as they were of trees. That's what the story is. And that's why, when they want to get rid of anyone, they usually bring him down here (like they were doing with me) and say they'll leave him to the ghosts. But I always wondered if they didn't really drown 'em or cut their throats. I never quite believed in the ghosts. But those two cowards you've just shot believed all right. They were more frightened of taking me to my death than I was of going!"

"Oh," said Susan. "So that's why they both ran away."

"Eh? What's that?" said the Dwarf.

"They got away," said Edmund. "To the mainland."

"I wasn't shooting to kill, you know," said Susan. She would not have liked anyone to think she could miss at such a short range.

"H'm," said the Dwarf. "That's not so good. That may mean trouble later on. Unless they hold their tongues for their own sake."

"What were they going to drown you for?" asked Peter.

"Oh, I'm a dangerous criminal, I am," said the Dwarf cheerfully. "But that's a long story. Meantime, I was wondering if perhaps you were going to ask me to breakfast? You've no idea what an appetite it gives one, being executed."

"There's only apples," said Lucy dolefully.

"Better than nothing, but not so good as fresh fish," said the Dwarf. "It looks as if I'll have to ask you to breakfast instead. I saw some fishing tackle in that boat. And anyway, we must take her round to the other side of the island. We don't want anyone from the mainland coming down and seeing her."

"I ought to have thought of that myself," said Peter.

The four children and the Dwarf went down to the water's edge, pushed off the boat with some difficulty, and scrambled aboard. The Dwarf at once took charge. The oars were of course too big for him to use, so Peter rowed and the Dwarf steered them north along the channel and presently eastward round the tip of the island. From here the children could see right up the river, and all the bays and headlands of the coast beyond it. They thought they could recognize bits of it, but the woods, which had grown up since their time, made everything look very different.

When they had come round into open sea on the east of the island, the Dwarf took to fishing. They had an excellent catch of pavenders, a beautiful rainbow-coloured fish which they all remembered eating in Cair Paravel in the old days. When they had caught enough they ran the boat up into a little creek and moored her to a tree. The Dwarf, who was a most capable person (and, indeed, though one meets bad Dwarfs, I never heard of a Dwarf who was a fool), cut the fish open, cleaned them, and said:

"Now, what we want next is some firewood."

"We've got some up at the castle," said Edmund.

The Dwarf gave a low whistle. "Beards and bedsteads!" he said. "So there really is a castle, after all?"

"It's only a ruin," said Lucy.

The Dwarf stared round at all four of them with a very curious expression on his face. "And who on earth——?" he began, but then broke off and said, "No matter. Breakfast first. But one thing before we go on. Can you lay your hand on your hearts and tell me I'm really alive? Are you sure I wasn't drowned and we're not all ghosts together?"

When they had all reassured him, the next question was how to carry the fish. They had nothing to string them on and no basket. They had to use Edmund's hat in the end because no one else had a hat. He would have made much more fuss about this if he had not by now been so ravenously hungry.

At first the Dwarf did not seem very comfortable in the castle. He kept looking round and sniffing and saying, "H'm. Looks a bit spooky after all. Smells like ghosts, too." But he cheered up when it came to lighting the fire and showing them how to roast the fresh pavenders in the embers. Eating hot fish with no forks, and one pocket knife between five people, is a messy business and there were several burnt fingers before the meal was ended; but, as it was now nine o'clock and they had been up since five, nobody minded the burns so much as you might have expected. When everyone had finished off with a drink from the well and an apple or so, the Dwarf produced a pipe about the size of his own arm, filled it, lit it, blew a great cloud of fragrant smoke, and said, "Now."

"You tell us your story first," said Peter. "And then we'll tell you ours."

"Well," said the Dwarf, "as you've saved my life it is only fair you should have your own way. But I hardly know where to begin. First of all I'm a messenger of King Caspian's."

"Who's he?" asked four voices all at once.

"Caspian the Tenth, King of Narnia, and long may he reign!" answered the Dwarf. "That is to say, he ought to be King of Narnia and we hope he will be. At present he is only King of us Old Narnians—"

"What do you mean by *old* Narnians, please?" asked Lucy.

"Why, that's us," said the Dwarf. "We're a kind of rebellion, I suppose."

"I see," said Peter. "And Caspian is the chief Old Narnian."

"Well, in a manner of speaking," said the Dwarf, scratching his head. "But he's really a New Narnian himself, a Telmarine, if you follow me."

"I don't," said Edmund.

"It's worse than the Wars of the Roses," said Lucy.

"Oh dear," said the Dwarf. "I'm doing this very badly. Look here: I think I'll have to go right back to the beginning and tell you how Caspian grew up in his uncle's court and how he came to be on our side at all. But it'll be a long story."

"All the better," said Lucy. "We love stories."

So the Dwarf settled down and told his tale. I shall not give it to you in his words, putting in all the children's questions and interruptions, because it would take too long and be confusing and, even so, it would leave out some points that the children only heard later. But the gist of the story, as they knew it in the end, was as follows.

CHAPTER FOUR

THE DWARF TELLS OF PRINCE CASPIAN

Prince Caspian lived in a great castle in the centre of Narnia with his uncle, Miraz, the King of Narnia, and his aunt, who had red hair and was called Queen Prunaprismia. His father and mother were dead and the person whom Caspian loved best was his nurse, and though (being a prince) he had wonderful toys which would do almost anything but talk, he liked best the last hour of the day when the toys had all been put back in their cupboards and Nurse would tell him stories.

He did not care much for his uncle and aunt, but about twice a week his uncle would send for him and they would walk up and down together for half an hour on the terrace at the south side of the castle. One day, while they were doing this, the King said to him,

"Well, boy, we must soon teach you to ride and use a sword. You know that your aunt and I have no children, so it looks as if you might have to be King when I'm gone. How shall you like that, eh?"

"I don't know, Uncle," said Caspian.

"Don't know, eh?" said Miraz. "Why, I should like to know what more anyone could wish for!"

"All the same, I *do* wish," said Caspian.

"What do you wish?" asked the King.

"I wish – I wish – I wish I could have lived in the Old Days," said Caspian. (He was only a very little boy at the time.)

Up till now King Miraz had been talking in the tiresome way that some grown-ups have, which makes it quite clear that they are not really interested in what you are saying, but now he suddenly gave Caspian a very sharp look.

"Eh? What's that?" he said. "What old days do you mean?"

"Oh, don't you know, Uncle?" said Caspian. "When everything was quite different. When all the animals could talk, and there were nice people who lived in the streams and the trees. Naiads and Dryads, they were called. And there were Dwarfs. And there were lovely little Fauns in all the woods. They had feet like goats. And—"

"That's all nonsense, for babies," said the King sternly. "Only fit for babies, do you hear? You're getting too old for that sort of stuff. At your age you ought to be thinking of battles and adventures, not fairy tales."

"Oh, but there *were* battles and adventures in those days," said Caspian. "Wonderful adventures. Once there was a White Witch and she made herself queen of the whole country. And she made it so that it was always winter. And then two boys and two girls came from somewhere and so they killed the Witch and they were made Kings and Queens of Narnia, and their names were Peter and Susan and Edmund and Lucy. And so they reigned for ever so long and everyone had a lovely time, and it was all because of Aslan—"

"Who's he?" said Miraz. And if Caspian had been a very little older, the tone of his uncle's voice would have warned him that it would be wiser to shut up. But he babbled on:

"Oh, don't you know?" he said. "Aslan is the great Lion who comes from over the sea."

"Who has been telling you all this nonsense?" said the King in a voice of thunder. Caspian was frightened and said nothing.

"Your Royal Highness," said King Miraz, letting go of Caspian's hand, which he had been holding till now, "I insist upon being answered. Look me in the face. Who has been telling you this pack of lies?"

"N – Nurse," faltered Caspian, and burst into tears.

"Stop that noise," said his uncle, taking Caspian by the shoulders and giving him a shake. "Stop it. And never let me catch you talking – or *thinking* either – about all those silly stories again. There never were those Kings and Queens. How could there be two Kings at the same time? And there's no such person as Aslan. And there are no such things as lions. And there never was a time when animals could talk. Do you hear?"

"Yes, Uncle," sobbed Caspian.

"Then let's have no more of it," said the King. Then he called to one of the gentlemen-in-waiting who were standing at the far end of the terrace and said in a cold voice, "Conduct His Royal Highness to his apartments and send His Royal Highness's nurse to me AT ONCE."

Next day Caspian found what a terrible thing he had done, for Nurse had been sent away without even being allowed to say goodbye to him, and he was told he was to have a Tutor.

Caspian missed his nurse very much and shed many tears; and because he was so miserable, he thought about the old stories of Narnia far more than before. He dreamed of Dwarfs and Dryads every night and tried very hard to make the dogs and cats in the castle talk to him. But the dogs only wagged their tails and the cats only purred.

Caspian felt sure that he would hate the new Tutor, but when the new Tutor arrived about a week later he turned out to be the sort of person it is almost impossible not to like. He was the smallest, and also the fattest, man Caspian had ever seen. He had a long, silvery, pointed beard which came down to his waist, and his face, which was brown and covered with wrinkles, looked very wise, very ugly, and very kind. His voice was grave and his eyes were merry so that, until you got to know him really well, it was hard to know when he was joking and when he was serious. His name was Doctor Cornelius.

Of all his lessons with Doctor Cornelius the one that Caspian liked best was History. Up till now, except for Nurse's stories, he had known nothing about the History of Narnia, and he was very surprised to learn that the royal family were newcomers in the country.

"It was your Highness's ancestor, Caspian the First," said Doctor Cornelius, "who first con-quered Narnia and made it his kingdom. It was he who brought all your nation into the country. You are not native Narnians at all. You are all Telmarines – that is, you all came from the Land of Telmar, far beyond the Western Mountains. That is why Caspian the First is called Caspian the Conqueror."

"Please, Doctor," asked Caspian one day, "who lived in Narnia before we all came here out of Telmar?"

"No men – or very few – lived in Narnia before the Telmarines took it," said Doctor Cornelius.

"Then who did my great-great-grandcesters conquer?"

"*Whom*, not *who*, your Highness," said Doctor Cornelius. "Perhaps it is time to turn from History to Grammar."

"Oh, please, not yet," said Caspian. "I mean, wasn't there a battle? Why is he called Caspian the Conqueror if there was nobody to fight with him?"

"I said there were very few *men* in Narnia," said the Doctor, looking at the little boy very strangely through his great spectacles.

For a moment Caspian was puzzled and then suddenly his heart gave a leap. "Do you mean," he gasped, "that there were other things? Do you mean it was like in the stories? Were there—?"

"Hush!" said Doctor Cornelius, laying his head very close to Caspian's. "Not a word more. Don't you know your Nurse was sent away for telling you about Old Narnia? The King doesn't like it. If he found me telling you secrets, you'd be whipped and I should have my head cut off."

"But why?" asked Caspian.

"It is high time we turned to Grammar now," said Doctor Cornelius in a loud voice. "Will your Royal Highness be pleased to open Pulverulentus Siccus at the fourth page of his *Grammatical garden or the Arbour of Accidence pleasantlie open'd to Tender Wits?*"

After that it was all nouns and verbs till lunchtime, but I don't think Caspian learned much. He was too excited. He felt sure that Doctor Cornelius would not have said so much unless he meant to tell him more sooner or later.

In this he was not disappointed. A few days later his Tutor said, "Tonight I am going to give you a lesson in Astronomy. At the dead of night two noble planets, Tarva and Alambil, will pass within one degree of each other. Such a conjunction has not occurred for two hundred years, and your Highness will not live to see it again. It will be best if you go to bed a little earlier than usual. When the time of the conjunction draws near I will come and wake you."

This didn't seem to have anything to do with Old Narnia, which was what Caspian really wanted to hear about, but getting up in the middle of the night is always interesting and he was moderately pleased. When he went to bed that night, he thought at first that he would not be able to sleep; but he soon dropped off and it seemed only a few minutes before he felt someone gently shaking him.

He sat up in bed and saw that the room was full of moonlight. Doctor Cornelius, muffled in a hooded robe and holding a small lamp in his hand, stood by the bedside. Caspian remembered at once what they were going to do. He got up and put on some clothes. Although it was a summer night he felt colder than he had expected and was quite glad when the Doctor wrapped him in a robe like his own and gave him a pair of warm, soft buskins for his feet. A moment later, both muffled so that they could hardly be seen in the dark corridors, and both shod so that they made almost no noise, master and pupil left the room.

Caspian followed the Doctor through many passages and up several staircases, and at last, through a little door in a turret, they came out upon the leads. On one side were the battlements, on the other a steep roof; below them, all shadowy and shimmery, the castle gardens; above them, stars and moon. Presently they came to another door which led into the great central tower of the whole castle: Doctor Cornelius unlocked it and they began to climb the dark winding stair of the tower. Caspian was becoming excited; he had never been allowed up this stair before.

It was long and steep, but when they came out on the roof of the tower and Caspian had got his breath, he felt that it had been well worth it. Away on his right he could see, rather indistinctly, the Western Mountains. On his left was the gleam of the Great River, and everything was so quiet that he could hear the sound of the waterfall at Beaversdam, a mile away. There was no difficulty in picking out the two stars they had come to see. They hung rather low in the southern sky, almost as bright as two little moons and very close together.

"Are they going to have a collision?" he asked in an awestruck voice.

"Nay, dear Prince," said the doctor (and he too spoke in a whisper). "The great lords of the upper sky know the steps of their dance too well for that. Look well upon them. Their meeting is fortunate and means some great good for the sad realm of Narnia. Tarva, the Lord of Victory, salutes Alambil, the Lady of Peace. They are just coming to their nearest."

"It's a pity that tree gets in the way," said Caspian. "We'd really see better from the West Tower, though it is not so high."

Doctor Cornelius said nothing for about two minutes, but stood still with his eyes fixed on Tarva and Alambil. Then he drew a deep breath and turned to Caspian.

"There," he said. "You have seen what no man now alive has seen, nor will see again. And you are right. We should have seen it even better from the smaller tower. I brought you here for another reason."

Caspian looked up at him, but the Doctor's hood concealed most of his face.

"The virtue of this tower," said Doctor Cornelius, "is that we have six empty rooms beneath us, and a long stair, and the door at the bottom of the stair is locked. We cannot be overheard."

"Are you going to tell me what you wouldn't tell me the other day?" said Caspian.

"I am," said the Doctor. "But remember. You and I must never talk about these things except here – on the very top of the Great Tower."

"No. That's a promise," said Caspian. "But do go on, please."

"Listen," said the Doctor. "All you have heard about Old Narnia is true. It is not the land of Men. It is the country of Aslan, the country of the Waking Trees and Visible Naiads, of Fauns and Satyrs, of Dwarfs and Giants, of the gods and the Centaurs, of Talking Beasts. It was against these that the first Caspian fought. It is you Telmarines who silenced the beasts and the trees and the fountains, and who killed and drove away the Dwarfs and Fauns, and are now trying to cover up even the memory of them. The King does not allow them to be spoken of."

"Oh, I do wish we hadn't," said Caspian. "And I *am* glad it was all true, even if it is all over."

"Many of your race wish that in secret," said Doctor Cornelius.

"But, Doctor," said Caspian, "why do you say *my* race? After all, I suppose you're a Telmarine too."

"Am I ?" said the Doctor.

"Well, you're a Man anyway," said Caspian.

"Am I?" repeated the Doctor in a deeper voice, at the same moment throwing back his hood so that Caspian could see his face clearly in the moonlight.

All at once Caspian realized the truth and felt that he ought to have realized it long before. Doctor Cornelius was so small and so fat, and had such a very long beard. Two thoughts came into his head at the same moment. One was a thought of terror – "He's not a real man, not a man at all, he's a *Dwarf*, and he's brought me up here to kill me." The other was sheer delight – "There are real Dwarfs still, and I've seen one at last."

"So you've guessed it in the end," said Doctor Cornelius. "Or guessed it nearly right. I'm not a pure Dwarf. I have human blood in me too. Many Dwarfs escaped in the great battles and lived on, shaving their beards and wearing high-heeled shoes and pretending to be men. They have mixed with your Telmarines. I am one of those, only a half-Dwarf, and if any of my kindred, the true Dwarfs, are still alive anywhere in the world, doubtless they would despise me and call me a traitor. But never in all these years have we forgotten our own people and all the other happy creatures of Narnia, and the long-lost days of freedom."

"I'm – I'm sorry, Doctor," said Caspian. "It wasn't my fault, you know."

"I am not saying these things in blame of you, dear Prince," answered the Doctor. "You may well ask why I say them at all. But I have two reasons. Firstly, because my old heart has carried these secret memories so long that it aches with them and would burst if I did not whisper them to you. But secondly, for this: that when you become King you may help us, for I know that you also, Telmarine though you are, love the Old Things."

"I do, I do," said Caspian. "But how can I help?"

"You can be kind to the poor remnants of the Dwarf people, like myself. You can gather learned magicians and try to find a way of awakening the trees once more. You can search through all the nooks and wild places of the land to see if any Fauns or Talking Beasts or Dwarfs are perhaps still alive in hiding."

"Do you think there are any?" asked Caspian eagerly.

"I don't know – I don't know," said the Doctor with a deep sigh. "Sometimes I am afraid there can't be. I have been looking for traces of them all my life. Sometimes I have thought I heard a Dwarf-drum in the mountains. Sometimes at night, in the woods, I thought I had caught a glimpse of Fauns and Satyrs dancing a long way off; but when I came to the place, there was never anything there. I have often despaired; but something always happens to start me hoping again. I don't know. But at least you can try to be a King like the High King Peter of old, and not like your uncle."

"Then it's true about the Kings and Queens too, and about the White Witch?" said Caspian.

"Certainly it is true," said Cornelius. "Their reign was the Golden Age in Narnia and the land has never forgotten them."

"Did they live in this castle, Doctor?"

"Nay, my dear," said the old man. "This castle is a thing of yesterday. Your great-great-grand-father built it. But when the two sons of Adam and the two daughters of Eve were made Kings and Queens of Narnia by Aslan himself, they lived in the castle of Cair Paravel. No man alive has seen that blessed place and perhaps even the ruins of it have now vanished. But we believe it was far from here, down at the mouth of the Great River, on the very shore of the sea."

"Ugh!" said Caspian with a shudder. "Do you mean in the Black Woods? Where all the – the – you know, the ghosts live?"

"Your Highness speaks as you have been taught," said the Doctor. "But it is all lies. There are no ghosts there. That is a story invented by the Telmarines. Your Kings are in deadly fear of the sea because they can never quite forget that in all stories Aslan comes from over the sea. They don't want to go near it and they don't want anyone else to go near it. So they have let great woods grow up to cut their people off from the coast. But because they have quarrelled with the trees, they are afraid of the woods. And because they are afraid of the woods they imagine that they are full of ghosts. And the Kings and great men, hating both the sea and the wood, partly believe these stories, and partly encourage them. They feel safer if no one in Narnia dares to go down to the coast and look out to sea – towards Aslan's land and the morning and the eastern end of the world."

There was a deep silence between them for a few minutes. Then Doctor Cornelius said, "Come. We have been here long enough. It is time to go down and to bed."

"Must we?" said Caspian. "I'd like to go on talking about these things for hours and hours and hours."

"Someone might begin looking for us, if we did that," said Doctor Cornelius.

Chapter Five

Caspian's Adventure in the Mountains

After this, Caspian and his Tutor had many more secret conversations on the top of the Great Tower, and at each conversation Caspian learned more about Old Narnia, so that thinking and dreaming about the old days, and longing that they might come back, filled nearly all his spare hours. But of course he had not many hours to spare, for now his education was beginning in earnest. He learned sword-fighting and riding, swimming and diving, how to shoot with the bow and play on the recorder and the theorbo, how to hunt the stag and cut him up when he was dead, besides Cosmography, Rhetoric, Heraldry, Versification, and of course History, with a little Law, Physics, Alchemy, and Astronomy. Of Magic he learned only the theory, for Doctor Cornelius said the practical part was not proper study for princes. "And I myself," he added, "am only a very imperfect magician and can do only the smallest experiments." Of Navigation ("Which is a noble and heroical art," said the Doctor) he was taught nothing, because King Miraz disapproved of ships and the sea.

He also learned a great deal by using his own eyes and ears. As a little boy he had often wondered why he disliked his aunt, Queen Prunaprismia; he now saw that it was because she disliked him. He also began to see that Narnia was an unhappy country. The taxes were high and the laws were stern and Miraz was a cruel man.

After some years there came a time when the Queen seemed to be ill and there was a great deal of bustle and pother about her in the castle and doctors came and the courtiers whispered. This was in early summertime. And one night, while all this fuss was going on, Caspian was unexpectedly wakened by Doctor Cornelius after he had been only a few hours in bed.

"Are we going to do a little Astronomy, Doctor?" said Caspian.

"Hush!" said the Doctor. "Trust me and do exactly as I tell you. Put on all your clothes; you have a long journey before you."

Caspian was very surprised, but he had learned to have confidence in his Tutor and he began doing what he was told at once. When he was dressed, the Doctor said, "I have a wallet for you. We must go into the next room and fill it with victuals from your Highness's supper table."

"My gentlemen-in-waiting will be there," said Caspian.

"They are fast asleep and will not wake," said the doctor. "I am a very minor magician but I *can* at least contrive a charmed sleep."

They went into the antechamber and there, sure enough, the two gentlemen-in-waiting were, sprawling on chairs and snoring hard. Doctor Cornelius quickly cut up the remains of a cold chicken and some slices of venison and put them, with bread and an apple or so and a little flask of good wine, into the wallet which he then gave to Caspian. It fitted on by a strap over Caspian's shoulder, like a satchel you would use for taking books to school.

"Have you your sword?" asked the Doctor.

"Yes," said Caspian.

"Then put this mantle over all to hide the sword and the wallet. That's right. And now we must go to the Great Tower and talk."

When they had reached the top of the tower (it was a cloudy night, not at all like the night when they had seen the conjunction of Tarva and Alambil), Doctor Cornelius said,

"Dear Prince, you must leave this castle at once and go to seek your fortune in the wide world. Your life is in danger here."

"Why?" asked Caspian.

"Because you are the true King of Narnia: Caspian the Tenth, the true son and heir of Caspian the Ninth. Long life to your Majesty" – and suddenly, to Caspian's great surprise, the little man dropped down on one knee and kissed his hand.

"What does it all mean? I don't understand," said Caspian.

"I wonder you have never asked me before," said the Doctor, "why, being the son of King Caspian, you are not King Caspian yourself. Everyone except your Majesty knows that Miraz is a usurper. When he first began to rule he did not even pretend to be the King: he called himself Lord Protector. But then your royal mother died, the good Queen and the only Telmarine who was ever kind to me. And then, one by one, all the great lords, who had known your father, died or disappeared. Not by accident, either. Miraz weeded them out. Belisar and Uvilas were shot with arrows on a hunting party: by chance, it was pretended. All the great house of the Passarids he sent to fight giants on the northern frontier till one by one they fell. Arlian and Erimon and a dozen more he executed for treason on a false charge. The two brothers of Beaversdam he shut up as madmen. And finally he persuaded the seven noble lords, who alone among all the Telmarines did not fear the sea, to sail away and look for new lands beyond the Eastern Ocean and, as he intended, they never came back. And when there was no one left who could speak a word for you, then his flatterers (as he had instructed them) begged him to become King. And of course he did."

"Do you mean he now wants to kill me too?" said Caspian.

"That is almost certain," said Doctor Cornelius.

"But why now?" said Caspian. "I mean, why didn't he do it long ago if he wanted to? And what harm have I done him?"

"He has changed his mind about you because of something that happened only two hours ago. The Queen has had a son."

"I don't see what that's got to do with it," said Caspian.

"Don't see!" exclaimed the Doctor. "Have all my lessons in History and Politics taught you no more than that? Listen. As long as he had no children of his own, he was willing enough that you should be King after he died. He may not have cared much about you, but he would rather you should have the throne than a stranger. Now that he has a son of his own he will want his own son to be the next King. You are in the way. He'll clear you out of the way."

"Is he really as bad as that?" said Caspian. "Would he really murder me?"

"He murdered your Father," said Doctor Cornelius.

Caspian felt very strange and said nothing.

"I can tell you the whole story," said the Doctor. "But not now. There is no time. You must fly at once."

"You'll come with me?" said Caspian.

"I dare not," said the Doctor. "It would make your danger greater. Two are more easily tracked than one. Dear Prince, dear King Caspian, you must be very brave. You must go alone and at once. Try to get across the southern border to the court of King Nain of Archenland. He will be good to you."

"Shall I never see you again?" said Caspian in a quavering voice.

"I hope so, dear King," said the Doctor. "What friend have I in the wide world except your Majesty? And I have a little magic. But in the meantime, speed is everything. Here are two gifts before you go. This is a little purse of gold – alas, all the treasure in this castle should be your own by rights. And here is something far better."

He put in Caspian's hands something which he could hardly see but which he knew by the feel to be a horn.

"That," said Doctor Cornelius, "is the greatest and most sacred treasure of Narnia. Many terrors I endured, many spells did I utter, to find it, when I was still young. It is the magic horn of Queen Susan herself which she left behind her when she vanished from Narnia at the end of the Golden Age. It is said that whoever blows it shall have strange help — no one can say how strange. It may have the power to call Queen Lucy and King Edmund and Queen Susan and High King Peter back from the past, and they will set all to rights. It may be that it will call up Aslan himself. Take it, King Caspian: but do not use it except at your greatest need. And now, haste, haste, haste. The little door at the very bottom of the Tower, the door into the garden, is unlocked. There we must part."

"Can't I get my horse, Destrier?" said Caspian.

"He is already saddled and waiting for you just at the corner of the orchard."

During the long climb down the winding staircase Cornelius whispered many more words of direction and advice. Caspian's heart was sinking, but he tried to take it all in. Then came the fresh air in the garden, a fervent handclasp with the Doctor, a run across the lawn, a welcoming whinny from Destrier, and so King Caspian the Tenth left the castle of his fathers. Looking back, he saw fireworks going up to celebrate the birth of the new prince.

All night he rode southward, choosing by-ways and bridle paths through woods as long as he was in country that he knew; but afterwards he kept to the high road. Destrier was as excited as his master at this unusual journey, and Caspian, though tears had come into his eyes at saying goodbye to Doctor Cornelius, felt brave and, in a way, happy, to think that he was King Caspian riding to seek adventures, with his sword on his left hip and Queen Susan's magic horn on his right. But when day came, with a sprinkle of rain, and he looked about him and saw on every side unknown woods, wild heaths, and blue mountains, he thought how large and strange the world was and felt frightened and small.

As soon as it was full daylight he left the road and found an open grassy place amid a wood where he could rest. He took off Destrier's bridle and let him graze, ate some cold chicken and drank a little wine, and presently fell asleep. It was late afternoon when he awoke. He ate a morsel and continued his journey, still southward, by many unfrequented lanes. He was now in a land of hills, going up and down, but always more up than down. From every ridge he could see the mountains growing bigger and blacker ahead. As the evening closed in, he was riding their lower slopes. The wind rose. Soon rain fell in torrents. Destrier became uneasy; there was thunder in the air. And now they entered a dark and seemingly endless pine forest, and all the stories Caspian had ever heard of trees being unfriendly to Man crowded into his mind. He remembered that he was, after all, a Telmarine, one of the race who cut down trees wherever they could and were at war with all wild things; and though he himself might be unlike other Telmarines, the trees could not be expected to know this.

Nor did they. The wind became a tempest, the woods roared and creaked all round them. There came a crash. A tree fell right across the road just behind him. "Quiet, Destrier, quiet!" said Caspian, patting his horse's neck; but he was trembling himself and knew that he had escaped death by an inch. Lightning flashed and a great crack of thunder seemed to break the sky in two just overhead. Destrier bolted in good earnest. Caspian was a good rider, but he had not the strength to hold him back. He kept his seat, but he knew that his life hung by a thread during the wild career that followed. Tree after tree rose up before them in the dusk and was only just avoided. Then, almost too suddenly to hurt (and yet it did hurt him too) something struck Caspian on the forehead and he knew no more.

When he came to himself he was lying in a firelit place with bruised limbs and a bad headache. Low voices were speaking close at hand.

"And now," said one, "before it wakes up we must decide what to do with it."

"Kill it," said another. "We can't let it live. It would betray us."

"We ought to have killed it at once, or else let it alone," said a third voice. "We can't kill it now. Not after we've taken it in and bandaged its head and all. It would be murdering a guest."

"Gentlemen," said Caspian in a feeble voice, "whatever you do to me, I hope you will be kind to my poor horse."

"Your horse had taken flight long before we found you," said the first voice – a curiously husky, earthy voice, as Caspian now noticed.

"Now don't let it talk you round with its pretty words," said the second voice. "I still say——"

"Horns and halibuts!" exclaimed the third voice. "Of course we're not going to murder it. For shame, Nikabrik. What do you say, Trufflehunter? What shall we do with it?"

"I shall give it a drink," said the first voice, presumably Trufflehunter's. A dark shape approached the bed. Caspian felt an arm slipped gently under his shoulders – if it was exactly an arm. The shape somehow seemed wrong. The face that bent towards him seemed wrong too. He got the impression that it was very hairy and very long nosed, and there were odd white patches on each side of it. "It's a mask of some sort," thought Caspian. "Or perhaps I'm in a fever and imagining it all." A cupful of something sweet and hot was set to his lips and he drank. At that moment one of the others poked the fire. A blaze sprang up and Caspian almost screamed with the shock as the sudden light revealed the face that was looking into his own. It was not a man's face but a badger's, though larger and friendlier and more intelligent than the face of any badger he had seen before. And it had certainly been talking. He saw, too, that he was on a bed of heather, in a cave. By the fire sat two little bearded men, so much wilder and shorter and hairier and thicker than Doctor Cornelius that he knew them at once for real Dwarfs, ancient Dwarfs with not a drop of human blood in their veins. And Caspian knew that he had found the Old Narnians at last. Then his head began to swim again.

In the next few days he learned to know them by names. The Badger was called Trufflehunter; he was the oldest and kindest of the three. The Dwarf who had wanted to kill Caspian was a sour Black Dwarf (that is, his hair and beard were black and thick and hard like horsehair). His name was Nikabrik. The other Dwarf was a Red Dwarf with hair rather like a Fox's and he was called Trumpkin.

"And now," said Nikabrik on the first evening when Caspian was well enough to sit up and talk, "we still have to decide what to do with this Human. You two think you've done it a great kindness by not letting me kill it. But I suppose the upshot is that we have to keep it a prisoner for life. I'm certainly not going to let it go alive – to go back to its own kind and betray us all."

"Bulbs and bolsters, Nikabrik!" said Trumpkin. "Why need you talk so unhandsomely? It isn't the creature's fault that it bashed its head against a tree outside our hole. And I don't think it looks like a traitor."

"I say," said Caspian, "you haven't yet found out whether I *want* to go back. I don't. I want to stay with you – if you'll let me. I've been looking for people like you all my life."

"That's a likely story," growled Nikabrik. "You're a Telmarine and a Human, aren't you? Of course you want to go back to your own kind."

"Well, even if I did, I couldn't," said Caspian. "I was flying for my life when I had my accident. The King wants to kill me. If you'd killed me, you'd have done the very thing to please him."

"Well, now," said Trufflehunter, "you don't say so!"

"Eh?" said Trumpkin. "What's that? What have you been doing, Human, to fall foul of Miraz at your age?"

"He's my uncle," began Caspian, when Nikabrik jumped up with his hand on his dagger.

"There you are!" he cried. "Not only a Telmarine but close kin and heir to our greatest enemy. Are you still mad enough to let this creature live?" He would have stabbed Caspian then and there, if the Badger and Trumpkin had not got in the way and forced him back to his seat and held him down.

"Now, once and for all, Nikabrik," said Trumpkin. "Will you contain yourself, or must Trufflehunter and I sit on your head?"

Nikabrik sulkily promised to behave, and the other two asked Caspian to tell his whole story. When he had done so there was a moment's silence.

"This is the queerest thing I ever heard," said Trumpkin.

"I don't like it," said Nikabrik. "I didn't know there were stories about us still told among the Humans. The less they know about us the better. That old nurse, now. She'd better have held her tongue. And it's all mixed up with that Tutor: a renegade Dwarf. I hate 'em. I hate 'em worse than the Humans. You mark my words – no good will come of it."

"Don't you go talking about things you don't understand, Nikabrik," said Trufflehunter. "You Dwarfs are as forgetful and changeable as the Humans themselves. I'm a beast, I am, and a Badger what's more. We don't change. We hold on. I say great good will come of it. This is the true King of Narnia. And we beasts remember, even if Dwarfs forget, that Narnia was never right except when a son of Adam was King."

"Whistles and whirligigs, Trufflehunter!" said Trumpkin. "You don't mean you want to give the country to the Humans?"

"I said nothing about that," answered the Badger. "It's not Man's country (who should know that better than me?) but it's a country for a man to be King of. We badgers have long enough memories to know that. Why, bless us all, wasn't the High King Peter a Man?"

"Do you believe all those old stories?" asked Trumpkin.

"I tell you, we don't change, we beasts," said Trufflehunter. "We don't forget. I believe in the High King Peter and the rest that reigned at Cair Paravel, as firmly as I believe in Aslan himself."

"As firmly as *that*, I dare say," said Trumpkin. "But who believes in Aslan nowadays?"

"I do," said Caspian. "And if I hadn't believed in him before, I would now. Back there among the Humans, the people who laughed at Aslan would have laughed at stories about Talking Beasts and Dwarfs. Sometimes I did wonder if there really was such a person as Aslan; but then sometimes I wondered if there were really people like you. Yet there you are."

"That's right," said Trufflehunter. "You're right, King Caspian. And as long as you will be true to Old Narnia you shall be *my* King, whatever they say. Long life to your Majesty."

"You make me sick, Badger," growled Nikabrik. "The High King Peter and the rest may have been Men, but they were a different sort of men. This is one of the cursed Telmarines. He has *hunted* beasts for sport. Haven't you, now?" he added, rounding suddenly on Caspian.

"Well, to tell you the truth, I have," said Caspian. "But they weren't Talking Beasts."

"It's all the same thing," said Nikabrik.

"No, no, no," said Trufflehunter. "You know it isn't. You know very well that the beasts in Narnia nowadays are different and are no more than the poor dumb, witless creatures you'd find in Calormen or Telmar. They're smaller too. They're far more different from us than the half-Dwarfs are from you."

There was a great deal more talk, but it all ended with the agreement that Caspian should stay and even the promise that, as soon as he was able to go out, he should be taken to see what Trumpkin called "the Others"; for apparently in these wild parts all sorts of creatures from the Old Days of Narnia still lived on in hiding.

CHAPTER SIX

THE PEOPLE THAT LIVED IN HIDING

Now began the happiest times that Caspian had ever known. On a fine summer morning when the dew lay on the grass he set off with the Badger and the two Dwarfs, up through the forest to a high saddle in the mountains and down on to their sunny southern slopes where one looked across the green wolds of Archenland.

"We will go first to the Three Bulgy Bears," said Trumpkin.

They came in a glade to an old hollow oak tree covered with moss, and Trufflehunter tapped with his paw three times on the trunk and there was no answer. Then he tapped again and a woolly sort of voice from inside said, "Go away. It's not time to get up yet." But when he tapped the third time there was a noise like a small earthquake from inside and a sort of door opened and out came three brown bears, very bulgy indeed and blinking their little eyes. And when everything had been explained to them (which took a long time because they were so sleepy) they said, just as Trufflehunter had said, that a Son of Adam ought to be King of Narnia and all kissed Caspian — very wet, snuffly kisses they were — and offered him some honey. Caspian did not really want honey, without bread, at that time in the morning, but he thought it polite to accept. It took him a long time afterwards to get unsticky.

After that they went on till they came among tall beech trees, and Trufflehunter called out, "Pattertwig! Pattertwig! Pattertwig!" and almost at once, bounding down from branch to branch till he was just above their heads, came the most magnificent red Squirrel that Caspian had ever seen. He was far bigger than the ordinary dumb squirrels which he had sometimes seen in the castle gardens; indeed he was nearly the size of a terrier and the moment you looked in his face you saw that he could talk. Indeed the difficulty was to get him to stop talking, for, like all squirrels, he was a chatterer. He welcomed Caspian at once and asked if he would like a nut and Caspian said thanks, he would. But as Pattertwig went bounding away to fetch it, Trufflehunter whispered in Caspian's ear, "Don't look. Look the other way. It's very bad manners among squirrels to watch anyone going to his store or to look as if you wanted to know where it was." Then Pattertwig came back with the nut and Caspian ate it and after that Pattertwig asked if he could take any messages to other friends. "For I can go nearly everywhere without setting foot to ground," he said. Trufflehunter and the Dwarfs thought this a very good idea and gave Pattertwig messages to all sorts of people with queer names telling them all to come to a feast and council on Dancing Lawn at midnight three nights ahead. "And you'd better tell the three Bulgies too," added Trumpkin. "We forgot to mention it to them."

Their next visit was to the Seven Brothers of Shuddering Wood. Trumpkin led the way back to the saddle and then down eastward on the northern slope of the mountains till they came to a very solemn place among rocks and fir trees. They went very quietly and presently Caspian could feel the ground shake under his feet as if someone were hammering down below. Trumpkin went to a flat stone about the size of the top of a water-butt, and stamped on it with his foot. After a long pause it was moved away by someone or something underneath, and there was a dark, round hole with a good deal of heat and steam coming out of it and in the middle of the hole the head of a Dwarf very like Trumpkin himself. There was a long talk here and the Dwarf seemed more suspicious than the Squirrel or the Bulgy Bears had been, but in the end the whole party was invited to come down. Caspian found himself descending a dark stairway into the earth, but when he came to the bottom he saw firelight. It was the light of a furnace. The whole place was a smithy. A subterranean stream ran past on one side of it. Two Dwarfs were at the bellows, another was holding a piece of red-hot metal on the anvil with a pair of tongs, a fourth was hammering it, and two, wiping their horny little hands on a greasy cloth, were coming forward to meet the visitors. It took some time to satisfy them that Caspian was a friend and not an enemy, but when they did, they all cried, "Long live the King," and their gifts were noble – mail shirts and helmets and swords for Caspian and Trumpkin and Nikabrik. The Badger could have had the same if he had liked, but he said he was a beast, he was, and if his claws and teeth could not keep his skin whole, it wasn't worth keeping. The workmanship of the arms was far finer than any Caspian had ever seen, and he gladly accepted the Dwarf-made sword instead of his own, which looked, in comparison, as feeble as a toy and as clumsy as a stick. The seven brothers (who were all Red Dwarfs) promised to come to the feast at Dancing Lawn.

A little farther on, in a dry, rocky ravine, they reached the cave of five Black Dwarfs. They looked suspiciously at Caspian, but in the end the eldest of them said, "If he is against Miraz, we'll have him for King." And the next oldest said, "Shall we go farther up for you, up to the crags? There's an Ogre or two and a Hag that we could introduce you to, up there."

"Certainly not," said Caspian.

"I should think not, indeed," said Trufflehunter. "We want none of that sort on our side." Nikabrik disagreed with this, but Trumpkin and the Badger overruled him. It gave Caspian a shock to realize that the horrible creatures out of the old stories, as well as the nice ones, had some descendants in Narnia still.

"We should not have Aslan for a friend if we brought in *that* rabble," said Trufflehunter as they came away from the cave of the Black Dwarfs.

"Oh, Aslan!" said Trumpkin, cheerily but contemptuously. "What matters much more is that you wouldn't have me."

"Do *you* believe in Aslan?" said Caspian to Nikabrik.

"I'll believe in anyone or anything," said Nikabrik, "that'll batter these cursed Telmarine barbarians to pieces or drive them out of Narnia. Anyone or anything, Aslan *or* the White Witch, do you understand?"

"Silence, silence," said Trufflehunter. "You do not know what you are saying. She was a worse enemy than Miraz and all his race."

"Not to Dwarfs, she wasn't," said Nikabrik.

Their next visit was a pleasanter one. As they came lower down, the mountains opened out into a great glen or wooded forge with a swift river running at the bottom. The open places near the river's edge were a mass of foxgloves and wild roses and the air was buzzing with bees. Here Trufflehunter called again, "Glenstorm! Glenstorm!" and after a pause Caspian heard the sound of hoofs. It grew louder till the valley trembled and at last, breaking and trampling the thickets, there came in sight the noblest creatures that Caspian had yet seen, the great Centaur Glenstorm and his three sons. His flanks were glossy chestnut and the beard that covered his broad chest was golden-red. He was a prophet and a star-gazer and knew what they had come about.

"Long live the King," he cried. "I and my sons are ready for war. When is the battle to be joined?"

Up till now neither Caspian nor the others had really been thinking of a war. They had some vague idea, perhaps, of an occasional raid on some Human farmstead or of attacking a party of hunters, if it ventured too far into these southern wilds. But, in the main, they had thought only of living to themselves in woods and caves and building up an attempt at Old Narnia in hiding. As soon as Glenstorm had spoken everyone felt much more serious.

"Do you mean a real war to drive Miraz out of Narnia?" asked Caspian.

"What else?" said the Centaur. "Why else does your Majesty go clad in mail and girt with sword?"

"Is it possible, Glenstorm?" said the Badger.

"The time is ripe," said Glenstorm. "I watch the skies, Badger, for it is mine to watch, as it is yours to remember. Tarva and Alambil have met in the halls of high heaven, and on earth a Son of Adam has once more arisen to rule and name the creatures. The hour has struck. Our council at the Dancing Lawn must be a council of war." He spoke in such a voice that neither Caspian nor the others hesitated for a moment: it now seemed to them quite possible that they might win a war and quite certain that they must wage one.

As it was now past the middle of the day, they rested with the Centaurs and ate such food as the centaurs provided – cakes of oaten meal, and apples, and herbs, and wine, and cheese.

The next place they were to visit was quite near at hand, but they had to go a long way round in order to avoid a region in which Men lived. It was well into the afternoon before they found themselves in level fields, warm between hedgerows. There Trufflehunter called at the mouth of a little hole in a green bank and out popped the last thing Caspian expected – a Talking Mouse. He was of course bigger than a common mouse, well over a foot high when he stood on his hind legs, and with ears nearly as long as (though broader than) a rabbit's. His name was Reepicheep and he was a gay and martial mouse. He wore a tiny little rapier at his side and twirled his long whiskers as if they were a moustache. "There are twelve of us, Sire," he said with a dashing and graceful bow, "and I place all the resources of my people unreservedly at your Majesty's disposal." Caspian tried hard (and successfully) not to laugh, but he couldn't help thinking that Reepicheep and all his people could very easily be put in a washing basket and carried home on one's back.

It would take too long to mention all the creatures whom Caspian met that day – Clodsley Shovel the Mole, the three Hardbiters (who were badgers like Trufflehunter), Camillo the Hare, and Hogglestock the Hedgehog. They rested at last beside a well at the edge of a wide and level circle of grass, bordered with tall elms which now threw long shadows across it, for the sun was setting, the daisies closing, and the rooks flying home to bed. Here they supped on food they had brought with them and Trumpkin lit his pipe (Nikabrik was not a smoker).

"Now," said the Badger, "if only we could wake the spirits of these trees and this well, we should have done a good day's work."

"Can't we?" said Caspian.

"No," said Trufflehunter. "We have no power over them. Since the Humans came into the land, felling forests and defiling streams, the Dryads and Naiads have sunk into a deep sleep. Who knows if ever they will stir again? And that is a great loss to our side. The Telmarines are horribly afraid of the woods, and once the Trees moved in anger, our enemies would go mad with fright and be chased out of Narnia as quick as their legs could carry them."

"What imaginations you Animals have!" said Trumpkin, who didn't believe in such things. "But why stop at Trees and Waters? Wouldn't it be even nicer if the stones started throwing themselves at old Miraz?"

The Badger only grunted at this, and after that there was such a silence that Caspian had nearly dropped off to sleep when he thought he heard a faint musical sound from the depth of the woods at his back. Then he thought it was only a dream and turned over again; but as soon as his ear touched the ground he felt or heard (it was hard to tell which) a faint beating or drumming. He raised his head. The beating noise at once became fainter, but the music returned, clearer this time. It was like flutes. He saw that Trufflehunter was sitting up staring into the wood. The moon was bright; Caspian had been asleep longer than he thought. Nearer and nearer came the music, a tune wild and yet dreamy, and the noise of many light feet, till at last, out from the wood into the moonlight, came dancing shapes such as Caspian had been thinking of all his life. They were not much taller than dwarfs, but far slighter and more graceful. Their curly heads had little horns, the upper part of their bodies gleamed naked in the pale light, but their legs and feet were those of goats.

"Fauns!" cried Caspian, jumping up, and in a moment they were all round him. It took next to no time to explain the whole situation to them and they accepted Caspian at once. Before he knew what he was doing he found himself joining in the dance. Trumpkin, with heavier and jerkier movements, did likewise and even Trufflehunter hopped and lumbered about as best he could. Only Nikabrik stayed where he was, looking on in silence. The Fauns footed it all round Caspian to their reedy pipes. Their strange faces, which seemed mournful and merry all at once, looked into his; dozens of fauns, Mentius and Obentinus and Dumnus, Voluns, Voltinus, Girbius, Nimienus, Nausus, and Oscuns. Pattertwig had sent them all.

When Caspian awoke next morning he could hardly believe that it had not all been a dream; but the grass was covered with little cloven hoof-marks.

CHAPTER SEVEN

OLD NARNIA IN DANGER

The place where they had met the Fauns was, of course, Dancing Lawn itself, and here Caspian and his friends remained till the night of the great Council. To sleep under the stars, to drink nothing but well water and to live chiefly on nuts and wild fruit, was a strange experience for Caspian after his bed with silken sheets in a tapestried chamber at the castle, with meals laid out on gold and silver dishes in the anteroom, and attendants ready at his call. But he had never enjoyed himself more. Never had sleep been more refreshing nor food tasted more savoury, and he began already to harden and his face wore a kinglier look.

When the great night came, and his various strange subjects came stealing into the lawn by ones and twos and threes or by sixes and sevens – the moon then shining almost at her full – his heart swelled as he saw their numbers and heard their greetings. All whom he had met were there: Bulgy Bears and Red Dwarfs and Black Dwarfs, Moles and Badgers, Hares and Hedgehogs, and others whom he had not yet seen – five Satyrs as red as foxes, the whole contingent of Talking Mice, armed to the teeth and following a shrill trumpet, some Owls, the Old Raven of Ravenscaur. Last of all (and this took Caspian's breath away), with the Centaurs came a small but genuine Giant, Wimbleweather of Deadman's Hill, carrying on his back a basketful of rather sea-sick Dwarfs who had accepted his offer of a lift and were now wishing they had walked instead.

The Bulgy Bears were very anxious to have the feast first and leave the council till afterwards; perhaps till tomorrow. Reepicheep and his Mice said that councils and feasts could both wait, and proposed storming Miraz in his own castle that very night. Pattertwig and the other Squirrels said they could talk and eat at the same time, so why not have the council and feast all at once? The Moles proposed throwing up entrenchments round the Lawn before they did anything else. The Fauns thought it would be better to begin with a solemn dance. The Old Raven, while agreeing with the Bears that it would take too long to have a full council before supper, begged to be allowed to give a brief address to the whole company. But Caspian and the Centaurs and the Dwarfs overruled all these suggestions and insisted on holding a real council of war at once.

When all the other creatures had been persuaded to sit down quietly in a great circle, and when (with more difficulty) they had got Pattertwig to stop running to and fro and saying, "Silence! Silence, everyone, for the King's speech", Caspian, feeling a little nervous, got up. "Narnians!" he began, but he never got any further, for at that very moment Camillo the Hare said, "Hush! There's a Man somewhere near."

They were all creatures of the wild, accustomed to being hunted, and they all became still as statues. The beasts all turned their noses in the direction which Camillo had indicated.

"Smells like Man and yet not quite like Man," whispered Trufflehunter.

"It's getting steadily nearer," said Camillo.

"Two badgers and you three Dwarfs, with your bows at the ready, go softly off to meet it," said Caspian.

"We'll settle 'un," said a Black Dwarf grimly, fitting a shaft to his bowstring.

"Don't shoot if it is alone," said Caspian. "Catch it."

"Why?" asked the Dwarf.

"Do as you're told," said Glenstorm the Centaur.

Everyone waited in silence while the three Dwarfs and two Badgers trotted stealthily across to the trees on the north-west side of the Lawn. Then came a sharp dwarfish cry, "Stop! Who goes there?" and a sudden spring. A moment later a voice, which Caspian knew well, could be heard saying, "All right, all right, I'm unarmed. Take my wrists if you like, worthy Badgers, but don't bite right through them. I want to speak to the King."

"Doctor Cornelius!" cried Caspian with joy, and rushed forward to greet his old tutor. Everyone else crowded round.

"Pah!" said Nikabrik. "A renegade Dwarf. A half-and-halfer! Shall I pass my sword through its throat?"

"Be quiet, Nikabrik," said Trumpkin. "The creature can't help its ancestry."

"This is my greatest friend and the saviour of my life," said Caspian. "And anyone who doesn't like his company may leave my army at once. Dearest Doctor, I *am* glad to see you again. How ever did you find us out?"

"By a little use of simple magic, your Majesty," said the Doctor, who was still puffing and blowing from having walked so fast. "But there's no time to go into that now. We must all fly from this place at once. You are already betrayed and Miraz is on the move. Before midday tomorrow you will be surrounded."

"Betrayed!" said Caspian. "And by whom?"

"Another renegade Dwarf, no doubt," said Nikabrik.

"By your horse Destrier," said Doctor Cornelius. "The poor brute knew no better. When you were knocked off, of course, he went dawdling back to his stable in the castle. Then the secret of your flight was known. I made myself scarce, having no wish to be questioned about it in Miraz's torture chamber. I had a pretty good guess from my crystal as to where I should find you. But all day – that was the day before yesterday – I saw Miraz's tracking parties out in the woods. Yesterday I learned that his army is out. I don't think some of your – um – pure-blooded Dwarfs have as much woodcraft as might be expected. You've left tracks all over the place. Great carelessness. At any rate something has warned Miraz that Old Narnia is not so dead as he had hoped, and he is on the move."

"Hurray!" said a very shrill and small voice from somewhere at the Doctor's feet. "Let them come! All I ask is that the King will put me and my people in the front."

"What on earth?" said Doctor Cornelius. "Has your Majesty got grasshoppers – or mosquitoes – in your army?" Then after stooping down and peering carefully through his spectacles, he broke into a laugh.

"By the Lion," he swore, "it's a mouse. Signior Mouse, I desire your better acquaintance. I am honoured by meeting so valiant a beast."

"My friendship you shall have, learned Man," piped Reepicheep. "And any Dwarf – or Giant – in the army who does not give you good language shall have my sword to reckon with."

"Is there time for this foolery?" asked Nikabrik. "What are our plans? Battle or flight?"

"Battle if need be," said Trumpkin. "But we are hardly ready for it yet, and this is no very defensible place."

"I don't like the idea of running away," said Caspian.

"Hear him! Hear him!" said the Bulgy Bears. "Whatever we do, don't let's have any *running*. Especially not before supper; and not too soon after it neither."

"Those who run first do not always run last," said the Centaur. "And why should we let the enemy choose our position instead of choosing it ourselves? Let us find a strong place."

"That's wise, your Majesty, that's wise," said Trufflehunter.

"But where are we to go?" asked several voices.

"Your Majesty," said Doctor Cornelius, "and all you variety of creatures, I think we must fly east and down the river to the great woods. The Telmarines hate that region. They have always been afraid of the sea and of something that may come over the sea. That is why they have let the great woods grow up. If traditions speak true, the ancient Cair Paravel was at the river-mouth. All that part is friendly to us and hateful to our enemies. We must go to Aslan's How."

"Aslan's How?" said several voices. "We do not know what it is."

"It lies within the skirts of the Great Woods and it is a huge mound which Narnians raised in very ancient times over a very magical place, where there stood – and perhaps still stands – a very magical Stone. The Mound is all hollowed out within into galleries and caves, and the Stone is in the central cave of all. There is room in the mound for all our stores, and those of us who have most need of cover and are most accustomed to underground life can be lodged in the caves. The rest of us can lie in the wood. At a pinch all of us (except this worthy Giant) could retreat into the Mound itself, and there we should be beyond the reach of every danger except famine."

"It is a good thing we have a learned man among us," said Trufflehunter; but Trumpkin muttered under his breath, "Soup and celery! I wish our leaders would think less about these old wives' tales and more about victuals and arms." But all approved of Cornelius's proposal and that very night, half an hour later, they were on the march. Before sunrise they arrived at Aslan's How.

It was certainly an awesome place, a round green hill on top of another hill, long since grown over with trees, and one little, low doorway leading into it. The tunnels inside were a perfect maze till you got to know them, and they were lined and roofed with smooth stones, and on the stones, peering in the twilight, Caspian saw strange characters and snaky patterns, and pictures in which the form of a Lion was repeated again and again. It all seemed to belong to an even older Narnia than the Narnia of which his nurse had told him.

It was after they had taken up their quarters in and around the How that fortune began to turn against them. King Miraz's scouts soon found their new lair, and he and his army arrived on the edge of the woods. And as so often happens, the enemy turned out stronger than they had reckoned. Caspian's heart sank as he saw company after company arriving. And though Miraz's men may have been afraid of going into the wood, they were even more afraid of Miraz, and with him in command they carried battle deeply into it and sometimes almost to the How itself. Caspian and other captains of course made many sorties into the open country. Thus there was fighting on most days and sometimes by night as well; but

Caspian's party had on the whole the worst of it.

At last there came a night when everything had gone as badly as possible, and the rain which had been falling heavily all day had ceased at nightfall only to give place to raw cold. That morning Caspian had arranged what was his biggest battle yet, and all had hung their hopes on it. He, with most of the Dwarfs, was to have fallen on the King's right wing at daybreak, and then, when they were heavily engaged, Giant Wimbleweather, with the Centaurs and some of the fiercest beasts, was to have broken out from another place and endeavoured to cut the King's right off from the rest of the army. But it had all failed. No one had warned Caspian (because no one in these later days of Narnia remembered) that Giants are not at all clever. Poor Wimbleweather, though as brave as a lion, was a true Giant in that respect. He had broken out at the wrong time and from the wrong place, and both his party and Caspian's had suffered badly and done the enemy little harm. The best of the Bears had been hurt, a Centaur terribly wounded, and there were few in Caspian's party who had not lost blood. It was a gloomy company that huddled under the dripping trees to eat their scanty supper.

The gloomiest of all was Giant Wimbleweather. He knew it was all his fault. He sat in silence shedding big tears which collected on the end of his nose and then fell off with a huge splash on the whole bivouac of the Mice, who had just been beginning to get warm and drowsy.

They all jumped up, shaking the water out of their ears and wringing their little blankets, and asked the Giant in shrill but forcible voices whether he thought they weren't wet enough without this sort of thing. And then other people woke up and told the Mice they had been enrolled as scouts and not as a concert party, and asked why they couldn't keep quiet. And Wimbleweather tiptoed away to find some place where he could be miserable in peace, and stepped on somebody's tail and somebody (they said afterwards it was a fox) bit him. And so everyone was out of temper.

But in the secret and magical chamber at the heart of the How, King Caspian, with Cornelius and the Badger and Nikabrik and Trumpkin, were at council. Thick pillars of ancient workmanship supported the roof. In the centre was the Stone itself – a stone table, split right down the centre, and covered with what had once been writing of some kind; but ages of wind and rain and snow had almost worn it away in old times when the Stone Table had stood on the hilltop, and the Mound had not yet been built above it. They were not using the Table nor sitting round it: it was too magic a thing for any common use. They sat on logs a little way from it, and between them was a rough wooden table, on which stood a rude clay lamp lighting up their pale faces and throwing big shadows on the walls.

"If your Majesty is ever to use the Horn," said Trufflehunter, "I think the time has now come." Caspian had of course told them of his treasure several days ago.

"We are certainly in great need," answered Caspian. "But it is hard to be sure we are at our greatest. Supposing there came an even worse need and we had already used it?"

"By that argument," said Nikabrik, "your Majesty will never use it until it is too late."

"I agree with that," said Doctor Cornelius.

"And what do you think, Trumpkin?" asked Caspian.

"Oh, as for me," said the Red Dwarf, who had been listening with complete indifference, "your Majesty knows I think the Horn – and that bit of broken stone over there – and your great King Peter – and your Lion Aslan – are all eggs in moonshine. It's all one to me when your Majesty blows the Horn. All I insist on is that the army is told nothing about it. There's no good raising hopes of magical help which (as I think) are sure to be disappointed."

"Then in the name of Aslan we will wind Queen Susan's horn," said Caspian.

"There is one thing, Sire," said Doctor Cornelius, "that should perhaps be done first. We do not know what form the help will take. It might call Aslan himself from overseas. But I think it is more likely to call Peter the High King and his mighty consorts down from the high past. But in either case, I do not think we can be sure that the help will come to this very spot—"

"You never said a truer word," put in Trumpkin.

"I think," went on the learned man, "that they – or he – will come back to one or other of the Ancient Places of Narnia. This, where we now sit, is the most ancient and most deeply magical of all, and here, I think, the answer is likeliest to come. But there are two others. One is Lantern Waste, up-river, west of Beaversdam, where the Royal Children first appeared in Narnia, as the records tell. The other is down at the river-mouth, where their castle of Cair Paravel once stood. And if Aslan himself comes, that would be the best place for meeting him too, for every story says that he is the son of the great Emperor-over-Sea, and over the sea he will pass. I should like very much to send messengers to both places, to Lantern Waste and the river-mouth, to receive them – or him – or it."

"Just as I thought," muttered Trumpkin. "The first result of all this foolery is not to bring us help but to lose us two fighters."

"Who would you think of sending, Doctor Cornelius?" asked Caspian.

"Squirrels are best for getting through enemy country without being caught," said Trufflehunter.

"All *our* squirrels (and we haven't many)," said Nikabrik, "are rather flighty. The only one I'd trust on a job like that would be Pattertwig."

"Let it be Pattertwig, then," said King Caspian. "And who for our other messenger? I know you'd go, Trufflehunter, but you haven't the speed. Nor you, Doctor Cornelius."

"I *won't* go," said Nikabrik. "With all these Humans and beasts about, there must be a Dwarf here to see that the Dwarfs are fairly treated."

"Thimbles and thunderstorms!" cried Trumpkin in a rage. "Is that how you speak to the King? Send me, Sire, I'll go."

"But I thought you didn't believe in the Horn, Trumpkin," said Caspian.

"No more I do, your Majesty. But what's that got to do with it? I might as well die on a wild goose chase as die here. You are my King. I know the difference between giving advice and taking orders. You've had my advice, and now it's the time for orders."

"I will never forget this, Trumpkin," said Caspian. "Send for Pattertwig, one of you. And when shall I blow the Horn?"

"I would wait for sunrise, your Majesty," said Doctor Cornelius. "That sometimes has an effect in operations of White Magic."

A few minutes later Pattertwig arrived and had his task explained to him. As he was, like many squirrels, full of courage and dash and energy and excitement and mischief (not to say conceit), he no sooner heard it than he was eager to be off. It was arranged that he should run for Lantern Waste while Trumpkin made the shorter journey to the river-mouth. After a hasty meal they both set off with fervent thanks and good wishes of the King, the Badger, and Cornelius.

CHAPTER EIGHT

HOW THEY LEFT THE ISLAND

"And so," said Trumpkin (for, as you have realized, it was he who had been telling all this story to the four children, sitting on the grass in the ruined hall of Cair Paravel) – "and so I put a crust or two in my pocket, left behind all weapons but my dagger, and took to the woods in the grey of the morning. I'd been plugging away for many hours when there came a sound that I'd never heard the like of in my born days. Eh, I won't forget that. The whole air was full of it, loud as thunder but far longer, cool and sweet as music over water, but strong enough to shake the woods. And I said to myself, 'If that's not the Horn, call me a rabbit.' And a moment later I wondered why he hadn't blown it sooner—"

"What time was it?" asked Edmund.

"Between nine and ten of the clock," said Trumpkin.

"Just when we were at the railway station!" said all the children, and looked at one another with shining eyes.

"Please go on," said Lucy to the Dwarf.

"Well, as I was saying, I wondered, but I went on as hard as I could pelt. I kept on all night – and then, when it was half light this morning, as if I'd no more sense than a Giant, I risked a short cut across open country to cut off a big loop of the river, and was caught. Not by the army, but by a pompous old fool who has charge of a little castle which is Miraz's last stronghold towards the coast. I needn't tell you they got no true tale out of me, but I was a Dwarf and that was enough. But, lobsters and lollipops! It is a good thing the seneschal *was* a pompous fool. Anyone else would have run me through there and then. But nothing would do for him short of a grand execution: sending me down 'to the ghosts' in the full ceremonial way. And then this young lady" (he nodded at Susan) "does her bit of archery – and it was pretty shooting, let me tell you – and here we are. And without my armour, for of course they took that." He knocked out and refilled his pipe.

"Great Scott!" said Peter. "So it was the horn – your own horn, Su – that dragged us all off that seat on the platform yesterday morning! I can hardly believe it; yet it all fits in."

"I don't know why you shouldn't believe it," said Lucy, "if you believe in magic at all. Aren't there lots of stories about magic forcing people out of one place – out of one world – into another? I mean, when a magician in *The Arabian Nights* calls up a Jinn, it has to come. We had to come, just like that."

"Yes," said Peter, "I suppose what makes it feel so queer is that in the stories it's always someone in our world who does the calling. One doesn't really think about where the Jinn's coming *from*."

"And now we know what it feels like for the Jinn," said Edmund with a chuckle. "Golly! It's a bit uncomfortable to know that *we* can be whistled for like that. It's worse than what Father says about living at the mercy of the telephone."

"But we want to be here, don't we," said Lucy, "if Aslan wants us?"

"Meanwhile," said the Dwarf, "what are we to do? I suppose I'd better go back to King Caspian and tell him no help has come."

"No help?" said Susan. "But it *has* worked. And here we are."

"Um – um – yes, to be sure. I see that," said the Dwarf, whose pipe seemed to be blocked (at any rate he made himself very busy cleaning it). "But – well – I mean——"

"But don't you yet see who we are?" shouted Lucy. "You *are* stupid."

"I suppose you are the four children out of the old stories," said Trumpkin. "And I'm very glad to meet you of course. And it's very interesting, no doubt. But – no offence?" – and he hesitated again.

"Do get on and say whatever you're going to say," said Edmund.

"Well, then – no offence," said Trumpkin. "But, you know, the King and Trufflehunter and Doctor Cornelius were expecting – well, if you see what I mean, help. To put it in another way, I think they'd been imagining you as great warriors. As it is – we're awfully fond of children and all that, but just at the moment, in the middle of a war – but I'm sure you understand."

"You mean you think we're no good," said Edmund, getting red in the face.

"Now pray don't be offended," interrupted the Dwarf. "I assure you, my dear little friends——"

"*Little* from you is really a bit too much," said Edmund, jumping up. "I suppose you don't believe we won the Battle of Beruna? Well, you can say what you like about me because I know——"

"There's no good losing our tempers," said Peter. "Let's fit him out with fresh armour and fit ourselves out from the treasure chamber, and have a talk after that."

"I don't quite see the point——" began Edmund, but Lucy whispered in his ear, "Hadn't we better do what Peter says? He is the High King, you know. And I think he has an idea." So Edmund agreed and by the aid of his torch they all, including Trumpkin, went down the steps again into the dark coldness and dusty splendour of the treasure house.

The Dwarf's eyes glistened as he saw the wealth that lay on the shelves (though he had to stand on tiptoe to do so) and he muttered to himself, "It would never do to let Nikabrik see this; never." They found easily enough a mail shirt for him, a sword, a helmet, a shield, a bow and quiverful of arrows, all of dwarfish size. The helmet was of copper, set with rubies, and there was gold on the hilt of the sword: Trumpkin had never seen, much less carried, so much wealth in all his life. The children also put on mail shirts and helmets; a sword and shield were found for Edmund and a bow for Lucy – Peter and Susan were of course already carrying their gifts. As they came back up the stairway, jingling in their mail, and already looking and feeling more like Narnians and less like schoolchildren, the two boys were behind, apparently making some plan. Lucy heard Edmund say, "No, let me do it. It will be more of a sucks for him if I win, and less of a let-down for us all if I fail."

"All right, Ed," said Peter.

When they came out into the daylight Edmund turned to the Dwarf very politely and said, "I've got something to ask you. Kids like us don't often have the chance of meeting a great warrior like you. Would you have a little fencing match with me? It would be frightfully decent."

"But, lad," said Trumpkin, "these swords are sharp."

"I know," said Edmund. "But I'll never get anywhere near you and you'll be quite clever enough to disarm me without doing me any damage."

"It's a dangerous game," said Trumpkin. "But since you make such a point of it, I'll try a pass or two."

Both swords were out in a moment and the three others jumped off the dais and stood watching. It was well worth it. It was not like the silly fighting you see with broadswords on the stage. It was not even like the rapier fighting which you sometimes see rather better done. This was real broadsword fighting. The great thing is to slash at your enemy's legs and feet because they are the part that have no armour. And when he slashes at yours you jump with both feet off the ground so that his blow goes under them. This gave the Dwarf an advantage because Edmund, being much taller, had to be always stooping. I don't think Edmund would have had a chance if he had fought Trumpkin twenty-four hours earlier. But the air of Narnia had been working upon him ever since they arrived on the island, and all his old battles came back to him, and his arms and fingers remembered their old skill. He was King Edmund once more. Round and round the two combatants circled, stroke after stroke they gave, and Susan (who never could learn to like this sort of thing) shouted out, "Oh, *do* be careful." And then, so quickly that no one (unless they knew, as Peter did) could quite see how it happened, Edmund flashed his sword round with a peculiar twist, the Dwarf's sword flew out of his grip, and Trumpkin was wringing his empty hand as you do after a "sting" from a cricket bat.

"Not hurt, I hope, my dear little friend?" said Edmund, panting a little and returning his own sword to its sheath.

"I see the point," said Trumpkin drily. "You know a trick I never learned."

"That's quite true," put in Peter. "The best swordsman in the world may be disarmed by a trick that's new to him. I think it's only fair to give Trumpkin a chance at something else. Will you have a shooting match with my sister? There are no tricks in archery, you know."

"Ah, you're jokers, you," said the Dwarf. "I begin to see. As if I didn't know how she can shoot, after what happened this morning. All the same, I'll have a try." He spoke gruffly, but his eyes brightened, for he was a famous bowman among his own people.

All five of them came out into the courtyard.

"What's to be the target?" asked Peter.

"I think that apple hanging over the wall on the branch there would do," said Susan.

"That'll do nicely, lass," said Trumpkin. "You mean the yellow one near the middle of the arch?"

"No, not that," said Susan. "The red one up above — over the battlement."

The Dwarf's face fell. "Looks more like a cherry than an apple," he muttered, but he said nothing out loud.

They tossed up for the first shot (greatly to the interest of Trumpkin, who had never seen a coin tossed before) and Susan lost. They were to shoot from the top of the steps that led from the hall into the courtyard. Everyone could see from the way the Dwarf took his position and handled his bow that he knew what he was about.

Twang went the string. It was an excellent shot. The tiny apple shook as the arrow passed, and a leaf came fluttering down. Then Susan went to the top of the steps and strung her bow. She was not enjoying her match half so much as Edmund had enjoyed his; not because she had any doubt about hitting the apple but because Susan was so tender-hearted that she almost hated to beat someone who had been beaten already. The Dwarf watched her keenly as she drew the shaft to her ear. A moment later, with a little soft thump which they could all hear in that quiet place, the apple fell to the grass with Susan's arrow in it.

"Oh, well done, Su," shouted the other children.

"It wasn't really any better than yours," said Susan to the Dwarf. "I think there was a tiny breath of wind as you shot."

"No, there wasn't," said Trumpkin. "Don't tell me. I know when I am fairly beaten. I won't even say that the scar of my last wound catches me a bit when I get my arm well back—"

"Oh, are you wounded?" asked Lucy. "Do let me look."

"It's not a sight for little girls," began Trumpkin, but then he suddenly checked himself. "There I go talking like a fool again," he said. "I suppose you're as likely to be a great surgeon as your brother was to be a great swordsman or your sister to be a great archer." He sat down on the steps and took off his hauberk and slipped down his little shirt, showing an arm as hairy and muscular (in proportion) as a sailor's though not much bigger than a child's. There was a clumsy bandage on the shoulder which Lucy proceeded to unroll. Underneath, the cut looked very nasty and there was a good deal of swelling. "Oh, poor Trumpkin," said Lucy. "How horrid." Then she carefully dripped on to it one single drop of the cordial from her flask.

"Hullo. Eh? What have you done?" said Trumpkin. But however he turned his head and squinted and whisked his beard to and fro, he couldn't quite see his own shoulder. Then he felt it as well as he could, getting his arms and fingers into very difficult positions as you do when you're trying to scratch a place that is just out of reach. Then he swung his arm and raised it and tried the muscles, and finally jumped to his feet crying, "Giants and junipers! It's cured! It's as good as new." After that he burst into a great laugh and said, "Well, I've made as big a fool of myself as ever a Dwarf did. No offence, I hope? My humble duty to your Majesties all — humble duty. And thanks for my life, my cure, my breakfast — and my lesson."

The children all said it was quite all right and not to mention it.

"And now," said Peter, "if you've really decided to believe in us—"

"I have," said the Dwarf.

"It's quite clear what we have to do. We must join King Caspian at once."

"The sooner the better," said Trumpkin. "My being such a fool has already wasted about an hour."

"It's about two days' journey, the way you came," said Peter. "For us, I mean. We can't walk all day and night like you Dwarfs." Then he turned to the others. "What Trumpkin calls Aslan's How is obviously the Stone Table itself. You remember it was about half a day's march, or a little less, from there down to the Fords of Beruna—"

"Beruna's Bridge, we call it," said Trumpkin.

"There was no bridge in our time," said Peter. "And then from Beruna down to here was another day and a bit. We used to get home about teatime on the second day, going easily. Going hard, we could do the whole thing in a day and a half perhaps."

"But remember it's all woods now," said Trumpkin, "and there are enemies to dodge."

"Look here," said Edmund, "need we go by the same way that Our Dear Little Friend came?"

"No more of that, your Majesty, if you love me," said the Dwarf.

"Very well," said Edmund. "May I say our DLF?"

"Oh, Edmund," said Susan. "Don't keep *on* at him like that."

"That's all right, lass – I mean your Majesty," said Trumpkin with a chuckle. "A jibe won't raise a blister." (And after that they often called him the DLF till they'd almost forgotten what it meant.)

"As I was saying," continued Edmund, "we needn't go that way. Why shouldn't we row a little south till we come to Glasswater Creek and row up it? That brings us up behind the Hill of the Stone Table, and we'll be safe while we're at sea. If we start at once, we can be at the head of Glasswater before dark, get a few hours' sleep, and be with Caspian pretty early tomorrow."

"What a thing it is to know the coast," said Trumpkin. "None of us knows anything about Glasswater."

"What about food?" asked Susan.

"Oh, we'll have to do with apples," said Lucy. "Do let's get on. We've done nothing yet, and we've been here nearly two days."

"And anyway, no one's going to have my hat for a fish-basket again," said Edmund.

They used one of the raincoats as a kind of bag and put a good many apples in it. Then they all had a good long drink at the well (for they would meet no more fresh water till they landed at the head of the Creek) and went down to the boat. The children were sorry to leave Cair Paravel which, even in ruins, had begun to feel like home again.

"The DLF had better steer," said Peter, "and Ed and I will take an oar each. Half a moment, though. We'd better take off our mail: we're going to be pretty warm before we're done. The girls had better be in the bows and shout directions to the DLF because he doesn't know the way. You'd better get us a fair way out to sea till we've passed the island."

And soon the green, wooded coast of the island was falling away behind them, and its little bays and headlands were beginning to look flatter, and the boat was rising and falling in the gentle swell. The sea began to grow bigger around them and, in the distance, bluer, but close round the boat it was green and bubbly. Everything smelled salty and there was no noise except the swishing of water and the clop-clop of water against the sides and the splash of the oars and the jolting noise of the rowlocks. The sun grew hot.

It was delightful for Lucy and Susan in the bows, bending over the edge and trying to get their hands in the sea which they could never quite reach. The bottom, mostly pure, pale sand but with occasional patches of purple seaweed, could be seen beneath them.

"It's like old times," said Lucy. "Do you remember our voyage to Terebinthia – and Galma – and Seven Isles – and the Lone Islands?"

"Yes," said Susan, "and our great ship the *Splendour Hyaline*, with the swan's head at her prow and the carved swan's wings coming back almost to her waist?"

"And the silken sails, and the great stern lanterns?"

"And the feasts on the poop and the musicians."

"Do you remember when we had the musicians up in the rigging playing flutes so that it sounded like music out of the sky?"

Presently Susan took over Edmund's oar and he came forward to join Lucy. They had passed the island now and stood closer in to the shore – all wooded and deserted. They would have thought it very pretty if they had not remembered the time when it was open and breezy and full of merry friends.

"Phew! This is pretty gruelling work," said Peter.

"Can't I row for a bit?" said Lucy.

"The oars are too big for you," said Peter shortly, not because he was cross but because he had no strength to spare for talking.

CHAPTER NINE

WHAT LUCY SAW

Susan and the two boys were bitterly tired with rowing before they rounded the last headland and began the final pull up Glasswater itself, and Lucy's head ached from the long hours of sun and the glare on the water. Even Trumpkin longed for the voyage to be over. The seat on which he sat to steer had been made for men, not Dwarfs, and his feet did not reach the floorboards; and everyone knows how uncomfortable that is even for ten minutes. And as they all grew more tired, their spirits fell. Up till now the children had only been thinking of how to get to Caspian. Now they wondered what they would do when they found him, and how a handful of Dwarfs and woodland creatures could defeat an army of grown-up Humans.

Twilight was coming on as they rowed slowly up the windings of Glasswater Creek – a twilight which deepened as the banks drew closer together and the overhanging trees began almost to meet overhead. It was very quiet in here as the sound of the sea died away behind them; they could even hear the trickle of the little streams that poured down from the forest into Glasswater.

They went ashore at last, far too tired to attempt lighting a fire; and even a supper of apples (though most of them felt that they never wanted to see an apple again) seemed better than trying to catch or shoot anything. After a little silent munching they all huddled down together in the moss and dead leaves between four large beech trees.

Everyone except Lucy went to sleep at once. Lucy, being far less tired, found it hard to get comfortable. Also, she had forgotten till now that all Dwarfs snore. She knew that one of the best ways of getting to sleep is to stop trying, so she opened her eyes. Through a gap in the bracken and branches she could just see a patch of water in the Creek and the sky above it. Then, with a thrill of memory, she saw again, after all those years, the bright Narnian stars. She had once known them better than the stars of our own world, because as a queen in Narnia she had gone to bed much later than as a child in England. And there they were – at least, three of the summer constellations could be seen from where she lay: the Ship, the Hammer, and the Leopard. "Dear old Leopard," she murmured happily to herself.

Instead of getting drowsier she was getting more awake – with an odd, night-time, dreamish kind of wakefulness. The Creek was growing brighter. She knew now that the moon was on it, though she couldn't see the moon. And now she began to feel that the whole forest was coming awake like herself. Hardly knowing why she did it, she got up quickly and walked a little distance away from their bivouac.

"This is lovely," said Lucy to herself. It was cool and fresh; delicious smells were floating everywhere. Somewhere close by she heard the twitter of a nightingale beginning to sing, then stopping, then beginning again. It was a little lighter ahead. She went towards the light and came to a place where there were fewer trees, and whole patches or pools of moonlight, but the moonlight and the shadows so mixed that you could hardly be sure where anything was or what it was. At the same moment the nightingale, satisfied at last with his tuning up, burst into full song.

Lucy's eyes began to grow accustomed to the light, and she saw the trees that were nearest her more distinctly. A great longing for the old days when the trees could talk in Narnia came over her. She knew exactly how each of these trees would talk if only she could wake them, and what sort of human form it would put on. She looked at a silver birch: it would have a soft, showery voice and would look like a slender girl, with hair blown all about her face, and fond of dancing. She looked at the oak: he would be a wizened, but hearty old man with a frizzled beard and warts on his face and hands, and hair growing out of the warts. She looked at the beech under which she was standing. Ah! – she would be the best of all. She would be a gracious goddess, smooth and stately, the lady of the wood.

"Oh, Trees, Trees, Trees," said Lucy (though she had not been intending to speak at all). "Oh, Trees, wake, wake, wake. Don't you remember it? Don't you remember me? Dryads and Hamadryads, come out, come to me."

Though there was not a breath of wind they all stirred about her. The rustling noise of the leaves was almost like words. The nightingale stopped singing as if to listen to it. Lucy felt that at any moment she would begin to understand what the trees were trying to say. But the moment did not come. The rustling died away. The nightingale resumed its song. Even in the moonlight the wood looked more ordinary again. Yet Lucy had the feeling (as you sometimes have when you are trying to remember a name or a date and almost get it, but it vanishes before you really do) that she had just missed something: as if she had spoken to the trees a split second too soon or a split second too late, or used all the right words except one, or put in one word that was just wrong.

Quite suddenly she began to feel tired. She went back to the bivouac, snuggled down between Susan and Peter, and was asleep in a few minutes.

It was a cold and cheerless waking for them all next morning, with a grey twilight in the wood (for the sun had not yet risen) and everything damp and dirty.

"Apples, heigh-ho," said Trumpkin with a rueful grin. "I must say, you ancient kings and queens don't overfeed your courtiers!"

They stood up and shook themselves and looked about. The trees were thick and they could see no more than a few yards in any direction.

"I suppose your Majesties know the way all right?" said the Dwarf.

"I don't," said Susan. "I've never seen these woods in my life before. In fact I thought all along that we ought to have gone by the river."

"Then I think you might have said so at the time," answered Peter, with pardonable sharpness.

"Oh, don't take any notice of her," said Edmund. "She always is a wet blanket. You've got that pocket compass of yours, Peter, haven't you? Well, then, we're as right as rain. We've only got to keep on going northwest — cross that little river, the what-do-you-call-it? — the Rush—"

"I know," said Peter. "The one that joins the big river at the Fords of Beruna, or Beruna's Bridge, as the DLF calls it."

"That's right. Cross it and strike uphill, and we'll be at the Stone Table (Aslan's How, I mean) by eight or nine o'clock. I hope King Caspian will give us a good breakfast!"

"I hope you're right," said Susan. "I can't remember all that at all."

"That's the worst of girls," said Edmund to Peter and the Dwarf. "They never carry a map in their heads."

"That's because our heads have something inside them," said Lucy.

At first, things seemed to be going pretty well. They even thought they had struck an old path, but if you know anything about woods, you will know that one is always finding imaginary paths. They disappear after about five minutes and then you think you have found another (and hope it is not another but more of the same one) and it also disappears, and after you have been well lured out of your right direction you realize that none of them were paths at all. The boys and the Dwarf, however, were used to woods and were not taken in for more than a few seconds.

They had plodded on for about half an hour (three of them very stiff from yesterday's rowing) when Trumpkin suddenly whispered, "Stop". They all stopped. "There's something following us," he said in a low voice. "Or rather, something keeping up with us: over there on the left." They all stood still, listening and staring till their ears and eyes ached. "You and I'd better each have an Arrow on the string," said Susan to Trumpkin. The Dwarf nodded, and when both bows were ready for action the party went on again.

They went a few dozen yards through fairly open woodland, keeping a sharp look-out. Then they came to a place where the undergrowth thickened and they had to pass nearer to it. Just as they were passing the place, there came a sudden something that snarled and flashed, rising out from the breaking twigs like a thunderbolt. Lucy was knocked down and winded, hearing the twang of a bowstring as she fell. When she was able to take notice of things again, she saw a great grim-looking grey bear lying dead with Trumpkin's arrow in its side.

"The DLF beat you in *that* shooting match, Su," said Peter, with a slightly forced smile. Even he had been shaken by this adventure.

"I – I left it too late," said Susan, in an embarrassed voice. "I was so afraid it might be, you know – one of our kind of bears, a *talking* bear." She hated killing things.

"That's the trouble of it," said Trumpkin, "when most of the beasts have gone enemy and gone dumb, but there are still some of the other kind left. You never know, and you daren't wait to see."

"Poor old Bruin," said Susan. "You don't think he *was*?"

"Not he," said the Dwarf. "I saw the face and I heard the snarl. He only wanted Little Girl for his breakfast. And talking of breakfast, I didn't want to discourage your Majesties when you said you hoped King Caspian would give you a good one: but meat's precious scarce in camp. And there's good eating on a bear. It would be a shame to leave the carcass without taking a bit, and it won't delay us more than half an hour. I dare say you two youngsters – Kings, I should say – know how to skin a bear?"

"Let's go and sit down a fair way off," said Susan to Lucy. "I know what a horrid messy business *that* will be."

Lucy shuddered and nodded. When they had sat down she said: "Such a horrible idea has come into my head, Su."

"What's that?"

"Wouldn't it be dreadful if some day, in our own world, at home, men started going wild inside, like the animals here, and still looked like men, so that you'd never know which were which?"

"We've got enough to bother about here and now in Narnia," said the practical Susan, "without imagining things like that."

When they rejoined the boys and the Dwarf, as much as they thought they could carry of the best meat had been cut off. Raw meat is not a nice thing to fill one's pockets with, but they folded it up in fresh leaves and made the best of it. They were all experienced enough to know that they would feel quite differently about these squashy and unpleasant parcels when they had walked long enough to be really hungry.

On they trudged again (stopping to wash three pairs of hands that needed it in the first stream they passed) until the sun rose and the birds began to sing, and more flies than they wanted were buzzing in the bracken. The stiffness from yesterday's rowing began to wear off. Everybody's spirits rose. The sun grew warmer and they took their helmets off and carried them.

"I suppose we *are* going right?" said Edmund about an hour later.

"I don't see how we can go wrong as long as we don't bear too much to the left," said Peter. "If we bear too much to the right, the worst that can happen is wasting a little time by striking the Great River too soon and not cutting off the corner."

And again they trudged on with no sound except the thud of their feet and the jingle of their chain shirts.

"Where's this bally Rush got to?" said Edmund a good deal later.

"I certainly thought we'd have struck it by now," said Peter. "But there's nothing to do but keep on." They both knew that the Dwarf was looking anxiously at them, but he said nothing.

And still they trudged on and their mail shirts began to feel very hot and heavy.

"What on earth?" said Peter suddenly.

They had come, without seeing it, almost to the edge of a small precipice from which they looked down into a gorge with a river at the bottom. On the far side the cliffs rose much higher. None of the party except Edmund (and perhaps Trumpkin) was a rock climber.

"I'm sorry," said Peter. "It's my fault for coming this way. We're lost. I've never seen this place in my life before."

The Dwarf gave a low whistle between his teeth.

"Oh, do let's go back and go the other way," said Susan. "I knew all along we'd get lost in these woods."

"Susan!" said Lucy, reproachfully. "Don't nag at Peter like that. It's so rotten, and he's doing all he can."

"And don't you snap at Su like that, either," said Edmund. "I think she's quite right."

"Tubs and tortoiseshells!" exclaimed Trumpkin. "If we've got lost coming, what chance have we of finding our way back? And if we're to go back to the Island and begin all over again – even supposing we could – we might as well give the whole thing up. Miraz will have finished with Caspian before we get there at that rate."

"You think we ought to go on?" said Lucy.

"I'm not sure the High King *is* lost," said Trumpkin. "What's to hinder this river being the Rush?"

"Because the Rush is not in a gorge," said Peter, keeping his temper with some difficulty.

"Your Majesty says *is*," replied the Dwarf, "but oughtn't you to say *was*? You knew this country hundreds – it may be a thousand – years ago. Mayn't it have changed? A landslide might have pulled off half the side of that hill, leaving bare rock, and there are your precipices beyond the gorge. Then the Rush might go on deepening its course year after year till you get the little precipices this side. Or there might have been an earthquake, or anything."

"I never thought of that," said Peter.

"And anyway," continued Trumpkin, "even if this is not the Rush, it's flowing roughly north and so it must fall into the Great River anyway. I think I passed something that might have been it, on my way down. So if we go downstream, to our right, we'll hit the Great River. Perhaps not so high as we'd hoped, but at least we'll be no worse off than if you'd come my way."

"Trumpkin, you're a brick," said Peter. "Come on, then. Down this side of the gorge."

"Look! Look! Look!" cried Lucy.

"Where? What?" said everyone.

"The Lion," said Lucy. "Aslan himself. Didn't you see?" Her face had changed completely and her eyes shone.

"Do you really mean—?" began Peter.

"Where did you think you saw him?" asked Susan.

"Don't talk like a grown-up," said Lucy, stamping her foot. "I didn't *think* I saw him. I saw him."

"Where, Lu?" asked Peter.

"Right up there between those mountain ashes. No, this side of the gorge. And up, not down. Just the opposite of the way you want to go. And he wanted us to go where he was – up there."

"How do you know that was what he wanted?" asked Edmund.

"He – I – I just know," said Lucy, "by his face."

The others all looked at each other in puzzled silence.

"Her Majesty may well have seen a lion," put in Trumpkin. "There are lions in these woods, I've been told. But it needn't have been a friendly and talking lion any more than the bear was a friendly and talking bear."

"Oh, don't be so stupid," said Lucy. "Do you think I don't know Aslan when I see him?"

"He'd be a pretty elderly lion by now," said Trumpkin, "if he's one you knew when you were here before! And if it could be the same one, what's to prevent him having gone wild and witless like so many others?"

Lucy turned crimson and I think she would have flown at Trumpkin, if Peter had not laid his hand on her arm. "The DLF doesn't understand. How could he? You must just take it, Trumpkin, that we do really know about Aslan; a little bit about him, I mean. And you mustn't talk about him like that again. It isn't lucky for one thing, and it's all nonsense for another. The only question is whether Aslan was really there."

"But I know he was," said Lucy, her eyes filling with tears.

"Yes, Lu, but we don't, you see," said Peter.

"There's nothing for it but a vote," said Edmund.

"All right," replied Peter. "You're the eldest, DLF. What do you vote for? Up or down?"

"Down," said the Dwarf. "I know nothing about Aslan. But I do know that if we turn left and follow the gorge up, it might lead us all day before we found a place where we could cross it. Whereas if we turn right and go down, we're bound to reach the Great River in about a couple of hours. And if there *are* any real lions about, we want to go away from them, not towards them."

"What do you say, Susan?"

"Don't be angry, Lu," said Susan, "but I do think we should go down. I'm dead tired. Do let's get out of this wretched wood into the open as quick as we can. And none of us except you saw *anything*."

"Edmund?" said Peter.

"Well, there's just this," said Edmund, speaking quickly and turning a little red. "When we first discovered Narnia a year ago — or a thousand years ago, whichever it is — it was Lucy who discovered it first and none of us would believe her. I was the worst of the lot, I know. Yet she was right after all. Wouldn't it be fair to believe her this time? I vote for going up."

"Oh, Ed!" said Lucy and seized his hand.

"And now it's your turn, Peter," said Susan, "and I do hope—"

"Oh, shut up, shut up and let a chap think," interrupted Peter. "I'd much rather not have to vote."

"You're the High King," said Trumpkin sternly.

"Down," said Peter after a long pause. "I know Lucy may be right after all, but I can't help it. We must do one or the other."

So they set off to their right along the edge, downstream. And Lucy came last of the party, crying bitterly.

CHAPTER TEN

THE RETURN OF THE LION

To keep along the edge of the gorge was not so easy as it had looked. Before they had gone many yards they were confronted with young fir woods growing on the very edge, and after they had tried to go through these, stooping and pushing for about ten minutes, they realized that, in there, it would take them an hour to do half a mile. So they came back and out again and decided to go round the fir wood. This took them much farther to their right than they wanted to go, far out of sight of the cliffs and out of sound of the river, till they began to be afraid they had lost it altogether. Nobody knew the time, but it was getting to the hottest part of the day.

When they were able at last to go back to the edge of the gorge (nearly a mile below the point from which they had started) they found the cliffs on their side of it a good deal lower and more broken. Soon they found a way down into the gorge and continued the journey at the river's edge. But first they had a rest and a long drink. No one was talking any more about breakfast, or even dinner, with Caspian.

They may have been wise to stick to the Rush instead of going along the top. It kept them sure of their direction: and ever since the fir wood they had all been afraid of being forced too far out of their course and losing themselves in the wood. It was an old and pathless forest, and you could not keep anything like a straight course in it. Patches of hopeless brambles, fallen trees, boggy places and dense undergrowth would be always getting in your way. But the gorge of the Rush was not at all a nice place for travelling either. I mean, it was not a nice place for people in a hurry. For an afternoon's ramble ending in a picnic tea it would have been delightful. It had everything you could want on an occasion of that sort – rumbling waterfalls, silver cascades, deep, amber-coloured pools, mossy rocks, and deep moss on the banks in which you could sink over your ankles, every kind of fern, jewel-like dragonflies, sometimes a hawk overhead and once (Peter and Trumpkin both thought) an eagle. But of course what the children and the Dwarf wanted to see as soon as possible was the Great River below them, and Beruna, and the way to Aslan's How.

As they went on, the Rush began to fall more and more steeply. Their journey became more and more of a climb and less and less of a walk – in places even a dangerous climb over slippery rock with a nasty drop into dark chasms, and the river roaring angrily at the bottom.

You may be sure they watched the cliffs on their left eagerly for any sign of a break or any place where they could climb them; but those cliffs remained cruel. It was maddening, because everyone knew that once they were out of the gorge on that side, they would have only a smooth slope and a fairly short walk to Caspian's headquarters.

The boys and the Dwarf were now in favour of lighting a fire and cooking their bear-meat. Susan didn't want this; she only wanted, as she said, "to get *on* and finish it and get out of these beastly woods". Lucy was far too tired and miserable to have any opinion about anything. But as there was no dry wood to be had, it mattered very little what anyone thought. The boys began to wonder if raw meat was really as nasty as they had always been told. Trumpkin assured them it was.

Of course, if the children had attempted a journey like this a few days ago in England, they would have been knocked up. I think I have explained before how Narnia was altering them. Even Lucy was by now, so to speak, only one-third of a little girl going to boarding school for the first time, and two-thirds of Queen Lucy of Narnia.

"At last!" said Susan.

"Oh, hurray!" said Peter.

The river gorge had just made a bend and the whole view spread out beneath them. They could see open country stretching before them to the horizon and, between it and them, the broad silver ribbon of the Great River. They could see the specially broad and shallow place which had once been the Fords of Beruna but was now spanned by a long, many-arched bridge. There was a little town at the far end of it.

"By Jove," said Edmund. "We fought the Battle of Beruna just where that town is!"

This cheered the boys more than anything. You can't help feeling stronger when you look at a place where you won a glorious victory not to mention a kingdom, hundreds of years ago. Peter and Edmund were soon so busy talking about the battle that they forgot their sore feet and the heavy drag of their mail shirts on their shoulders. The Dwarf was interested too.

They were all getting on at a quicker pace now. The going became easier. Though there were still sheer cliffs on their left, the ground was becoming lower on their right. Soon it was no longer a gorge at all, only a valley. There were no more waterfalls and presently they were in fairly thick woods again.

Then — all at once — *whizz*, and a sound rather like the stroke of a woodpecker. The children were still wondering where (ages ago) they had heard a sound just like that and why they disliked it so, when Trumpkin shouted, "Down", at the same moment forcing Lucy (who happened to be next to him) flat down into the bracken. Peter, who had been looking up to see if he could spot a squirrel, had seen what it was — a long cruel arrow had sunk into a tree-trunk just above his head. As he pulled Susan down and dropped himself, another came rasping over his shoulder and struck the ground at his side.

"Quick! Quick! Get back! *Crawl!*" panted Trumpkin.

They turned and wriggled along uphill, under the bracken amid clouds of horribly buzzing flies. Arrows whizzed round them. One struck Susan's helmet with a sharp ping and glanced off. They crawled quicker. Sweat poured off them. Then they ran, stooping nearly double. The boys held their swords in their hands for fear they would trip them up.

It was heartbreaking work — all uphill again, back over the ground they had already travelled. When they felt that they really couldn't run any more, even to save their lives, they all dropped down in the damp moss beside a waterfall and behind a big boulder, panting. They were surprised to see how high they had already got.

They listened intently and heard no sound of pursuit.

"So *that's* all right," said Trumpkin, drawing a deep breath. "They're not searching the wood. Only sentries, I expect. But it means that Miraz has an outpost down there. Bottles and battledores, though, it was a near thing."

"I ought to have my head smacked for bringing us this way at all," said Peter.

"On the contrary, your Majesty," said the Dwarf. "For one thing it wasn't you, it was your royal brother, King Edmund, who first suggested going by Glasswater."

"I'm afraid the DLF's right," said Edmund, who had quite honestly forgotten this ever since things began going wrong.

"And for another," continued Trumpkin, "if we'd gone my way, we'd have walked straight into that new outpost, most likely; or at least had just the same trouble avoiding it. I think this Glasswater route has turned out for the best."

"A blessing in disguise," said Susan.

"Some disguise!" said Edmund.

"I suppose we'll have to go right up the gorge again now," said Lucy.

"Lu, you're a hero," said Peter. "That's the nearest you've got today to saying *I told you so*. Let's get on."

"And as soon as we're well up into the forest," said Trumpkin, "whatever anyone says, I'm going to light a fire and cook supper. But we must get well away from here."

There is no need to describe how they toiled back up the gorge. It was pretty hard work, but oddly enough everyone felt more cheerful. They were getting their second wind; and the word *supper* had had a wonderful effect.

They reached the fir wood which had caused them so much trouble while it was still daylight, and bivouacked in a hollow just above it. It was tedious gathering the firewood; but it was grand when the fire blazed up and they began producing the damp and smeary parcels of bear-meat which would have been so very unattractive to anyone who had spent the day indoors. The Dwarf had splendid ideas about cookery. Each apple (they still had a few of these) was wrapped up in bear's meat — as if it was to be apple dumpling with meat instead of pastry, only much thicker — and spiked on a sharp stick and then roasted. And the juice of the apple worked all through the meat, like apple sauce with roast pork. Bear that has lived too much on other animals is not very nice, but bear that has had plenty of honey and fruit is excellent, and this turned out to be that sort of bear. It was a truly glorious meal. And, of course, no washing up — only lying back and watching the smoke from Trumpkin's pipe and stretching one's tired legs and chatting. Everyone felt quite hopeful now about finding King Caspian tomorrow and defeating Miraz in a few days. It may not have been sensible of them to feel like this, but they did.

They dropped off to sleep one by one, but all pretty quickly.

Lucy woke out of the deepest sleep you can imagine, with the feeling that the voice she liked best in the world had been calling her name. She thought at first it was her father's voice, but that did not seem quite right. Then she thought it was Peter's voice, but that did not seem to fit either. She did not want to get up; not because she was still tired — on the contrary she was wonderfully rested and all the aches had gone from her bones — but because she felt so extremely happy and comfortable. She was looking straight up at the Narnian moon, which is larger than ours, and at the starry sky, for the place where they had bivouacked was comparatively open.

"Lucy," came the call again, neither her father's voice nor Peter's. She sat up, trembling with excitement but not with fear. The moon was so bright that the whole forest landscape around her was almost as clear as day, though it looked wilder. Behind her was the fir wood; away to her right the jagged cliff-tops on the far side of the gorge; straight ahead, open grass to where a glade of trees began about a bow-shot away. Lucy looked very hard at the trees of that glade.

"Why, I do believe they're moving," she said to herself. "They're walking about."

She got up, her heart beating wildly, and walked towards them. There was certainly a noise in the glade, a noise such as trees make in a high wind, though there was no wind tonight. Yet it was not exactly an ordinary tree-noise either. Lucy felt there was a tune in it, but she could not catch the tune any more than she had been able to catch the words when the trees had so nearly talked to her the night before. But there was, at least, a lilt; she felt her own feet wanting to dance as she got nearer. And now there was no doubt that the trees were really moving – moving in and out through one another as if in a complicated country dance. ("And I suppose," thought Lucy, "when trees dance, it must be a very, very country dance indeed.") She was almost among them now.

The first tree she looked at seemed at first glance to be not a tree at all but a huge man with a shaggy beard and great bushes of hair. She was not frightened: she had seen such things before. But when she looked again he was only a tree, though he was still moving. You couldn't see whether he had feet or roots, of course, because when trees move they don't walk on the surface of the earth; they wade in it as we do in water. The same thing happened with every tree she looked at. At one moment they seemed to be the friendly, lovely giant and giantess forms which the tree-people put on when some good magic has called them into full life: next moment they all looked like trees again. But when they looked like trees, it was like strangely human trees, and when they looked like people, it was like strangely branchy and leafy people – and all the time that queer lilting, rustling, cool, merry noise.

"They are almost awake, not quite," said Lucy. She knew she herself was wide awake, wider than anyone usually is.

She went fearlessly in among them, dancing herself as she leapt this way and that to avoid being run into by these huge partners. But she was only half interested in them. She wanted to get beyond them to something else; it was from beyond them that the dear voice had called.

She soon got through them (half wondering whether she had been using her arms to push branches aside, or to take hands in a Great Chain with big dancers who stooped to reach her) for they were really a ring of trees round a central open place. She stepped out from among their shifting confusion of lovely lights and shadows.

A circle of grass, smooth as a lawn, met her eyes, with dark trees dancing all round it. And then – oh joy! For *he* was there: the huge Lion, shining white in the moonlight, with his huge black shadow underneath him.

But for the movement of his tail he might have been a stone lion, but Lucy never thought of that. She never stopped to think whether he was a friendly lion or not. She rushed to him. She felt her heart would burst if she lost a moment. And the next thing she knew was that she was kissing him and putting her arms as far round his neck as she could and burying her face in the beautiful rich silkiness of his mane.

"Aslan, Aslan. Dear Aslan," sobbed Lucy. "At last."

The great beast rolled over on his side so that Lucy fell, half sitting and half lying between his front paws. He bent forward and just touched her nose with his tongue. His warm breath came all round her. She gazed up into the large wise face.

"Welcome, child," he said.

"Aslan," said Lucy, "you're bigger."

"That is because you are older, little one," answered he.

"Not because you are?"

"I am not. But every year you grow, you will find me bigger."

For a time she was so happy that she did not want to speak. But Aslan spoke.

"Lucy," he said, "we must not lie here for long. You have work in hand, and much time has been lost today."

"Yes, wasn't it a shame?" said Lucy. "*I* saw you all right. They wouldn't believe me. They're all so—"

From somewhere deep inside Aslan's body there came the faintest suggestion of a growl.

"I'm sorry," said Lucy, who understood some of his moods. "I didn't mean to start slanging the others. But it wasn't my fault anyway, was it?"

The Lion looked straight into her eyes.

"Oh, Aslan," said Lucy. "You don't mean it was? How could I – I couldn't have left the others and come up to you alone, how could I? Don't look at me like that... oh well, I suppose I *could*. Yes, and it wouldn't have been alone, I know, not if I was with you. But what would have been the good?"

Aslan said nothing.

"You mean," said Lucy rather faintly, "that it would have turned out all right – somehow? But how? Please, Aslan! Am I not to know?"

"To know what *would* have happened, child?" said Aslan. "No. Nobody is ever told that."

"Oh dear," said Lucy.

"But anyone can find out what *will* happen," said Aslan. "If you go back to the others now, and wake them up; and tell them you have seen me again; and that you must all get up at once and follow me – what will happen? There is only one way of finding out."

"Do you mean that is what you want me to do?" gasped Lucy.

"Yes, little one," said Aslan.

"Will the others see you too?" asked Lucy.

"Certainly not at first," said Aslan. "Later on, it depends."

"But they won't believe me!" said Lucy.

"It doesn't matter," said Aslan.

"Oh dear, oh dear," said Lucy. "And I was so pleased at finding you again. And I thought you'd let me stay. And I thought you'd come roaring in and frighten all the enemies away – like last time. And now everything is going to be horrid."

"It is hard for you, little one," said Aslan. "But things never happen the same way twice. It has been hard for us all in Narnia before now."

Lucy buried her head in his mane to hide from his face. But there must have been magic in his mane. She could feel lion-strength going into her. Quite suddenly she sat up. "I'm sorry, Aslan," she said. "I'm ready now."

"Now you are a lioness," said Aslan. "And now all Narnia will be renewed. But come. We have no time to lose."

He got up and walked with stately, noiseless paces back to the belt of dancing trees through which she had just come: and Lucy went with him, laying a rather tremulous hand on his mane. The trees parted to let them through and for one second assumed their human forms completely. Lucy had a glimpse of tall and lovely wood-gods and wood-goddesses all bowing to the Lion; the next moment they were trees again, but still bowing, with such graceful sweeps of branch and trunk that their bowing was itself a kind of dance.

"Now, child," said Aslan, when they had left the trees behind them, "I will wait here. Go and wake the others and tell them to follow. If they will not, then you at least must follow me alone."

It is a terrible thing to have to wake four people, all older than yourself and all very tired, for the purpose of telling them something they probably won't believe and making them do something they certainly won't like. "I mustn't think about it, I must just do it," thought Lucy.

She went to Peter first and shook him. "Peter," she whispered in his ear, "wake up. Quick! Aslan is here. He says we've got to follow him at once."

"Certainly, Lu. Whatever you like," said Peter unexpectedly. This was encouraging, but as Peter instantly rolled round and went to sleep again it wasn't much use.

Then she tried Susan. Susan did really wake up, but only to say in her most annoying grown-up voice, "You've been dreaming, Lucy. Go to sleep again."

She tackled Edmund next. It was very difficult to wake him, but when at last she had done it he was really awake and sat up.

"Eh?" he said in a grumpy voice. "What are you talking about?"

She said it all over again. This was one of the worst parts of her job, for each time she said it, it sounded less convincing.

"Aslan!" said Edmund, jumping up. "Hurray! Where?"

Lucy turned back to where she could see the Lion waiting, his patient eyes fixed upon her. "There," she said, pointing.

"Where?" asked Edmund again.

"There. There. Don't you see? Just this side of the trees."

Edmund stared hard for a while and then said, "No. There's nothing there. You've got dazzled and muddled with the moonlight. One does, you know. I thought I saw something for a moment myself. It's only an optical what-do-you-call-it."

"I can see him all the time," said Lucy. "He's looking straight at us."

"Then why can't I see him?"

"He said you mightn't be able to."

"Why?"

"I don't know. That's what he said."

"Oh, bother it all," said Edmund. "I do wish you wouldn't keep on seeing things. But I suppose we'll have to wake the others."

CHAPTER ELEVEN

THE LION ROARS

When the whole party was finally awake Lucy had to tell her story for the fourth time. The blank silence which followed it was as discouraging as anything could be.

"I can't see anything," said Peter after he had stared his eyes sore. "Can you, Susan?"

"No, of course I can't," snapped Susan. "Because there isn't anything to see. She's been dreaming. Do lie down and go to sleep, Lucy."

"And I do hope," said Lucy in a tremulous voice, "that you will all come with me. Because – because I'll have to go with him whether anyone else does or not."

"Don't talk nonsense, Lucy," said Susan. "Of course you can't go off on your own. Don't let her, Peter. She's being downright naughty."

"I'll go with her, if she *must* go," said Edmund. "She's been right before."

"I know she has," said Peter. "And she may have been right this morning. We certainly had no luck going down the gorge. Still – at this hour of the night. And why should Aslan be invisible to us? He never used to be. It's not like him. What does the DLF say?"

"Oh, I say nothing at all," answered the dwarf. "If you all go, of course, I'll go with you; and if your party splits up, I'll go with the High King. That's my duty to him and King Caspian. But, if you ask my private opinion, I'm a plain dwarf who doesn't think there's much chance of finding a road by night where you couldn't find one by day. And I have no use for magic lions which are talking lions and don't talk, and friendly lions though they don't do us any good, and whopping big lions though nobody can see them. It's all bilge and beanstalks as far as I can see."

"He's beating his paw on the ground for us to hurry," said Lucy. "We must go *now*. At least I must."

"You've no right to try to force the rest of us like that. It's four to one and you're the youngest," said Susan.

"Oh, come on," growled Edmund. "We've got to go. There'll be no peace till we do." He fully intended to back Lucy up, but he was annoyed at losing his night's sleep and was making up for it by doing everything as sulkily as possible.

"On the march, then," said Peter, wearily fitting his arm into his shield-strap and putting his helmet on. At any other time he would have said something nice to Lucy, who was his favourite sister, for he knew how wretched she must be feeling, and he knew that, whatever had happened, it was not her fault. But he couldn't help being a little annoyed with her all the same.

Susan was the worst. "Supposing I started behaving like Lucy," she said. "I might threaten to stay here whether the rest of you went on or not. I jolly well think I shall."

"Obey the High King, your Majesty," said Trumpkin, "and let's be off. If I'm not to be allowed to sleep, I'd as soon march as stand here talking."

And so at last they got on the move. Lucy went first, biting her lip and trying not to say all the things she thought of saying to Susan. But she forgot them when she fixed her eyes on Aslan. He turned and walked at a slow pace about thirty yards ahead of them. The others had only Lucy's directions to guide them, for Aslan was not only invisible to them but silent as well. His big cat-like paws made no noise on the grass.

He led them to the right of the dancing trees — whether they were still dancing nobody knew, for Lucy had her eyes on the Lion and the rest had their eyes on Lucy — and nearer the edge of the gorge. "Cobbles and kettledrums!" thought Trumpkin. "I hope this madness isn't going to end in a moonlight climb and broken necks."

For a long way Aslan went along the top of the precipices. Then they came to a place where some little trees grew right on the edge. He turned and disappeared among them. Lucy held her breath, for it looked as if he had plunged over the cliff; but she was too busy keeping him in sight to stop and think about this. She quickened her pace and was soon among the trees herself. Looking down, she could see a steep and narrow path going slantwise down into the gorge between rocks, and Aslan descending it. He turned and looked at her with his happy eyes. Lucy clapped her hands and began to scramble down after him. From behind her she heard the voices of the others shouting, "Hi! Lucy! Look out, for goodness' sake. You're right on the edge of the gorge. Come back—" and then, a moment later, Edmund's voice saying, "No, she's right. There *is* a way down."

Halfway down the path Edmund caught up with her.

"Look!" he said in great excitement. "Look! What's that shadow crawling down in front of us?"

"It's *his* shadow," said Lucy.

"I do believe you're right, Lu," said Edmund. "I can't think how I didn't see it before. But where is he?"

"With his shadow, of course. Can't you see him?"

"Well, I almost thought I did – for a moment. It's such a rum light."

"Get on, King Edmund, get on," came Trumpkin's voice from behind and above: and then, farther behind and still nearly at the top, Peter's voice saying, "Oh, buck up, Susan. Give me your hand. Why, a baby could get down here. And do stop grousing."

In a few minutes they were at the bottom, and the roaring of water filled their ears. Treading delicately, like a cat, Aslan stepped from stone to stone across the stream. In the middle he stopped, bent down to drink, and as he raised his shaggy head, dripping from the water, he turned to face them again. This time Edmund saw him. "Oh, Aslan!" he cried, darting forward. But the Lion whisked round and began padding up the slope on the far side of the Rush.

"Peter, Peter," cried Edmund. "Did you see?"

"I saw something," said Peter. "But it's so tricky in this moonlight. On we go, though, and three cheers for Lucy. I don't feel half so tired now, either."

Aslan without hesitation led them to their left, farther up the gorge. The whole journey was odd and dream-like – the roaring stream, the wet grey grass, the glimmering cliffs which they were approaching, and always the glorious, silently pacing Beast ahead. Everyone except Susan and the Dwarf could see him now.

Presently they came to another steep path, up the face of the farther precipices. These were far higher than the ones they had just descended, and the journey up them was a long and tedious zigzag. Fortunately the Moon shone right above the gorge so that neither side was in shadow.

Lucy was nearly blown when the tail and hind legs of Aslan disappeared over the top: but with one last effort she scrambled after him and came out, rather shaky-legged and breathless, on the hill they had been trying to reach ever since they left Glasswater. The long gentle slope (heather and grass and a few very big rocks that shone white in the moonlight) stretched up to where it vanished in a glimmer of trees about half a mile away. She knew it. It was the hill of the Stone Table.

With a jingling of mail the others climbed up behind her. Aslan glided on before them and they walked after him.

"Lucy," said Susan in a very small voice.

"Yes?" said Lucy.

"I see him now. I'm sorry."

"That's all right."

"But I've been far worse than you know. I really believed it was him — he, I mean — yesterday. When he warned us not to go down to the fir wood. And I really believed it was him tonight, when you woke us up. I mean, deep down inside. Or I could have, if I'd let myself. But I just wanted to get out of the woods and — and — oh, I don't know. And whatever am I to say to him?"

"Perhaps you won't need to say much," suggested Lucy.

Soon they reached the trees and through them the children could see the Great Mound, Aslan's How, which had been raised over the Table since their days.

"Our side don't keep very good watch," muttered Trumpkin. "We ought to have been challenged before now—"

"Hush!" said the other four, for now Aslan had stopped and turned and stood facing them, looking so majestic that they felt as glad as anyone can who feels afraid, and as afraid as anyone can who feels glad. The boys strode forward: Lucy made way for them: and Susan and the Dwarf shrank back.

"Oh, Aslan," said King Peter, dropping on one knee and raising the Lion's heavy paw to his face, "I'm so glad. And I'm so sorry. I've been leading them wrong ever since we started and especially yesterday morning."

"My dear son," said Aslan.

Then he turned and welcomed Edmund. "Well done," were his words.

Then, after an awful pause, the deep voice said, "Susan". Susan made no answer but the others thought she was crying. "You have listened to fears, child," said Aslan. "Come, let me breathe on you. Forget them. Are you brave again?"

"A little, Aslan," said Susan.

"And now!" said Aslan in a much louder voice with just a hint of roar in it, while his tail lashed his flanks. "And now, where is this little Dwarf, this famous swordsman and archer, who doesn't believe in lions? Come here, Son of Earth, come HERE!" — and the last word was no longer the hint of a roar but almost the real thing.

"Wraiths and wreckage!" gasped Trumpkin in the ghost of a voice. The children, who knew Aslan well enough to see that he liked the Dwarf very much, were not disturbed; but it was quite another thing for Trumpkin, who had never seen a lion before, let alone this Lion. He did the only sensible thing he could have done; that is, instead of bolting, he tottered towards Aslan.

Aslan pounced. Have you ever seen a very young kitten being carried in the mother cat's mouth? It was like that. The Dwarf, hunched up in a little, miserable ball, hung from Aslan's mouth. The Lion gave him one shake and all his armour rattled like a tinker's pack and then – hey-presto – the Dwarf flew up in the air. He was as safe as if he had been in bed, though he did not feel so. As he came down the huge velvety paws caught him as gently as a mother's arms and set him (right way up, too) on the ground.

"Son of Earth, shall we be friends?" asked Aslan.

"Ye – he – he – hes," panted the Dwarf, for he had not yet got his breath back.

"Now," said Aslan. "The Moon is setting. Look behind you: there is the dawn beginning. We have no time to lose. You three, you sons of Adam and son of Earth, hasten into the mound and deal with what you will find there."

The Dwarf was still speechless and neither of the boys dared to ask if Aslan would follow them. All three drew their swords and saluted, then turned and jingled away into the dusk. Lucy noticed that there was no sign of weariness in their faces: both the High King and King Edmund looked more like men than boys.

The girls watched them out of sight, standing close beside Aslan. The light was changing. Low down in the east, Aravir, the morning star of Narnia, gleamed like a little moon. Aslan, who seemed larger than before, lifted his head, shook his mane, and roared.

The sound, deep and throbbing at first like an organ beginning on a low note, rose and became louder, and then far louder again, till the earth and air were shaking with it. It rose up from that hill and floated across all Narnia. Down in Miraz's camp men woke, stared palely in one another's faces, and grasped their weapons. Down below that in the Great River, now at its coldest hour, the heads and shoulders of the nymphs, and the great weedy-bearded head of the river-god, rose from the water. Beyond it, in every field and wood, the alert ears of rabbits rose from their holes, the sleepy heads of birds came out from under wings, owls hooted, vixens barked, hedgehogs grunted, the trees stirred. In towns and villages mothers pressed babies close to their breasts, staring with wild eyes, dogs whimpered, and men leapt up groping for lights. Far away on the northern frontier the mountain giants peered from the dark gateways of their castles.

What Lucy and Susan saw was a dark something coming to them from almost every direction across the hills. It looked first like a black mist creeping on the ground, then like the stormy waves of a black sea rising higher and higher as it came on, and then, at last, like what it was – woods on the move. All the trees of the world appeared to be rushing towards Aslan. But as they drew nearer they looked less like trees, and when the whole crowd, bowing and curtsying and waving thin long arms to Aslan, were all around Lucy, she saw that it was a crowd of human shapes. Pale birch-girls were tossing their heads, willow-women pushed back their hair from their brooding faces to gaze on Aslan, the queenly beeches stood still and adored him, shaggy oak-men, lean and melancholy elms, shock-headed hollies (dark themselves, but their wives all bright with berries) and gay rowans, all bowed and rose again, shouting, "Aslan, Aslan!" in their various husky or creaking or wave-like voices.

The crowd and the dance round Aslan (for it had become a dance once more) grew so thick and rapid that Lucy was confused. She never saw where certain other people came from who were soon capering about among the trees. One was a youth, dressed only in a fawn-skin, with vine-leaves wreathed in his curly hair. His face would have been almost too pretty for a boy's, if it had not looked so extremely wild. You felt, as Edmund said when he saw him a few days later, "There's a chap who might do anything – absolutely anything." He seemed to have a great many names – Bromios, Bassareus, and the Ram were three of them. There were a lot of girls with him, as wild as he. There was even, unexpectedly, someone on a donkey. And everybody was laughing: and everybody was shouting out, "Euan, euan, eu-oi-oi-oi."

"Is it a Romp, Aslan?" cried the youth. And apparently it was. But nearly everyone seemed to have a different idea as to what they were playing. It may have been Tig, but Lucy never discovered who was It. It was rather like Blind Man's Buff, only everyone behaved as if they were blindfolded. It was not unlike Hunt the Slipper, but the slipper was never found. What made it more complicated was that the man on the donkey, who was old and enormously fat, began calling out at once, "Refreshments! Time for refreshments," and falling off his donkey and being bundled on to it again by the others, while the donkey was under the impression that the whole thing was a circus and tried to give a display of walking on its hind legs. And all the time there were more and more vine leaves everywhere. And soon not only leaves but vines. They were climbing up everything. They were running up the legs of the tree people and circling round their necks. Lucy put up her hands to push back her hair and found she was pushing back vine branches. The donkey was a mass of them. His tail was completely entangled and something dark was nodding between his ears. Lucy looked again and saw it was a bunch of grapes. After that it was mostly grapes – overhead and underfoot and all around.

"Refreshments! Refreshments," roared the old man. Everyone began eating, and whatever hothouses your people may have, you have never tasted such grapes. Really good grapes, firm and tight on the outside, but bursting into cool sweetness when you put them into your mouth, were one of the things the girls had never had quite enough of before. Here, there were more than anyone could possibly want, and no table-manners at all. One saw sticky and stained fingers everywhere and, though mouths were full, the laughter never ceased nor the yodelling cries of *Euan, euan, eu-oi-oi-oi-oi*, till all of a sudden everyone felt at the same moment that the game (whatever it was), and the feast, ought to be over, and everyone flopped down breathless on the ground and turned their faces to Aslan to hear what he would say next.

At that moment the sun was just rising and Lucy remembered something and whispered to Susan,

"I say, Su, I know who they are."

"Who?"

"The boy with the wild face is Bacchus and the old one on the donkey is Silenus. Don't you remember Mr Tumnus telling us about them long ago?"

"Yes, of course. But I say, Lu—"

"What?"

"I wouldn't have felt safe with Bacchus and all his wild girls if we'd met them without Aslan."

"I should think not," said Lucy.

CHAPTER TWELVE

SORCERY AND SUDDEN VENGEANCE

Meanwhile Trumpkin and the two boys arrived at the dark little stone archway which led into the inside of the Mound, and two sentinel badgers (the white patches on their cheeks were all Edmund could see of them) leapt up with bared teeth and asked them in snarling voices, "Who goes there?"

"Trumpkin," said the Dwarf. "Bringing the High King of Narnia out of the far past."

The badgers nosed at the boys' hands. "At last," they said. "At last."

"Give us a light, friends," said Trumpkin.

The badgers found a torch just inside the arch and Peter lit it and handed it to Trumpkin. "The DLF had better lead," he said. "We don't know our way about this place."

Trumpkin took the torch and went ahead into the dark tunnel. It was a cold, black, musty place, with an occasional bat fluttering in the torchlight, and plenty of cobwebs. The boys, who had been mostly in the open air since that morning at the railway station, felt as if they were going into a trap or a prison.

"I say, Peter," whispered Edmund. "Look at those carvings on the walls. Don't they look old? And yet we're older than that. When we were last here, they hadn't been made."

"Yes," said Peter. "That makes one think."

The Dwarf went on ahead and then turned to the right, and then to the left, and then down some steps, and then to the left again. Then at last they saw a light ahead – light from under a door. And now for the first time they heard voices, for they had come to the door of the central chamber. The voices inside were angry ones. Someone was talking so loudly that the approach of the boys and the Dwarf had not been heard.

"Don't like the sound of that," whispered Trumpkin to Peter. "Let's listen for a moment." All three stood perfectly still on the outside of the door.

"You know well enough," said a voice ("That's the King," whispered Trumpkin), "why the Horn was not blown at sunrise this morning. Have you forgotten that Miraz fell upon us almost before Trumpkin had gone, and we were fighting for our lives for the space of three hours and more? I blew it when first I had a breathing space."

"I'm not likely to forget it," came the angry voice, "when my Dwarfs bore the brunt of the attack and one in five of them fell." ("That's Nikabrik," whispered Trumpkin.)

"For shame, Dwarf," came a thick voice ("Trufflehunter's," said Trumpkin). "We all did as much as the Dwarfs and none more than the King."

"Tell that tale your own way for all I care," answered Nikabrik. "But whether it was that the Horn was blown too late, or whether there was no magic in it, no help has come. You, you great clerk, you master magician, you know-all; are you still asking us to hang our hopes on Aslan and King Peter and all the rest of it?"

"I must confess – I cannot deny it – that I am deeply disappointed in the result of the operation," came the answer. ("That'll be Doctor Cornelius," said Trumpkin.)

"To speak plainly," said Nikabrik, "your wallet's empty, your eggs addled, your fish uncaught, your promises broken. Stand aside then and let others work. And that is why—"

"The help will come," said Trufflehunter. "I stand by Aslan. Have patience, like us beasts. The help will come. It may be even now at the door."

"Pah!" snarled Nikabrik. "You badgers would have us wait till the sky falls and we can all catch larks. I tell you we *can't* wait. Food is running short; we lose more than we can afford at every encounter; our followers are slipping away."

"And why?" asked Trufflehunter. "I'll tell you why. Because it is noised among them that we have called on the Kings of old and the Kings of old have not answered. The last words Trumpkin spoke before he went (and went, most likely, to his death) were, 'If you must blow the Horn, do not let the army know why you blow it or what you hope from it.' But that same evening everyone seemed to know."

"You'd better have shoved your grey snout in a hornets' nest, Badger, than suggest that I am the blab," said Nikabrik. "Take it back, or—"

"Oh, stop it, both of you," said King Caspian. "I want to know what it is that Nikabrik keeps on hinting we should do. But before that, I want to know who those two strangers are whom he has brought into our council and who stand there with their ears open and their mouths shut."

"They are friends of mine," said Nikabrik. "And what better right have you yourself to be here than that you are a friend of Trumpkin's and the Badger's? And what right has that old dotard in the black gown to be here except that he is your friend? Why am I to be the only one who can't bring in his friends?"

"His Majesty is the King to whom you have sworn allegiance," said Trufflehunter sternly.

"Court manners, court manners," sneered Nikabrik. "But in this hole we may talk plainly. You know – and he knows – that this Telmarine boy will be king of nowhere and nobody in a week unless we can help him out of the trap in which he sits."

"Perhaps," said Cornelius, "your new friends would like to speak for themselves? You there, who and what are you?"

"Worshipful Master Doctor," came a thin, whining voice. "So please you, I'm only a poor old woman, I am, and very obliged to his Worshipful Dwarfship for his friendship, I'm sure. His Majesty, bless his handsome face, has no need to be afraid of an old woman that's nearly doubled up with the rheumatics and hasn't two sticks to put under her kettle. I have some poor little skill – not like yours, Master Doctor, of course – in small spells and cantrips that I'd be glad to use against our enemies if it was agreeable to all concerned. For I hate 'em. Oh, yes. No one hates better than me."

"That is all most interesting and – er – satisfactory," said Doctor Cornelius. "I think I now know what you are, madam. Perhaps your other friend, Nikabrik, would give some account of himself?"

A dull, grey voice at which Peter's flesh crept replied, "I'm hunger. I'm thirst. Where I bite, I hold till I die, and even after death they must cut out my mouthful from my enemy's body and bury it with me. I can fast a hundred years and not die. I can lie a hundred nights on the ice and not freeze. I can drink a river of blood and not burst. Show me your enemies."

"And it is in the presence of these two that you wish to disclose your plan?" said Caspian.

"Yes," said Nikabrik. "And by their help that I mean to execute it."

There was a minute or two during which Trumpkin and the boys could hear Caspian and his two friends speaking in low voices but could not make out what they were saying. Then Caspian spoke aloud.

"Well, Nikabrik," he said, "we will hear your plan."

There was a pause so long that the boys began to wonder if Nikabrik was ever going to begin; when he did, it was in a lower voice, as if he himself did not much like what he was saying.

"All said and done," he muttered, "none of us knows the truth about the ancient days in Narnia. Trumpkin believed none of the stories. I was ready to put them to the trial. We tried first the Horn and it has failed. If there ever was a High King Peter and a Queen Susan and a King Edmund and a Queen Lucy, then either they have not heard us, or they cannot come, or they are our enemies—"

"Or they are on the way," put in Trufflehunter.

"You can go on saying that till Miraz has fed us all to his dogs. As I was saying, we have tried one link in the chain of old legends, and it has done us no good. Well. But when your sword breaks, you draw your dagger. The stories tell of other powers beside the ancient Kings and Queens. How if we could call *them* up?"

"If you mean Aslan," said Trufflehunter, "it's all one calling on him and on the Kings. They were his servants. If he will not send them (but I make no doubt he will), is he more likely to come himself?"

"No. You're right there," said Nikabrik. "Aslan and the Kings go together. Either Aslan is dead, or he is not on our side. Or else something stronger than himself keeps him back. And if he did come – how do we know he'd be our friend? He was not always a good friend to Dwarfs by all that's told. Not even to all beasts. Ask the Wolves. And anyway, he was in Narnia only once that I ever heard of, and he didn't stay long. You may drop Aslan out of the reckoning. I was thinking of someone else."

There was no answer, and for a few minutes it was so still that Edmund could hear the wheezy and snuffling breath of the Badger.

"Who do you mean?" said Caspian at last.

"I mean a power so much greater than Aslan's that it held Narnia spellbound for years and years, if the stories are true."

"The White Witch!" cried three voices all at once, and from the noise Peter guessed that three people had leapt to their feet.

"Yes," said Nikabrik very slowly and distinctly, "I mean the Witch. Sit down again. Don't all take fright at a name as if you were children. We want power: and we want a power that will be on our side. As for power, do not the stories say that the Witch defeated Aslan, and bound him, and killed him on that very Stone which is over there, just beyond the light?"

"But they also say that he came to life again," said the Badger sharply.

"Yes, they *say*," answered Nikabrik, "but you'll notice that we hear precious little about anything he did afterwards. He just fades out of the story. How do you explain that, if he really came to life? Isn't it much more likely that he didn't, and that the stories say nothing more about him because there was nothing more to say?"

"He established the Kings and Queens," said Caspian.

"A King who has just won a great battle can usually establish himself without the help of a performing lion," said Nikabrik. There was a fierce growl, probably from Trufflehunter.

"And anyway," Nikabrik continued, "what came of the Kings and their reign? They faded too. But it's very different with the Witch. They say she ruled for a hundred years: a hundred years of winter. There's power, if you like. There's something practical."

"But, heaven and earth!" said the King. "Haven't we always been told that she was the worst enemy of all? Wasn't she a tyrant ten times worse than Miraz?"

"Perhaps," said Nikabrik in a cold voice. "Perhaps she *was* for you Humans, if there were any of you in those days. Perhaps she was for some of the beasts. She stamped out the Beavers, I dare say; at least there are none of them in Narnia now. But she got on all right with us Dwarfs. I'm a Dwarf and I stand by my own people. *We're* not afraid of the Witch."

"But you've joined with us," said Trufflehunter.

"Yes, and a lot of good it has done my people, so far," snapped Nikabrik. "Who is sent on all the dangerous raids? The Dwarfs. Who goes short when the rations fail? The Dwarfs. Who——?"

"Lies! All lies!" said the Badger.

"And so," said Nikabrik, whose voice now rose to a scream, "if you can't help my people, I'll go to someone who can."

"Is this open treason, Dwarf?" asked the King.

"Put that sword back in its sheath, Caspian," said Nikabrik. "Murder at council, eh? Is that your game? Don't be fool enough to try it. Do you think I'm afraid of you? There's three on my side, and three on yours."

"Come on, then," snarled Trufflehunter, but he was immediately interrupted.

"Stop, stop, stop," said Doctor Cornelius. "You go on too fast. The Witch is dead. All the stories agree on that. What does Nikabrik mean by calling on the Witch?"

That grey and terrible voice which had spoken only once before said, "Oh, *is* she?"

And then the shrill, whining voice began, "Oh, bless his heart, his dear little Majesty needn't mind about the White Lady – that's what *we* call her – being dead. The Worshipful Master Doctor is only making game of a poor old woman like me when he says that. Sweet Master Doctor, learned Master Doctor, who ever heard of a witch that really died? You can always get them back."

"Call her up," said the grey voice. "We are all ready. Draw the circle. Prepare the blue fire."

Above the steadily increasing growl of the Badger, and Cornelius's sharp, "What?" rose the voice of King Caspian like thunder.

"So that is your plan, Nikabrik! Black sorcery and the calling up of an accursed ghost. And I see who your companions are — a Hag and a Wer-Wolf!"

The next minute or so was very confused. There was an animal roaring, a clash of steel; and the boys and Trumpkin rushed in; Peter had a glimpse of a horrible, grey, gaunt creature, half man and half wolf, in the very act of leaping upon a boy about his own age, and Edmund saw a badger and a Dwarf rolling on the floor in a sort of cat fight. Trumpkin found himself face to face with the Hag. Her nose and chin stuck out like a pair of nut-crackers, her dirty grey hair was flying about her face and she had just got Doctor Cornelius by the throat. At one slash of Trumpkin's sword her head rolled on the floor. Then the light was knocked over and it was all swords, teeth, claws, fists, and boots for about sixty seconds. Then silence.

"Are you all right, Ed?"

"I — I think so," panted Edmund. "I've got that brute Nikabrik, but he's still alive."

"Weights and water-bottles!" came an angry voice. "It's *me* you're sitting on. Get off. You're like a young elephant."

"Sorry, D.L.F," said Edmund. "Is that better?"

"Ow! No!" bellowed Trumpkin. "You're putting your boot in my mouth. Go away."

"Is King Caspian anywhere?" asked Peter.

"I'm here," said a rather faint voice. "Something bit me."

They all heard the noise of someone striking a match. It was Edmund. The little flame showed his face, looking pale and dirty. He blundered about for a little, found the candle (they were no longer using the lamp, for they had run out of oil), set it on the table, and lit it. When the flame rose clear, several people scrambled to their feet. Six faces blinked at one another in the candlelight.

"We don't seem to have any enemies left," said Peter. "There's the Hag, dead." (He turned his eyes quickly away from her.) "And Nikabrik, dead too. And I suppose this thing is a Wer-Wolf. It's so long since I've seen one. Wolf's head and man's body. That means he was just turning from man into wolf at the moment he was killed. And you, I suppose, are King Caspian?"

"Yes," said the other boy. "But I've no idea who you are."

"It's the High King, King Peter," said Trumpkin.

"Your Majesty is very welcome," said Caspian.

"And so is *your* Majesty," said Peter. "I haven't come to take your place, you know, but to put you into it."

"Your Majesty," said another voice at Peter's elbow. He turned and found himself face to face with the Badger. Peter leaned forward, put his arms round the beast and kissed the furry head: it wasn't a girlish thing for him to do, because he was the High King.

"Best of badgers," he said. "You never doubted us all through."

"No credit to me, your Majesty," said Trufflehunter. "I'm a beast and we don't change. I'm a badger, what's more, and we hold on."

"I am sorry for Nikabrik," said Caspian, "though he hated me from the first moment he saw me. He had gone sour inside from long suffering and hating. If we had won quickly he might have become a good Dwarf in the days of peace. I don't know which of us killed him. I'm glad of that."

"You're bleeding," said Peter.

"Yes, I'm bitten," said Caspian. "It was that – that wolf thing." Cleaning and bandaging the wound took a long time, and when it was done Trumpkin said, "Now. Before everything else we want some breakfast."

"But not here," said Peter.

"No," said Caspian with a shudder. "And we must send someone to take away the bodies."

"Let the vermin be flung into a pit," said Peter. "But the Dwarf we will give to his people to be buried in their own fashion."

They breakfasted at last in another of the dark cellars of Aslan's How. It was not such a breakfast as they would have chosen, for Caspian and Cornelius were thinking of venison pasties, and Peter and Edmund of buttered eggs and hot coffee, but what everyone got was a little bit of cold bear-meat (out of the boys' pockets), a lump of hard cheese, an onion, and a mug of water. But, from the way they fell to, anyone would have supposed it was delicious.

Chapter Thirteen

The High King in Command

"Now," said Peter, as they finished their meal, "Aslan and the girls (that's Queen Susan and Queen Lucy, Caspian) are somewhere close. We don't know when he will act. In his time, no doubt, not ours. In the meantime he would like us to do what we can on our own. You say, Caspian, we are not strong enough to meet Miraz in pitched battle."

"I'm afraid not, High King," said Caspian. He was liking Peter very much, but was rather tongue-tied. It was much stranger for him to meet the great Kings out of the old stories than it was for them to meet him.

"Very well, then," said Peter, "I'll send him a challenge to a single combat." No one had thought of this before.

"Please," said Caspian, "could it not be me? I want to avenge my father."

"You're wounded," said Peter. "And anyway, wouldn't he just laugh at a challenge from you? I mean, we have seen that you are a king and a warrior but he thinks of you as a kid."

"But, Sire," said the Badger, who sat very close to Peter and never took his eyes off him. "Will he accept a challenge even from you? He knows he has the stronger army."

"Very likely he won't," said Peter, "but there's always the chance. And even if he doesn't, we shall spend the best part of the day sending heralds to and fro and all that. By then Aslan may have done something. And at least I can inspect the army and strengthen the position. I will send the challenge. In fact I will write it at once. Have you pen and ink, Master Doctor?"

"A scholar is never without them, Your Majesty," answered Doctor Cornelius.

"Very well, I will dictate," said Peter. And while the Doctor spread out a parchment and opened his ink-horn and sharpened his pen, Peter leant back with half-closed eyes and recalled to his mind the language in which he had written such things long ago in Narnia's golden age.

"Right," he said at last. "And now, if you are ready, Doctor?"

Doctor Cornelius dipped his pen and waited. Peter dictated as follows:

"Peter, by the gift of Aslan, by election, by prescription, and by conquest, High King over all Kings in Narnia, Emperor of the Lone Islands and Lord of Cair Paravel, Knight of the Most Noble Order of the Lion, to Miraz, Son of Caspian the Eighth, sometime Lord Protector of Narnia and now styling himself King of Narnia, Greeting. Have you got that?"

"*Narnia, comma, Greeting,*" muttered the Doctor. "Yes, Sire."

"Then begin a new paragraph," said Peter. "*For to prevent the effusion of blood, and for the avoiding of all other inconveniences likely to grow from the wars now levied in our realm of Narnia, it is our pleasure to adventure our royal person on behalf of our trusty and well-beloved Caspian in clean wager of battle to prove upon your Lordship's body that the said Caspian is lawful King under us in Narnia both by our gift and by the laws of the Telmarines, and your Lordship twice guilty of treachery both in withholding the dominion of Narnia from the said Caspian and in the most abhominable,* — don't forget to spell it with an H, Doctor — *bloody, and unnatural murder of your kindly lord and brother King Caspian Ninth of that name. Wherefore we most heartily provoke, challenge, and defy your Lordship to the said combat and monomachy, and have sent these letters by the hand of our well-beloved and royal brother Edmund, sometime King under us in Narnia, Duke of Lantern Waste and Count of the Western March, Knight of the Noble Order of the Table, to whom we have given full power of determining with your Lordship all the conditions of the said battle. Given at our lodging in Aslan's How this XII day of the month Greenroof in the first year of Caspian Tenth of Narnia.*

"That ought to do," said Peter, drawing a deep breath. "And now we must send two others with King Edmund. I think the Giant ought to be one."

"He's — he's not very clever, you know," said Caspian.

"Of course not," said Peter. "But any giant looks impressive if only he will keep quiet. And it will cheer him up. But who for the other?"

"Upon my word," said Trumpkin, "if you want someone who can kill with looks, Reepicheep would be the best."

"He would indeed, from all I hear," said Peter with a laugh. "If only he wasn't so small. They wouldn't even see him till he was close!"

"Send Glenstorm, Sire," said Trufflehunter. "No one ever laughed at a Centaur."

An hour later two great lords in the army of Miraz, the Lord Glozelle and the Lord Sopespian, strolling along their lines and picking their teeth after breakfast, looked up and saw coming down to them from the wood the

Centaur and Giant Wimbleweather, whom they had seen before in battle, and between them a figure they could not recognize. Nor indeed would the other boys at Edmund's school have recognized him if they could have seen him at that moment. For Aslan had breathed on him at their meeting and a kind of greatness hung about him.

"What's to do?" said the Lord Glozelle. "An attack?"

"A parley, rather," said Sopespian. "See, they carry green branches. They are coming to surrender most likely."

"He that is walking between the Centaur and the Giant has no look of surrender in his face," said Glozelle. "Who can he be? It is not the boy Caspian."

"No indeed," said Sopespian. "This is a fell warrior, I warrant you, wherever the rebels have got him from. He is (in your Lordship's private ear) a kinglier man than ever Miraz was. And what mail he wears! None of our smiths can make the like."

"I'll wager my dappled Pomely he brings a challenge, not a surrender," said Glozelle.

"How then?" said Sopespian. "We hold the enemy in our fist here. Miraz would never be so harebrained as to throw away his advantage on a combat."

"He might be brought to it," said Glozelle in a much lower voice.

"Softly," said Sopespian. "Step a little aside here out of earshot of those sentries. Now. Have I taken your Lordship's meaning aright?"

"If the King undertook wager of battle," whispered Glozelle, "why, either he would kill or be killed."

"So," said Sopespian, nodding his head.

"And if he killed we should have won this war."

"Certainly. And if not?"

"Why, if not, we should be as able to win it without the King's grace as with him. For I need not tell your Lordship that Miraz is no very great captain. And after that, we should be both victorious and kingless."

"And it is your meaning, my Lord, that you and I could hold this land quite as conveniently without a King as with one?"

Glozelle's face grew ugly. "Not forgetting," said he, "that it was we who first put him on the throne. And in all the years that he has enjoyed it, what fruits have come our way? What gratitude has he shown us?"

"Say no more," answered Sopespian. "But look — here comes one to fetch us to the King's tent."

When they reached Miraz's tent they saw Edmund and his two companions seated outside it and being entertained with cakes and wine, having already delivered the challenge, and withdrawn while the King was considering it. When they saw them thus at close quarters the two

Telmarine lords thought all three of them very alarming.

Inside, they found Miraz, unarmed and finishing his breakfast. His face was flushed and there was a scowl on his brow.

"There!" he growled, flinging the parchment across the table to them. "See what a pack of nursery tales our jackanapes of a nephew has sent us."

"By your leave, Sire," said Glozelle. "If the young warrior whom we have just seen outside is the King Edmund mentioned in the writing, then I would not call him a nursery tale but a very dangerous knight."

"King Edmund, pah!" said Miraz. "Does your Lordship believe those old wives' fables about Peter and Edmund and the rest?"

"I believe my eyes, your Majesty," said Glozelle.

"Well, this is to no purpose," said Miraz, "but as touching the challenge, I suppose there is only one opinion between us?"

"I suppose so, indeed, Sire," said Glozelle.

"And what is that?" asked the King.

"Most infallibly to refuse it," said Glozelle. "For though I have never been called a coward, I must plainly say that to meet that young man in battle is more than my heart would serve me for. And if (as is likely) his brother, the High King, is more dangerous than he – why, on your life, my Lord King, have nothing to do with him."

"Plague on you!" cried Miraz. "It was not that sort of counsel I wanted. Do you think I am asking you if I should be afraid to meet this Peter (if there is such a man)? Do you think I fear him? I wanted your counsel of the policy of the matter; whether we, having the advantage, should hazard it on a wager of battle."

"To which I can only answer, your Majesty," said Glozelle, "that for all reasons the challenge should be refused. There is death in the strange knight's face."

"There you are again!" said Miraz, now thoroughly angry. "Are you trying to make it appear that I am as great a coward as your Lordship?"

"Your Majesty may say your pleasure," said Glozelle sulkily.

"You talk like an old woman, Glozelle," said the King. "What say you, my Lord Sopespian?"

"Do not touch it, Sire," was the reply. "And what your Majesty says of the policy of the thing comes in very happily. It gives your Majesty excellent grounds for a refusal without any cause for questioning your Majesty's honour or courage."

"Great Heaven!" exclaimed Miraz, jumping to his feet. "Are *you* also bewitched today? Do you think I am *looking* for grounds to refuse it? You might as well call me coward to my face."

The conversation was going exactly as the two lords wished, so they said nothing.

"I see what it is," said Miraz, after staring at them as if his eyes would start out of his head, "you are as lily-livered as hares yourselves and have the effrontery to imagine my heart after the likeness of yours! Grounds for a refusal, indeed! Excuses for not fighting! Are you soldiers? Are you Telmarines? Are you men? And if I do refuse it (as all good reasons of captaincy and martial policy urge me to do) you will think, and teach others to think, I was afraid. Is it not so?"

"No man of your Majesty's age," said Glozelle, "would be called coward by any wise soldier for refusing the combat with a great warrior in the flower of his youth."

"So I'm to be a dotard with one foot in the grave, as well as a dastard," roared Miraz. "I'll tell you what it is, my Lords. With your womanish counsels (ever shying from the true point, which is one of policy) you have done the very opposite of your intent. I had meant to refuse it. But I'll accept it. Do you hear, accept it! I'll not be shamed because some witchcraft or treason has frozen both your bloods."

"We beseech your Majesty—" said Glozelle, but Miraz had flung out of the tent and they could hear him bawling out his acceptance to Edmund.

The two lords looked at one another and chuckled quietly.

"I knew he'd do it if he were properly chafed," said Glozelle. "But I'll not forget he called me coward. It shall be paid for."

There was a great stirring at Aslan's How when the news came back and was communicated to the various creatures. Edmund, with one of Miraz's captains, had already marked out the place for the combat, and ropes and stakes had been put round it. Two Telmarines were to stand at two of the corners, and one in the middle of one side, as marshals of the lists. Three marshalls for the other two corners and the other side were to be furnished by the High King. Peter was just explaining to Caspian that he could not be one, because his right to the throne was what they were fighting about, when suddenly a thick, sleepy voice said, "Your Majesty, please." Peter turned and there stood the eldest of the Bulgy Bears. "If you please, your Majesty," he said, "I'm a bear, I am."

"To be sure, so you are, and a good bear too, I don't doubt," said Peter.

"Yes," said the Bear. "But it was always a right of the bears to supply one marshal of the lists."

"Don't let him," whispered Trumpkin to Peter. "He's a good creature, but he'll shame us all. He'll go to sleep and he *will* suck his paws. In front of the enemy too."

"I can't help that," said Peter. "Because he's quite right. The Bears had that privilege. I can't imagine how it has been remembered all these years, when so many other things have been forgotten."

"Please, your Majesty," said the Bear.

"It is your right," said Peter. "And you shall be one of the marshals. But you *must* remember not to suck your paws."

"Of course not," said the Bear in a very shocked voice.

"Why, you're doing it this minute!" bellowed Trumpkin.

The Bear whipped his paw out of his mouth and pretended he hadn't heard.

"Sire!" came a shrill voice from near the ground.

"Ah – Reepicheep!" said Peter, after looking up and down and round as people usually did when addressed by the Mouse.

"Sire," said Reepicheep. "My life is ever at your command, but my honour is my own. Sire, I have among my people the only trumpeter in your Majesty's army. I had thought, perhaps, we might have been sent with the challenge. Sire, my people are grieved. Perhaps if it were your pleasure that I should be a marshal of the lists, it would content them."

A noise not unlike thunder broke out from somewhere overhead at this point, as Giant Wimbleweather burst into one of those not very intelligent laughs to which the nicer sorts of Giant are so liable. He checked himself at once and looked as grave as a turnip by the time Reepicheep discovered where the noise came from.

"I am afraid it would not do," said Peter very gravely. "Some humans are afraid of mice—"

"I had observed it, Sire," said Reepicheep.

"And it would not be quite fair to Miraz," Peter continued, "to have in sight anything that might abate the edge of his courage."

"Your Majesty is the mirror of honour," said the Mouse with one of his admirable bows. "And on this matter we have but a single mind... I thought I heard someone laughing just now. If anyone present wishes to make me the subject of his wit, I am very much at his service – with my sword – whenever he has leisure."

An awful silence followed this remark, which was broken by Peter saying, "Giant Wimble-weather and the Bear and the Centaur Glenstorm shall be our marshals. The combat will be at two hours after noon. Dinner at noon precisely."

"I say," said Edmund as they walked away, "I suppose it *is* all right. I mean, I suppose you can beat him?"

"That's what I'm fighting him to find out," said Peter.

CHAPTER FOURTEEN

HOW ALL WERE VERY BUSY

A little before two o'clock, Trumpkin and the Badger sat with the rest of the creatures at the wood's edge looking across at the gleaming line of Miraz's army which was about two arrow-shots away. In between, a square space of level grass had been staked for the combat. At the two far corners stood Glozelle and Sopespian with drawn swords. At the near corners were Giant Wimbleweather and the Bulgy Bear, who in spite of all their warnings was sucking his paws and looking, to tell the truth, uncommonly silly. To make up for this, Glenstorm on the right of the lists, stock-still except when he stamped a hind hoof occasionally on the turf, looked much more imposing than the Telmarine baron who faced him on the left. Peter had just shaken hands with Edmund and the Doctor, and was now walking down to the combat. It was like the moment before the pistol goes at an important race, but very much worse.

"I wish Aslan had turned up before it came to this," said Trumpkin.

"So do I," said Trufflehunter. "But look behind you."

"Crows and crockery!" muttered the Dwarf as soon as he had done so. "What are they? Huge people – beautiful people – like gods and goddesses and giants. Hundreds and thousands of them, closing in behind us. What are they?"

"It's the Dryads and Hamadryads and Silvans," said Trufflehunter. "Aslan has wakened them."

"Humph!" said the Dwarf. "That'll be very useful if the enemy try any treachery. But it won't help the High King very much if Miraz proves handier with his sword."

The Badger said nothing, for now Peter and Miraz were entering the lists from opposite ends, both on foot, both in chain shirts, with helmets and shields. They advanced till they were close together. Both bowed and seemed to speak, but it was impossible to hear what they said. Next moment the two swords flashed in the sunlight. For a second the clash could be heard but it was immediately drowned because both armies began shouting like crowds at a football match.

"Well done, Peter, oh, well done!" shouted Edmund as he saw Miraz reel back a whole pace and a half. "Follow it up, quick!" And Peter did, and for a few seconds it looked as if the fight might be won. But then Miraz pulled himself together – began to make real use of his height and weight. "Miraz! Miraz! The King! The King!" came the roar of the Telmarines. Caspian and Edmund grew white with sickening anxiety.

"Peter is taking some dreadful knocks," said Edmund.

"Hullo!" said Caspian. "What's happening now?"

"Both falling apart," said Edmund. "A bit blown, I expect. Watch. Ah, now they're beginning again, more scientifically this time. Circling round and round, feeling each other's defences."

"I'm afraid this Miraz knows his work," muttered the Doctor. But hardly had he said this when there was such a clapping and baying and throwing up of hoods among the Old Narnians that it was nearly deafening.

"What was it? What was it?" asked the Doctor. "My old eyes missed it."

"The High King has pricked him in the armpit," said Caspian, still clapping. "Just where the arm-hole of the hauberk let the point through. First blood."

"It's looking ugly again, now, though," said Edmund. "Peter's not using his shield properly. He must be hurt in the left arm."

It was only too true. Everyone could see that Peter's shield hung limp. The shouting of the Telmarines redoubled.

"You've seen more battles than I," said Caspian. "Is there any chance now?"

"Precious little," said Edmund. "I suppose he might *just* do it. With luck."

"Oh, why did we let it happen at all?" said Caspian.

Suddenly all the shouting on both sides died down. Edmund was puzzled for a moment. Then he said, "Oh, I see. They've both agreed to a rest. Come on, Doctor. You and I may be able to do something for the High King." They ran down to the lists and Peter came outside the ropes to meet them, his face red and sweaty, his chest heaving.

"Is your left arm wounded?" asked Edmund.

"It's not exactly a wound," Peter said. "I got the full weight of his shoulder on my shield – like a load of bricks – and the rim of the shield drove into my wrist. I don't think it's broken, but it might be a sprain. If you could tie it up very tight I think I could manage."

While they were doing this, Edmund asked anxiously, "What do you think of him, Peter?"

"Tough," said Peter. "Very tough. I have a chance if I can keep him on the hop till his weight and short wind come against him – in this hot sun too. To tell the truth, I haven't much chance else. Give my love to – to everyone at home, Ed, if he gets me. Here he comes into the lists again. So long, old chap. Goodbye, Doctor. And I say, Ed, say something specially nice to Trumpkin. He's been a brick."

Edmund couldn't speak. He walked back with the Doctor to his own lines with a sick feeling in his stomach.

But the new bout went well. Peter now seemed to be able to make some use of his shield, and he certainly made good use of his feet. He was almost playing Tig with Miraz now, keeping out of range, shifting his ground, making the enemy work.

"Coward!" booed the Telmarines. "Why don't you stand up to him? Don't you like it, eh? Thought you'd come to fight, not dance. Yah!"

"Oh, I do hope he won't listen to them," said Caspian.

"Not he," said Edmund. "You don't know him – Oh!" – for Miraz had got in a blow at last, on Peter's helmet. Peter staggered, slipped sideways, and fell on one knee. The roar of the Telmarines rose like the noise of the sea. "Now, Miraz," they yelled. "Now. Quick! Quick! Kill him." But indeed there was no need to egg the usurper on. He was on top of Peter already. Edmund bit his lips till the blood came, as the sword flashed down on Peter. It looked as if it would slash off his head. Thank heavens! It had glanced down his right shoulder. The Dwarf-wrought mail was sound and did not break.

"Great Scott!" cried Edmund. "He's up again. Peter, go it, Peter!"

"I couldn't see what happened," said the Doctor. "How did he do it?"

"Grabbed Miraz's arm as it came down," said Trumpkin, dancing with delight. "There's a man for you! Uses his enemy's arm as a ladder. The High King! The High King! Up, Old Narnia!"

"Look," said Trufflehunter. "Miraz is angry. It is good."

They were certainly at it hammer and tongs now: such a flurry of blows that it seemed impossible for either not to be killed. As the excitement grew, the shouting almost died away. The spectators were holding their breath. It was most horrible and most magnificent.

A great shout arose from the Old Narnians. Miraz was down – not struck by Peter, but face downwards, having tripped on a tussock. Peter stepped back, waiting for him to rise.

"Oh, bother, bother, bother," said Edmund to himself. "Need he be as gentlemanly as all that? I suppose he must. Comes of being a Knight *and* a

High King. I suppose it is what Aslan would like. But that brute will be up again in a minute and then—"

But "that brute" never rose. The Lords Glozelle and Sopespian had their own plans ready. As soon as they saw their King down they leapt into the lists crying, "Treachery! Treachery! The Narnian traitor has stabbed him in the back while he lay helpless. To arms! To arms, Telmar!"

Peter hardly understood what was happening. He saw two big men running towards him with drawn swords. Then the third Telmarine had leapt over the ropes on his left.

"To arms, Narnia! Treachery!" Peter shouted. If all three had set upon him at once he would never have spoken again. But Glozelle stopped to stab his own King dead where he lay: "That's for your insult, this morning," he whispered as the blade went home. Peter swung to face Sopespian, slashed his legs from under him and, with the back-cut of the same stroke, walloped off his head. Edmund was now at his side crying, "Narnia, Narnia! The Lion!" The whole Telmarine army was rushing towards them. But now the Giant was stamping forward, stooping low and swinging his club. The Centaurs charged. *Twang, twang* behind and *hiss, hiss* overhead came the archery of Dwarfs. Trumpkin was fighting at his left. Full battle was joined.

"Come back, Reepicheep, you little ass!" shouted Peter. "You'll only be killed. This is no place for mice." But the ridiculous little creatures were dancing in and out among the feet of both armies, jabbing with their swords. Many a Telmarine warrior that day felt his foot suddenly pierced as if by a dozen skewers, hopped on one leg cursing the pain, and fell as often as not. If he fell, the mice finished him off; if he did not, someone else did.

But almost before the Old Narnians were really warmed to their work they found the enemy giving way. Tough-looking warriors turned white, gazed in terror not on the Old Narnians but on something behind them, and then flung down their weapons, shrieking, "The Wood! The Wood! The end of the world!"

But soon neither their cries nor the sound of weapons could be heard any more, for both were drowned in the ocean-like roar of the Awakened Trees as they plunged through the ranks of Peter's army, and then on, in pursuit of the Telmarines. Have you ever stood at the edge of a great wood on a high ridge when a wild southwester broke over it in full fury on an autumn evening? Imagine that sound. And then imagine that the wood, instead of being fixed to one place, was rushing *at* you; and was no longer trees but huge people; yet still like trees because their long arms waved like branches and their heads tossed and leaves fell round them in showers. It was like that for the Telmarines. It was a little alarming even for the Narnians. In a few minutes all Miraz's followers were running down to the

Great River in the hope of crossing the bridge to the town of Beruna and there defending themselves behind ramparts and closed gates.

They reached the river, but there was no bridge. It had disappeared since yesterday. Then utter panic and horror fell upon them and they all surrendered.

But what had happened to the bridge?

Early that morning, after a few hours' sleep, the girls had woken, to see Aslan standing over them and to hear his voice saying, "We will make holiday." They rubbed their eyes and looked round them. The trees had all gone but could still be seen moving away towards Aslan's How in a dark mass. Bacchus and the Maenads – his fierce, madcap girls – and Silenus were still with them. Lucy, fully rested, jumped up. Everyone was awake, everyone was laughing, flutes were playing, cymbals clashing. Animals, not Talking Animals, were crowding in upon them from every direction.

"What is it, Aslan?" said Lucy, her eyes dancing and her feet wanting to dance.

"Come, children," said he. "Ride on my back again today."

"Oh, lovely!" cried Lucy, and both girls climbed on to the warm golden back as they had done no one knew how many years before. Then the whole party moved off – Aslan leading, Bacchus and his Maenads leaping, rushing, and turning somersaults, the beasts frisking round them, and Silenus and his donkey bringing up the rear.

They turned a little to the right, raced down a steep hill, and found the long Bridge of Beruna in front of them. Before they had begun to cross it, however, up out of the water came a great wet, bearded head, larger than a man's, crowned with rushes. It looked at Aslan and out of its mouth a deep voice came.

"Hail, Lord," it said. "Loose my chains."

"Who on earth is *that*?" whispered Susan.

"I think it's the river-god, but hush," said Lucy.

"Bacchus," said Aslan. "Deliver him from his chains."

"That means the bridge, I expect," thought Lucy. And so it did. Bacchus and his people splashed forward into the shallow water, and a minute later the most curious things began happening. Great, strong trunks of ivy came curling up all the piers of the bridge, growing as quickly as a fire grows, wrapping the stones round, splitting, breaking, separating them. The walls of the bridge turned into hedges gay with hawthorn for a moment and then disappeared as the whole thing with a rush and a rumble collapsed into the swirling water. With much splashing, screaming, and laughter the revellers waded or swam or danced across the ford ("Hurray! It's the Ford of Beruna again now!" cried the girls) and up the bank on the far side and into the town.

Everyone in the streets fled before their faces. The first house they came to was a school: a girls' school, where a lot of Narnian girls, with their hair done very tight and ugly tight collars round their necks and thick tickly stockings on their legs, were having a History lesson. The sort of History that was taught in Narnia under Miraz's rule was duller than the truest History you ever read and less true than the most exciting adventure story.

"If you don't attend, Gwendolen," said the mistress, "and stop looking out of the window, I shall have to give you an order-mark."

"But please, Miss Prizzle—" began Gwendolen.

"Did you hear what I said, Gwendolen?" asked Miss Prizzle.

"But please, Miss Prizzle," said Gwendolen, "there's a LION!"

"Take two order-marks for talking nonsense," said Miss Prizzle. "And now——" A roar interrupted her. Ivy came curling in at the windows of the classroom. The walls became a mass of shimmering green, and leafy branches arched overhead where the ceiling had been. Miss Prizzle found she was standing on grass in a forest glade. She clutched at her desk to steady herself, and found that the desk was a rose-bush. Wild people such as she had never even imagined were crowding round her. Then she saw the Lion, screamed and fled, and with her fled her class, who were mostly dumpy, prim little girls with fat legs. Gwendolen hesitated.

"You'll stay with us, sweetheart?" said Aslan.

"Oh, *may* I? Thank you, thank you," said Gwendolen. Instantly she joined hands with two of the Maenads, who whirled her round in a merry dance and helped her take off some of the unnecessary and uncomfortable clothes that she was wearing.

Wherever they went in the little town of Beruna it was the same. Most of the people fled, a few joined them. When they left the town they were a larger and a merrier company.

They swept on across the level fields on the north bank, or left bank, of the river. At every farm, animals came out to join them. Sad old donkeys who had never known joy grew suddenly young again; chained dogs broke their chains; horses kicked their carts to pieces and came trotting along with them – clop-clop – kicking up the mud and whinnying.

At a well in a yard they met a man who was beating a boy. The stick burst into flower in the man's hand. He tried to drop it, but it stuck to his hand. His arm became a branch, his body the trunk of a tree, his feet took root. The boy, who had been crying a moment before, burst out laughing and joined them.

At a little town halfway to Beaversdam, where two rivers met, they came to another school, where a tired-looking girl was teaching arithmetic to a number of boys who looked very like pigs. She looked out of the window and saw the divine revellers singing up the street and a stab of joy went through her heart. Aslan stopped right under the window and looked up at her.

"Oh, don't, don't," she said. "I'd love to. But I mustn't. I must stick to my work. And the children would be frightened if they saw you."

"Frightened?" said the most pig-like of the boys. "Who's she talking to out of the window? Let's tell the inspector she talks to people out of the window when she ought to be teaching us."

"Let's go and see who it is," said another boy, and they all came crowding to the window. But as soon as their mean little faces looked out, Bacchus gave a great cry of *Euan, euoi-oi-oi-oi* and the boys all began howling with fright and trampling one another down to get out of the door and jumping out of the windows. And it was said afterwards (whether truly or not) that those particular little boys were never seen again, but that there were a lot of very fine little pigs in that part of the country which had never been there before.

"Now, Dear Heart," said Aslan to the Mistress: and she jumped down and joined them.

At Beaversdam they re-crossed the river and came east again along the southern bank. They came to a little cottage where a child stood in the doorway crying.

"Why are you crying, my love?" asked Aslan. The child, who had never seen a picture of a lion, was not afraid of him.

"Auntie's very ill," she said. "She's going to die."

Then Aslan went to go in at the door of the cottage, but it was too small for him. So, when he had got his head through, he pushed with his shoulders (Lucy and Susan fell off when he did this) and lifted the whole house up and it fell backwards and apart. And there, still in her bed, though the bed was now in the open air, lay a little old woman who looked as if she had dwarf blood in her. She was at death's door, but when she opened her eyes and saw the bright, hairy head of the lion staring into her face, she did not scream or faint. She said, "Oh, Aslan! I knew it was true. I've been waiting for this all my life. Have you come to take me away?"

"Yes, Dearest," said Aslan. "But not the long journey yet." And as he spoke, like the flush creeping along the underside of a cloud at sunrise, the colour came back to her white face and her eyes grew bright and she sat up and said, "Why, I do declare I feel *that* better. I think I could take a little breakfast this morning."

"Here you are, mother," said Bacchus, dipping a pitcher in the cottage well and handing it to her. But what was in it now was not water but the richest wine, red as redcurrant jelly, smooth as oil, strong as beef, warming as tea, cool as dew.

"Eh, you've done something to our well," said the old woman. "That makes a nice change, that does." And she jumped out of bed.

"Ride on me," said Aslan, and added to Susan and Lucy, "You two queens will have to run now."

"But we'd like that just as well," said Susan. And off they went again.

And so at last, with leaping and dancing and singing, with music and laughter and roaring and barking and neighing, they all came to the place where Miraz's army stood flinging down their swords and holding up their hands, and Peter's army, still holding their weapons and breathing hard, stood round them with stern and glad faces. And the first thing that happened was that the old woman slipped off Aslan's back and ran across to Caspian and they embraced one another; for she was his old nurse.

CHAPTER FIFTEEN

ASLAN MAKES A DOOR IN THE AIR

At the sight of Aslan the cheeks of the Telmarine soldiers became the colour of cold gravy, their knees knocked together, and many fell on their faces. They had not believed in lions and this made their fear greater. Even the Red Dwarfs, who knew that he came as a friend, stood with open mouths and could not speak. Some of the Black Dwarfs, who had been of Nikabrik's party, began to edge away. But all the Talking Beasts surged round the Lion, with purrs and grunts and squeaks and whinnies of delight, fawning on him with their tails, rubbing against him, touching him reverently with their noses and going to and fro under his body and between his legs. If you have ever seen a little cat loving a big dog whom it knows and trusts, you will have a pretty good picture of their behaviour. Then Peter, leading Caspian, forced his way through the crowd of animals.

"This is Caspian, Sir," he said. And Caspian knelt and kissed the Lion's paw.

"Welcome, Prince," said Aslan. "Do you feel yourself sufficient to take up the Kingship of Narnia?"

"I – I don't think I do, Sir," said Caspian. "I'm only a kid."

"Good," said Aslan. "If you had felt yourself sufficient, it would have been a proof that you were not. Therefore, under us and under the High King, you shall be King of Narnia, Lord of Cair Paravel, and Emperor of the Lone Islands. You and your heirs while your race lasts. And your coronation – but what have we here?" For at that moment a curious little procession was approaching – eleven Mice, six of whom carried between them something on a litter made of branches, but the litter was no bigger than a large atlas. No one has ever seen mice more woebegone than these.

They were plastered with mud – some with blood too – and their ears were down and their whiskers drooped and their tails dragged in the grass, and their leader piped on his slender pipe a melancholy tune. On the litter lay what seemed little better than a damp heap of fur; all that was left of Reepicheep. He was still breathing, but more dead than alive, gashed with innumerable wounds, one paw crushed and, where his tail had been, a bandaged stump.

"Now, Lucy," said Aslan.

Lucy had her diamond bottle out in a moment. Though only a drop was needed on each of Reepicheep's wounds, the wounds were so many that there was a long and anxious silence before she had finished and the Mouse sprang from the litter. His hand went at once to his sword hilt, with the other he twirled his whiskers. He bowed.

"Hail, Aslan!" came his shrill voice. "I have the honour—" But then he suddenly stopped.

The fact was that he still had no tail – whether that Lucy had forgotten it or that her cordial, though it could heal wounds, could not make things grow again. Reepicheep became aware of his loss as he made his bow; perhaps it altered something in his balance. He looked over his right shoulder. Failing to see his tail, he strained his neck further till he had to turn his shoulders and his whole body followed. But by that time his hindquarters had turned too and were out of sight. Then he strained his neck looking over his shoulder again, with the same result. Only after he had turned completely round three times did he realize the dreadful truth.

"I am confounded," said Reepicheep to Aslan. "I am completely out of countenance. I must crave your indulgence for appearing in this unseemly fashion."

"It becomes you very well, Small One," said Aslan.

"All the same," replied Reepicheep, "if anything could be done… Perhaps her Majesty?" and here he bowed to Lucy.

"But what do you want with a tail?" asked Aslan.

"Sir," said the Mouse, "I can eat and sleep and die for my King without one. But a tail is the honour and glory of a Mouse."

"I have sometimes wondered, friend," said Aslan, "whether you do not think too much about your honour."

"Highest of all High Kings," said Reepicheep, "permit me to remind you that a very small size has been bestowed on us Mice, and if we did not guard our dignity, some (who weigh worth by inches) would allow themselves very unsuitable pleasantries at our expense. That is why I have been at some pains to make it known that no one who does not wish to feel this sword as near his heart as I can reach shall talk in my presence about Traps or Toasted Cheese or Candles: no, sir – not the tallest fool in

Narnia!" Here he glared very fiercely up at Wimbleweather, but the Giant, who was always a stage behind everyone else, had not yet discovered what was being talked about down at his feet, and so missed the point.

"Why have your followers all drawn *their* swords, may I ask?" said Aslan.

"May it please your High Majesty," said the second Mouse, whose name was Peepiceek, "we are all waiting to cut off our own tails if our Chief must go without his. We will not bear the shame of wearing an honour which is denied to the High Mouse."

"Ah!" roared Aslan. "You have conquered me. You have great hearts. Not for the sake of your dignity, Reepicheep, but for the love that is between you and your people, and still more for the kindness your people showed me long ago when you ate away the cords that bound me on the Stone Table (and it was then, though you have long forgotten it, that you began to be *Talking* Mice), you shall have your tail again."

Before Aslan had finished speaking the new tail was in its place. Then, at Aslan's command, Peter bestowed the Knighthood of the Order of the Lion on Caspian, and Caspian, as soon as he was knighted, himself bestowed it on Trufflehunter and Trumpkin and Reepicheep, and made Doctor Cornelius his Lord Chancellor, and confirmed the Bulgy Bear in his hereditary office of Marshal of the Lists. And there was great applause.

After this the Telmarine soldiers, firmly but without taunts or blows, were taken across the ford and all put under lock and key in the town of Beruna and given beef and beer. They made a great fuss about wading in the river, for they all hated and feared running water just as much as they hated and feared woods and animals. But in the end the nuisance was over: and then the nicest parts of that long day began.

Lucy, sitting close to Aslan and divinely comfortable, wondered what the trees were doing. At first she thought they were merely dancing; they were certainly going round slowly in two circles, one from left to right and the other from right to left. Then she noticed that they kept throwing something down in the centre of both circles. Sometimes she thought they were cutting off long strands of their hair; at other times it looked as if they were breaking off bits of their fingers – but, if so, they had plenty of fingers to spare and it did not hurt them. But whatever they were throwing down, when it reached the ground, it became brushwood or dry sticks. Then three or four of the Red Dwarfs came forward with their tinder boxes and set light to the pile, which first crackled, and then blazed, and finally roared as a woodland bonfire on midsummer night ought to do. And everyone sat down in a wide circle round it.

Then Bacchus and Silenus and the Maenads began a dance, far wilder than the dance of the trees; not merely a dance for fun and beauty (though it was that too) but a magic dance of plenty, and where their hands touched, and where their feet fell, the feast came into existence – sides of roasted meat that filled the grove with delicious smells, and wheaten cakes and oaten cakes, honey and many-coloured sugars and cream as thick as porridge and as smooth as still water, peaches, nectarines, pomegranates, pears, grapes, straw-berries, raspberries – pyramids and cataracts of fruit. Then, in great wooden cups and bowls and mazers, wreathed with ivy, came the wines; dark, thick ones like syrups of mulberry juice, and clear red ones like red jellies liquefied, and yellow wines and green wines and yellow-green and greenish-yellow.

But for the tree people different fare was provided. When Lucy saw Clodsley Shovel and his moles scuffling up the turf in various places (which Bacchus had pointed out to them) and realized that the trees were going to eat *earth* it gave her rather a shudder. But when she saw the earths that were actually brought to them she felt quite different. They began with a rich brown loam that looked almost exactly like chocolate; so like chocolate, in fact, that Edmund tried a piece of it, but he did not find it at all nice. When the rich loam had taken the edge off their hunger, the trees turned to an earth of the kind you see in Somerset, which is almost pink. They said it was lighter and sweeter. At the cheese stage they had a chalky soil, and then went on to delicate confections of the finest gravels powdered with choice silver sand. They drank very little wine, and it made the Hollies very talkative: for the most part they quenched their thirst with deep draughts of mingled dew and rain, flavoured with forest flowers and the airy taste of the thinnest clouds.

Thus Aslan feasted the Narnians till long after the sunset had died away, and the stars had come out: and the great fire, now hotter but less noisy, shone like a beacon in the dark woods, and the frightened Telmarines saw it from far away and wondered what it might mean. The best thing of all about this feast was that there was no breaking up or going away, but as the talk grew quieter and slower, one after another would begin to nod and finally drop off to sleep with feet towards the fire and good friends on either side, till at last there was silence all round the circle, and the chattering of water over stone at the Ford of Beruna could be heard once more. But all night Aslan and the Moon gazed upon each other with joyful and unblinking eyes.

Next day messengers (who were chiefly squirrels and birds) were sent all over the country with a proclamation to the scattered Telmarines – including, of course, the prisoners in Beruna. They were told that Caspian was now King and that Narnia would henceforth belong to the Talking Beasts and the Dwarfs and Dryads and Fauns and other creatures quite as much as to the men. Any who chose to stay under the new conditions might do so; but for those who did not like the idea, Aslan would provide another home. Anyone who wished to go there must come to Aslan and the Kings at the Ford of Beruna by noon on the fifth day. You may imagine that this caused plenty of head-scratching among the Telmarines. Some of them, chiefly the young ones, had, like Caspian, heard stories of the Old Days and were delighted that they had come back. They were already making friends with the creatures. These all decided to stay in Narnia. But most of the older men, especially those who had been important under Miraz, were sulky and had no wish to live in a country where they could not rule the roost. "Live here with a lot of blooming performing animals! No fear," they said. "And ghosts too," some added with a shudder. "That's what those there Dryads really are. It's not canny." They were also suspicious. "I don't trust 'em," they said. "Not with that awful Lion and all. He won't keep his claws off us long, *you'll* see." But then they were equally suspicious of his offer to give them a new home. "Take us off to his den and eat us one by one most likely," they muttered. And the more they talked to one another the sulkier and more suspicious they became. But on the appointed day more than half of them turned up.

At one end of the glade Aslan had caused to be set up two stakes of wood, higher than a man's head and about three feet apart. A third, and lighter, piece of wood was bound across them at the top, uniting them, so that the whole thing looked like a doorway from nowhere into nowhere. In front of this stood Aslan himself with Peter on his right and Caspian on his left. Grouped round them were Susan, Edmund and Lucy, Trumpkin and Trufflehunter, the Lord Cornelius, Glenstorm, Reepicheep, and others. The children and the Dwarfs had made good use of the royal wardrobes in what had been the castle of Miraz and was now the castle of Caspian, and what with silk and cloth of gold, with snowy linen glancing through slashed sleeves, with silver mail shirts and jewelled sword-hilts, with gilt helmets and feathered bonnets, they were almost too bright to look at. Even the beasts wore rich chains about their necks. Yet nobody's eyes were on them or the children. The living and strokable gold of Aslan's mane outshone them all. The rest of the Old Narnians stood down each side of the glade. At the far end stood the Telmarines. The sun shone brightly and pennants fluttered in the light wind.

"Men of Telmar," said Aslan, "you who seek a new land, hear my words. I will send you all to your own country, which I know and you do not."

"We don't remember Telmar. We don't know where it is. We don't know what it is like," grumbled the Telmarines.

"You came into Narnia out of Telmar," said Aslan. "But you came into Telmar from another place. You do not belong to this world at all. You came hither, certain generations ago, out of that same world to which the High King Peter belongs."

At this, half the Telmarines began whimpering, "There you are. Told you so. He's going to kill us all, send us right out of the world," and the other half began throwing out their chests and slapping one another on the back and whispering, "There you are. Might have guessed we didn't belong to this place with all its queer, nasty, unnatural creatures. We're of royal blood, you'll see." And even Caspian and Cornelius and the children turned to Aslan with looks of amazement on their faces.

"Peace," said Aslan in the low voice which was nearest to his growl. The earth seemed to shake a little and every living thing in the grove became still as stone.

"You, Sir Caspian," said Aslan, "might have known that you could be no true King of Narnia unless, like the Kings of old, you were a son of Adam and came from the world of Adam's sons. And so you are. Many years ago in that world, in a deep sea of that world which is called the South Sea, a shipload of pirates were driven by storm on an island. And there they did as pirates would: killed the natives and took the native women for wives, and made palm wine, and drank and were drunk, and lay in the shade of the palm trees, and woke up and quarrelled, and sometimes killed one another. And in one of these frays six were put to flight by the rest and fled with their women into the centre of the island and up a mountain and went, as they thought, into a cave to hide. But it was one of the magical places of that world, one of the chinks or chasms between worlds in old times, but they have grown rarer. This was one of the last: I do not say *the* last. And so they fell, or rose, or blundered, or dropped right through, and found themselves in this world, in the Land of Telmar which was then unpeopled. But why it was unpeopled is a long story: I will not tell it now. And in Telmar their descendants lived and became a fierce and proud people; and after many generations there was a famine in Telmar and they invaded Narnia, which was then in some disorder (but that also would be a long story), and conquered it and ruled it. Do you mark all this well, King Caspian?"

"I do indeed, Sir," said Caspian. "I was wishing that I came of a more honourable lineage."

"You come of the Lord Adam and the Lady Eve," said Aslan. "And that is both honour enough to erect the head of the poorest beggar, and shame enough to bow the shoulders of the greatest emperor on earth. Be content."

Caspian bowed.

"And now," said Aslan, "you men and women of Telmar, will you go back to that island in the world of men from which your fathers first came? It is no bad place. The race of those pirates who first found it has died out, and it is without inhabitants. There are good wells of fresh water, and fruitful soil, and timber for building, and fish in the lagoons; and the other men of that world have not yet discovered it. The chasm is open for your return; but this I must warn you, that once you have gone through, it will close behind you for ever. There will be no more commerce between the worlds by that door."

There was silence for a moment. Then a burly, decent-looking fellow among the Telmarine soldiers pushed forward and said:

"Well, I'll take the offer."

"It is well chosen," said Aslan. "And because you have spoken first, strong magic is upon you. Your future in that world shall be good. Come forth."

The man, now a little pale, came forward. Aslan and his court drew aside, leaving him free access to the empty doorway of the stakes.

"Go through it, my son," said Aslan, bending towards him and touching the man's nose with his own. As soon as the Lion's breath came about him, a new look came into the man's eyes – startled, but not unhappy – as if he were trying to remember something. Then he squared his shoulders and walked through the Door.

Everyone's eyes were fixed on him. They saw the three pieces of wood, and through them the trees and grass and sky of Narnia. They saw the man between the doorposts: then, in one second, he had vanished utterly.

From the other end of the glade the remaining Telmarines set up a wailing. "Ugh! What's happened to him? Do you mean to murder us? We won't go that way." And then one of the clever Telmarines said:

"We don't see any other world through those sticks. If you want us to believe in it, why doesn't one of *you* go? All your own friends are keeping well away from the sticks."

Instantly Reepicheep stood forward and bowed. "If *my* example can be of any service, Aslan," he said, "I will take eleven mice through that arch at your bidding without a moment's delay."

"Nay, little one," said Aslan, laying his velvety paw ever so lightly on Reepicheep's head. "They would do dreadful things to you in that world. They would show you at fairs. It is others who must lead."

"Come on," said Peter suddenly to Edmund and Lucy. "Our time's up."

"What do you mean?" said Edmund.

"This way," said Susan, who seemed to know all about it. "Back into the trees. We've got to change."

"Change what?" asked Lucy.

"Our clothes, of course," said Susan. "Nice fools we'd look on the platform of an English station in *these*."

"But our other things are at Caspian's castle," said Edmund.

"No, they're not," said Peter, still leading the way into the thickest wood. "They're all here. They were brought down in bundles this morning. It's all arranged."

"Was that what Aslan was talking to you and Susan about this morning?" asked Lucy.

"Yes — that and other things," said Peter, his face very solemn. "I can't tell it all to you. There were things he wanted to say to Su and me because we're not coming back to Narnia."

"Never?" cried Edmund and Lucy in dismay.

"Oh, you two are," answered Peter. "At least, from what he said, I'm pretty sure he means you to get back some day. But not Su and me. He says we're getting too old."

"Oh, Peter," said Lucy. "What awful bad luck. Can you bear it?"

"Well, I think I can," said Peter. "It's all rather different from what I thought. You'll understand when it comes to your last time. But, quick, here are our things."

It was odd, and not very nice, to take off their royal clothes and to come back in their school things (not very fresh now) into that great assembly. One or two of the nastier Telmarines jeered. But the other creatures all cheered and rose up in honour of Peter the High King, and Queen Susan of the Horn, and King Edmund, and Queen Lucy. There were affectionate and (on Lucy's part) tearful farewells with all their old friends — animal kisses, and hugs from Bulgy Bears, and hands wrung by Trumpkin, and a last tickly, whiskerish embrace with Trufflehunter. And of course Caspian offered the Horn back to Susan and of course Susan told him to keep it. And then, wonderfully and terribly, it was farewell to Aslan himself, and Peter took his place with Susan's hands on his shoulders and Edmund's on hers and Lucy's on his and the first of the Telmarines' on Lucy's, and so in a long line they moved forward to the Door. After that came a moment which is hard to describe, for the children seemed to be seeing three things at once. One was the mouth of a cave opening into the glaring green and blue of an island in the Pacific, where all the Telmarines would find themselves the moment they were through the door. The second was a glade in Narnia, the faces of Dwarfs and Beasts, the deep eyes of Aslan, and the white patches on the Badger's cheeks. But the third (which rapidly swallowed up the other two) was the grey, gravelly surface of a platform in a country station, and a seat with luggage round it, where they were all sitting as if they had never moved from it — a little flat and dreary for a moment after all they had been through, but also, unexpectedly, nice in its own way, what with the familiar railway smell and the English sky and the summer term before them.

"Well!" said Peter. "We *have* had a time."

"Bother!" said Edmund. "I've left my new torch in Narnia."

THE VOYAGE OF THE

DAWN TREADER

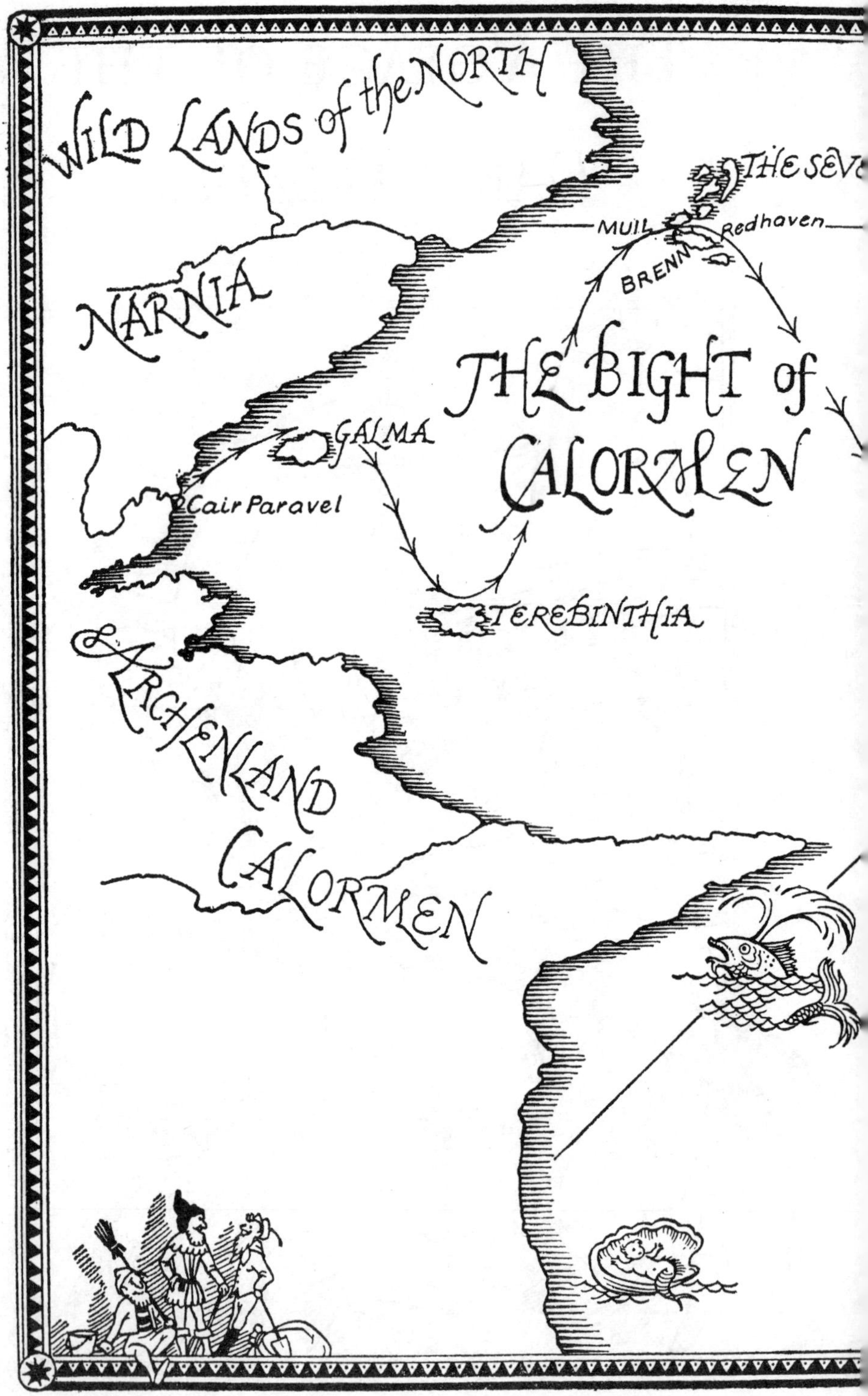

WILD LANDS of the NORTH

NARNIA

THE SEV

MUIL   Redhaven

BRENN

THE BIGHT of
CALORMEN

GALMA

Cair Paravel

TEREBINTHIA

ARCHENLAND

CALORMEN

ISLES

N

W E

S

The first
part of the
VOYAGE

About here they
joined the ship

FELIMATH THE LONE ISLANDS

DOORN AVRA

THE GREAT EASTERN OCEAN

The Voyage of the Dawn Treader

Contents

To Geoffrey Barfield

Plan of the
Dawn Treader

FORECASTLE

POOP

tiller

poop deck

lookout man

hatch

boat

hen coop

Lucy's cabin

Drinian's cabin

stern cabin

Caspian's cabin

galley

quarters

starboard

port

Chapter One

The Picture in the Bedroom

There was a boy called Eustace Clarence Scrubb, and he almost deserved it. His parents called him Eustace Clarence and masters called him Scrubb. I can't tell you how his friends spoke to him for he had none. He didn't call his Father and Mother "Father" and "Mother", but Harold and Alberta. They were very up-to-date and advanced people. They were vegetarians, non-smokers and tee-totallers, and wore a special kind of underclothes. In their house there was very little furniture and very few clothes on beds and the windows were always open.

Eustace Clarence liked animals, especially beetles, if they were dead and pinned on a card. He liked books if they were books of information and had pictures of grain elevators or of fat foreign children doing exercises in model schools.

Eustace Clarence disliked his cousins, the four Pevensies – Peter, Susan, Edmund and Lucy. But he was quite glad when he heard that Edmund and Lucy were coming to stay. For deep down inside him he liked bossing and bullying; and, though he was a puny little person who couldn't have stood up even to Lucy, let alone Edmund, in a fight, he knew that there are dozens of ways to give people a bad time if you are in your own home and they are only visitors.

Edmund and Lucy did not at all want to come and stay with Uncle Harold and Aunt Alberta. But it really couldn't be helped. Father had got a job lecturing in America for sixteen weeks that summer, and Mother was to go with him because she hadn't had a real holiday for ten years. Peter was working very hard for an exam and he was to spend the holidays being coached by old Professor Kirke in whose house these four children had had wonderful adventures long ago in the war years. If he had still been in that house he would have had them all to stay. But he had somehow become poor since the old days and was living in a small cottage with only one bedroom to spare. It would have cost too much money to take the other three all to America, and so only Susan had gone.

Grown-ups thought her the pretty one of the family and she was no good at school work (though otherwise very old for her age) and Mother said she "would get far more out of a trip to America than the youngsters". Edmund and Lucy tried not to grudge Susan her luck, but it was dreadful having to spend the summer holidays at their Aunt's. "But it's far worse for me," said Edmund, "because you'll at least have a room of your own and I shall have to share a bedroom with that record stinker, Eustace."

The story begins on an afternoon when Edmund and Lucy were stealing a few precious minutes alone together. And of course they were talking about Narnia, which was the name of their own private and secret country. Most of us, I suppose, have a secret country, but for most of us it is only an imaginary country. Edmund and Lucy were luckier than other people in that respect. Their secret country was real. They had already visited it twice; not in a game or a dream but in reality. They had got there of course by Magic, which is the only way of getting to Narnia. And a promise, or very nearly a promise, had been made them in Narnia itself that they would some day get back. You may imagine that they talked about it a good deal, when they got the chance.

They were in Lucy's room, sitting on the edge of her bed and looking at a picture on the opposite wall. It was the only picture in the house that they liked. Aunt Alberta didn't like it at all (that was why it was put away in a little back room upstairs), but she couldn't get rid of it because it had been a wedding present from someone she did not want to offend.

It was a picture of a ship – a ship sailing straight towards you. Her prow was gilded and shaped like the head of a dragon with a wide-open mouth. She had only one mast and one large, square sail which was a rich purple. The sides of the ship – what you could see of them where the gilded wings of the dragon ended – were green. She had just run up to the top of one glorious blue wave, and the nearer slope of that wave came down towards you, with streaks and bubbles on it. She was obviously running fast before a gay wind, listing over a little on her port side. (By the way, if you are going to read this story at all, and if you don't know already, you had better get it into your head that the left of a ship when you are looking ahead is *port*, and the right is *starboard*.) All the sunlight fell on her from that side, and the water on that side was full of greens and purples. On the other, it was darker blue from the shadow of the ship.

"The question is," said Edmund, "whether it doesn't make things worse, *looking* at a Narnian ship when you can't get there."

"Even looking is better than nothing," said Lucy. "And she is such a very Narnian ship."

"Still playing your old game?" said Eustace Clarence, who had been listening outside the door and now came grinning into the room. Last year, when he had been staying with the Pevensies, he had managed to hear them all talking of Narnia and he loved teasing them about it. He thought of course that they were making it all up; and as he was far too stupid to make anything up himself, he did not approve of that.

"You're not wanted here," said Edmund curtly.

"I'm trying to think of a limerick," said Eustace. "Something like this:

> Some kids who played games about Narnia
> Got gradually balmier and balmier—"

"Well, *Narnia* and *balmier* don't rhyme, to begin with," said Lucy.

"It's an assonance," said Eustace.

"Don't ask him what an assy-thingummy is," said Edmund. "He's only longing to be asked. Say nothing and perhaps he'll go away."

Most boys, on meeting a reception like this, would either have cleared out or flared up. Eustace did neither. He just hung about grinning, and presently began talking again.

"Do you like that picture?" he asked.

"For Heaven's sake don't let him get started about Art and all that," said Edmund hurriedly, but Lucy, who was very truthful, had already said, "Yes, I do. I like it very much."

"It's a rotten picture," said Eustace.

"You won't see it if you step outside," said Edmund.

"Why do you like it?" said Eustace to Lucy.

"Well, for one thing," said Lucy, "I like it because the ship looks as if it were really moving. And the water looks as if it were really wet. And the waves look as if they were really going up and down."

Of course Eustace knew lots of answers to this, but he didn't say anything. The reason was that at that very moment he looked at the waves and saw that they did look very much indeed as if they were going up and down. He had only once been in a ship (and then only as far as the Isle of Wight) and had been horribly seasick. The look of the waves in the picture made him feel sick again. He turned rather green and tried another look. And then all three children were staring with open mouths.

What they were seeing may be hard to believe when you read it in print, but it was almost as hard to believe when you saw it happening. The things in the picture were moving. It didn't look at all like a cinema either; the colours were too real and clean and out-of-doors for that. Down went the prow of the ship into the wave and up went a great shock of spray. And then up went the wave behind her, and her stern and her deck became visible for the first time, and then disappeared as the next wave came to meet her and her bows went up again. At the same moment an exercise book which had been lying beside Edmund on the bed flapped, rose and sailed through the air to the wall behind him, and Lucy felt all her hair whipping round her face as it does on a windy day. And this was a windy day; but the wind was blowing out of the picture towards them. And suddenly with the wind came the noises – the swishing of waves and the slap of water against the ship's sides and the creaking and the overall high steady roar of air and water. But it was the smell, the wild, briny smell, which really convinced Lucy that she was not dreaming.

"Stop it," came Eustace's voice, squeaky with fright and bad temper. "It's some silly trick you two are playing. Stop it. I'll tell Alberta – Ow!"

The other two were much more accustomed to adventures but, just exactly as Eustace Clarence said, "Ow," they both said, "Ow" too. The reason was that a great cold, salt splash had broken right out of the frame and they were breathless from the smack of it, besides being wet through.

"I'll smash the rotten thing," cried Eustace; and then several things happened at the same time. Eustace rushed towards the picture. Edmund, who knew something about magic, sprang after him, warning him to look out and not to be a fool. Lucy grabbed at him from the other side and was dragged forward. And by this time either they had grown much smaller or the picture had grown bigger. Eustace jumped to try to pull it off the wall and found himself standing on the frame; in front of him was not glass but real sea, and wind and waves rushing up to the frame as they might to a rock. He lost his head and clutched at the other two who had jumped up beside him. There was a second of struggling and shouting, and just as they thought they had got their balance a great blue roller surged up round them, swept them off their feet, and drew them down into the sea. Eustace's despairing cry suddenly ended as the water got into his mouth.

Lucy thanked her stars that she had worked hard at her swimming in the summer term. It is true that she would have got on much better if she had used a slower stroke, and also that the water felt a great deal colder than it had looked while it was only a picture. Still, she kept her head and kicked her shoes off, as everyone ought to do who falls into deep water in their clothes. She even kept her mouth shut and her eyes open. They were still quite near the ship; she saw its green side towering high above them, and people looking at her from the deck. Then, as one might have expected, Eustace clutched at her in a panic and down they both went.

When they came up again she saw a white figure diving off the ship's side. Edmund was close beside her now, treading water, and had caught the arms of the howling Eustace. Then someone else, whose face was vaguely familiar, slipped an arm under her from the other side. There was a lot of shouting going on from the ship, heads crowding together above the bulwarks, ropes being thrown. Edmund and the stranger were fastening ropes round her. After that followed what seemed a very long delay during which her face got blue and her teeth began chattering. In reality the delay was not very long; they were waiting till the moment when she could be got on board ship without being dashed against its side. Even with all their best endeavours she had a bruised knee when she finally stood, dripping and shivering, on the deck. After her Edmund was heaved up, and then the miserable Eustace. Last of all came the stranger – a golden-headed boy some years older than herself.

"Ca – Ca – Caspian!" gasped Lucy as soon as she had breath enough. For Caspian it was; Caspian, the boy king of Narnia whom they had helped to set on the throne during their last visit. Immediately Edmund recognized him too. All three shook hands and clapped one another on the back with great delight.

"But who is your friend?" said Caspian almost at once, turning to Eustace with his cheerful smile. But Eustace was crying much harder than any boy of his age has a right to cry when nothing worse than a wetting has happened to him, and would only yell out, "Let me go. Let me go back. I don't *like* it."

"Let you go?" said Caspian. "But where?"

Eustace rushed to the ship's side, as if he expected to see the picture frame hanging above the sea, and perhaps a glimpse of Lucy's bedroom. What he saw was blue waves flecked with foam, and paler blue sky, both spreading without a break to the horizon. Perhaps we can hardly blame him if his heart sank. He was promptly sick.

"Hey! Rynelf," said Caspian to one of the sailors. "Bring spiced wine for their Majesties. You'll need something to warm you after that dip." He called Edmund and Lucy their Majesties because they and Peter and Susan had all been Kings and Queens of Narnia long before his time. Narnian time flows differently from ours. If you spent a hundred years in Narnia, you would still come back to our world at the very same hour of the very same day on which you left. And then, if you went back to Narnia after spending a week here, you might find that a thousand Narnian years had passed, or only a day, or no time at all. You never know till you get there. Consequently, when the Pevensie children had returned to Narnia last time for their second visit, it was (for the Narnians) as if King Arthur came back to Britain, as some people say he will. And I say the sooner the better.

Rynelf returned with the spiced wine steaming in a flagon, and four silver cups. It was just what one wanted, and as Lucy and Edmund sipped it they could feel the warmth going right down to their toes. But Eustace made faces and spluttered and spat it out and was sick again and began to cry again and asked if they hadn't any Plumptree's Vitaminized Nerve Food and could it be made with distilled water and anyway he insisted on being put ashore at the next station.

"This is a merry shipmate you've brought us, Brother," whispered Caspian to Edmund with a chuckle; but before he could say anything more, Eustace burst out again.

"Oh! Ugh! What on earth's *that*? Take it away, the horrid thing."

He really had some excuse this time for feeling a little surprised. Something very curious indeed had come out of the cabin in the poop and was slowly approaching them. You might call it — and indeed it was — a Mouse. But then it was a Mouse on its hind legs and stood about two feet high. A thin band of gold passed round its head under one ear and over the other and in this was stuck a long crimson feather. (As the Mouse's fur was very dark, almost black, the effect was bold and striking.) Its left paw rested on the hilt of a sword very nearly as long as its tail. Its balance, as it paced gravely along the swaying deck, was perfect, and its manners courtly. Lucy and Edmund recognized it at once — Reepicheep, the most valiant of all the Talking Beasts of Narnia, and the Chief Mouse. He had won undying glory in the second Battle of Beruna. Lucy longed, as she had always done, to take Reepicheep up in her arms and cuddle him. But this, as she well knew, was a pleasure she could never have: it would have offended him deeply. Instead, she went down on one knee to talk to him.

Reepicheep put forward his left leg, drew back his right, bowed, kissed her hand, straightened himself, twirled his whiskers, and said in his shrill, piping voice:

"My humble duty to your Majesty. And to King Edmund, too." (Here he bowed again.) "Nothing except your Majesties' presence was lacking to this glorious venture."

"Ugh, take it away," wailed Eustace. "I hate mice. And I never could bear performing animals. They're silly and vulgar and — and sentimental."

"Am I to understand," said Reepicheep to Lucy after a long stare at Eustace, "that this singularly discourteous person is under your Majesty's protection? Because, if not—"

At this moment Lucy and Edmund both sneezed.

"What a fool I am to keep you all standing here in your wet things," said Caspian. "Come on below and get changed. I'll give you my cabin of course, Lucy, but I'm afraid we have no women's clothes on board. You'll have to make do with some of mine. Lead the way, Reepicheep, like a good fellow."

"To the convenience of a lady," said Reepicheep, "even a question of honour must give way – at least for the moment—" and here he looked very hard at Eustace. But Caspian hustled them on and in a few minutes Lucy found herself passing through the door into the stern cabin. She fell in love with it at once – the three square windows that looked out on the blue, swirling water astern, the low cushioned benches round three sides of the table, the swinging silver lamp overhead (Dwarfs' work, she knew at once by its exquisite delicacy) and the flat gold image of Aslan the Lion on the forward wall above the door. All this she took in in a flash, for Caspian immediately opened a door on the starboard side, and said, "This'll be your room, Lucy. I'll just get some dry things for myself" – he was rummaging in one of the lockers while he spoke – "and then leave you to change. If you'll fling your wet things outside the door I'll get them taken to the galley to be dried."

Lucy found herself as much at home as if she had been in Caspian's cabin for weeks, and the motion of the ship did not worry her, for in the old days when she had been a queen in Narnia she had done a good deal of voyaging. The cabin was very tiny but bright with painted panels (all birds and beasts and crimson dragons and vines) and spotlessly clean. Caspian's clothes were too big for her, but she could manage. His shoes, sandals and sea-boots were hopelessly big but she did not mind going barefoot on board ship. When she had finished dressing she looked out of her window at the water rushing past and took a long deep breath. She felt quite sure they were in for a lovely time.

Chapter Two

On Board the *Dawn Treader*

"Ah, there you are, Lucy," said Caspian. "We were just waiting for you. This is my captain, the Lord Drinian."

A dark-haired man went down on one knee and kissed her hand. The only others present were Reepicheep and Edmund.

"Where is Eustace?" asked Lucy.

"In bed," said Edmund, "and I don't think we can do anything for him. It only makes him worse if you try to be nice to him."

"Meanwhile," said Caspian, "we want to talk."

"By Jove, we do," said Edmund. "And first, about time. It's a year ago by our time since we left you just before your coronation. How long has it been in Narnia?"

"Exactly three years," said Caspian.

"All going well?" asked Edmund.

"You don't suppose I'd have left my kingdom and put to sea unless all was well," answered the King. "It couldn't be better. There's no trouble at all now between Telmarines, Dwarfs, Talking Beasts, Fauns and the rest. And we gave those troublesome giants on the frontier such a good beating last summer that they pay us tribute now. And I had an excellent person to leave as Regent while I'm away – Trumpkin, the Dwarf. You remember him?"

"Dear Trumpkin," said Lucy, "of course I do. You couldn't have made a better choice."

"Loyal as a badger, Ma'am, and valiant as – as a Mouse," said Drinian. He had been going to say "as a lion" but had noticed Reepicheep's eyes fixed on him.

"And where are we heading for?" asked Edmund.

"Well," said Caspian, "that's rather a long story. Perhaps you remember that when I was a child my usurping uncle Miraz got rid of seven friends of my father's (who might have taken my part) by sending them off to explore the unknown Eastern Seas beyond the Lone Islands."

"Yes," said Lucy, "and none of them ever came back."

"Right. Well, on my coronation day, with Aslan's approval, I swore an oath that, if once I established peace in Narnia, I would sail east myself for a year and a day to find my father's friends or to learn of their deaths and avenge them if I could. These were their names – the Lord Revilian, the Lord Bern, the Lord Argoz, the Lord Mavramorn, the Lord Octesian, the Lord Restimar, and – oh, that other one who's so hard to remember."

"The Lord Rhoop, Sire," said Drinian.

"Rhoop, Rhoop, of course," said Caspian. "That is my main intention. But Reepicheep here has an even higher hope." Everyone's eyes turned to the Mouse.

"As high as my spirit," he said. "Though perhaps as small as my stature. Why should we not come to the very eastern end of the world? And what might we find there? I expect to find Aslan's own country. It is always from the east, across the sea, that the great Lion comes to us."

"I say, that *is* an idea," said Edmund in an awed voice.

"But do you think," said Lucy, "Aslan's country would be that sort of country – I mean, the sort you could ever *sail* to?"

"I do not know, Madam," said Reepicheep. "But there is this. When I was in my cradle, a wood woman, a Dryad, spoke this verse over me:

> Where sky and water meet,
> Where the waves grow sweet,
> Doubt not, Reepicheep,
> To find all you seek,
> There is the utter east.

"I do not know what it means. But the spell of it has been on me all my life."

After a short silence Lucy asked, "And where are we now, Caspian?"

"The Captain can tell you better than I," said Caspian, so Drinian got out his chart and spread it on the table.

"That's our position," he said, laying his finger on it. "Or was at noon today. We had a fair wind from Cair Paravel and stood a little north for Galma, which we made on the next day. We were in port for a week, for the Duke of Galma made a great tournament for his Majesty and there he unhorsed many knights—"

"And got a few nasty falls myself, Drinian. Some of the bruises are there still," put in Caspian.

"—and unhorsed many knights," repeated Drinian with a grin. "We thought the duke would have been pleased if the King's Majesty would have married his daughter, but nothing came of that—"

"Squints, and has freckles," said Caspian.

"Oh, poor girl," said Lucy.

"And we sailed from Galma," continued Drinian, "and ran into a calm for the best part of two days and had to row, and then had wind again and did not make Terebinthia till the fourth day from Galma. And there their King sent out a warning not to land for there was sickness in Terebinthia, but we doubled the cape and put in at a little creek far from the city and watered. Then we had to lie off for three days before we got a south-east wind and stood out for Seven Isles. The third day out a pirate (Terebinthian by her rig) overhauled us, but when she saw us well armed she stood off after some shooting of arrows on either part—"

"And we ought to have given her chase and boarded her and hanged every mother's son of them," said Reepicheep.

"—and in five days more we were in sight of Muil which, as you know, is the westernmost of the Seven Isles. Then we rowed through the straits and came about sundown into Redhaven on the isle of Brenn, where we were very lovingly feasted and had victuals and water at will. We left Redhaven six days ago and have made marvellously good speed, so that I hope to see the Lone Islands the day after tomorrow. The sum is, we are now nearly thirty days at sea and have sailed more than four hundred leagues from Narnia."

"And after the Lone Islands?" said Lucy.

"No one knows, your Majesty," answered Drinian. "Unless the Lone Islanders themselves can tell us."

"They couldn't in our days," said Edmund.

"Then," said Reepicheep, "it is after the Lone Islands that the adventure really begins."

Caspian now suggested that they might like to be shown over the ship before supper, but Lucy's conscience smote her and she said, "I think I really must go and see Eustace. Seasickness is horrid, you know. If I had my old cordial with me I could cure him."

"But you have," said Caspian. "I'd quite forgotten about it. As you left it behind I thought it might be regarded as one of the royal treasures and so I brought it—if you think it ought to be wasted on a thing like seasickness."

"It'll only take a drop," said Lucy.

Caspian opened one of the lockers beneath the bench and brought out the beautiful little diamond flask which Lucy remembered so well. "Take back your own, Queen," he said. They then left the cabin and went out into the sunshine.

In the deck there were two large, long hatches, fore and aft of the mast, and both open, as they always were in fair weather, to let light and air into the belly of the ship. Caspian led them down a ladder into the after hatch. Here they found themselves in a place where benches for rowing ran from side to side and the light came in through the oar-holes and danced on the roof. Of course Caspian's ship was not that horrible thing, a galley rowed by slaves. Oars were used only when wind failed or for getting in and out of harbour and everyone (except Reepicheep whose legs were too short) had often taken a turn. At each side of the ship the space under the benches was left clear for the rowers' feet, but all down the centre there was a kind of pit which went down to the very keel and this was filled with all kinds of things – sacks of flour, casks of water and beer, barrels of pork, jars of honey, skin bottles of wine, apples, nuts, cheese, biscuits, turnips, sides of bacon. From the roof – that is, from the under side of the deck – hung hams and strings of onions, and also the men of the watch off-duty in their hammocks. Caspian led them aft, stepping from bench to bench; at least, it was stepping for him, and something between a step and a jump for Lucy, and a real long jump for Reepicheep. In this way they came to a partition with a door in it. Caspian opened the door and led them into a cabin which filled the stern underneath the deck cabins in the poop. It was of course not so nice. It was very low and the sides sloped together as they went down so that there was hardly any floor; and though it had windows of thick glass, they were not made to open because they were under water. In fact at this very moment, as the ship pitched, they were alternately golden with sunlight and dim green with the sea.

"You and I must lodge here, Edmund," said Caspian. "We'll leave your kinsman the bunk and sling hammocks for ourselves."

"I beseech your Majesty—" said Drinian.

"No, no, shipmate," said Caspian, "we have argued all that out already. You and Rhince" (Rhince was the mate) "are sailing the ship and will have cares and labours many a night when we are singing catches or telling stories, so you and he must have the port cabin above. King Edmund and I can lie very snug here below. But how is the stranger?"

Eustace, very green in the face, scowled and asked whether there was any sign of the storm getting less. But Caspian said, "What storm?" and Drinian burst out laughing.

"Storm, young master!" he roared. "This is as fair weather as a man could ask for."

"Who's that?" said Eustace irritably. "Send him away. His voice goes through my head."

"I've brought you something that will make you feel better, Eustace," said Lucy.

"Oh, go away and leave me alone," growled Eustace. But he took a drop from her flask, and though he said it was beastly stuff (the smell in the cabin when she opened it was delicious), it is certain that his face came the right colour a few moments after he had swallowed it, and he must have felt better because, instead of wailing about the storm and his head, he began demanding to be put ashore and said that at the first port he would "lodge a disposition" against them all with the British Consul. But when Reepicheep asked what a disposition was and how you lodged it (Reepicheep thought it was some new way of arranging a single combat) Eustace could only reply, "Fancy not knowing that." In the end they succeeded in convincing Eustace that they were already sailing as fast as they could towards the nearest land they knew, and that they had no more power of sending him back to Cambridge – which was where Uncle Harold lived – than of sending him to the moon. After that he sulkily agreed to put on the fresh clothes which had been put out for him and come on deck.

Caspian now showed them over the ship, though indeed they had seen most of it already. They went up on the forecastle and saw the look-out man standing on a little shelf inside the gilded dragon's neck and peering through its open mouth. Inside the forecastle was the galley (or ship's kitchen) and quarters for such people as the boatswain, the carpenter, the cook and the master archer. If you think it odd to have the galley in the bows and imagine the smoke from its chimney streaming back over the ship, that is because you are thinking of steamships where there is always a headwind. On a sailing ship the wind is coming from behind, and anything smelly is put as far forward as possible. They were taken up to the fighting top, and at first it was rather alarming to rock to and fro there and see the deck looking small and far away beneath. You realized that if you fell there was no particular reason why you should fall on board rather than in the sea. Then they were taken to the poop, where Rhince was on duty with another man at the great tiller, and behind that the dragon's tail rose up, covered with gilding, and round inside it ran a little bench. The name of the ship was *Dawn Treader*. She was only a little bit of a thing compared with one of our ships, or even with the cogs, dromonds, carracks and galleons which Narnia had owned when Lucy and Edmund had reigned there under Peter as the High King, for nearly all navigation had died out in the reigns of Caspian's ancestors. When his uncle, Miraz the usurper, had sent the seven lords to sea, they had had to buy a Galmian ship and man it with hired Galmian sailors. But now Caspian had begun to teach the Narnians to be sea-faring folk once more, and the *Dawn*

Treader was the finest ship he had built yet. She was so small that, forward of the mast, there was hardly any deck room between the central hatch and the ship's boat on one side and the hen-coop (Lucy fed the hens) on the other. But she was a beauty of her kind, a "lady", as sailors say, her lines perfect, her colours pure, and every spar and rope and pin lovingly made. Eustace of course would be pleased with nothing, and kept on boasting about liners and motor-boats and aeroplanes and submarines ("As if *he* knew anything about them," muttered Edmund), but the other two were delighted with the *Dawn Treader*, and when they returned aft to the cabin and supper, and saw the whole western sky lit up with an immense crimson sunset, and felt the quiver of the ship, and tasted the salt on their lips, and thought of unknown lands on the Eastern rim of the world, Lucy felt that she was almost too happy to speak.

What Eustace thought had best be told in his own words, for when they all got their clothes back, dried, next morning, he at once got out a little black notebook and a pencil and started to keep a diary. He always had this notebook with him and kept a record of his marks in it, for though he didn't care much about any subject for its own sake, he cared a great deal about marks and would even go to people and say, "I got so much. What did you get?" But as he didn't seem likely to get many marks on the *Dawn Treader* he now started a diary. This was the first entry:

August 7

Have now been twenty-four hours on this ghastly boat if it isn't a dream. All the time a frightful storm has been raging (it's a good thing I'm not seasick). Huge waves keep coming in over the front and I have seen the boat nearly go under any number of times. All the others pretend to take no notice of this, either from swank or because Harold says one of the most cowardly things ordinary people do is to shut their eyes to Facts. It's madness to come out into the sea in a rotten little thing like this. Not much bigger than a lifeboat. And, of course, absolutely primitive indoors. No proper saloon, no radio, no bathrooms, no deck-chairs. I was dragged all over it yesterday evening and it would make anyone sick to hear Caspian showing off his funny little toy boat as if it was the *Queen Mary*. I tried to tell him what real ships are like, but he's too dense. E. and L., *of course*, didn't back me up. I suppose a kid like L. doesn't realize the danger and E. is buttering up C. as everyone does here. They call him a king. I said I was a republican but he had to ask me what that meant! He doesn't seem to know anything at all. *Needless to say* I've been put in the worst cabin of the boat, a perfect dungeon, and Lucy has been given a whole room on deck to herself, almost a nice room compared with the rest of this place. C. says that's because she's a girl. I tried to make him see what Alberta says, that all that sort of thing is really lowering girls, but he was too dense. Still, he might see that I shall be ill if I'm kept in that *hole* any longer. E. says we mustn't grumble because C. is sharing it with us himself to make room for L. As if that didn't make it more crowded and far worse. Nearly forgot to say that there is also a kind of Mouse thing that gives everyone the most frightful cheek. The others can put up with it if they like but I shall twist his tail pretty soon if he tries it on me. The food is frightful too.

The trouble between Eustace and Reepicheep arrived even sooner than might have been expected. Before dinner the next day, when the others were sitting round the table waiting (being at sea gives one a magnificent appetite), Eustace came rushing in, wringing his hands and shouting out:

"That little brute has half killed me. I insist on it being kept under control. I could bring an action against you, Caspian. I could order you to have it destroyed."

At the same moment Reepicheep appeared. His sword was drawn and his whiskers looked very fierce but he was as polite as ever.

"I ask your pardons all," he said, "and especially her Majesty's. If I had known that he would take refuge here I would have awaited a more reasonable time for his correction."

"What on earth's up?" asked Edmund.

What had really happened was this. Reepicheep, who never felt that the ship was getting on fast enough, loved to sit on the bulwarks far forwards just beside the dragon's head, gazing out at the eastern horizon and singing softly in his little chirruping voice the song the Dryad had made for him. He never held on to anything, however the ship pitched, and kept his balance with perfect ease; perhaps his long tail, hanging down to the deck inside the bulwarks, made this easier. Everyone on board was familiar with this habit, and the sailors liked it because when one was on look-out duty it gave one somebody to talk to. Why exactly Eustace had slipped and reeled and stumbled all the way forward to the forecastle (he had not yet got his sea-legs) I never heard. Perhaps he hoped he would see land, or perhaps he wanted to hang about the galley and scrounge something. Anyway, as soon as he saw that long tail hanging down – and perhaps it was rather tempting – he thought it would be delightful to catch hold of it, swing Reepicheep round by it once or twice upside-down, then run away and laugh. At first the plan seemed to work beautifully. The Mouse was not much heavier than a very large cat. Eustace had him off the rail in a trice and very silly he looked (thought Eustace) with his little limbs all splayed out and his mouth open. But unfortunately

Reepicheep, who had fought for his life many a time, never lost his head even for a moment. Nor his skill. It is not very easy to draw one's sword when one is swinging round in the air by one's tail, but he did. And the next thing Eustace knew was two agonizing jabs in his hand which made him let go of the tail; and the next thing after that was that the Mouse had picked itself up again as if it were a ball bouncing off the deck, and there it was facing him, and a horrid long, bright, sharp thing like a skewer was waving to and fro within an inch of his stomach. (This doesn't count as below the belt for mice in Narnia because they can hardly be expected to reach higher.)

"Stop it," spluttered Eustace, "go away. Put that thing away. It's not safe. Stop it, I say. I'll tell Caspian. I'll have you muzzled and tied up."

"Why do you not draw your own sword, poltroon?" cheeped the Mouse. "Draw and fight or I'll beat you black and blue with the flat."

"I haven't got one," said Eustace. "I'm a pacifist. I don't believe in fighting."

"Do I understand," said Reepicheep, with-drawing his sword for a moment and speaking very sternly, "that you do not intend to give me satisfaction?"

"I don't know what you mean," said Eustace, nursing his hand. "If you don't know how to take a joke I shan't bother my head about you."

"Then take that," said Reepicheep, "and that — to teach you manners — and the respect due to a knight — and a Mouse — and a Mouse's tail—" and at each word he gave Eustace a blow with the side of his rapier, which was thin, fine, dwarf-tempered steel, and as supple and effective as a birch rod. Eustace (of course) was at a school where they didn't have corporal punishment, so the sensation was quite new to him. That was why, in spite of having no sea-legs, it took him less than a minute to get off that forecastle and cover the whole length of the deck and burst in at the cabin door — still hotly pursued by Reepicheep. Indeed it seemed to Eustace that the rapier as well as the pursuit was hot. It might have been red-hot by the feel.

There was not much difficulty in settling the matter once Eustace realized that everyone took the idea of a duel seriously and heard Caspian offering to lend him a sword, and Drinian and Edmund discussing whether he ought to be handicapped in some way to make up for his being so much bigger than Reepicheep. He apologized sulkily and went off with Lucy to have his hand bathed and bandaged and then went to his bunk. He was careful to lie on his side.

CHAPTER THREE

THE LONE ISLANDS

"Land in sight," shouted the man in the bows.

Lucy, who had been talking to Rhince on the poop, came pattering down the ladder and raced forward. As she went she was joined by Edmund, and they found Caspian, Drinian and Reepicheep already on the forecastle. It was a coldish morning, the sky very pale and the sea very dark blue with little white caps of foam, and there, a little way off on the starboard bow, was the nearest of the Lone Islands, Felimath, like a low green hill in the sea, and behind it, further off, the grey slopes of its sister Doorn.

"Same old Felimath! Same old Doorn," said Lucy, clapping her hands. "Oh – Edmund, how long it is since you and I saw them last!"

"I've never understood why they belong to Narnia," said Caspian. "Did Peter the High King conquer them?"

"Oh, no," said Edmund. "They were Narnian before our time – in the days of the White Witch."

(By the way, I have never yet heard how these remote islands became attached to the crown of Narnia; if I ever do, and if the story is at all interesting, I may put it in some other book.)

"Are we to put in here, Sire?" asked Drinian.

"I shouldn't think it would be much good landing on Felimath," said Edmund. "It was almost uninhabited in our days and it looks as if it is the same still. The people lived mostly on Doorn and a little on Avra – that's the third one; you can't see it yet. They only kept sheep on Felimath."

"Then we'll have to double that cape, I suppose," said Drinian, "and land on Doorn. That'll mean rowing."

440

"I'm sorry we're not landing on Felimath," said Lucy. "I'd like to walk there again. It was so lonely — a nice kind of loneliness, and all grass and clover and soft sea air."

"I'd love to stretch my legs now too," said Caspian. "I tell you what. Why shouldn't we go ashore in the boat and send it back, and then we could walk across Felimath and let the *Dawn Treader* pick us up on the other side?"

If Caspian had been as experienced then as he became later on in this voyage he would not have made this suggestion; but at the moment it seemed an excellent one. "Oh, do let's," said Lucy.

"You'll come, will you?" said Caspian to Eustace, who had come on deck with his hand bandaged.

"Anything to get off this blasted boat," said Eustace.

"Blasted?" said Drinian. "How do you mean?"

"In a civilized country like where I come from," said Eustace, "the ships are so big that when you're inside you wouldn't know you were at sea at all."

"In that case you might just as well stay ashore," said Caspian. "Will you tell them to lower the boat, Drinian?"

The King, the Mouse, the two Pevensies, and Eustace all got into the boat and were pulled to the beach of Felimath. When the boat had left them and was being rowed back they all turned and looked round. They were surprised at how small the *Dawn Treader* looked.

Lucy was of course barefoot, having kicked off her shoes while swimming, but that is no hardship if one is going to walk on downy turf. It was delightful to be ashore again and to smell the earth and grass, even if at first the ground seemed to be pitching up and down like a ship, as it usually does for a while if one has been at sea. It was much warmer here than it had been on board and Lucy found the sand pleasant to her feet as they crossed it. There was a lark singing.

They struck inland and up a fairly steep, though low, hill. At the top of course they looked back, and there was the *Dawn Treader* shining like a great bright insect and crawling slowly northwestward with her oars. Then they went over the ridge and could see her no longer.

Doorn now lay before them, divided from Felimath by a channel about a mile wide; behind it and to the left lay Avra. The little white town of Narrowhaven on Doorn was easily seen.

"Hullo! What's this?" said Edmund suddenly.

In the green valley to which they were descending, six or seven rough-looking men, all armed, were sitting by a tree.

"Don't tell them who we are," said Caspian.

"And pray, your Majesty, why not?" said Reepicheep, who had consented to ride on Lucy's shoulder.

"It just occurred to me," replied Caspian, "that no one here can have heard from Narnia for a long time. It's just possible they may not still acknowledge our over-lordship. In which case it might not be quite safe to be known as the King."

"We have our swords, Sire," said Reepicheep.

"Yes, Reep, I know we have," said Caspian. "But if it is a question of re-conquering the three islands, I'd prefer to come back with a rather larger army."

By this time they were quite close to the strangers, one of whom – a big black-haired fellow – shouted out, "A good morning to you."

"And a good morning to you," said Caspian. "Is there still a Governor of the Lone Islands?"

"To be sure there is," said the man, "Governor Gumpas. His Sufficiency is at Narrowhaven. But you'll stay and drink with us."

Caspian thanked him, though neither he nor the others much liked the look of their new acquaintance, and all of them sat down. But hardly had they raised their cups to their lips when the black-haired man nodded to his companions and, as quick as lightning, all the five visitors found themselves wrapped in strong arms. There was a moment's struggle but all the advantages were on one side, and soon everyone was disarmed and had their hands tied behind their backs – except Reepicheep, writhing in his captor's grip and biting furiously.

"Careful with that beast, Tacks," said the Leader. "Don't damage him. He'll fetch the best price of the lot, I shouldn't wonder."

"Coward! Poltroon!" squeaked Reepicheep. "Give me my sword and free my paws if you dare."

"Whew!" whistled the slave merchant (for that is what he was). "It can talk! Well, I never did. Blowed if I take less than two hundred crescents for him." The Calormen crescent, which is the chief coin in those parts, is worth about a third of a pound.

"So that's what you are," said Caspian. "A kidnapper and slaver. I hope you're proud of it."

"Now, now, now, now," said the slaver. "Don't you start any jaw. The easier you take it, the pleasanter all round, see? I don't do this for fun. I've got my living to make same as anyone else."

"Where will you take us?" asked Lucy, getting the words out with some difficulty.

"Over to Narrowhaven," said the slaver. "For market day tomorrow."

"Is there a British Consul there?" asked Eustace.

"Is there a which?" said the man.

But long before Eustace was tired of trying to explain, the slaver simply said, "Well, I've had enough of this jabber. The Mouse is a fair treat but this one would talk the hind leg off a donkey. Off we go, mates."

Then the four human prisoners were roped together, not cruelly but securely, and made to march down to the shore. Reepicheep was carried. He had stopped biting on a threat of having his mouth tied up, but he had a great deal to say, and Lucy really wondered how any man could bear to have the things said to him which were said to the slave dealer by the Mouse. But the slave dealer, far from objecting, only said, "Go on" whenever Reepicheep paused for breath, occasionally adding, "It's as good as a play," or, "Blimey, you can't help almost thinking it knows what it's saying!" or, "Was it one of you what trained it?" This so infuriated Reepicheep that in the end the number of things he thought of saying all at once nearly suffocated him and he became silent.

When they got down to the shore that looked towards Doorn they found a little village and a longboat on the beach and, lying a little further out, a dirty, bedraggled-looking ship.

"Now, youngsters," said the slave dealer, "let's have no fuss and then you'll have nothing to cry about. All aboard."

At that moment a fine-looking bearded man came out of one of the houses (an inn, I think) and said:

"Well, Pug. More of your usual wares?"

The slaver, whose name seemed to be Pug, bowed very low, and said in a wheedling kind of voice, "Yes, if it please your Lordship."

"How much do you want for that boy?" asked the other, pointing to Caspian.

"Ah," said Pug, "I knew your Lordship would pick on the best. No deceiving your Lordship with anything second-rate. That boy, now, I've taken a fancy to him myself. Got kind of fond of him, I have. I'm that tender-hearted I didn't ever ought to have taken up this job. Still, to a customer like your Lordship—"

"Tell me your price, carrion," said the Lord sternly. "Do you think I want to listen to the rigmarole of your filthy trade?"

"Three hundred crescents, my Lord, to your honourable Lordship, but to anyone else—"

"I'll give you a hundred and fifty."

"Oh, please, please," broke in Lucy. "Don't separate us, whatever you do. You don't know—" But then she stopped for she saw that Caspian didn't even now want to be known.

"A hundred and fifty, then," said the Lord. "As for you, little maiden, I am sorry I cannot buy you all. Unrope my boy, Pug. And look – treat these others well while they are in your hands or it'll be the worse for you."

"Well!" said Pug. "Now who ever heard of a gentleman in my way of business who treated his stock better than what I do? Well? Why, I treat 'em like my own children."

"That's likely enough to be true," said the other grimly.

The dreadful moment had now come. Caspian was untied and his new master said, "This way, lad," and Lucy burst into tears and Edmund looked very blank. But Caspian looked over his shoulder and said, "Cheer up. I'm sure it will come all right in the end. So long."

"Now, missie," said Pug. "Don't you start taking on and spoiling your looks for the market tomorrow. You be a good girl and then you won't have nothing to cry *about*, see?"

Then they were rowed out to the slave-ship and taken below into a long, rather dark place, none too clean, where they found many other unfortunate prisoners; for Pug was of course a pirate and had just returned from cruising among the islands and capturing what he could. The children didn't meet anyone whom they knew; the prisoners were mostly Galmians and Terebinthians. And there they sat in the straw and wondered what was happening to Caspian, and tried to stop Eustace talking as if everyone except himself was to blame.

Meanwhile Caspian was having a much more interesting time. The man who had bought him led him down a little lane between two of the village houses and so out into an open place behind the village. Then he turned and faced him.

"You needn't be afraid of me, boy," he said. "I'll treat you well. I bought you for your face. You reminded me of someone."

"May I ask of whom, my Lord?" said Caspian.

"You remind me of my master, King Caspian of Narnia."

Then Caspian decided to risk everything on one stroke.

"My Lord," he said, "I *am* your master. I am Caspian, King of Narnia."

"You make very free," said the other. "How shall I know this is true?"

"Firstly by my face," said Caspian. "Secondly because I know within six guesses who you are. You are one of those seven lords of Narnia whom my Uncle Miraz sent to sea and whom I have come out to look for – Argoz, Bern, Octesian, Restimar, Mavramorn, or – or – I have forgotten the others. And finally, if your Lordship will give me a sword I will prove on any man's body in clean battle that I am Caspian, the son of Caspian, lawful King of Narnia, Lord of Cair Paravel, and Emperor of the Lone Islands."

"By heaven," exclaimed the man, "it is his father's very voice and trick of speech. My liege – your Majesty—" And there in the field he knelt and kissed the King's hand.

"The moneys your Lordship disbursed for our person will be made good from our own treasury," said Caspian.

"They're not in Pug's purse yet, Sire," said the Lord Bern, for he it was.

"And never will be, I trust. I have moved his Sufficiency the Governor a hundred times to crush this vile traffic in man's flesh."

"My Lord Bern," said Caspian, "we must talk of the state of these islands. But first, what is your Lordship's own story?"

"Short enough, Sire," said Bern. "I came thus far with my six fellows, loved a girl of the islands, and felt I had had enough of the sea. And there was no purpose in returning to Narnia while your Majesty's uncle held the reins. So I married and have lived here ever since."

"And what is this governor, this Gumpas, like? Does he still acknowledge the King of Narnia for his lord?"

"In words, yes. All is done in the King's name. But he would not be best pleased to find a real, live King of Narnia coming in upon him. And if your Majesty came before him alone and unarmed – well, he would not deny his allegiance, but he would pretend to disbelieve you. Your Grace's life would be in danger. What following has your Majesty in these waters?"

"There is my ship just rounding the point," said Caspian. "We are about thirty swords if it came to fighting. Shall we not have my ship in and fall upon Pug and free my friends whom he holds captive?"

"Not by my counsel," said Bern. "As soon as there was a fight, two or three ships would put out from Narrowhaven to rescue Pug. Your Majesty must work by a show of more power than you really have, and by the terror of the King's name. It must not come to plain battle. Gumpas is a chicken-hearted man and can be overawed."

After a little more conversation Caspian and Bern walked down to the coast a little west of the village, and there Caspian winded his horn. (This was not the great magic horn of Narnia, Queen Susan's Horn: he had left that at home for his regent Trumpkin to use if any great need fell upon the land in the King's absence.) Drinian, who was on the look-out for a signal, recognized the royal horn at once and the *Dawn Treader* began standing in to shore. Then the boat put off again and in a few moments Caspian and the Lord Bern were on deck explaining the situation to Drinian. He, just like Caspian, wanted to lay the *Dawn Treader* alongside the slave-ship at once and board her, but Bern made the same objection.

"Steer straight down this channel, Captain," said Bern, "and then round to Avra where my own estates are. But first run up the King's banner, hang out all the shields, and send as many men to the fighting top as you can. And about five bowshots hence, when you get open sea on your port bow, run up a few signals."

"Signals? To whom?" said Drinian.

"Why, to all the other ships we haven't got but which it might be well that Gumpas thinks we have."

"Oh, I see," said Drinian rubbing his hands. "And they'll read our signals.

What shall I say? *Whole fleet round the South of Avra and assemble at——?"*

"Bernstead," said the Lord Bern. "That'll do excellently. Their whole journey — if there *were* any ships — would be out of sight from Narrowhaven."

Caspian was sorry for the others languishing in the hold of Pug's slave-ship, but he could not help finding the rest of that day enjoyable. Late in the afternoon (for they had to do all by oar), having turned to starboard round the northeast end of Doorn and port again round the point of Avra, they entered into a good harbour on Avra's southern shore where Bern's pleasant lands sloped down to the water's edge. Bern's people, many of whom they saw working in the fields, were all freemen and it was a happy and prosperous fief. Here they all went ashore and were royally feasted in a low, pillared house overlooking the bay. Bern and his gracious wife and merry daughters made them good cheer. But after dark Bern sent a messenger over by boat to Doorn to order some preparations (he did not say exactly what) for the following day.

CHAPTER FOUR

WHAT CASPIAN DID THERE

Next morning the Lord Bern called his guests early, and after breakfast he asked Caspian to order every man he had into full armour. "And above all," he added, "let everything be as trim and scoured as if it were the morning of the first battle in a great war between noble kings with all the world looking on." This was done; and then in three boatloads Caspian and his people, and Bern with a few of his, put out for Narrowhaven. The king's flag flew in the stern of his boat and his trumpeter was with him.

When they reached the jetty at Narrowhaven, Caspian found a considerable crowd assembled to meet them. "This is what I sent word about last night," said Bern. "They are all friends of mine and honest people." And as soon as Caspian stepped ashore the crowd broke out into hurrays and shouts of, "Narnia! Narnia! Long live the king." At the same moment — and this was also due to Bern's messengers — bells began ringing from many parts of the town. Then Caspian caused his banner to be advanced and his trumpet to be blown, and every man drew his sword and set his face into a joyful sternness, and they marched up the street so that the street shook, and their armour shone (for it was a sunny morning) so that one could hardly look at it steadily.

At first, the only people who cheered were those who had been warned by Bern's messenger and knew what was happening and wanted it to happen. But then all the children joined in because they liked a procession and had seen very few. And then all the schoolboys joined in because they also liked processions and felt that the more noise and disturbance there was, the less likely they would be to have any school that morning. And then all the old women put their heads out of doors and windows and began chattering and cheering because it was a king, and what is a governor compared with that? And all the young women joined in for the same reason and also because Caspian and Drinian and the rest were so handsome. And then all the young men came to see what the young women were looking at, so that by the time Caspian reached the castle gates, nearly the whole town was shouting; and where Gumpas sat in the castle, muddling and messing about with accounts and forms and rules and regulations, he heard the noise.

At the castle gate Caspian's trumpeter blew a blast and cried, "Open for the king of Narnia, come to visit his trusty and well-beloved servant the governor of the Lone Islands." In those days everything in the islands was done in a slovenly, slouching manner. Only the little postern opened, and out came a tousled fellow with a dirty old hat on his head instead of a helmet, and a rusty old pike in his hand. He blinked at the flashing figures before him. "Carn — seez — fishansy," he mumbled (which was his way of saying, "You can't see his Sufficiency"). "No interviews without 'pointments 'cept 'tween nine 'n' ten p.m. second Saturday every month."

"Uncover before Narnia, you dog," thundered the Lord Bern, and dealt him a rap with his gauntleted hand which sent his hat flying from his head.

"'Ere? Wot's it all about?" began the door-keeper, but no one took any notice of him. Two of Caspian's men stepped through the postern and after some struggling with bars and bolts (for everything was rusty), flung both wings of the gate wide open. Then the King and his followers strode into the courtyard. Here a number of the governor's guards were lounging about and several more (they were mostly wiping their mouths) came tumbling out of various doorways. Though their armour was in a disgraceful condition, these were fellows who might have fought if they had been led or had known what was happening; so this was the dangerous moment. Caspian gave them no time to think.

"Where is the captain?" he asked.

"I am, more or less, if you know what I mean," said a languid and rather dandified young person without any armour at all.

"It is our wish," said Caspian, "that our royal visitation to our realm of the Lone Islands should, if possible, be an occasion of joy and not of terror to our loyal subjects. If it were not for that, I should have something to say about the state of your men's armour and weapons. As it is, you are pardoned. Command a cask of wine to be opened that your men may drink our health. But at noon tomorrow I wish to see them here in this courtyard looking like men-at-arms and not like vagabonds. See to it on pain of our extreme displeasure."

The captain gaped but Bern immediately cried, "Three cheers for the king," and the soldiers, who had understood about the cask of wine even if they understood nothing else, joined in. Caspian then ordered most of his own men to remain in the courtyard. He, with Bern and Drinian and four others, went into the hall.

Behind a table at the far end with various secretaries about him sat his Sufficiency, the governor of the Lone Islands. Gumpas was a bilious-looking man with hair that had once been red and was now mostly grey. He glanced up as the strangers entered and then looked down at his papers saying automatically, "No interviews without appointments except between nine and ten p.m. on second Saturdays."

Caspian nodded to Bern and then stood aside. Bern and Drinian took a step forward and each seized one end of the table. They lifted it, and flung it on one side of the hall where it rolled over, scattering a cascade of letters, dossiers, ink-pots, pens, sealing-wax and documents. Then, not roughly but as firmly as if their hands were pincers of steel, they plucked Gumpas out of his chair and deposited him, facing it, about four feet away. Caspian at once sat down in the chair and laid his naked sword across his knees.

"My Lord," said he, fixing his eyes on Gumpas, "you have not given us quite the welcome we expected. I am the King of Narnia."

"Nothing about it in the correspondence," said the governor. "Nothing in the minutes. We have not been notified of any such thing. All irregular. Happy to consider any applications—"

"And we are come to enquire into your Sufficiency's conduct of your office," continued Caspian. "There are two points especially on which I require an explanation. Firstly I find no record that the tribute due from these Islands to the crown of Narnia has been received for about a hundred and fifty years."

"That would be a question to raise at the Council next month," said Gumpas. "If anyone moves that a commission of enquiry be set up to report on the financial history of the islands at the first meeting next year, why then…"

"I also find it very clearly written in our laws," Caspian went on, "that if the tribute is not delivered, the whole debt has to be paid by the governor of the Lone Islands out of his private purse."

At this Gumpas began to pay real attention. "Oh, that's quite out of the question," he said. "It is an economic impossibility – er – your Majesty must be joking."

Inside, he was wondering if there were any way of getting rid of these unwelcome visitors. Had he known that Caspian had only one ship and one ship's company with him, he would have spoken soft words for the moment, and hoped to have them all surrounded and killed during the night. But he had seen a ship of war sail down the straits yesterday and seen it signalling, as he supposed, to its consorts. He had not then known it was the King's ship for there was not wind enough to spread the flag out and make the golden lion visible, so he had waited further developments. Now he imagined that Caspian had a whole fleet at Bernstead. It would never have occurred to Gumpas that anyone would walk into Narrowhaven to take the islands with fewer than fifty men; it was certainly not at all the kind of thing he could imagine doing himself.

"Secondly," said Caspian, "I want to know why you have permitted this abominable and unnatural traffic in slaves to grow up here, contrary to the ancient custom and usage of our dominions."

"Necessary, unavoidable," said his Sufficiency. "An essential part of the economic development of the islands, I assure you. Our present burst of prosperity depends on it."

"What need have you of slaves?"

"For export, your Majesty. Sell 'em to Calormen mostly; and we have other markets. We are a great centre of the trade."

"In other words," said Caspian, "you don't need them. Tell me what purpose they serve except to put money into the pockets of such as Pug?"

"Your Majesty's tender years," said Gumpas, with what was meant to be a fatherly smile, "hardly make it possible that you should understand the economic problem involved. I have statistics, I have graphs, I have——"

"Tender as my years may be," said Caspian, "I believe I understand the slave trade from within quite as well as your Sufficiency. And I do not see that it brings into the islands meat or bread or beer or wine or timber or cabbages or books or instruments of music or horses or armour or anything else worth having. But whether it does or not, it must be stopped."

"But that would be putting the clock back," gasped the governor. "Have you no idea of progress, of development?"

"I have seen them both in an egg," said Caspian. "We call it 'Going Bad' in Narnia. This trade must stop."

"I can take no responsibility for any such measure," said Gumpas.

"Very well, then," answered Caspian, "we relieve you of your office. My Lord Bern, come here." And before Gumpas quite realized what was happening, Bern was kneeling with his hands between the King's hands and taking the oath to govern the Lone Islands in accordance with the old customs, rights, usages and laws of Narnia. And Caspian said, "I think we have had enough of governors," and made Bern a Duke, the Duke of the Lone Islands.

"As for you, my Lord," he said to Gumpas, "I forgive you your debt for the tribute. But before noon tomorrow you and yours must be out of the castle, which is now the Duke's residence."

"Look here, this is all very well," said one of Gumpas's secretaries, "but suppose all you gentlemen stop playacting and we do a little business. The question before us really is—"

"The question is," said the Duke, "whether you and the rest of the rabble will leave without a flogging or with one. You may choose which you prefer."

When all this had been pleasantly settled, Caspian ordered horses, of which there were a few in the castle, though very ill-groomed and he, with Bern and Drinian and a few others, rode out into the town and made for the slave market. It was a long low building near the harbour and the scene which they found going on inside was very much like any other auction; that is to say, there was a great crowd and Pug, on a platform, was roaring out in a raucous voice:

"Now, gentlemen, lot twenty-three. Fine Terebinthian agricultural labourer, suitable for the mines or the galleys. Under twenty-five years of age. Not a bad tooth in his head. Good, brawny fellow. Take off his shirt, Tacks, and let the gentlemen see. There's muscle for you! Look at the chest on him. Ten crescents from the gentleman in the corner. You must be joking, Sir. Fifteen! Eighteen! Eighteen is bid for lot twenty-three. Any advance on eighteen? Twenty-one. Thank you, Sir. Twenty-one is bid—"

But Pug stopped and gaped when he saw the mail-clad figures who had clanked up to the platform.

"On your knees, every man of you, to the King of Narnia," said the Duke. Everyone heard the horses jingling and stamping outside and many had heard some rumour of the landing and the events at the castle. Most obeyed. Those who did not were pulled down by their neighbours. Some cheered.

"Your life is forfeit, Pug, for laying hands on our royal person yesterday," said Caspian. "But your ignorance is pardoned. The slave trade was forbidden in all our dominions quarter of an hour ago. I declare every slave in this market free."

He held up his hand to check the cheering of the slaves and went on, "Where are my friends?"

"That dear little gel and the nice young gentleman?" said Pug with an ingratiating smile. "Why, they were snapped up at once—"

"We're here, we're here, Caspian," cried Lucy and Edmund together and, "At your service, Sire," piped Reepicheep from another corner. They had all been sold but the men who had bought them were staying to bid for other slaves and so they had not yet been taken away. The crowd parted to let the three of them out and there was great hand-clasping and greeting between them and Caspian. Two merchants of Calormen at once approached. The Calormen have dark faces and long beards. They wear flowing robes and orange-coloured turbans, and they are a wise, wealthy, courteous, cruel and ancient people. They bowed most politely to Caspian and paid him long compliments, all about the fountains of prosperity irrigating the gardens of prudence and virtue – and things like that – but of course what they wanted was the money they had paid.

"That is only fair, Sirs," said Caspian. "Every man who has bought a slave today must have his money back. Pug, bring out your takings to the last minim." (A minim is the fortieth part of a crescent.)

"Does your good Majesty mean to beggar me?" whined Pug.

"You have lived on broken hearts all your life," said Caspian, "and if you *are* beggared, it is better to be a beggar than a slave. But where is my other friend?"

"Oh, *him*?" said Pug. "Oh, take *him* and welcome. Glad to have him off my hands. I've never seen such a drug in the market in all my born days. Priced him at five crescents in the end and even so nobody'd have him. Threw him in free with other lots and still no one would have him. Wouldn't touch him. Wouldn't look at him. Tacks, bring out Sulky."

Thus Eustace was produced, and sulky he certainly looked; for though no one would want to be sold as a slave, it is perhaps even more galling to be a sort of utility slave whom no one will buy. He walked up to Caspian and said, "I see. As usual. Been enjoying yourself somewhere while the rest of us were prisoners. I suppose you haven't even found out about the British Consul. Of course not."

That night they had a great feast in the castle of Narrowhaven and then, "Tomorrow for the beginning of our real adventures!" said Reepicheep when he had made his bows to everyone and went to bed. But it could not really be tomorrow or anything like it. For now they were preparing to leave all known lands and seas behind them, and the fullest preparations had to be made. The *Dawn Treader* was emptied and drawn on land by eight horses over rollers and every bit of her was gone over by the most skilled shipwrights. Then she was launched again and victualled and watered as full as she could hold – that is to say, for twenty-eight days. Even this, as Edmund noticed with disappointment, only gave them a fortnight's eastward sailing before they had to abandon their quest.

While all this was being done Caspian missed no chance of questioning all the oldest sea captains whom he could find in Narrowhaven to learn if they had any knowledge or even any rumours of land further to the east. He poured out many a flagon of the castle ale to weather-beaten men with short grey beards and clear blue eyes, and many a tall yarn he heard in return. But those who seemed the most truthful could tell of no lands beyond the Lone Islands, and many thought that if you sailed too far east you would come into the surges of a sea without lands that swirled perpetually round the rim of the world — "And that, I reckon, is where your Majesty's friends went to the bottom." The rest had only wild stories of islands inhabited by headless men, floating islands, waterspouts, and a fire that burned along the water. Only one, to Reepicheep's delight, said, "And beyond that, Aslan country. But that's beyond the end of the world and you can't get there." But when they questioned him he could only say that he'd heard it from his father.

Bern could only tell them that he had seen his six companions sail away eastward and that nothing had ever been heard of them again. He said this when he and Caspian were standing on the highest point of Avra looking down on the Eastern Ocean. "I've often been up here of a morning," said the Duke, "and seen the sun come up out of the sea, and sometimes it looked as if it were only a couple of miles away. And I've wondered about my friends and wondered what there really is behind that horizon. Nothing, most likely, yet I am always half ashamed that I stayed behind. But I wish your Majesty wouldn't go. We may need your help here. This closing the slave market might make a new world; war with Calormen is what I foresee. My liege, think again."

"I have an oath, my lord Duke," said Caspian. "And anyway, what *could* I say to Reepicheep?"

Chapter Five

The Storm and What Came of It

It was nearly three weeks after their landing that the *Dawn Treader* was towed out of Narrowhaven harbour. Very solemn farewells had been spoken and a great crowd had assembled to see her departure. There had been cheers, and tears too, when Caspian made his last speech to the Lone Islanders and parted from the Duke and his family, but as the ship, her purple sail still flapping idly, drew further from the shore, and the sound of Caspian's trumpet from the poop came fainter across the water, everyone became silent. Then she came into the wind. The sail swelled out, the tug cast off and began rowing back, the first real wave ran up under the *Dawn Treader*'s prow, and she was a live ship again. The men off duty went below, Drinian took the first watch on the poop, and she turned her head eastward round the south of Avra.

The next few days were delightful. Lucy thought she was the most fortunate girl in the world as she woke each morning to see the reflections of the sunlit water dancing on the ceiling of her cabin, and looked round on all the nice new things she had got in the Lone Islands – seaboots and buskins and cloaks and jerkins and scarves. And then she would go on deck and take a look from the forecastle at a sea which was a brighter blue each morning and drink in an air that was a little warmer day by day. After that came breakfast and such an appetite as one only has at sea.

She spent a good deal of time sitting on the little bench in the stern playing chess with Reepicheep. It was amusing to see him lifting the pieces, which were far too big for him, with both paws and standing on tiptoe if he made a move near the centre of the board. He was a good player and when he remembered what he was doing he usually won. But every now and then Lucy won because the Mouse did something quite ridiculous like sending a knight into the danger of a queen and castle combined. This happened because he had momentarily forgotten it was a game of chess and was thinking of a real battle and making the knight do what he would certainly have done in its place. For his mind was full of forlorn hopes, death-or-glory charges, and last stands.

But this pleasant time did not last. There came an evening when Lucy, gazing idly astern at the long furrow or wake they were leaving behind them, saw a great rack of clouds building itself up in the west with amazing speed. Then a gap was torn in it and a yellow sunset poured through the gap. All the waves behind them seemed to take on unusual shapes and the sea was a drab or yellowish colour like dirty canvas. The air grew cold. The ship seemed to move uneasily as if she felt danger behind her. The sail would be flat and limp one minute and wildly full the next. While she was noting these things and wondering at a sinister change which had come over the very noise of the wind, Drinian cried, "All hands on deck." In a moment everyone became frantically busy. The hatches were battened down, the galley fire was put out, men went aloft to reef the sail. Before they had finished, the storm struck them. It seemed to Lucy that a great valley in the sea opened just before their bows, and they rushed down into it, deeper down than she would have believed possible. A great grey hill of water, far higher than the mast, rushed to meet them; it looked like certain death but they were tossed to the top of it. Then the ship seemed to spin round. A cataract of water poured over the deck; the poop and forecastle were like two islands with a fierce sea between them. Up aloft the sailors were lying out along the yard desperately trying to get control of the sail. A broken rope stood out sideways in the wind as straight and stiff as if it were a poker.

"Get below, Ma'am," bawled Drinian. And Lucy, knowing that landsmen – and landswomen – are a nuisance to the crew, began to obey. It was not easy. The *Dawn Treader* was listing terribly to starboard and the deck sloped like the roof of a house. She had to clamber round to the top of the ladder, holding on to the rail, and then stand by while two men climbed up it, and then get down it as best she could. It was as well she was already holding on tight for at the foot of the ladder another wave roared across the deck, up to her shoulders. She was already almost wet through with spray and rain but this was colder. Then she made a dash for the cabin door and got in and shut out for a moment the appalling sight of the speed with which they were rushing into the dark, but not of course the horrible confusion of creakings, groanings, snappings, clatterings, roarings and boomings which only sounded more alarming below than they had done on the poop.

And all the next day and all the next it went on. It went on till one could hardly even remember a time before it had begun. And there always had to be three men at the tiller and it was as much as three could do to keep any kind of a course. And there always had to be men at the pump. And there was hardly any rest for anyone, and nothing could be cooked and nothing could be dried, and one man was lost overboard, and they never saw the sun.

When it was over, Eustace made the following entry in his diary:

September 3

The first day for ages when I have been able to write. We had been driven before a hurricane for thirteen days and nights. I know that because I kept a careful count, though the others all say it was only twelve. *Pleasant* to be embarked on a dangerous voyage with people who can't even count right! I have had a ghastly time, up and down enormous waves hour after hour, usually wet to the skin, and not even an *attempt* at giving us proper meals. Needless to say there's no wireless or even a rocket, so no chance of signalling anyone for help. It all proves what I keep on telling them, the madness of setting out in a rotten little tub like this. It would be bad enough even if one was with decent people instead of fiends in human form. Caspian and Edmund are simply brutal to me. The night we lost our mast (there's only a stump left now), though I was *not at all* well, they forced me to come on deck and work like a slave. Lucy shoved her oar in by saying that Reepicheep was longing to go only he was too small. I wonder she doesn't see that everything that little beast does is all for the sake of *showing off*. Even at her age she ought to have that amount of sense. Today the beastly boat is level at last and the sun's out and we have all been jawing about what to do. We have food enough, pretty beastly stuff most of it, to last for sixteen days. (The poultry were all washed overboard. Even if they hadn't been, the storm would have stopped them laying.) The real trouble is water. Two casks seem to have got a leak knocked in them and are empty. (Narnian efficiency again.) On short rations, half a pint a day each, we've got enough for twelve days. (There's still lots of rum and wine but even *they* realize that would only make them thirstier.)

"If we could, of course, the sensible thing would be to turn west at once and make for the Lone Islands. But it took us eighteen days to get where we are, running like mad with a gale behind us. Even if we got an east wind it might take us far longer to get back. And at present there's no sign of an east wind – in fact there's no wind at all. As for rowing back, it would take far too long and Caspian says the men couldn't row on half a pint of water a day. I'm pretty sure this is wrong. I tried to explain that perspiration really cools people down, so the men would need less water if they were working. He didn't take any notice of this, which is always his way when he can't think of an answer. The others all voted for going *on* in the hope of finding land. I felt it my duty to point out that we didn't know there *was* any land ahead and tried to get them to see the dangers of *wishful thinking*. Instead of producing a better plan they had the cheek to ask me what I proposed. So I just explained coolly and quietly that I had been kidnapped and brought away on this *idiotic* voyage without my consent, and it was hardly *my* business to get *them* out of their scrape.

September 4

Still becalmed. Very short rations for dinner and I got less than anyone. Caspian is very clever at helping and thinks I don't see! Lucy for some reason tried to make up to me by offering me some of hers but that *interfering prig* Edmund wouldn't let her. Pretty hot sun. Terribly thirsty all evening.

September 5

Still becalmed and very hot. Feeling rotten all day and sure I've got a temperature. Of course they haven't the sense to keep a thermometer on board.

September 6

A horrible day. Woke up in the night *knowing* I was feverish and *must* have a drink of water. Any doctor would have said so. Heaven knows I'm the last person to try to get any unfair advantage but I never *dreamed* that this water-rationing would be meant to apply to a sick man. In fact I would have woken the others up and asked for some only I thought it would be selfish to wake them. So I got up and took my cup and tiptoed out of the Black Hole we sleep in, taking great care not to disturb Caspian and Edmund, for they've been sleeping badly since the heat and the short water began. I always try to consider others whether they are nice to me or not. I got out all right into the big room, if you can call it a room, where the rowing benches and the luggage are. The thing of water is at this end. All was going beautifully, but before I'd drawn a cupful who should catch me but that *little spy*, Reep. I tried to explain that I was going on deck for a breath of air (the business about the water had nothing to do with him) and he asked me why I had a cup. He made such a noise that the whole ship was roused. They treated me scandalously. I asked, as I think anyone would have, why Reepicheep was sneaking about the water cask in the middle of the night. He said that as he was too small to be any use on deck, he did sentry over the water every night so that one more man could go to sleep. Now comes their rotten unfairness: they all believed *him*. Can you beat it?

"I had to apologize or the dangerous little brute would have been at me with his sword. And then Caspian showed up in his true colours as a brutal tyrant and said out loud for everyone to hear that anyone found 'stealing' water in future would 'get two dozen'. I didn't know what this meant till Edmund explained to me. It comes in the sort of books those Pevensie kids read.

"After this cowardly threat Caspian changed his tune and started being *patronizing*. Said he was sorry for me and that everyone felt just as feverish as I did and we must all make the best of it, etc., etc. Odious, stuck-up prig. Stayed in bed all day today.

September 7

A little wind today but still from the west. Made a few miles eastward with part of the sail, set on what Drinian calls the jury-mast – that means the bowsprit set upright and tied (they call it 'lashed') to the stump of the real mast. Still terribly thirsty.

September 8

Still sailing east. I stay in my bunk all day now and see no one except Lucy till the two *fiends* come to bed. Lucy gives me a little of her water ration. She says girls don't get as thirsty as boys. I had often thought this but it ought to be more generally known at sea.

September 9

Land in sight; a very high mountain a long way off to the south-east.

September 10

The mountain is bigger and clearer but still a long way off. Gulls again today for the first time since I don't know how long.

September 11

Caught some fish and had them for dinner. Dropped anchor at about 7 p.m. in three fathoms of water in a bay of this mountainous island. That idiot Caspian wouldn't let us go ashore because it was getting dark and he was afraid of savages and wild beasts. Extra water ration tonight.

What awaited them on this island was going to concern Eustace more than anyone else, but it cannot be told in his words because after September 11 he forgot about keeping his diary for a long time.

When morning came, with a low, grey sky but very hot, the adventurers found they were in a bay encircled by such cliffs and crags that it was like a Norwegian fjord. In front of them, at the head of the bay, there was some level land heavily overgrown with trees that appeared to be cedars, through which a rapid stream came out. Beyond that was a steep ascent ending in a jagged ridge and behind that a vague darkness of mountains which ran into dull-coloured clouds so that you could not see their tops. The nearer cliffs, at each side of the bay, were streaked here and there with lines of white which everyone knew to be waterfalls, though at that distance they did not show any movement or make any noise. Indeed the whole place was very silent and the water of the bay as smooth as glass. It reflected every detail of the cliffs. The scene would have been pretty in a picture but was rather oppressive in real life. It was not a country that welcomed visitors.

The whole ship's company went ashore in two boatloads and everyone drank and washed deliciously in the river and had a meal and a rest before Caspian sent four men back to keep the ship, and the day's work began. There was everything to be done. The casks must be brought ashore and the faulty ones mended if possible and all refilled; a tree – a pine if they could get it – must be felled and made into a new mast; sails must be repaired; a hunting party organized to shoot any game the land might yield; clothes to be washed and mended; and countless small breakages on board to be set right. For the *Dawn Treader* herself – and this was more obvious now that they saw her at a distance – could hardly be recognized as the same gallant ship which had left Narrowhaven. She looked a crippled, discoloured hulk which anyone might have taken for a wreck. And her officers and crew were no better – lean, pale, red-eyed from lack of sleep, and dressed in rags.

As Eustace lay under a tree and heard all these plans being discussed, his heart sank. Was there going to be no rest? It looked as if their first day on the longed-for land was going to be quite as hard work as a day at sea. Then a delightful idea occurred to him. Nobody was looking – they were all chattering about their ship as if they actually liked the beastly thing. Why shouldn't he simply slip away? He would take a stroll inland, find a cool, airy place up in the mountains, have a good long sleep, and not rejoin the others till the day's work was over. He felt it would do him good. But he would take great care to keep the bay and the ship in sight so as to be sure of his way back. He wouldn't like to be left behind in this country.

He at once put his plan into action. He rose quietly from his place and walked away among the trees, taking care to go slowly and in an aimless manner so that anyone who saw him would think he was merely stretching his legs. He was surprised to find how quickly the noise of conversation died away behind him and how very silent and warm and dark green the wood became. Soon he felt he could venture on a quicker and more determined stride.

This soon brought him out of the wood. The ground began sloping steeply up in front of him. The grass was dry and slippery but manageable if he used his hands as well as his feet, and though he panted and mopped his forehead a good deal, he plugged away steadily. This showed, by the way, that his new life, little as he suspected it, had already done him some good; the old Eustace, Harold and Alberta's Eustace, would have given up the climb after about ten minutes.

Slowly, and with several rests, he reached the ridge. Here he had expected to have a view into the heart of the island, but the clouds had now come lower and nearer and a sea of fog was rolling to meet him. He sat down and looked back. He was now so high that the bay looked small beneath him and miles of sea were visible. Then the fog from the mountains closed in all round him, thick but not cold, and he lay down and turned this way and that to find the most comfortable position to enjoy himself.

But he didn't enjoy himself, or not for very long. He began, almost for the first time in his life, to feel lonely. At first this feeling grew very gradually. And then he began to worry about the time. There was not the slightest sound. Suddenly it occurred to him that he might have been lying there for hours. Perhaps the others had gone! Perhaps they had let him wander away on purpose simply in order to leave him behind! He leapt up in a panic and began the descent.

At first he tried to do it too quickly, slipped on the steep grass, and slid for several feet. Then he thought this had carried him too far to the left – and as he came up he had seen precipices on that side. So he clambered up again, as near as he could guess to the place he had started from, and began the descent afresh, bearing to his right. After that things seemed to be going better. He went very cautiously, for he could not see more than a yard ahead, and there was still perfect silence all around him. It is very unpleasant to have to go cautiously when there is a voice inside you saying all the time, "Hurry, hurry, hurry." For every moment the terrible idea of being left behind grew stronger. If he had understood Caspian and the Pevensies at all he would have known, of course, that there was not the least chance of their doing any such thing. But he had persuaded himself that they were all fiends in human form.

"At last!" said Eustace as he came slithering down a slide of loose stones (*scree*, they call it) and found himself on the level. "And now, where are those trees? There *is* something dark ahead. Why, I do believe the fog is clearing."

It was. The light increased every moment and made him blink. The fog lifted. He was in an utterly unknown valley and the sea was nowhere in sight.

CHAPTER SIX

THE ADVENTURES OF EUSTACE

At that very moment the others were washing hands and faces in the river and generally getting ready for dinner and a rest. The three best archers had gone up into the hills north of the bay and returned laden with a pair of wild goats which were now roasting over a fire. Caspian had ordered a cask of wine ashore, strong wine of Archenland which had to be mixed with water before you drank it, so there would be plenty for all. The work had gone well so far and it was a merry meal. Only after the second helping of goat did Edmund say, "Where's that blighter Eustace?"

Meanwhile Eustace stared round the unknown valley. It was so narrow and deep, and the precipices which surrounded it so sheer, that it was like a huge pit or trench. The floor was grassy though strewn with rocks, and here and there Eustace saw black burnt patches like those you see on the sides of a railway embankment in a dry summer. About fifteen yards away from him was a pool of clear smooth water. There was, at first, nothing else at all in the valley; not an animal, not a bird, not an insect. The sun beat down, and grim peaks and horns of mountains peered over the valley's edge.

Eustace realized of course that in the fog he had come down the wrong side of the ridge, so he turned at once to see about getting back. But as soon as he had looked he shuddered. Apparently he had by amazing luck found the only possible way down – a long green spit of land, horribly steep and narrow, with precipices on either side. There was no other possible way of getting back. But could he do it, now that he saw what it was really like? His head swam at the very thought of it.

He turned round again, thinking that at any rate he'd better have a good drink from the pool first. But as soon as he had turned and before he had taken a step forward into the valley he heard a noise behind him. It was only a small noise but it sounded loud in that immense silence. It froze him dead-still where he stood for a second. Then he slewed round his neck and looked.

At the bottom of the cliff a little on his left hand was a low, dark hole – the entrance to a cave perhaps. And out of this two thin wisps of smoke were coming. And the loose stones just beneath the dark hollow were moving (that was the noise he had heard) just as if something were crawling in the dark behind them.

Something *was* crawling. Worse still, something was coming out. Edmund or Lucy or you would have recognized it at once, but Eustace had read none of the right books. The thing that came out of the cave was something he had never even imagined – a long lead-coloured snout, dull red eyes, no feathers or fur, a long lithe body that trailed on the ground, legs whose elbows went up higher than its back like a spider's, cruel claws, bat's wings that made a rasping noise on the stone, yards of tail. And the lines of smoke were coming from its two nostrils. He never said the word *dragon* to himself. Nor would it have made things any better if he had.

But perhaps if he had known something about dragons he would have been a little surprised at this dragon's behaviour. It did not sit up and clap its wings, nor did it shoot out a stream of flame from its mouth. The smoke from its nostrils was like the smoke of a fire that will not last much longer. Nor did it seem to have noticed Eustace. It moved very slowly towards the pool – slowly and with many pauses. Even in his fear Eustace felt that it was an old, sad creature. He wondered if he dared make a dash for the ascent. But it might look round if he made any noise. It might come more to life. Perhaps it was only shamming. Anyway, what was the use of trying to escape by climbing from a creature that could fly?

It reached the pool and slid its horrible scaly chin down over the gravel to drink: but before it had drunk there came from it a great croaking or clanging cry and after a few twitches and convulsions it rolled round on its side and lay perfectly still with one claw in the air. A little dark blood gushed from its wide-opened mouth. The smoke from its nostrils turned black for a moment and then floated away. No more came.

For a long time Eustace did not dare to move. Perhaps this was the brute's trick, the way it lured travellers to their doom. But one couldn't wait for ever. He took a step nearer, then two steps, and halted again. The dragon remained motionless; he noticed too that the red fire had gone out of its eyes. At last he came up to it. He was quite sure now that it was dead. With a shudder he touched it; nothing happened.

The relief was so great that Eustace almost laughed out loud. He began to feel as if he had fought and killed the dragon instead of merely seeing it die. He stepped over it and went to the pool for his drink, for the heat was getting unbearable. He was not surprised when he heard a peal of thunder. Almost immediately afterwards, the sun disappeared and before he had finished his drink big drops of rain were falling.

The climate of this island was a very unpleasant one. In less than a minute Eustace was wet to the skin and half blinded with such rain as one never sees in Europe. There was no use trying to climb out of the valley as long as this lasted. He bolted for the only shelter in sight – the dragon's cave. There he lay down and tried to get his breath.

Most of us know what we should expect to find in a dragon's lair but, as I said before, Eustace had read only the wrong books. They had a lot to say about exports and imports and governments and drains, but they were weak on dragons. That is why he was so puzzled at the surface on which he was lying. Parts of it were too prickly to be stones and too hard to be thorns, and there seemed to be a great many round, flat things, and it all clinked when he moved. There was light enough at the cave's mouth to examine it by. And of course Eustace found it to be what any of us could have told him in advance – treasure. There were crowns (those were the prickly things), coins, rings, bracelets, ingots, cups, plates and gems.

Eustace (unlike most boys) had never thought much of treasure but he saw at once the use it would be in this new world which he had so foolishly stumbled into through the picture in Lucy's bedroom at home. "They don't have any tax here," he said. "And you don't have to give treasure to the government. With some of this stuff I could have quite a decent time here – perhaps in Calormen. It sounds the least phoney of these countries. I wonder how much I can carry? That bracelet now – those things in it are probably diamonds – I'll slip that on my own wrist. Too big, but not if I push it right up here above my elbow. Then fill my pockets with diamonds – that's easier than gold. I wonder when this infernal rain's going to let up?" He got into a less uncomfortable part of the pile, where it was mostly coins, and settled down to wait. But a bad fright, when once it is over, and especially a bad fright following a mountain walk, leaves you very tired. Eustace fell asleep.

By the time he was sound asleep and snoring the others had finished dinner and became seriously alarmed about him. They shouted, "Eustace! Eustace! Coo-ee!" till they were hoarse, and Caspian blew his horn.

"He's nowhere near or he'd have heard that," said Lucy with a white face.

"Confound the fellow," said Edmund. "What on earth did he want to slink away like this for?"

"But we must do something," said Lucy. "He may have got lost, or fallen into a hole, or been captured by savages."

"Or killed by wild beasts," said Drinian.

"And a good riddance if he has, *I* say," muttered Rhince.

"Master Rhince," said Reepicheep, "you never spoke a word that became you less. The creature is no friend of mine but he is of the Queen's blood, and while he is one of our fellowship it concerns our honour to find him and to avenge him if he is dead."

"Of course we've got to find him (if we *can*)," said Caspian wearily. "That's the nuisance of it. It means a search party and endless trouble. Bother Eustace."

Meanwhile Eustace slept and slept – and slept. What woke him was a pain in his arm. The moon was shining in at the mouth of the cave, and the bed of treasures seemed to have grown much more comfortable: in fact he could hardly feel it at all. He was puzzled by the pain in his arm at first, but presently it occurred to him that the bracelet which he had shoved up above his elbow had become strangely tight. His arm must have swollen while he was asleep (it was his left arm).

He moved his right arm in order to feel his left, but stopped before he had moved it an inch and bit his lip in terror. For just in front of him, and a little on his right, where the moonlight fell clear on the floor of the cave, he saw a hideous shape moving. He knew that shape: it was a dragon's claw. It had moved as he moved his hand and became still when he stopped moving his hand.

"Oh, what a fool I've been," thought Eustace. "Of course, the brute had a mate and it's lying beside me."

For several minutes he did not dare to move a muscle. He saw two thin columns of smoke going up before his eyes, black against the moonlight; just as there had been smoke coming from the other dragon's nose before it died. This was so alarming that he held his breath. The two columns of smoke vanished. When he could hold his breath no longer he let it out stealthily; instantly two jets of smoke appeared again. But even yet he had no idea of the truth.

Presently he decided that he would edge very cautiously to his left and try to creep out of the cave. Perhaps the creature was asleep – and anyway it was his only chance. But of course before he edged to the left he looked to the left. Oh, horror! There was a dragon's claw on that side too.

No one will blame Eustace if at this moment he shed tears. He was surprised at the size of his own tears as he saw them splashing on to the treasure in front of him. They also seemed strangely hot; steam went up from them.

But there was no good crying. He must try to crawl out from between the two dragons. He began extending his right arm. The dragon's fore-leg and claw on his right went through exactly the same motion. Then he thought he would try his left. The dragon limb on that side moved too.

Two dragons, one on each side, mimicking whatever he did! His nerve broke and he simply made a bolt for it.

There was such a clatter and rasping, and clinking of gold, and grinding of stones, as he rushed out of the cave that he thought they were both following him. He daren't look back. He rushed to the pool. The twisted shape of the dead dragon lying in the moonlight would have been enough to frighten anyone but now he hardly noticed it. His idea was to get into the water.

But just as he reached the edge of the pool two things happened. First of all it came over him like a thunder-clap that he had been running on all fours – and why on earth had he been doing that? And secondly, as he bent towards the water, he thought for a second that yet another dragon was staring up at him out of the pool. But in an instant he realized the truth. The dragon face in the pool was his own reflection. There was no doubt of it. It moved as he moved: it opened and shut its mouth as he opened and shut his.

He had turned into a dragon while he was asleep. Sleeping on a dragon's hoard with greedy, dragonish thoughts in his heart, he had become a dragon himself.

That explained everything. There had been no two dragons beside him in the cave. The claws to right and left had been his own right and left claw. The two columns of smoke had been coming from his own nostrils. As for the pain in his left arm (or what had been his left arm) he could now see what had happened by squinting with his left eye. The bracelet which had fitted very nicely on the upper arm of a boy was far too small for the thick, stumpy foreleg of a dragon. It had sunk deeply into his scaly flesh and there was a throbbing bulge on each side of it. He tore at the place with his dragon's teeth but could not get it off.

In spite of the pain, his first feeling was one of relief. There was nothing to be afraid of any more. He was a terror himself and nothing in the world but a knight (and not all of those) would dare to attack him. He could get even with Caspian and Edmund now –

But the moment he thought this he realized that he didn't want to. He wanted to be friends. He wanted to get back among humans and talk and laugh and share things. He realized that he was a monster cut off from the whole human race. An appalling loneliness came over him. He began to see that the others had not really been fiends at all. He began to wonder if he himself had been such a nice person as he had always supposed. He longed for their voices. He would have been grateful for a kind word even from Reepicheep.

When he thought of this the poor dragon that had been Eustace lifted up its voice and wept. A powerful dragon crying its eyes out under the moon in a deserted valley is a sight and a sound hardly to be imagined.

At last he decided he would try to find his way back to the shore. He realized now that Caspian would never have sailed away and left him. And he felt sure that somehow or other he would be able to make people understand who he was.

He took a long drink and then (I know this sounds shocking, but it isn't if you think it over) he ate nearly all the dead dragon. He was halfway through it before he realized what he was doing; for, you see, though his mind was the mind of Eustace, his tastes and his digestion were dragonish. And there is nothing a dragon likes so well as fresh dragon. That is why you so seldom find more than one dragon in the same county.

Then he turned to climb out of the valley. He began the climb with a jump and as soon as he jumped he found that he was flying. He had quite forgotten about his wings and it was a great surprise to him — the first pleasant surprise he had had for a long time. He rose high into the air and saw innumerable mountain-tops spread out beneath him in the moonlight. He could see the bay like a silver slab and the *Dawn Treader* lying at anchor, and camp fires twinkling in the woods beside the beach. From a great height he launched himself down towards them in a single glide.

Lucy was sleeping very soundly for she had sat up till the return of the search party in the hope of good news about Eustace. It had been led by Caspian and had come back late and weary. Their news was disquieting. They had found no trace of Eustace but had seen a dead dragon in a valley. They tried to make the best of it and everyone assured everyone else that there were not likely to be more dragons about, and that one which was dead at about three o'clock that afternoon (which was when they had seen it) would hardly have been killing people a very few hours before.

"Unless it ate the little brat and died of him: he'd poison anything," said Rhince. But he said this under his breath and no one heard it.

But later in the night Lucy was wakened, very softly, and found the whole company gathered close together and talking in whispers.

"What is it?" said Lucy.

"We must all show great constancy," Caspian was saying. "A dragon has just flown over the tree-tops and lighted on the beach. Yes, I am afraid it is between us and the ship. And arrows are no use against dragons. And they're not at all afraid of fire."

"With your Majesty's leave——" began Reepicheep.

"No, Reepicheep," said the King very firmly, "you are *not* to attempt a single combat with it. And unless you promise to obey me in this matter I'll have you tied up. We must just keep close watch and, as soon as it is light, go down to the beach and give it battle. I will lead. King Edmund will be on my right and the Lord Drinian on my left. There are no other arrangements to be made. It will be light in a couple of hours. In an hour's time let a meal be served out and what is left of the wine. And let everything be done silently."

"Perhaps it will go away," said Lucy.

"It'll be worse if it does," said Edmund, "because then we shan't know where it is. If there's a wasp in the room I like to be able to see it."

The rest of the night was dreadful, and when the meal came, though they knew they ought to eat, many found that they had very poor appetites. And endless hours seemed to pass before the darkness thinned and birds began chirping here and there and the world got colder and wetter than it had been all night and Caspian said, "Now for it, friends."

They got up, all with swords drawn, and formed themselves into a solid mass with Lucy in the middle and Reepicheep on her shoulder. It was nicer than the waiting about and everyone felt fonder of everyone else than at ordinary times. A moment later they were marching. It grew lighter as they came to the edge of the wood. And there on the sand, like a giant lizard, or a flexible crocodile, or a serpent with legs, huge and horrible and humpy, lay the dragon.

But when it saw them, instead of rising up and blowing fire and smoke, the dragon retreated — you could almost say it waddled — back into the shallows of the bay.

"What's it wagging its head like that for?" said Edmund.

"And now it's nodding," said Caspian.

"And there's something coming from its eyes," said Drinian.

"Oh, can't you see?" said Lucy. "It's crying. Those are tears."

"I shouldn't trust to that, Ma'am," said Drinian. "That's what crocodiles do, to put you off your guard."

"It wagged its head when you said that," remarked Edmund. "Just as if it meant 'No'. Look, there it goes again."

"Do you think it understands what we're saying?" asked Lucy.

The dragon nodded its head violently.

Reepicheep slipped off Lucy's shoulder and stepped to the front.

"Dragon," came his shrill voice, "can you understand speech?"

The dragon nodded.

"Can you speak?"

It shook its head.

"Then," said Reepicheep, "it is idle to ask you your business. But if you will swear friendship with us raise your left foreleg above your head."

It did so, but clumsily because that leg was sore and swollen with the golden bracelet.

"Oh, look," said Lucy, "there's something wrong with its leg. The poor thing — that's probably what it was crying about. Perhaps it came to us to be cured like in *Androcles and the Lion*."

"Be careful, Lucy," said Caspian. "It's a very clever dragon but it may be a liar."

Lucy had, however, already run forward, followed by Reepicheep, as fast as his short legs could carry him, and then of course the boys and Drinian came too.

"Show me your poor paw," said Lucy. "I might be able to cure it."

The dragon-that-had-been-Eustace held out its sore leg gladly enough, remembering how Lucy's cordial had cured him of sea-sickness before he became a dragon. But he was disappointed. The magic fluid reduced the swelling and eased the pain a little but it could not dissolve the gold.

Everyone had now crowded round to watch the treatment, and Caspian suddenly exclaimed, "Look!" He was staring at the bracelet.

CHAPTER SEVEN

HOW THE ADVENTURE ENDED

"Look at what?" said Edmund.

"Look at the device on the gold," said Caspian.

"A little hammer with a diamond above it like a star," said Drinian. "Why, I've seen that before."

"Seen it!" said Caspian. "Why, of course you have. It is the sign of a great Narnian house. This is the Lord Octesian's arm-ring."

"Villain," said Reepicheep to the dragon, "have you devoured a Narnian lord?" But the dragon shook his head violently.

"Or perhaps," said Lucy, "this is the Lord Octesian, turned into a dragon – under an enchantment, you know."

"It needn't be either," said Edmund. "All dragons collect gold. But I think it's a safe guess that Octesian got no further than this island."

"Are you the Lord Octesian?" said Lucy to the dragon, and then, when it sadly shook its head, "Are you someone enchanted – someone human, I mean?"

It nodded violently.

And then someone said – people disputed afterwards whether Lucy or Edmund said it first – "You're not – not Eustace by any chance?"

And Eustace nodded his terrible dragon head and thumped his tail in the sea and everyone skipped back (some of the sailors with ejaculations I will not put down in writing) to avoid the enormous and boiling tears which flowed from his eyes.

Lucy tried hard to console him and even screwed up her courage to kiss the scaly face, and nearly everyone said, "Hard luck" and several assured Eustace that they would all stand by him and many said there was sure to be some way of disenchanting him and they'd have him as right as rain in a day or two. And of course they were all very anxious to hear his story, but he couldn't speak. More than once in the days that followed he attempted to write it for them on the sand. But this never succeeded. In the first place Eustace (never having read the right books) had no idea how to tell a story straight. And for another thing, the muscles and nerves of the dragon-claws that he had to use had never learned to write and were not built for writing anyway. As a result he never got nearly to the end before the tide came in and washed away all the writing except the bits he had already trodden on or accidentally swished out with his tail. And all that anyone had seen would be something like this – the dots are for the bits he had smudged out –

I WNET TO SLEE... RGOS AGRONS I MEAN DRANGONS CAVE CAUSE ITWAS DEAD AND AINING SO HAR... WOKE UP AND COU... GET OFFF MI ARM OH BOTHER...

It was, however, clear to everyone that Eustace's character had been rather improved by becoming a dragon. He was anxious to help. He flew over the whole island and found it was all mountainous and inhabited only by wild goats and droves of wild swine. Of these he brought back many carcases as provisions for this ship. He was a very humane killer too, for he could dispatch a beast with one blow of his tail so that it didn't know (and presumably still doesn't know) it had been killed. He ate a few himself, of course, but always alone, for now that he was a dragon he liked his food raw but he could never bear to let others see him at his messy meals. And one day, flying slowly and wearily but in great triumph, he bore back to camp a great tall pine tree which he had torn up by the roots in a distant valley and which could be made into a capital mast. And in the evening if it turned chilly, as it sometimes did after the heavy rains, he was a comfort to everyone, for the whole party would come and sit with their backs against his hot sides and get well warmed and dried; and one puff of his fiery breath would light the most obstinate fire. Sometimes he would take a select party for a fly on his back, so that they could see wheeling below them the green slopes, the rocky heights, the narrow pit-like valleys and far out over the sea to the eastward a spot of darker blue on the blue horizon which might be land.

The pleasure (quite new to him) of being liked and, still more, of liking other people, was what kept Eustace from despair. For it was very dreary being a dragon. He shuddered whenever he caught sight of his own reflection as he flew over a mountain lake. He hated the huge batlike wings, the saw-edged ridge on his back, and the cruel, curved claws. He was almost afraid to be alone with himself and yet he was ashamed to be with the others. On the evenings when he was not being used as a hot-water bottle he would slink away from the camp and lie curled up like a snake between the wood and the water. On such occasions, greatly to his surprise, Reepicheep was his most constant comforter. The noble Mouse would creep away from the merry circle at the camp fire and sit down by the dragon's head, well to the windward to be out of the way of his smoky breath. There he would explain that what had happened to Eustace was a striking illustration of the turn of Fortune's wheel, and that if he had Eustace at his own house in Narnia (it was really a hole not a house and the dragon's head, let alone his body, would not have fitted in) he could show him more than a hundred examples of emperors, kings, dukes, knights, poets, lovers, astronomers, philosophers, and magicians, who had fallen from prosperity into the most distressing circumstances, and of whom many had recovered and lived happily ever afterwards. It did not, perhaps, seem so very comforting at the time, but it was kindly meant and Eustace never forgot it.

But of course what hung over everyone like a cloud was the problem of what to do with their dragon when they were ready to sail. They tried not to talk of it when he was there, but he couldn't help overhearing things like, "Would he fit all along one side of the deck? And we'd have to shift all the stores to the other side down below so as to balance," or, "Would towing him be any good?" or, "Would he be able to keep up by flying?" and (most often of all), "But how are we to feed him?" And poor Eustace realized more and more that since the first day he came on board he had been an unmitigated nuisance and that he was now a greater nuisance still. And this ate into his mind, just as that bracelet ate into his foreleg. He knew that it only made it worse to tear at it with his great teeth, but he couldn't help tearing now and then, especially on hot nights.

About six days after they had landed on Dragon Island, Edmund happened to wake up very early one morning. It was just getting grey so that you could see the tree-trunks if they were between you and the bay but not in the other direction. As he woke he thought he heard something moving, so he raised himself on one elbow and looked about him: and presently he thought he saw a dark figure moving on the seaward side of the wood. The idea that at once occurred to his mind was, "Are we so sure there are no natives on this island after all?" Then he thought it was Caspian – it was about the right size – but he knew that Caspian had been sleeping next to him and could see that he hadn't moved. Edmund made sure that his sword was in its place and then rose to investigate.

He came down softly to the edge of the wood and the dark figure was still there. He saw now that it was too small for Caspian and too big for Lucy. It did not run away. Edmund drew his sword and was about to challenge the stranger when the stranger said in a low voice, "Is that you, Edmund?"

"Yes. Who are you?" said he.

"Don't you know me?" said the other. "It's me – Eustace."

"By jove," said Edmund, "so it is. My dear chap—"

"Hush," said Eustace, and lurched as if he were going to fall.

"Hello!" said Edmund, steadying him. "What's up? Are you ill?"

Eustace was silent for so long that Edmund thought he was fainting; but at last he said, "It's been ghastly. You don't know... but it's all right now. Could we go and talk somewhere? I don't want to meet the others just yet."

"Yes, rather, anywhere you like," said Edmund. "We can go and sit on the rocks over there. I say, I *am* glad to see you – er – looking yourself again. You must have had a pretty beastly time."

They went to the rocks and sat down looking out across the bay while the sky got paler and paler and the stars disappeared except for one very bright one low down and near the horizon.

"I won't tell you how I became a – a dragon till I can tell the others and get it all over," said Eustace. "By the way, I didn't even know it *was* a dragon till I heard you all using the word when I turned up here the other morning. I want to tell you how I stopped being one."

"Fire ahead," said Edmund.

"Well, last night I was more miserable than ever. And that beastly arm-ring was hurting like anything—"

"Is that all right now?"

Eustace laughed – a different laugh from any Edmund had heard him give before – and slipped the bracelet easily off his arm. "There it is," he said, "and anyone who likes can have it as far as I'm concerned. Well, as I say, I was lying awake and wondering what on earth would become of me. And then – but, mind you, it may have been all a dream. I don't know."

"Go on," said Edmund, with considerable patience.

"Well, anyway, I looked up and saw the very last thing I expected: a huge lion coming slowly towards me. And one queer thing was that there was no moon last night, but there was moonlight where the lion was. So it came nearer and nearer. I was terribly afraid of it. You may think that, being a dragon, I could have knocked any lion out easily enough. But it wasn't that kind of fear. I wasn't afraid of it eating me, I was just afraid of *it* – if you can understand. Well, it came close up to me and looked straight into my eyes. And I shut my eyes tight. But that wasn't any good because it told me to follow it."

"You mean it spoke?"

"I don't know. Now that you mention it, I don't think it did. But it told me all the same. And I knew I'd have to do what it told me, so I got up and followed it. And it led me a long way into the mountains. And there was always this moonlight over and round the lion wherever we went. So at last we came to the top of a mountain I'd never seen before and on the top of this mountain there was a garden – trees and fruit and everything. In the middle of it there was a well.

"I knew it was a well because you could see the water bubbling up from the bottom of it: but it was a lot bigger than most wells – like a very big, round bath with marble steps going down into it. The water was as clear as anything and I thought if I could get in there and bathe, it would ease the pain in my leg. But the lion told me I must undress first. Mind you, I don't know if he said any words out loud or not.

"I was just going to say that I couldn't undress because I hadn't any clothes on when I suddenly thought that dragons are snaky sort of things and snakes can cast their skins. Oh, of course, thought I, that's what the lion means. So I started scratching myself and my scales began coming off all over the place. And then I scratched a little deeper and, instead of just scales coming off here and there, my whole skin started peeling off beautifully, like it does after an illness, or as if I was a banana. In a minute or two I just stepped out of it. I could see it lying there beside me, looking rather nasty. It was a most lovely feeling. So I started to go down into the well for my bathe.

"But just as I was going to put my feet into the water I looked down and saw that they were all hard and rough and wrinkled and scaly just as they had been before. Oh, that's all right, said I, it only means I had another smaller suit on underneath the first one, and I'll have to get out of it too. So I scratched and tore again and this underskin peeled off beautifully and out I stepped and left it lying beside the other one and went down to the well for my bathe.

"Well, exactly the same thing happened again. And I thought to myself, oh dear, how ever many skins have I got to take off? For I was longing to bathe my leg. So I scratched away for the third time and got off a third skin, just like the two others, and stepped out of it. But as soon as I looked at myself in the water I knew it had been no good.

"Then the lion said – but I don't know if it spoke – 'You will have to let me undress you.' I was afraid of his claws, I can tell you, but I was pretty nearly desperate now. So I just lay flat down on my back to let him do it.

"The very first tear he made was so deep that I thought it had gone right into my heart. And when he began pulling the skin off, it hurt worse than anything I've ever felt. The only thing that made me able to bear it was just the pleasure of feeling the stuff peel off. You know — if you've ever picked the scab off a sore place. It hurts like billy-oh but it *is* fun to see it coming away."

"I know exactly what you mean," said Edmund.

"Well, he peeled the beastly stuff right off — just as I thought I'd done it myself the other three times, only they hadn't hurt — and there it was, lying on the grass: only ever so much thicker, and darker, and more knobbly-looking than the others had been. And there was I as smooth and soft as a peeled switch and smaller than I had been. Then he caught hold of me — I didn't like that much for I was very tender underneath now that I'd no skin on — and threw me into the water. It smarted like anything but only for a moment. After that it became perfectly delicious and as soon as I started swimming and splashing I found that all the pain had gone from my arm. And then I saw why. I'd turned into a boy again. You'd think me simply phoney if I told you how I felt about my own arms. I know they've no muscle and are pretty mouldy compared with Caspian's, but I was so glad to see them.

"After a bit the lion took me out and dressed me—"

"Dressed you? With his paws?"

"Well, I don't exactly remember that bit. But he did somehow or other: in new clothes — the same I've got on now, as a matter of fact. And then suddenly I was back here. Which is what makes me think it must have been a dream."

"No. It wasn't a dream," said Edmund.

"Why not?"

"Well, there are the clothes, for one thing. And you have been — well, un-dragoned, for another."

"What do you think it was, then?" asked Eustace.

"I think you've seen Aslan," said Edmund.

"Aslan!" said Eustace. "I've heard that name mentioned several times since we joined the *Dawn Treader*. And I felt — I don't know what — I hated it. But I was hating everything then. And by the way, I'd like to apologize. I'm afraid I've been pretty beastly."

"That's all right," said Edmund. "Between ourselves, you haven't been as bad as I was on my first trip to Narnia. You were only an ass, but I was a traitor."

"Well, don't tell me about it, then," said Eustace. "But who is Aslan? Do you know him?"

"Well — he knows me," said Edmund. "He is the great Lion, the son of the Emperor-over-Sea, who saved me and saved Narnia. We've all seen him. Lucy sees him most often. And it may be Aslan's country we are sailing to."

Neither said anything for a while. The last bright star had vanished and though they could not see the sunrise because of the mountains on their right, they knew it was going on because the sky above them and the bay before them turned the colour of roses. Then some bird of the parrot kind screamed in the wood behind them, and they heard movements among the trees, and finally a blast on Caspian's horn. The camp was astir.

Great was the rejoicing when Edmund and the restored Eustace walked into the breakfast circle round the camp fire. And now of course everyone heard the earlier part of his story. People wondered whether the other dragon had killed the Lord Octesian several years ago or whether Octesian himself had been the old dragon. The jewels with which Eustace had crammed his pockets in the cave had disappeared along with the clothes he had then been wearing: but no one, least of all Eustace himself, felt any desire to go back to that valley for more treasure.

In a few days now the *Dawn Treader*, remasted, re-painted, and well stored, was ready to sail. Before they embarked, Caspian caused to be cut on a smooth cliff facing the bay the words:

DRAGON ISLAND
DISCOVERED BY CASPIAN X,
KING OF NARNIA, ETC.
IN THE FOURTH
YEAR OF HIS REIGN.
HERE, AS WE SUPPOSE,
THE LORD OCTESIAN
HAD HIS DEATH.

It would be nice, and fairly true, to say that "from that time forth Eustace was a different boy". To be strictly accurate, he began to be a different boy. He had relapses. There were still many days when he could be very tiresome. But most of those I shall not notice. The cure had begun.

The Lord Octesian's arm-ring had a curious fate. Eustace did not want it and offered it to Caspian, and Caspian offered it to Lucy. She did not care about having it. "Very well, then, catch as catch can," said Caspian and flung it up in the air. This was when they were all standing looking at the inscription. Up went the ring, flashing in the sunlight, and caught, and hung, as neatly as a well-thrown quoit, on a little projection on the rock. No one could climb up to get it from below and no one could climb down to get it from above. And there, for all I know, it is hanging still and may hang till that world ends.

CHAPTER EIGHT

TWO NARROW ESCAPES

Everyone was cheerful as the *Dawn Treader* sailed from Dragon Island. They
had fair winds as soon as they were out of the bay and came early the next
morning to the unknown land which some of them had seen when flying
over the mountains while Eustace was still a dragon. It was a low green
island inhabited by nothing but rabbits and a few goats, but from the ruins
of stone huts, and from blackened places where fires had been, they judged
that it had been peopled not long before. There were also some bones and
broken weapons.

"Pirates' work," said Caspian.

"Or the dragon's," said Edmund.

The only other thing they found there was a little skin boat, or coracle,
on the sands. It was made of hide stretched over a wicker framework. It was
a tiny boat, barely four feet long, and the paddle which still lay in it was in
proportion. They thought that either it had been made for a child or else
that the people of that country had been Dwarfs. Reepicheep decided to
keep it, as it was just the right size for him; so it was taken on board. They
called that land Burnt Island, and sailed away before the noon.

For some five days they ran before a south-south-east wind, out of sight
of all lands and seeing neither fish nor gull. Then they had a day when it
rained hard till the afternoon. Eustace lost two games of chess to
Reepicheep and began to get like his old and disagreeable self again, and
Edmund said he wished they could have gone to America with Susan.
Then Lucy looked out of the stern windows and said:

"Hullo! I do believe it's stopping. And what's *that*?"

They all tumbled up to the poop at this and found that the rain had stopped and that Drinian, who was on watch, was also staring hard at something astern. Or rather, at several things. They looked a little like smooth rounded rocks, a whole line of them with intervals of about forty feet in between.

"But they can't be rocks," Drinian was saying, "because they weren't there five minutes ago."

"And one's just disappeared," said Lucy.

"Yes, and there's another one coming up," said Edmund.

"And nearer," said Eustace.

"Hang it!" said Caspian. "The whole thing is moving this way."

"And moving a great deal quicker than we can sail, Sire," said Drinian. "It'll be up with us in a minute."

They all held their breath, for it is not at all nice to be pursued by an unknown something either on land or sea. But what it turned out to be was far worse than anyone had suspected. Suddenly, only about the length of a cricket pitch from their port side, an appalling head reared itself out of the sea. It was all greens and vermilions with purple blotches – except where shellfish clung to it – and shaped rather like a horse's, though without ears. It had enormous eyes, eyes made for staring through the dark depths of the ocean, and a gaping mouth filled with double rows of sharp fish-like teeth. It came up on what they first took to be a huge neck, but as more and more of it emerged, everyone knew that this was not its neck but its body and that at last they were seeing what so many people have foolishly wanted to see – the great Sea Serpent. The folds of its gigantic tail could be seen far away, rising at intervals from the surface. And now its head was towering up higher than the mast.

Every man rushed to his weapon, but there was nothing to be done, the monster was out of reach. "Shoot! Shoot!" cried the Master Bowman, and several obeyed, but the arrows glanced off the Sea Serpent's hide as if it were iron-plated. Then, for a dreadful minute, everyone was still, staring up at its eyes and mouth and wondering where it would pounce.

But it didn't pounce. It shot its head forward across the ship on a level with the yard of the mast. Now its head was just beside the fighting top. Still it stretched and stretched till its head was over the starboard bulwark. Then down it began to come – not onto the crowded deck but into the water, so that the whole ship was under an arch of serpent. And almost at once that arch began to get smaller: indeed on the starboard the Sea Serpent was now almost touching the *Dawn Treader*'s side.

Eustace (who had really been trying very hard to behave well, till the rain and the chess put him back) now did the first brave thing he had ever done. He was wearing a sword that Caspian had lent him. As soon as the serpent's body was near enough on the starboard side he jumped onto the bulwark and began hacking at it with all his might. It is true that he accomplished nothing beyond breaking Caspian's second-best sword into bits, but it was a fine thing for a beginner to have done.

Others would have joined him if at that moment Reepicheep had not called out, "Don't fight! Push!" It was so unusual for the Mouse to advise anyone not to fight that, even in that terrible moment, every eye turned to him. And when he jumped up onto the bulwark, forward of the snake, and set his little furry back against its huge scaly, slimy back, and began pushing as hard as he could, quite a number of people saw what he meant and rushed to both sides of the ship to do the same. And when, a moment later, the Sea Serpent's head appeared again, this time on the port side, and this time with its back to them, then everyone understood.

The brute had made a loop of itself round the *Dawn Treader* and was beginning to draw the loop tight. When it got quite tight — snap! — there would be floating matchwood where the ship had been and it could pick them out of the water one by one. Their only chance was to push the loop backward till it slid over the stern; or else (to put the same thing another way) to push the ship forward out of the loop.

Reepicheep alone had, of course, no more chance of doing this than of lifting up a cathedral, but he had nearly killed himself with trying before others shoved him aside. Very soon the whole ship's company except Lucy and the Mouse (who was fainting) was in two long lines along the two bulwarks, each man's chest to the back of the man in front, so that the weight of the whole line was in the last man, pushing for their lives. For a few sickening seconds (which seemed like hours) nothing appeared to happen. Joints cracked, sweat dropped, breath came in grunts and gasps. Then they felt that the ship was moving. They saw that the snake-loop was further from the mast than it had been. But they also saw that it was smaller. And now the real danger was at hand. Could they get it over the poop, or was it already too tight? Yes. It would just fit. It was resting on the poop rails. A dozen or more sprang up on the poop. This was far better. The Sea Serpent's body was so low now that they could make a line across the poop and push side by side. Hope rose high till everyone remembered the high carved stern, the dragon tail, of the *Dawn Treader*. It would be quite impossible to get the brute over that.

"An axe," cried Caspian hoarsely, "and still shove."

Lucy, who knew where everything was, heard him where she was standing on the main deck staring up at the poop. In a few seconds she had been below, got the axe, and was rushing up the ladder to the poop. But just as she reached the top there came a great crashing noise like a tree coming down and the ship rocked and darted forward. For at that very moment, whether because the Sea Serpent was being pushed so hard, or because it foolishly decided to draw the noose tight, the whole of the carved stern broke off and the ship was free.

The others were too exhausted to see what Lucy saw. There, a few yards behind them, the loop of Sea Serpent's body got rapidly smaller and disappeared into a splash. Lucy always said (but of course she was very excited at the moment, and it may have been only imagination) that she saw a look of idiotic satisfaction on the creature's face. What is certain is that it was a very stupid animal, for instead of pursuing the ship it turned its head round and began nosing all along its own body as if it expected to find the wreckage of the *Dawn Treader* there. But the *Dawn Treader* was already well away, running before a fresh breeze, and the men lay and sat panting and groaning all about the deck, till presently they were able to talk about it, and then to laugh about it. And when some rum had been served out they even raised a cheer; and everyone praised the valour of Eustace (though it hadn't done any good) and of Reepicheep.

After this they sailed for three days more and saw nothing but sea and sky. On the fourth day the wind changed to the north and the seas began to rise; by the afternoon it had nearly become a gale. But at the same time they sighted land on their port bow.

"By your leave, Sire," said Drinian, "we will try to get under the lee of that country by rowing and lie in harbour, maybe till this is over." Caspian agreed, but a long row against the gale did not bring them to the land before evening. By the last light of that day they steered into a natural harbour and anchored, but no one went ashore that night. In the morning they found themselves in the green bay of a rugged, lonely-looking country which sloped up to a rocky summit. From the windy north beyond that summit, clouds came streaming rapidly. They lowered the boat and loaded her with any of the water casks which were now empty.

"Which stream shall we water at, Drinian?" said Caspian as he took his seat in the stern-sheets of the boat. "There seem to be two coming down into the bay."

"It makes little odds, Sire," said Drinian. "But I think it's a shorter pull to that on the starboard – the eastern one."

"Here comes the rain," said Lucy.

"I should think it does!" said Edmund, for it was already pelting hard. "I say, let's go to the other stream. There are trees there and we'll have some shelter."

"Yes, let's," said Eustace. "No point in getting wetter than we need."

But all the time Drinian was steadily steering to the starboard, like tiresome people in cars who continue at forty miles an hour while you are explaining to them that they are on the wrong road.

"They're right, Drinian," said Caspian. "Why don't you bring her head round and make for the western stream?"

"As your Majesty pleases," said Drinian a little shortly. He had had an anxious day with the weather yesterday, and he didn't like advice from landsmen. But he altered course; and it turned out afterwards that it was a good thing he did.

By the time they had finished watering, the rain was over and Caspian, with Eustace, the Pevensies, and Reepicheep decided to walk up to the top of the hill and see what could be seen. It was a stiffish climb through coarse grass and heather and they saw neither man nor beast, except seagulls. When they reached the top they saw that it was a very small island, not more than twenty acres; and from this height the sea looked larger and more desolate than it did from the deck, or even the fighting top, of the *Dawn Treader*.

"Crazy, you know," said Eustace to Lucy in a low voice, looking at the eastern horizon. "Sailing on and on into *that* with no idea what we may get to." But he only said it out of habit, not really nastily as he would have done at one time.

It was too cold to stay long on the ridge for the wind still blew freshly from the north.

"Don't let's go back the same way," said Lucy as they turned. "Let's go along a bit and come down by the other stream, the one Drinian wanted to go to."

Everyone agreed to this and after about fifteen minutes they were at the source of the second river. It was a more interesting place than they had expected; a deep little mountain lake, surrounded by cliffs except for a narrow channel on the seaward side out of which the water flowed. Here at last they were out of the wind, and all sat down in the heather above the cliff for a rest.

All sat down, but one (it was Edmund) jumped up again very quickly.

"They go in for sharp stones on this island," he said, groping about in the heather. "Where is the wretched thing?... Ah, now I've got it... Hullo! It wasn't a stone at all, it's a sword-hilt. No, by jove, it's a whole sword; what the rust has left of it. It must have lain here for ages."

"Narnian, too, by the look of it," said Caspian, as they all crowded round.

"I'm sitting on something too," said Lucy. "Something hard." It turned out to be the remains of a mail-shirt. By this time everyone was on hands and knees, feeling in the thick heather in every direction. Their search revealed, one by one, a helmet, a dagger, and a few coins; not Calormen crescents but genuine Narnian "Lions" and "Trees" such as you might see any day in the market place of Beaversdam or Beruna.

"Looks as if this might be all that's left of one of our seven lords," said Edmund.

"Just what I was thinking," said Caspian. "I wonder which it was. There's nothing on the dagger to show. And I wonder how he died."

"And how we are to avenge him," added Reepicheep.

Edmund, the only one of the party who had read several detective stories, had meanwhile been thinking.

"Look here," he said, "there's something very fishy about this. He can't have been killed in a fight."

"Why not?" asked Caspian.

"No bones," said Edmund. "An enemy might take the armour and leave the body. But who ever heard of a chap who'd won a fight carrying away the body and leaving the armour?"

"Perhaps he was killed by a wild animal," Lucy suggested.

"It'd be a clever animal," said Edmund, "that would take a man's mail-shirt off."

"Perhaps a dragon?" said Caspian.

"Nothing doing," said Eustace. "A dragon couldn't do it. I ought to know."

"Well, let's get away from the place, anyway," said Lucy. She had not felt like sitting down again since Edmund had raised the question of bones.

"If you like," said Caspian, getting up. "I don't think any of this stuff is worth taking away."

They came down and round to the little opening where the stream came out of the lake, and stood looking at the deep water within the circle of cliffs. If it had been a hot day, no doubt some would have been tempted to bathe and everyone would have had a drink. Indeed, even as it was, Eustace was on the very point of stooping down and scooping up some water in his hands when Reepicheep and Lucy both at the same moment cried, "Look," so he forgot about his drink and looked.

The bottom of the pool was made of large greyish-blue stones and the water was perfectly clear, and on the bottom lay a life-size figure of a man, made apparently of gold. It lay face downwards with its arms stretched out above its head. And it so happened that as they looked at it, the clouds parted and the sun shone out. The golden shape was lit up from end to end. Lucy thought it was the most beautiful statue she had ever seen.

"Well!" whistled Caspian. "That was worth coming to see! I wonder, can we get it out?"

"We can dive for it, Sire," said Reepicheep.

"No good at all," said Edmund. "At least, if it's really gold – solid gold – it'll be far too heavy to bring up. And that pool's twelve or fifteen feet deep if it's an inch. Half a moment, though. It's a good thing I've brought a hunting spear with me. Let's see what the depth *is* like. Hold on to my hand, Caspian, while I lean out over the water a bit." Caspian took his hand and Edmund, leaning forward, began to lower his spear into the water.

Before it was halfway in Lucy said, "I don't believe the statue is gold at all. It's only the light. Your spear looks just the same colour."

"What's wrong?" asked several voices at once, for Edmund had suddenly let go of the spear.

"I couldn't hold it," gasped Edmund, "it seemed so *heavy*."

"And there it is on the bottom now," said Caspian, "and Lucy is right. It looks just the same colour as the statue."

But Edmund, who appeared to be having some trouble with his boots – at least he was bending down and looking at them – straightened himself all at once and shouted out in the sharp voice which people hardly ever disobey:

"Get back! Back from the water. All of you. At once!!"

They all did and stared at him.

"Look," said Edmund, "look at the toes of my boots."

"They look a bit yellow," began Eustace.

"They're gold, solid gold," interrupted Edmund. "Look at them. Feel them. The leather's pulled away from it already. And they're as heavy as lead."

"By Aslan!" said Caspian. "You don't mean to say——?"

"Yes, I do," said Edmund. "That water turns things into gold. It turned the spear into gold, that's why it got so heavy. And it was just lapping against my feet (it's a good thing I wasn't barefoot) and it turned the toe-caps into gold. And that poor fellow on the bottom – well, you see."

"So it isn't a statue at all," said Lucy in a low voice.

"No. The whole thing is plain now. He was here on a hot day. He undressed on top of the cliff – where we were sitting. The clothes have rotted away or been taken by birds to line nests with; the armour's still there. Then he dived and——"

"Don't," said Lucy. "What a horrible thing."

"And what a narrow shave *we've* had," said Edmund.

"Narrow indeed," said Reepicheep. "Anyone's finger, anyone's foot, anyone's whisker, or anyone's tail, might have slipped into the water at any moment."

"All the same," said Caspian, "we may as well test it." He stooped down and wrenched up a spray of heather. Then, very cautiously, he knelt beside the pool and dipped it in. It was heather that he dipped; what he drew out was a perfect model of heather made of the purest gold, heavy and soft as lead.

"The King who owned this island," said Caspian slowly, and his face flushed as he spoke, "would soon be the richest of all the Kings of the world. I claim this land for ever as a Narnian possession. It shall be called Goldwater Island. And I bind all of you to secrecy. No one must know of this. Not even Drinian – on pain of death, do you hear?"

"Who are you talking to?" said Edmund. "I'm no subject of yours. If anything it's the other way round. I am one of the four ancient sovereigns of Narnia and you are under allegiance to the High King my brother."

"So it has come to that, King Edmund, has it?" said Caspian, laying his hand on his sword-hilt.

"Oh, stop it, both of you," said Lucy. "That's the worst of doing anything with boys. You're all such swaggering, bullying idiots – oooh!—" Her voice died away into a gasp. And everyone else saw what she had seen.

Across the grey hillside above them – grey, for the heather was not yet in bloom – without noise, and without looking at them, and shining as if he were in bright sunlight though the sun had in fact gone in, passed with slow pace the hugest lion that human eyes have ever seen. In describing the scene Lucy said afterwards, "He was the size of an elephant," though at another time she only said, "The size of a cart-horse." But it was not the size that mattered. Nobody dared to ask what it was. They knew it was Aslan.

And nobody ever saw how or where he went. They looked at one another like people waking from sleep.

"What were we talking about?" said Caspian. "Have I been making rather an ass of myself?"

"Sire," said Reepicheep, "this is a place with a curse on it. Let us get back on board at once. And if I might have the honour of naming this island, I should call it Deathwater."

"That strikes me as a very good name, Reep," said Caspian, "though now that I come to think of it, I don't know why. But the weather seems to be settling and I dare say Drinian would like to be off. What a lot we shall have to tell him."

But in fact they had not much to tell for the memory of the last hour had all become confused.

"Their Majesties all seemed a bit bewitched when they came aboard," said Drinian to Rhince some hours later when the *Dawn Treader* was once more under sail and Deathwater Island already below the horizon. "Something happened to them in that place. The only thing I could get clear was that they think they've found the body of one of these lords we're looking for."

"You don't say so, Captain," answered Rhince. "Well, that's three. Only four more. At this rate we might be home soon after the New Year. And a good thing too. My baccy's running a bit low. Good night, Sir."

Chapter Nine

The Island of the Voices

And now the winds which had so long been from the north-west began to blow from the west itself and every morning when the sun rose out of the sea the curved prow of the *Dawn Treader* stood up right across the middle of the sun. Some thought that the sun looked larger than it looked from Narnia, but others disagreed. And they sailed and sailed before a gentle yet steady breeze and saw neither fish nor gull nor ship nor shore. And stores began to get low again, and it crept into their hearts that perhaps they might have come to a sea which went on for ever. But when the very last day on which they thought they could risk continuing their eastward voyage dawned, it showed, right ahead between them and the sunrise, a low land lying like a cloud.

They made harbour in a wide bay about the middle of the afternoon and landed. It was a very different country from any they had yet seen. For when they had crossed the sandy beach they found all silent and empty as if it were an uninhabited land, but before them there were level lawns in which the grass was as smooth and short as it used to be in the grounds of a great English house where ten gardeners were kept. The trees, of which there were many, all stood well apart from one another, and there were no broken branches and no leaves lying on the ground. Pigeons sometimes cooed but there was no other noise.

Presently they came to a long, straight, sanded path with not a weed growing on it and trees on either hand. Far off at the other end of this avenue they now caught sight of a house – very long and grey and quiet-looking in the afternoon sun.

Almost as soon as they entered this path Lucy noticed that she had a little stone in her shoe. In that unknown place it might have been wiser for her to ask the others to wait while she took it out. But she didn't; she just dropped quietly behind and sat down to take off her shoe. Her lace had got into a knot.

Before she had undone the knot the others were a fair distance ahead. By the time she had got the stone out and was putting the shoe on again she could no longer hear them. But almost at once she heard something else. It was not coming from the direction of the house.

What she heard was a thumping. It sounded as if dozens of strong workmen were hitting the ground as hard as they could with great wooden mallets. And it was very quickly coming nearer. She was already sitting with her back to a tree, and as the tree was not one she could climb, there was really nothing to do but to sit dead still and press herself against the tree and hope she wouldn't be seen.

Thump, thump, thump... and whatever it was must be very close now for she could feel the ground shaking. But she could see nothing. She thought the thing – or things – must be just behind her. But then there came a thump on the path right in front of her. She knew it was on the path not only by the sound but because she saw the sand scatter as if it had been struck a heavy blow. But she could see nothing that had struck it. Then all the thumping noises drew together about twenty feet away from her and suddenly ceased. Then came the voice.

It was really very dreadful because she could still see nobody at all. The whole of that park-like country still looked as quiet and empty as it had looked when they first landed. Nevertheless, only a few feet away from her, a voice spoke. And what it said was:

"Mates, now's our chance."

Instantly a whole chorus of other voices replied, "Hear him. Hear him. Now's our chance, he said. Well done, Chief. You never said a truer word."

"What I say," continued the first voice, "is, get down to the shore between them and their boat, and let every mother's son look to his weapons. Catch 'em when they try to put to sea."

"Eh, that's the way," shouted all the other voices. "You never made a better plan, Chief. Keep it up, Chief. You couldn't have a better plan than that."

"Lively, then, mates, lively," said the first voice. "Off we go."

"Right again, Chief," said the others. "Couldn't have a better order. Just what we were going to say ourselves. Off we go."

Immediately the thumping began again – very loud at first but soon fainter and fainter, till it died out in the direction of the sea.

Lucy knew there was no time to sit puzzling as to what these invisible creatures might be. As soon as the thumping noise had died away she got up and ran along the path after the others as quickly as her legs would carry her. They must at all costs be warned.

While this had been happening the others had reached the house. It was a low building – only two stories high – made of a beautiful mellow stone, many-windowed, and partially covered with ivy. Everything was so still that Eustace said, "I think it's empty," but Caspian silently pointed to the column of smoke which rose from one chimney.

They found a wide gateway open and passed through it into a paved courtyard. And it was here that they had their first indication that there was something odd about this island. In the middle of the courtyard stood a pump, and beneath the pump a bucket. There was nothing odd about that. But the pump handle was moving up and down, though there seemed to be no one moving it.

"There's some magic at work here," said Caspian.

"Machinery!" said Eustace. "I do believe we've come to a civilized country at last."

At that moment Lucy, hot and breathless, rushed into the courtyard behind them. In a low voice she tried to make them understand what she had overheard. And when they had partly understood it even the bravest of them did not look very happy.

"Invisible enemies," muttered Caspian. "And cutting us off from the boat. This is an ugly furrow to plough."

"You've no idea what *sort* of creatures they are, Lu?" asked Edmund.

"How can I, Ed, when I couldn't see them?"

"Did they sound like humans from their footsteps?"

"I didn't hear any noise of feet – only voices and this frightful thudding and thumping – like a mallet."

"I wonder," said Reepicheep, "do they become visible when you drive a sword into them?"

"It looks as if we shall find out," said Caspian. "But let's get out of this gateway. There's one of these gentry at that pump listening to all we say."

They came out and went back on to the path where the trees might possibly make them less conspicuous. "Not that it's any good *really*," said Eustace, "trying to hide from people you can't see. They may be all round us."

"Now, Drinian," said Caspian. "How would it be if we gave up the boat for lost, went down to another part of the bay, and signalled to the *Dawn Treader* to stand in and take us aboard?"

"Not depth enough for her, Sire," said Drinian.

"We could swim," said Lucy.

"Your Majesties all," said Reepicheep, "hear me. It is folly to think of avoiding an invisible enemy by any amount of creeping and skulking. If these creatures mean to bring us to battle, be sure they will succeed. And whatever comes of it I'd sooner meet them face to face than be caught by the tail."

"I really think Reep is in the right this time," said Edmund.

"Surely," said Lucy, "if Rhince and the others on the *Dawn Treader* see us fighting on the shore they'll be able to do *something*."

"But they won't see us fighting if they can't see any enemy," said Eustace miserably. "They'll think we're just swinging our swords in the air for fun."

There was an uncomfortable pause.

"Well," said Caspian at last, "let's get on with it. We must go and face them. Shake hands all round — arrow on the string, Lucy — swords out, everyone else — and now for it. Perhaps they'll parley."

It was strange to see the lawns and the great trees looking so peaceful as they marched back to the beach. And when they arrived there, and saw the boat lying where they had left her, and the smooth sand with no one to be seen on it, more than one doubted whether Lucy had not merely imagined all she had told them. But before they reached the sand, a voice spoke out of the air.

"No further, masters, no further now," it said. "We've got to talk with you first. There's fifty of us and more here with weapons in our fists."

"Hear him, hear him," came the chorus. "That's our chief. You can depend on what he says. He's telling you the truth, he is."

"I do not see these fifty warriors," observed Reepicheep.

"That's right, that's right," said the Chief Voice. "You don't see us. And why not? Because we're invisible."

"Keep it up, Chief, keep it up," said the Other Voices. "You're talking like a book. They couldn't ask for a better answer than that."

"Be quiet, Reep," said Caspian, and then added in a louder voice, "You invisible people, what do you want with us? And what have we done to earn your enmity?"

"We want something that little girl can do for us," said the Chief Voice. (The others explained that this was just what they would have said themselves.)

"Little girl!" said Reepicheep. "The lady is a queen."

"We don't know about queens," said the Chief Voice. ("No more we do, no more we do," chimed in the others.) "But we want something she can do."

"What is it?" said Lucy.

"And if it is anything against her Majesty's honour or safety," added Reepicheep, "you will wonder to see how many we can kill before we die."

"Well," said the Chief Voice. "It's a long story. Suppose we all sit down?"

The proposal was warmly approved by the other voices but the Narnians remained standing.

"Well," said the Chief Voice. "It's like this. This island has been the property of a great magician time out of mind. And we all are – or perhaps in a manner of speaking, I might say, we were – his servants. Well, to cut a long story short, this magician that I was speaking about, he told us to do something we didn't like. And why not? Because we didn't want to. Well, then, this same magician he fell into a great rage; for I ought to tell you he owned the island and he wasn't used to being crossed. He was terribly downright, you know. But let me see, where am I? Oh, yes, this magician then, he goes upstairs (for you must know he kept all his magic things up there and we all lived down below), I say he goes upstairs and puts a spell on us. An uglifying spell. If you saw us now, which in my opinion you may thank your stars you can't, you wouldn't believe what we looked like before we were uglified. You wouldn't, really. So there we all were so ugly we couldn't bear to look at one another. So then what did we do? Well, I'll tell you what we did. We waited till we thought this same magician would be asleep in the afternoon and we creep upstairs and go to his magic book, as bold as brass, to see if we can do anything about this uglification. But we were all of a sweat and a tremble, so I won't deceive you. But, believe me or believe me not, I do assure you that we couldn't find anything in the way of a spell for taking off the ugliness. And what with time getting on and being afraid that the old gentleman might wake up any minute – I was all of a muck sweat, so I won't deceive you – well, to cut a long story short, whether we did right or whether we did wrong, in the end we see a spell for making people invisible. And we thought we'd rather be invisible than go on being as ugly as all that. And why? Because we'd like it better. So my little girl, who's just about your little girl's age, and a sweet child she was before she was uglified, though now – but least said soonest mended – I say, my little girl she says the spell, for it's got to be a little girl or else the magician himself, if you see my meaning, for otherwise it won't work. And why not? Because nothing happens. So my Clipsie says the spell, for I ought to have told you she reads beautifully, and there we all were as invisible as you could wish to see. And I do assure you it was a relief not to see one another's faces. At first, anyway. But the long and the short of it is we're mortal tired of being invisible. And there's another thing. We never reckoned on this magician (the one I was telling you about before) going invisible too. But we haven't ever seen him since. So we don't know if he's dead, or gone away, or whether he's just sitting upstairs being invisible, and perhaps coming down and being invisible there. And, believe me, it's no manner of use listening because he always did go about with his bare feet on, making no more noise than a great big cat. And I'll tell all you gentlemen straight, it's getting more than what our nerves can stand."

Such was the Chief Voice's story, but very much shortened, because I have left out what the other voices said. Actually he never got out more than six or seven words without being interrupted by their agreements and encouragements, which drove the Narnians nearly out of their minds with impatience. When it was over there was a very long silence.

"But," said Lucy at last, "what's all this got to do with us? I don't understand."

"Why, bless me, if I haven't gone and left out the whole point," said the Chief Voice.

"That you have, that you have," roared the Other Voices with great enthusiasm. "No one couldn't have left it out cleaner and better. Keep it up, Chief, keep it up."

"Well, I needn't go over the whole story again," began the Chief Voice.

"No. Certainly not," said Caspian and Edmund.

"Well, then, to put it in a nutshell," said the Chief Voice, "we've been waiting for ever so long for a nice little girl from foreign parts, like it might be you, Missie – that would go upstairs and go to the magic book and find the spell that takes off the invisibleness, and say it. And we all swore that the first strangers as landed on this island (having a nice little girl with them, I mean, for if they hadn't it'd be another matter) we wouldn't let them go away alive unless they'd done the needful for us. And that's why, gentlemen, if your little girl doesn't come up to scratch, it will be our painful duty to cut all your throats. Merely in the way of business, as you might say, and no offence, I hope."

"I don't see all your weapons," said Reepicheep. "Are they invisible too?" The words were scarcely out of his mouth before they heard a whizzing sound and next moment a spear had stuck, quivering, in one of the trees behind them.

"That's a spear, that is," said the Chief Voice.

"That it is, Chief, that it is," said the others. "You couldn't have put it better."

"And it came from my hand," the Chief Voice continued. "They get visible when they leave us."

"But why do you want *me* to do this?" asked Lucy. "Why can't one of your own people? Haven't you got any girls?"

"We dursen't, we dursen't," said all the Voices. "We're not going upstairs again."

"In other words," said Caspian, "you are asking this lady to face some danger which you daren't ask your own sisters and daughters to face!"

"That's right, that's right," said all the Voices cheerfully. "You couldn't have said it better. Eh, you've had some education, you have. Anyone can see that."

"Well, of all the outrageous—" began Edmund, but Lucy interrupted.

"Would I have to go upstairs at night, or would it do in the daylight?"

"Oh, daylight, daylight, to be sure," said the Chief Voice. "Not at night. No one's asking you to do that. Go upstairs in the dark? Ugh."

"All right, then, I'll do it," said Lucy. "No," she said, turning to the others, "don't try to stop me. Can't you see it's no use? There are dozens of them there. We can't fight them. And the other way there *is* a chance."

"But a magician!" said Caspian.

"I know," said Lucy. "But he mayn't be as bad as they make out. Don't you get the idea that these people are not very brave?"

"They're certainly not very clever," said Eustace.

"Look here, Lu," said Edmund. "We really can't let you do a thing like this. Ask Reep, I'm sure he'll say just the same."

"But it's to save my own life as well as yours," said Lucy. "I don't want to be cut to bits with invisible swords any more than anyone else."

"Her Majesty is in the right," said Reepicheep. "If we had any assurance of saving *her* by battle, our duty would be very plain. It appears to me that we have none. And the service they ask of her is in no way contrary to her Majesty's honour, but a noble and heroical act. If the Queen's heart moves her to risk the magician, I will not speak against it."

As no one had ever known Reepicheep to be afraid of anything, he could say this without feeling at all awkward. But the boys, who had all been afraid quite often, grew very red. None the less, it was such obvious sense that they had to give in. Loud cheers broke from the invisible people when their decision was announced, and the Chief Voice (warmly supported by all the others) invited the Narnians to come to supper and spend the night. Eustace didn't want to accept, but Lucy said, "I'm sure they're not treacherous. They're not like that at all," and the others agreed. And so, accompanied by an enormous noise of thumpings (which became louder when they reached the flagged and echoing courtyard) they all went back to the house.

CHAPTER TEN

THE MAGICIAN'S BOOK

The invisible people feasted their guests royally. It was very funny to see the plates and dishes coming to the table and not to see anyone carrying them. It would have been funny even if they had moved along level with the floor, as you would expect things to do in invisible hands. But they didn't. They progressed up the long dining-hall in a series of bounds or jumps. At the highest point of each jump a dish would be about fifteen feet up in the air; then it would come down and stop quite suddenly about three feet from the floor. When the dish contained anything like soup or stew the result was rather disastrous.

"I'm beginning to feel very inquisitive about these people," whispered Eustace to Edmund. "Do you think they're human at all? More like huge grasshoppers or giant frogs, I should say."

"It does look like it," said Edmund. "But don't put the idea of the grasshoppers into Lucy's head. She's not too keen on insects; especially big ones."

The meal would have been pleasanter if it had not been so exceedingly messy, and also if the conversation had not consisted entirely of agreements. The invisible people agreed about everything. Indeed most of their remarks were the sort it would not be easy to disagree with: "What I always say is, when a chap's hungry, he likes some victuals," or, "Getting dark now; always does at night," or even, "Ah, you've come over the water. Powerful wet stuff, ain't it?" And Lucy could not help looking at the dark yawning entrance to the foot of the staircase — she could see it from where she sat — and wondering what she would find when she went up those stairs the next morning. But it was a good meal otherwise, with mushroom soup and boiled chickens and hot boiled ham and gooseberries, redcurrants, curds, cream, milk, and mead. The others liked the mead but Eustace was sorry afterwards that he had drunk any.

When Lucy woke up the next morning it was like waking up on the day of an examination or a day when you are going to the dentist. It was a lovely morning with bees buzzing in and out of her open window and the lawn outside looking very like somewhere in England. She got up and dressed and tried to talk and eat ordinarily at breakfast. Then, after being instructed by the Chief Voice about what she was to do upstairs, she bid goodbye to the others, said nothing, walked to the bottom of the stairs, and began going up them without once looking back.

It was quite light, that was one good thing. There was, indeed, a window straight ahead of her at the top of the first flight. As long as she was on that flight she could hear the *tick-tock-tick-tock* of a grandfather clock in the hall below. Then she came to the landing and had to turn to her left up the next flight; after that she couldn't hear the clock any more.

Now she had come to the top of the stairs. Lucy looked and saw a long, wide passage with a large window at the far end. Apparently the passage ran the whole length of the house. It was carved and panelled and carpeted and very many doors opened off it on each side. She stood still and couldn't hear the squeak of a mouse, or the buzzing of a fly, or the swaying of a curtain, or anything – except the beating of her own heart.

"The last doorway on the left," she said to herself. It did seem a bit hard that it should be the last. To reach it she would have to walk past room after room. And in any room there might be the magician – asleep, or awake, or invisible, or even dead. But it wouldn't do to think about that. She set out on her journey. The carpet was so thick that her feet made no noise.

"There's nothing whatever to be afraid of yet," Lucy told herself. And certainly it was a quiet, sunlit passage; perhaps a bit too quiet. It would have been nicer if there had not been strange signs painted in scarlet on the doors – twisty, complicated things which obviously had a meaning and it mightn't be a very nice meaning either. It would have been nicer still if there weren't those masks hanging on the wall. Not that they were exactly ugly – or not so very ugly – but the empty eye-holes did look queer, and if you let yourself you would soon start imagining that the masks were doing things as soon as your back was turned to them.

After about the sixth door she got her first real fright. For one second she felt almost certain that a wicked little bearded face had popped out of the wall and made a grimace at her. She forced herself to stop and look at it. And it was not a face at all. It was a little mirror just the size and shape of her own face, with hair on the top of it and a beard hanging down from it, so that when you looked in the mirror your own face fitted into the hair and beard and it looked as if they belonged to you. "I just caught my own reflection with the tail of my eye as I went past," said Lucy to herself. "That was all it was. It's quite harmless." But she didn't like the look of her own face with that hair and beard, and went on. (I don't know what the Bearded Glass was for because I am not a magician.)

Before she reached the last door on the left, Lucy was beginning to wonder whether the corridor had grown longer since she began her journey and whether this was part of the magic of the house. But she got to it at last. And the door was open.

It was a large room with three big windows, and it was lined from floor to ceiling with books; more books than Lucy had ever seen before, tiny little books, fat and dumpy books, and books bigger than any church Bible you have ever seen, all bound in leather and smelling old and learned and magical. But she knew from her instructions that she need not bother about any of these. For *the* Book, the Magic Book, was lying on a reading-desk in the very middle of the room. She saw she would have to read it standing (and anyway there were no chairs) and also that she would have to stand with her back to the door while she read it. So at once she turned to shut the door.

It wouldn't shut.

Some people may disagree with Lucy about this, but I think she was quite right. She said she wouldn't have minded if she could have shut the door, but that it was unpleasant to have to stand in a place like that with an open doorway right behind your back. I should have felt just the same. But there was nothing else to be done.

One thing that worried her a good deal was the size of the Book. The Chief Voice had not been able to give her any idea whereabouts in the Book the spell for making things visible came. He even seemed rather surprised at her asking. He expected her to begin at the beginning and go on till she came to it; obviously he had never thought that there was any other way of finding a place in a book. "But it might take me days and weeks!" said Lucy, looking at the huge volume. "And I feel already as if I've been in this place for hours."

She went up to the desk and laid her hand on the book; her fingers tingled when she touched it as if it were full of electricity. She tried to open it but couldn't at first; this, however, was only because it was fastened by two leaden clasps, and when she had undone these it opened easily enough. And what a book it was!

It was written, not printed; written in a clear, even hand, with thick downstrokes and thin upstrokes, very large, easier than print, and so beautiful that Lucy stared at it for a whole minute and forgot about reading it. The paper was crisp and smooth and a nice smell came from it; and in the margins, and round the big coloured capital letters at the beginning of each spell, there were pictures.

There was no title page or title; the spells began straight away, and at first there was nothing very important in them. They were cures for warts (by washing your hands in moonlight in a silver basin) and toothache and cramp, and a spell for taking a swarm of bees. The picture of the man with toothache was so lifelike that it would have set your own teeth aching if you looked at it too long, and the golden bees which were dotted all round the fourth spell looked for a moment as if they were really flying.

Lucy could hardly tear herself away from that first page, but when she turned over, the next was just as interesting. "But I must get on," she told herself. And on she went for about thirty pages which, if she could have remembered them, would have taught her how to find buried treasure, how to remember things forgotten, how to forget things you wanted to forget, how to tell whether anyone was speaking the truth, how to call up (or prevent) wind, fog, snow, sleet or rain, how to produce enchanted sleeps and how to give a man an ass's head (as they did to poor Bottom). And the longer she read the more wonderful and more real the pictures became.

Then she came to a page which was such a blaze of pictures that one hardly noticed the writing. Hardly — but she *did* notice the first words. They were, *An infallible spell to make beautiful her that uttereth it beyond the lot of mortals.* Lucy peered at the pictures with her face close to the page, and though they had seemed crowded and muddlesome before, she found she could now see them quite clearly. The first was a picture of a girl standing at a reading-desk reading in a huge book. And the girl was dressed exactly like Lucy. In the next picture Lucy (for the girl in the picture was Lucy herself) was standing up with her mouth open and a rather terrible expression on her face, chanting or reciting something. In the third picture the beauty beyond the lot of mortals had come to her. It was strange, considering how small the pictures had looked at first, that the Lucy in the picture now seemed quite as big as the real Lucy; and they looked into each other's eyes and the real Lucy looked away after a few minutes because she was dazzled by the beauty of the other Lucy; though she could still see a sort of likeness to herself in that beautiful face. And now the pictures came crowding on her thick and fast. She saw herself throned on high at a great tournament in Calormen and all the Kings of the world fought because of her beauty. After that it turned from tournaments to real wars, and all Narnia and Archenland, Telmar and Calormen, Galma and Terebinthia, were laid waste with the fury of the kings and dukes and great lords who fought for her favour. Then it changed and Lucy, still beautiful beyond the lot of mortals, was back in England. And Susan (who had always been the beauty of the family) came home from America. The Susan in the picture looked exactly like the real Susan only plainer and with a nasty expression. And Susan was jealous of the dazzling beauty of Lucy, but that didn't matter a bit because no one cared anything about Susan now.

"I *will* say the spell," said Lucy. "I don't care. I will." She said *I don't care* because she had a strong feeling that she mustn't.

But when she looked back at the opening words of the spell, there in the middle of the writing, where she felt quite sure there had been no picture before, she found the great face of a lion, of The Lion, Aslan himself, staring into hers. It was painted such a bright gold that it seemed to be coming towards her out of the page; and indeed she never was quite sure afterwards that it hadn't really moved a little. At any rate she knew the expression on his face quite well. He was growling and you could see most of his teeth. She became horribly afraid and turned over the page at once.

A little later she came to a spell which would let you know what your friends thought about you. Now Lucy had wanted very badly to try the other spell, the one that made you beautiful beyond the lot of mortals. So she felt that to make up for not having said it, she really would say this one. And all in a hurry, for fear her mind would change, she said the words (nothing will induce me to tell you what they were). Then she waited for something to happen.

As nothing happened she began looking at the pictures. And all at once she saw the very last thing she expected – a picture of a third-class carriage in a train, with two schoolgirls sitting in it. She knew them at once. They were Marjorie Preston and Anne Featherstone. Only now it was much more than a picture. It was alive. She could see the telegraph posts flicking past outside the window. Then gradually (like when the radio is "coming on") she could hear what they were saying.

"Shall I see anything of you this term?" said Anne. "Or are you still going to be all taken up with Lucy Pevensie?"

"Don't know what you mean by *taken up*," said Marjorie.

"Oh yes, you do," said Anne. "You were crazy about her last term."

"No, I wasn't," said Marjorie. "I've got more sense than that. Not a bad little kid in her way. But I was getting pretty tired of her before the end of term."

"Well, you jolly well won't have the chance any other term!" shouted Lucy. "Two-faced little beast." But the sound of her own voice at once reminded her that she was talking to a picture and that the real Marjorie was far away in another world.

"Well," said Lucy to herself, "I did think better of her than that. And I did all sorts of things for her last term, and I stuck to her when not many other girls would. And she knows it too. And to Anne Featherstone of all people! I wonder, are all my friends the same? There are lots of other pictures. No. I won't look at any more. I won't, I won't" — and with a great effort she turned over the page, but not before a large, angry tear had splashed on it.

On the next page she came to a spell "for the refreshment of the spirit". The pictures were fewer here but very beautiful. And what Lucy found herself reading was more like a story than a spell. It went on for three pages and before she had read to the bottom of the page she had forgotten that she was reading at all. She was living in the story as if it were real, and all the pictures were real too. When she had got to the third page and come to the end, she said, "That is the loveliest story I've ever read or ever shall read in my whole life. Oh, I wish I could have gone on reading it for ten years. At least I'll read it over again."

But here part of the magic of the Book came into play. You couldn't turn back. The right-hand pages, the ones ahead, could be turned; the left-hand pages could not.

"Oh, what a shame!" said Lucy. "I did so want to read it again. Well, at least I must remember it. Let's see… it was about… about… oh dear, it's all fading away again. And even this last page is going blank. This is a very strange book. How can I have forgotten? It was about a cup and a sword and a tree and a green hill, I know that much. But I can't remember, and what *shall* I do?"

And she never could remember; and ever since that day, what Lucy means by a good story is a story which reminds her of the forgotten story in the Magician's Book.

She turned on and found to her surprise a page with no pictures at all, but the first words were *A spell to make hidden things visible*. She read it through to make sure of all the hard words and then said it out loud. And she knew at once that it was working because as she spoke, the colours came into the capital letters at the top of the page and the pictures began appearing in the margins. It was like when you hold to the fire something written in Invisible Ink and the writing gradually shows up; only instead of the dingy colour of lemon juice (which is the easiest Invisible Ink) this was all gold and blue and scarlet. They were odd pictures and contained many figures that Lucy did not much like the look of. And then she thought, "I suppose I've made everything visible, and not only the Thumpers. There might be lots of other invisible things hanging about a place like this. I'm not sure that I want to see them all."

At that moment she heard soft, heavy footfalls coming along the corridor behind her; and of course she remembered what she had been told about the Magician walking in his bare feet and making no more noise than a cat. It is always better to turn round than to have anything creeping up behind your back. Lucy did so.

Then her face lit up till, for a moment (but of course she didn't know it), she looked almost as beautiful as that other Lucy in the picture, and she ran forward with a little cry of delight and with her arms stretched out. For what stood in the doorway was Aslan himself, the Lion, the highest of all High Kings. And he was solid and real and warm and he let her kiss him and bury herself in his shining mane. And from the low, earthquake-like sound that came from inside him, Lucy even dared to think that he was purring.

"Oh, Aslan," said she, "it was kind of you to come."

"I have been here all the time," said he, "but you have just made me visible."

"Aslan!" said Lucy almost a little reproachfully. "Don't make fun of me. As if anything *I* could do would make *you* visible!"

"It did," said Aslan. "Do you think I wouldn't obey my own rules?"

After a little pause he spoke again.

"Child," he said, "I think you have been eavesdropping."

"Eavesdropping?"

"You listened to what your two schoolfellows were saying about you."

"Oh, that? I never thought that was eavesdropping, Aslan. Wasn't it magic?"

"Spying on people by magic is the same as spying on them in any other way. And you have misjudged your friend. She is weak, but she loves you. She was afraid of the older girl and said what she does not mean."

"I don't think I'll ever be able to forget what I heard her say."

"No, you won't."

"Oh dear," said Lucy. "Have I spoiled everything? Do you mean we would have gone on being friends if it hadn't been for this — and been really great friends — all our lives perhaps — and now we never shall?"

"Child," said Aslan, "did I not explain to you once before that no one is ever told what *would have happened*?"

"Yes, Aslan, you did," said Lucy. "I'm sorry. But please——"

"Speak on, dear heart."

"Shall I ever be able to read that story again; the one I couldn't remember? Will you tell it to me, Aslan? Oh do, do, do."

"Indeed, yes, I will tell it to you for years and years. But now, come. We must meet the master of this house."

CHAPTER ELEVEN

THE DUFFLEPUDS MADE HAPPY

Lucy followed the great Lion out into the passage and at once she saw coming towards them an old man, barefoot, dressed in a red robe. His white hair was crowned with a chaplet of oak leaves, his beard fell to his girdle, and he supported himself with a curiously carved staff. When he saw Aslan he bowed low and said,

"Welcome, Sir, to the least of your houses."

"Do you grow weary, Coriakin, of ruling such foolish subjects as I have given you here?"

"No," said the Magician, "they are very stupid but there is no real harm in them. I begin to grow rather fond of the creatures. Sometimes, perhaps, I am a little impatient, waiting for the day when they can be governed by wisdom instead of this rough magic."

"All in good time, Coriakin," said Aslan.

"Yes, all in very good time, Sir," was the answer. "Do you intend to show yourself to them?"

"Nay," said the Lion, with a little half-growl that meant (Lucy thought) the same as a laugh. "I should frighten them out of their senses. Many stars will grow old and come to take their rest in islands before your people are ripe for that. And today before sunset I must visit Trumpkin the Dwarf where he sits in the castle of Cair Paravel counting the days till his master Caspian comes home. I will tell him all your story, Lucy. Do not look so sad. We shall meet soon again."

"Please, Aslan," said Lucy, "what do you call *soon*?"

"I call all times soon," said Aslan; and instantly he was vanished away and Lucy was alone with the Magician.

"Gone!" said he. "And you and I quite crestfallen. It's always like that, you can't keep him; it's not as if he were a *tame* lion. And how did you enjoy my book?"

"Parts of it very much indeed," said Lucy. "Did you know I was there all the time?"

"Well, of course I knew when I let the Duffers make themselves invisible that you would be coming along presently to take the spell off. I wasn't quite sure of the exact day. And I wasn't especially on the watch this morning. You see they had made me invisible too and being invisible always makes me so sleepy. Heigh-ho – there, I'm yawning again. Are you hungry?"

"Well, perhaps I am a little," said Lucy. "I've no idea what the time is."

"Come," said the Magician. "All times may be soon to Aslan, but in my home all hungry times are one o'clock."

He led her a little way down the passage and opened a door. Passing in, Lucy found herself in a pleasant room full of sunlight and flowers. The table was bare when they entered, but it was of course a magic table, and at a word from the old man the tablecloth, silver, plates, glasses and food appeared.

"I hope that is what you would like," said he. "I have tried to give you food more like the food of your own land than perhaps you have had lately."

"It's lovely," said Lucy, and so it was; an omelette, piping hot, cold lamb and green peas, a strawberry ice, lemon squash to drink with the meal and a cup of chocolate to follow. But the Magician himself drank only wine and ate only bread. There was nothing alarming about him, and Lucy and he were soon chatting away like old friends.

"When will the spell work?" asked Lucy. "Will the Duffers be visible again at once?"

"Oh yes, they're visible now. But they're probably all asleep still; they always take a rest in the middle of the day."

"And now that they're visible, are you going to let them off being ugly? Will you make them as they were before?"

"Well, that's rather a delicate question," said the Magician. "You see, it's only *they* who think they were so nice to look at before. They say they've been uglified, but that isn't what I called it. Many people might say the change was for the better."

"Are they awfully conceited?"

"They are. Or at least the Chief Duffer is, and he's taught all the rest to be. They always believe every word he says."

"We'd noticed that," said Lucy.

"Yes – we'd get on better without him, in a way. Of course I could turn him into something else, or even put a spell on him which would make them not believe a word he said. But I don't like to do that. It's better for them to admire him than to admire nobody."

"Don't they admire *you*?" asked Lucy.

"Oh, not *me*," said the Magician. "They wouldn't admire *me*."

"What was it you uglified them for – I mean, what *they* call uglified?"

"Well, they wouldn't do what they were told. Their work is to mind the garden and raise food – not for me, as they imagine, but for themselves. They wouldn't do it at all if I didn't make them. And of course, for a garden you want water. There is a beautiful spring about half a mile away up the hill. And from that spring there flows a stream which comes right past the garden. All I asked them to do was to take their water from the stream instead of trudging up to the spring with their buckets two or three times a day and tiring themselves out besides spilling half of it on the way back. But they wouldn't see it. In the end they refused point blank."

"Are they as stupid as all that?" asked Lucy.

The Magician sighed. "You wouldn't believe the troubles I've had with them. A few months ago they were all for washing up the plates and knives before dinner: they said it saved time afterwards. I've caught them planting boiled potatoes to save cooking them when they were dug up. One day the cat got into the dairy and twenty of them were at work moving all the milk out; no one thought of moving the cat. But I see you've finished. Let's go and look at the Duffers now they can be looked at."

They went into another room which was full of polished instruments hard to understand – such as Astrolabes, Orreries, Chronoscopes, Poesimeters, Choriambuses and Theodolinds – and here, when they had come to the window, the Magician said, "There. There are your Duffers."

"I don't see anybody," said Lucy. "And what are those mushroom things?"

The things she pointed at were dotted all over the level grass. They were certainly very like mushrooms, but far too big – the stalks about three feet high and the umbrellas about the same length from edge to edge. When she looked carefully she noticed too that the stalks joined the umbrellas not in the middle but at one side which gave an unbalanced look to them. And there was something – a sort of little bundle – lying on the grass at the foot of each stalk. In fact the longer she gazed at them the less like mushrooms they appeared. The umbrella part was not really round as she had thought at first. It was longer than it was broad, and it widened at one end. There were a great many of them, fifty or more.

The clock struck three.

Instantly a most extraordinary thing happened. Each of the "mushrooms" suddenly turned upside-down. The little bundles which had lain at the bottom of the stalks were heads and bodies. The stalks themselves were legs. But not two legs to each body. Each body had a single thick leg right under it (not to one side like the leg of a one-legged man) and at the end of it, a single enormous foot – a broad-toed foot with the toes curling up a little so that it looked rather like a small canoe. She saw in a moment why they had looked like mushrooms. They had been lying flat on their backs each with its single leg straight up in the air and its enormous foot spread out above it. She learned afterwards that this was their ordinary way of resting; for the foot kept off both rain and sun, and for a Monopod to lie under its own foot is almost as good as being in a tent.

"Oh, the funnies, the funnies," cried Lucy, bursting into laughter. "Did *you* make them like that?"

"Yes, yes. I made the Duffers into Monopods," said the Magician. He too was laughing till the tears ran down his cheeks. "But watch," he added.

It was worth watching. Of course these little one-footed men couldn't walk or run as we do. They got about by jumping, like fleas or frogs. And what jumps they made! – as if each big foot were a mass of springs. And with what a bounce they came down; that was what made the thumping noise which had so puzzled Lucy yesterday. For now they were jumping in all directions and calling out to one another, "Hey, lads! We're visible again."

"Visible we are," said one in a tasselled red cap who was obviously the Chief Monopod. "And what I say is, when chaps are visible, why, they can see one another."

"Ah, there it is, there it is, Chief," cried all the others. "There's the point. No one's got a clearer head than you. You couldn't have made it plainer."

"She caught the old man napping, that little girl did," said the Chief Monopod. "We've beaten him this time."

"Just what we were going to say ourselves," chimed the chorus. "You're going stronger than ever today, Chief. Keep it up, keep it up."

"But do they dare to talk about you like that?" said Lucy. "They seemed to be so afraid of you yesterday. Don't they know you might be listening?"

"That's one of the funny things about the Duffers," said the Magician. "One minute they talk as if I ran everything and overheard everything and was extremely dangerous. The next moment they think they can take me in by tricks that a baby would see through – bless them!"

"Will they have to be turned back into their proper shapes?" asked Lucy. "Oh, I do hope it wouldn't be unkind to leave them as they are. Do they really mind very much? They seem pretty happy. I say – look at that jump. What were they like before?"

"Common little dwarfs," said he. "Nothing like so nice as the sort you have in Narnia."

"It *would* be a pity to change them back," said Lucy. "They're so funny: and they're rather nice. Do you think it would make any difference if I told them that?"

"I'm sure it would – if you could get it into their heads."

"Will you come with me and try?"

"No, no. You'll get on far better without me."

"Thanks awfully for the lunch," said Lucy and turned quickly away. She ran down the stairs which she had come up so nervously that morning and cannoned into Edmund at the bottom. All the others were there with him waiting, and Lucy's conscience smote her when she saw their anxious faces and realized how long she had forgotten them.

"It's all right," she shouted. "Everything's all right. The Magician's a brick – and I've seen *him* – Aslan."

After that she went from them like the wind and out into the garden. Here the earth was shaking with the jumps, and the air ringing with the shouts of the Monopods. Both were redoubled when they caught sight of her.

"Here she comes, here she comes," they cried. "Three cheers for the little girl. Ah! She put it across the old gentleman properly, she did."

"And we're extremely regrettable," said the Chief Monopod, "that we can't give you the pleasure of seeing us as we were before we were uglified, for you wouldn't believe the difference, and that's the truth, for there's no denying we're mortal ugly now, so we won't deceive you."

"Eh, that we are, Chief, that we are," echoed the others, bouncing like so many toy balloons. "You've said it, you've said it."

"But I don't think you are at all," said Lucy, shouting to make herself heard. "I think you look very nice."

"Hear her, hear her," said the Monopods. "True for you, Missie. Very nice we look. You couldn't find a handsomer lot." They said this without any surprise and did not seem to notice that they had changed their minds.

"She's a-saying," remarked the Chief Monopod, "as how we looked very nice before we were uglified."

"True for you, Chief, true for you," chanted the others. "That's what she says. We heard her ourselves."

"I did *not*," bawled Lucy. "I said you're very nice *now*."

"So she did, so she did," said the Chief Monopod, "said we were very nice then."

"Hear 'em both, hear 'em both," said the Monopods. "There's a pair for you. Always right. They couldn't have put it better."

"But we're saying just the opposite," said Lucy, stamping her foot with impatience.

"So you are, to be sure, so you are," said the Monopods. "Nothing like

503

an opposite. Keep it up, both of you."

"You're enough to drive anyone mad," said Lucy, and gave it up. But the Monopods seemed perfectly contented, and she decided that on the whole the conversation had been a success.

And before everyone went to bed that evening something else happened which made them even more satisfied with their one-legged condition. Caspian and all the Narnians went back as soon as possible to the shore to give their news to Rhince and the others on board the *Dawn Treader*, who were by now very anxious. And, of course, the Monopods went with them, bouncing like footballs and agreeing with one another in loud voices till Eustace said, "I wish the Magician would make them inaudible instead of invisible." (He was soon sorry he had spoken because then he had to explain that an inaudible thing is something you can't hear, and though he took a lot of trouble he never felt sure that the Monopods had really understood, and what especially annoyed him was that they said in the end, "Eh, he can't put things the way our Chief does. But you'll learn, young man. Hark to *him*. He'll show you how to say things. There's a speaker for you!") When they reached the bay, Reepicheep had a brilliant idea. He had his little coracle lowered and paddled himself about in it till the Monopods were thoroughly interested. He then stood up in it and said, "Worthy and intelligent Monopods, you do not need boats. Each of you has a foot that will do instead. Just jump as lightly as you can on the water and see what happens."

The Chief Monopod hung back and warned the others that they'd find the water powerful wet, but one or two of the younger ones tried it almost at once; and then a few others followed their example, and at last the whole lot did the same. It worked perfectly. The huge single foot of a Monopod acted as a natural raft or boat, and when Reepicheep had taught them how to cut rude paddles for themselves, they all paddled about the bay and round the *Dawn Treader*, looking for all the world like a fleet of little canoes with a fat dwarf standing up in the extreme stern of each. And they had races, and bottles of wine were lowered down to them from the ship as prizes, and the sailors stood leaning over the ship's sides and laughed till their own sides ached.

The Duffers were also very pleased with their new name of Monopods, which seemed to them a magnificent name though they never got it right. "That's what we are," they bellowed, "Moneypuds, Pomonods, Poddymons. Just what it was on the tips of our tongues to call ourselves." But they soon got it mixed up with their old name of Duffers and finally settled down to calling themselves the Dufflepuds; and that is what they will probably be called for centuries.

That evening all the Narnians dined upstairs with the Magician, and

Lucy noticed how different the whole top floor looked now that she was no longer afraid of it. The mysterious signs on the doors were still mysterious but now looked as if they had kind and cheerful meanings, and even the bearded mirror now seemed funny rather than frightening. At dinner everyone had by magic what everyone liked best to eat and drink, and after dinner the Magician did a very useful and beautiful piece of magic. He laid two blank sheets of parchment on the table and asked Drinian to give him an exact account of their voyage up to date: and as Drinian spoke, everything he described came out on the parchment in fine clear lines till at last each sheet was a splendid map of the Eastern Ocean, showing Galma, Terebinthia, the Seven Isles, the Lone Islands, Dragon Island, Burnt Island, Deathwater, and the land of the Duffers itself, all exactly the right sizes and in the right positions. They were the first maps ever made of those seas and better than any that have been made since without magic. For on these, though the towns and mountains looked at first just as they would on an ordinary map, when the Magician lent them a magnifying glass you saw that they were perfect little pictures of the real things, so that you could see the very castle and slave market and streets in Narrowhaven, all very clear though very distant, like things seen through the wrong end of a telescope. The only drawback was that the coastline of most of the islands was incomplete, for the map showed only what Drinian had seen with his own eyes. When they were finished the Magician kept one himself and presented the other to Caspian: it still hangs in his Chamber of Instruments at Cair Paravel. But the Magician could tell them nothing about seas or lands further east. He did, however, tell them that about seven years before a Narnian ship had put in at his waters and that she had on board the Lords Revilian, Argoz, Mavramorn and Rhoop: so they judged that the golden man they had seen lying in Deathwater must be the Lord Restimar.

Next day, the Magician magically mended the stern of the *Dawn Treader* where it had been damaged by the sea serpent and loaded her with useful gifts. There was a most friendly parting, and when she sailed, two hours after noon, all the Dufflepuds paddled out with her to the harbour mouth, and cheered until she was out of sound of their cheering.

Chapter Twelve

The Dark Island

After this adventure they sailed on south and a little east for twelve days with a gentle wind, the skies being mostly clear and the air warm, and saw no bird or fish, except that once there were whales spouting a long way to starboard. Lucy and Reepicheep played a good deal of chess at this time. Then on the thirteenth day, Edmund, from the fighting top, sighted what looked like a great dark mountain rising out of the sea on their port bow.

They altered course and made for this land, mostly by oar, for the wind would not serve them to sail north-east. When evening fell they were still a long way from it and rowed all night. The next morning the weather was fair but a flat calm prevailed. The dark mass lay ahead, much nearer and larger, but still very dim, so that some thought it was still a long way off and others thought they were running into a mist.

About nine that morning, very suddenly, it was so close that they could see that it was not land at all, nor even, in an ordinary sense, a mist. It was a Darkness. It is rather hard to describe, but you will see what it was like if you imagine yourself looking into the mouth of a railway tunnel — a tunnel either so long or so twisty that you cannot see the light at the far end. And you know what it would be like. For a few feet you would see the rails and sleepers and gravel in broad daylight; then there would come a place where they were in twilight; and then, pretty suddenly, but of course without a sharp dividing line, they would vanish altogether into smooth, solid blackness. It was just so here. For a few feet in front of their bows they could see the swell of the bright greenish-blue water. Beyond that, they could see the water looking pale and grey as it would look late in the evening. But beyond that again, utter blackness as if they had come to the edge of moonless and starless night.

Caspian shouted to the boatswain to keep her back, and all except the rowers rushed forward and gazed from the bows. But there was nothing to be seen by gazing. Behind them was the sea and the sun, before them the darkness.

"Do we go into this?" asked Caspian at length.

"Not by my advice," said Drinian.

"The Captain's right," said several sailors.

"I almost think he is," said Edmund.

Lucy and Eustace didn't speak but they felt very glad inside at the turn things seemed to be taking. But all at once the clear voice of Reepicheep broke in upon the silence.

"And why not?" he said. "Will someone explain to me why not?"

No one was anxious to explain, so Reepicheep continued:

"If I were addressing peasants or slaves," he said, "I might suppose that this suggestion proceeded from cowardice. But I hope it will never be told in Narnia that a company of noble and royal persons in the flower of their age turned tail because they were afraid of the dark."

"But what manner of use would it be ploughing through that blackness?" asked Drinian.

"Use?" replied Reepicheep. "Use, Captain? If by use you mean filling our bellies or our purses, I confess it will be no use at all. So far as I know we did not set sail to look for things useful but to seek honour and adventure. And here is as great an adventure as ever I heard of, and here, if we turn back, no little impeachment of all our honours."

Several of the sailors said things under their breath that sounded like, "Honour be blowed", but Caspian said:

"Oh, *bother* you, Reepicheep. I almost wish we'd left you at home. All right! If you put it that way, I suppose we shall have to go on. Unless Lucy would rather not?"

Lucy felt that she would very much rather not, but what she said out loud was, "I'm game."

"Your Majesty will at least order lights?" said Drinian.

"By all means," said Caspian. "See to it, Captain."

So the three lanterns, at the stern, and the prow and the masthead, were all lit, and Drinian ordered two torches amidships. Pale and feeble they looked in the sunshine. Then all the men except some who were left below at the oars were ordered on deck and fully armed and posted in their battle stations with swords drawn. Lucy and two archers were posted on the fighting top with bows bent and arrows on the string. Rynelf was in the bows with his line ready to take sounding. Reepicheep, Edmund, Eustace and Caspian, glittering in mail, were with him. Drinian took the tiller.

"And now, in Aslan's name, forward!" cried Caspian. "A slow, steady stroke. And let every man be silent and keep his ears open for orders."

With a creak and a groan the *Dawn Treader* started to creep forward as the men began to row. Lucy, up in the fighting top, had a wonderful view of the exact moment at which they entered the darkness. The bows had already disappeared before the sunlight had left the stern. She saw it go. At one minute the gilded stern, the blue sea, and the sky, were all in broad daylight: next minute the sea and sky had vanished, the stern lantern – which had been hardly noticeable before – was the only thing to show where the ship ended. In front of the lantern she could see the black shape of Drinian crouching at the tiller. Down below her the two torches made visible two small patches of deck, and gleamed on swords and helmets, and forward there was another island of light on the forecastle. Apart from that, the fighting top, lit by the masthead light which was only just above her, seemed to be a little lighted world of its own floating in lonely darkness. And the lights themselves, as always happens with lights when you have to have them at the wrong time of day, looked lurid and unnatural. She also noticed that she was very cold.

How long this voyage into the darkness lasted, nobody knew. Except for the creak of the rowlocks and the splash of the oars there was nothing to show that they were moving at all. Edmund, peering from the bows, could see nothing except the reflection of the lantern in the water before him. It looked a greasy sort of reflection, and the ripple made by their advancing prow appeared to be heavy, small, and lifeless. As time went on everyone except the rowers began to shiver with cold.

Suddenly, from somewhere – no one's sense of direction was very clear by now – there came a cry, either of some inhuman voice or else a voice of one in such extremity of terror that he had almost lost his humanity.

Caspian was still trying to speak – his mouth was too dry – when the shrill voice of Reepicheep, which sounded louder than usual in that silence, was heard.

"Who calls?" it piped. "If you are a foe we do not fear you, and if you are a friend your enemies shall be taught the fear of us."

"Mercy!" cried the voice. "Mercy! Even if you are only one more dream, have mercy. Take me on board. Take me, even if you strike me dead. But in the name of all mercies do not fade away and leave me in this horrible land."

"Where are you?" shouted Caspian. "Come aboard and welcome."

There came another cry, whether of joy or terror, and then they knew that someone was swimming towards them.

"Stand by to heave him up, men," said Caspian.

"Aye, aye, your Majesty," said the sailors. Several crowded to the port bulwark with ropes and one, leaning far out over the side, held the torch. A wild, white face appeared in the blackness of the water, and then, after some scrambling and pulling, a dozen friendly hands had heaved the stranger on board.

Edmund thought he had never seen a wilder-looking man. Though he did not otherwise look very old, his hair was an untidy mop of white, his face was thin and drawn and, for clothing, only a few wet rags hung about him. But what one mainly noticed were his eyes, which were so widely opened that he seemed to have no eyelids at all, and stared as if in an agony of pure fear. The moment his feet reached the deck he said:

"Fly! Fly! About with your ship and fly! Row, row, row for your lives away from this accursed shore."

"Compose yourself," said Reepicheep, "and tell us what the danger is. We are not used to flying."

The stranger started horribly at the voice of the Mouse, which he had not noticed before.

"Nevertheless you will fly from here," he gasped. "This is the Island where Dreams come true."

"That's the island I've been looking for this long time," said one of the sailors. "I reckoned I'd find I was married to Nancy if we landed here."

"And I'd find Tom alive again," said another.

"Fools!" said the man, stamping his foot with rage. "That is the sort of talk that brought me here, and I'd better have been drowned or never born. Do you hear what I say? This is where dreams – dreams, do you understand – come to life, come real. Not daydreams: dreams."

There was about half a minute's silence and then, with a great clatter of armour, the whole crew were tumbling down the main hatch as quick as they could and flinging themselves on the oars to row as they had never rowed before; and Drinian was swinging round the tiller, and the boatswain was giving out the quickest stroke that had ever been heard at sea. For it had taken everyone just that half-minute to remember certain dreams they had had – dreams that make you afraid of going to sleep again – and to realize what it would mean to land on a country where dreams come true.

Only Reepicheep remained unmoved.

"Your Majesty, your Majesty," he said, "are you going to tolerate this mutiny, this poltroonery? This is a panic, this is a rout."

"Row, row," bellowed Caspian. "Pull for all our lives. Is her head right, Drinian? You can say what you like, Reepicheep. There are some things no man can face."

"It is, then, my good fortune not to be a man," replied Reepicheep with a very stiff bow.

Lucy from up aloft had heard it all. In an instant that one of her own dreams which she had tried hardest to forget came back to her as vividly as if she had only just woken from it. So *that* was what was behind them, on the island, in the darkness! For a second she wanted to go down to the deck and be with Edmund and Caspian. But what was the use? If dreams began coming true, Edmund and Caspian themselves might turn into something horrible just as she reached them. She gripped the rail of the fighting top and tried to steady herself. They were rowing back to the light as hard as they could: it would be all right in a few seconds. But oh, if only it could be all right now!

Though the rowing made a good deal of noise it did not quite conceal the total silence which surrounded the ship. Everyone knew it would be better not to listen, not to strain his ears for any sound from the darkness. But no one could help listening. And soon everyone was hearing things. Each one heard something different.

"Do you hear a noise like... like a huge pair of scissors opening and shutting... over there?" Eustace asked Rynelf.

"Hush!" said Rynelf. "I can hear *them* crawling up the sides of the ship."

"*It's* just going to settle on the mast," said Caspian.

"Ugh!" said a sailor. "There are the gongs beginning. I knew they would."

Caspian, trying not to look at anything (especially not to keep looking behind him), went aft to Drinian.

"Drinian," he said in a very low voice. "How long did we take rowing in? – I mean rowing to where we picked up the stranger?"

"Five minutes, perhaps," whispered Drinian. "Why?"

"Because we've been more than that already trying to get out."

Drinian's hand shook on the tiller and a line of cold sweat ran down his face. The same idea was occurring to everyone on board. "We shall never get out, never get out," moaned the rowers. "He's steering us wrong. We're going round and round in circles. We shall never get out." The stranger, who had been lying in a huddled heap on the deck, sat up and burst out into a horrible screaming laugh.

"Never get out!" he yelled. "That's it. Of course. We shall never get out. What a fool I was to have thought they would let me go as easily as that. No, no, we shall never get out."

Lucy leant her head on the edge of the fighting top and whispered, "Aslan, Aslan, if ever you loved us at all, send us help now." The darkness did not grow any less, but she began to feel a little – a very, very little – better. "After all, nothing has really happened to us yet," she thought.

"Look!" cried Rynelf's voice hoarsely from the bows. There was a tiny speck of light ahead, and while they watched, a broad beam of light fell from it upon the ship. It did not alter the surrounding darkness, but the whole ship was lit up as if by searchlight. Caspian blinked, stared round, saw the faces of his companions all with wild, fixed expressions. Everyone was staring in the same direction: behind everyone lay his black, sharply-edged shadow.

Lucy looked along the beam and presently saw something in it. At first it looked like a cross, then it looked like an aeroplane, then it looked like a kite, and at last with a whirring of wings it was right overhead and was an albatross. It circled three times round the mast and then perched for an instant on the crest of the gilded dragon at the prow. It called out in a strong sweet voice what seemed to be words though no one understood them. After that it spread its wings, rose, and began to fly slowly ahead, bearing a little to starboard. Drinian steered after it not doubting that it offered good guidance. But no one except Lucy knew that as it circled the mast it had whispered to her, "Courage, dear heart," and the voice, she felt sure, was Aslan's, and with the voice a delicious smell breathed in her face.

In a few moments the darkness turned into a greyness ahead, and then, almost before they dared to begin hoping, they had shot out into the sunlight and were in the warm, blue world again. And all at once everybody realized that there was nothing to be afraid of and never had been. They blinked their eyes and looked about them. The brightness of the ship herself astonished them: they had half expected to find that the darkness would cling to the white and the green and the gold in the form of some grime or scum. And then first one, and then another, began laughing.

"I reckon we've made pretty good fools of ourselves," said Rynelf.

Lucy lost no time in coming down to the deck, where she found the others all gathered round the newcomer. For a long time he was too happy to speak, and could only gaze at the sea and the sun and feel the bulwarks and the ropes, as if to make sure he was really awake, while tears rolled down his cheeks.

"Thank you," he said at last. "You have saved me from... but I won't talk of that. And now let me know who you are. I am a Telmarine of Narnia, and when I was worth anything men called me the Lord Rhoop."

"And I," said Caspian, "am Caspian, King of Narnia, and I sail to find you and your companions who were my father's friends."

Lord Rhoop fell on his knees and kissed the King's hand. "Sire," he said, "you are the man in all the world I most wished to see. Grant me a boon."

"What is it?" asked Caspian.

"Never to bring me back there," he said. He pointed astern. They all looked. But they saw only bright blue sea and bright blue sky. The Dark Island and the darkness had vanished for ever.

"Why!" cried Lord Rhoop. "You have destroyed it!"

"I don't think it was us," said Lucy.

"Sire," said Drinian, "this wind is fair for the south-east. Shall I have our poor fellows up and set sail? And after that, every man who can be spared, to his hammock."

"Yes," said Caspian, "and let there be grog all round. Heigh-ho, I feel I could sleep the clock round myself."

So all afternoon with great joy they sailed south-east with a fair wind. But nobody noticed when the albatross had disappeared.

CHAPTER THIRTEEN

THE THREE SLEEPERS

The wind never failed but it grew gentler every day till at length the waves were little more than ripples, and the ship glided on hour after hour almost as if they were sailing on a lake. And every night they saw that there rose in the east new constellations which no one had ever seen in Narnia and perhaps, as Lucy thought with a mixture of joy and fear, no living eye had seen at all. Those new stars were big and bright and the nights were warm. Most of them slept on deck and talked far into the night or hung over the ship's side watching the luminous dance of the foam thrown up by their bows.

On an evening of startling beauty, when the sunset behind them was so crimson and purple and widely spread that the very sky itself seemed to have grown larger, they came in sight of land on their starboard bow. It came slowly nearer and the light behind them made it look as if the capes and headlands of this new country were all on fire. But presently they were sailing along its coast and its western cape now rose up astern of them, black against the red sky and sharp as if it was cut out of cardboard, and then they could see better what this country was like. It had no mountains but many gentle hills with slopes like pillows. An attractive smell came from it – what Lucy called "a dim, purple kind of smell", which Edmund said (and Rhince thought) was rot, but Caspian said, "I know what you mean."

They sailed on a good way, past point after point, hoping to find a nice deep harbour, but had to content themselves in the end with a wide and shallow bay. Though it had seemed calm out at sea there was of course surf breaking on the sand and they could not bring the *Dawn Treader* as far in as they would have liked. They dropped anchor a good way from the beach and had a wet and tumbling landing in the boat. The Lord Rhoop remained on board the *Dawn Treader*. He wished to see no more islands. All the time that they remained in this country the sound of the long breakers was in their ears.

Two men were left to guard the boat and Caspian led the others inland, but not far because it was too late for exploring and the light would soon go. But there was no need to go far to find an adventure. The level valley which lay at the head of the bay showed no road or track or other sign of habitation. Underfoot was fine springy turf dotted here and there with a low bushy growth which Edmund and Lucy took for heather. Eustace, who was really rather good at Botany, said it wasn't, and he was probably right; but it was something of very much the same kind.

When they had gone less than a bowshot from the shore, Drinian said, "Look! What's that?" and everyone stopped.

"Are they great trees?" said Caspian

"Towers, I think," said Eustace.

"It might be giants," said Edmund in a lower voice.

"The way to find out is to go right in among them," said Reepicheep, drawing his sword and pattering off ahead of everyone else.

"I think it's a ruin," said Lucy when they had got a good deal nearer, and her guess was the best so far. What they now saw was a wide oblong space flagged with smooth stones and surrounded by grey pillars but unroofed. And from end to end of it ran a long table laid with a rich crimson cloth that came down nearly to the pavement. At either side of it were many chairs of stone, richly carved and with silken cushions upon the seats. But on the table itself there was set out such a banquet as had never been seen, not even when Peter the High King kept his court at Cair Paravel. There were turkeys and geese and peacocks, there were boars' heads and sides of venison, there were pies shaped like ships under full sail or like dragons and elephants, there were ice puddings and bright lobsters and gleaming salmon, there were nuts and grapes, pineapples and peaches, pomegranates and melons and tomatoes. There were flagons of gold and silver and curiously-wrought glass; and the smell of the fruit and the wine blew towards them like a promise of all happiness.

"I *say!*" said Lucy.

They came nearer and nearer, all very quietly.

"But where are the guests?" asked Eustace.

"We can provide that, Sir," said Rhince.

"Look!" said Edmund sharply. They were actually within the pillars now and standing on the pavement. Everyone looked where Edmund had pointed. The chairs were not all empty. At the head of the table and in the two places beside it there was something – or possibly three somethings.

"What are *those*?" asked Lucy in a whisper. "It looks like three beavers sitting on the table."

"Or a huge bird's nest," said Edmund.

"It looks more like a haystack to me," said Caspian.

Reepicheep ran forward, jumped on a chair and thence onto the table, and ran along it, threading his way as nimbly as a dancer between jewelled cups and pyramids of fruit and ivory salt-cellars. He ran right up to the mysterious grey mass at the end: peered, touched, and then called out:

"These will not fight, I think."

Everyone now came close and saw that what sat in those three chairs was three men, though hard to recognize as men till you looked closely. Their hair, which was grey, had grown over their eyes till it almost concealed their faces, and their beards had grown over the table, climbing round and entwining plates and goblets as brambles entwine a fence until, all mixed in one great mat of hair, they flowed over the edge and down to the floor. And from their heads the hair hung over the backs of their chairs so that they were wholly hidden. In fact the three men were nearly all hair.

"Dead?" said Caspian.

"I think not, Sire," said Reepicheep, lifting one of their hands out of its tangle of hair in his two paws. "This one is warm and his pulse beats."

"This one, too, and this," said Drinian.

"Why, they're only asleep," said Eustace.

"It's been a long sleep, though," said Edmund, "to let their hair grow like this."

"It must be an enchanted sleep," said Lucy. "I felt the moment we landed on this island that it was full of magic. Oh! Do you think we have perhaps come here to break it?"

"We can try," said Caspian, and began shaking the nearest of the three sleepers. For a moment everyone thought he was going to be successful, for the man breathed hard and muttered, "I'll go eastward no more. Out oars for Narnia." But he sank back almost at once into a yet deeper sleep than before: that is, his heavy head sagged a few inches lower towards the table and all efforts to rouse him again were useless.

With the second it was much the same: "Weren't born to live like animals. Get to the east while you've a chance – lands behind the sun," and sank down. And the third only said, "Mustard, please," and slept hard.

"*Out oars for Narnia*, eh?" said Drinian.

"Yes," said Caspian, "you are right, Drinian. I think our quest is at an end. Let's look at their rings. Yes, these are their devices. This is the Lord Revilian. This is the Lord Argoz: and this, the Lord Mavramorn."

"But we can't wake them," said Lucy. "What are we to do?"

"Begging your Majesties' pardons all," said Rhince, "but why not fall to while you're discussing it? We don't see a dinner like this every day."

"Not for your life!" said Caspian.

"That's right, that's right," said several of the sailors. "Too much magic about here. The sooner we're back on board the better."

"Depend upon it," said Reepicheep, "it was from eating this food that these three lords came by a seven years' sleep."

"I wouldn't touch it to save my life," said Drinian.

"The light's going uncommon quick," said Rynelf.

"Back to ship, back to ship," muttered the men.

"I really think," said Edmund, "they're right. We can decide what to do with the three sleepers tomorrow. We daren't eat the food and there's no point in staying here for the night. The whole place smells of magic – and danger."

"I am entirely of King Edmund's opinion," said Reepicheep, "as far as concerns the ship's company in general. But I myself will sit at this table till sunrise."

"Why on earth?" said Eustace.

"Because," said the Mouse, "this is a very great adventure, and no danger seems to me so great as that of knowing when I get back to Narnia that I left a mystery behind me through fear."

"I'll stay with you, Reep," said Edmund.

"And I too," said Caspian.

"And me," said Lucy. And then Eustace volunteered also. This was very brave of him because never having read of such things or even heard of them till he joined the *Dawn Treader* made it worse for him than for the others.

"I beseech your Majesty—" began Drinian.

"No, my Lord," said Caspian. "Your place is with the ship, and you have had a day's work while we five have idled." There was a lot of argument about this but in the end Caspian had his way. As the crew marched off to the shore in the gathering dusk none of the five watchers, except perhaps Reepicheep, could avoid a cold feeling in the stomach.

They took some time choosing their seats at the perilous table. Probably everyone had the same reason but no one said it out loud. For it was really a rather nasty choice. One could hardly bear to sit all night next to those three terrible hairy objects which, if not dead, were certainly not alive in the ordinary sense. On the other hand, to sit at the far end, so that you would see them less and less as the night grew darker, and wouldn't know if they were moving, and perhaps wouldn't see them at all by about two o'clock – no, it was not to be thought of. So they sauntered round and round the table saying, "What about here?" and, "Or perhaps a bit further on," or, "Why not on this side?" till at last they settled down somewhere about the middle but nearer to the sleepers than to the other end. It was about ten by now and almost dark. Those strange new constellations burned in the east. Lucy would have liked it better if they had been the Leopard and the Ship and other old friends of the Narnian sky.

They wrapped themselves in their sea cloaks and sat still and waited. At first there was some attempt at talk but it didn't come to much. And they sat and sat. And all the time they heard the waves breaking on the beach.

After hours that seemed like ages there came a moment when they all knew they had been dozing a moment before but were all suddenly wide awake. The stars were all in quite different positions from those they had last noticed. The sky was very black except for the faintest possible greyness in the east. They were cold, though thirsty, and stiff, and none of them spoke because now at last something was happening.

Before them, beyond the pillars, there was the slope of a low hill. And now a door opened in the hillside, and light appeared in the doorway, and a figure came out, and the door shut behind it. The figure carried a light, and this light was really all that they could see distinctly. It came slowly nearer and nearer till at last it stood right at the table opposite to them. Now they could see that it was a tall girl, dressed in a single long garment of clear blue which left her arms bare. She was bareheaded and her yellow hair hung down her back. And when they looked at her they thought they had never before known what beauty meant.

The light which she had been carrying was a tall candle in a silver candlestick which she now set upon the table. If there had been any wind off the sea earlier in the night it must have died down by now, for the flame of the candle burned as straight and still as if it were in a room with the windows shut and the curtains drawn. Gold and silver on the table shone in its light.

Lucy now noticed something lying lengthwise on the table which had escaped her attention before. It was a knife of stone, sharp as steel, a cruel-looking, ancient-looking thing.

No one had yet spoken a word. Then — Reepicheep first, and Caspian next — they all rose to their feet, because they felt that she was a great lady.

"Travellers who have come from far to Aslan's table," said the girl. "Why do you not eat and drink?"

"Madam," said Caspian, "we feared the food because we thought it had cast our friends into an enchanted sleep."

"They have never tasted it," she said.

"Please," said Lucy, "what happened to them?"

"Seven years ago," said the girl, "they came here in a ship whose sails were rags and her timbers ready to fall apart. There were a few others with them, sailors, and when they came to this table one said, 'Here is the good place. Let us set sail and reef sail and row no longer but sit down and end our days in peace!' And the second said, 'No, let us re-embark and sail for Narnia and the west; it may be that Miraz is dead.' But the third, who was a very masterful man, leapt up and said, 'No, by heaven. We are men and Telmarines, not brutes. What should we do but seek adventure after adventure? We have not long to live in any event. Let us spend what is left in seeking the unpeopled world behind the sunrise.' And as they quarrelled he caught up the Knife of Stone which lies there on the table and would have fought with his comrades. But it is a thing not right for him to touch. And as his fingers closed upon the hilt, deep sleep fell upon all the three. And till the enchantment is undone they will never wake."

"What is this Knife of Stone?" asked Eustace.

"Do none of you know it?" said the girl.

"I — I think," said Lucy, "I've seen something like it before. It was a knife like it that the White Witch used when she killed Aslan at the Stone Table long ago."

"It was the same," said the girl, "and it was brought here to be kept in honour while the world lasts."

Edmund, who had been looking more and more uncomfortable for the last few minutes, now spoke.

"Look here," he said, "I hope I'm not a coward — about eating this food, I mean — and I'm sure I don't mean to be rude. But we have had a lot of queer adventures on this voyage of ours and things aren't always what they seem. When I look in your face I can't help believing all you say: but then that's just what might happen with a witch too. How are we to know you're a friend?"

"You can't know," said the girl. "You can only believe — or not."

After a moment's pause Reepicheep's small voice was heard.

"Sire," he said to Caspian, "of your courtesy fill my cup with wine from that flagon: it is too big for me to lift. I will drink to the lady."

Caspian obeyed and the Mouse, standing on the table, held up a golden cup between its tiny paws and said, "Lady, I pledge you." Then it fell to on cold peacock, and in a short while everyone else followed its example. All were very hungry and the meal, if not quite what you wanted for a very early breakfast, was excellent as a very late supper.

"Why is it called Aslan's table?" asked Lucy presently.

"It is set here by his bidding," said the girl, "for those who come so far. Some call this island the World's End, for though you can sail further, this is the beginning of the end."

"But how does the food *keep*?" asked the practical Eustace.

"It is eaten, and renewed every day," said the girl. "This you will see."

"And what are we to do about the Sleepers?" asked Caspian. "In the world from which my friends come" (here he nodded at Eustace and the Pevensies) "they have a story of a prince or a king coming to a castle where all the people lay in an enchanted sleep. In that story he could not dissolve the enchantment until he had kissed the Princess."

"But here," said the girl, "it is different. Here he cannot kiss the Princess till he has dissolved the enchantment."

"Then," said Caspian, "in the name of Aslan, show me how to set about that work at once."

"My father will teach you that," said the girl.

"Your father!" said everyone. "Who is he? And where?"

"Look," said the girl, turning round and pointing at the door in the hillside. They could see it more easily now, for while they had been talking the stars had grown fainter and great gaps of white light were appearing in the greyness of the eastern sky.

CHAPTER FOURTEEN

THE BEGINNING OF THE END OF THE WORLD

Slowly the door opened again and out there came a figure as tall and straight as the girl's but not so slender. It carried no light but light seemed to come from it. As it came nearer, Lucy saw that it was like an old man. His silver beard came down to his bare feet in front and his silver hair hung down to his heels behind and his robe appeared to be made from the fleece of silver sheep. He looked so mild and grave that once more all the travellers rose to their feet and stood in silence.

But the old man came on without speaking to the travellers and stood on the other side of the table opposite to his daughter. Then both of them held up their arms before them and turned to face the east. In that position they began to sing. I wish I could write down the song, but no one who was present could remember it. Lucy said afterwards that it was high, almost shrill, but very beautiful – "A cold kind of song, an early morning kind of song." And as they sang, the grey clouds lifted from the eastern sky and the white patches grew bigger and bigger till it was all white, and the sea began to shine like silver. And long afterwards (but those two sang all the time) the east began to turn red and at last, unclouded, the sun came up out of the sea and its long level ray shot down the length of the table on the gold and silver and on the Stone Knife.

Once or twice before, the Narnians had wondered whether the sun at its rising did not look bigger in these seas than it had looked at home. This time they were certain. There was no mistaking it. And the brightness of its rays on the dew and on the table was far beyond any morning brightness they had ever seen. And as Edmund said afterwards, "Though lots of things happened on that trip which *sound* more exciting, that

moment was really the most exciting." For now they knew that they had truly come to the beginning of the End of the World.

Then something seemed to be flying at them out of the very centre of the rising sun: but of course one couldn't look steadily in that direction to make sure. But presently the air became full of voices — voices which took up the same song that the Lady and her Father were singing, but in far wilder tones and in a language which no one knew. And soon after that the owners of these voices could be seen. They were birds, large and white, and they came by hundreds and thousands and alighted on everything; on the grass, and the pavement, on the table, on your shoulders, your hands, and your head, till it looked as if heavy snow had fallen. For, like snow, they not only made everything white, but blurred and blunted all shapes. But Lucy, looking out from between the wings of the birds that covered her, saw one bird fly to the Old Man with something in its beak that looked like a little fruit, unless it was a little live coal, which it might have been, for it was too bright to look at. And the bird laid it in the Old Man's mouth.

Then the birds stopped their singing and appeared to be very busy about the table. When they rose from it again everything on the table that could be eaten or drunk had disappeared. These birds rose from their meal in their thousands and hundreds and carried away all the things that could not be eaten or drunk, such as bones, rinds, and shells, and took their flight back to the rising sun. But now, because they were not singing, the whirr of their wings seemed to set the whole air a-tremble. And there was the table pecked clean and empty, and the three old Lords of Narnia still fast asleep.

Now at last the Old Man turned to the travellers and bade them welcome.

"Sir," said Caspian, "will you tell us how to undo the enchantment which holds these three Narnian Lords asleep?"

"I will gladly tell you that, my son," said the Old Man. "To break this enchantment you must sail to the World's End, or as near as you can come to it, and you must come back having left at least one of your company behind."

"And what must happen to that one?" asked Reepicheep.

"He must go on into the utter east and never return into the world."

"That is my heart's desire," said Reepicheep.

"And are we near the World's End now, Sir?" asked Caspian. "Have you any knowledge of the seas and lands further east than this?"

"I saw them long ago," said the Old Man, "but it was from a great height. I cannot tell you such things as sailors need to know."

"Do you mean you were flying in the air?" Eustace blurted out.

"I was a long way above the air, my son," replied the Old Man. "I am Ramandu. But I see that you stare at one another and have not heard this name. And no wonder, for the days when I was a star had ceased long before any of you knew this world, and all the constellations have changed."

"Golly," said Edmund under his breath. "He's a *retired* star."

"Aren't you a star any longer?" asked Lucy.

"I am a star at rest, my daughter," answered Ramandu. "When I set for the last time, decrepit and old beyond all that you can reckon, I was carried to this island. I am not so old now as I was then. Every morning a bird brings me a fire-berry from the valleys in the sun, and each fire-berry takes away a little of my age. And when I have become as young as the child that was born yesterday, then I shall take my rising again (for we are at earth's eastern rim) and once more tread the great dance."

"In our world," said Eustace, "a star is a huge ball of flaming gas."

"Even in your world, my son, that is not what a star is but only what it is made of. And in this world you have already met a star: for I think you have been with Coriakin."

"Is he a retired star, too?" said Lucy.

"Well, not quite the same," said Ramandu. "It was not quite as a rest that he was set to govern the Duffers. You might call it a punishment. He might have shone for thousands of years more in the southern winter sky if all had gone well."

"What did he do, Sir?" asked Caspian.

"My son," said Ramandu, "it is not for you, a son of Adam, to know what faults a star can commit. But come, we waste time in such talk. Are you yet resolved? Will you sail further east and come again, leaving one to return no more, and so break the enchantment? Or will you sail westward?"

"Surely, Sire," said Reepicheep, "there is no question about that? It is very plainly part of our quest to rescue these three lords from enchantment."

"I think the same, Reepicheep," replied Caspian. "And even if it were not so, it would break my heart not to go as near the World's End as the *Dawn Treader* will take us. But I am thinking of the crew. They signed on to seek the seven lords, not to reach the rim of the earth. If we sail east from here we sail to find the edge, the utter east. And no one knows how far it is. They're brave fellows, but I see signs that some of them are weary of the voyage and long to have our prow pointing to Narnia. I don't think I should take them further without their knowledge and consent. And then there's the poor Lord Rhoop. He's a broken man."

"My son," said the star, "it would be no use, even though you wished it, to sail for the World's End with men unwilling or men deceived. That is not how great unenchantments are achieved. They must know where they go and why. But who is this broken man you speak of?"

Caspian told Ramandu the story of Rhoop.

"I can give him what he needs most," said Ramandu. "In this island there is sleep without stint or measure, and sleep in which no faintest footfall of a dream was ever heard. Let him sit beside these other three and drink oblivion till your return."

"Oh, do let's do that, Caspian," said Lucy. "I'm sure it's just what he would love."

At that moment they were interrupted by the sound of many feet and voices: Drinian and the rest of the ship's company were approaching. They halted in surprise when they saw Ramandu and his daughter; and then, because these were obviously great people, every man uncovered his head. Some sailors eyed the empty dishes and flagons on the table with regret.

"My lord," said the King to Drinian, "pray send two men back to the *Dawn Treader* with a message to the Lord Rhoop. Tell him that the last of his old shipmates are here asleep – a sleep without dreams – and that he can share it."

When this had been done, Caspian told the rest to sit down and laid the whole situation before them. When he had finished there was a long silence and some whispering until presently the Master Bowman got to his feet, and said:

"What some of us have been wanting to ask for a long time, your Majesty, is how we're ever to get home when we do turn, whether we turn here or somewhere else. It's been west and north-west winds all the way, barring an occasional calm. And if that doesn't change, I'd like to know what hopes we have of seeing Narnia again. There's not much chance of supplies lasting while we *row* all that way."

"That's landsman's talk," said Drinian. "There's always a prevailing west wind in these seas all through the late summer, and it always changes after the New Year. We'll have plenty of wind for sailing westward; more than we shall like, from all accounts."

"That's true, Master," said an old sailor who was a Galmian by birth. "You get some ugly weather rolling up from the east in January and February. And by your leave, Sire, if I was in command of this ship I'd say to winter here and begin the voyage home in March."

"What'd you eat while you were wintering here?" asked Eustace.

"This table," said Ramandu, "will be filled with a king's feast every day at sunset."

"Now you're talking!" said several sailors.

"Your Majesties and gentlemen and ladies all," said Rynelf, "there's just one thing I want to say. There's not one of us chaps as was pressed on this journey. We're volunteers. And there's some here that are looking very hard at that table and thinking about king's feasts who were talking very loud about adventures on the day we sailed from Cair Paravel, and swearing they wouldn't come home till we'd found the end of the world. And there were some standing on the quay who would have given all they had to come with us. It was thought a finer thing then to have a cabin-boy's berth on the *Dawn Treader* than to wear a knight's belt. I don't know if you get the hang of what I'm saying. But what I mean is that I think chaps who set out like us will look as silly as — as those Dufflepuds — if we come home and say we got to the beginning of the World's End and hadn't the heart to go further."

Some of the sailors cheered at this but some said that that was all very well.

"This isn't going to be much fun," whispered Edmund to Caspian. "What are we to do if half those fellows hang back?"

"Wait," Caspian whispered back. "I've still a card to play."

"Aren't you going to say anything, Reep?" whispered Lucy.

"No. Why should your Majesty expect it?" answered Reepicheep in a voice that most people heard. "My own plans are made. While I can, I sail east in the *Dawn Treader*. When she fails me, I paddle east in my coracle. When she sinks, I shall swim east with my four paws. And when I can swim no longer, if I have not reached Aslan's country, or shot over the edge of the world in some vast cataract, I shall sink with my nose to the sunrise and Peepiceek will be head of the talking mice in Narnia."

"Hear, hear," said a sailor, "I'll say the same, barring the bit about the coracle, which wouldn't bear me." He added in a lower voice, "I'm not going to be outdone by a mouse."

At this point Caspian jumped to his feet. "Friends," he said, "I think you have not quite understood our purpose. You talk as if we had come to you with our hat in our hand, begging for shipmates. It isn't like that at all. We and our royal brother and sister and their kinsman and Sir Reepicheep, the good knight, and the Lord Drinian have an errand to the world's edge. It is our pleasure to choose from among such of you as are willing, those whom we deem worthy of so high an enterprise. We have not said that any can come for the asking. That is why we shall now command the Lord Drinian and Master Rhince to consider carefully what men among you are the hardest in battle, the most skilled seamen, the purest in blood, the most loyal to our person, and the cleanest of life and manners; and to give their names to us in a schedule." He paused and went on in a quicker voice: "Aslan's mane!" he exclaimed. "Do you think that the privilege of seeing the last things is to be bought for a song? Why, every man that comes with us shall bequeath the title of *Dawn Treader* to all his descendants, and when we land at Cair Paravel on the homeward voyage he shall have either gold or land enough to make him rich all his life. Now – scatter over the island, all of you. In half an hour's time I shall receive the names that Lord Drinian brings me."

There was rather a sheepish silence and then the crew made their bows and moved away, one in this direction and one in that, but mostly in little knots or bunches, talking.

"And now for the Lord Rhoop," said Caspian.

But turning to the head of the table he saw that Rhoop was already there. He had arrived, silent and unnoticed, while the discussion was going on, and was seated beside the Lord Argoz. The daughter of Ramandu stood beside him as if she had just helped him into his chair; Ramandu stood behind him and laid both his hands on Rhoop's grey head. Even in daylight a faint silver light came from the hands of the star. There was a smile on Rhoop's haggard face. He held out one of his hands to Lucy and the other to Caspian. For a moment it looked as if he were going to say something. Then his smile brightened as if he were feeling some delicious sensation, a long sigh of contentment came from his lips, his head fell forward, and he slept.

"Poor Rhoop," said Lucy. "I *am* glad. He must have had terrible times."

"Don't let's even think of it," said Eustace.

Meanwhile Caspian's speech, helped perhaps by some magic of the island, was having just the effect he intended. A good many who had been anxious enough to *get* out of the voyage felt quite differently about being *left* out of it. And of course whenever any one sailor announced that he had made up his mind to ask for permission to sail, the ones who hadn't said this felt that they were getting fewer and more uncomfortable. So that before the half-hour was nearly over several people were positively "sucking up" to Drinian and Rhince (at least that was what they called it at my school) to get a good report. And soon there were only three left who didn't want to go, and those three were trying very hard to persuade others to stay with them. And very shortly after that there was only one left. And in the end he began to be afraid of being left behind all on his own and changed his mind.

At the end of the half-hour they all came trooping back to Aslan's Table and stood at one end while Drinian and Rhince went and sat down with Caspian and made their report; and Caspian accepted all the men but that one who had changed his mind at the last moment. His name was Pittencream and he stayed on the Island of the Star all the time the others were away looking for the World's End, and he very much wished he had gone with them. He wasn't the sort of man who could enjoy talking to Ramandu and Ramandu's daughter (nor they to him), and it rained a good deal, and though there was a wonderful feast on the Table every night, he didn't very much enjoy it. He said it gave him the creeps sitting there alone (and in the rain as likely as not) with those four Lords asleep at the end of the Table. And when the others returned he felt so out of things that he deserted on the voyage home at the Lone Islands, and went and lived in Calormen, where he told wonderful stories about his adventures at the End of the World, until at last he came to believe them himself. So you may say, in a sense, that he lived happily ever after. But he could never bear mice.

That night they all ate and drank together at the great Table between the pillars where the feast was magically renewed: and the next morning the *Dawn Treader* set sail once more just when the great birds had come and gone again.

"Lady," said Caspian, "I hope to speak with you again when I have broken the enchantments." And Ramandu's daughter looked at him and smiled.

CHAPTER FIFTEEN

THE WONDERS OF THE LAST SEA

Very soon after they had left Ramandu's country they began to feel that they had already sailed beyond the world. All was different. For one thing they all found that they were needing less sleep. One did not want to go to bed nor to eat much, nor even to talk except in low voices. Another thing was the light. There was too much of it. The sun when it came up each morning looked twice, if not three times, its usual size. And every morning (which gave Lucy the strangest feeling of all) the huge white birds, singing their song with human voices in a language no one knew, streamed overhead and vanished astern on their way to their breakfast at Aslan's Table. A little later they came flying back and vanished into the east.

"How beautifully clear the water is!" said Lucy to herself, as she leant over the port side early in the afternoon of the second day.

And it was. The first thing that she noticed was a little black object, about the size of a shoe, travelling along at the same speed as the ship. For a moment she thought it was something floating on the surface. But then there came floating past a bit of stale bread which the cook had just thrown out of the galley. And the bit of bread looked as if it were going to collide with the black thing, but it didn't. It passed above it, and Lucy now saw that the black thing could not be on the surface. Then the black thing suddenly got very much bigger and flicked back to normal size a moment later.

Now Lucy knew she had seen something just like that happen somewhere else – if only she could remember where. She held her hand to her head and screwed up her face and put out her tongue in the effort to remember. At last she did. Of course! It was like what you saw from a train on a bright sunny day. You saw the black shadow of your own coach running along the fields at the same pace as the train. Then you went into a cutting; and immediately the same shadow flicked close up to you and got big, racing along the grass of the cutting-bank. Then you came out of the cutting and – flick! – once more the black shadow had gone back to its normal size and was running along the fields.

"It's our shadow! The shadow of the *Dawn Treader*," said Lucy. "Our shadow running along on the bottom of the sea. That time when it got bigger it went over a hill. But in that case the water must be clearer than I thought! Good gracious, I must be seeing the bottom of the sea, fathoms and fathoms down."

As soon as she had said this she realized that the great silvery expanse which she had been seeing (without noticing) for some time was really the sand on the sea-bed and that all sorts of darker or brighter patches were not lights and shadows on the surface but real things on the bottom. At present, for instance, they were passing over a mass of soft purply green with a broad, winding strip of pale grey in the middle of it. But now that she knew it was on the bottom she saw it much better. She could see that bits of the dark stuff were much higher than other bits and were waving gently. "Just like trees in a wind," said Lucy. "And I do believe that's what they are. It's a submarine forest."

They passed on above it and presently the pale streak was joined by another pale streak. "If I was down there," thought Lucy, "that streak would be just like a road through the wood. And that place where it joins the other would be a crossroads. Oh, I do wish I was. Hullo! The forest is coming to an end. And I do believe the streak really was a road! I can still see it going on across the open sand. It's a different colour. And it's marked out with something at the edges – dotted lines. Perhaps they are stones. And now it's getting wider."

But it was not really getting wider, it was getting nearer. She realized this because of the way in which the shadow of the ship came rushing up towards her. And the road – she felt sure it was a road now – began to go in zigzags. Obviously it was climbing up a steep hill. And when she held her head sideways and looked back, what she saw was very like what you see when you look down a winding road from the top of a hill. She could even see the shafts of sunlight falling through the deep water onto the wooded valley – and, in the extreme distance, everything melting away into a dim greenness. But some places – the sunny ones, she thought – were ultramarine blue.

She could not, however, spend much time looking back; what was coming into view in the forward direction was too exciting. The road had apparently now reached the top of the hill and ran straight forward. Little specks were moving to and fro on it. And now something most wonderful, fortunately in full sunlight – or as full as it can be when it falls through fathoms of water – flashed into sight. It was knobbly and jagged and of a pearly, or perhaps an ivory, colour. She was so nearly straight above it that at first she could hardly make out what it was. But everything became plain when she noticed its shadow. The sunlight was falling across Lucy's shoulders, so the shadow of the thing lay stretched out on the sand behind it. And by its shape she saw clearly that it was a shadow of towers and pinnacles, minarets and domes.

"Why! – It's a city or a huge castle," said Lucy to herself. "But I wonder why they've built it on top of a high mountain?"

Long afterwards when she was back in England and talked all these adventures over with Edmund, they thought of a reason and I am pretty sure it is the true one. In the sea, the deeper you go, the darker and colder it gets, and it is down there, in the dark and cold, that dangerous things live – the squid and the Sea Serpent and the Kraken. The valleys are the wild, unfriendly places. The sea people feel about their valleys as we do about the mountains, and feel about their mountains as we feel about valleys. It is on the heights (or, as we would say, "in the shallows") that there is warmth and peace. The reckless hunters and brave knights of the sea go down into the depths on quests and adventures, but return home to the heights for rest and peace, courtesy and council, the sports, the dances and the songs.

They had passed the city and the sea-bed was still rising. It was only a few hundred feet below the ship now. The road had disappeared. They were sailing above an open, park-like country, dotted with little groves of brightly-coloured vegetation. And then – Lucy nearly squealed aloud with excitement – she had seen People.

There were between fifteen and twenty of them, and all mounted on sea-horses – not the tiny little sea-horses which you may have seen in museums but horses rather bigger than themselves. They must be noble and lordly people, Lucy thought, for she could catch the gleam of gold on some of their foreheads, and streamers of emerald- or orange-coloured stuff fluttered from their shoulders in the current. Then:

"Oh, bother these fish!" said Lucy, for a whole shoal of small fat fish, swimming quite close to the surface, had come between her and the Sea People. But though this spoiled her view it led to the most interesting thing of all. Suddenly a fierce little fish of a kind she had never seen before came darting up from below, snapped, grabbed, and sank rapidly with one of the fat fish in its mouth. And all the Sea People were sitting on their horses staring up at what had happened. They seemed to be talking and laughing. And before the hunting fish had got back to them with its prey, another of the same kind came up from the Sea People. And Lucy was almost certain that one big Sea Man who sat on his sea-horse in the middle of the party had sent it or released it; as if he had been holding it back till then in his hand or on his wrist.

"Why, I do declare," said Lucy, "it's a hunting party. Or more like a hawking party. Yes, that's it. They ride out with these little fierce fish on their wrists just as we used to ride out with falcons on our wrists when we were Kings and Queens at Cair Paravel long ago. And then they fly them – or I suppose I should say *swim* them – at the others. How—"

She stopped suddenly because the scene was changing. The Sea People had noticed the *Dawn Treader*. The shoal of fish had scattered in every direction: the People themselves were coming up to find out the meaning of this big, black thing which had come between them and the sun. And now they were so close to the surface that if they had been in air, instead of water, Lucy could have spoken to them. There were men and women both. All wore coronets of some kind and many had chains of pearls. They wore no other clothes. Their bodies were the colour of old ivory, their hair dark purple. The King in the centre (no one could mistake him for anything but the King) looked proudly and fiercely into Lucy's face and shook a spear in his hand. His knights did the same. The faces of the ladies were filled with astonishment. Lucy felt sure they had never seen a ship or a human before – and how should they, in seas beyond the World's End where no ship ever came?

"What are you staring at, Lu?" said a voice close beside her.

Lucy had been so absorbed in what she was seeing that she started at the sound, and when she turned she found that her arm had gone "dead" from leaning so long on the rail in one position. Drinian and Edmund were beside her.

"Look," she said.

They both looked, but almost at once Drinian said in a low voice:

"Turn round at once, your Majesties – that's right, with your backs to the sea. And don't look as if we were talking about anything important."

"Why, what's the matter?" said Lucy as she obeyed.

"It'll never do for the sailors to see *all that*," said Drinian. "We'll have men falling in love with a sea-woman, or falling in love with the under-sea country itself, and jumping overboard. I've heard of that kind of thing happening before in strange seas. It's always unlucky to see *these* people."

"But we used to know them," said Lucy. "In the old days at Cair Paravel when my brother Peter was High King. They came to the surface and sang at our coronation."

"I think that must have been a different kind, Lu," said Edmund. "They could live in the air as well as under water. I rather think these can't. By the look of them they'd have surfaced and started attacking us long ago if they could. They seem very fierce."

"At any rate," said Drinian, but at that moment two sounds were heard. One was a plop. The other was a voice from the fighting top shouting, "Man overboard!" Then everyone was busy. Some of the sailors hurried aloft to take in the sail; others hurried below to get out the oars; and Rhince, who was on duty on the poop, began to put the helm hard over so as to come round and back to the man who had gone overboard. But by now everyone knew that it wasn't strictly a man. It was Reepicheep.

"Drat that mouse!" said Drinian. "He's more trouble than all the rest of the ship's company put together. If there is any scrape to be got into, in he will get! He ought to be put in irons – keel-hauled – marooned – have his whiskers cut off. Can anyone see the little blighter?"

All this didn't mean that Drinian really disliked Reepicheep. On the contrary he liked him very much and was therefore frightened about him, and being frightened put him in a bad temper – just as your mother is much angrier with you for running out into the road in front of a car than a stranger would be. No one, of course, was afraid of Reepicheep's drowning, for he was an excellent swimmer; but the three who knew what was going on below the water were afraid of those long, cruel spears in the hands of the Sea People.

In a few minutes the *Dawn Treader* had come round and everyone could see the black blob in the water which was Reepicheep. He was chattering with the greatest excitement but as his mouth kept on getting filled with water nobody could understand what he was saying.

"He'll blurt the whole thing out if we don't shut him up," cried Drinian. To prevent this he rushed to the side and lowered a rope himself, shouting to the sailors, "All right, all right. Back to your places. I hope I can heave a *mouse* up without help." And as Reepicheep began climbing up the rope – not very nimbly because his wet fur made him heavy – Drinian leant over and whispered to him,

"Don't tell. Not a word."

But when the dripping Mouse had reached the deck he turned out not to be at all interested in the Sea People.

"Sweet!" he cheeped. "Sweet, sweet!"

"What are you talking about?" asked Drinian crossly. "And you needn't shake yourself all over *me*, either."

"I tell you the water's sweet," said the Mouse. "Sweet, fresh. It isn't salt."

For a moment no one quite took in the importance of this. But then Reepicheep once more repeated the old prophecy:

"Where the waves grow sweet,
    Doubt not, Reepicheep,
    There is the utter east."

Then at last everyone understood.

"Let me have a bucket, Rynelf," said Drinian.

It was handed him and he lowered it and up it came again. The water shone in it like glass.

"Perhaps your Majesty would like to taste it first?" said Drinian to Caspian.

The King took the bucket in both hands, raised it to his lips, sipped, then drank deeply and raised his head. His face was changed. Not only his eyes but everything about him seemed to be brighter.

"Yes," he said, "it is sweet. That's real water, that. I'm not sure that it isn't going to kill me. But it is the death I would have chosen – if I'd known about it till now."

"What do you mean?" asked Edmund.

"It – it's like light more than anything else," said Caspian.

"That is what it is," said Reepicheep. "Drinkable light. We must be very near the end of the world now."

There was a moment's silence and then Lucy knelt down on the deck and drank from the bucket.

"It's the loveliest thing I have ever tasted," she said with a kind of gasp. "But oh – it's strong. We shan't need to *eat* anything now."

And one by one everybody on board drank. And for a long time they were all silent. They felt almost too well and strong to bear it; and presently they began to notice another result. As I have said before, there had been too much light ever since they left the island of Ramandu – the sun too large (though not too hot), the sea too bright, the air too shining. Now, the light grew no less – if anything, it increased – but they could bear it. They could look straight up at the sun without blinking. They could see more light than they had ever seen before. And the deck and the sail and their own faces and bodies became brighter and brighter and every rope shone. And the next morning, when the sun rose, now five or six times its old size, they stared hard into it and could see the very feathers of the birds that came flying from it.

Hardly a word was spoken on board all that day, till about dinner-time (no one wanted any dinner, the water was enough for them), when Drinian said:

"I can't understand this. There is not a breath of wind. The sail hangs dead. The sea is as flat as a pond. And yet we drive on as fast as if there were a gale behind us."

"I've been thinking that, too," said Caspian. "We must be caught in some strong current."

"H'm," said Edmund. "That's not so nice if the World really has an edge and we're getting near it."

"You mean," said Caspian, "that we might be just – well, poured over it?"

"Yes, yes," cried Reepicheep, clapping his paws together. "That's how I've always imagined it – the World like a great round table and the waters of all the oceans endlessly pouring over the edge. The ship will tip up – stand on her head – for one moment we shall see over the edge – and then, down, down, the rush, the speed—"

"And what do you think will be waiting for us at the bottom, eh?" said Drinian.

"Aslan's country perhaps," said the Mouse, his eyes shining. "Or perhaps there isn't any bottom. Perhaps it goes down for ever and ever. But whatever it is, won't it be worth anything just to have looked for one moment beyond the edge of the world?"

"But look here," said Eustace, "this is all rot. The world's round – I mean, round like a ball, not like a table."

"*Our* world is," said Edmund. "But is this?"

"Do you mean to say," asked Caspian, "that you three come from a round world (round like a ball) and you've never told me! It's really too bad of you. Because we have fairy-tales in which there are round worlds and I always loved them. I never believed there were any real ones. But I've always wished there were and I've always longed to live in one. Oh, I'd give anything – I wonder why you can get into our world and we never get into yours? If only I had the chance! It must be exciting to live on a thing like a ball. Have you ever been to the parts where people walk about upside-down?"

Edmund shook his head. "And it isn't like that," he added. "There's nothing particularly exciting about a round world when you're there."

CHAPTER SIXTEEN

THE VERY END OF THE WORLD

Reepicheep was the only person on board besides Drinian and the two Pevensies who had noticed the Sea People. He had dived in at once when he saw the Sea King shaking his spear, for he regarded this as a sort of threat or challenge and wanted to have the matter out there and then. The excitement of discovering that the water was now fresh had distracted his attention, and before he remembered the Sea People again, Lucy and Drinian had taken him aside and warned him not to mention what he had seen.

As things turned out they need hardly have bothered, for by this time the *Dawn Treader* was gliding over a part of the sea which seemed to be uninhabited. No one except Lucy saw anything more of the People, and even she had only one short glimpse. All morning on the following day they sailed in fairly shallow water and the bottom was weedy. Just before midday Lucy saw a large shoal of fishes grazing on the weed. They were all eating steadily and all moving in the same direction. "Just like a flock of sheep," thought Lucy. Suddenly she saw a little Sea Girl of about her own age in the middle of them – a quiet, lonely-looking girl with a sort of crook in her hand. Lucy felt sure that this girl must be a shepherdess – or perhaps a fish-herdess – and that the shoal was really a flock at pasture. Both the fishes and the girl were quite close to the surface. And just as the girl, gliding in the shallow water, and Lucy, leaning over the bulwark, came opposite to one another, the girl looked up and stared straight into Lucy's face. Neither could speak to the other and in a moment the Sea Girl dropped astern. But Lucy will never forget her face. It did not look frightened or angry like those of the other Sea People. Lucy had liked that girl and she felt certain the girl had liked her. In that one moment they had somehow become friends. There does not seem to be much chance of their meeting again in that world or any other. But if ever they do they will rush together with their hands held out.

After that, for many days, without wind in her shrouds or foam at her bows, across a waveless sea, the *Dawn Treader* glided smoothly east. Every day and every hour the light became more brilliant and still they could bear it. No one ate or slept and no one wanted to, but they drew buckets of dazzling water from the sea, stronger than wine and somehow wetter, more liquid, than ordinary water, and pledged one another silently in deep draughts of it. And one or two of the sailors who had been oldish men when the voyage began now grew younger every day. Everyone on board was filled with joy and excitement, but not an excitement that made one talk. The further they sailed the less they spoke, and then almost in a whisper. The stillness of that last sea laid hold on them.

"My Lord," said Caspian to Drinian one day, "what do you see ahead?"

"Sire," said Drinian, "I see whiteness. All along the horizon from north to south, as far as my eyes can reach."

"That is what I see too," said Caspian, "and I cannot imagine what it is."

"If we were in higher latitudes, your Majesty," said Drinian, "I would say it was ice. But it can't be that; not here. All the same, we'd better get men to the oars and hold the ship back against the current. Whatever the stuff is, we don't want to crash into it at this speed!"

They did as Drinian said, and so continued to go slower and slower. The whiteness did not get any less mysterious as they approached it. If it was land it must be a very strange land, for it seemed just as smooth as the water and on the same level with it. When they got very close to it Drinian put the helm hard over and turned the *Dawn Treader* south so that she was broadside on to the current and rowed a little way southward along the edge of the whiteness. In so doing they accidentally made the important discovery that the current was only about forty feet wide and the rest of the sea as still as a pond. This was good news for the crew, who had already begun to think that the return journey to Ramandu's land, rowing against stream all the way, would be pretty poor sport. (It also explained why the shepherd girl had dropped so quickly astern. She was not in the current. If she had been she would have been moving east at the same speed as the ship.)

And still no one could make out what the white stuff was. Then the boat was lowered and it put off to investigate. Those who remained on the *Dawn Treader* could see that the boat pushed right in amidst the whiteness. Then they could hear the voices of the party in the boat (clear across the still water) talking in a shrill and surprised way. Then there was a pause while

Rynelf in the bows of the boat took a sounding; and when, after that, the boat came rowing back there seemed to be plenty of the white stuff inside her. Everyone crowded to the side to hear the news.

"Lilies, your Majesty!" shouted Rynelf, standing up in the bows.

"*What* did you say?" asked Caspian.

"Blooming lilies, your Majesty," said Rynelf. "Same as in a pool or in a garden at home."

"Look!" said Lucy, who was in the stern of the boat. She held up her wet arms full of white petals and broad flat leaves.

"What's the depth, Rynelf?" asked Drinian.

"That's the funny thing, Captain," said Rynelf. "It's still deep. Three and a half fathoms clear."

"They can't be real lilies – not what we call lilies," said Eustace.

Probably they were not, but they were very like them. And when, after some consultation, the *Dawn Treader* turned back into the current and began to glide eastward through the Lily Lake or the Silver Sea (they tried both these names but it was the Silver Sea that stuck and is now on Caspian's map) the strangest part of their travels began. Very soon the open sea which they were leaving was only a thin rim of blue on the western horizon. Whiteness, shot with faintest colour of gold, spread round them on every side, except just astern where their passage had thrust the lilies apart and left an open lane of water that shone like dark green glass. To look at, this last sea was very like the Arctic; and if their eyes had not by now grown as strong as eagles', the sun on all that whiteness – especially at early morning when the sun was hugest – would have been unbearable. And every evening the same whiteness made the daylight last longer. There seemed no end to the lilies. Day after day from all those miles and leagues of flowers there rose a smell which Lucy found very hard to describe; sweet – yes, but not at all sleepy or overpowering, a fresh, wild, lonely smell that seemed to get into your brain and make you feel that you could go up mountains at a run or wrestle with an elephant. She and Caspian said to one another, "I feel that I can't stand much more of this, yet I don't want it to stop."

They took soundings very often but it was only several days later that the water became shallower. After that it went on getting shallower. There came a day when they had to row out of the current and feel their way forward at a snail's pace, rowing. And soon it was clear that the *Dawn Treader* could sail no further east. Indeed it was only by very clever handling that they saved her from grounding.

"Lower the boat," cried Caspian, "and then call the men aft. I must speak to them."

"What's he going to do?" whispered Eustace to Edmund. "There's a queer look in his eyes."

"I think we probably all look the same," said Edmund.

They joined Caspian on the poop and soon all the men were crowded together at the foot of the ladder to hear the King's speech.

"Friends," said Caspian, "we have now fulfilled the quest on which you embarked. The seven lords are all accounted for, and as Sir Reepicheep has sworn never to return, when you reach Ramandu's land you will doubtless find the Lords Revilian and Argoz and Mavramorn awake. To you, my Lord Drinian, I entrust this ship bidding you sail to Narnia with all the speed you may, and above all not to land on the Island of Deathwater. And instruct my regent, the Dwarf Trumpkin, to give to all these, my shipmates, the rewards I promised them. They have been earned well. And if I come not again it is my will that the Regent, and Master Cornelius, and Trufflehunter the Badger, and the Lord Drinian choose a King of Narnia with the consent—"

"But, Sire," interrupted Drinian, "are you abdicating?"

"I am going with Reepicheep to see the World's End," said Caspian.

A low murmur of dismay ran through the sailors.

"We will take the boat," said Caspian. "You will have no need of it in these gentle seas and you must build a new one in Ramandu's Island. And now—"

"Caspian," said Edmund suddenly and sternly, "you can't do this."

"Most certainly," said Reepicheep, "his Majesty cannot."

"No, indeed," said Drinian.

"Can't?" said Caspian sharply, looking for a moment not unlike his uncle Miraz.

"Begging your Majesty's pardon," said Rynelf from the deck below, "but if one of us did the same it would be called deserting."

"You presume too much on your long service, Rynelf," said Caspian.

"No, Sire! He's perfectly right," said Drinian.

"By the mane of Aslan," said Caspian, "I had thought you were all my subjects here, not my schoolmasters."

"I'm not," said Edmund, "and I say you can *not* do this."

"Can't again," said Caspian. "What do you mean?"

"If it please your Majesty, we mean *shall not*," said Reepicheep with a very low bow. "You are the King of Narnia. You break faith with all your subjects, and especially Trumpkin, if you do not return. You shall not please yourself with adventures as if you were a private person. And if your Majesty will not hear reason it will be the truest loyalty of every man on board to follow me in disarming and binding you till you come to your senses."

"Quite right," said Edmund. "Like they did with Ulysses when he wanted to go near the Sirens."

Caspian's hand had gone to his sword hilt, when Lucy said, "And you've almost promised Ramandu's daughter to go back."

Caspian paused. "Well, yes. There is that," he said. He stood irresolute for a moment and then shouted out to the ship in general:

"Well, have your way. The quest is ended. We all return. Get the boat up again."

"Sire," said Reepicheep, "we do not *all* return. I, as I explained before——"

"Silence!" thundered Caspian. "I've been lessoned but I'll not be baited. Will no one silence that Mouse?"

"Your Majesty promised," said Reepicheep, "to be a good lord to the Talking Beasts of Narnia."

"Talking beasts, yes," said Caspian. "I said nothing about beasts that never stop talking." And he flung down the ladder in a temper and went into the cabin, slamming the door.

But when the others rejoined him a little later they found him changed; he was white and there were tears in his eyes.

"It's no good," he said. "I might as well have behaved decently for all the good I did with my temper and swagger. Aslan has spoken to me. No – I don't mean he was actually here. He wouldn't fit into the cabin, for one thing. But that gold lion's head on the wall came to life and spoke to me. It was terrible – his eyes. Not that he was at all rough with me – only a bit stern at first. But it was terrible all the same. And he said – he said – oh, I can't bear it. The worst thing he could have said. You're to go on – Reep and Edmund, and Lucy, and Eustace; and I'm to go back. Alone. And at once. And what is the good of anything?"

"Caspian, dear," said Lucy. "You knew we'd have to go back to our own world sooner or later."

"Yes," said Caspian with a sob, "but this is sooner."

"You'll feel better when you get back to Ramandu's Island," said Lucy.

He cheered up a little later on, but it was a grievous parting on both sides and I will not dwell on it. About two o'clock in the afternoon, well victualled and watered (though they thought they would need neither food nor drink) and with Reepicheep's coracle on board, the boat pulled away from the *Dawn Treader* to row through the endless carpet of lilies. The *Dawn Treader* flew all her flags and hung out her shields to honour their departure. Tall and big and homelike she looked from their low position with the lilies all round them. And before she was out of sight they saw her turn and begin rowing slowly westward. Yet though Lucy shed a few tears, she could not feel it as much as you might have expected. The light, the silence, the tingling smell of the Silver Sea, even (in some odd way) the loneliness itself, were too exciting.

There was no need to row, for the current drifted them steadily to the east. None of them slept or ate. All that night and all next day they glided eastward, and when the third day dawned – with a brightness you or I could not bear even if we had dark glasses on – they saw a wonder ahead. It was as if a wall stood up between them and the sky, a greenish-grey, trembling, shimmering wall. Then up came the sun, and at its first rising they saw it through the wall and it turned into wonderful rainbow colours. Then they knew that the wall was really a long, tall wave – a wave endlessly fixed in one place as you may often see at the edge of a waterfall. It seemed to be about thirty feet high, and the current was gliding them swiftly towards it. You might have supposed they would have thought of their danger. They didn't. I don't think anyone could have in their position. For now they saw something not only behind the wave but behind the sun. They could not have seen even the sun if their eyes had not been strengthened by the water of the Last Sea. But now they could look at the rising sun and see it clearly and see things beyond it. What they saw – eastward, beyond the sun – was a range of mountains. It was so high that either they never saw the top of it or they forgot it. None of them remembers seeing any sky in that direction. And the mountains must really have been outside the world. For any mountains even a quarter of a twentieth of that height ought to have had ice and snow on them. But these were warm and green and full of forests and waterfalls however high you looked. And suddenly there came a breeze from the east, tossing the top of the wave into foamy shapes and ruffling the smooth water all round them. It lasted only a second or so but what it brought them in that second none of those three children will ever forget. It brought both a smell and a sound, a musical sound. Edmund and Eustace would never talk about it afterwards. Lucy could only say, "It would break your heart." "Why," said I, "was it so sad?" "Sad!! No," said Lucy.

No one in that boat doubted that they were seeing beyond the End of the World into Aslan's country.

At that moment, with a crunch, the boat ran aground. The water was too shallow now for it. "This," said Reepicheep, "is where I go on alone."

They did not even try to stop him, for everything now felt as if it had been fated or had happened before. They helped him to lower his little coracle. Then he took off his sword ("I shall need it no more," he said) and flung it far away across the lilied sea. Where it fell it stood upright with the hilt above the surface. Then he bade them goodbye, trying to be sad for their sakes; but he was quivering with happiness. Lucy, for the first and last time, did what she had always wanted to do, taking him in her arms and caressing him. Then hastily he got into his coracle and took his paddle, and the current caught it and away he went, very black against the lilies. But no lilies grew on the wave; it was a smooth green slope. The coracle went more and more quickly, and beautifully it rushed up the wave's side. For one split second they saw its shape and Reepicheep's on the very top. Then it vanished, and since that moment no one can truly claim to have seen Reepicheep the Mouse. But my belief is that he came safe to Aslan's country and is alive there to this day.

As the sun rose, the sight of those mountains outside the world faded away. The wave remained but there was only blue sky behind it.

The children got out of the boat and waded – not towards the wave but southward with the wall of water on their left. They could not have told you why they did this; it was their fate. And though they had felt – and been – very grown-up on the *Dawn Treader*, they now felt just the opposite and held hands as they waded through the lilies. They never felt tired. The water was warm and all the time it got shallower. At last they were on dry sand, and then on grass – a huge plain of very fine short grass, almost level with the Silver Sea and spreading in every direction without so much as a molehill.

And of course, as it always does in a perfectly flat place without trees, it looked as if the sky came down to meet the grass in front of them. But as they went on they got the strangest impression that here at last the sky did really come down and join the earth – a blue wall, very bright, but real and solid: more like glass than anything else. And soon they were quite sure of it. It was very near now.

But between them and the foot of the sky there was something so white on the green grass that even with their eagles' eyes they could hardly look at it. They came on and saw that it was a Lamb.

"Come and have breakfast," said the Lamb in its sweet milky voice.

Then they noticed for the first time that there was a fire lit on the grass and fish roasting on it. They sat down and ate the fish, hungry now for the first time for many days. And it was the most delicious food they had ever tasted.

"Please, Lamb," said Lucy, "is this the way to Aslan's country?"

"Not for you," said the Lamb. "For you the door into Aslan's country is from your own world."

"What!" said Edmund. "Is there a way into Aslan's country from our world too?"

"There is a way into my country from all the worlds," said the Lamb; but as he spoke, his snowy white flushed into tawny gold and his size changed and he was Aslan himself, towering above them and scattering light from his mane.

"Oh, Aslan," said Lucy. "Will you tell us how to get into your country from our world?"

"I shall be telling you all the time," said Aslan. "But I will not tell you how long or short the way will be; only that it lies across a river. But do not fear that, for I am the great Bridge Builder. And now come; I will open the door in the sky and send you to your own land."

"Please, Aslan," said Lucy. "Before we go, will you tell us when we can come back to Narnia again? Please. And oh, do, do, do make it soon."

"Dearest," said Aslan very gently, "you and your brother will never come back to Narnia."

"Oh, *Aslan*!!" said Edmund and Lucy both together in despairing voices.

"You are too old, children," said Aslan, "and you must begin to come close to your own world now."

"It isn't Narnia, you know," sobbed Lucy. "It's you. We shan't meet you there. And how can we live, never meeting you?"

"But you shall meet me, dear one," said Aslan.

"Are – are you there too, Sir?" said Edmund.

"I am," said Aslan. "But there I have another name. You must learn to know me by that name. This was the very reason why you were brought to Narnia, that by knowing me here for a little, you may know me better there."

"And is Eustace never to come back here either?" said Lucy.

"Child," said Aslan, "do you really need to know that? Come, I am opening the door in the sky." Then all in one moment there was a rending of the blue wall (like a curtain being torn) and a terrible white light from beyond the sky, and the feel of Aslan's mane and a Lion's kiss on their foreheads and then – the back bedroom in Aunt Alberta's home in Cambridge.

Only two more things need to be told. One is that Caspian and his men all came safely back to Ramandu's Island. And the three lords woke from their sleep. Caspian married Ramandu's daughter and they all reached Narnia in the end, and she became a great queen and the mother and grandmother of great kings. The other is that back in our own world everyone soon started saying how Eustace had improved, and how "You'd never know him for the same boy": everyone except Aunt Alberta, who said he had become very commonplace and tiresome and it must have been the influence of those Pevensie children.

THE SILVER CHAIR

A MAP OF THE
WILD LANDS
OF THE NORTH

N

W

E

S

LANTERN

WASTE

GREAT RIVER

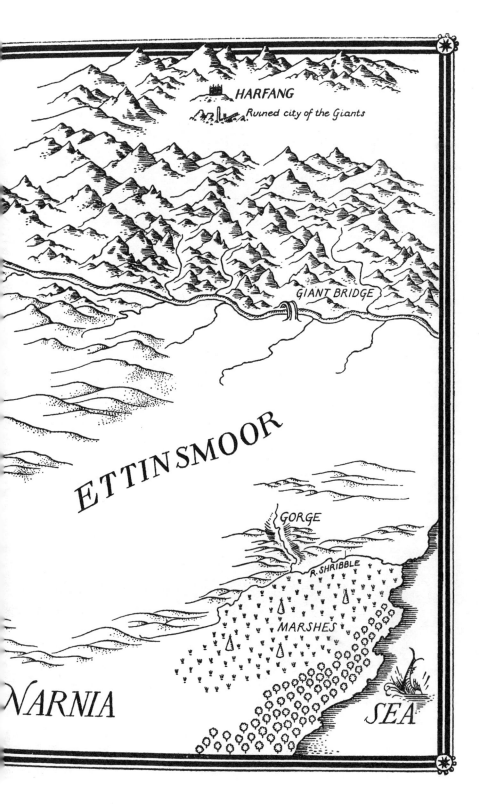

HARFANG

Ruined city of the Giants

GIANT BRIDGE

ETTINSMOOR

GORGE

R. SHRIBBLE

MARSHES

NARNIA

SEA

THE SILVER CHAIR

CONTENTS

To Nicholas Hardie

CHAPTER ONE

BEHIND THE GYM

It was a dull autumn day and Jill Pole was crying behind the gym.

She was crying because they had been bullying her. This is not going to be a school story, so I shall say as little as possible about Jill's school, which is not a pleasant subject. It was Co-educational, a school for both boys and girls, what used to be called a "mixed" school; some said it was not nearly so mixed as the minds of the people who ran it. These people had the idea that boys and girls should be allowed to do what they liked. And unfortunately what ten or fifteen of the biggest boys and girls liked best was bullying the others. All sorts of things, horrid things, went on which at an ordinary school would have been found out and stopped in half a term; but at this school they weren't. Or even if they were, the people who did them were not expelled or punished. The Head said they were interesting psychological cases and sent for them and talked to them for hours. And if you knew the right sort of things to say to the Head, the main result was that you became rather a favourite than otherwise.

That was why Jill Pole was crying on that dull autumn day on the damp little path which runs between the back of the gym and the shrubbery. And she hadn't nearly finished her cry when a boy came round the corner of the gym whistling, with his hands in his pockets. He nearly ran into her.

"Can't you look where you're going?" said Jill Pole.

"All *right*," said the boy, "you needn't start—" and then he noticed her face. "I say, Pole," he said, "what's up?"

Jill only made faces; the sort you make when you're trying to say something but find that if you speak you'll start crying again.

"It's *Them*, I suppose – as usual," said the boy grimly, digging his hands further into his pockets.

Jill nodded. There was no need for her to say any-thing, even if she could have said it. They both knew.

"Now, look here," said the boy, "there's no good us all—"

He meant well, but he *did* talk rather like someone beginning a lecture. Jill suddenly flew into a temper (which is quite a likely thing to happen if you have been interrupted in a cry).

"Oh, go away and mind your own business," she said. "Nobody asked you to come barging in, did they? And you're a nice person to start telling us what we all ought to do, aren't you? I suppose you mean we ought to spend all our time sucking up to Them, and currying favour, and dancing attendance on Them like you do."

"Oh, Lor!" said the boy, sitting down on the grassy bank at the edge of the shrubbery and very quickly getting up again because the grass was soaking wet. His name unfortunately was Eustace Scrubb, but he wasn't a bad sort.

"Pole!" he said. "Is that fair? Have I been doing anything of the sort this term? Didn't I stand up to Carter about the rabbit? And didn't I keep the secret about Spivvins – under torture too? And didn't I—"

"I d-don't know and I don't care," sobbed Jill.

Scrubb saw that she wasn't quite herself yet and very sensibly offered her a peppermint. He had one too. Presently Jill began to see things in a clearer light.

"I'm sorry, Scrubb," she said presently. "I wasn't fair. You have done all that – this term."

"Then wash out last term if you can," said Eustace. "I was a different chap then. I was – gosh! What a little tick I was."

"Well, honestly, you were," said Jill.

"You think there has been a change, then?" said Eustace.

"It's not only me," said Jill. "Everyone's been saying so. *They've* noticed it. Eleanor Blakiston heard Adela Pennyfather talking about it in our changing room yesterday. She said, 'Someone's got hold of that Scrubb kid. He's quite unmanageable this term. We shall have to attend to *him* next.'"

Eustace gave a shudder. Everyone at Experiment House knew what it was like being "attended to" by *Them*.

Both children were quiet for a moment. The drops dripped off the laurel leaves.

"Why were you so different last term?" said Jill presently.

"A lot of queer things happened to me in the hols," said Eustace mysteriously.

"What sort of things?" asked Jill.

Eustace didn't say anything for quite a long time. Then he said: "Look here, Pole, you and I hate this place about as much as anybody can hate anything, don't we?"

"I know I do," said Jill.

"Then I really think I can trust you."

"Dam' good of you," said Jill.

"Yes, but this is a really terrific secret. Pole, I say, are you good at believing things? I mean things that everyone here would laugh at?"

"I've never had the chance," said Jill, "but I think I would be."

"Could you believe me if I said I'd been right out of the world – outside this world – last hols?"

"I wouldn't know what you meant."

"Well, don't let's bother about worlds, then. Supposing I told you I'd been in a place where animals can talk and where there are – er – enchantments and dragons – and – well, all the sorts of things you have in fairy tales." Scrubb felt terribly awkward as he said this and got red in the face.

"How did you get there?" said Jill. She also felt curiously shy.

"The only way you can – by Magic," said Eustace almost in a whisper. "I was with two cousins of mine. We were just – whisked away. They'd been there before."

Now that they were talking in whispers Jill somehow felt it easier to believe. Then suddenly a horrible suspicion came over her and she said (so fiercely that for the moment she looked like a tigress):

"If I find you've been pulling my leg I'll never speak to you again; never, never, never."

"I'm not," said Eustace. "I swear I'm not. I swear by – by everything."

(When I was at school one would have said, "I swear by the Bible." But Bibles were not encouraged at Experiment House.)

"All right," said Jill, "I'll believe you."

"And tell nobody?"

"What do you take me for?"

They were very excited as they said this. But when they had said it and Jill looked round and saw the dull autumn sky and heard the drip off the leaves and thought of all the hopelessness of Experiment House (it was a thirteen-week term and there were still eleven weeks to come) she said:

"But after all, what's the good? We're not there; we're here. And we jolly well can't get *there*. Or can we?"

"That's what I've been wondering," said Eustace. "When we came back from That Place, Someone said that the two Pevensie kids (that's my two cousins) could never go there again. It was their third time, you see. I suppose they've had their share. But he never said I couldn't. Surely he would have said so, unless he meant that I was to get back? And I can't help wondering, can we – could we—?"

"Do you mean, do something to make it happen?"

Eustace nodded.

"You mean we might draw a circle on the ground – and write things in queer letters in it – and stand inside it – and recite charms and spells?"

"Well," said Eustace after he had thought hard for a bit. "I believe that was the sort of thing I was thinking of, though I never did it. But now that it comes to the point, I've an idea that all those circles and things are rather rot. I don't think he'd like them. It would look as if we thought we could make him do things. But really, we can only ask him."

"Who is this person you keep on talking about?"

"They call him Aslan in That Place," said Eustace.

"What a curious name!"

"Not half so curious as himself," said Eustace solemnly. "But let's get on. It can't do any harm, just asking. Let's stand side by side, like this. And we'll hold out our arms in front of us with the palms down: like they did in Ramandu's Island—"

"Whose island?"

"I'll tell you about that another time. And he might like us to face the east. Let's see, where is the east?"

"I don't know," said Jill.

"It's an extraordinary thing about girls that they never know the points of the compass," said Eustace.

"You don't know either," said Jill indignantly.

"Yes I do, if only you didn't keep on interrupting. I've got it now. That's the east, facing up into the laurels. Now, will you say the words after me?"

"What words?" asked Jill.

"The words I'm going to say, of course," answered Eustace. "Now—"

And he began, "Aslan, Aslan, Aslan!"

"Aslan, Aslan, Aslan," repeated Jill.

"Please let us two go into—"

At that moment a voice from the other side of the gym was heard shouting out, "Pole? Yes, I know where she is. She's blubbing behind the gym. Shall I fetch her out?"

Jill and Eustace gave one glance at each other, dived under the laurels, and began scrambling up the steep, earthy slope of the shrubbery at a speed which did them great credit. (Owing to the curious methods of teaching at Experiment House, one did not learn much French or Maths or Latin or things of that sort; but one did learn a lot about getting away quickly and quietly when They were looking for one.)

After about a minute's scramble they stopped to listen, and knew by the noises they heard that they were being followed.

"If only the door was open again!" said Scrubb as they went on, and Jill nodded. For at the top of the shrubbery was a high stone wall and in that wall a door by which you could get out on to open moor. This door was nearly always locked. But there had been times when people had found it open; or perhaps there had been only one time. But you may imagine how the memory of even one time kept people hoping, and trying the door; for if it should happen to be unlocked it would be a splendid way of getting outside the school grounds without being seen.

Jill and Eustace, now both very hot and very grubby from going along bent almost double under the laurels, panted up to the wall. And there was the door, shut as usual.

"It's sure to be no good," said Eustace with his hand on the handle; and then, "O-o-oh, by Gum!!" For the handle turned and the door opened.

A moment before, both of them had meant to get through that doorway in double quick time, if by any chance the door was not locked. But when the door actually opened, they both stood stock still. For what they saw was quite different from what they had expected.

They had expected to see the grey, heathery slope of the moor going up and up to join the dull autumn sky. Instead, a blaze of sunshine met them. It poured through the doorway as the light of a June day pours into a garage when you open the door. It made the drops of water on the grass glitter like beads and showed up the dirtiness of Jill's tear-stained face. And the sunlight was coming from what certainly did look like a different world — what they could see of it. They saw smooth turf, smoother and brighter than Jill had ever seen before, and blue sky and, darting to and fro, things so bright that they might have been jewels or huge butterflies.

Although she had been longing for something like this, Jill felt frightened. She looked at Scrubb's face and saw that he was frightened too.

"Come on, Pole," he said in a breathless voice.

"Can we get back? Is it safe?" asked Jill.

At that moment a voice shouted from behind, a mean, spiteful little voice. "Now then, Pole," it squeaked. "Everyone knows you're there. Down you come." It was the voice of Edith Jackle, not one of Them herself but one of their hangers-on and tale-bearers.

"Quick!" said Scrubb. "Here. Hold hands. We mustn't get separated." And before she quite knew what was happening, he had grabbed her hand and pulled her through the door, out of the school grounds, out of England, out of our whole world into That Place.

The sound of Edith Jackle's voice stopped as suddenly as the voice on the radio when it is switched off. Instantly there was a quite different sound all about them. It came from those bright things overhead, which now turned out to be birds. They were making a riotous noise, but it was much more like music – rather advanced music which you don't quite take in at the first hearing – than birds' songs ever are in our world. Yet, in spite of the singing, there was a sort of background of immense silence. That silence, combined with the freshness of the air, made Jill think they must be on the top of a very high mountain.

Scrubb still had her by the hand and they were walking forward, staring about them on every side. Jill saw that huge trees, rather like cedars but bigger, grew in every direction. But as they did not grow close together, and as there was no under-growth, this did not prevent one from seeing a long way into the forest to left and right. And as far as Jill's eye could reach, it was all the same – level turf, darting birds with yellow, or dragonfly blue, or rainbow plumage, blue shadows, and emptiness. There was not a breath of wind in that cool, bright air. It was a very lonely forest.

Right ahead there were no trees: only blue sky. They went straight on without speaking till suddenly Jill heard Scrubb say, "Look out!" and felt herself jerked back. They were at the very edge of a cliff.

Jill was one of those lucky people who have a good head for heights. She didn't mind in the least standing on the edge of a precipice. She was rather annoyed with Scrubb for pulling her back – "just as if I was a kid", she said – and she wrenched her hand out of his. When she saw how very white he had turned, she despised him.

"What's the matter?" she said. And to show that she was not afraid, she stood very near the edge indeed; in fact, a good deal nearer than even she liked. Then she looked down.

She now realized that Scrubb had some excuse for looking white, for no cliff in our world is to be compared with this. Imagine yourself at the top of the very highest cliff you know. And imagine yourself looking down to the very bottom. And then imagine that the precipice goes on below that, as far again, ten times as far, twenty times as far. And when you've looked down all that distance imagine little white things that might, at first glance, be mistaken for sheep, but presently you realize that they are clouds – not little wreaths of mist but the enormous white, puffy clouds which are themselves as big as most mountains. And at last, in between those clouds, you get your first glimpse of the real bottom, so far away that you can't make out whether it's field or wood, or land or water: further below those clouds than you are above them.

Jill stared at it. Then she thought that perhaps, after all, she would step back a foot or so from the edge; but she didn't like to for fear of what Scrubb would think. Then she suddenly decided that she didn't care what he thought, and that she would jolly well get away from that horrible edge and never laugh at anyone for not liking heights again. But when she tried to move, she found she couldn't. Her legs seemed to have turned into putty. Everything was swimming before her eyes.

"What are you doing, Pole? Come back — blithering little idiot!" shouted Scrubb. But his voice seemed to be coming from a long way off. She felt him grabbing at her. But by now she had no control over her own arms and legs. There was a moment's struggling on the cliff edge. Jill was too frightened and dizzy to know quite what she was doing, but two things she remembered as long as she lived (they often came back to her in dreams). One was that she had wrenched herself free of Scrubb's clutches; the other was that, at the same moment, Eustace himself, with a terrified scream, had lost his balance and gone hurtling to the depths.

Fortunately, she was given no time to think over what she had done. Some huge, brightly coloured animal had rushed to the edge of the cliff. It was lying down, leaning over, and (this was the odd thing) blowing. Not roaring or snorting, but just blowing from its wide-opened mouth; blowing out as steadily as a vacuum cleaner sucks in. Jill was lying so close to the creature that she could feel the breath vibrating steadily through its body. She was lying still because she couldn't get up. She was nearly fainting; indeed, she wished she could really faint, but faints don't come for the asking. At last she saw, far away below her, a tiny black speck floating away from the cliff and slightly upwards. As it rose, it also got further away. By the time it was nearly on a level with the cliff-top it was so far off that she lost sight of it. It was obviously moving away from them at a great speed. Jill couldn't help thinking that the creature at her side was blowing it away.

So she turned and looked at the creature. It was a lion.

CHAPTER TWO

JILL IS GIVEN A TASK

Without a glance at Jill, the lion rose to its feet and gave one last blow. Then, as if satisfied with its work, it turned and stalked slowly away, back into the forest.

"It must be a dream, it must, it must," said Jill to herself. "I'll wake up in a moment." But it wasn't, and she didn't.

"I do wish we'd never come to this dreadful place," said Jill. "I don't believe Scrubb knew any more about it than I do. Or if he did, he had no business to bring me here without warning me what it was like. It's not my fault he fell over that cliff. If he'd left me alone we should both be all right." Then she remembered again the scream that Scrubb had given when he fell, and burst into tears.

Crying is all right in its way while it lasts. But you have to stop sooner or later, and then you still have to decide what to do. When Jill stopped, she found she was dreadfully thirsty. She had been lying face downward, and now she sat up. The birds had ceased singing and there was perfect silence except for one small, persistent sound, which seemed to come from a good distance away. She listened carefully, and felt almost sure it was the sound of running water.

Jill got up and looked round her very carefully. There was no sign of the lion; but there were so many trees about that it might easily be quite close without her seeing it. For all she knew, there might be several lions. But her thirst was very bad now, and she plucked up her courage to go and look for that running water. She went on tiptoes, stealing cautiously from tree to tree, and stopping to peer round her at every step.

The wood was so still that it was not difficult to decide where the sound was coming from. It grew clearer every moment and, sooner than she expected, she came to an open glade and saw the stream, bright as glass, running across the turf a stone's throw away from her. But although the sight of the water made her feel ten times thirstier than before, she didn't rush forward and drink. She stood as still as if she had been turned into stone, with her mouth wide open. And she had a very good reason; just on this side of the stream lay the lion.

It lay with its head raised and its two fore-paws out in front of it, like the lions in Trafalgar Square. She knew at once that it had seen her, for its eyes looked straight into hers for a moment and then turned away – as if it knew her quite well and didn't think much of her.

"If I run away, it'll be after me in a moment," thought Jill. "And if I go on, I shall run straight into its mouth." Anyway, she couldn't have moved if she had tried, and she couldn't take her eyes off it. How long this lasted, she could not be sure; it seemed like hours. And the thirst became so bad that she almost felt she would not mind being eaten by the lion if only she could be sure of getting a mouthful of water first.

"If you're thirsty, you may drink."

They were the first words she had heard since Scrubb had spoken to her on the edge of the cliff. For a second she stared here and there, wondering who had spoken. Then the voice said again, "If you are thirsty, come and drink," and of course she remembered what Scrubb had said about animals talking in that other world, and realized that it was the lion speaking. Anyway, she had seen its lips move this time, and the voice was not like a man's. It was deeper, wilder, and stronger; a sort of heavy, golden voice. It did not make her any less frightened than she had been before, but it made her frightened in rather a different way.

"Are you not thirsty?" said the lion.

"I'm *dying* of thirst," said Jill.

"Then drink," said the lion.

"May I – could I – would you mind going away while I do?" said Jill.

The Lion answered this only by a look and a very low growl. And as Jill gazed at its motionless bulk, she realized that she might as well have asked the whole mountain to move aside for her convenience.

The delicious rippling noise of the stream was driving her nearly frantic.

"Will you promise not to – do anything to me, if I do come?" said Jill.

"I make no promise," said the Lion.

Jill was so thirsty now that, without noticing it, she had come a step nearer.

"*Do* you eat girls?" she said.

"I have swallowed up girls and boys, women and men, kings and emperors, cities and realms," said the Lion. It didn't say this as if it were boasting, nor as if it were sorry, nor as if it were angry. It just said it.

"I daren't come and drink," said Jill.

"Then you will die of thirst," said the Lion.

"Oh dear!" said Jill, coming another step nearer. "I suppose I must go and look for another stream then."

"There is no other stream," said the Lion.

It never occurred to Jill to disbelieve the Lion – no one who had seen his stern face could do that – and her mind suddenly made itself up. It was the worst thing she had ever had to do, but she went forward to the stream, knelt down, and began scooping up water in her hand. It was the coldest, most refreshing water she had ever tasted. You didn't need to drink much of it, for it quenched your thirst at once. Before she tasted it she had been intending to make a dash away from the Lion the moment she had finished. Now, she realized that this would be on the whole the most dangerous thing of all. She got up and stood there with her lips still wet from drinking.

"Come here," said the Lion. And she had to. She was almost between its front paws now, looking straight into its face. But she couldn't stand that for long; she dropped her eyes.

"Human Child," said the Lion. "Where is the boy?"

"He fell over the cliff," said Jill, and added, "Sir". She didn't know what else to call him, and it sounded cheek to call him nothing.

"How did he come to do that, Human Child?"

"He was trying to stop me from falling, Sir."

"Why were you so near the edge, Human Child?"

"I was showing off, Sir."

"That is a very good answer, Human Child. Do so no more. And now" (here for the first time the Lion's face became a little less stern) "the Boy is safe. I have blown him to Narnia. But your task will be the harder because of what you have done."

"Please, what task, Sir?" said Jill.

"The task for which I called you and him here out of your own world."

This puzzled Jill very much. "It's mistaking me for someone else," she thought. She didn't dare to tell the Lion this, though she felt things would get into a dreadful muddle unless she did.

"Speak your thought, Human Child," said the Lion.

"I was wondering – I mean – could there be some mistake? Because nobody called me and Scrubb, you know. It was we who asked to come here. Scrubb said we were to call to – to Somebody – it was a name I wouldn't know – and perhaps the Somebody would let us in. And we did, and then we found the door open."

"You would not have called to me unless I had been calling to you," said the Lion.

"Then you are Somebody, sir?" said Jill.

"I am. And now hear your task. Far from here in the land of Narnia there lives an aged king who is sad because he has no prince of his blood to be king after him. He has no heir because his only son was stolen from him many years ago, and no one in Narnia knows where that prince went or whether he is still alive. But he is. I lay on you this command, that you seek this lost prince until either you have found him and brought him to his father's house, or else died in the attempt, or else gone back into your own world."

"How, please?" said Jill.

"I will tell you, child," said the Lion. "These are the signs by which I will guide you in your quest. First; as soon as the boy Eustace sets foot in Narnia, he will meet an old and dear friend. He must greet that friend at once; if he does, you will both have good help. Second; you must journey out of Narnia to the north till you come to the ruined city of the ancient giants. Third; you shall find a writing on a stone in that ruined city, and you must do what the writing tells you. Fourth; you will know the lost prince (if you find him) by this, that he will be the first person you have met in your travels who will ask you to do something in my name, in the name of Aslan."

As the Lion seemed to have finished, Jill thought she should say something. So she said, "Thank you very much. I see."

"Child," said Aslan, in a gentler voice than he had yet used, "perhaps you do not see quite as well as you think. But the first step is to remember. Repeat to me, in order, the four signs."

Jill tried, and didn't get them quite right. So the Lion corrected her, and made her repeat them again and again till she could say them perfectly. He was very patient over this, so that when it was done, Jill plucked up courage to ask:

"Please, how am I to get to Narnia?"

"On my breath," said the Lion. "I will blow you into the west of the world as I blew Eustace."

"Shall I catch him in time to tell him the first sign? But I suppose it won't matter. If he sees an old friend, he's sure to go and speak to him, isn't he?"

"You will have no time to spare," said the Lion. "That is why I must send you at once. Come. Walk before me to the edge of the cliff."

Jill remembered very well that if there was no time to spare, that was her own fault. "If I hadn't made such a fool of myself, Scrubb and I would have been going together. And he'd have heard all the instructions as well as me," she thought. So she did as she was told. It was very alarming walking back to the edge of the cliff, especially as the Lion did not walk with her but behind her — making no noise on his soft paws.

But long before she had got anywhere near the edge, the voice behind her said, "Stand still. In a moment I will blow. But first, remember, remember, remember the signs. Say them to yourself when you wake in the morning and when you lie down at night, and when you wake in the middle of the night. And whatever strange things may happen to you, let nothing turn your mind from following the signs. And secondly, I give you a warning. Here on the mountain I have spoken to you clearly: I will not often do so down in Narnia. Here on the mountain, the air is clear and your mind is clear; as you drop down into Narnia, the air will thicken. Take great care that it does not confuse your mind. And the signs which you have learned here will not look at all as you expect them to look, when you meet them there. That is why it is so important to know them by heart and pay no attention to appearances. Remember the signs and believe the signs. Nothing else matters. And now, Daughter of Eve, farewell—"

The voice had been growing softer towards the end of this speech and now it faded away altogether. Jill looked behind her. To her astonishment she saw the cliff already more than a hundred yards behind her, and the Lion himself a speck of bright gold on the edge of it. She had been setting her teeth and clenching her fists for a terrible blast of lion's breath; but the breath had really been so gentle that she had not even noticed the moment at which she left the earth. And now, there was nothing but air for thousands upon thousands of feet below her.

She felt frightened only for a second. For one thing, the world beneath her was so very far away that it seemed to have nothing to do with her. For another, floating on the breath of the Lion was so extremely comfortable. She found she could lie on her back or on her face and twist any way she pleased, just as you can in water (if you've learned to float really well). And because she was moving at the same pace as the breath, there was no wind, and the air seemed beautifully warm. It was not in the least like being in an aeroplane, because there was no noise and no vibration. If Jill had ever been in a balloon she might have thought it more like that; only better.

When she looked back now she could take in for the first time the real size of the mountain she was leaving. She wondered why a mountain so huge as that was not covered with snow and ice – "but I suppose all that sort of thing is different in this world," thought Jill. Then she looked below her; but she was so high that she couldn't make out whether she was floating over land or sea, nor what speed she was going at.

"By Jove! The signs!" said Jill suddenly. "I'd better repeat them." She was in a panic for a second or two, but she found she could still say them all correctly. "So that's all right," she said, and lay back on the air as if it was a sofa, with a sigh of contentment.

"Well, I do declare," said Jill to herself some hours later, "I've been asleep. Fancy sleeping on air. I wonder if anyone's done it before. I don't suppose they have. Oh, bother — Scrubb probably has! On this same journey, a little bit before me. Let's see what it looks like down below."

What it looked like was an enormous, very dark blue plain. There were no hills to be seen, but there were biggish white things moving slowly across it. "Those must be clouds," she thought. "But far bigger than the ones we saw from the cliff. I suppose they're bigger because they're nearer. I must be getting lower. Bother this sun."

The sun which had been high overhead when she began her journey was now getting in her eyes. This meant that it was getting lower, ahead of her. Scrubb was quite right in saying that Jill (I don't know about girls in general) didn't think much about points of the compass. Otherwise she would have known, when the sun began getting in her eyes, that she was travelling pretty nearly due west.

Staring at the blue plain below her, she presently noticed that there were little dots of brighter, paler colour in it here and there. "It's the sea!" thought Jill. "I do believe those are islands." And so they were. She might have felt rather jealous if she had known that some of them were islands which Scrubb had seen from a ship's deck and even landed on; but she didn't know this. Then, later on, she began to see that there were little wrinkles on the blue flatness; little wrinkles which must be quite big ocean waves if you were down among them. And now, all along the horizon there was a thick dark line which grew thicker and darker so quickly that you could see it growing. That was the first sign she had had of the great speed at which she was travelling. And she knew that the thickening line must be land.

Suddenly from her left (for the wind was in the south) a great white cloud came rushing towards her, this time on the same level as herself. And before she knew where she was, she had shot right into the middle of its cold, wet fogginess. That took her breath away, but she was in it only for a moment. She came out blinking in the sunlight and found her clothes wet. (She had on a blazer and sweater and shorts and stockings and pretty thick shoes; it had been a muddy sort of day in England.) She came out lower than she had gone in; and as soon as she did so she noticed something which, I suppose, she ought to have been expecting, but which came as a surprise and a shock. It was Noises. Up till then she had travelled in total silence. Now, for the first time, she heard the noise of waves and the crying of seagulls. And now, too, she smelled the smell of the sea. There was no mistake about her speed now. She saw two waves meet with a smack and a spout of foam go up between them; but she had hardly seen it before it was a hundred yards behind her.

The land was getting nearer at a great pace. She could see mountains far inland, and other nearer mountains on her left. She could see bays and headlands, woods and fields, stretches of sandy beach. The sound of waves breaking on the shore was growing louder every second and drowning the other sea noises.

Suddenly the land opened right ahead of her. She was coming to the mouth of a river. She was very low now, only a few feet above the water. A wave-top came against her toe and a great splash of foam spurted up, drenching her nearly to the waist. Now she was losing speed. Instead of being carried up the river she was gliding in to the river bank on her left. There were so many things to notice that she could hardly take them all in; a smooth, green lawn, a ship so brightly coloured that it looked like an enormous piece of jewellery, towers and battlements, banners fluttering in the air, a crowd, gay clothes, armour, gold, swords, a sound of music. But this was all jumbled. The first thing that she knew clearly was that she had alighted and was standing under a thicket of trees close by the river side, and there, only a few feet away from her, was Scrubb.

The first thing she thought was how very grubby and untidy and generally unimpressive he looked. And the second was "How wet I am!"

CHAPTER THREE

THE SAILING OF THE KING

What made Scrubb look so dingy (and Jill too, if she could only have seen herself) was the splendour of their surroundings. I had better describe them at once.

Through a cleft in those mountains which Jill had seen far inland as she approached the land, the sunset light was pouring over a level lawn. On the far side of the lawn, its weather-vanes glittering in the light, rose a many-towered and many-turreted castle; the most beautiful castle Jill had ever seen. On the near side was a quay of white marble and, moored to this, the ship: a tall ship with high forecastle and high poop, gilded and crimson, with a great flag at the mast-head, and many banners waving from the decks, and a row of shields, bright as silver, along the bulwarks. The gangplank was laid to her, and at the foot of it, just ready to go on board, stood an old, old man. He wore a rich mantle of scarlet which opened in front to show his silver mail shirt. There was a thin circlet of gold on his head. His beard, white as wool, fell nearly to his waist. He stood straight enough, leaning one hand on the shoulder of a richly dressed lord who seemed younger than himself: but you could see he was very old and frail. He looked as if a puff of wind could blow him away, and his eyes were watery.

Immediately in front of the King – who had turned round to speak to his people before going on board the ship – there was a little chair on wheels and, harnessed to it, a little donkey: not much bigger than a big retriever. In this chair sat a fat little dwarf. He was as richly dressed as the King, but because of his fatness and because he was sitting hunched up among cushions, the effect was quite different: it made him look like a shapeless little bundle of fur and silk and velvet. He was as old as the King, but more hale and hearty, with very keen eyes. His bare head, which was bald and extremely large, shone like a gigantic billiard ball in the sunset light.

Further back, in a half-circle, stood what Jill at once knew to be the courtiers. They were well worth looking at for their clothes and armour alone. As far as that went, they looked more like a flower-bed than a crowd. But what really made Jill open her eyes and mouth as wide as they would go, was the people themselves. If "people" was the right word. For only about one in every five was human. The rest were things you never see in our world. Fauns, satyrs, centaurs: Jill could give a name to these, for she had seen pictures of them. Dwarfs, too. And there were a lot of animals she knew as well; bears, badgers, moles, leopards, mice and various birds. But then they were so very different from the animals which one called by the same names in England. Some of them were much bigger — the mice, for instance, stood on their hind legs and were over two feet high. But quite apart from that, they all looked different. You could see by the expression in their faces that they could talk and think just as well as you could.

"Golly!" thought Jill. "So it's true after all." But next moment she added, "I wonder, are they friendly?" For she had just noticed, on the outskirts of the crowd, one or two giants and some people whom she couldn't give a name to at all.

At that moment Aslan and the signs rushed back into her mind. She had forgotten all about them for the last half-hour.

"Scrubb!" she whispered, grabbing his arm. "Scrubb, quick! Do you see anyone you know?"

"So *you've* turned up again, have you?" said Scrubb disagreeably (for which he had some reason). "Well, keep quiet, can't you? I want to listen."

"Don't be a fool," said Jill. "There isn't a moment to lose. Don't you see some old friend here? Because you've got to go and speak to him at once."

"What are you talking about?" said Scrubb.

"It's Aslan — the Lion — says you've got to," said Jill despairingly. "I've seen him."

"Oh, you have, have you? What did he say?"

"He said the very first person you saw in Narnia would be an old friend, and you'd got to speak to him at once."

"Well, there's nobody here I've ever seen in my life before; and anyway, I don't know whether this is Narnia."

"Thought you said you'd been here before," said Jill.

"Well, you thought wrong then."

"Well, I like that! You told me——"

"For heaven's sake dry up and let's hear what they're saying."

The King was speaking to the Dwarf, but Jill couldn't hear what he said. And, as far as she could make out, the Dwarf made no answer, though he nodded and wagged his head a great deal. Then the King raised his voice and addressed the whole court: but his voice was so old and cracked that she could understand very little of his speech — especially since it was all about people and places she had never heard of.

When the speech was over, the King stooped down and kissed the Dwarf on both cheeks, straightened himself, raised his right hand as if in blessing, and went, slowly and with feeble steps, up the gangway and on board the ship. The courtiers appeared to be greatly moved by his departure. Handkerchiefs were got out, sounds of sobbing were heard in every direction. The gangway was cast off, trumpets sounded from the poop, and the ship moved away from the quay. (It was being towed by a rowing-boat, but Jill didn't see that.)

"Now—" said Scrubb, but he didn't get any further, because at that moment a large white object — Jill thought for a second that it was a kite — came gliding through the air and alighted at his feet. It was a white owl, but so big that it stood as high as a good-sized dwarf.

It blinked and peered as if it were short-sighted, and put its head a little on one side, and said in a soft, hooting kind of voice:

"Tu-whoo, tu-whoo! Who are you two?"

"My name's Scrubb, and this is Pole," said Eustace. "Would you mind telling us where we are?"

"In the land of Narnia, at the King's castle of Cair Paravel."

"Is that the King who's just taken ship?"

"Too true, too true," said the Owl sadly, shaking its big head. "But who are you? There's something magic about you two. I saw you arrive: you *flew*. Everyone else was so busy seeing the King off that nobody knew. Except me. I happened to notice you, you flew."

"We were sent here by Aslan," said Eustace in a low voice.

"Tu-whoo, tu-whoo!" said the Owl, ruffling out its feathers. "This is almost too much for me, so early in the evening. I'm not quite myself till the sun's down."

"And we've been sent to find the lost Prince," said Jill, who had been anxiously waiting to get into the conversation.

"It's the first I've heard about it," said Eustace. "What prince?"

"You had better come and speak to the Lord Regent at once," it said. "That's him, over there in the donkey carriage; Trumpkin the Dwarf." The bird turned and began leading the way, muttering to itself, "Whoo! Tu-whoo! What a to-do! I can't think clearly yet. It's too early."

"What is the King's name?" asked Eustace.

"Caspian the Tenth," said the Owl. And Jill wondered why Scrubb had suddenly pulled up short in his walk and turned an extraordinary colour. She thought she had never seen him look so sick about anything. But before she had time to ask any questions they had reached the dwarf, who was just gathering up the reins of his donkey and preparing to drive back to the castle. The crowd of courtiers had broken up and were going in the same direction, by ones and twos and little knots, like people coming away from watching a game or a race.

"Tu-whoo! Ahem! Lord Regent," said the Owl, stooping down a little and holding its beak near the Dwarf's ear.

"Heh? What's that?" said the Dwarf.

"Two strangers, my lord," said the Owl.

"Rangers! What d'ye mean?" said the Dwarf. "I see two uncommonly grubby man-cubs. What do they want?"

"My name's Jill," said Jill, pressing forward. She was very eager to explain the important business on which they had come.

"The girl's called Jill," said the Owl, as loud as it could.

"What's that?" said the Dwarf. "The girls are all killed! I don't believe a word of it. What girls? Who killed 'em?"

"Only one girl, my lord," said the Owl. "Her name is Jill."

"Speak up, speak up," said the Dwarf. "Don't stand there buzzing and twittering in my ear. Who's been killed?"

"Nobody's been killed," hooted the Owl.

"Who?"

"NOBODY."

"All right, all right. You needn't shout. I'm not so deaf as all that. What do you mean by coming here to tell me that nobody's been killed? Why should anyone have been killed?"

"Better tell him I'm Eustace," said Scrubb.

"The boy's Eustace, my lord," hooted the Owl as loud as it could.

"Useless?" said the Dwarf irritably. "I dare say he is. Is that any reason for bringing him to court? Hey?"

"Not useless," said the Owl. "EUSTACE."

"Used to it, is he? I don't know what you're talking about, I'm sure. I tell you what it is, Master Glimfeather; when I was a young Dwarf there used to be *talking* beasts and birds in this country who really could talk. There wasn't all this mumbling and muttering and whispering. It wouldn't have been tolerated for a moment. Not for a moment, sir. Urnus, my trumpet please—"

A little Faun who had been standing quietly beside the Dwarf's elbow all this time now handed him a silver ear-trumpet. It was made like the musical instrument called a serpent, so that the tube curled right round the Dwarf's neck. While he was getting it settled, the Owl, Glimfeather, suddenly said to the children in a whisper:

"My brain's a bit clearer now. Don't say anything about the lost Prince. I'll explain later. It wouldn't do, wouldn't do, Tu-Whoo! Oh, *what* a to-do!"

"Now," said the Dwarf, "if you *have* anything sensible to say, Master Glimfeather, try and say it. Take a deep breath and don't attempt to speak too quickly."

With help from the children, and in spite of a fit of coughing on the part of the Dwarf, Glimfeather explained that the strangers had been sent by Aslan to visit the court of Narnia. The Dwarf glanced quickly up at them with a new expression in his eyes.

"Sent by the Lion himself, hey?" he said. "And from — m'm — from that other Place — beyond the World's End, hey?"

"Yes, my lord," bawled Eustace into the trumpet.

"Son of Adam and Daughter of Eve, hey?" said the Dwarf. But people at Experiment House haven't heard of Adam and Eve, so Jill and Eustace couldn't answer this. But the Dwarf didn't seem to notice.

"Well, my dears," he said, taking first one and then the other by the hand and bowing his head a little. "You are very heartily welcome. If the good King, my poor Master, had not this very hour set sail for Seven Isles, he would have been glad of your coming. It would have brought back his youth to him for a moment — for a moment. And now, it is high time for supper. You shall tell me your business in full council tomorrow morning. Master Glimfeather, see that bedchambers and suitable clothes and all else are provided for these guests in the most honourable fashion. And — Glimfeather — in your ear—"

Here the Dwarf put his mouth close to the Owl's head and, no doubt, intended to whisper: but, like other deaf people, he wasn't a very good judge of his own voice, and both children heard him say, "See that they're properly washed."

After that, the Dwarf touched up his donkey and it set off towards the castle at something between a trot and a waddle (it was a very fat little beast), while the Faun, the Owl, and the children followed at a rather slower pace. The sun had set and the air was growing cool.

They went across the lawn and then through an orchard and so to the North Gate of Cair Paravel, which stood wide open. Inside, they found a grassy courtyard. Lights were already showing from the windows of the great hall on their right and from a more complicated mass of buildings straight ahead. Into these the Owl led them, and there a most delightful person was called to look after Jill. She was not much taller than Jill herself, and a good deal slenderer, but obviously full grown, graceful as a willow, and her hair was willowy too, and there seemed to be moss in it.

She brought Jill to a round room in one of the turrets, where there was a little bath sunk in the floor and a fire of sweet-smelling woods burning on the flat hearth and a lamp hanging by a silver chain from the vaulted roof. The window looked west into the strange land of Narnia, and Jill saw the red remains of the sunset still glowing behind distant mountains. It made her long for more adventures and feel sure that this was only the beginning.

When she had had her bath, and brushed her hair, and put on the clothes that had been laid out for her – they were the kind that not only felt nice, but looked nice and smelt nice and made nice sounds when you moved as well – she would have gone back to gaze out of that exciting window, but she was interrupted by a bang on the door.

"Come in," said Jill. And in came Scrubb, also bathed and splendidly dressed in Narnian clothes. But his face didn't look as if he were enjoying it.

"Oh, here you are at last," he said crossly, flinging himself into a chair. "I've been trying to find you for ever so long."

"Well, now you have," said Jill. "I say, Scrubb, isn't it all simply too exciting and scrumptious for words?" She had forgotten all about the signs and the lost Prince for the moment.

"Oh! That's what you think, is it?" said Scrubb: and then, after a pause, "I wish to goodness we'd never come."

"Why on earth?"

"I can't bear it," said Scrubb. "Seeing the King – Caspian – a doddering old man like that. It's – it's frightful."

"Why, what harm does it do you?"

"Oh, you don't understand. Now that I come to think of it, you couldn't. I didn't tell you that this world has a different time from ours."

"How do you mean?"

"The time you spend here doesn't take up any of our time. Do you see? I mean, however long we spend here, we shall still get back to Experiment House at the moment we left it—"

"That won't be much fun—"

"Oh, dry up! Don't keep interrupting. And when you're back in England – in our world – you can't tell how time is going here. It might be any number of years in Narnia while we're having one year at home. The Pevensies explained it all to me, but, like a fool, I forgot about it. And now apparently it's been about seventy years – Narnian years – since I was here last. Do you see now? And I come back and find Caspian an old, old man."

"Then the King *was* an old friend of yours!" said Jill. A horrid thought had struck her.

"I should jolly well think he was," said Scrubb miserably. "About as good a friend as a chap could have. And last time he was only a few years older than me. And to see that old man with a white beard, and to remember Caspian as he was the morning we captured the Lone Islands, or in the fight with the Sea Serpent — oh, it's frightful. It's worse than coming back and finding him dead."

"Oh, shut up," said Jill impatiently. "It's far worse than you think. We've muffed the first sign." Of course Scrubb did not understand this. Then Jill told him about her conversation with Aslan and the four signs and the task of finding the lost prince which had been laid upon them.

"So you see," she wound up, "you did see an old friend, just as Aslan said, and you ought to have gone and spoken to him at once. And now you haven't, and everything is going wrong from the very beginning."

"But how was I to know?" said Scrubb.

"If you'd only listened to me when I tried to tell you, we'd be all right," said Jill.

"Yes, and if you hadn't played the fool on the edge of that cliff and jolly nearly murdered me — all right, I said *murder*, and I'll say it again as often as I like, so keep your hair on — we'd have come together and both known what to do."

"I suppose he *was* the very first person you saw?" said Jill. "You must have been here hours before me. Are you sure you didn't see anyone else first?"

"I was only here about a minute before you," said Scrubb. "He must have blown you quicker than me. Making up for lost time: the time *you* lost."

"Don't be a perfect beast, Scrubb," said Jill. "Hullo! What's that?"

It was the castle bell ringing for supper, and thus what looked like turning into a first-rate quarrel was happily cut short. Both had a good appetite by this time.

Supper in the great hall of the castle was the most splendid thing either of them had ever seen; for though Eustace had been in that world before, he had spent his whole visit at sea and knew nothing of the glory and courtesy of the Narnians at home in their own land.

The banners hung from the roof, and each course came in with trumpeters and kettledrums. There were soups that would make your mouth water to think of, and the lovely fishes called pavenders, and venison and peacock and pies, and ices and jellies and fruit and nuts, and all manner of wines and fruit drinks. Even Eustace cheered up and admitted that it was "something like". And when all the serious eating and drinking was over, a blind poet came forward and struck up the grand old tale of Prince Cor and Aravis and the horse Bree, which is called *The Horse and His Boy* and tells of an adventure that happened in Narnia and Calormen and the lands between, in the golden Age when Peter was High King in Cair Paravel. (I haven't time to tell it now, though it is well worth hearing.)

When they were dragging themselves upstairs to bed, yawning their heads off, Jill said, "I bet we sleep well, tonight"; for it had been a full day. Which just shows how little anyone knows what is going to happen to them next.

CHAPTER FOUR

A PARLIAMENT OF OWLS

It is a very funny thing that the sleepier you are, the longer you take about getting to bed; especially if you are lucky enough to have a fire in your room. Jill felt she couldn't even start undressing unless she sat down in front of the fire for a bit first. And once she had sat down, she didn't want to get up again. She had already said to herself about five times, "I must go to bed", when she was startled by a tap on the window.

She got up, pulled the curtain, and at first saw nothing but darkness. Then she jumped and started backwards, for something very large had dashed itself against the window, giving a sharp tap on the glass as it did so. A very unpleasant idea came into her head – "Suppose they have giant moths in this country! Ugh!" But then the thing came back, and this time she was almost sure she saw a beak, and that the beak had made the tapping noise. "It's some huge bird," thought Jill. "Could it be an eagle?" She didn't very much want a visit even from an eagle, but she opened the window and looked out. Instantly, with a great whirring noise, the creature alighted on the window-sill and stood there filling up the whole window, so that Jill had to step back to make room for it. It was the Owl.

"Hush, hush! Tu-whoo, tu-whoo," said the Owl. "Don't make a noise. Now, are you two really in earnest about what you've got to do?"

"About the lost Prince, you mean?" said Jill. "Yes, we've got to be." For now she remembered the Lion's voice and face, which she had nearly forgotten during the feasting and storytelling in the hall.

"Good!" said the Owl. "Then there's no time to waste. You must get away from here at once. I'll go and wake the other human. Then I'll come back for you. You'd better change those court clothes and put on something you can travel in. I'll be back in two twos. Tu-whoo!" And without waiting for an answer, he was gone.

If Jill had been more used to adventures, she might have doubted the Owl's word, but this never occurred to her: and in the exciting idea of a midnight escape she forgot her sleepiness. She changed back into sweater and shorts — there was a guide's knife on the belt of the shorts which might come in useful — and added a few of the things that had been left in the room for her by the girl with the willowy hair. She chose a short cloak that came down to her knees and had a hood ("just the thing, if it rains," she thought), a few handkerchiefs and a comb. Then she sat down and waited.

She was getting sleepy again when the Owl returned.

"Now we're ready," it said.

"You'd better lead the way," said Jill. "I don't know all these passages yet."

"Tu-whoo!" said the Owl. "We're not going through the castle. That would never do. You must ride on me. We shall fly."

"Oh!" said Jill, and stood with her mouth open, not much liking the idea. "Shan't I be far too heavy for you?"

"Tu-whoo, tu-whoo! Don't you be a fool. I've already carried the other one. Now. But we'll put out that lamp first."

As soon as the lamp was out, the bit of the night which you saw through the window looked less dark — no longer black, but grey. The Owl stood on the window-sill with his back to the room and raised his wings. Jill had to climb on to his short fat body and get her knees under the wings and grip tight. The feathers felt beautifully warm and soft but there was nothing to hold on by. "I wonder how Scrubb liked *his* ride!" thought Jill. And just as she was thinking this, with a horrid plunge they had left the window-sill, and the wings were making a flurry round her ears, and the night air, rather cool and damp, was flying in her face.

It was much lighter than she expected, and though the sky was overcast, one patch of watery silver showed where the moon was hiding above the clouds. The fields beneath her looked grey, and the trees black. There was a certain amount of wind — a hushing, ruffling sort of wind which meant that rain was coming soon.

The Owl wheeled round so that the castle was now ahead of them. Very few of the windows showed lights. They flew right over it, northwards, crossing the river: the air grew colder, and Jill thought she could see the white reflection of the Owl in the water beneath her. But soon they were on the north bank of the river, flying above wooded country.

The Owl snapped at something which Jill couldn't see.

"Oh, don't, please!" said Jill. "Don't jerk like that. You nearly threw me off."

"I beg your pardon," said the Owl. "I was just nabbing a bat. There's nothing so sustaining, in a small way, as a nice plump little bat. Shall I catch you one?"

"No, thanks," said Jill with a shudder.

He was flying a little lower now and a large, black-looking object was looming up towards them. Jill had just time to see that it was a tower – a partly ruinous tower, with a lot of ivy on it, she thought – when she found herself ducking to avoid the archway of a window, as the Owl squeezed with her through the ivied and cobwebby opening, out of the fresh, grey night into a dark place inside the top of the tower.

It was rather fusty inside and, the moment she slipped off the Owl's back, she knew (as one usually does somehow) that it was quite crowded. And when voices began saying out of the darkness from every direction "Tu-whoo! Tu-whoo!" she knew it was crowded with owls. She was rather relieved when a very different voice said: "Is that you, Pole?"

"Is that you, Scrubb?" said Jill.

"Now," said Glimfeather, "I think we're all here. Let us hold a parliament of owls."

"Tu-whoo, tu-whoo. True for you. That's the right thing to do," said several voices.

"Half a moment," said Scrubb's voice. "There's something I want to say first."

"Do, do, do," said the owls; and Jill said, "Fire ahead."

"I suppose all you chaps – owls, I mean," said Scrubb, "I suppose you all know that King Caspian the Tenth, in his young days, sailed to the eastern end of the world. Well, I was with him on that journey; with him and Reepicheep the Mouse, and the Lord Drinian and all of them. I know it sounds hard to believe, but people don't grow older in our world at the same speed as they do in yours. And what I want to say is this, that I'm the King's man; and if this parliament of owls is any sort of plot against the King, I'm having nothing to do with it."

"Tu-whoo, tu-whoo, we're all the King's owls too," said the owls.

"What's it all about then?" said Scrubb.

"It's only this," said Glimfeather. "That if the Lord Regent, the Dwarf Trumpkin, hears you are going to look for the lost Prince, he won't let you start. He'd keep you under lock and key sooner."

"Great Scott!" said Scrubb. "You don't mean that Trumpkin is a traitor? I used to hear a lot about him in the old days, at sea. Caspian – the King, I mean – trusted him absolutely."

"Oh, no," said a voice. "Trumpkin's no traitor. But more than thirty champions (knights, centaurs, good giants, and all sorts) have at one time or another set out to look for the lost Prince, and none of them have ever come back. And at last the King said he was not going to have all the bravest Narnians destroyed in the search for his son. And now nobody is allowed to go."

"But surely he'd let *us* go," said Scrubb. "When he knew who I was and who had sent me."

("Sent both of us," put in Jill.)

"Yes," said Glimfeather, "I think, very likely, he would. But the King's away. And Trumpkin will stick to the rules. He's as true as steel, but he's deaf as a post and very peppery. You could never make him see that this might be the time for making an exception to the rule."

"You might think he'd take some notice of *us*, because we're owls and everyone knows how wise owls are," said someone else. "But he's so old now he'd only say, 'You're a mere chick. I remember you when you were an egg. Don't come trying to teach *me*, Sir. Crabs and crumpets!'"

This owl imitated Trumpkin's voice rather well, and there were sounds of owlish laughter all round. The children began to see that the Narnians all felt about Trumpkin as people feel at school about some crusty teacher, whom everyone is a little afraid of and everyone makes fun of and nobody really dislikes.

"How long is the King going to be away?" asked Scrubb.

"If only we knew!" said Glimfeather. "You see, there has been a rumour lately that Aslan himself has been seen in the islands – in Terebinthia, I think it was. And the King said he would make one more attempt before he died to see Aslan face to face again, and ask his advice about who is to be King after him. But we're all afraid that, if he doesn't meet Aslan in Terebinthia, he'll go on east, to Seven Isles and the Lone Islands – and on and on. He never talks about it, but we all know he has never forgotten that voyage to the world's end. I'm sure in his heart of hearts he wants to go there again."

"Then there's no good waiting for him to come back?" said Jill.

"No, no good," said the Owl. "Oh, what a to-do! If only you two had known and spoken to him at once! He'd have arranged everything – probably given you an army to go with you in search of the Prince."

Jill kept quiet at this and hoped Scrubb would be sporting enough not to tell all the owls why this hadn't happened. He was, or very nearly. That is, he only muttered under his breath, "Well, it wasn't *my* fault," before saying out loud:

"Very well. We'll have to manage without it. But there's just one thing more I want to know. If this owls' parliament, as you call it, is all fair and above board and means no mischief, why does it have to be so jolly secret – meeting in a ruin at the dead of night, and all that?"

"Tu-whoo! Tu-whoo!" hooted several owls. "Where should we meet? When would anyone meet except at night?"

"You see," explained Glimfeather, "most of the creatures in Narnia have such unnatural habits. They do things by day, in broad blazing sunlight (ugh!) when everyone ought to be asleep. And, as a result, at night they're so blind and stupid that you can't get a word out of them. So we owls have got into the habit of meeting at sensible hours, on our own, when we want to talk about things."

"I see," said Scrubb. "Well now, let's get on. Tell us all about the lost Prince." Then an old owl, not Glimfeather, related the story.

About ten years ago, it appeared, when Rilian, the son of Caspian, was a very young knight, he rode with the Queen his mother on a May morning in the north parts of Narnia. They had many squires and ladies with them and all wore garlands of fresh leaves on their heads, and horns at their sides; but they had no hounds with them, for they were maying, not hunting.

In the warm part of the day they came to a pleasant glade where a fountain flowed freshly out of the earth, and there they dismounted and ate and drank and were merry. After a time the Queen felt sleepy, and they spread cloaks for her on the grassy bank, and Prince Rilian with the rest of the party went a little way from her, that their tales and laughter might not wake her.

And so, presently, a great serpent came out of the thick wood and stung the Queen in her hand. All heard her cry out and rushed towards her, and Rilian was first at her side. He saw the worm gliding away from her and made after it with his sword drawn. It was great, shining, and as green as poison, so that he could see it well: but it glided away into thick bushes and he could not come at it. So he returned to his mother, and found them all busy about her. But they were busy in vain, for at the first glance of her face Rilian knew that no physic in the world would do her good. As long as the life was in her she seemed to be trying hard to tell him something. But she could not speak clearly and, whatever her message was, she died without delivering it. It was then hardly ten minutes since they had heard her cry.

They carried the dead Queen back to Cair Paravel, and she was bitterly mourned by Rilian and by the King, and by all Narnia. She had been a great lady, wise and gracious and happy, King Caspian's bride whom he had brought home from the eastern end of the world. And men said that the blood of the stars flowed in her veins.

The Prince took his mother's death very hardly, as well he might. After that, he was always riding on the northern marches of Narnia, hunting for that venomous worm, to kill it and be avenged. No one remarked much on this, though the Prince came home from these wanderings looking tired and distraught. But about a month after the Queen's death, some said they could see a change in him. There was a look in his eyes as of a man who has seen visions, and though he would be out all day, his horse did not bear the signs of hard riding. His chief friend among the older courtiers was the Lord Drinian, he who had been his father's captain on that great voyage to the east parts of the earth.

One evening Drinian said to the Prince, "Your Highness must soon give over seeking the worm. There is no true vengeance on a witless brute as there might be on a man. You weary yourself in vain." The Prince answered him, "My Lord, I have almost forgotten the worm this seven days." Drinian asked him why, if that were so, he rode so continually in the northern woods. "My lord," said the Prince, "I have seen there the most beautiful thing that was ever made." "Fair Prince," said Drinian, "of your courtesy let me ride with you tomorrow, that I also may see this fair thing." "With a good will," said Rilian.

Then in good time on the next day they saddled their horses and rode a great gallop into the northern woods and alighted at that same fountain where the Queen got her death. Drinian thought it strange that the Prince should choose that place of all places, to linger in. And there they rested till it came to high noon: and at noon Drinian looked up and saw the most beautiful lady he had ever seen; and she stood at the north side of the fountain and said no word but beckoned to the Prince with her hand as if she bade him come to her. And she was tall and great, shining, and wrapped in a thin garment as green as poison. And the Prince stared at her like a man out of his wits. But suddenly the lady was gone, Drinian knew not where; and the two returned to Cair Paravel. It stuck in Drinian's mind that this shining green woman was evil.

Drinian doubted very much whether he ought not to tell this adventure to the King, but he had little wish to be a blab and a tale-bearer and so he held his tongue. But afterwards he wished he had spoken. For next day Prince Rilian rode out alone. That night he came not back, and from that hour no trace of him was ever found in Narnia nor any neighbouring land, and neither his horse nor his hat nor his cloak nor anything else was ever found.

Then Drinian in the bitterness of his heart went to Caspian and said, "Lord King, slay me speedily as a great traitor: for by my silence I have destroyed your son." And he told him the story.

Then Caspian caught up a battle-axe and rushed upon the Lord Drinian to kill him, and Drinian stood still as a stock for the death blow. But when the axe was raised, Caspian suddenly threw it away and cried out, "I have lost my queen and my son: shall I lose my friend also?" And he fell upon the Lord Drinian's neck and embraced him and both wept, and their friendship was not broken.

Such was the story of Rilian. And when it was over, Jill said, "I bet that serpent and that woman were the same person."

"True, true, we think the same as you," hooted the owls.

"But we don't think she killed the Prince," said Glimfeather, "because no bones—"

"We know she didn't," said Scrubb. "Aslan told Pole he was still alive somewhere."

"That almost makes it worse," said the oldest owl. "It means she has some use for him, and some deep scheme against Narnia. Long, long ago, at the very beginning, a White Witch came out of the north and bound our land in snow and ice for a hundred years. And we think this may be one of the same crew."

"Very well, then," said Scrubb. "Pole and I have got to find this Prince. Can you help us?"

"Have you any clue, you two?" asked Glimfeather.

"Yes," said Scrubb. "We know we've got to go north. And we know we've got to reach the ruins of a giant city."

At this there was a greater tu-whooing than ever, and noises of birds shifting their feet and ruffling their feathers, and then all the owls started speaking at once. They all explained how very sorry they were that they themselves could not go with the children on their search for the lost Prince.

"You'd want to travel by day, and we'd want to travel by night," they said. "It wouldn't do, wouldn't do." One or two owls added that even here in the ruined tower it wasn't nearly so dark as it had been when they began, and that the parliament had been going on quite long enough. In fact, the mere mention of a journey to the ruined city of giants seemed to have damped the spirits of those birds.

But Glimfeather said: "If they want to go that way — into Ettinsmoor — we must take them to one of the Marsh-wiggles. They're the only people who can help them much."

"True, true. Do," said the owls.

"Come on, then," said Glimfeather. "I'll take one. Who'll take the other? It must be done tonight."

"I will: as far as the Marsh-wiggles," said another owl.

"Are you ready?" said Glimfeather to Jill.

"I think Pole's asleep," said Scrubb.

CHAPTER FIVE

PUDDLEGLUM

Jill *was* asleep. Ever since the owls' parliament began she had been yawning terribly and now she had dropped off. She was not at all pleased at being waked again, and at finding herself lying on bare boards in a dusty belfry sort of place, completely dark, and almost completely full of owls. She was even less pleased when she heard that they had to set off for somewhere else – and not, apparently, for bed – on the Owl's back.

"Oh, come on, Pole, buck up," said Scrubb's voice. "After all, it *is* an adventure."

"I'm sick of adventures," said Jill crossly.

She did, however, consent to climb on to Glimfeather's back, and was thoroughly waked up (for a while) by the unexpected coldness of the air when he flew out with her into the night. The moon had disappeared and there were no stars. Far behind her she could see a single lighted window well above the ground; doubtless, in one of the towers of Cair Paravel. It made her long to be back in that delightful bedroom, snug in bed, watching the firelight on the walls.

She put her hands under her cloak and wrapped it tightly round her. It was uncanny to hear two voices in the dark air a little distance away; Scrubb and his owl were talking to one another. "*He* doesn't sound tired," thought Jill. She did not realize that he had been on great adventures in that world before and that the Narnian air was bringing back to him a strength he had won when he sailed the Eastern Seas with King Caspian.

Jill had to pinch herself to keep awake, for she knew that if she dozed on Glimfeather's back she would probably fall off. When at last the two owls ended their flight, she climbed stiffly off Glimfeather and found herself on flat ground. A chilly wind was blowing and they appeared to be in a place without trees. "Tu-whoo, tu-whoo!" Glimfeather was calling. "Wake up, Puddleglum. Wake up. It is on the Lion's business."

For a long time there was no reply. Then, a long way off, a dim light appeared and began to come nearer. With it came a voice.

"Owls ahoy!" it said. "What is it? Is the King dead? Has an enemy landed in Narnia? Is it a flood? Or dragons?"

When the light reached them, it turned out to be that of a large lantern. Jill could see very little of the person who held it. He seemed to be all legs and arms. The owls were talking to him, explaining everything, but she was too tired to listen. She tried to wake herself up a bit when she realized that they were saying goodbye to her. But she could never afterwards remember much except that, sooner or later, she and Scrubb were stooping to enter a low doorway and then (oh, thank heavens) were lying down on something soft and warm, and a voice was saying:

"There you are. Best we can do. You'll lie cold and hard. Damp too, I shouldn't wonder. Won't sleep a wink, most likely; even if there isn't a thunderstorm or a flood or the wigwam doesn't fall down on top of us all, as I've known them do. Must make the best of it—" But she was fast asleep before the voice had ended.

When the children woke late the next morning they found that they were lying, very dry and warm, on beds of straw in a dark place. A triangular opening let in the daylight.

"Where on earth are we?" asked Jill.

"In the wigwam of a Marsh-wiggle," said Eustace.

"A what?"

"A Marsh-wiggle. Don't ask me what it is. I couldn't see it last night. I'm getting up. Let's go and look for it."

"How beastly one feels after sleeping in one's clothes," said Jill, sitting up.

"I was just thinking how nice it was not to have to dress," said Eustace.

"Or wash either, I suppose," said Jill scornfully. But Scrubb had already got up, yawned, shaken himself, and crawled out of the wigwam. Jill did the same.

What they found outside was quite unlike the bit of Narnia they had seen on the day before. They were on a great flat plain which was cut into countless little islands by countless channels of water. The islands were covered with coarse grass and bordered with reeds and rushes. Sometimes there were beds of rushes about an acre in extent. Clouds of birds were constantly alighting in them and rising from them again – duck, snipe, bitterns, herons. Many wigwams like that in which they had passed the night could be seen dotted about, but all at a good distance from one another; for Marsh-wiggles are people who like privacy.

Except for the fringe of the forest several miles to the south and west of them, there was not a tree in sight. Eastward the flat marsh stretched to low sand-hills on the horizon, and you could tell by the salt tang in the wind which blew from that direction that the sea lay over there. To the North there were low pale-coloured hills, in places bastioned with rock. The rest was all flat marsh. It would have been a depressing place on a wet evening. Seen under a morning sun, with a fresh wind blowing, and the air filled with the crying of birds, there was something fine and fresh and clean about its loneliness. The children felt their spirits rise.

"Where has the thingummy got to, I wonder?" said Jill.

"The Marsh-wiggle," said Scrubb, as if he were rather proud of knowing the word. "I expect – hullo, that must be him." And then they both saw him, sitting with his back to them, fishing, about fifty yards away. He had been hard to see at first because he was nearly the same colour as the marsh and because he sat so still.

"I suppose we'd better go and speak to him," said Jill. Scrubb nodded. They both felt a little nervous.

As they drew nearer, the figure turned its head and showed them a long thin face with rather sunken cheeks, a tightly shut mouth, a sharp nose, and no beard. He was wearing a high, pointed hat like a steeple, with an enormously wide flat brim. The hair, if it could be called hair, which hung over his large ears was greeny-grey, and each lock was flat rather than round, so that they were like tiny reeds. His expression was solemn, his complexion muddy, and you could see at once that he took a serious view of life.

"Good morning, Guests," he said. "Though when I say *good* I don't mean it won't probably turn to rain or it might be snow, or fog, or thunder. You didn't get any sleep, I dare say."

"Yes we did, though," said Jill. "We had a lovely night."

"Ah," said the Marsh-wiggle, shaking his head. "I see you're making the best of a bad job. That's right. You've been well brought up, you have. You've learned to put a good face on things."

"Please, we don't know your name," said Scrubb.

"Puddleglum's my name. But it doesn't matter if you forget it. I can always tell you again."

The children sat down on each side of him. They now saw that he had very long legs and arms, so that although his body was not much bigger than a dwarf's, he would be taller than most men when he stood up. The fingers of his hands were webbed like a frog's, and so were his bare feet which dangled in the muddy water. He was dressed in earth-coloured clothes that hung loose about him.

"I'm trying to catch a few eels to make an eel stew for our dinner," said Puddleglum. "Though I shouldn't wonder if I didn't get any. And you won't like them much if I do."

"Why not?" asked Scrubb.

"Why, it's not in reason that you should like our sort of victuals, though I've no doubt you'll put a bold face on it. All the same, while I am a-catching of them, if you two could try to light the fire — no harm in trying! The wood's behind the wigwam. It may be wet. You could light it inside the wigwam, and then we'd get all the smoke in our eyes. Or you could light it outside, and then the rain would come and put it out. Here's my tinder-box. You won't know how to use it, I expect."

But Scrubb had learnt that sort of thing on his last adventure. The children ran back together to the wigwam, found the wood (which was perfectly dry) and succeeded in lighting a fire with rather less than the usual difficulty. Then Scrubb sat and took care of it while Jill went and had some sort of wash — not a very nice one — in the nearest channel. After that she saw to the fire and he had a wash. Both felt a good deal fresher, but very hungry.

Presently the Marsh-wiggle joined them. In spite of his expectation of catching no eels, he had a dozen or so, which he had already skinned and cleaned. He put a big pot on, mended the fire, and lit his pipe. Marsh-wiggles smoke a very strange, heavy sort of tobacco (some people say they mix it with mud) and the children noticed the smoke from Puddleglum's pipe hardly rose in the air at all. It trickled out of the bowl and downwards and drifted along the ground like a mist. It was very black and set Scrubb coughing.

"Now," said Puddleglum. "Those eels will take a mortal long time to cook, and either of you might faint with hunger before they're done. I knew a little girl — but I'd better not tell you that story. It might lower your spirits, and that's a thing I never do. So, to keep your minds off your hunger, we may as well talk about our plans."

"Yes, do let's," said Jill. "Can you help us to find Prince Rilian?"

The Marsh-wiggle sucked in his cheeks till they were hollower than you would have thought possible. "Well, I don't know that you'd call it *help*," he said. "I don't know that anyone can exactly *help*. It stands to reason we're not likely to get very far on a journey to the north, not at this time of the year, with the winter coming on soon and all. And an early winter too, by the look of things. But you mustn't let that make you down-hearted. Very likely, what with enemies, and mountains, and rivers to cross, and losing our way, and next to nothing to eat, and sore feet, we'll hardly notice the weather. And if we don't get far enough to do any good, we may get far enough not to get back in a hurry."

Both children noticed that he said "we", not "you", and both exclaimed at the same moment, "Are you coming with us?"

"Oh yes, I'm coming of course. Might as well, you see. I don't suppose we shall ever see the King back in Narnia, now that he's once set off for foreign parts; and he had a nasty cough when he left. Then there's Trumpkin. He's failing fast. And you'll find there'll have been a bad harvest after this terrible dry summer. And I shouldn't wonder if some enemy attacked us. Mark my words."

"And how shall we start?" said Scrubb.

"Well," said the Marsh-wiggle very slowly, "all the others who ever went looking for Prince Rilian started from that same fountain where the Lord Drinian saw the lady. They went north, mostly. And as none of them ever came back, we can't exactly say how they got on."

"We've got to start by finding a ruined city of giants," said Jill. "Aslan said so."

"Got to start by *finding* it, have we?" answered Puddleglum. "Not allowed to start by *looking* for it, I suppose?"

"That's what I meant, of course," said Jill. "And then, when we've found it—"

"Yes, when!" said Puddleglum very drily.

"Doesn't anyone know where it is?" asked Scrubb.

"I don't know about Anyone," said Puddleglum. "And I won't say I haven't heard of that Ruined City. You wouldn't start from the fountain, though. You'd have to go across Ettinsmoor. That's where the Ruined City is, if it's anywhere. But I've been as far in that direction as most people and I never got to any ruins, so I won't deceive you."

"Where's Ettinsmoor?" said Scrubb.

"Look over there northward," said Puddleglum, pointing with his pipe. "See those hills and bits of cliff? That's the beginning of Ettinsmoor. But there's a river between it and us; the river Shribble. No bridges, of course."

"I suppose we can ford it, though," said Scrubb.

"Well, it *has* been forded," admitted the Marsh-wiggle.

"Perhaps we shall meet people on Ettinsmoor who can tell us the way," said Jill.

"You're right about meeting people," said Puddleglum.

"What sort of people live there?" she asked.

"It's not for me to say they aren't all right in their own way," answered Puddleglum. "If you like their way."

"Yes, but what *are* they?" pressed Jill. "There are so many strange creatures in this country. I mean, are they animals, or birds, or dwarfs, or what?"

The Marsh-wiggle gave a long whistle. "Phew!" he said. "Don't you know? I thought the owls had told you. They're giants."

Jill winced. She had never liked giants even in books, and she had once met one in a nightmare. Then she saw Scrubb's face, which had turned rather green, and thought to herself, "I bet he's in a worse funk than I am." That made her feel braver.

"The King told me long ago," said Scrubb – "that time when I was with him at sea – that he'd jolly well beaten those giants in war and made them pay him tribute."

"That's true enough," said Puddleglum. "They're at peace with us all right. As long as we stay on our own side of the Shribble, they won't do us any harm. Over on their side, on the moor – Still, there's always a chance. If we don't get near any of them, and if none of them forget themselves, and if we're not seen, it's just possible we might get a long way."

"Look here!" said Scrubb, suddenly losing his temper, as people so easily do when they have been frightened. "I don't believe the whole thing can be half as bad as you're making out; any more than the beds in the wigwam were hard or the wood was wet. I don't think Aslan would ever have sent us if there was so little chance as all that."

He quite expected the Marsh-wiggle to give him an angry reply, but he only said, "That's the spirit, Scrubb. That's the way to talk. Put a good face on it. But we all need to be very careful about our tempers, seeing all the hard times we shall have to go through together. Won't do to quarrel, you know. At any rate, don't begin it too soon. I know these expeditions usually *end* that way: knifing one another, I shouldn't wonder, before all's done. But the longer we can keep off it—"

"Well, if you feel it's so hopeless," interrupted Scrubb, "I think you'd better stay behind. Pole and I can go on alone, can't we, Pole?"

"Shut up and don't be an ass, Scrubb," said Jill hastily, terrified lest the Marsh-wiggle should take him at his word.

"Don't you lose heart, Pole," said Puddleglum. "I'm coming, sure and certain. I'm not going to lose an opportunity like this. It will do me good. They all say – I mean, the other wiggles all say – that I'm too flighty; don't take life seriously enough. If they've said it once, they've said it a thousand times. 'Puddleglum,' they've said, 'you're altogether too full of bobance and bounce and high spirits. You've got to learn that life isn't all fricasseed frogs and eel pie. You want something to sober you down a bit. We're only saying it for your own good, Puddleglum.' That's what they say. Now a job like this – a journey up north just as winter's beginning, looking for a prince who probably isn't there, by way of a ruined city that no one has ever seen – will be just the thing. If that doesn't steady a chap, I don't know what will." And he rubbed his big frog-like hands together as if he were talking of going to a party or a pantomime. "And now," he added, "let's see how those eels are getting on."

When the meal came it was delicious and the children had two large helpings each. At first the Marsh-wiggle wouldn't believe that they really liked it, and when they had eaten so much that he had to believe them, he fell back on saying that it would probably disagree with them horribly. "What's food for wiggles may be poison for humans, I shouldn't wonder," he said. After the meal they had tea, in tins (as you've seen men having it who are working on the road), and Puddleglum had a good many sips out of a square black bottle. He offered the children some of it, but they thought it very nasty.

The rest of the day was spent in preparations for an early start the next morning. Puddleglum, being far the biggest, said he would carry three blankets, with a large bit of bacon rolled up inside them. Jill was to carry the remains of the eels, some biscuit, and the tinder-box. Scrubb was to carry both his own cloak and Jill's when they didn't want to wear them. Scrubb (who had learned some shooting when he sailed to the east under Caspian) had Puddleglum's second-best bow, and Puddleglum had his best one; though he said that what with winds, and damp bowstrings, and bad light, and cold fingers, it was a hundred to one against either of them hitting anything. He and Scrubb both had swords – Scrubb had brought the one which had been left out for him in his room at Cair Paravel – but Jill had to be content with her knife. There would have been a quarrel about this, but as soon as they started sparring the wiggle rubbed his hands and said, "Ah, there you are. I thought as much. That's what usually happens on adventures." This made them both shut up.

All three went to bed early in the wigwam. This time the children really had a rather bad night. That was because Puddleglum, after saying, "You'd better try for some sleep, you two; not that I suppose any of us will close an eye tonight," instantly went off into such a loud, continuous snore that, when Jill at last got to sleep, she dreamed all night about road-drills and waterfalls and being in express trains in tunnels.

CHAPTER SIX

THE WILD WASTELANDS OF THE NORTH

At about nine o'clock the next morning three lonely figures might have been seen picking their way across the Shribble by the shoals and stepping-stones. It was a shallow, noisy stream, and even Jill was not wet above her knees when they reached the northern bank. About fifty yards ahead, the land rose up to the beginning of the moor, everywhere steeply, and often in cliffs.

"I suppose *that's* our way!" said Scrubb, pointing left and west to where a stream flowed down from the moor through a shallow gorge. But the Marsh-wiggle shook his head.

"The giants mainly live along the side of that gorge," he said. "You might say the gorge was like a street to them. We'll do better straight ahead, even though it's a bit steep."

They found a place where they could scramble up, and in about ten minutes stood panting at the top. They cast a longing look back at the valley-land of Narnia and then turned their faces to the North. The vast, lonely moor stretched on and up as far as they could see. On their left was rockier ground. Jill thought that must be the edge of the giants' gorge and did not much care about looking in that direction. They set out.

It was good, springy ground for walking, and a day of pale winter sunlight. As they got deeper into the moor, the loneliness increased: one could hear peewits and see an occasional hawk. When they halted in the middle of the morning for a rest and a drink in a little hollow by a stream, Jill was beginning to feel that she might enjoy adventures after all, and said so.

"We haven't had any yet," said the Marsh-wiggle.

Walks after the first halt – like school mornings after break or railway journeys after changing trains – never go on as they were before. When they set out again, Jill noticed that the rocky edge of the gorge had drawn nearer. And the rocks were less flat, more upright, than they had been. In fact they were like little towers of rock. And what funny shapes they were!

"I do believe," thought Jill, "that all the stories about giants might have come from those funny rocks. If you were coming along here when it was half dark, you could easily think those piles of rock were giants. Look at that one, now! You could almost imagine that the lump on top was a head. It would be rather too big for the body, but it would do well enough for an ugly giant. And all that bushy stuff – I suppose it's heather and birds' nests, really – would do quite well for hair and beard. And the things sticking out on each side are quite like ears. They'd be horribly big, but then I dare say giants would have big ears, like elephants. And – o-o-oh!—"

Her blood froze. The thing moved. It was a real giant. There was no mistaking it; she had seen it turn its head. She had caught a glimpse of the great, stupid, puff-cheeked face. All the things were giants, not rocks. There were forty or fifty of them, all in a row; obviously standing with their feet on the bottom of the gorge and their elbows resting on the edge of the gorge, just as men might stand leaning on a wall – lazy men, on a fine morning after breakfast.

"Keep straight on," whispered Puddleglum, who had noticed them too. "Don't look at them. And whatever you do, don't *run*. They'd all be after us in a moment."

So they kept on, pretending not to have seen the giants. It was like walking past the gate of a house where there is a fierce dog, only far worse. There were dozens and dozens of these giants. They didn't look angry – or kind – or interested at all. There was no sign that they had seen the travellers.

Then – whizz-whizz-whizz – some heavy object came hurtling through the air, and with a crash a big boulder fell about twenty paces ahead of them. And then – thud! – another fell twenty feet behind.

"Are they aiming at us?" asked Scrubb.

"No," said Puddleglum. "We'd be a good deal safer if they were. They're trying to hit *that* – that cairn over there to the right. They won't hit *it*, you know. *It's* safe enough; they're such very bad shots. They play cock-shies most fine mornings. About the only game they're clever enough to understand."

It was a horrible time. There seemed no end to the line of giants, and they never ceased hurling stones, some of which fell extremely close. Quite apart from the real danger, the very sight and sound of their faces and voices were enough to scare anyone. Jill tried not to look at them.

After about twenty-five minutes the giants apparently had a quarrel. This put an end to the cock-shies, but it is not pleasant to be within a mile of quarrelling giants. They stormed and jeered at one another in long, meaningless words of about twenty syllables each. They foamed and gibbered and jumped in their rage, and each jump shook the earth like a bomb. They lammed each other on the head with great, clumsy stone hammers; but their skulls were so hard that the hammers bounced off again, and then the monster who had given the blow would drop his hammer and howl with pain because it had stung his fingers. But he was so stupid that he would do exactly the same thing a minute later. This was a good thing in the long run, for by the end of an hour all the giants were so hurt that they sat down and began to cry. When they sat down, their heads were below the edge of the gorge, so that you saw them no more; but Jill could hear them howling and blubbering and boo-hooing like great babies even after the place was a mile behind.

That night they bivouacked on the bare moor, and Puddleglum showed the children how to make the best of their blankets by sleeping back to back. (The backs keep each other warm and you can then have both blankets on top.) But it was chilly even so, and the ground was hard and lumpy. The Marsh-wiggle told them they would feel more comfortable if only they thought how very much colder it would be later on and further north; but this didn't cheer them up at all.

They travelled across Ettinsmoor for many days, saving the bacon and living chiefly on the moor-fowl (they were not, of course, *talking* birds) which Eustace and the wiggle shot. Jill rather envied Eustace for being able to shoot; he had learned it on his voyage with King Caspian. As there were countless streams on the moor, they were never short of water. Jill thought that when, in books, people live on what they shoot, it never tells you what a long, smelly, messy job it is plucking and cleaning dead birds, and how cold it makes your fingers. But the great thing was that they met hardly any giants. One giant saw them, but he only roared with laughter and stumped away about his own business.

About the tenth day, they reached a place where the country changed. They came to the northern edge of the moor and looked down a long, steep slope into a different, and grimmer, land. At the bottom of the slope were cliffs: beyond these, a country of high mountains, dark precipices, stony valleys, ravines so deep and narrow that one could not see far into them, and rivers that poured out of echoing gorges to plunge sullenly into black depths. Needless to say, it was Puddleglum who pointed out a sprinkling of snow on the more distant slopes.

"But there'll be more on the north side of them, I shouldn't wonder," he added.

It took them some time to reach the foot of the slope and, when they did, they looked down from the top of the cliffs at a river running below them from west to east. It was walled in by precipices on the far side as well as on their own, and it was green and sunless, full of rapids and waterfalls. The roar of it shook the earth even where they stood.

"The bright side of it is," said Puddleglum, "that if we break our necks getting down the cliff, then we're safe from being drowned in the river."

"What about *that*?" said Scrubb suddenly, pointing upstream to their left. Then they all looked and saw the last thing they were expecting – a bridge. And what a bridge, too! It was a huge, single arch that spanned the gorge from cliff-top to cliff-top; and the crown of that arch was as high above the cliff-tops as the dome of St Paul's is above the street.

"Why, it must be a giants' bridge!" said Jill.

"Or a sorcerer's, more likely," said Puddleglum. "We've got to look out for enchantments in a place like this. I think it's a trap. I think it'll turn into mist and melt away just when we're out on the middle of it."

"Oh, for goodness' sake, don't be such a wet blanket," said Scrubb. "Why on earth shouldn't it be a proper bridge?"

"Do you think any of the giants we've seen would have sense to build a thing like that?" said Puddleglum.

"But mightn't it have been built by other giants?" said Jill. "I mean, by giants who lived hundreds of years ago, and were far cleverer than the modern kind? It might have been built by the same ones who built the giant city we're looking for. And that would mean we were on the right track – the old bridge leading to the old city!"

"That's a real brainwave, Pole," said Scrubb. "It must be that. Come on."

So they turned and went to the bridge. And when they reached it, it certainly seemed solid enough. The single stones were as big as those at Stonehenge and must have been squared by good masons once, though now they were cracked and crumbled. The balustrade had apparently been covered with rich carvings, of which some traces remained; mouldering faces and forms of giants, minotaurs, squids, centipedes, and dreadful gods. Puddleglum still didn't trust it, but he consented to cross it with the children.

The climb up to the crown of the arch was long and heavy. In many places the great stones had dropped out, leaving horrible gaps through which you looked down on the river foaming thousands of feet below. They saw an eagle fly through under their feet. And the higher they went, the colder it grew, and the wind blew so that they could hardly keep their footing. It seemed to shake the bridge.

When they reached the top and could look down the further slope of the bridge, they saw what looked like the remains of an ancient giant road stretching away before them into the heart of the mountains. Many stones of its pavement were missing and there were wide patches of grass between those that remained. And riding towards them on that ancient road were two people of normal grown-up human size.

"Keep on. Move towards them," said Puddleglum. "Anyone you meet in a place like this is as likely as not to be an enemy, but we mustn't let them think we're afraid."

By the time they had stepped off the end of the bridge on to the grass, the two strangers were quite close. One was a knight in complete armour with his visor down. His armour and his horse were black; there was no device on his shield and no banneret on his spear. The other was a lady on a white horse, a horse so lovely that you wanted to kiss its nose and give it a lump of sugar at once. But the lady, who rode side-saddle and wore a long, fluttering dress of dazzling green, was lovelier still.

"Good day, t-r-r-avellers," she cried out in a voice as sweet as the sweetest bird's song, trilling her R's delightfully. "Some of you are young pilgrims to walk this rough waste."

"That's as may be, Ma'am," said Puddleglum very stiffly and on his guard.

"We're looking for the ruined city of the giants," said Jill.

"The r-r-ruined city?" said the Lady. "That is a strange place to be seeking. What will you do if you find it?"

"We've got to——" began Jill, but Puddleglum interrupted.

"Begging your pardon, Ma'am. But we don't know you or your friend — a silent chap, isn't he? — and you don't know us. And we'd as soon not talk to strangers about our business, if you don't mind. Shall we have a little rain soon, do you think?"

The Lady laughed: the richest, most musical laugh you can imagine. "Well, children," she said, "you have a wise, solemn old guide with you. I think none the worse of him for keeping his own counsel, but I'll be free with mine. I have often heard the name of the giantish City Ruinous, but never met any who would tell me the way thither. This road leads to the burgh and castle of Harfang, where dwell the Gentle Giants. They are as mild, civil, prudent, and courteous as those of Ettinsmoor are foolish, fierce, savage, and given to all beastliness. And in Harfang you may or may not hear tidings of the City Ruinous, but certainly you shall find good lodgings and merry hosts. You would be wise to winter there or, at the least, to tarry certain days for your ease and refreshment. There you shall have steaming baths, soft beds, and bright hearths; and the roast and the baked and the sweet and the strong will be on the table four times in a day."

"I say!" exclaimed Scrubb. "That's something like! Think of sleeping in a bed again."

"Yes, and having a hot bath," said Jill. "Do you think they'll ask us to stay? We don't know them, you see."

"Only tell them," answered the Lady, "that She of the Green Kirtle salutes them by you, and has sent them two fair Southern children for the Autumn Feast."

"Oh, thank you, thank you ever so much," said Jill and Scrubb.

"But have a care," said the Lady. "On whatever day you reach Harfang, that you come not to the door too late. For they shut their gates a few hours after noon, and it is the custom of the castle that they open to none when once they have drawn bolt, how hard so ever he knock."

The children thanked her again, with shining eyes, and the Lady waved to them. The Marsh-wiggle took off his steeple-hat and bowed very stiffly. Then the silent Knight and the Lady started walking their horses up the slope of the bridge with a great clatter of hoofs.

"Well!" said Puddleglum. "I'd give a good deal to know where *she's* coming from and where she's going. Not the sort you expect to meet in the wilds of Giantland, is she? Up to no good, I'll be bound."

"Oh, rot!" said Scrubb. "I thought she was simply super. And think of hot meals and warm rooms. I do hope Harfang isn't a long way off."

"Same here," said Jill. "And hadn't she a scrumptious dress? And the horse!"

"All the same," said Puddleglum, "I wish we knew a bit more about her."

"I *was* going to ask her all about herself," said Jill. "But how could I when you wouldn't tell her anything about us?"

"Yes," said Scrubb. "And why were you so stiff and unpleasant? Didn't you like them?"

"Them?" said the wiggle. "Who's *them*? I only saw one."

"Didn't you see the Knight?" asked Jill.

"I saw a suit of armour," said Puddleglum. "Why didn't he speak?"

"I expect he was shy," said Jill. "Or perhaps he just wants to look at her and listen to her lovely voice. I'm sure I would if I was him."

"I was wondering," remarked Puddleglum, "what you'd really see if you lifted up the visor of that helmet and looked inside."

"Hang it all," said Scrubb. "Think of the shape of the armour! What *could* be inside it except a man?"

"How about a skeleton?" asked the Marsh-wiggle with ghastly cheerfulness. "Or perhaps," he added as an afterthought, "nothing at all. I mean, nothing you could see. Someone invisible."

"Really, Puddleglum," said Jill with a shudder, "you do have the most horrible ideas. How do you think of them all?"

"Oh, bother his ideas!" said Scrubb. "He's always expecting the worst, and he's always wrong. Let's think about those Gentle Giants and get on to Harfang as quickly as we can. I wish I knew how far it is."

And now they nearly had the first of those quarrels which Puddleglum had foretold: not that Jill and Scrubb hadn't been sparring and snapping at each other a good deal before, but this was the first really serious disagreement. Puddleglum didn't want them to go to Harfang at all. He said that he didn't know what a giant's idea of being "gentle" might be, and that, anyway, Aslan's signs had said nothing about staying with giants, gentle or otherwise.

The children, on the other hand, who were sick of wind and rain, and skinny fowl roasted over campfires, and hard, cold earth to sleep on, were absolutely dead set to visit the Gentle Giants. In the end, Puddleglum agreed to do so, but only on one condition. The others must give an absolute promise that, unless he gave them leave, they would not tell the Gentle Giants that they came from Narnia or that they were looking for Prince Rilian. And they gave him this promise, and went on.

After that talk with the Lady things got worse in two different ways. In the first place the country was much harder. The road led through endless, narrow valleys down which a cruel north wind was always blowing in their faces. There was nothing that could be used for firewood, and there were no nice little hollows to camp in, as there had been on the moor. And the ground was all stony, and made your feet sore by day and every bit of you sore by night.

In the second place, whatever the Lady had intended by telling them about Harfang, the actual effect on the children was a bad one. They could think about nothing but beds and baths and hot meals and how lovely it would be to get indoors. They never talked about Aslan, or even about the lost Prince, now. And Jill gave up her habit of repeating the signs over to herself every night and morning. She said to herself, at first, that she was too tired, but she soon forgot all about it. And though you might have expected that the idea of having a good time at Harfang would have made them more cheerful, it really made them more sorry for themselves and more grumpy and snappy with each other and with Puddleglum.

At last they came one afternoon to a place where the gorge in which they were travelling widened out, and dark fir woods rose on either side. They looked ahead and saw that they had come through the mountains. Before them lay a desolate, rocky plain: beyond it, further mountains capped with snow. But between them and those further mountains rose a low hill with an irregular flattish top.

"Look! Look!" cried Jill, and pointed across the plain; and there, through the gathering dusk, from beyond the flat hill, everyone saw lights. Lights! Not moonlight, nor fires, but a homely cheering row of lighted windows.

If you have never been in the wild wilderness, day and night, for weeks, you will hardly understand how they felt.

"Harfang!" cried Scrubb and Jill in glad, excited voices; and, "Harfang," repeated Puddleglum in a dull, gloomy voice. But he added, "Hullo! Wild geese!" and had the bow off his shoulder in a second. He brought down a good fat goose. It was far too late to think of reaching Harfang that day. But they had a hot meal and a fire, and started the night warmer than they had been for over a week. After the fire had gone out, the night grew bitterly cold, and when they woke next morning, their blankets were stiff with frost.

"Never mind!" said Jill, stamping her feet. "Hot baths tonight!"

CHAPTER SEVEN

THE HILL OF THE STRANGE TRENCHES

There is no denying it was a beast of a day. Overhead was a sunless sky, muffled in clouds that were heavy with snow; underfoot, a black frost; blowing over it, a wind that felt as if it would take your skin off. When they got down into the plain they found that this part of the ancient road was much more ruinous than any they had yet seen. They had to pick their way over great broken stones and between boulders and across rubble: hard going for sore feet. And, however tired they got, it was far too cold for a halt.

At about ten o'clock the first tiny snowflakes came loitering down and settled on Jill's arm. Ten minutes later they were falling quite thickly. In twenty minutes the ground was noticeably white. And by the end of half an hour a good steady snowstorm, which looked as if it meant to last all day, was driving in their faces so that they could hardly see.

In order to understand what followed, you must keep on remembering how little they could see. As they drew near the low hill which separated them from the place where the lighted windows had appeared, they had no general view of it at all. It was a question of seeing the next few paces ahead, and, even for that, you had to screw up your eyes. Needless to say, they were not talking.

When they reached the foot of the hill they caught a glimpse of what might be rocks on each side – squarish rocks, if you looked at them carefully, but no one did. All were more concerned with the ledge right in front of them which barred their way. It was about four feet high. The Marsh-wiggle, with his long legs, had no difficulty in jumping onto the top of it, and he then helped the others up. It was a nasty wet business for

593

them, though not for him, because the snow now lay quite deep on the ledge. They then had a stiff climb – Jill fell once – up very rough ground for about a hundred yards, and came to a second ledge. There were four of these ledges altogether, at quite irregular intervals.

As they struggled on to the fourth ledge, there was no mistaking the fact that they were now at the top of the flat hill. Up till now the slope had given them some shelter; here, they got the full fury of the wind. For the hill, oddly enough, was quite as flat on top as it had looked from a distance: a great level tableland which the storm tore across without resistance. In most places the snow was still hardly lying at all, for the wind kept catching it up off the ground in sheets and clouds, and hurling it in their faces. And round their feet little eddies of snow ran about as you sometimes see them doing over ice. And, indeed, in many places, the surface was almost as smooth as ice. But to make matters worse it was crossed and criss-crossed with curious banks or dykes, which sometimes divided it up into squares and oblongs. All these of course had to be climbed; they varied from two to five feet in height and were about a couple of yards thick. On the north side of each bank the snow already lay in deep drifts; and after each climb you came down into a drift and got wet.

Fighting her way forward with hood up and head down and numb hands inside her cloak, Jill had glimpses of other odd things on that horrible tableland – things on her right that looked vaguely like factory chimneys, and, on her left, a huge cliff, straighter than any cliff ought to be. But she wasn't at all interested and didn't give them a thought. The only things she thought about were her cold hands (and nose and chin and ears) and hot baths and beds at Harfang.

Suddenly she skidded, slid about five feet, and found herself to her horror sliding down into a dark, narrow chasm which seemed that moment to have appeared in front of her. Half a second later she had reached the bottom. She appeared to be in a kind of trench or groove, only about three feet wide. And though she was shaken by the fall, almost the first thing she noticed was the relief of being out of the wind; for the walls of the trench rose high above her. The next thing she noticed was, naturally, the anxious faces of Scrubb and Puddleglum looking down at her from the edge.

"Are you hurt, Pole?" shouted Scrubb.

"*Both* legs broken, I shouldn't wonder," shouted Puddleglum.

Jill stood up and explained that she was all right, but they'd have to help her out.

"What is it you've fallen into?" asked Scrubb.

"It's a kind of trench, or it might be a kind of sunken lane or something," said Jill. "It runs quite straight."

"Yes, by Jove," said Scrubb. "And it runs due north! I wonder, is it a sort of road? If it was, we'd be out of this infernal wind down there. Is there a lot of snow at the bottom?"

"Hardly any. It all blows over the top, I suppose."

"What happens further on?"

"Half a sec. I'll go and see," said Jill. She got up and walked along the trench; but before she had gone far, it turned sharply to the right. She shouted this information back to the others.

"What's round the corner?" asked Scrubb.

Now it happened that Jill had the same feeling about twisty passages and dark places underground, or even nearly underground, that Scrubb had about the edges of cliffs. She had no intention of going round that corner alone; especially when she heard Puddleglum bawling out from behind her:

"Be careful, Pole. It's just the sort of place that might lead to a dragon's cave. And in a giant country, there might be giant earthworms or giant beetles."

"I don't think it goes anywhere much," said Jill, coming hastily back.

"I'm jolly well going to have a look," said Scrubb. "What do you mean by *anywhere much*, I should like to know?" So he sat down on the edge of the trench (everyone was too wet by now to bother about being a bit wetter) and then dropped in. He pushed past Jill and, though he didn't say anything, she felt sure that he knew she had funked it. So she followed him closely, but took care not to get in front of him.

It proved, however, a disappointing exploration. They went round the right-hand turn and straight on for a few paces. Here there was a choice of ways: straight on again, or sharp to the right. "That's no good," said Scrubb, glancing down the right-hand turn, "that would be taking us back – south." He went straight on, but once more, in a few steps, they found a second turn to the right. But this time there was no choice of ways, for the trench they had been following here came to a dead end.

"No good," grunted Scrubb. Jill lost no time in turning and leading the way back. When they returned to the place where Jill had first fallen in, the Marsh-wiggle with his long arms had no difficulty in pulling them out.

But it was dreadful to be out on top again. Down in those narrow slits of trenches, their ears had almost begun to thaw. They had been able to see clearly and breathe easily and hear each other speak without shouting. It was absolute misery to come back into the withering coldness. And it did seem hard when Puddleglum chose that moment for saying:

"Are you still sure of those signs, Pole? What's the one we ought to be after, now?"

"Oh, come *on*! Bother the signs," said Pole. "Something about someone mentioning Aslan's name, I think. But I'm jolly well not going to give a recitation here."

As you see, she had got the order wrong. That was because she had given up saying the signs over every night. She still really knew them, if she troubled to think: but she was no longer so "pat" in her lesson as to be sure of reeling them off in the right order at a moment's notice and without thinking. Puddleglum's question annoyed her because, deep down inside her, she was already annoyed with herself for not knowing the Lion's lesson quite so well as she felt she ought to have known it. This annoyance, added to the misery of being very cold and tired, made her say, "Bother the signs". She didn't perhaps quite mean it.

"Oh, that was next, was it?" said Puddleglum. "Now I wonder, are you right? Got 'em mixed, I shouldn't wonder. It seems to me, this hill, this flat place we're on, is worth stopping to have a look at. Have you noticed——"

"Oh, Lor!" said Scrubb. "Is this a time for stopping to admire the view? For goodness' sake let's get on."

"Oh, look, look, look," cried Jill and pointed. Everyone turned, and everyone saw. Some way off to the north, and a good deal higher up than the tableland on which they stood, a line of lights had appeared. This time, even more obviously than when the travellers had seen them the night before, they were windows: smaller windows that made one think deliciously of bedrooms, and larger windows that made one think of great halls with fires roaring on the hearth and hot soup or juicy sirloins smoking on the table.

"Harfang!" exclaimed Scrubb.

"That's all very well," said Puddleglum. "But what I was saying was——"

"Oh, shut up," said Jill crossly. "We haven't a moment to lose. Don't you remember what the Lady said about their locking up so early? We must get there in time, we must, we must. We'll *die* if we're shut out on a night like this."

"Well, it isn't exactly a night, not yet," began Puddleglum; but the two children both said, "Come on," and began stumbling forward on the slippery tableland as quickly as their legs would carry them. The Marshwiggle followed them: still talking, but now that they were forcing their way into the wind again, they could not have heard him even if they had wanted to. And they didn't want. They were thinking of baths and beds and hot drinks; and the idea of coming to Harfang too late and being shut out was almost unbearable.

In spite of their haste, it took them a long time to cross the flat top of that hill. And even when they had crossed it, there were still several ledges to climb down on the far side. But at last they reached the bottom and could see what Harfang was like.

It stood on a high crag, and in spite of its many towers was more a huge house than a castle. Obviously, the Gentle Giants feared no attack. There were windows in the outside wall quite close to the ground – a thing no one would have in a serious fortress. There were even odd little doors here and there, so that it would be quite easy to get in and out of the castle without going through the courtyard. This raised the spirits of Jill and Scrubb. It made the whole place look more friendly and less forbidding.

At first the height and steepness of the crag frightened them, but presently they noticed that there was an easier way up on the left and that the road wound up towards it. It was a terrible climb, after the journey they had already had, and Jill nearly gave up. Scrubb and Puddleglum had to help her for the last hundred yards. But in the end they stood before the castle gate. The portcullis was up and the gate open.

However tired you are, it takes some nerve to walk up to a giant's front door. In spite of all his previous warnings against Harfang, it was Puddleglum who showed most courage.

"Steady pace, now," he said. "Don't look frightened, whatever you do. We've done the silliest thing in the world by coming at all: but now that we *are* here, we'd best put a bold face on it."

With these words he strode forward into the gateway, stood still under the arch where the echo would help his voice, and called out as loud as he could.

"Ho! Porter! Guests who seek lodging."

And while he was waiting for something to happen, he took off his hat and knocked off the heavy mass of snow which had gathered on its wide brim.

"I say," whispered Scrubb to Jill. "He may be a wet blanket, but he has plenty of pluck – and cheek."

A door opened, letting out a delicious glow of firelight, and the Porter appeared. Jill bit her lips for fear she should scream. He was not a perfectly enormous giant; that is to say, he was rather taller than an apple tree but nothing like so tall as a telegraph pole. He had bristly red hair, a leather jerkin with metal plates fastened all over it so as to make a kind of mail shirt, bare knees (very hairy indeed) and things like puttees on his legs. He stooped down and goggled at Puddleglum.

"And what sort of creature do you call yourself?" he said.

Jill took her courage in both hands. "Please," she said, shouting up at the Giant. "The Lady of the Green Kirtle salutes the King of the Gentle Giants, and has sent us two Southern children and this Marsh-wiggle (his name's Puddleglum) to your Autumn Feast. – If it's quite convenient, of course," she added.

"O-ho!" said the Porter. "That's quite a different story. Come in, little people, come in. You'd best come into the lodge while I'm sending word to his Majesty." He looked at the children with curiosity. "Blue faces," he said. "I didn't know they were that colour. Don't care about it myself. But I dare say you look quite nice to one another. Beetles fancy other beetles, they do say."

"Our faces are only blue with cold," said Jill. "We're not this colour *really*."

"Then come in and get warm. Come in, little shrimps," said the Porter. They followed him into the lodge. And though it was rather terrible to hear such a big door clang shut behind them, they forgot about it as soon as they saw the thing they had been longing for ever since supper time the previous night – a fire. And such a fire! It looked as if four or five whole trees were blazing on it, and it was so hot they couldn't go within yards of it. But they all flopped down on the brick floor, as near as they could bear the heat, and heaved great sighs of relief.

"Now, youngster," said the Porter to another giant who had been sitting in the back of the room, staring at the visitors till it looked as if his eyes would start out of his head, "run across with this message to the House." And he repeated what Jill had said to him. The younger Giant, after a final stare, and a great guffaw, left the room.

"Now, Froggy," said the Porter to Puddleglum, "you look as if you wanted some cheering up." He produced a black bottle very like Puddleglum's own, but about twenty times larger. "Let me see, let me see," said the Porter. "I can't give you a cup or you'll drown yourself. Let me see. This salt-cellar will be just the thing. You needn't mention it over at the House. The silver *will* keep on getting over here, and it's not my fault."

The salt-cellar was not very like one of ours, being narrower and more upright, and made quite a good cup for Puddleglum, when the giant set it down on the floor beside him.

The children expected Puddleglum to refuse it, distrusting the Gentle Giants as he did. But he muttered, "It's rather late to be thinking of precautions now that we're inside and the door shut behind us." Then he sniffed at the liquor. "Smells all right," he said. "But that's nothing to go by. Better make sure," and took a sip. "Tastes all right, too," he said. "But it might do that at the *first* sip. How does it go on?" He took a larger sip. "Ah!" he said. "But is it the same all the way down?" and took another. "There'll be something nasty at the bottom, I shouldn't wonder," he said, and finished the drink. He licked his lips and remarked to the children, "This'll be a test, you see. If I curl up, or burst, or turn into a lizard, or something, then you'll know not to take anything they offer you."

But the giant, who was too far up to hear the things Puddleglum had been saying under his breath, roared with laughter and said, "Why, Froggy, you're a man. See him put it away!"

"Not a man... Marsh-wiggle," replied Puddleglum in a somewhat indistinct voice. "Not frog either: Marsh-wiggle."

At that moment the door opened behind them and the younger giant came in saying, "They're to go to the throne-room at once."

The children stood up but Puddleglum remained sitting and said, "Marsh-wiggle. Marsh-wiggle. Very respectable Marsh-wiggle. Respectowiggle."

"Show them the way, young 'un," said the giant Porter. "You'd better carry Froggy. He's had a drop more than's good for him."

"Nothing wrong with me," said Puddleglum. "Not a frog. Nothing frog with me. I'm a respectabiggle."

But the young giant caught him up by the waist and signed to the children to follow. In this undignified way they crossed the courtyard. Puddleglum, held in the giant's fist, and vaguely kicking the air, did certainly look very like a frog. But they had little time to notice this, for they soon entered the great doorway of the main castle – both their hearts were beating faster than usual – and, after pattering along several corridors at a trot to keep up with the giant's paces, found themselves blinking in the light of an enormous room, where lamps glowed and a fire roared on the hearth and both were reflected from the gilding of roof and cornice. More giants than they could count stood on their left and right, all in magnificent robes; and on two thrones at the far end sat two huge shapes that appeared to be the King and Queen.

About twenty feet from the thrones, they stopped. Scrubb and Jill made an awkward attempt at a bow (girls are not taught how to curtsey at Experiment House) and the young Giant carefully put Puddleglum down on the floor, where he collapsed into a sort of sitting position. With his long limbs he looked, to tell the truth, uncommonly like a large spider.

CHAPTER EIGHT

THE HOUSE OF HARFANG

"Go on, Pole, do your stuff," whispered Scrubb.

Jill found that her mouth was so dry that she couldn't speak a word. She nodded savagely at Scrubb.

Thinking to himself that he would never forgive her (or Puddleglum either), Scrubb licked his lips and shouted up to the King giant.

"If you please, Sire, the Lady of the Green Kirtle salutes you by us and said you'd like to have us for your Autumn Feast."

The giant King and Queen looked at each other, nodded to each other, and smiled in a way that Jill didn't exactly like. She liked the King better than the Queen. He had a fine, curled beard and a straight eagle-like nose, and was really rather good-looking as giants go. The Queen was dreadfully fat and had a double chin and a fat, powdered face – which isn't a very nice thing at the best of times, and of course looks much worse when it is ten times too big. Then the King put out his tongue and licked his lips. Anyone might do that: but his tongue was so very large and red, and came out so unexpectedly, that it gave Jill quite a shock.

"Oh, what *good* children!" said the Queen. ("Perhaps she's the nice one after all," thought Jill.)

"Yes indeed," said the King. "Quite excellent children. We welcome you to our court. Give me your hands."

He stretched down his great right hand – very clean and with any number of rings on the fingers, but also with terrible pointed nails. He was much too big to shake the hands which the children, in turn, held up to him; but he shook the arms.

"And what's *that*?" asked the King, pointing to Puddleglum.

"Reshpeckobiggle," said Puddleglum.

"Oh!" screamed the Queen, gathering her skirts close about her ankles. "The horrid thing! It's alive."

"He's quite all right, your Majesty, really, he is," said Scrubb hastily. "You'll like him much better when you get to know him. I'm sure you will."

I hope you won't lose all interest in Jill for the rest of the book if I tell you that at this moment she began to cry. There was a good deal of excuse for her. Her feet and hands and ears and nose were still only just beginning to thaw; melted snow was trickling off her clothes; she had had hardly anything to eat or drink that day; and her legs were aching so that she felt she could not go on standing much longer. Anyway, it did more good at the moment than anything else would have done, for the Queen said:

"Ah, the poor child! My lord, we do wrong to keep our guests standing. Quick, some of you! Take them away. Give them food and wine and baths. Comfort the little girl. Give her lollipops, give her dolls, give her physics, give her all you can think of – possets and comfits and caraways and lullabies and toys. Don't cry, little girl, or you won't be good for anything when the feast comes."

Jill was just as indignant as you and I would have been at the mention of toys and dolls; and, though lollipops and comfits might be all very well in their way, she very much hoped that something more solid would be provided. The Queen's foolish speech, however, produced excellent results, for Puddleglum and Scrubb were at once picked up by gigantic gentlemen-in-waiting, and Jill by a gigantic maid of honour, and carried off to their rooms.

Jill's room was about the size of a church, and would have been rather grim if it had not had a roaring fire on the hearth and a very thick crimson carpet on the floor. And here delightful things began to happen to her. She was handed over to the Queen's old Nurse, who was, from the giants' point of view, a little old woman almost bent double with age, and, from the human point of view, a giantess small enough to go about an ordinary room without knocking her head on the ceiling. She was very capable, though Jill did wish she wouldn't keep on clicking her tongue and saying things like "Oh la, la! Ups-a-daisy" and "There's a duck" and "Now we'll be all right, my poppet".

She filled a giant foot-bath with hot water and helped Jill into it. If you can swim (as Jill could) a giant bath is a lovely thing. And giant towels, though a bit rough and coarse, are lovely too, because there are acres of them. In fact you don't need to dry at all, you just roll about on them in front of the fire and enjoy yourself. And when that was over, clean, fresh, warmed clothes were put on Jill: very splendid clothes and a little too big for her, but clearly made for humans not giantesses. "I suppose if that woman in the green kirtle comes here, they must be used to guests of our size," thought Jill.

She soon saw that she was right about this, for a table and chair of the right height for an ordinary grown-up human were placed for her, and the knives and forks and spoons were the proper size too. It was delightful to sit down, feeling warm and clean at last. Her feet were still bare and it was lovely to tread on the giant carpet. She sank in it well over her ankles and it was just the thing for sore feet. The meal – which I suppose we must call dinner, though it was nearer tea time – was cock-a-leekie soup, and hot roast turkey, and a steamed pudding, and roast chestnuts, and as much fruit as you could eat.

The only annoying thing was that the Nurse kept coming in and out, and every time she came in, she brought a gigantic toy with her – a huge doll, bigger than Jill herself, a wooden horse on wheels, about the size of an elephant, a drum that looked like a young gasometer, and a woolly lamb. They were crude, badly made things, painted in very bright colours, and Jill hated the sight of them. She kept on telling the Nurse she didn't want them, but the Nurse said:

"Tut-tut-tut-tut. You'll want 'em all right when you've had a bit of a rest, I know! Te-he-he! Beddy bye, now. A precious poppet!"

The bed was not a giant bed but only a big four-poster, like what you might see in an old-fashioned hotel; and very small it looked in that enormous room. She was very glad to tumble into it.

"Is it still snowing, Nurse?" she asked sleepily.

"No. Raining now, ducky!" said the giantess. "Rain'll wash away all the nasty snow. Precious poppet will be able to go out and play tomorrow!" And she tucked Jill up and said good night.

I know nothing so disagreeable as being kissed by a giantess. Jill thought the same, but was asleep in five minutes.

The rain fell steadily all the evening and all the night, dashing against the windows of the castle, and Jill never heard it but slept deeply, past supper time and past midnight. And then came the deadest hour of the night and nothing stirred but mice in the house of the giants. At that hour there came to Jill a dream.

It seemed to her that she awoke in the same room and saw the fire, sunk low and red, and in the firelight the great wooden horse. And the horse came of its own will, rolling on its wheels across the carpet, and stood at her head. And now it was no longer a horse, but a lion as big as the horse. And then it was not a toy lion, but a real lion, The Real Lion, just as she had seen him on the mountain beyond the World's End. And a smell of all sweet-smelling things there are filled the room. But there was some trouble in Jill's mind, though she could not think what it was, and the tears streamed down her face and wet the pillow. The Lion told her to repeat the signs, and she found that she had forgotten them all. At that, a great horror came over her. And Aslan took her up in his jaws (she could feel his lips and his breath but not his teeth) and carried her to the window and made her look out. The moon shone bright; and written in great letters across the world or the sky (she did not know which) were the words UNDER ME. After that, the dream faded away, and when she woke, very late next morning, she did not remember that she had dreamed at all.

She was up and dressed and had finished breakfast in front of the fire when the Nurse opened the door and said: "Here's pretty poppet's little friends come to play with her."

In came Scrubb and the Marsh-wiggle.

"Hullo! Good morning," said Jill. "Isn't this fun? I've slept about fifteen hours, I believe. I do feel better, don't you?"

"I do," said Scrubb, "but Puddleglum says he has a headache. Hullo! – your window has a window seat. If we got up on that, we could see out." And at once they all did so: and at the first glance Jill said, "Oh, how perfectly dreadful!"

The sun was shining and, except for a few drifts, the snow had been almost completely washed away by the rain. Down below them, spread out like a map, lay the flat hill-top which they had struggled over yesterday afternoon; seen from the castle, it could not be mistaken for anything but the ruins of a gigantic city. It had been flat, as Jill now saw, because it was still, on the whole, paved, though in places the pavement was broken. The criss-cross banks were what was left of the walls of huge buildings which might once have been giants' palaces and temples. One bit of wall, about five hundred feet high, was still standing; it was that which she had thought was a cliff. The things that had looked like factory chimneys were enormous pillars, broken off at unequal heights; their fragments lay at their bases like felled trees of monstrous stone. The ledges which they had climbed down on the north side of the hill – and also, no doubt the other ledges which they had climbed up on the south side – were the remaining steps of giant stairs. To crown all, in large, dark lettering across the centre of the pavement, ran the words UNDER ME.

The three travellers looked at each other in dismay and, after a short whistle, Scrubb said what they were all thinking, "The second and third signs muffed". And at that moment Jill's dream rushed back into her mind.

"It's my fault," she said in despairing tones. "I – I'd given up repeating the signs every night. If I'd been thinking about them I could have seen it was the city, even *in* all that snow."

"I'm worse," said Puddleglum. "I *did* see, or nearly. I thought it looked uncommonly like a ruined city."

"You're the only one who isn't to blame," said Scrubb. "You *did* try to make us stop."

"Didn't try hard enough, though," said the Marsh-wiggle. "And I'd no call to be trying. I ought to have done it. As if I couldn't have stopped you two with one hand each!"

"The truth is," said Scrubb, "we were so jolly keen on getting to this place that we weren't bothering about anything else. At least I know I was. Ever since we met that woman with the knight who didn't talk, we've been thinking of nothing else. We'd nearly forgotten about Prince Rilian."

"I shouldn't wonder," said Puddleglum, "if that wasn't exactly what she intended."

"What I don't quite understand," said Jill, "is how we didn't see the lettering? Or could it have come there since last night. Could he – Aslan – have put it there in the night? I had such a strange dream." And she told them all about it.

"Why, you chump!" said Scrubb. "We did see it. We got into the lettering. Don't you see? We got into the letter E in ME. That was your sunk lane. We walked along the bottom stroke of the E, due north – turned to our right along the upright – came to another turn to the right – that's the middle stroke – and then went on to the top left-hand corner, or (if you like) the north-eastern corner of the letter, and came back. Like the bally idiots we are." He kicked the window seat savagely, and went on, "So it's no good, Pole. I know what you were thinking because I was thinking the same. You were thinking how nice it would have been if Aslan hadn't put the instructions on the stones of the ruined city till after we'd passed it. And then it would have been his fault, not ours. So likely, isn't it? No. We must just own up. We've only four signs to go by, and we've muffed the first three."

"You mean I have," said Jill. "It's quite true. I've spoilt everything ever since you brought me here. All the same – I'm frightfully sorry and all that – all the same, what *are* the instructions? UNDER ME doesn't seem to make much sense."

"Yes it does, though," said Puddleglum. "It means we've got to look for the Prince under that city."

"But how can we?" asked Jill.

"That's the question," said Puddleglum, rubbing his big, frog-like hands together. "How can we *now*? No doubt, if we'd had our minds on our job when we were at the Ruinous City, we'd have been shown how – found a little door, or a cave, or a tunnel, met someone to help us. Might have been (you never know) Aslan himself. We'd have got down under those paving-stones somehow or other. Aslan's instructions always work: there are no exceptions. But how to do it *now* – that's another matter."

"Well, we shall just have to go back, I suppose," said Jill.

"Easy, isn't it?" said Puddleglum. "We might try opening that door to begin with." And they all looked at the door and saw that none of them could reach the handle, and that almost certainly no one could turn it if they did.

"Do you think they won't let us out if we ask?" said Jill. And nobody said, but everyone thought, "Supposing they don't."

It was not a pleasant idea. Puddleglum was dead against any idea of telling the giants their real business and simply asking to be let out; and of course the children couldn't tell without his permission, because they had promised. And all three felt pretty sure that there would be no chance of escaping from the castle by night. Once they were in their rooms with the doors shut, they would be prisoners till morning. They might, of course, ask to have their doors left open, but that would rouse suspicions.

"Our only chance," said Scrubb, "is to try to sneak away by daylight. Mightn't there be an hour in the afternoon when most of the giants are asleep? – and if we could steal down into the kitchen, mightn't there be a back door open?"

"It's hardly what I call a Chance," said the Marsh-wiggle. "But it's all the chance we're likely to get." As a matter of fact, Scrubb's plan was not quite so hopeless as you might think. If you want to get out of a house without being seen, the middle of the afternoon is in some ways a better time to try it than the middle of the night. Doors and windows are more likely to be open; and if you *are* caught, you can always pretend you weren't meaning to go far and had no particular plans. (It is very hard to make either giants or grown-ups believe this if you're found climbing out of a bedroom window at one o'clock in the morning.)

"We must put them off their guard, though," said Scrubb. "We must pretend we love being here and are longing for this Autumn Feast."

"That's tomorrow night," said Puddleglum. "I heard one of them say so."

"I see," said Jill. "We must pretend to be awfully excited about it, and keep on asking questions. They think we're absolute infants anyway, which will make it easier."

"Gay," said Puddleglum with a deep sigh. "That's what we've got to be. Gay. As if we hadn't a care in the world. Frolicsome. You two youngsters haven't always got very high spirits, I've noticed. You must watch me, and do as I do. I'll be gay. Like this" – and he assumed a ghastly grin. "And frolicsome" – here he cut a most mournful caper. "You'll soon get into it, if you keep your eyes on me. They think I'm a funny fellow already, you see. I dare say you two thought I was a trifle tipsy last night, but I do assure you it was – well, most of it was – put on. I had an idea it would come in useful, somehow."

The children, when they talked over their adventures afterwards, could never feel sure whether this last statement was quite strictly true; but they were sure that Puddleglum thought it was true when he made it.

"All right. Gay's the word," said Scrubb. "Now, if we could only get someone to open this door. While we're fooling about and being gay, we've got to find out all we can about this castle."

Luckily, at that very moment the door opened, and the giant Nurse bustled in saying, "Now, my poppets. Like to come and see the King and all the court setting out on the hunting? Such a pretty sight!"

They lost no time in rushing out past her and climbing down the first staircase they came to. The noise of hounds and horns and giant voices guided them, so that in a few minutes they reached the courtyard. The giants were all on foot, for there are no giant horses in that part of the world, and the giants' hunting is done on foot; like beagling in England. The hounds also were of normal size.

When Jill saw that there were no horses she was at first dreadfully disappointed, for she felt sure that the great fat Queen would never go after hounds on foot; and it would never do to have her about the house all day. But then she saw the Queen in a kind of litter supported on the shoulders of six young giants. The silly old creature was all got up in green and had a horn at her side. Twenty or thirty giants, including the King, were assembled, ready for the sport, all talking and laughing fit to deafen you: and down below, nearer Jill's level, there were wagging tails, and barking, and loose, slobbery mouths and noses of dogs thrust into your hand.

Puddleglum was just beginning to strike what he thought a gay and gamesome attitude (which might have spoiled everything if it had been noticed) when Jill put on her most attractively childish smile, rushed across to the Queen's litter and shouted up to the Queen.

"Oh, please! You're not going *away*, are you? You will come back?"

"Yes, my dear," said the Queen. "I'll be back tonight."

"Oh, *good*. How lovely!" said Jill. "And we *may* come to the feast tomorrow night, mayn't we? We're so longing for tomorrow night! And we do love being here. And while you're out, we may run over the whole castle and see everything, mayn't we? Do say yes."

The Queen did say yes, but the laughter of all the courtiers nearly drowned her voice.

CHAPTER NINE

HOW THEY DISCOVERED SOMETHING WORTH KNOWING

The others admitted afterwards that Jill had been wonderful that day. As soon as the King and the rest of the hunting party had set off, she began making a tour of the whole castle and asking questions, but all in such an innocent, babyish way that no one could suspect her of any secret design. Though her tongue was never still, you could hardly say she talked: she *prattled* and giggled. She made love to everyone – the grooms, the porters, the housemaids, the ladies-in-waiting, and the elderly giant lords whose hunting days were past. She submitted to being kissed and pawed about by any number of giantesses, many of whom seemed sorry for her and called her "a poor little thing" though none of them explained why. She made especial friends with the cook and discovered the all-important fact there was a scullery door which let you out through the outer wall, so that you did not have to cross the courtyard or pass the great gatehouse. In the kitchen she pretended to be greedy, and ate all sorts of scraps which the cook and scullions delighted to give her. But upstairs among the ladies she asked questions about how she would be dressed for the great feast, and how long she would be allowed to sit up, and whether she would dance with some very, very small giant. And then (it made her hot all over when she remembered it afterwards) she would put her head on one side in an idiotic fashion which grown-ups, giant and otherwise, thought very fetching, and shake her curls, and fidget, and say, "Oh, I do wish it was tomorrow night, don't you? Do you think the time will go quickly till then?" And all the giantesses said she was a perfect little darling; and some of them dabbed their eyes with enormous handkerchiefs as if they were going to cry.

"They're dear little things at that age," said one giantess to another. "It seems almost a pity…"

Scrubb and Puddleglum both did their best, but girls do that kind of thing better than boys. Even boys do it better than Marsh-wiggles.

At lunchtime something happened which made all three of them more anxious than ever to leave the castle of the Gentle Giants. They had lunch in the great hall at a little table of their own, near the fireplace. At a bigger table, about twenty yards away, half a dozen old giants were lunching. Their conversation was so noisy, and so high up in the air, that the children soon took no more notice of it than you would of hooters outside the window or traffic noises in the street. They were eating cold venison, a kind of food which Jill had never tasted before, and she was liking it.

Suddenly Puddleglum turned to them, and his face had gone so pale that you could see the paleness under the natural muddiness of his complexion. He said:

"Don't eat another bite."

"What's wrong?" asked the other two in a whisper.

"Didn't you hear what those giants were saying? 'That's a nice tender haunch of venison,' said one of them. 'Then that stag was a liar,' said another. 'Why?' said the first one. 'Oh,' said the other. 'They say that when he was caught he said, "Don't kill me, I'm tough. You won't like me."'"

For a moment Jill did not realize the full meaning of this. But she did when Scrubb's eyes opened wide with horror and he said, "So we've been eating a *Talking* stag."

This discovery didn't have exactly the same effect on all of them. Jill, who was new to that world, was sorry for the poor stag and thought it rotten of the giants to have killed him. Scrubb, who had been in that world before and had at least one Talking beast as his dear friend, felt horrified; as you might feel about a murder. But Puddleglum, who was Narnian born, was sick and faint, and felt as you would feel if you found you had eaten a baby.

"We've brought the anger of Aslan on us," he said. "That's what comes of not attending to the signs. We're under a curse, I expect. If it was allowed, it would be the best thing we could do, to take these knives and drive them into our own hearts."

And gradually even Jill came to see it from his point of view. At any rate, none of them wanted any more lunch. And as soon as they thought it safe they crept quietly out of the hall.

It was now drawing near to that time of the day on which their hopes of escape depended, and all became nervous. They hung about in passages and waited for things to become quiet. The giants in the hall sat on a dreadfully long time after the meal was over. The bald one was telling a story. When that was over, the three travellers dawdled down to the kitchen. But there were still plenty of giants there, or at least in the scullery, washing up and putting things away. It was agonizing, waiting till these finished their jobs and, one by one, wiped their hands and went away. At last only one old giantess was left in the room. She pottered about, and pottered about, and at last the three travellers realized with horror that she did not intend to go away at all.

"Well, dearies," she said to them. "That job's about through. Let's put the kettle there. That'll make a nice cup of tea presently. Now I can have a little bit of a rest. Just look into the scullery, like good poppets, and tell me if the back door is open."

"Yes, it is," said Scrubb.

"That's right. I always leave it open so as Puss can get in and out, the poor thing."

Then she sat down on one chair and put her feet up on another.

"I don't know as I mightn't have forty winks," said the giantess. "If only that blamey hunting party doesn't come back too soon."

All their spirits leapt up when she mentioned forty winks, and flopped down again when she mentioned the return of the hunting party.

"When do they usually come back?" asked Jill.

"You never can tell," said the giantess. "But there; go and be quiet for a bit, my dearies."

They retreated to the far end of the kitchen, and would have slipped out into the scullery there and then if the giantess had not sat up, opened her eyes, and brushed away a fly.

"Don't try it till we're sure she's really asleep," whispered Scrubb. "Or it'll spoil everything."

So they all huddled at the kitchen end, waiting and watching. The thought that the hunters might come back at any moment was terrible. And the giantess was fidgety. Whenever they thought she had really gone to sleep, she moved.

"I can't bear this," thought Jill. To distract her mind, she began looking about her. Just in front of her was a clean wide table with two clean pie-dishes on it, and an open book. They were giant pie-dishes of course. Jill thought that she could lie down just comfortably in one of them. Then she climbed up on the bench beside the table to look at the book. She read:

MALLARD. This delicious bird can be cooked in a variety of ways.

"It's a cookery book," thought Jill without much interest, and glanced over her shoulder. The giantess's eyes were shut but she didn't look as if she were properly asleep. Jill glanced back at the book. It was arranged alphabetically: and at the very next entry her heart seemed to stop beating; it ran —

> *MAN. This elegant little biped has long been valued as a delicacy. It forms
> a traditional part of the Autumn Feast, and is served between the fish and the
> joint. Each Man—*

but she could not bear to read any more. She turned round. The giantess
had woken up and was having a fit of coughing. Jill nudged the other two
and pointed to the book. They also mounted the bench and bent over the
huge pages. Scrubb was still reading about how to cook Men when
Puddleglum pointed to the next entry below it. It was like this:

> *MARSH-WIGGLE. Some authorities reject this animal altogether as unfit
> for giants' consumption because of its stringy consistency and muddy flavour.
> The flavour can, however, be greatly reduced if—*

Jill touched his feet, and Scrubb's, gently. All three looked back at the
giantess. Her mouth was slightly open and from her nose there came a
sound which at that moment was more welcome to them than any
music; she snored. And now it was a question of tiptoe work, not daring
to go too fast, hardly daring to breathe, out through the scullery (giant
sculleries smell horrid), out at last into the pale sunlight of a winter
afternoon.

They were at the top of a rough little path which ran steeply down.
And, thank heavens, on the right side of the castle; the City Ruinous was
in sight. In a few minutes they were back on the broad, steep road which
led down from the main gate of the castle. They were also in full view
from every single window on that side. If it had been one, or two, or five
windows there'd be a reasonable chance that no one might be looking out.
But there were nearer fifty than five. They now realized, too, that the road
on which they were, and indeed all the ground between them and the City
Ruinous, didn't offer as much cover as would hide a fox; it was all coarse
grass and pebbles and flat stones. To make matters worse, they were now
in the clothes that the giants had provided for them the previous night:
except Puddleglum, whom nothing would fit. Jill wore a vivid green robe,
rather too long for her, and over that a scarlet mantle fringed with white
fur. Scrubb had scarlet stockings, blue tunic and cloak, a gold-hilted
sword, and a feathered bonnet.

"Nice bits of colour, you two are," muttered Puddleglum. "Show up
very prettily on a winter day. The worst archer in the world couldn't miss
either of you if you were in range. And talking of archers, we'll be sorry not
to have our own bows before long, I shouldn't wonder. Bit thin, too, those
clothes of yours, are they?"

"Yes, I'm freezing already," said Jill.

A few minutes ago when they had been in the kitchen, she had thought that if only they could once get out of the castle, their escape would be almost complete. She now realized that the most dangerous part of it was still to come.

"Steady, steady," said Puddleglum. "Don't look back. Don't walk too quickly. Whatever you do, don't run. Look as if we were just taking a stroll, and then, if anyone sees us, he might, just possibly, not bother. The moment we look like people running away, we're done."

The distance to the City Ruinous seemed longer than Jill would have believed possible. But bit by bit they were covering it. Then came a noise. The other two gasped. Jill, who didn't know what it was, said, "What's that?"

"Hunting horn," whispered Scrubb.

"But don't run even now," said Puddleglum. "Not till I give the word."

This time Jill couldn't help glancing over her shoulder. There, about half a mile away, was the hunt returning from behind them on the left.

They walked on. Suddenly a great clamour of giant voices arose: then shouts and hollers.

"They've seen us. Run," said Puddleglum.

Jill gathered up her long skirts – horrible things for running in – and ran. There was no mistaking the danger now. She could hear the music of the hounds. She could hear the King's voice roaring out, "After them, after them, or we'll have no man-pies tomorrow."

She was last of the three now, cumbered with her dress, slipping on loose stones, her hair getting in her mouth, running-pains across her chest. The hounds were much nearer. Now she had to run uphill, up the stony slope which led to the lowest step of the giant stairway. She had no idea what they would do when they got there, or how they would be any better off even if they reached the top. But she didn't think about that. She was like a hunted animal now; as long as the pack was after her, she must run till she dropped.

The Marsh-wiggle was ahead. As he came to the lowest step he stopped, looked a little to his right, and all of a sudden darted into a little hole or crevice at the bottom of it. His long legs, disappearing into it, looked very like those of a spider. Scrubb hesitated and then vanished after him. Jill, breathless and reeling, came to the place about a minute later. It was an unattractive hole – a crack between the earth and the stone about three feet long and hardly more than a foot high. You had to fling yourself flat on your face and crawl in. You couldn't do it so very quickly either. She felt sure that a dog's teeth would close on her heel before she had got inside.

"Quick, quick. Stones. Fill up the opening," came Puddleglum's voice in the darkness beside her. It was pitch black in there, except for the grey light in the opening by which they had crawled in. The other two were working hard. She could see Scrubb's small hands and the Marsh-wiggle's big, frog-like hands black against the light, working desperately to pile up stones. Then she realized how important this was and began groping for large stones herself, and handing them to the others. Before the dogs were baying and yelping at the cave mouth, they had it pretty well filled; and now, of course, there was no light at all.

"Further in, quick," said Puddleglum's voice.

"Let's all hold hands," said Jill.

"Good idea," said Scrubb. But it took them quite a long time to find one another's hands in the darkness. The dogs were sniffing at the other side of the barrier now.

"Try if we can stand up," suggested Scrubb. They did and found that they could. Then, Puddleglum holding out a hand behind him to Scrubb, and Scrubb holding a hand out behind him to Jill (who wished very much that she was the middle one of the party and not the last), they began groping with their feet and stumbling forwards into the blackness. It was all loose stones underfoot. Then Puddleglum came up to a wall of rock. They turned a little to their right and went on. There were a good many more twists and turns. Jill had now no sense of direction at all, and no idea where the mouth of the cave lay.

"The question is," came Puddleglum's voice out of the darkness ahead, "whether, taking one thing with another, it wouldn't be better to go back (if we *can*) and give the giants a treat at that feast of theirs, instead of losing our way in the guts of a hill where, ten to one, there's dragons and deep holes and gases and water and— Ow! Let go! Save yourselves. I'm—"

After that all happened quickly. There was a wild cry, a swishing, dusty, gravelly noise, a rattle of stones, and Jill found herself sliding, sliding, hopelessly sliding, and sliding quicker every moment down a slope that grew steeper every moment. It was not a smooth, firm slope, but a slope of small stones and rubbish. Even if you could have stood up, it would have been no use. Any bit of that slope you had put your foot on would have slid away from under you and carried you down with it. But Jill was more lying than standing. And the further they all slid, the more they disturbed all the stones and earth, so that the general downward rush of everything (including themselves) got faster and louder and dustier and dirtier. From the sharp cries and swearing of the other two, Jill got the idea that many of the stones which she was dislodging were hitting Scrubb and Puddleglum pretty hard. And now she was going at a furious rate and felt sure she would be broken to bits at the bottom.

Yet somehow they weren't. They were a mass of bruises, and the wet sticky stuff on her face appeared to be blood. And such a mass of loose earth, shingle, and larger stones was piled up round her (and partly over her) that she couldn't get up. The darkness was so complete that it made no difference at all whether you had your eyes open or shut. There was no noise. And that was the very worst moment Jill had ever known in her life. Supposing she was alone: supposing the others... Then she heard movements around her. And presently all three, in shaken voices, were explaining that none of them seemed to have any broken bones.

"We can never get up that again," said Scrubb's voice.

"And have you noticed how warm it is?" said the voice of Puddleglum. "That means we're a long way down. Might be nearly a mile."

No one said anything. Some time later Puddleglum added: "My tinder-box has gone."

After another long pause Jill said, "I'm terribly thirsty."

No one suggested doing anything. There was so obviously nothing to be done. For the moment, they did not feel it quite so badly as one might have expected; that was because they were so tired.

Long, long afterwards, without the slightest warning, an utterly strange voice spoke. They knew at once that it was not the one voice in the whole world for which each had secretly been hoping; the voice of Aslan. It was a dark, flat voice – almost, if you know what that means, a pitch-black voice. It said:

"What make you here, creatures of the Overworld?"

CHAPTER TEN

TRAVELS WITHOUT THE SUN

"Who's there?" shouted the three travellers.

"I am the Warden of the Marches of Underland, and with me stand a hundred Earthmen in arms," came the reply. "Tell me quickly who you are and what is your errand in the Deep Realm?"

"We fell down by accident," said Puddleglum, truthfully enough.

"Many fall down, and few return to the sunlit lands," said the voice. "Make ready now to come with me to the Queen of the Deep Realm."

"What does she want with us?" asked Scrubb cautiously.

"I do not know," said the voice. "Her will is not to be questioned but obeyed."

While he said these words there was a noise like a soft explosion and immediately a cold light, grey with a little blue in it, flooded the cavern. All hope that the speaker had been idly boasting when he spoke of his hundred armed followers died at once. Jill found herself blinking and staring at a dense crowd. They were of all sizes, from little gnomes barely a foot high to stately figures taller than men. All carried three-pronged spears in their hands, and all were dreadfully pale, and all stood as still as statues. Apart from that, they were very different; some had tails and others not, some wore great beards and others had very round, smooth faces, big as pumpkins. There were long, pointed noses, and long, soft noses like small trunks, and great blobby noses. Several had single horns in the middle of their foreheads. But in one respect they were all alike: every face in the whole hundred was as sad as a face could be. They were so sad that, after the first glance, Jill almost forgot to be afraid of them. She felt she would like to cheer them up.

"Well!" said Puddleglum, rubbing his hands. "This is just what I needed. If these chaps don't teach me to take a serious view of life, I don't know what will. Look at that fellow with the walrus moustache – or that one with the——"

"Get up," said the leader of the Earthmen.

There was nothing else to be done. The three travellers scrambled to their feet and joined hands. One wanted the touch of a friend's hand at a moment like that. And the Earthmen came all round them, padding on large, soft feet, on which some had ten toes, some twelve, and others none.

"March," said the Warden: and march they did.

The cold light came from a large ball on the top of a long pole, and the tallest of the gnomes carried this at the head of the procession. By its cheerless rays they could see that they were in a natural cavern; the walls and roof were knobbed, twisted, and gashed into a thousand fantastic shapes, and the stony floor sloped downward as they proceeded. It was worse for Jill than for the others, because she hated dark, underground places. And when, as they went on, the cave got lower and narrower, and when, at last, the light-bearer stood aside, and the gnomes, one by one, stooped down (all except the very smallest ones) and stepped into a little dark crack and disappeared, she felt she could bear it no longer.

"I can't go in there, I can't! I can't! I won't!" she panted. The Earthmen said nothing but they all lowered their spears and pointed them at her.

"Steady, Pole," said Puddleglum. "Those big fellows wouldn't be crawling in there if it didn't get wider later on. And there's one thing about this underground work, we shan't get any rain."

"Oh, you don't understand. I can't," wailed Jill.

"Think how *I* felt on that cliff, Pole," said Scrubb. "You go first, Puddleglum, and I'll come after her."

"That's right," said the Marsh-wiggle, getting down on his hands and knees. "You keep a grip of my heels, Pole, and Scrubb will hold on to yours. Then we'll all be comfortable."

"Comfortable!" said Jill. But she got down and they crawled in on their elbows. It was a nasty place. You had to go flat on your face for what seemed like half an hour, though it may really have been only five minutes. It was hot. Jill felt she was being smothered. But at last a dim light showed ahead, the tunnel grew wider and higher, and they came out, hot, dirty, and shaken, into a cave so large that it scarcely seemed like a cave at all.

It was full of a dim, drowsy radiance, so that here they had no need of the Earthmen's strange lantern. The floor was soft with some kind of moss and out of this grew many strange shapes, branched and tall like trees, but flabby like mushrooms. They stood too far apart to make a forest; it was more like a park. The light (a greenish grey) seemed to come both from them and from the moss, and it was not strong enough to reach the roof of the cave, which must have been a long way overhead. Across the mild, soft, sleepy place they were now made to march. It was very sad, but with a quiet sort of sadness like soft music.

Here they passed dozens of strange animals lying on the turf, either dead or asleep, Jill could not tell which. These were mostly of a dragonish or bat-like sort; Puddleglum did not know what any of them were.

"Do they grow here?" Scrubb asked the Warden. He seemed very surprised at being spoken to, but replied, "No. They are all beasts that have found their way down by chasms and caves, out of Overland into the Deep Realm. Many come down, and few return to the sunlit lands. It is said that they will all wake at the end of the world."

His mouth shut like a box when he had said this, and in the great silence of that cave the children felt that they would not dare to speak again. The bare feet of the gnomes, padding on the deep moss, made no sound. There was no wind, there were no birds, there was no sound of water. There was no sound of breathing from the strange beasts.

When they had walked for several miles, they came to a wall of rock, and in it a low archway leading into another cavern. It was not, however, so bad as the last entrance and Jill could go through it without bending her head. It brought them into a smaller cave, long and narrow, about the shape and size of a cathedral. And here, filling almost the whole length of it, lay an enormous man fast asleep. He was far bigger than any of the giants, and his face was not like a giant's, but noble and beautiful. His breast rose and fell gently under the snowy beard which covered him to the waist. A pure, silver light (no one saw where it came from) rested upon him.

"Who's that?" asked Puddleglum. And it was so long since anyone had spoken, that Jill wondered how he had the nerve.

"That is old Father Time, who once was a King in Overland," said the Warden. "And now he has sunk down into the Deep Realm and lies dreaming of all the things that are done in the upper world. Many sink down, and few return to the sunlit lands. They say he will wake at the end of the world."

And out of that cave they passed into another, and then into another and another, and so on till Jill lost count, but always they were going downhill and each cave was lower than the last, till the very thought of the weight and depth of earth above you was suffocating. At last they came to a place where the Warden commanded his cheerless lantern to be lit again. Then they passed into a cave so wide and dark that they could see nothing of it except that right in front of them a strip of pale sand ran down into still water. And there, beside a little jetty, lay a ship without mast or sail but with many oars. They were made to go on board her and led forward to the bows where there was a clear space in front of the rowers' benches and a seat running round inside the bulwarks.

"One thing I'd like to know," said Puddleglum, "is whether anyone from our world – from up-a-top, I mean – has ever done this trip before?"

"Many have taken ship at the pale beaches," replied the Warden, "and—"

"Yes, I know," interrupted Puddleglum. "*And few return to the sunlit lands.* You needn't say it again. You *are* a chap of one idea, aren't you?"

The children huddled close together on each side of Puddleglum. They had thought him a wet blanket while they were still above ground, but down here he seemed the only comforting thing they had. Then the pale lantern was hung up amidships, the Earthmen sat to the oars, and the ship began to move. The lantern cast its light only a very short way. Looking ahead, they could see nothing but smooth, dark water, fading into absolute blackness.

"Oh, whatever will become of us?" said Jill despairingly.

"Now, don't you let your spirits down, Pole," said the Marsh-wiggle. "There's one thing you've got to remember. We're back on the right lines. We were to go under the Ruined City, and we *are* under it. We're following the instructions again."

Presently they were given food – flat, flabby cakes of some sort which had hardly any taste. And after that, they gradually fell asleep. But when they woke, everything was just the same; the gnomes still rowing, the ship still gliding on, still dead blackness ahead. How often they woke and slept and ate and slept again, none of them could ever remember. And the worst thing about it was that you began to feel as if you had always lived on that ship, in that darkness, and to wonder whether sun and blue skies and wind and birds had not been only a dream.

They had almost given up hoping or being afraid about anything when at last they saw lights ahead: dreary lights, like that of their own lantern. Then, quite suddenly, one of these lights came close and they saw that they were passing another ship. After that they met several ships. Then, staring till their eyes hurt, they saw that some of the lights ahead were shining on what looked like wharfs, walls, towers, and moving crowds. But still there was hardly any noise.

"By Jove," said Scrubb. "A city!" and soon they all saw that he was right.

But it was a queer city. The lights were so few and far apart that they would hardly have done for scattered cottages in our world. But the little bits of the place which you could see by the lights were like glimpses of a great seaport. You could make out in one place a whole crowd of ships loading or unloading; in another, bales of stuff and warehouses; in a third, walls and pillars that suggested great palaces or temples; and always, wherever the light fell, endless crowds — hundreds of Earthmen, jostling one another as they padded softly about their business in narrow streets, broad squares, or up great flights of steps. Their continued movement made a sort of soft, murmuring noise as the ship drew nearer and nearer; but there was not a song or a shout or a bell or the rattle of a wheel anywhere. The City was as quiet, and nearly as dark, as the inside of an ant-hill.

At last their ship was brought alongside a quay and made fast. The three travellers were taken ashore and marched up into the City. Crowds of Earthmen, no two alike, rubbed shoulders with them in the crowded streets, and the sad light fell on many sad and grotesque faces. But no one showed any interest in the strangers. Every gnome seemed to be as busy as it was sad, though Jill never found what they were so busy about. But the endless moving, shoving, hurrying, and the soft pad-pad-pad went on.

At last they came to what appeared to be a great castle, though few of the windows in it were lighted. Here they were taken in and made to cross a courtyard, and to climb many staircases. This brought them in the end to a great murkily lit room. But in one corner of it — oh joy! — there was an archway filled with a quite different sort of light; the honest, yellowish, warm light of such a lamp as humans use. What showed by this light inside the archway was the foot of a staircase which wound upward between walls of stone. The light seemed to come from the top. Two Earthmen stood one on each side of the arch like sentries, or footmen.

The Warden went up to these two, and said, as if it were a password:

"Many sink down to the Underworld."

"And few return to the sunlit lands," they answered, as if it were the countersign. Then all three put their heads together and talked. At last one of the two gnomes-in-waiting said, "I tell you, the Queen's grace is gone from hence on her great affair. We had best keep these topdwellers in strait prison till her homecoming. Few return to the sunlit lands."

At that moment the conversation was interrupted by what seemed to Jill the most delightful noise in the world. It came from above, from the top of the staircase; and it was a clear, ringing, perfectly human voice, the voice of a young man.

"What coil are you keeping down there, Mullugutherum?" it shouted. "Overworlders, ha! Bring them up to me, and that presently."

"Please it your Highness to remember," began Mullugutherum, but the voice cut him short.

"It pleases my Highness principally to be obeyed, old mutterer. Bring them up," it called.

Mullugutherum shook his head, motioned to the travellers to follow and began going up the staircase. At every step the light increased. There were rich tapestries hanging on the walls. The lamplight shone golden through thin curtains at the staircase-head.

The Earthmen parted the curtains and stood aside. The three passed in. They were in a beautiful room, richly tapestried, with a bright fire on a clean hearth, and red wine and cut glass sparkling on the table. A young man with fair hair rose to greet them. He was handsome and looked both bold and kind, though there was something about his face that didn't seem quite right. He was dressed in black and altogether looked a little bit like Hamlet.

"Welcome, Overworlders," he cried. "But stay a moment! I cry you mercy! I have seen you two fair children, and this, your strange governor, before. Was it not you three that met me by the bridge on the borders of Ettinsmoor when I rode there by my Lady's side?"

"Oh… you were the black knight who never spoke?" exclaimed Jill.

"And was that lady the Queen of Underland?" asked Puddleglum, in no very friendly voice. And Scrubb, who was thinking the same, burst out, "Because if it was, I think she was jolly mean to send us off to a castle of giants who intended to eat us. What harm had we ever done her, I should like to know?"

"How?" said the Black Knight with a frown. "If you were not so young a warrior, Boy, you and I must have fought to the death on this quarrel. I can hear no words against my Lady's honour. But of this you may be assured, that whatever she said to you, she said of a good intent. You do not know her. She is a nosegay of all virtues, as truth, mercy, constancy, gentleness, courage, and the rest. I say what I know. Her kindness to me alone, who can in no way reward her, would make an admirable history. But you shall know and love her hereafter. Meanwhile, what is your errand in the Deep Lands?"

And before Puddleglum could stop her, Jill blurted out, "Please, we are trying to find Prince Rilian of Narnia." And then she realized what a frightful risk she had taken; these people might be enemies. But the Knight showed no interest.

"Rilian? Narnia?" he said carelessly. "Narnia? What land is that? I have never heard the name. It must be a thousand leagues from those parts of the Overworld that I know. But it was a strange fantasy that brought you seeking this – how do you call him? – Billian? Trillian? in my Lady's realm. Indeed, to my certain knowledge, there is no such man here." He laughed very loudly at this, and Jill thought to herself, "I wonder is *that* what's wrong with his face? Is he a bit silly?"

"We had been told to look for a message on the stones of the City Ruinous," said Scrubb. "And we saw the words UNDER ME."

The Knight laughed even more heartily than before. "You were the more deceived," he said. "Those words meant nothing to your purpose. Had you but asked my Lady, she could have given you better counsel. For those words are all that is left of a longer script, which in ancient times, as she well remembers, expressed this verse:

> Though under Earth and throneless now I be,
> Yet, while I lived, all Earth was under me.

From which it is plain that some great king of the ancient giants, who lies buried there, caused this boast to be cut in the stone over his sepulchre; though the breaking up of some stones, and the carrying away of others for new buildings, and the filling up of the cuts with rubble, has left only two words that can still be read. Is it not the merriest jest in the world that you should have thought they were written to you?"

This was like cold water down the back to Scrubb and Jill; for it seemed to them very likely that the words had nothing to do with their quest at all, and that they had been taken in by a mere accident.

"Don't you mind him," said Puddleglum. "There *are* no accidents. Our guide is Aslan; and he was there when the giant King caused the letters to be cut, and he knew already all things that would come of them; including *this*."

"This guide of yours must be a long liver, friend," said the Knight with another of his laughs.

Jill began to find them a little irritating.

"And it seems to me, Sir," answered Puddleglum, "that this Lady of yours must be a long liver too, if she remembers the verse as it was when they first cut it."

"Very shrewd, Frog-face," said the Knight, clapping Puddleglum on the shoulder and laughing again. "And you have hit the truth. She is of divine race, and knows neither age nor death. I am the more thankful to her for all her infinite bounty to such a poor mortal wretch as I. For you must know, Sirs, I am a man under most strange afflictions, and none but the Queen's grace would have had patience with me. Patience, said I? But it goes far beyond that. She has promised me a great kingdom in Overland and, when I am king, her own most gracious hand in marriage. But the tale is too long for you to hear fasting and standing. Hi there, some of you! Bring wine and Updwellers' food for my guests. Please you, be seated, gentlemen. Little maiden, sit in this chair. You shall hear it all."

CHAPTER ELEVEN

IN THE DARK CASTLE

When the meal (which was pigeon pie, cold ham, salad, and cakes) had been brought, and all had drawn their chairs up to the table and begun, the Knight continued:

"You must understand, friends, that I know nothing of who I was and whence I came into this Dark World. I remember no time when I was not dwelling, as now, at the court of this all but heavenly Queen; but my thought is that she saved me from some evil enchantment and brought me hither of her exceeding bounty. (Honest Frogfoot, your cup is empty. Suffer me to refill it.) And this seems to me the likelier because even now I am bound by a spell, from which my Lady alone can free me.

"Every night there comes an hour when my mind is most horribly changed and, after my mind, my body. For first I become furious and wild and would rush upon my dearest friends to kill them, if I were not bound. And soon after that, I turn into the likeness of a great serpent, hungry, fierce, and deadly. (Sir, be pleased to take another breast of pigeon, I entreat you.) So they tell me, and they certainly speak truth, for my Lady says the same. I myself know nothing of it, for when my hour is past I awake forgetful of all that vile fit and in my proper shape and sound mind – saving that I am somewhat wearied. (Little lady, eat one of these honey cakes, which are brought for me from some barbarous land in the far south of the world.)

"Now the Queen's majesty knows by her art that I shall be freed from this enchantment when once she has made me king of a land in the Overworld and set its crown upon my head. The land is already chosen and the very place of our breaking out. Her Earthmen have worked day and night digging a way beneath it, and have now gone so far and so high that they tunnel not a score of feet beneath the very grass on which the Updwellers of that country walk. It will be very soon now that those Uplanders' fate will come upon them. She herself is at the diggings tonight, and I expect a message to go to her. Then the thin roof of earth which still keeps me from my kingdom will be broken through, and with her to guide me and a thousand Earthmen at my back, I shall ride forth in arms, fall suddenly on our enemies, slay their chief men, cast down their strong places, and doubtless be their crowned king within four and twenty hours."

"It's a bit rough luck on *them*, isn't it?" said Scrubb.

"Thou art a lad of a wondrous, quick-working wit!" exclaimed the Knight. "For, on my honour, I had never thought of it so before. I see your meaning."

He looked slightly, very slightly troubled for a moment or two; but his face soon cleared and he broke out, with another of his loud laughs, "But fie on gravity! Is it not the most comical and ridiculous thing in the world to think of them all going about their business and never dreaming that under their peaceful fields and floors, only a fathom down, there is a great army ready to break out upon them like a fountain! And they never to have suspected! Why, they themselves, when once the first smart of their defeat is over, can hardly choose but laugh at the thought!"

"I don't think it's funny at all," said Jill. "I think you'll be a wicked tyrant."

"What?" said the Knight, still laughing and patting her head in a quite infuriating fashion. "Is our little maid a deep politician? But never fear, sweetheart. In ruling that land, I shall do all by the counsel of my Lady, who will then be my Queen too. Her word shall be my law, even as my word will be law to the people we have conquered."

"Where I come from," said Jill, who was disliking him more every minute, "they don't think much of men who are bossed about by their wives."

"Shalt think otherwise when thou hast a man of thine own, I warrant you," said the Knight, apparently thinking this very funny. "But with my Lady, it is another matter. I am well content to live by her word, who has already saved me from a thousand dangers. No mother has taken pains more tenderly for her child, than the Queen's grace has for me. Why, look you, amid all her cares and business, she rideth out with me in the Overworld many a time and oft to accustom my eyes to the sunlight. And then I must go fully armed and with visor down, so that no man may see my face, and I must speak to no one. For she has found out by art magical that this would hinder my deliverance from the grievous enchantment I lie under. Is not that a lady worthy of a man's whole worship?"

"Sounds a very nice lady indeed," said Puddleglum in a voice which meant exactly the opposite.

They were thoroughly tired of the Knight's talk before they had finished supper. Puddleglum was thinking, "I wonder what game that witch is really playing with this young fool." Scrubb was thinking, "He's a great baby, really: tied to that woman's apron strings; he's a sap." And Jill was thinking, "He's the silliest, most conceited, selfish pig I've met for a long time." But when the meal was over, the knight's mood had changed. There was no more laughter about him.

"Friends," he said, "my hour is now very near. I am ashamed that you should see me yet I dread being left alone. They will come in presently and bind me hand and foot to yonder chair. Alas, so it must be; for in my fury, they tell me, I would destroy all that I could reach."

"I say," said Scrubb, "I'm awfully sorry about your enchantment of course, but what will those fellows do to *us* when they come to bind you? They talked of putting us in prison. And we don't like all those dark places very much. We'd much rather stay here till you're... better... if we may."

"It is well thought of," said the Knight. "By custom none but the Queen herself remains with me in my evil hour. Such is her tender care for my honour that she would not willingly suffer any ears but her own to hear the words I utter in that frenzy. But I could not easily persuade my attendant gnomes that you should be left with me. And I think I hear their soft feet even now upon the stairs. Go through yonder door: it leads into my other apartments. And there, either await my coming when they have unbound me; or, if you will, return and sit with me in my ravings."

They followed his directions and passed out of the room by a door which they had not yet seen opened. It brought them, they were pleased to see, not into darkness but into a lighted corridor. They tried various doors and found (what they very badly needed) water for washing and even a looking glass. "He never offered us a wash before supper," said Jill, drying her face. "Selfish, self-centred pig."

"Are we going back to watch the enchantment, or shall we stay here?" said Scrubb.

"Stay here, I vote," said Jill. "I'd much rather not see it." But she felt a little inquisitive all the same.

"No, go back," said Puddleglum. "We may pick up some information, and we need all we can get. I am sure that Queen is a witch and an enemy. And those Earthmen would knock us on the head as soon as look at us. There's a stronger smell of danger and lies and magic and treason about this land than I've ever smelled before. We need to keep our eyes and ears open."

They went back down the corridor and gently pushed the door open. "It's all right," said Scrubb, meaning that there were no Earthmen about. Then they all came back into the room where they had supped.

The main door was now shut, concealing the curtain between which they had first entered. The Knight was seated in a curious silver chair, to which he was bound by his ankles, his knees, his elbows, his wrists, and his waist. There was sweat on his forehead and his face was filled with anguish.

"Come in, friends," he said, glancing quickly up. "The fit is not yet upon me. Make no noise, for I told that prying chamberlain that you were in bed. Now... I can feel it coming. Quick! Listen while I am master of myself. When the fit is upon me, it well may be that I shall beg and implore you, with entreaties and threatenings, to loosen my bonds. They say I do. I shall call upon you by all that is most dear and most dreadful. But do not listen to me. Harden your hearts and stop your ears. For while I am bound you are safe. But if once I were up and out of this chair, then first would come my fury, and after that" – he shuddered – "the change into a loathsome serpent."

"There's no fear of our loosing you," said Puddleglum. "We've no wish to meet wild men; or serpents either."

"I should think not," said Scrubb and Jill together.

"All the same," added Puddleglum in a whisper. "Don't let's be too sure. Let's be on our guard. We've muffed everything else, you know. He'll be cunning, I shouldn't wonder, once he gets started. Can we trust one another? Do we all promise that whatever he says we don't touch those cords? *Whatever* he says, mind you?"

"Rather!" said Scrubb.

"There's nothing in the world he can say or do that'll make me change my mind," said Jill.

"Hush! Something's happening," said Puddleglum.

The Knight was moaning. His face was as pale as putty, and he writhed in his bonds. And whether because she was sorry for him, or for some other reason, Jill thought that he looked a nicer sort of man than he had looked before.

"Ah," he groaned. "Enchantments, enchant-ments... the heavy, tangled, cold, clammy web of evil magic. Buried alive. Dragged down under the earth, down into the sooty blackness... how many years is it?... Have I lived ten years, or a thousand years, in the pit? Maggotmen all around me. Oh, have mercy. Let me out, let me go back. Let me feel the wind and see the sky... There used to be a little pool. When you looked down into it you could see all the trees growing upside-down in the water, all green, and below them, deep, very deep, the blue sky."

He had been speaking in a low voice; now he looked up, fixed his eyes upon them, and said loud and clear:

"Quick! I am sane now. Every night I am sane. If only I could get out of this enchanted chair, it would last. I should be a man again. But every night they bind me, and so every night my chance is gone. But you are not enemies. I am not *your* prisoner. Quick! Cut these cords."

"Stand fast! Steady," said Puddleglum to the two children.

"I beseech you to hear me," said the Knight, forcing himself to speak calmly. "Have they told you that if I am released from this chair I shall kill you and become a serpent? I see by your faces that they have. It is a lie. It is at this hour that I am in my right mind: it is all the rest of the day that I am enchanted. You are not Earthmen nor witches. Why should you be on their side? Of your courtesy, cut my bonds."

"Steady! Steady! Steady!" said the three travellers to one another.

"Oh, you have hearts of stone," said the Knight. "Believe me, you look upon a wretch who has suffered almost more than any mortal heart can bear. What wrong have I ever done you, that you should side with my enemies to keep me in such miseries? And the minutes are slipping past. *Now* you can save me; when this hour has passed, I shall be witless again – the toy and lap-dog, nay, more likely the pawn and tool, of the most devilish sorceress that ever planned the woe of men. And this night, of all nights, when she is away! You take from me a chance that may never come again."

"This is dreadful. I do wish we'd stayed away till it was over," said Jill.

"Steady!" said Puddleglum.

The prisoner's voice was now rising into a shriek. "Let me go, I say. Give me my sword. My sword! Once I am free I shall take such revenge on Earthmen that Underland will talk of it for a thousand years!"

"Now the frenzy is beginning," said Scrubb. "I hope those knots are all right."

"Yes," said Puddleglum. "He'd have twice his natural strength if he got free now. And I'm not clever with my sword. He'd get us both, I shouldn't wonder; and then Pole on her own would be left to tackle the snake."

The prisoner was now so straining at his bonds that they cut into his wrists and ankles. "Beware," he said. "Beware. One night I *did* break them. But the witch was there that time. You will not have her to help you tonight. Free me now, and I am your friend. I'm your mortal enemy else."

"Cunning, isn't he?" said Puddleglum.

"Once and for all," said the prisoner, "I adjure you to set me free. By all fears and all loves, by the bright skies of Overland, by the great Lion, by Aslan himself, I charge you—"

"Oh!" cried the three travellers as though they had been hurt.

"It's the sign," said Puddleglum.

"It was the *words* of the sign," said Scrubb more cautiously.

"Oh, what *are* we to do?" said Jill.

It was a dreadful question. What had been the use of promising one another that they would not on any account set the Knight free, if they were now to do so the first time he happened to call upon a name they really cared about? On the other hand, what had been the use of learning the signs if they weren't going to obey them? Yet could Aslan have really meant them to unbind anyone – even a lunatic – who asked it in his name? Could it be a mere accident? Or how if the Queen of the Underworld knew all about the signs and had made the Knight learn this name simply in order to entrap them? But then, supposing this was the real sign? They had muffed three already; they daren't muff the fourth.

"Oh, if only we knew!" said Jill.

"I think we do know," said Puddleglum.

"Do you mean you think everything will come right if we do untie him?" said Scrubb.

"I don't know about that," said Puddleglum. "You see, Aslan didn't tell Pole what would happen. He only told her what to do. That fellow will be the death of us once he's up, I shouldn't wonder. But that doesn't let us off following the sign."

They all stood looking at one another with bright eyes. It was a sickening moment. "All right!" said Jill suddenly. "Let's get it over. Goodbye, everyone!" They all shook hands. The Knight was screaming by now; there was foam on his cheeks.

"Come on, Scrubb," said Puddleglum. He and Scrubb drew their swords and went over to the captive.

"In the name of Aslan," they said and began methodically cutting the cords. The instant the prisoner was free, he crossed the room in a single bound, seized his own sword (which had been taken from him and laid on the table), and drew it.

"You first!" he cried and fell upon the silver chair. That must have been a good sword. The silver gave way before its edge like string, and in a moment a few twisted fragments, shining on the floor, were all that was left. But as the chair broke, there came from it a bright flash, a sound like small thunder, and (for one moment) a loathsome smell.

"Lie there, vile engine of sorcery," he said, "lest your mistress should ever use you for another victim." Then he turned and surveyed his rescuers; and the something wrong, whatever it was, had vanished from his face.

"What?" he cried, turning to Puddleglum. "Do I see before me a Marsh-wiggle – a real, live, honest, Narnian Marsh-wiggle?"

"Oh, so you *have* heard of Narnia after all?" said Jill.

"Had I forgotten it when I was under the spell?" asked the Knight. "Well, that and all other bedevilments are now over. You may well believe that I know Narnia, for I am Rilian, Prince of Narnia, and Caspian the great King is my father."

"Your Royal Highness," said Puddleglum, sinking on one knee (and the children did the same), "we have come hither for no other end than to seek you."

"And who are you, my other deliverers?" said the Prince to Scrubb and Jill.

"We were sent by Aslan himself from beyond the world's end to seek your Highness," said Scrubb. "I am Eustace who sailed with him to the island of Ramandu."

"I owe all three of you a greater debt than I can ever pay," said Prince Rilian. "But my father? Is he yet alive?"

"He sailed east again before we left Narnia, my lord," said Puddleglum. "But your Highness must consider that the King is very old. It is ten to one his Majesty must die on the voyage."

"He is old, you say. How long then have I been in the power of the witch?"

"It is more than ten years since your Highness was lost in the woods at the north side of Narnia."

"Ten years!" said the Prince, drawing his hand across his face as if to rub away the past. "Yes, I believe you. For now that I am myself I can remember that enchanted life, though while I was enchanted I could not remember my true self. And now, fair friends – but wait! I hear their feet (does it not sicken a man, that padding woolly tread! Faugh!) on the stairs. Lock the door, boy. Or stay. I have a better thought than that. I will fool these Earthmen, if Aslan gives me the wit. Take your cue from me."

He walked resolutely to the door and flung it wide open.

CHAPTER TWELVE

THE QUEEN OF UNDERLAND

Two Earthmen entered, but instead of advancing into the room, they placed themselves one on each side of the door, and bowed deeply. They were followed immediately by the last person whom anyone had expected or wished to see: the Lady of the Green Kirtle, the Queen of Underland. She stood dead still in the doorway, and they could see her eyes moving as she took in the whole situation – the three strangers, the silver chair destroyed, and the Prince free, with his sword in his hand.

She turned very white; but Jill thought it was the sort of whiteness that comes over some people's faces not when they are frightened but when they are angry. For a moment the Witch fixed her eyes on the Prince, and there was murder in them. Then she seemed to change her mind.

"Leave us," she said to the two Earthmen. "And let none disturb us till I call, on pain of death." The gnomes padded away obediently, and the Witch-queen shut and locked the door.

"How now, my lord Prince," she said. "Has your nightly fit not yet come upon you, or is it over so soon? Why stand you here unbound? Who are these aliens? And is it they who have destroyed the chair which was your only safety?"

Prince Rilian shivered as she spoke to him. And no wonder: it is not easy to throw off in half an hour an enchantment which has made one a slave for ten years. Then, speaking with a great effort, he said:

"Madam, there will be no more need of that chair. And you, who have told me a hundred times how deeply you pitied me for the sorceries by which I was bound, will doubtless hear with joy that they are now ended for ever. There was, it seems, some small error in your Ladyship's way of treating them. These, my true friends, have delivered me. I am now in my right mind, and there are two things I will say to you. First — as for your Ladyship's design of putting me at the head of an army of Earthmen so that I may break out into the Overworld and there, by main force, make myself king over some nation that never did me wrong — murdering their natural lords and holding their throne as a bloody and foreign tyrant — now that I know myself, I do utterly abhor and renounce it as plain villainy. And second: I am the King's son of Narnia, Rilian, the only child of Caspian, Tenth of that name, whom some call Caspian the Seafarer. Therefore, Madam, it is my purpose, as it is also my duty, to depart suddenly from your Highness's court into my own country. Please it you to grant me and my friends safe conduct and a guide through your dark realm."

Now the Witch said nothing at all, but moved gently across the room, always keeping her face and eyes very steadily towards the Prince. When she had come to a little ark set in the wall not far from the fireplace, she opened it, and took out first a handful of a green powder. This she threw on the fire. It did not blaze much, but a very sweet and drowsy smell came from it. And all through the conversation which followed, that smell grew stronger, and filled the room, and made it harder to think. Secondly, she took out a musical instrument rather like a mandolin. She began to play it with her fingers — a steady, monotonous thrumming that you didn't notice after a few minutes. But the less you noticed it, the more it got into your brain and your blood. This also made it hard to think. After she had thrummed for a time (and the sweet smell was now strong) she began speaking in a sweet, quiet voice.

"Narnia?" she said. "Narnia? I have often heard your Lordship utter that name in your ravings. Dear Prince, you are very sick. There is no land called Narnia."

"Yes, there is, though, Ma'am," said Puddleglum. "You see, I happen to have lived there all my life."

"Indeed," said the Witch. "Tell me, I pray you, where that country is?"

"Up there," said Puddleglum, stoutly, pointing overhead. "I — I don't know exactly where."

"How?" said the Queen, with a kind, soft, musical laugh. "Is there a country up among the stones and mortar of the roof?"

"No," said Puddleglum, struggling a little to get his breath. "It's in the Overworld."

"And what, or where, pray is this... how do you call it... *Overworld?*"

"Oh, don't be so silly," said Scrubb, who was fighting hard against the enchantment of the sweet smell and the thrumming. "As if you didn't know! It's up above, up where you can see the sky and the sun and the stars. Why, you've been there yourself. We met you there."

"I cry you mercy, little brother," laughed the Witch (you couldn't have heard a lovelier laugh). "I have no memory of that meeting. But we often meet our friends in strange places when we dream. And unless all dreamed alike, you must not ask them to remember it."

"Madam," said the Prince sternly, "I have already told your Grace that I am the King's son of Narnia."

"And shalt be, dear friend," said the Witch in a soothing voice, as if she were humouring a child, "shalt be king of many imagined lands in thy fancies."

"We've been there, too," snapped Jill. She was very angry because she could feel enchantment getting hold of her every moment. But of course the very fact that she could still feel it, showed that it had not yet fully worked.

"And thou art Queen of Narnia too, I doubt not, pretty one," said the Witch in the same coaxing, half-mocking tone.

"I'm nothing of the sort," said Jill, stamping her foot. "*We* come from another world."

"Why, this is a prettier game than the other," said the Witch. "Tell us, little maid, where is this other world? What ships and chariots go between it and ours?"

Of course a lot of things darted into Jill's head at once: Experiment House, Adela Pennyfather, her own home, radio-sets, cinemas, cars, aeroplanes, ration-books, queues. But they seemed dim and far away. (*Thrum — thrum — thrum* — went the strings of the Witch's instrument.) Jill couldn't remember the names of the things in our world. And this time it didn't come into her head that she was being enchanted, for now the magic was in its full strength; and of course, the more enchanted you get, the more certain you feel that you are not enchanted at all.

She found herself saying (and at the moment it was a relief to say): "No. I suppose that other world must be all a dream."

"Yes. It *is* all a dream," said the Witch, always thrumming.

"Yes, all a dream," said Jill.

"There never was such a world," said the Witch.

"No," said Jill and Scrubb, "never was such a world."

"There never was any world but mine," said the Witch.

"There never was any world but yours," said they.

Puddleglum was still fighting hard. "I don't know rightly what you all mean by a world," he said, talking like a man who hasn't enough air. "But you can play that fiddle till your fingers drop off, and still you won't make me forget Narnia; and the whole Overworld too. We'll never see it *again*, I shouldn't wonder. You may have blotted it out and turned it dark like this, for all I know. Nothing more likely. But I know I was there once. I've seen the sky full of stars. I've seen the sun coming up out of the sea of a morning and sinking behind the mountains at night. And I've seen him up in the midday sky when I couldn't look at him for brightness."

Puddleglum's words had a very rousing effect. The other three all breathed again and looked at one another like people newly awaked.

"Why, there it is!" cried the Prince. "Of course! The blessing of Aslan upon this honest Marsh-wiggle. We have all been dreaming, these last few minutes. How could we have forgotten it? Of course we've all seen the sun."

"By Jove, so we have!" said Scrubb. "Good for you, Puddleglum! You're the only one of us with any sense, I do believe."

Then came the Witch's voice, cooing softly like the voice of a wood-pigeon from the high elms in an old garden at three o'clock in the middle of a sleepy, summer afternoon; and it said:

"What is this *sun* that you all speak of? Do you mean anything by the word?"

"Yes, we jolly well do," said Scrubb.

"Can you tell me what it's like?" asked the Witch (*thrum, thrum, thrum*, went the strings).

"Please it your Grace," said the Prince, very coldly and politely. "You see that lamp. It is round and yellow and gives light to the whole room, and hangeth moreover from the roof. Now that thing which we call the sun is like the lamp, only far greater and brighter. It giveth light to the whole Overworld and hangeth in the sky."

"Hangeth from what, my lord?" asked the Witch; and then, while they were all still thinking how to answer her, she added, with another of her soft, silver laughs: "You see? When you try to think out clearly what this *sun* must be, you cannot tell me. You can only tell me it is like the lamp. Your *sun* is a dream; and there is nothing in that dream that was not copied from the lamp. The lamp is the real thing; the *sun* is but a tale, a children's story."

"Yes, I see now," said Jill in a heavy, hopeless tone. "It must be so." And while she said this, it seemed to her to be very good sense.

Slowly and gravely the Witch repeated, "There is no *sun*." And they all said nothing. She repeated, in a softer and deeper voice. "There is no *sun*." After a pause, and after a struggle in their minds, all four of them said together, "You are right. There is no sun." It was such a relief to give in and say it.

"There never was a *sun*," said the Witch.

"No. There never was a sun," said the Prince, and the Marsh-wiggle, and the children.

For the last few minutes Jill had been feeling that there was something she must remember at all costs. And now she did. But it was dreadfully hard to say it. She felt as if huge weights were laid on her lips. At last, with an effort that seemed to take all the good out of her, she said:

"There's Aslan."

"Aslan?" said the Witch, quickening ever so slightly the pace of her thrumming. "What a pretty name! What does it mean?"

"He is the great Lion who called us out of our own world," said Scrubb, "and sent us into this to find Prince Rilian."

"What is a *lion*?" asked the Witch.

"Oh, hang it all!" said Scrubb. "Don't you know? How can we describe it to her? Have you ever seen a cat?"

"Surely," said the Queen. "I love cats."

"Well, a lion is a little bit – only a little bit, mind you – like a huge cat – with a mane. At least, it's not like a horse's mane, you know, it's more like a judge's wig. And it's yellow. And terrifically strong."

The Witch shook her head. "I see," she said, "that we should do no better with your *lion*, as you call it, than we did with your *sun*. You have seen lamps, and so you imagined a bigger and better lamp and called it the *sun*. You've seen cats, and now you want a bigger and better cat, and it's to be called a *lion*. Well, 'tis a pretty make-believe, though, to say truth, it would suit you all better if you were younger. And look how you can put nothing into your make-believe without copying it from the real world of mine, which is the only world. But even you children are too old for such play. As for you, my lord Prince, that art a man full grown, fie upon you! Are you not ashamed of such toys? Come, all of you. Put away these childish tricks. I have work for you all in the real world. There is no Narnia, no Overworld, no sky, no sun, no Aslan. And now, to bed all. And let us begin a wiser life tomorrow. But, first, to bed; to sleep; deep sleep, soft pillows, sleep without foolish dreams."

The Prince and the two children were standing with their heads hung down, their cheeks flushed, their eyes half closed; the strength all gone from them; the enchantment almost complete. But Puddleglum, desperately gathering all his strength, walked over to the fire. Then he did a very brave thing. He knew it wouldn't hurt him quite as much as it would hurt a human; for his feet (which were bare) were webbed and hard and cold-blooded like a duck's. But he knew it would hurt him badly enough; and so it did. With his bare foot he stamped on the fire, grinding a large part of it into ashes on the flat hearth. And three things happened at once.

First, the sweet heavy smell grew very much less. For though the whole fire had not been put out, a good bit of it had, and what remained smelled very largely of burnt Marsh-wiggle, which is not at all an enchanting smell. This instantly made everyone's brain far clearer. The Prince and the children held up their heads again and opened their eyes.

Secondly, the Witch, in a loud, terrible voice, utterly different from all the sweet tones she had been using up till now, called out, "What are you doing? Dare to touch my fire again, mud-filth, and I'll turn the blood to fire inside your veins."

Thirdly, the pain itself made Puddleglum's head for a moment perfectly clear and he knew exactly what he really thought. There is nothing like a good shock of pain for dissolving certain kinds of magic.

"One word, Ma'am," he said, coming back from the fire; limping because of the pain. "One word. All you've been saying is quite right, I shouldn't wonder. I'm a chap who always liked to know the worst and then put the best face I can on it. So I won't deny any of what you said. But there's one thing more to be said, even so. Suppose we *have* only dreamed, or made up, all those things – trees and grass and sun and moon and stars and Aslan himself. Suppose we have. Then all I can say is that, in that case, the made-up things seem a good deal more important than the real ones. Suppose this black pit of a kingdom of yours *is* the only world. Well, it strikes me as a pretty poor one. And that's a funny thing, when you come to think of it. We're just babies making up a game, if you're right. But four babies playing a game can make a play-world which licks your real world hollow. That's why I'm going to stand by the play-world. I'm on Aslan's side even if there isn't any Aslan to lead it. I'm going to live as like a Narnian as I can even if there isn't any Narnia. So, thanking you kindly for our supper, if these two gentlemen and the young lady are ready, we're leaving your court at once and setting out in the dark to spend our lives looking for the Overland. Not that our lives will be very long, I should think; but that's a small loss if the world's as dull a place as you say."

"Oh, hurray! Good old Puddleglum!" cried Scrubb and Jill.

But the Prince shouted suddenly, "Ware! Look to the Witch."

When they did look their hair nearly stood on end.

The instrument dropped from her hands. Her arms appeared to be fastened to her sides. Her legs were intertwined with each other, and her feet had disappeared. The long green train of her skirt thickened and grew solid, and seemed to be all one piece with the writhing green pillar of her interlocked legs. And that writhing green pillar was curving and swaying as if it had no joints, or else were all joints. Her head was thrown far back and while her nose grew longer and longer, every other part of her face seemed to disappear, except her eyes. Huge flaming eyes they were now, without brows or lashes. All this takes time to write down; it happened so quickly that there was only just time to see it. Long before there was time to do anything, the change was complete, and the great serpent which the Witch had become, green as poison, thick as Jill's waist, had flung two or three coils of its loathsome body round the Prince's legs. Quick as lightning another great loop darted round, intending to pinion his sword-arm to his side. But the Prince was just in time. He raised his arms and got them clear: the living knot closed only round his chest – ready to crack his ribs like firewood when it drew tight.

The Prince caught the creature's neck in his left hand, trying to squeeze it till it choked. This held its face (if you could call it a face) about five inches from his own. The forked tongue flickered horribly in and out, but could not reach him. With his right hand he drew back his sword for the strongest blow he could give. Meanwhile Scrubb and Puddleglum had drawn their weapons and rushed to his aid. All three blows fell at once: Scrubb's (which did not even pierce the scales and did no good) on the body of the snake below the Prince's hand, but the Prince's own blow and Puddleglum's both on its neck. Even that did not quite kill it, though it began to loosen its hold on Rilian's legs and chest. With repeated blows they hacked off its head. The horrible thing went on coiling and moving like a bit of wire long after it had died; and the floor, as you may imagine, was a nasty mess.

The Prince, when he had breath, said, "Gentlemen, I thank you." Then the three conquerors stood staring at one another and panting, without another word, for a long time. Jill had very wisely sat down and was keeping quiet; she was saying to herself, "I do hope I don't faint – or blub – or do anything idiotic."

"My royal mother is avenged," said Rilian presently. "This is undoubtedly the same worm that I pursued in vain by the fountain in the forest of Narnia, so many years ago. All these years I have been the slave of my mother's slayer. Yet I am glad, gentlemen, that the foul Witch took to her serpent form at the last. It would not have suited well either with my heart or with my honour to have slain a woman. But look to the lady." He meant Jill.

"I'm all right, thanks," said she.

"Damsel," said the Prince, bowing to her. "You are of a high courage, and therefore, I doubt not, you come of a noble blood in your own world. But come, friends. Here is some wine left. Let us refresh ourselves and each pledge his fellows. After that, to our plans."

"A jolly good idea, Sir," said Scrubb.

CHAPTER THIRTEEN

UNDERLAND WITHOUT THE QUEEN

All felt that they had earned what Scrubb called a "breather". The Witch had locked the door and told the Earthmen not to disturb her, so there was no danger of interruption for the present. Their first business was, of course, Puddleglum's burnt foot. A couple of clean shirts from the Prince's bedroom, torn into strips, and well greased on the inside with butter and salad oil off the supper table, made a fairly good dressing. When this had been applied, they all sat down and had a little refreshment, and discussed plans for escaping from the Underworld.

Rilian explained that there were quite a lot of outlets by which one could get to the surface – he had been taken out through most of them at one time or another. But he had never gone out alone, only with the Witch; and he had always reached these outlets by going in a ship across the Sunless Sea. What the Earthmen would say if he went down to the harbour without the Witch, and with four strangers, and simply ordered a ship, no one could guess. But most likely they would ask awkward questions. On the other hand the new outlet, the one for the invasion of Overworld, was on this side of the sea, and only a few miles away. The Prince knew that it was nearly finished; only a few feet of earth divided the diggings from the outer air. It was even possible that it had now been quite finished. Perhaps the Witch had come back to tell him this and to start the attack. Even if it was not, they could probably dig themselves out by that route in a few hours – if they could only get there without being stopped, and if only they found the diggings unguarded. But those were the difficulties.

"If you ask me——" began Puddleglum, when Scrubb interrupted.

"I say," he asked, "what's that noise?"

"I've been wondering that for some time!" said Jill.

They had all, in fact, been hearing the noise but it had begun and increased so gradually that they did not know when they had first noticed it. For a time it had been only a vague disquiet like gentle winds, or traffic very far away. Then it swelled to a murmur like the sea. Then came rumblings and rushings. Now there seemed to be voices as well and also a steady roaring that was not voices.

"By the Lion," said Prince Rilian, "it seems this silent land has found a tongue at last." He rose, walked to the window, and drew aside the curtains. The others crowded round him to look out.

The very first thing they noticed was a great red glow. Its reflection made a red patch on the roof of the Underworld thousands of feet above them, so that they could see a rocky ceiling which had perhaps been hidden in darkness ever since the world was made. The glow itself came from the far side of the city so that many buildings, grim and great, stood up blackly against it. But it also cast its light down many streets that ran from it towards the castle. And in those streets something very strange was going on. The closely-packed, silent crowds of Earthmen had vanished. Instead, there were figures darting about by ones, or twos, or threes. They behaved like people who do not want to be seen: lurking in shadow behind buttresses or in doorways, and then moving quickly across the open into fresh places of hiding. But the strangest thing of all, to anyone who knew the gnomes, was the noise. Shouts and cries came from all directions. But from the harbour there came a low, rumbling roar which grew steadily louder and was already shaking the whole city.

"What's happened to the Earthmen?" said Scrubb. "Is it *them* shouting?"

"'Tis hardly possible," said the Prince. "I never heard one of the rascals so much as speak with a loud voice in all the weary years of my bondage. Some new devilry, I don't doubt."

"And what is that red light over there?" asked Jill. "Is something on fire?"

"If you ask me," said Puddleglum, "I should say that was the central fires of the Earth breaking out to make a new volcano. We'll be in the middle of it, I shouldn't wonder."

"Look at that ship!" said Scrubb. "Why's it coming on so quickly? No one's rowing it."

"Look, look!" said the Prince. "The ship is already far this side of the harbour – it is in the street. Look! All the ships are driving into the city! By my head, the sea's rising. The flood is upon us. Aslan be praised, this castle stands on high ground. But the water comes on grimly fast."

"Oh, what *can* be happening?" cried Jill. "Fire and water and all those people dodging about the streets."

"I'll tell you what it is," said Puddleglum. "That Witch has laid a train of magic spells so that whenever she was killed, at that same moment her whole kingdom would fall to pieces. She's the sort that wouldn't so much mind dying herself if she knew that the chap who killed her was going to be burned, or buried, or drowned five minutes later."

"Hast hit it, friend wiggle," said the Prince. "When our swords hacked off the Witch's head, that stroke ended all her magic works, and now the Deep Lands are falling to pieces. We are looking on the end of the Underworld."

"That's it, Sir," said Puddleglum. "Unless it should happen to be the end of the whole world."

"But are we just going to stay here and – wait?" gasped Jill.

"Not by my counsel," said the Prince. "I would save my horse, Coalblack, and the Witch's Snowflake (a noble beast and worthy of a better mistress) which are both stabled in the courtyard. After that, let us make shift to get out to high ground and pray that we shall find an outlet. The horses can carry two each at need, and if we put them to it they may outstrip the flood."

"Will your Highness not put on armour?" asked Puddleglum. "I don't like the look of *those*" – and he pointed down to the street. Everyone looked down. Dozens of creatures (and now that they were close, they obviously were Earthmen) were coming up from the direction of the harbour. But they were not moving like an aimless crowd. They behaved like modern soldiers in an attack, making rushes and taking cover, anxious not to be seen from the castle windows.

"I dare not see the inside of that armour again," said the Prince. "I rode in it as in a movable dungeon, and it stinks of magic and slavery. But I will take the shield."

He left the room and returned with a strange light in his eyes a moment later.

"Look, friends," he said, holding out the shield towards them. "An hour ago it was black and without device; and now, this." The shield had turned bright as silver, and on it, redder than blood or cherries, was the figure of the Lion.

"Doubtless," said the Prince, "this signifies that Aslan will be our good lord, whether he means us to live or die. And all's one, for that. Now, by my counsel, we shall all kneel and kiss his likeness, and then all shake hands one with another, as true friends that may shortly be parted. And then, let us descend into the city and take the adventure that is sent us."

And they all did as the Prince had said. But when Scrubb shook hands with Jill, he said, "So long, Jill. Sorry I've been a funk and so ratty. I hope you get safe home," and Jill said, "So long, Eustace. And I'm sorry I've been such a pig." And this was the first time they had ever used Christian names, because one didn't do it at school.

The Prince unlocked the door and they all went down the stairs: three of them with drawn swords, and Jill with drawn knife. The attendants had vanished and the great room at the foot of the Prince's stairs was empty. The grey, doleful lamps were still burning and by their light they had no difficulty in passing gallery after gallery and descending stairway after stairway. The noises from outside the castle were not so easily heard here as they had been in the room above. Inside the house all was still as death, and deserted. It was as they turned a corner into the great hall on the ground floor that they met their first Earthman – a fat, whitish creature with a very pig-like face who was gobbling up all the remains of food on the tables. It squealed (the squeal also was very like a pig's) and darted under a bench, whisking its long tail out of Puddleglum's reach in the nick of time. Then it rushed away through the far door too quickly to be followed.

From the hall they came out into the courtyard. Jill, who went to a riding school in the holidays, had just noticed the smell of a stable (a very nice, honest, homely smell it is to meet in a place like Underland) when Eustace said, "Great Scott! Look at that!" A magnificent rocket had risen from somewhere beyond the castle walls and broken into green stars.

"Fireworks!" said Jill in a puzzled voice.

"Yes," said Eustace, "but you can't imagine those Earth people letting them off for fun! It must be a signal."

"And means no good to us, I'll be bound," said Puddleglum.

"Friends," said the Prince, "when once a man is launched on such an adventure as this, he must bid farewell to hopes and fears, otherwise death or deliverance will both come too late to save his honour and his reason. Ho, my beauties" (he was now opening the stable door). "Hey, cousins! Steady, Coalblack! Softly now, Snowflake! You are not forgotten."

The horses were both frightened by the strange lights and the noises. Jill, who had been so cowardly about going through a black hole between one cave and another, went in without fear between the stamping and snorting beasts, and she and the Prince had them saddled and bridled in a few minutes. Very fine they looked as they came out into the courtyard, tossing their heads. Jill mounted Snowflake, and Puddleglum got up behind her. Eustace got up behind the Prince on Coalblack. Then, with a great echo of hooves, they rode out of the main gateway into the street.

"Not much danger of being burnt. That's the bright side of it," observed Puddleglum, pointing to their right. There, hardly a hundred yards away, lapping against the walls of the houses, was water.

"Courage!" said the Prince. "The road there goes down steeply. That water has climbed only half up the greatest hill in the city. It might come so near in the first half-hour and come no nearer in the next two. My fear is more of that—" and he pointed with his sword to a great tall Earthman with boar's tusks, followed by six others of assorted shapes and sizes who had just dashed out of a side street and stepped into the shadow of the houses where no one could see them.

The Prince led them, aiming always in the direction of the glowing red light but a little to the left of it. His plan was to get round the fire (if it was a fire) on to high ground, in hope that they might find their way to the new diggings. Unlike the other three, he seemed to be almost enjoying himself. He whistled as he rode, and sang snatches of an old song about Corin Thunder-fist of Archenland. The truth is, he was so glad at being free from his long enchantment that all dangers seemed a game in comparison. But the rest found it an eerie journey.

Behind them was the sound of clashing and entangled ships, and the rumble of collapsing buildings. Overhead was the great patch of lurid light on the roof of the Underworld. Ahead was the mysterious glow, which did not seem to grow any bigger. From the same direction came a continual hubbub of shouts, screams, cat-calls, laughter, squeals, and bellowings; and fireworks of all sorts rose in the dark air. No one could guess what they meant. Nearer to them, the city was partly lit up by the red glow, and partly by the very different light of the dreary Gnome lamps. But there were many places where neither of these lights fell, and those places were jet black. And in and out of those places the shapes of Earthmen were darting and slipping all the time, always with their eyes fixed on the travellers, always trying to keep out of sight themselves. There were big faces and little faces, huge eyes like fishes' eyes and little eyes like bears'. There were feathers and bristles, horns and tusks, noses like whipcord, and chins so long that they looked like beards. Every now and then a group of them would get too big or come too near. Then the Prince would brandish his sword and make a show of charging them. And the creatures, with all manner of hootings, squeakings, and cluckings, would dive away into the darkness.

But when they had climbed many steep streets and were far away from the flood, and almost out of the town on the inland side, it began to be more serious. They were now close to the red glow and nearly on a level with it, though they still could not see what it really was. But by its light they could see their enemies more clearly. Hundreds − perhaps a few thousands – of gnomes were all moving towards it. But they were doing so in short rushes, and whenever they stopped, they turned and faced the travellers.

"If your Highness asked me," said Puddleglum, "I'd say those fellows were meaning to cut us off in front."

"That was my thought too, Puddleglum," said the Prince. "And we can never fight our way through so many. Hark you! Let us ride forth close by the edge of yonder house. And even as we reach it, do you slip off into its shadow. The Lady and I will go forward a few paces. Some of these devils will follow us, I doubt not; they are thick behind us. Do you, who have long arms, take one alive if you may, as it passes your ambush. We may get a true tale of it or learn what is their quarrel against us."

"But won't the others all come rushing at us to rescue the one we catch?" said Jill in a voice not so steady as she tried to make it.

"Then, Madam," said the Prince, "you shall see us die fighting around you, and you must commend yourself to the Lion. Now, good Puddleglum."

The Marsh-wiggle slipped off into the shadow as quickly as a cat. The others, for a sickening minute or so, went forward at a walk. Then suddenly from behind them there broke out a series of blood-curdling screams, mixed with the familiar voice of Puddleglum, saying, "Now then! Don't cry out before you're hurt, or you *will* be hurt, see? Anyone would think it was a pig being killed."

"That was good hunting," exclaimed the Prince, immediately turning Coalblack and coming back to the corner of her house. "Eustace," he said, "of your courtesy, take Coalblack's head." Then he dismounted, and all three gazed in silence while Puddleglum pulled his catch out into the light. It was a most miserable little gnome, only about three feet long. It had a sort of ridge, like a cock's comb (only hard), on the top of its head, little pink eyes, and a mouth and chin so large and round that its face looked like that of a pigmy hippopotamus. If they had not been in such a tight place, they would have burst into laughter at the sight of it.

"Now, Earthman," said the Prince, standing over it and holding his sword point very near the prisoner's neck, "speak up, like an honest gnome, and you shall go free. Play the knave with us, and you are but a dead Earthman. Good Puddleglum, how can it speak while you hold its mouth tight shut?"

"No, and it can't bite either," said Puddleglum. "If I had the silly soft hands that you humans have (saving your Highness's reverence) I'd have been all over blood by now. Yet even a Marsh-wiggle gets tired of being chewed."

"Sirrah," said the Prince to the gnome, "one bite and you die. Let its mouth open, Puddleglum."

"Oo-ee-ee," squealed the Earthman. "Let me go, let me go. It isn't me. I didn't do it."

"Didn't do what?" asked Puddleglum.

"Whatever your Honours say I *did* do," answered the creature.

"Tell me your name," said the Prince, "and what you Earthmen are all about today."

"Oh please, your Honours, please, kind gentlemen," whimpered the gnome. "Promise you will not tell the Queen's grace anything I say."

"The Queen's grace, as you call her," said the Prince sternly, "is dead. I killed her myself."

"What!" cried the gnome, opening its ridiculous mouth wider and wider in astonishment. "Dead? The Witch dead? And by your Honour's hand?" It gave a huge sigh of relief and added, "Why, then your Honour is a friend!"

The Prince withdrew his sword an inch or so. Puddleglum let the creature sit up. It looked round on the four travellers with its twinkling, red eyes, chuckled once or twice, and began.

CHAPTER FOURTEEN

THE BOTTOM OF THE WORLD

"My name is Golg," said the gnome. "And I'll tell your Honours all I know. About an hour ago we were all going about our work – *her* work, I should say – sad and silent, same as we've done any other day for years and years. Then there came a great crash and bang. As soon as they heard it, everyone says to himself, I haven't had a song or a dance or let off a squib for a long time; why's that? And everyone thinks to himself, Why, I must have been enchanted. And then everyone says to himself, I'm blessed if I know why I'm carrying this load, and I'm not going to carry it any further: that's that. And down we all throw our sacks and bundles and tools. Then everyone turns and sees the great red glow over yonder. And everyone says to himself, What's that? And everyone answers himself and says, There's a crack or chasm split open and a nice warm glow coming up through it from the Really Deep Land, a thousand fathoms under us."

"Great Scott," exclaimed Eustace, "are there other lands still lower down?"

"Oh yes, your Honour," said Golg. "Lovely places; what we call the Land of Bism. This country where we are now, the Witch's country, is what *we* call the Shallow Lands. It's a good deal too near the surface to suit us. Ugh! You might almost as well be living outside, on the surface itself. You see, we're all poor gnomes from Bism whom the Witch has called up here by magic to work for her. But we'd forgotten all about it till that crash came and the spell broke. We didn't know who we were or where we belonged. We couldn't do anything, or think anything, except what she put into our heads. And it was glum and gloomy things she put there all those years. I've nearly forgotten how to make a joke or dance a jig. But the moment the bang came and the chasm opened and the sea began rising, it all came back. And of course we all set off as quick as we could to get down the crack and home to our own place. And you can see them over there all letting off rockets and standing on their heads for joy. And I'll be very obliged to your Honours if you'll soon let me go and join in."

"I think this is simply splendid," said Jill. "I'm so glad we freed the gnomes as well as ourselves when we cut off the Witch's head! And I'm so glad they aren't really horrid and gloomy any more than the Prince really was – well, what he seemed like."

"That's all very well, Pole," said Puddleglum cautiously. "But those gnomes didn't look to me like chaps who were just running away. It looked more like military formations, if you ask me. Do you look me in the face, Mr Golg, and tell me you weren't preparing for battle?"

"Of course we were, your Honour," said Golg. "You see, we didn't know the Witch was dead. We thought she'd be watching from the castle. We were trying to slip away without being seen. And then when you four came out with swords and horses, of course everyone says to himself, Here it comes; not knowing that his Honour wasn't on the Witch's side. And we were determined to fight like anything rather than give up the hope of going back to Bism."

"I'll be sworn 'tis an honest gnome," said the Prince. "Let go of it, friend Puddleglum. As for me, good Golg, I have been enchanted like you and your fellows, and have but newly remembered myself. And now, one question more. Do you know the way to those new diggings, by which the sorceress meant to lead out an army against Overland?"

"Ee-ee-ee!" squeaked Golg. "Yes, I know that terrible road. I will show you where it begins. But it is no manner of use your Honour asking me to go with you on it. I'll die rather."

"Why?" asked Eustace anxiously. "What's so dreadful about it?"

"Too near the top, the outside," said Golg, shuddering. "That was the worst thing the Witch did to us. We were going to be led out into the open – on to the outside of the world. They say there's no roof at all there; only a horrible great emptiness called the sky. And the diggings have gone so far that a few strokes of the pick would bring you out to it. I wouldn't dare go near them."

"Hurray! Now you're talking!" cried Eustace, and Jill said, "But it's not horrid at all up there. We like it. We live there."

"I know you Overlanders live there," said Golg. "But I thought it was because you couldn't find your way down inside. You can't really *like* it – crawling about like flies on the top of the world!"

"What about showing us the road at once?" said Puddleglum.

"In a good hour," cried the Prince. The whole party set out. The Prince remounted his charger, Puddleglum climbed up behind Jill, and Golg led the way. As he went, he kept shouting out the good news that the Witch was dead and that the four Overlanders were not dangerous. And those who heard him shouted it on to others, so that in a few minutes the whole of Underland was ringing with shouts and cheers, and gnomes by hundreds and thousands, leaping, turning cartwheels, standing on their heads, playing leapfrog, and letting off huge crackers, came pressing round Coalblack and Snowflake. And the Prince had to tell the story of his own enchantment and deliverance at least ten times.

In this way they came to the edge of the chasm. It was about a thousand feet long and perhaps two hundred wide. They dismounted from their horses and came to the edge, and looked down into it. A strong heat smote up into their faces, mixed with a smell which was quite unlike any they had ever smelled. It was rich, sharp, exciting, and made you sneeze. The depth of the chasm was so bright that at first it dazzled their eyes and they could see nothing. When they got used to it they thought they could make out a river of fire, and, on the banks of that river, what seemed to be fields and groves of an unbearable, hot brilliance – though they were dim compared with the river. There were blues, reds, greens, and whites all jumbled together: a very good stained-glass window with the tropical sun staring straight through it at midday might have some-thing of the same effect. Down the rugged sides of the chasm, looking black like flies against all that fiery light, hundreds of Earthmen were climbing.

"Your honours," said Golg (and when they turned to look at him they could see nothing but blackness for a few minutes, their eyes were so dazzled). "Your honours, why don't you come down to Bism? You'd be happier there than in that cold, unprotected, naked country out on top. Or at least come down for a short visit."

Jill took it for granted that none of the others would listen to such an idea for a moment. To her horror she heard the Prince saying:

"Truly, friend Golg, I have half a mind to come down with you. For this is a marvellous adventure, and it may be no mortal man has ever looked into Bism before or will ever have the chance again. And I know not how, as the years pass, I shall bear to remember that it was once in my power to have probed the uttermost pit of Earth and that I forbore. But could a man live there? You do not swim in the fire-river itself?"

"Oh no, your Honour. Not we. It's only salamanders live in the fire itself."

"What kind of beast is your salamander?" asked the Prince.

"It is hard to tell their kind, your Honour," said Golg. "For they are too white-hot to look at but they are most like small dragons. They speak to us out of the fire. They are wonderfully clever with their tongues: very witty and eloquent."

Jill glanced hastily at Eustace. She had felt sure that he would like the idea of climbing down that chasm even less than she did. Her heart sank as she saw that his face was quite changed. He looked much more like the Prince than like the old Scrubb at Experiment House. For all his adventures, and the days when he had sailed with King Caspian, were coming back to him.

"Your Highness," he said. "If my old friend Reepicheep the Mouse were here, he would say we could not now refuse the adventures of Bism without a great impeachment to our honour."

"Down there," said Golg, "I could show you real gold, real silver, real diamonds."

"Bosh!" said Jill rudely. "As if we didn't know that we're below the deepest mines even here."

"Yes," said Golg. "I have heard of those little scratches in the crust that you Topdwellers call mines. But that's where you get dead gold, dead silver, dead gems. Down in Bism we have them alive and growing. There I'll pick you bunches of rubies that you can eat and squeeze you a cup full of diamond-juice. You won't care much about fingering the cold, dead treasures of your shallow mines after you have tasted the live ones of Bism."

"My father went to the world's end," said Rilian thoughtfully. "It would be a marvellous thing if his son went to the bottom of the world."

"If your Highness wants to see your father while he's still alive, which I think he'd prefer," said Puddleglum, "it's about time we were getting on to that road to the diggings."

"And I won't go down that hole, whatever anyone says," added Jill.

"Why, if your Honours are really set to go back to the Overworld," said Golg, "there *is* one bit of the road that's rather lower than this. And perhaps, if that flood's still rising—"

"Oh, do, do, do come *on*!" begged Jill.

"I fear it must be so," said the Prince with a deep sigh. "But I have left half of my heart in the land of Bism."

"Please!" begged Jill.

"Where is the road?" asked Puddleglum.

"There are lamps all the way," said Golg. "Your Honour can see the beginning of the road on the far side of the chasm."

"How long will the lamps burn for?" asked Puddleglum.

At that moment a hissing, scorching voice like the voice of fire itself (they wondered afterwards if it could have been a salamander's) came whistling up out of the very depths of Bism.

"Quick! Quick! Quick! To the cliffs, to the cliffs, to the cliffs!" it said. "The rift closes. It closes. It closes. Quick! Quick!" And at the same time, with ear-shattering cracks and creaks, the rocks moved. Already, while they looked, the chasm was narrower. From every side belated gnomes were rushing into it. They would not wait to climb down the rocks. They flung themselves headlong and, either because so strong a blast of hot air was beating up from the bottom, or for some other reason, they could be seen floating downwards like leaves. Thicker and thicker they floated, till their blackness almost blotted out the fiery river and the groves of live gems.

"Goodbye to your Honours. I'm off," shouted Golg, and dived. Only a few were left to follow him. The chasm was now no broader than a stream. Now it was narrow as the slit in a pillarbox. Now it was only an intensely bright thread. Then, with a shock like a thousand goods trains crashing into a thousand pairs of buffers, the lips of rock closed. The hot, maddening smell vanished. The travellers were alone in an Underworld which now looked far blacker than before. Pale, dim, and dreary, the lamps marked the direction of the road.

"Now," said Puddleglum, "it's ten to one we've already stayed too long, but we may as well make a try. Those lamps will give out in five minutes, I shouldn't wonder."

They urged the horses to a canter and thundered along the dusky road in fine style. But almost at once it began going downhill. They would have thought Golg had sent them the wrong way if they had not seen, on the other side of the valley, the lamps going on and upwards as far as the eye could reach. But at the bottom of the valley the lamps shone on moving water.

"Haste," cried the Prince. They galloped down the slope. It would have been nasty enough at the bottom even five minutes later for the tide was running up the valley like a millrace, and if it had come to swimming, the horses could hardly have won over. But it was still only a foot or two deep, and though it swished terribly round the horses' legs, they reached the far side in safety.

Then began the slow, weary march uphill with nothing ahead to look at but the pale lamps which went up and up as far as the eye could reach. When they looked back they could see the water spreading. All the hills of Underland were now islands, and it was only on those islands that the lamps remained. Every moment some distant light vanished. Soon there would be total darkness everywhere except on the road they were following; and even on the lower part of it behind them, though no lamps had yet gone out, the lamplight shone on water.

Although they had good reason for hurrying, the horses could not go on for ever without a rest. They halted; and in silence they could hear the lapping of water.

"I wonder, is what's his name – Father Time – flooded out now," said

Jill. "And all those strange sleeping animals."

"I don't think we're as high as that," said Eustace. "Don't you remember how we had to go downhill to reach the Sunless Sea? I shouldn't think the water has reached Father Time's cave yet."

"That's as may be," said Puddleglum. "I'm more interested in the lamps on this road. Look a bit sickly, don't they?"

"They always did," said Jill.

"Ah," said Puddleglum. "But they're greener now."

"You don't mean to say you think they're going out?" cried Eustace.

"Well, however they work, you can't expect them to last for ever, you know," replied the Marsh-wiggle. "But don't let your spirits down, Scrubb. I've got my eye on the water too, and I don't think it's rising so fast as it did."

"Small comfort, friend," said the Prince, "if we cannot find our way out. I cry you mercy, all. I am to blame for my pride and fantasy which delayed us by the mouth of the land of Bism. Now, let us ride on."

During the hour or so that followed Jill sometimes thought that Puddleglum was right about the lamps, and sometimes thought it was only her imagination. Meanwhile the land was changing. The roof of Underland was so near that even by that dull light they could now see it quite distinctly. And the great, rugged walls of Underland could be seen drawing closer on each side. The road, in fact, was leading them up into a steep tunnel. They began to pass picks and shovels and barrows and other signs that the diggers had recently been at work. If only one could be sure of getting out, all this was very cheering. But the thought of going on into a hole that would get narrower and narrower, and harder to turn back in, was very unpleasant.

At last the roof was so low that Puddleglum and the Prince knocked their heads against it. The party dismounted and led the horses. The road was uneven here and one had to pick one's steps with some care. That was how Jill noticed the growing darkness. There was no doubt about it now. The faces of the others looked strange and ghastly in the green glow. Then all at once (she couldn't help it) Jill gave a little scream. One light, the next one ahead, went out altogether. The one behind them did the same. Then they were in absolute darkness.

"Courage, friends," came Prince Rilian's voice. "Whether we live or die Aslan will be our good lord."

"That's right, Sir," said Puddleglum's voice. "And you must always remember there's one good thing about being trapped down here: it'll save funeral expenses."

Jill held her tongue. (If you don't want other people to know how frightened you are, this is always a wise thing to do; it's your voice that gives you away.)

"We might as well go on as stand here," said Eustace; and when she heard the tremble in *his* voice, Jill knew how wise she'd been not to trust her own.

Puddleglum and Eustace went first with their arms stretched out in front of them, for fear of blundering into anything; Jill and the Prince followed, leading the horses.

"I say," came Eustace's voice much later, "are my eyes going wrong, or is there a patch of light up there?"

Before anyone could answer him, Puddleglum called out: "Stop. I'm up against a dead end. And it's earth, not rock. What were you saying, Scrubb?"

"By the Lion," said the Prince, "Eustace is right. There is a sort of—"

"But it's not daylight," said Jill. "It's only a cold blue sort of light."

"Better than nothing, though," said Eustace. "Can we get up to it?"

"It's not right overhead," said Puddleglum. "It's above us, but it's in this wall that I've run into. How would it be, Pole, if you got on my shoulders and saw whether you could get up to it?"

CHAPTER FIFTEEN

THE DISAPPEARANCE OF JILL

The patch of light did not show up anything down in the darkness where they were standing. The others could only hear, not see, Jill's efforts to get on to the Marsh-wiggle's back. That is, they heard him saying, "You needn't put your finger in my eye," and, "Nor your foot in my mouth either," and, "That's more like it," and, "Now, I'll hold on to your legs. That'll leave your arms free to steady yourself against the earth."

Then they looked up and soon they saw the black shape of Jill's head against the patch of light.

"Well?" they all shouted up anxiously.

"It's a hole," called Jill's voice. "I could get through it if I was a little bit higher."

"What do you see through it?" asked Eustace.

"Nothing much yet," said Jill. "I say, Puddleglum, let go my legs so that I can stand on your shoulders instead of sitting on them. I can steady myself all right against the edge."

They could hear her moving and then much more of her came into sight against the greyness of the opening; in fact all of her down to the waist.

"I say—" began Jill, but suddenly broke off with a cry: not a sharp cry. It sounded more as if her mouth had been muffled up or had something pushed into it. After that she found her voice and seemed to be shouting out as loud as she could, but they couldn't hear the words. Two things then happened at the same moment. The patch of light was completely blocked up for a second or so; and they heard both a scuffling, struggling sound and the voice of the Marsh-wiggle gasping; "Quick! Help! Hold on to her legs. Someone's pulling her. There! No, here. Too late!"

The opening, and the cold light which filled it, were now perfectly clear again. Jill had vanished.

"Jill! Jill!" they shouted frantically, but there was no answer.

"Why the dickens couldn't you have held her feet?" said Eustace.

"I don't know, Scrubb," groaned Puddleglum. "Born to be a misfit, I shouldn't wonder. Fated. Fated to be Pole's death, just as I was fated to eat Talking Stag at Harfang. Not that it isn't my own fault as well, of course."

"This is the greatest shame and sorrow that could have fallen on us," said the Prince. "We have sent a brave lady into the hands of enemies and stayed behind in safety."

"Don't paint it *too* black, Sir," said Puddleglum. "We're not very safe except for death by starvation in this hole."

"I wonder, am *I* small enough to get through where Jill did?" said Eustace.

What had really happened to Jill was this. As soon as she got her head out of the hole she found that she was looking down as if from an upstairs window, not up as if through a trap-door. She had been so long in the dark that her eyes couldn't at first take in what they were seeing: except that she was not looking at the daylit, sunny world which she so wanted to see. The air seemed to be deadly cold, and the light was pale and blue. There was also a good deal of noise going on and a lot of white objects flying about in the air. It was at that moment that she had shouted down to Puddleglum to let her stand up on his shoulders.

When she had done this, she could see and hear a good deal better. The noises she had been hearing turned out to be of two kinds: the rhythmical thump of several feet, and the music of four fiddles, three flutes, and a drum. She also got her own position clear. She was looking out of a hole in a steep bank which sloped down and reached the level about fourteen feet below her. Everything was very white. A lot of people were moving about. Then she gasped! The people were trim little Fauns, and Dryads with leaf-crowned hair floating behind them. For a second they looked as if they were moving anyhow; then she saw that they were really doing a dance – a dance with so many complicated steps and figures that it took you some time to understand it. Then it came over her like a thunderclap that the pale, blue light was really moonlight, and the white stuff on the ground was really snow. And of course! There were the stars staring in a black frosty sky overhead. And the tall black things behind the dancers were trees. They had not only got out into the upper world at last, but had come out in the heart of Narnia. Jill felt she could have fainted with delight; and the music – the wild music, intensely sweet and yet just the least bit eerie too, and full of good magic as the Witch's thrumming had been full of bad magic – made her feel it all the more.

All this takes a long time to tell, but of course it took a very short time to see. Jill turned almost at once to shout down to the others, "I say! It's all right. We're out, and we're home." But the reason she never got further than "I say" was this. Circling round and round the dancers was a ring of Dwarfs, all dressed in their finest clothes; mostly scarlet with fur-lined hoods and golden tassels and big furry top-boots. As they circled round they were all diligently throwing snowballs. (Those were the white things that Jill had seen flying through the air.) They weren't throwing them *at* the dancers as silly boys might have been doing in England. They were throwing them through the dance in such perfect time with the music and with such perfect aim that if all the dancers were in exactly the right places at exactly the right moments, no one would be hit. This is called the Great Snow Dance and it is done every year in Narnia on the first moonlit night when there is snow on the ground. Of course it is a kind of game as well as a dance, because every now and then some dancer will be the least little bit wrong and get a snowball in the face, and then everyone laughs. But a good team of dancers, Dwarfs, and musicians will keep it up for hours without a single hit. On fine nights when the cold and the drum-taps, and the hooting of the owls, and the moonlight, have got into their wild, woodland blood and made it even wilder, they will dance till daybreak. I wish you could see it for yourselves.

What had stopped Jill when she got as far as the *say* of "I say" was of course simply a fine big snowball that came sailing through the dance from a Dwarf on the far side and got her fair and square in the mouth. She didn't in the least mind; twenty snowballs would not have damped her spirits at that moment. But however happy you are feeling, you can't talk with your mouth full of snow. And when, after considerable spluttering, she could speak again, she quite forgot in her excitement that the others, down in the dark, behind her, still didn't know the good news. She simply leaned as far out of the hole as she could, and yelled to the dancers.

"Help! Help! We're buried in the hill. Come and dig us out."

The Narnians, who had not even noticed the little hole in the hillside, were of course very surprised, and looked about in several wrong directions before they found out where the voice was coming from. But when they caught sight of Jill they all came running towards her, and as many as could scrambled up the bank, and a dozen or more hands were stretched up to help her. And Jill caught hold of them and thus got out of the hole and came slithering down the bank head first, and then picked herself up and said:

"Oh, do go and dig the others out. There are three others, besides the horses. And one of them is Prince Rilian."

She was already in the middle of a crowd when she said this, for besides the dancers all sorts of people who had been watching the dance, and whom she had not seen at first, came running up. Squirrels came out of the trees in showers, and so did owls. Hedgehogs came waddling as fast as their short legs would carry them. Bears and Badgers followed at a slower pace. A great Panther, twitching its tail in excitement, was the last to join the party.

But as soon as they understood what Jill was saying, they all became active. "Pick and shovel, boys, pick and shovel. Off for our tools!" said the Dwarfs, and dashed away into the woods at top speed. "Wake up some Moles, they're the chaps for digging. They're quite as good as Dwarfs," said a voice. "What was that she said about Prince Rilian?" said another. "Hush!" said the Panther. "The poor child's crazed, and no wonder after being lost inside the hill. She doesn't know what she's saying." "That's right," said an old Bear. "Why, she said Prince Rilian was a horse!" – "No, she didn't," said a Squirrel, very pert. – "Yes, she did," said another Squirrel, even perter.

"It's quite t-t-t-true. D-d-don't be so silly," said Jill. She spoke like that because her teeth were now chattering with the cold.

Immediately one of the Dryads flung round her a furry cloak which some Dwarf had dropped when he rushed to fetch his mining tools, and an obliging Faun trotted off among the trees to a place where Jill could see firelight in the mouth of a cave, to get her a hot drink. But before it came, all the Dwarfs reappeared with spades and pick-axes and charged at the hillside. Then Jill heard cries of "Hi! What are you doing? Put that sword down," and "Now, young 'un; none of that," and, "He's a vicious one, now, isn't he?" Jill hurried to the spot and didn't know whether to laugh or cry when she saw Eustace's face, very pale and dirty, projecting from the blackness of the hole, and Eustace's right hand brandishing a sword with which he made lunges at anyone who came near him.

For of course Eustace had been having a very different time from Jill during the last few minutes. He had heard Jill cry out and seen her disappear into the unknown. Like the Prince and Puddleglum, he thought that some enemies had caught her. And from down below he didn't see that the pale, blueish light was moonlight. He thought the hole would lead only into some other cave, lit by some ghostly phosphorescence and filled with goodness-knows-what evil creatures of the Underworld. So that when he had persuaded Puddleglum to give him a leg up, and drawn his sword, and poked out his head, he had really been doing a very brave thing. The others would have done it first if they could, but the hole was too small for them to climb through. Eustace was a little bigger, and a lot clumsier, than Jill, so that when he looked out he bumped his head against the top of the hole and brought a small avalanche of snow down on his face. And so, when he could see again, and saw dozens of figures coming at him as hard as they could run, it is not surprising that he tried to ward them off.

"Stop, Eustace, stop!" cried Jill. "They're all friends. Can't you see? We've come up in Narnia. Everything's all right."

Then Eustace did see, and apologized to the Dwarfs (and the Dwarfs said not to mention it), and dozens of thick, hairy, dwarfish hands helped him out just as they had helped Jill out a few minutes before. Then Jill scrambled up the bank and put her head in at the dark opening and shouted the good news in to the prisoners. As she turned away she heard Puddleglum mutter, "Ah, poor Pole. It's been too much for her, this last bit. Turned her head, I shouldn't wonder. She's beginning to see things."

Jill rejoined Eustace and they shook one another by both hands and took in great deep breaths of the free midnight air. And a warm cloak was brought for Eustace and hot drinks for both. While they were sipping it, the Dwarfs had already got all the snow and all the sods off a large strip of the hillside round the original hole, and the pickaxes and spades were now going as merrily as the feet of Fauns and Dryads had been going in the dance ten minutes before. Only ten minutes! Yet already it felt to Jill and Eustace as if all their dangers in the dark and heat and general smotheriness of the earth must have been only a dream. Out here, in the cold, with the moon and the huge stars overhead (Narnian stars are nearer than stars in our world) and with kind, merry faces all round them, one couldn't quite believe in Underland.

Before they had finished their hot drinks, a dozen or so Moles, newly waked and still very sleepy, and not well pleased, had arrived. But as soon as they understood what it was all about, they joined in with a will. Even the Fauns made themselves useful by carting away the earth in little barrows, and the Squirrels danced and leaped to and fro in great excitement, though Jill never found out exactly what they thought they were doing. The Bears and Owls contented themselves with giving advice, and kept on asking the children if they wouldn't like to come into the cave (that was where Jill had seen the firelight) and get warm and have supper. But the children couldn't bear to go without seeing their friends set free.

No one in our world can work at a job of that sort as Dwarfs and Talking Moles work in Narnia; but then, of course, Moles and Dwarfs don't look on it as work. They like digging. It was therefore not really long before they had opened a great black chasm in the hillside. And out from the blackness into the moonlight — this would have been rather dreadful if one hadn't known who they were — came, first, the long, leggy, steeple-hatted figure of the Marsh-wiggle, and then, leading two great horses, Rilian the Prince himself.

As Puddleglum appeared shouts broke out on every side: "Why, it's a Wiggle — why, it's old Puddleglum — old Puddleglum from the Eastern Marshes — what ever have you been doing, Puddleglum? — there've been search parties out for you — the Lord Trumpkin has been putting up notices — there's a reward offered!" But all this died away, all in one moment, into dead silence, as quickly as the noise dies away in a rowdy dormitory if the Headmaster opens the door. For now they saw the Prince.

No one doubted for a moment who he was. There were plenty of Beasts and Dryads and Dwarfs and Fauns who remembered him from the days before his enchanting. There were some old ones who could just remember how his father, King Caspian, had looked when he was a young man, and saw the likeness. But I think they would have known him anyway. Pale though he was from long imprisonment in the Deep Lands, dressed in black, dusty, dishevelled, and weary, there was something in his face and air which no one could mistake. That look is in the face of all true kings of Narnia, who rule by the will of Aslan and sit at Cair Paravel on the throne of Peter the High King. Instantly every head was bared and every knee was bent: a moment later, such cheering and shouting, such jumps and reels of joy, such hand-shakings and kissings and embracings of everybody by everybody else broke out that the tears came into Jill's eyes. Their quest had been worth all the pains it cost.

"Please it your Highness," said the oldest of the Dwarfs, "there is some attempt at a supper in the cave yonder, prepared against the ending of the snow-dance—"

"With a good will, Father," said the Prince. "For never had any Prince, Knight, Gentleman, or Bear so good a stomach to his victuals as we four wanderers have tonight."

The whole crowd began to move away through the trees towards the cave. Jill heard Puddleglum saying to those who pressed round him, "No, no, my story can wait. Nothing worth talking about has happened to me. I want to hear the news. Don't try breaking it to me gently, for I'd rather have it all at once. Has the King been shipwrecked? Any forest fires? No wars on the Calormen border? Or a few dragons, I shouldn't wonder?" And all the creatures laughed aloud and said, "Isn't that just like a Marsh-wiggle?"

The two children were nearly dropping with tiredness and hunger, but the warmth of the cave, and the very sight of it, with the firelight dancing on the walls and dressers and cups and saucers and plates and on the smooth stone floor, just as it does in a farmhouse kitchen, revived them a little. All the same they went fast asleep while supper was being got ready.

And while they slept Prince Rilian was talking over the whole adventure with the older and wiser Beasts and Dwarfs. And now they all saw what it meant; how a wicked Witch (doubtless the same kind as that White Witch who had brought the Great Winter on Narnia long ago) had contrived the whole thing, first killing Rilian's mother and enchanting Rilian himself. And they saw how she had dug right under Narnia and was going to break out and rule it through Rilian; and how he had never dreamed that the country of which she would make him king (king in name, but really her slave) was his own country. And from the children's part of the story they saw how she was in league and friendship with the dangerous giants of Harfang.

"And the lesson of it all is, your Highness," said the oldest Dwarf, "that those Northern Witches always mean the same thing, but in every age they have a different plan for getting it."

CHAPTER SIXTEEN

THE HEALING OF HARMS

When Jill woke the next morning and found herself in a cave, she thought for one horrid moment that she was back in the Underworld. But when she noticed that she was lying on a bed of heather with a furry mantle over her, and saw a cheery fire crackling (as if newly lit) on a stone hearth and, further off, morning sunlight coming in through the cave's mouth, she remembered all the happy truth. They had had a delightful supper, all crowded into that cave, in spite of being so sleepy before it was properly over. She had a vague impression of Dwarfs crowding round the fire with frying-pans rather bigger than themselves, and the hissing, and delicious smell of sausages, and more, and more, and more sausages. And not wretched sausages half full of bread and soya bean either, but real meaty, spicy ones, fat and piping hot and burst and just the tiniest bit burnt. And great mugs of frothy chocolate, and roast potatoes and roast chestnuts, and baked apples with raisins stuck in where the cores had been, and then ices just to freshen you up after all the hot things.

Jill sat up and looked around. Puddleglum and Eustace were lying not far away, both fast asleep.

"Hi, you two!" shouted Jill in a loud voice. "Aren't you ever going to get up?"

"Shoo, shoo!" said a sleepy voice somewhere above her. "Time to be settling down. Have a good snooze, do, do. Don't make a to-do. Tu-whoo!"

"Why, I do believe," said Jill, glancing up at a white bundle of fluffy feathers which was perched on top of a grandfather clock in one corner of the cave, "I do believe it's Glimfeather!"

"True, true," whirred the Owl, lifting its head out from under its wing and opening one eye. "I came up with a message for the Prince at about two. The squirrels brought us the good news. Message for the Prince. He's gone. You're to follow too. Good-day——" and the head disappeared again.

As there seemed no further hope of getting any information from the Owl, Jill got up and began looking round for any chance of a wash and some breakfast. But almost at once a little Faun came trotting into the cave with a sharp click-clack of his goaty hoofs on the stone floor.

"Ah! You've woken up at last, Daughter of Eve," he said. "Perhaps you'd better wake the Son of Adam. You've got to be off in a few minutes and two Centaurs have very kindly offered to let you ride on their backs down to Cair Paravel." He added in a lower voice, "Of course, you realize it is a most special and unheard-of honour to be allowed to ride a Centaur. I don't know that I ever heard of anyone doing it before. It wouldn't do to keep them waiting."

"Where's the Prince?" was the first question of Eustace and Puddleglum as soon as they had been wakened.

"He's gone down to meet the King, his father, at Cair Paravel," answered the Faun, whose name was Orruns. "His Majesty's ship is expected in harbour any moment. It seems that the King met Aslan – I don't know whether it was in a vision or face to face – before he had sailed far, and Aslan turned him back and told him he would find his long-lost son awaiting him when he reached Narnia."

Eustace was now up and he and Jill set about helping Orruns to get the breakfast. Puddleglum was told to stay in bed. A Centaur called Cloudbirth, a famous healer, or (as Orruns called it) a 'leech', was coming to see to his burnt foot.

"Ah!" said Puddleglum in a tone almost of contentment, "he'll want to have the leg off at the knee, I shouldn't wonder. You see if he doesn't." But he was quite glad to stay in bed.

Breakfast was scrambled eggs and toast and Eustace tackled it just as if he had not had a very large supper in the middle of the night.

"I say, Son of Adam," said the Faun, looking with a certain awe at Eustace's mouthfuls. "There's no need to hurry *quite* so dreadfully as that. I don't think the Centaurs have quite finished *their* breakfasts yet."

"Then they must have got up very late," said Eustace. "I bet it's after ten o'clock."

"Oh no," said Orruns. "They got up before it was light."

"Then they must have waited the dickens of a time for breakfast," said Eustace.

"No, they didn't," said Orruns. "They began eating the minute they woke."

"Golly!" said Eustace. "Do they eat a very big breakfast?"

"Why, Son of Adam, don't you understand? A Centaur has a man-stomach and a horse-stomach. And of course both want breakfast. So first of all he has porridge and pavenders and kidneys and bacon and omelette and cold ham and toast and marmalade and coffee and beer. And after that he attends to the horse part of himself by grazing for an hour or so and finishing up with a hot mash, some oats, and a bag of sugar. That's why it's such a serious thing to ask a Centaur to stay for the weekend. A very serious thing indeed."

At that moment there was a sound of horse-hooves tapping on rock from the mouth of the cave, and the children looked up. The two Centaurs, one with a black and one with a golden beard flowing over their magnificent bare chests, stood waiting for them, bending their heads a little so as to look into the cave. Then the children became very polite and finished their breakfast very quickly. No one thinks a Centaur funny when he sees it. They are solemn, majestic people, full of ancient wisdom which they learn from the stars, not easily made either merry or angry; but their anger is terrible as a tidal wave when it comes.

"Goodbye, dear Puddleglum," said Jill, going over to the Marsh-wiggle's bed. "I'm sorry we called you a wet blanket."

"So'm I," said Eustace. "You've been the best friend in the world."

"And I do hope we'll meet again," added Jill.

"Not much chance of that, I should say," replied Puddleglum. "I don't reckon I'm very likely to see my old wigwam again either. And that Prince – he's a nice chap – but do you think he's very strong? Constitution ruined with living underground, I shouldn't wonder. Looks the sort that might go off any day."

"Puddleglum!" said Jill. "You're a regular old humbug. You sound as doleful as a funeral and I believe you're perfectly happy. And you talk as if you were afraid of everything, when you're really as brave as – as a lion."

"Now, speaking of funerals," began Puddleglum, but Jill, who heard the Centaurs tapping with their hoofs behind her, surprised him very much by flinging her arms round his thin neck and kissing his muddy-looking face, while Eustace wrung his hand. Then they both rushed away to the centaurs, and the Marsh-wiggle, sinking back on his bed, remarked to himself, "Well, I wouldn't have dreamt of her doing that. Even though I *am* a good-looking chap."

To ride on a Centaur is, no doubt, a great honour (and except Jill and Eustace there is probably no one alive in the world today who has had it) but it is very uncomfortable. For no one who valued his life would suggest putting a saddle on a Centaur, and riding bareback is no fun; especially if, like Eustace, you have never learned to ride at all. The Centaurs were very polite in a grave, gracious, grown-up kind of way, and as they cantered through the Narnian woods they spoke, without turning their heads, telling the children about the properties of herbs and roots, the influences of the planets, the nine names of Aslan with their meanings, and things of that sort. But however sore and jolted the two humans were, they would now give anything to have that journey over again: to see those glades and slopes sparkling with the previous night's snow, to be met by rabbits and squirrels and birds that wished you good morning, to breathe again the air of Narnia and hear the voices of the Narnian trees.

They came down to the river, flowing bright and blue in winter sunshine, far below the last bridge (which is at the snug, red-roofed little town of Beruna) and were ferried across in a flat barge by the ferryman; or rather, by the ferry-wiggle, for it is Marsh-wiggles who do most of the watery and fishy kinds of work in Narnia. And when they had crossed they rode along the south bank of the river and presently came to Cair Paravel itself. And at the very moment of their arrival they saw that same bright ship which they had seen when they first set foot in Narnia, gliding up the river like a huge bird. All the court were once more assembled on the green between the castle and the quay to welcome King Caspian home again. Rilian, who had changed his black clothes and was now dressed in a scarlet cloak over silver mail, stood close to the water's edge, bare-headed, to receive his father; and the Dwarf Trumpkin sat beside him in his little donkey-chair. The children saw there would be no chance of reaching the Prince through all that crowd, and, anyway, they now felt rather shy. So they asked the Centaurs if they might go on sitting on their backs a little longer and thus see everything over the heads of the courtiers. And the Centaurs said they might.

A flourish of silver trumpets came over the water from the ship's deck: the sailors threw a rope; rats (Talking Rats, of course) and Marsh-wiggles made it fast ashore; and the ship was warped in. Musicians, hidden somewhere in the crowd, began to play solemn, triumphal music. And soon the King's galleon was alongside and the rats ran the gangway on board her.

Jill expected to see the old King come down it. But there appeared to be some hitch. A Lord with a pale face came ashore and knelt to the Prince and to Trumpkin. The three were talking with their heads close together for a few minutes, but no one could hear what they said. The music played on, but you could feel that everyone was becoming uneasy. Then four knights, carrying something and going very slowly, appeared on deck. When they started to come down the gangway you could see what they were carrying: it was the old King on a bed, very pale and still. They set him down. The Prince knelt beside him and embraced him. They could see King Caspian raising his hand to bless his son. And everyone cheered, but it was a half-hearted cheer, for they all felt that something was going wrong. Then suddenly the King's head fell back upon his pillows, the musicians stopped and there was a dead silence. The Prince, kneeling by the King's bed, laid down his head upon it and wept.

There were whisperings and goings to and fro. Then Jill noticed that all who wore hats, bonnets, helmets, or hoods were taking them off – Eustace included. Then she heard a rustling and flapping noise up above the castle; when she looked she saw that the great banner with the golden Lion on it was being brought down to half-mast. And after that, slowly, mercilessly, with wailing strings and disconsolate blowing of horns, the music began again: this time, a tune to break your heart.

They both slipped off their Centaurs (who took no notice of them).

"I wish I was at home," said Jill.

Eustace nodded, saying nothing, and bit his lip.

"I have come," said a deep voice behind them. They turned and saw the Lion himself, so bright and real and strong that everything else began at once to look pale and shadowy compared with him. And in less time than it takes to breathe Jill forgot about the dead King of Narnia and remembered only how she had made Eustace fall over the cliff, and how she had helped to muff nearly all the signs, and about all the snappings and quarrellings. And she wanted to say, "I'm sorry" but she could not speak. Then the Lion drew them towards him with his eyes, and bent down and touched their pale faces with his tongue, and said:

"Think of that no more. I will not always be scolding. You have done the work for which I sent you into Narnia."

"Please, Aslan," said Jill, "may we go home now?"

"Yes. I have come to bring you Home," said Aslan. Then he opened his mouth wide and blew. But this time they had no sense of flying through the air: instead, it seemed that they remained still, and the wild breath of Aslan blew away the ship and the dead King and the castle and the snow and the winter sky. For all these things floated off into the air like wreaths of smoke, and suddenly they were standing in a great brightness of mid-summer sunshine, on smooth turf, among mighty trees, and beside a fair, fresh stream. Then they saw that they were once more on the Mountain of Aslan, high up above and beyond the end of that world in which Narnia lies. But the strange thing was that the funeral music for King Caspian still went on, though no one could tell where it came from. They were walking beside the stream and the Lion went before them: and he became so beautiful, and the music so despairing, that Jill did not know which of them it was that filled her eyes with tears.

Then Aslan stopped, and the children looked into the stream. And there, on the golden gravel of the bed of the stream, lay King Caspian, dead, with the water flowing over him like liquid glass. His long white beard swayed in it like water-weed. And all three stood and wept. Even the Lion wept: great lion-tears, each tear more precious than the Earth would be if it was a single solid diamond. And Jill noticed that Eustace looked neither like a child crying, nor like a boy crying and wanting to hide it, but like a grown-up crying. At least, that is the nearest she could get to it; but really, as she said, people don't seem to have any particular ages on that mountain.

"Son of Adam," said Aslan, "go into that thicket and pluck the thorn that you will find there, and bring it to me."

Eustace obeyed. The thorn was a foot long and sharp as a rapier.

"Drive it into my paw, Son of Adam," said Aslan, holding up his right fore-paw and spreading out the great pad towards Eustace.

"Must I?" said Eustace.

"Yes," said Aslan.

Then Eustace set his teeth and drove the thorn into the Lion's pad. And there came out a great drop of blood, redder than all redness that you have ever seen or imagined. And it splashed into the stream over the dead body of the King. At the same moment the doleful music stopped. And the dead King began to be changed. His white beard turned to grey, and from grey to yellow, and got shorter and vanished altogether; and his sunken cheeks grew round and fresh, and the wrinkles were smoothed, and his eyes opened, and his eyes and lips both laughed, and suddenly he leaped up and stood before them – a very young man, or a boy. (But Jill couldn't say which, because of people having no particular ages in Aslan's country. Even in this world, of course, it is the stupidest children who are most childish and the stupidest grown-ups who are most grown-up.) And he rushed to Aslan and flung his arms as far as they would go round the huge neck; and he gave Aslan the strong kisses of a king, and Aslan gave him the wild kisses of a Lion.

At last Caspian turned to the others. He gave a great laugh of astonished joy.

"Why! Eustace!" he said. "Eustace! So you did reach the end of the world after all. What about my second-best sword that you broke on the sea serpent?"

Eustace made a step towards him with both hands held out, but then drew back with a somewhat startled expression.

"Look here! I say," he stammered. "It's all very well. But aren't you—? I mean, didn't you—?"

"Oh, don't be such an ass," said Caspian.

"But," said Eustace, looking at Aslan. "Hasn't he – er – died?"

"Yes," said the Lion in a very quiet voice, almost (Jill thought) as if he were laughing. "He has died. Most people have, you know. Even I have. There are very few who haven't."

"Oh," said Caspian. "I see what's bothering you. You think I'm a ghost, or some nonsense. But don't you see? I would be that if I appeared in Narnia now: because I don't belong there any more. But one can't be a ghost in one's own country. I might be a ghost if I got into your world. I don't know. But I suppose it isn't yours either, now you're here."

A great hope rose in the children's hearts. But Aslan shook his shaggy head. "No, my dears," he said. "When you meet me here again, you will have come to stay. But not now. You must go back to your own world for a while."

"Sir," said Caspian, "I've always wanted to have just one glimpse of *their* world. Is that wrong?"

"You cannot want wrong things any more, now that you have died, my son," said Aslan. "And you shall see their world – for five minutes of *their* time. It will take no longer for you to set things right there." Then Aslan explained to Caspian what Jill and Eustace were going back to and all about Experiment House: he seemed to know it quite as well as they did.

"Daughter," said Aslan to Jill, "pluck a switch off that bush." She did; and as soon as it was in her hand it turned into a fine new riding crop.

"Now, Sons of Adam, draw your swords," said Aslan. "But use only the flat, for it is cowards and children, not warriors, against whom I send you."

"Are you coming with us, Aslan?" said Jill.

"They shall see only my back," said Aslan.

He led them rapidly through the wood, and before they had gone many paces, the wall of Experiment House appeared before them. Then Aslan roared so that the sun shook in the sky and thirty feet of the wall fell down before them. They looked through the gap, down into the school shrubbery and on to the roof of the gym, all under the same dull autumn sky which they had seen before their adventures began. Aslan turned to Jill and Eustace and breathed upon them and touched their foreheads with his tongue. Then he lay down amid the gap he had made in the wall and turned his golden back to England, and his lordly face towards his own lands. At the same moment Jill saw figures whom she knew only too well running up through the laurels towards them.

Most of the gang were there – Adela Pennyfather and Cholmondely Major, Edith Winterblott, 'Spotty' Sorner, big Bannister, and the two loathsome Garrett twins. But suddenly they stopped. Their faces changed, and all the meanness, conceit, cruelty, and sneakishness almost disappeared in one single expression of terror. For they saw the wall fallen down, and a lion as large as a young elephant lying in the gap, and three figures in glittering clothes with weapons in their hands rushing down upon them. For, with the strength of Aslan in them, Jill plied her crop on the girls and Caspian and Eustace plied the flats of their swords on the boys so well that in two minutes all the bullies were running like mad, crying out, "Murder! Fascists! Lions! It isn't *fair*." And then the Head (who was, by the way, a woman) came running out to see what was happening. And when she saw the lion and the broken wall and Caspian and Jill and Eustace (whom she quite failed to recognize) she had hysterics and went back to the house and began ringing up the police with stories about a lion escaped from a circus, and escaped convicts who broke down walls and carried drawn swords. In the midst of all this fuss Jill and Eustace slipped quietly indoors and changed out of their bright clothes into ordinary things, and Caspian went back into his own world. And the wall, at Aslan's word, was made whole again. When the police arrived and found no lion, no broken wall, and no convicts, and the Head behaving like a lunatic, there was an inquiry into the whole thing. And in the inquiry all sorts of things about Experiment House came out, and about ten people got expelled. After that, the Head's friends saw that the Head was no use as a Head, so they got her made an Inspector to interfere with other Heads. And when they found she wasn't much good even at that, they got her into Parliament where she lived happily ever after.

Eustace buried his fine clothes secretly one night in the school grounds, but Jill smuggled hers home and wore them at a fancy-dress ball the next holidays. And from that day forth things changed for the better at Experiment House, and it became quite a good school. And Jill and Eustace were always friends.

But far off in Narnia, King Rilian buried his father, Caspian the Navigator, Tenth of that name, and mourned for him. He himself ruled Narnia well and the land was happy in his days, though Puddleglum (whose foot was as good as new in three weeks) often pointed out that bright mornings brought on wet afternoons, and that you couldn't expect good times to last. The opening into the hillside was left open, and often in hot summer days the Narnians go in there with ships and lanterns and down to the water and sail to and fro, singing, on the cool, dark underground sea, telling each other stories of the cities that lie fathoms deep below. If ever you have the luck to go to Narnia yourself, do not forget to have a look at those caves.

THE LAST BATTLE

THE LAST BATTLE

CONTENTS

Chapter One

By Caldron Pool

In the last days of Narnia, far up to the west beyond Lantern Waste and close beside the great waterfall, there lived an Ape. He was so old that no one could remember when he had first come to live in those parts, and he was the cleverest, ugliest, most wrinkled Ape you can imagine. He had a little house, built of wood and thatched with leaves, up in the fork of a great tree, and his name was Shift. There were very few Talking Beasts or Men or Dwarfs, or people of any sort, in that part of the wood, but Shift had one friend and neighbour who was a donkey called Puzzle. At least they both said they were friends, but from the way things went on you might have thought Puzzle was more like Shift's servant than his friend. He did all the work. When they went together to the river, Shift filled the big skin bottles with water but it was Puzzle who carried them back. When they wanted anything from the towns further down the river it was Puzzle who went down with empty panniers on his back and came back with the panniers full and heavy. And all the nicest things that Puzzle brought back were eaten by Shift; for as Shift said, "You see, Puzzle, I can't eat grass and thistles like you, so it's only fair I should make it up in other ways." And Puzzle always said, "Of course, Shift, of course. I see that."

Puzzle never complained, because he knew that Shift was far cleverer than himself and he thought it was very kind of Shift to be friends with him at all. And if ever Puzzle did try to argue about anything, Shift would always say, "Now, Puzzle, I understand what needs to be done better than you. You know you're not clever, Puzzle." And Puzzle always said, "No, Shift. It's quite true. I'm *not* clever." Then he would sigh and do whatever Shift had said.

One morning early in the year the pair of them were out walking along the shore of Caldron Pool. Caldron Pool is the big pool right under the cliffs at the western end of Narnia. The great waterfall pours down into it with a noise like everlasting thunder, and the River of Narnia flows out on the other side. The waterfall keeps the Pool always dancing and bubbling and churning round and round as if it were on the boil, and that of course is how it got its name of Caldron Pool. It is liveliest in the early spring when the waterfall is swollen with all the snow that has melted off the mountains from up beyond Narnia in the Western Wild from which the river comes. And as they looked at Caldron Pool, Shift suddenly pointed with his dark, skinny finger and said,

"Look! What's that?"

"What's what?" said Puzzle.

"That yellow thing that's just come down the waterfall. Look! There it is again, it's floating. We must find out what it is."

"Must we?" said Puzzle.

"Of course we must," said Shift. "It may be something useful. Just hop into the Pool like a good fellow and fish it out. Then we can have a proper look at it."

"Hop into the Pool?" said Puzzle, twitching his long ears.

"Well, how are we to get it if you don't?" said the Ape.

"But – but," said Puzzle, "wouldn't it be better if *you* went in? Because, you see, it's you who wants to know what it is, and I don't much. And you've got hands, you see. You're as good as a Man or a Dwarf when it comes to catching hold of things. I've only got hoofs."

"Really, Puzzle," said Shift, "I didn't think you'd ever say a thing like that. I didn't think it of you, really."

"Why, what have I said wrong?" said the Ass, speaking in rather a humble voice, for he saw that Shift was very deeply offended. "All I meant was—"

"Wanting *me* to go into the water," said the Ape. "As if you didn't know perfectly well what weak chests Apes always have and how easily they catch cold! Very well. I *will* go in. I'm feeling cold enough already in this cruel wind. But I'll go in. I shall probably die. Then you'll be sorry." And Shift's voice sounded as if he was just going to burst into tears.

"Please don't, please don't, please don't," said Puzzle, half braying and half talking. "I never meant anything of the sort, Shift, really I didn't. You know how stupid I am and how I can't think of more than one thing at a time. I'd forgotten about your weak chest. Of course I'll go in. You mustn't think of doing it yourself. Promise me you won't, Shift."

So Shift promised, and Puzzle went cloppety-clop on his four hoofs round the rocky edge of the Pool to find a place where he could get in.

Quite apart from the cold it was no joke getting into that quivering and foaming water, and Puzzle had to stand and shiver for a whole minute before he made up his mind to do it. But then Shift called out from behind him and said: "Perhaps I'd better do it after all, Puzzle." And when Puzzle heard that he said, "No, no. You promised. I'm in now," and in he went.

A great mass of foam got him in the face and filled his mouth with water and blinded him. Then he went under altogether for a few seconds, and when he came up again he was in quite another part of the Pool. Then the swirl caught him and carried him round and round and faster and faster till it took him right under the waterfall itself, and the force of the water plunged him down, deep down, so that he thought he would never be able to hold his breath till he came up again. And when he had come up and when at last he got somewhere near the thing he was trying to catch, it sailed away from him till it too got under the fall and was forced down to the bottom. When it came up again it was further from him than ever.

But at last, when he was almost tired to death, and bruised all over and numb with cold, he succeeded in gripping the thing with his teeth. And out he came carrying it in front of him and getting his front hoofs tangled up in it, for it was as big as a large hearthrug, and it was very heavy and cold and slimy.

He flung it down in front of Shift and stood dripping and shivering and trying to get his breath back. But the Ape never looked at him or asked him how he felt. The Ape was too busy going round and round the thing and spreading it out and patting it and smelling it. Then a wicked gleam came into his eye and he said: "It is a lion's skin."

"Ee – auh – auh – oh, is it?" gasped Puzzle.

"Now I wonder… I wonder… I wonder," said Shift to himself, for he was thinking very hard.

"I wonder who killed the poor lion," said Puzzle presently. "It ought to be buried. We must have a funeral."

"Oh, it wasn't a Talking Lion," said Shift. "You needn't bother about *that*. There are no Talking Beasts up beyond the Falls, up in the Western Wild. This skin must have belonged to a dumb, wild lion."

This, by the way, was true. A Hunter, a Man, had killed and skinned this lion somewhere up in the Western Wild several months before. But that doesn't come into this story.

"All the same, Shift," said Puzzle, "even if the skin only belonged to a dumb, wild lion, oughtn't we to give it a decent burial? I mean, aren't all lions rather – well, rather solemn? Because of you-know-who. Don't you see?"

"Don't you start getting ideas into your head, Puzzle," said Shift. "Because, you know, thinking isn't your strong point. We'll make this skin into a fine warm winter coat for you."

"Oh, I don't think I'd like that," said the Donkey. "It would look — I mean, the other Beasts might think — that is to say, I shouldn't feel—"

"What are you talking about?" said Shift, scratching himself the wrong way up as Apes do.

"I don't think it would be respectful to the Great Lion, to Aslan himself, if an ass like me went about dressed up in a lion-skin," said Puzzle.

"Now don't stand arguing, please," said Shift. "What does an ass like you know about things of that sort? You know you're no good at thinking, Puzzle, so why don't you let me do your thinking for you? Why don't you treat me as I treat you? *I* don't think I can do everything. I know you're better at some things than I am. That's why I let you go into the Pool; I knew you'd do it better than me. But why can't I have my turn when it comes to something I *can* do and you can't? Am I never to be allowed to do anything? Do be fair. Turn and turn about."

"Oh, well, of course, if you put it that way," said Puzzle.

"I tell you what," said Shift. "You'd better take a good brisk trot down river as far as Chippingford and see if they have any oranges or bananas."

"But I'm so tired, Shift," pleaded Puzzle.

"Yes, but you are very cold and wet," said the Ape. "You want something to warm you up. A brisk trot would be just the thing. Besides, it's market day at Chippingford today." And then of course Puzzle said he would go.

As soon as he was alone Shift went shambling along, sometimes on two paws and sometimes on four, till he reached his own tree. Then he swung himself up from branch to branch, chattering and grinning all the time, and went into his little house. He found needle and thread and a big pair of scissors there; for he was a clever Ape and the Dwarfs had taught him how to sew. He put the ball of thread (it was very thick stuff, more like cord than thread) into his mouth so that his cheek bulged out as if he were sucking a big bit of toffee. He held the needle between his lips and took the scissors in his left paw. Then he came down the tree and shambled across to the lion-skin. He squatted down and got to work.

He saw at once that the body of the lion-skin would be too long for Puzzle and its neck too short. So he cut a good piece out of the body and used it to make a long collar for Puzzle's long neck. Then he cut off the head and sewed the collar in between the head and the shoulders. He put threads on both sides of the skin so that it would tie up under Puzzle's chest and stomach. Every now and then a bird would pass overhead and Shift would stop his work, looking anxiously up. He did not want anyone to see what he was doing. But none of the birds he saw were Talking Birds, so it didn't matter.

Late in the afternoon Puzzle came back. He was not trotting but only plodding patiently along, the way donkeys do.

"There weren't any oranges," he said, "and there weren't any bananas. And I'm very tired." He lay down.

"Come and try on your beautiful new lion-skin coat," said Shift.

"Oh, bother that old skin," said Puzzle. "I'll try it on in the morning. I'm too tired tonight."

"You *are* unkind, Puzzle," said Shift. "If *you're* tired, what do you think *I* am? All day long, while you've been having a lovely refreshing walk down the valley, I've been working hard to make you a coat. My hands are so tired I can hardly hold these scissors. And now you won't say thank you – and you won't even look at the coat – and you don't care – and – and—"

"My dear Shift," said Puzzle, getting up at once, "I am so sorry. I've been horrid. Of course I'd love to try it on. And it looks simply splendid. Do try it on me at once. Please do."

"Well, stand still then," said the Ape. The skin was very heavy for him to lift, but in the end, with a lot of pulling and pushing and puffing and blowing, he got it on to the donkey. He tied it underneath Puzzle's body and he tied the legs to Puzzle's legs and the tail to Puzzle's tail. A good deal of Puzzle's grey nose and face could be seen through the open mouth of the lion's head. No one who had ever seen a real lion would have been taken in for a moment. But if someone who had never seen a lion looked at Puzzle in his lion-skin he just might mistake him for a lion, if he didn't come too close, and if the light was not too good, and if Puzzle didn't let out a bray and didn't make any noise with his hoofs.

"You look wonderful, wonderful," said the Ape. "If anyone saw you now, they'd think you were Aslan, the Great Lion, himself."

"That would be dreadful," said Puzzle.

"No, it wouldn't," said Shift. "Everyone would do whatever you told them."

"But I don't want to tell them anything."

"But think of the good we could do!" said Shift. "You'd have me to advise you, you know. I'd think of sensible orders for you to give. And everyone would have to obey us, even the King himself. We would set everything right in Narnia."

"But isn't everything right already?" said Puzzle.

"What!" cried Shift. "Everything right – when there are no oranges or bananas?"

"Well, you know," said Puzzle, "there aren't many people – in fact, I don't think there's anyone but yourself – who wants those sort of things."

"There's sugar too," said Shift.

"H'm, yes," said the Ass. "It would be nice if there was more sugar."

"Well then, that's settled," said the Ape. "You will pretend to be Aslan, and I'll tell you what to say."

"No, no, no," said Puzzle. "Don't say such dreadful things. It would be wrong, Shift. I may be not very clever but I know that much. What would become of us if the real Aslan turned up?"

"I expect he'd be very pleased," said Shift. "Probably he sent us the lion-skin on purpose, so that we could set things right. Anyway, he never *does* turn up, you know. Not nowadays."

At that moment there came a great thunderclap right overhead and the ground trembled with a small earthquake. Both the animals lost their balance and were flung on their faces.

"There!" gasped Puzzle, as soon as he had breath to speak. "It's a sign, a warning. I knew we were doing something dreadfully wicked. Take this wretched skin off me at once."

"No, no," said the Ape (whose mind worked very quickly). "It's a sign the other way. I was just going to say that if the real Aslan, as you call him, meant us to go on with this, he would send us a thunderclap and an earth-tremor. It was just on the tip of my tongue, only the sign itself came before I could get the words out. You've *got* to do it now, Puzzle. And please don't let us have any more arguing. You know you don't understand these things. What could a donkey know about signs?"

Chapter Two

The Rashness of the King

About three weeks later the last of the Kings of Narnia sat under the great oak which grew beside the door of his little hunting lodge, where he often stayed for ten days or so in the pleasant spring weather. It was a low, thatched building not far from the Eastern end of Lantern Waste and some way above the meeting of the two rivers. He loved to live there simply and at ease, away from the state and pomp of Cair Paravel, the royal city. His name was King Tirian, and he was between twenty and twenty-five years old, his shoulders were already broad and strong and his limbs full of hard muscle, but his beard was still scanty. He had blue eyes and a fearless, honest face.

There was no one with him that spring morning except his dearest friend, Jewel the Unicorn. They loved each other like brothers and each had saved the other's life in the wars. The lordly beast stood close beside the King's chair with its neck bent round, polishing its blue horn against the creamy whiteness of its flank.

"I cannot set myself to any work or sport today, Jewel," said the King. "I can think of nothing but this wonderful news. Think you we shall hear any more of it today?"

"They are the most wonderful tidings ever heard in our days or our fathers' or our grandfathers' days, Sire," said Jewel, "if they are true."

"How can they choose but be true?" said the King. "It is more than a week ago that the first birds came flying over us saying, Aslan is here, Aslan has come to Narnia again. And after that it was the squirrels. They had not seen him, but they said it was certain he was in the woods. Then came the Stag. He said he had seen him with his own eyes, a great way off, by moonlight, in Lantern Waste. Then came that dark Man with the beard, the merchant from Calormen. The Calormenes care nothing for Aslan as we do; but the man spoke of it as a thing beyond doubt. And there was the Badger last night; he too had seen Aslan."

"Indeed, Sire," answered Jewel, "I believe it all. If I seem not to, it is only that my joy is too great to let my belief settle itself. It is almost too beautiful to believe."

"Yes," said the King with a great sigh, almost a shiver, of delight. "It is beyond all that I ever hoped for in all my life."

"Listen!" said Jewel, putting his head on one side and cocking his ears forward.

"What is it?" asked the King.

"Hoofs, sire," said Jewel. "A galloping horse. A very heavy horse. It must be one of the Centaurs. And look, there he is."

A great, golden-bearded Centaur, with man's sweat on his forehead and horse's sweat on his chestnut flanks, dashed up to the King, stopped, and bowed low. "Hail, King," it cried in a voice as deep as a bull's.

"Ho, there!" said the King, looking over his shoulder towards the door of the hunting lodge. "A bowl of wine for the noble Centaur. Welcome, Roonwit. When you have found your breath you shall tell us your errand."

A page came out of the house carrying a great wooden bowl, curiously carved, and handed it to the Centaur. The Centaur raised the bowl and said,

"I drink first to Aslan and truth, Sire, and secondly to your Majesty."

He finished the wine (enough for six strong men) at one draught and handed the empty bowl back to the page.

"Now, Roonwit," said the King. "Do you bring us more news of Aslan?"

Roonwit looked very grave, frowning a little.

"Sire," he said. "You know how long I have lived and studied the stars; for we Centaurs live longer than you Men, and even longer than your kind, Unicorn. Never in all my days have I seen such terrible things written in the skies as there have been nightly since this year began. The stars say nothing of the coming of Aslan, nor of peace, nor of joy. I know by my art that there have not been such disastrous conjunctions of the planets for five hundred years.

"It was already in my mind to come and warn your Majesty that some great evil hangs over Narnia. But last night the rumour reached me that Aslan is abroad in Narnia. Sire, do not believe this tale. It cannot be. The stars never lie, but Men and Beasts do. If Aslan were really coming to Narnia the sky would have foretold it. If he were really come, all the most gracious stars would be assembled in his honour. It is all a lie."

"A lie!" said the King fiercely. "What creature in Narnia or all the world would dare to lie on such a matter?" And, without knowing it, he laid his hand on his sword hilt.

"That I know not, Lord King," said the Centaur. "But I know there are liars on earth; there are none among the stars."

"I wonder," said Jewel, "whether Aslan might not come though all the stars foretold otherwise. He is not the slave of the stars but their Maker. Is it not said in all the old stories that He is not a Tame Lion?"

"Well said, well said, Jewel," cried the King. "Those are the very words: *not a tame lion*. It comes in many tales."

Roonwit had just raised his hand and was leaning forward to say something very earnestly to the King when all three of them turned their heads to listen to a wailing sound that was quickly drawing nearer. The wood was so thick to the west of them that they could not see the newcomer yet. But they could soon hear the words.

"Woe, woe, woe!" called the voice. "Woe for my brothers and sisters! Woe for the holy trees! The woods are laid waste. The axe is loosed against us. We are being felled. Great trees are falling, falling, falling."

With the last "falling" the speaker came in sight. She was like a woman but so tall that her head was on a level with the Centaur's, yet she was like a tree too. It is hard to explain if you have never seen a Dryad but quite unmistakable once you have – something different in the colour, the voice, and the hair. King Tirian and the two Beasts knew at once that she was the nymph of a beech tree.

"Justice, Lord King!" she cried. "Come to our aid. Protect your people. They are felling us in Lantern Waste. Forty great trunks of my brothers and sisters are already on the ground."

"What, Lady! Felling Lantern Waste? Murdering the talking trees?" cried the King, leaping to his feet and drawing his sword. "How dare they? And who dares it? Now by the Mane of Aslan—"

"A-a-a-h," gasped the Dryad, shuddering as if in pain – shuddering time after time as if under repeated blows. Then all at once she fell sideways as suddenly as if both her feet had been cut from under her. For a second they saw her lying dead on the grass and then she vanished. They knew what had happened. Her tree, miles away, had been cut down.

For a moment the King's grief and anger were so great that he could not speak. Then he said: "Come, friends. We must go up river and find the villains who have done this, with all the speed we may. I will leave not one of them alive."

"Sire, with a good will," said Jewel.

But Roonwit said, "Sire, be wary even in your just wrath. There are strange doings on foot. If there should be rebels in arms further up the valley, we three are too few to meet them. If it would please you to wait while—"

"I will not wait the tenth part of a second," said the King. "But while Jewel and I go forward, do you gallop as hard as you may to Cair Paravel. Here is my ring for your token. Get me a score of men-at-arms, all well mounted, and a score of Talking Dogs, and ten Dwarfs (let them all be fell archers), and a Leopard or so, and Stonefoot the Giant. Bring all these after us as quickly as may be."

"With a good will, Sire," said Roonwit. And at once he turned and galloped Eastward down the valley.

The King strode on at a great pace, sometimes muttering to himself and sometimes clenching his fists. Jewel walked beside him, saying nothing; so there was no sound between them but the faint jingle of a rich gold chain that hung round the Unicorn's neck and the noise of two feet and four hoofs.

They soon reached the River and turned up it where there was a grassy road: they had the water on their left and the forest on their right. Soon after that they came to the place where the ground grew rougher and thick wood came down to the water's edge. The road, what there was of it, now ran on the southern bank and they had to ford the River to reach it. It was up to Tirian's armpits, but Jewel (who had four legs and was therefore steadier) kept on his right so as to break the force of the current, and Tirian put his strong arm round the Unicorn's strong neck and they both got safely over. The King was still so angry that he hardly noticed the cold of the water. But of course he dried his sword very carefully on the shoulder of his cloak, which was the only dry part of him, as soon as they came to shore.

They were now going westward with the River on their right and Lantern Waste straight ahead of them. They had not gone more than a mile when they both stopped and both spoke at the same moment. The King said "What have we here?" and Jewel said "Look!"

"It is a raft," said King Tirian.

And so it was. Half a dozen splendid tree-trunks, all newly cut and newly lopped of their branches, had been lashed together to make a raft, and were gliding swiftly down the river. On the front of the raft there was a water rat with a pole to steer it.

"Hey! Water Rat! What are you about?" cried the King.

"Taking logs down to sell to the Calormenes, Sire," said the Rat, touching his ear as he might have touched his cap if he had had one.

"Calormenes!" thundered Tirian. "What do you mean? Who gave order for these trees to be felled?"

The River flows so swiftly at that time of the year that the raft had already glided past the King and Jewel. But the Water Rat looked back over its shoulder and shouted out:

"The Lion's orders, Sire. Aslan himself." He added something more but they couldn't hear it.

The King and the Unicorn stared at one another and both looked more frightened than they had ever been in any battle.

"Aslan," said the King at last, in a very low voice. "Aslan. Could it be true? *Could* he be felling the holy trees and murdering the Dryads?"

"Unless the Dryads have all done something dreadfully wrong—" murmured Jewel.

"But selling them to Calormenes!" said the King. "Is it possible?"

"I don't know," said Jewel miserably. "He's not a *tame* Lion."

"Well," said the King at last, "we must go on and take the adventure that comes to us."

"It is the only thing left for us to do, Sire," said the Unicorn. He did not see at the moment how foolish it was for two of them to go on alone; nor did the King. They were too angry to think clearly. But much evil came of their rashness in the end.

Suddenly the King leaned hard on his friend's neck and bowed his head.

"Jewel," he said, "what lies before us? Horrible thoughts arise in my heart. If we had died before today we should have been happy."

"Yes," said Jewel. "We have lived too long. The worst thing in the world has come upon us." They stood like that for a minute or two and then went on.

Before long they could hear the hack-hack-hack of axes falling on timber, though they could see nothing yet because there was a rise of the ground in front of them. When they had reached the top of it they could see right into Lantern Waste itself. And the King's face turned white when he saw it.

Right through the middle of that ancient forest – that forest where the trees of gold and of silver had once grown and where a child from our world had once planted the Tree of Protection – a broad lane had already been opened. It was a hideous lane like a raw gash in the land, full of muddy ruts where felled trees had been dragged down to the river. There was a great crowd of people at work, and a cracking of whips, and horses tugging and straining as they dragged at the logs. The first thing that struck the King and the Unicorn was that about half the people in the crowd were not Talking Beasts but Men. The next thing was that these men were not the fair-haired men of Narnia: they were dark, bearded men from Calormen, that great and cruel country that lies beyond Archenland across the desert to the south.

There was no reason, of course, why one should not meet a Calormene or two in Narnia – a merchant or an ambassador – for there was peace between Narnia and Calormen in those days. But Tirian could not understand why there were so many of them: nor why they were cutting down a Narnian forest. He grasped his sword tighter and rolled his cloak round his left arm. They came quickly down among the men.

Two Calormenes were driving a horse which was harnessed to a log. Just as the King reached them the log had got stuck in a bad muddy place.

"Get on, son of sloth! Pull, you lazy pig!" cried the Calormenes, cracking their whips. The horse was already straining himself as hard as he could; his eyes were red and he was covered with foam.

"Work, lazy brute," shouted one of the Calormenes: and as he spoke he struck the horse savagely with his whip. It was then that the really dreadful thing happened.

Up till now Tirian had taken it for granted that the horses which the Calormenes were driving were their own horses; dumb, witless animals like the horses of our own world. And though he hated to see even a dumb horse overdriven, he was of course thinking more about the murder of the Trees. It had never crossed his mind that anyone would dare to harness one of the free Talking Horses of Narnia, much less to use a whip on it. But as that savage blow fell the horse reared up and said, half screaming:

"Fool and tyrant! Do you not see I am doing all I can?"

When Tirian knew that the Horse was one of his own Narnians, there came over him and over Jewel such a rage that they did not know what they were doing. The King's sword went up, the Unicorn's horn went down. They rushed forward together. Next moment both the Calormenes lay dead, the one beheaded by Tirian's sword and the other gored through the heart by Jewel's horn.

CHAPTER THREE

THE APE IN ITS GLORY

"Master Horse, Master Horse," said Tirian as he hastily cut its traces, "how came these aliens to enslave you? Is Narnia conquered? Has there been a battle?"

"No, Sire," panted the horse, "Aslan is here. It is all by his orders. He has commanded—"

"'Ware danger, King," said Jewel. Tirian looked up and saw that Calormenes (mixed with a few Talking Beasts) were beginning to run towards them from every direction. The two dead men had died without a cry and so it had taken a moment before the rest of the crowd knew what had happened. But now they did. Most of them had naked scimitars in their hands.

"Quick! On my back!" said Jewel.

The King flung himself astride of his old friend who turned and galloped away. He changed direction twice or thrice as soon as they were out of sight of their enemies, crossed a stream, and shouted without slackening his pace, "Whither away, Sire? To Cair Paravel?"

"Hold hard, friend," said Tirian. "Let me off." He slid off the Unicorn's back and faced him.

"Jewel," said the King. "We have done a dreadful deed."

"We were sorely provoked," said Jewel.

"But to leap on them unawares — without defying them — while they were unarmed — faugh! We are two murderers, Jewel. I am dishonoured for ever."

Jewel drooped his head. He too was ashamed.

"And then," said the King, "the Horse said it was by Aslan's orders. The Rat said the same. They all say Aslan is here. How if it were true?"

"But, Sire, how *could* Aslan be commanding such dreadful things?"

"He is not a *tame* Lion," said Tirian. "How should we know what he would do? We, who are murderers. Jewel, I will go back. I will give up my sword and put myself in the hands of these Calormenes and ask that they bring me before Aslan. Let him do justice on me."

"You will go to your death, then," said Jewel.

"Do you think I care if Aslan dooms me to death?" said the King. "That would be nothing, nothing at all. Would it not be better to be dead than to have this horrible fear that Aslan has come and is not like the Aslan we have believed in and longed for? It is as if the sun rose one day and were a black sun."

"I know," said Jewel. "Or as if you drank water and it were *dry* water. You are in the right, Sire. This is the end of all things. Let us go and give ourselves up."

"There is no need for both of us to go."

"If ever we loved one another, let me go with you now," said the Unicorn. "If you are dead and if Aslan is not Aslan, what life is left for me?"

They turned and walked back together, shedding bitter tears.

As soon as they came to the place where the work was going on the Calormenes raised a cry and came towards them with their weapons in hand. But the King held out his sword with the hilt towards them and said:

"I who was King of Narnia and am now a dishonoured knight give myself up to the justice of Aslan. Bring me before him."

"And I give myself up too," said Jewel.

Then the dark men came round them in a thick crowd, smelling of garlic and onions, their white eyes flashing dreadfully in their brown faces. They put a rope halter round Jewel's neck. They took the King's sword away and tied his hands behind his back. One of the Calormenes, who had a helmet instead of a turban and seemed to be in command, snatched the gold circlet off Tirian's head and hastily put it away somewhere among his clothes. They led the two prisoners uphill to a place where there was a big clearing. And this was what the prisoners saw.

At the centre of the clearing, which was also the highest point of the hill, there was a little hut like a stable, with a thatched roof. Its door was shut. On the grass in front of the door there sat an Ape. Tirian and Jewel, who had been expecting to see Aslan and had heard nothing about an Ape yet, were very bewildered when they saw it. The Ape was of course Shift himself, but he looked ten times uglier than when he lived by Caldron Pool, for he was now dressed up. He was wearing a scarlet jacket which did not fit him very well, having been made for a dwarf. He had jewelled slippers on his hind paws which would not stay on properly because, as you know, the hind paws of an Ape are really like hands. He wore what seemed to be a paper crown on his head. There was a great pile of nuts beside him and he kept cracking nuts with his jaws and spitting out the shells. And he also kept on pulling up the scarlet jacket to scratch himself. A great number of Talking Beasts stood facing him, and nearly every face in that crowd looked miserably worried and bewildered. When they saw who the prisoners were they all groaned and whimpered.

"O Lord Shift, mouthpiece of Aslan," said the chief Calormene. "We bring you prisoners. By our skill and courage and by the permission of the great god Tash we have taken alive these two desperate murderers."

"Give me that man's sword," said the Ape. So they took the King's sword and handed it, with the sword-belt and all, to the monkey. And he hung it round his own neck: and it made him look sillier than ever.

"We'll see about those two later," said the Ape, spitting out a shell in the direction of the two prisoners. "I got some other business first. They can wait. Now listen to me, everyone. The first thing I want to say is about nuts. Where's that Head Squirrel got to?"

"Here, sir," said a red squirrel, coming forward and making a nervous little bow.

"Oh you are, are you?" said the Ape with a nasty look. "Now attend to me. I want – I mean, Aslan wants – some more nuts. These you've brought aren't anything like enough. You must bring some more, do you hear? Twice as many. And they've got to be here by sunset tomorrow, and there mustn't be any bad ones or any small ones among them."

A murmur of dismay ran through the other squirrels, and the Head Squirrel plucked up courage to say: "Please, would Aslan himself speak to us about it? If we might be allowed to see him—"

"Well, you won't," said the Ape. "He may be very kind (though it's a lot more than most of you deserve) and come out for a few minutes tonight. Then you can all have a look at him. But he will *not* have you all crowding round him and pestering him with questions. Anything you want to say to him will be passed on through me: if I think it's worth bothering him about. In the meantime all you squirrels had better go and see about the nuts. And make sure they are here by tomorrow evening or, my word, you'll catch it!"

The poor squirrels all scampered away as if a dog were after them. This new order was terrible news for them. The nuts they had carefully hoarded for the winter had nearly all been eaten by now; and of the few that were left they had already given the Ape far more than they could spare.

Then a deep voice – it belonged to a great tusked and shaggy Boar – spoke from another part of the crowd.

"But *why* can't we see Aslan properly and talk to him?" it said. "When he used to appear in Narnia in the old days everyone could talk to him face to face."

"Don't you believe it," said the Ape. "And even if it was true, times have changed. Aslan says he's been far too soft with you before, do you see? Well, he isn't going to be soft any more. He's going to lick you into shape this time. He'll teach you to think he's a tame lion!"

A low moaning and whimpering was heard among the Beasts; and after that, a dead silence which was more miserable still.

"And now there's another thing you got to learn," said the Ape. "I hear some of you are saying I'm an Ape. Well, I'm not. I'm a Man. If I look like an Ape, that's because I'm so very old: hundreds and hundreds of years old. And it's because I'm so old that I'm so wise. And it's because I'm so wise that I'm the only one Aslan is ever going to speak to. He can't be bothered talking to a lot of stupid animals. He'll tell me what you've got to do, and I'll tell the rest of you. And take my advice, and see you do it in double quick time, for he doesn't mean to stand any nonsense."

There was a dead silence except for the noise of a very young badger crying and its mother trying to make it keep quiet.

"And now here's another thing," the Ape went on, fitting a fresh nut into its cheek, "I hear some of the horses are saying, 'Let's hurry up and get this job of carting timber over as quickly as we can, and then we'll be free again.' Well, you can get that idea out of your heads at once. And not only the Horses either. Everybody who can work is going to be made to work in future. Aslan has it all settled with the King of Calormen – the Tisroc, as our dark-faced friends the Calormenes call him. All you horses and bulls and donkeys are to be sent down into Calormen to work for your living – pulling and carrying the way horses and such-like do in other countries. And all you digging animals like moles and rabbits and Dwarfs are going down to work in the Tisroc's mines. And—"

"No, no, no," howled the Beasts. "It can't be true. Aslan would never sell us into slavery to the King of Calormen."

"None of that! Hold your noise!" said the Ape with a snarl. "Who said anything about slavery? You won't be slaves. You'll be paid – very good wages too. That is to say, your pay will be paid into Aslan's treasury and he will use it all for everybody's good." Then he glanced, and almost winked, at the chief Calormene.

The Calormene bowed and replied, in the pompous Calormene way:

"Most sapient Mouthpiece of Aslan, the Tisroc (may he live for ever) is wholly of one mind with your lordship in this judicious plan."

"There! You see!" said the Ape. "It's all arranged. And all for your own good. We'll be able, with the money you earn, to make Narnia a country worth living in. There'll be oranges and bananas pouring in – and roads and big cities and schools and offices and whips and muzzles and saddles and cages and kennels and prisons – oh, everything."

"But we don't want all those things," said an old Bear. "We want to be free. And we want to hear Aslan speak himself."

"Now don't you start arguing," said the Ape, "for it's a thing I won't stand. I'm a Man: you're only a fat, stupid old Bear. What do you know about freedom? You think freedom means doing what you like. Well, you're wrong. That isn't true freedom. True freedom means doing what I tell you."

"H-n-n-h," grunted the Bear and scratched its head; it found this sort of thing hard to understand.

"Please, please," said the high voice of a woolly lamb, who was so young that everyone was surprised he dared to speak at all.

"What is it now?" said the Ape. "Be quick."

"Please," said the Lamb, "I can't understand. What have we to do with the Calormenes? We belong to Aslan. They belong to Tash. They have a god called Tash. They say he has four arms and the head of a vulture. They kill Men on his altar. I don't believe there's any such person as Tash. But if there was, how could Aslan be friends with him?"

All the animals cocked their heads sideways and all their bright eyes flashed towards the Ape. They knew it was the best question anyone had asked yet.

The Ape jumped up and spat at the Lamb.

"Baby!" he hissed. "Silly little bleater! Go home to your mother and drink milk. What do you understand of such things? But you others, listen. Tash is only another name for Aslan. All that old idea of us being right and the Calormenes wrong is silly. We know better now. The Calormenes use different words but we all mean the same thing. Tash and Aslan are only two different names for you know Who. That's why there can never be any quarrel between them. Get that into your heads, you stupid brutes. Tash is Aslan: Aslan is Tash."

You know how sad your own dog's face can look sometimes. Think of that and then think of all the faces of those Talking Beasts – all those honest, humble, bewildered birds, bears, badgers, rabbits, moles, and mice – all far sadder than that. Every tail was down, every whisker drooped. It would have broken your heart with very pity to see their faces. There was only one who did not look at all unhappy.

It was a ginger cat – a great big Tom in the prime of life – who sat bolt upright with his tail curled round his toes, in the very front row of all the Beasts. He had been staring hard at the Ape and the Calormene captain all the time and had never once blinked his eyes.

"Excuse me," said the Cat very politely, "but this interests me. Does your friend from Calormen say the same?"

"Assuredly," said the Calormene. "The enlight-ened Ape – Man, I mean – is in the right. *Aslan* means neither less nor more than *Tash*."

"Especially, Aslan means *no more* than Tash?" suggested the Cat.

"No more at all," said the Calormene, looking the Cat straight in the face.

"Is that good enough for you, Ginger?" said the Ape.

"Oh certainly," said Ginger coolly. "Thank you very much. I only wanted to be quite clear. I think I am beginning to understand."

Up till now the King and Jewel had said nothing: they were waiting until the Ape should bid them speak, for they thought it was no use interrupting. But now, as Tirian looked round on the miserable faces of the Narnians, and saw how they would all believe that Aslan and Tash were one and the same, he could bear it no longer.

"Ape," he cried with a great voice, "you lie. You lie damnably. You lie like a Calormene. You lie like an Ape."

He meant to go on and ask how the terrible god Tash who fed on the blood of his people could possibly be the same as the good Lion by whose blood all Narnia was saved. If he had been allowed to speak, the rule of the Ape might have ended that day; the Beasts might have seen the truth and thrown the Ape down. But before he could say another word two Calormenes struck him in the mouth with all their force, and a third, from behind, kicked his feet from under him. And as he fell, the Ape squealed in rage and terror:

"Take him away. Take him away. Take him where he cannot hear us, nor we hear him. There tie him to a tree. I will – I mean, Aslan will – do justice on him later."

CHAPTER FOUR

WHAT HAPPENED THAT NIGHT

The King was so dizzy from being knocked down that he hardly knew what was happening until the Calormenes untied his wrists and put his arms straight down by his sides and set him with his back against an ash tree. Then they bound ropes round his ankles and his knees and his waist and his chest and left him there. What worried him worst at the moment – for it is often little things that are hardest to stand – was that his lip was bleeding where they had hit him and he couldn't wipe the little trickle of blood away although it tickled him.

From where he was he could still see the little stable on the top of the hill and the Ape sitting in front of it. He could just hear the Ape's voice still going on and, every now and then, some answer from the crowd, but he could not make out the words.

"I wonder what they've done to Jewel," thought the King.

Presently the crowd of Beasts broke up and began going away in different directions. Some passed close to Tirian. They looked at him as if they were both frightened and sorry to see him tied up but none of them spoke. Soon they had all gone and there was silence in the wood. Then hours and hours went past and Tirian became first very thirsty and then very hungry; and as the afternoon dragged on and turned into evening, he became cold too. His back was very sore. The sun went down and it began to be twilight.

When it was almost dark Tirian heard a light pitter-patter of feet and saw some small creatures coming towards him. The three on the left were Mice, and there was a Rabbit in the middle: on the right were two Moles. Both these were carrying little bags on their backs which gave them a curious look in the dark so that at first he wondered what kind of beasts they were. Then, in a moment, they were all standing up on their hind legs, laying their cool paws on his knees and giving his knees snuffly animal kisses. (They could reach his knees because Narnian Talking Beasts of that sort are bigger than the dumb beasts of the same kind in England.)

"Lord King! Dear Lord King," said their shrill voices, "we are so sorry for you. We daren't untie you because Aslan might be angry with us. But we've brought you your supper."

At once the first Mouse climbed nimbly up till he was perched on the rope that bound Tirian's chest and was wrinkling his blunt nose just in front of Tirian's face. Then the second Mouse climbed up and hung on just below the first Mouse. The other beasts stood on the ground and began handing things up.

"Drink, Sire, and then you'll find you are able to eat," said the topmost Mouse, and Tirian found that a little wooden cup was being held to his lips. It was only the size of an egg cup so that he had hardly tasted the wine in it before it was empty. But then the Mouse passed it down and the others refilled it and it was passed up again and Tirian emptied it a second time. In this way they went on till he had quite a good drink, which was all the better for coming in little doses, for that is more thirst-quenching than one long draught.

"Here is cheese, Sire," said the first Mouse, "but not very much, for fear it would make you too thirsty." And after the cheese they fed him with oatcakes and fresh butter, and then with some more wine.

"Now hand up the water," said the first Mouse, "and I'll wash the King's face. There is blood on it."

Then Tirian felt something like a tiny sponge dabbing his face, and it was most refreshing.

"Little friends," said Tirian, "how can I thank you for all this?"

"You needn't, you needn't," said the little voices. "What else could we do? We don't want any other King. We're your people. If it was only the Ape and the Calormenes who were against you we would have fought till we were cut into pieces before we'd have let them tie you up. We would, we would indeed. But we can't go against Aslan."

"Do you think it really is Aslan?" asked the King.

"Oh yes, yes," said the Rabbit. "He came out of the stable last night. We all saw him."

"What was he like?" said the King.

"Like a terrible, great Lion, to be sure," said one of the Mice.

"And you think it is really Aslan who is killing the Wood-Nymphs and making you all slaves to the King of Calormen?"

"Ah, that's bad, isn't it?" said the second Mouse. "It would have been better if we'd died before all this began. But there's no doubt about it. Everyone says it is Aslan's orders. And we've seen him. We didn't think Aslan would be like that. Why, we — we *wanted* him to come back to Narnia."

"He seems to have come back very angry this time," said the first Mouse. "We must all have done something dreadfully wrong without knowing it. He must be punishing us for something. But I do think we might be told what it was!"

"I suppose what we're doing now may be wrong," said the Rabbit.

"I don't care if it is," said one of the Moles. "I'd do it again."

But the others said, "Oh hush," and "Do be careful," and then they all said, "We're sorry, dear King, but we must go back now. It would never do for us to be caught here."

"Leave me at once, dear Beasts," said Tirian. "I would not for all Narnia bring any of you into danger."

"Goodnight, goodnight," said the Beasts, rubbing their noses against his knees. "We will come back — if we can." Then they all pattered away and the wood seemed darker and colder and lonelier than it had been before they came.

The stars came out and time went slowly on — imagine how slowly — while that last King of Narnia stood stiff and sore and upright against the tree in his bonds. But at last something happened.

Far away there appeared a red light. Then it disappeared for a moment and came back again, bigger and stronger. Then he could see dark shapes going to and fro on this side of the light and carrying bundles and throwing them down. He knew now what he was looking at. It was a bonfire, newly lit, and people were throwing bundles of brushwood on to it. Presently it blazed up and Tirian could see that it was on the very top of the hill. He could see quite clearly the stable behind it, all lit up in the red glow, and a great crowd of Beasts and Men between the fire and himself. A small figure, hunched up beside the fire, must have been the Ape. It was saying something to the crowd, but he could not hear what. Then it went and bowed three times to the ground in front of the door of the stable. Then it got up and opened the door. And something on four legs — something that walked rather stiffly — came out of the stable and stood facing the crowd.

A great wailing or howling went up, so loud that Tirian could hear some of the words.

"Aslan! Aslan! Aslan!" cried the Beasts. "Speak to us. Comfort us. Be angry with us no more."

From where Tirian was he could not make out very clearly what the thing was; but he could see that it was yellow and hairy. He had never seen the Great Lion. He had never seen a common lion. He couldn't be sure that what he saw was not the real Aslan. He had not expected Aslan to look like that stiff thing which stood and said nothing. But how could one be sure? For a moment horrible thoughts went through his mind: then he remembered the nonsense about Tash and Aslan being the same and knew that the whole thing must be a cheat.

The Ape put his head close up to the yellow thing's head as if he were listening to something it was whispering to him. Then he turned and spoke to the crowd, and the crowd wailed again. Then the yellow thing turned clumsily round and walked – you might almost say, waddled – back into the stable and the Ape shut the door behind it. After that the fire must have been put out for the light vanished quite suddenly, and Tirian was once more alone with the cold and the darkness.

He thought of other Kings who had lived and died in Narnia in old times and it seemed to him that none of them had ever been so unlucky as himself. He thought of his great-grandfather's great-grandfather King Rilian who had been stolen away by a Witch when he was only a young prince and kept hidden for years in the dark caves beneath the land of the Northern Giants. But then it had all come right in the end; for two mysterious children had suddenly appeared from the land beyond the world's end and had rescued him so that he came home to Narnia and had a long and prosperous reign. "It's not like that with me," said Tirian to himself.

Then he went further back and thought about Rilian's father, Caspian the Seafarer, whose wicked uncle King Miraz had tried to murder him and how Caspian had fled away into the woods and lived among the Dwarfs. But that story too had all come right in the end, for Caspian also had been helped by children – only there were four of them that time – who came from somewhere beyond the world and fought a great battle and set him on his father's throne. "But it was all long ago," said Tirian to himself. "That sort of thing doesn't happen now."

And then he remembered (for he had always been good at history when he was a boy) how those same four children who had helped Caspian had been in Narnia over a thousand years before; and it was then that they had done the most remarkable things of all. For then they had defeated the terrible White Witch and ended the Hundred Years of Winter, and after that they had reigned (all four of them together) at Cair Paravel, till they were no longer children but great Kings and lovely Queens, and their reign had been the Golden Age of Narnia. And Aslan had come into that story a lot. He had come into all the other stories too, as Tirian now remembered. "Aslan – and children from another world," thought Tirian. "They have always come in when things were at their worst. Oh, if only they could now."

And he called out "Aslan! Aslan! Aslan! Come and help us now."

But the darkness and the cold and the quietness went on just the same.

"Let *me* be killed," cried the King. "I ask nothing for myself. But come and save all Narnia."

And still there was no change in the night or the wood, but there began to be a kind of change inside Tirian. Without knowing why, he began to feel a faint hope. And he felt somehow stronger. "Oh, Aslan, Aslan," he whispered. "If you will not come yourself, at least send me the helpers from beyond the world. Or let me call them. Let my voice carry beyond the world." Then, hardly knowing that he was doing it, he suddenly cried out in a great voice:

"Children! Children! Friends of Narnia! Quick. Come to me. Across the worlds I call you; I, Tirian, King of Narnia, Lord of Cair Paravel, and Emperor of the Lone Islands!"

And immediately he was plunged into a dream (if it was a dream) more vivid than any he had had in his life.

He seemed to be standing in a lighted room where seven people sat round a table. It looked as if they had just finished their meal. Two of those people were very old, an old man with a white beard and an old woman with wise, merry, twinkling eyes. He who sat at the right hand of the old man was hardly full grown, certainly younger than Tirian himself, but his face had already the look of a king and a warrior. And you could almost say the same of the other youth who sat at the right hand of the old woman. Facing Tirian across the table sat a fair-haired girl younger than either of these, and on either side of her a boy and girl who were younger still. They were all dressed in what seemed to Tirian the oddest kind of clothes.

But he had no time to think about details like that, for instantly the youngest boy and both the girls started to their feet, and one of them gave a little scream. The old woman started and drew in her breath sharply. The old man must have made some sudden movement too for the wine glass which stood at his right hand was swept off the table: Tirian could hear the tinkling noise as it broke on the floor.

Then Tirian realized that these people could see him; they were staring at him as if they saw a ghost. But he noticed that the king-like one who sat at the old man's right never moved (though he turned pale) except that he clenched his hand very tight. Then he said:

"Speak, if you're not a phantom or a dream. You have a Narnian look about you and we are the seven friends of Narnia."

Tirian was longing to speak, and he tried to cry out aloud that he was Tirian of Narnia, in great need of help. But he found (as I have sometimes found in dreams too) that his voice made no noise at all.

The one who had already spoken to him rose to his feet. "Shadow or spirit or whatever you are," he said, fixing his eyes full upon Tirian. "If you are from Narnia, I charge you in the name of Aslan, speak to me. I am Peter the High King."

The room began to swim before Tirian's eyes. He heard the voices of those seven people all speaking at once, and all getting fainter every second, and they were saying things like, "Look! It's fading." "It's melting away." "It's vanishing."

Next moment he was wide awake, still tied to the tree, colder and stiffer than ever. The wood was full of the pale, dreary light that comes before sunrise, and he was soaking wet with dew; it was nearly morning.

That waking was about the worst moment he had ever had in his life.

CHAPTER FIVE

HOW HELP CAME TO THE KING

But his misery did not last long. Almost at once there came a bump, and then a second bump, and two children were standing before him. The wood in front of him had been quite empty a second before and he knew they had not come from behind his tree, for he would have heard them. They had in fact simply appeared from nowhere.

He saw at a glance that they were wearing the same queer, dingy sort of clothes as the people in his dream; and he saw, at a second glance, that they were the youngest boy and girl out of that party of seven.

"Gosh!" said the Boy, "that took one's breath away! I thought—"

"Hurry up and get him untied," said the girl. "We can talk, afterwards." Then she added, turning to Tirian, "I'm sorry we've been so long. We came the moment we could."

While she was speaking the Boy had produced a knife from his pocket and was quickly cutting the King's bonds: too quickly, in fact, for the King was so stiff and numb that when the last cord was cut he fell forward on his hands and knees. He couldn't get up again till he had brought some life back into his legs by a good rubbing.

"I say," said the girl. "It was you, wasn't it, who appeared to us that night when we were all at supper? Nearly a week ago."

"A week, fair maid?" said Tirian. "My dream led me into your world scarce ten minutes since."

"It's the usual muddle about times, Pole," said the Boy.

"I remember now," said Tirian. "That too comes in all the old tales. The time of your strange land is different from ours. But if we speak of time, 'tis time to be gone from here; for my enemies are close at hand. Will you come with me?"

"Of course," said the girl. "It's you we've come to help."

Tirian got to his feet and led them rapidly down hill, southward and away from the stable. He knew well where he meant to go but his first aim was to get to rocky places where they would leave no trail, and his second to cross some water so that they would leave no scent.

This took them about an hour's scrambling and wading and while that was going on nobody had any breath to talk. But even so, Tirian kept on stealing glances at his companions. The wonder of walking beside the creatures from another world made him feel a little dizzy: but it also made all the old stories seem far more real than they had ever seemed before... anything might happen now.

"Now," said Tirian as they came to the head of a little valley which ran down before them among young birch trees, "we are out of danger of those villains for a space and may walk more easily." The sun had risen, dewdrops were twinkling on every branch, and birds were singing.

"What about some grub? – I mean for you, Sir, we two have had our breakfast," said the Boy.

Tirian wondered very much what he meant by "grub", but when the Boy opened a bulgy satchel which he was carrying and pulled out a rather greasy and squashy packet, he understood. He was ravenously hungry, though he hadn't thought about it till that moment.

There were two hard-boiled egg sandwiches, and two cheese sandwiches, and two with some kind of paste in them. If he hadn't been so hungry he wouldn't have thought much of the paste, for that is a sort of food nobody eats in Narnia. By the time he had eaten all six sandwiches they had come to the bottom of the valley and there they found a mossy cliff with a little fountain bubbling out of it. All three stopped and drank and splashed their hot faces.

"And now," said the girl as she tossed her wet hair back from her forehead, "aren't you going to tell us who you are and why you were tied up and what it's all about?"

"With a good will, damsel," said Tirian. "But we must keep on the march." So while they went on walking he told them who he was and all the things that had happened to him. "And now," he said at the end, "I am going to a certain tower, one of three that were built in my grandsire's time to guard Lantern Waste against certain perilous outlaws who dwelled there in his day. By Aslan's goodwill I was not robbed of my keys. In that tower we shall find stores of weapons and mail and some victuals also, though no better than dry biscuit. There also we can lie safe while we make our plans. And now, prithee, tell me who you two are and all your story."

"I'm Eustace Scrubb and this is Jill Pole," said the boy. "And we were here once before, ages and ages ago, more than a year ago by our time, and there was a chap called Prince Rilian, and they were keeping this chap underground, and Puddleglum put his foot in—"

"Ha!" cried Tirian, "are you then that Eustace and that Jill who rescued King Rilian from his long enchantment?"

"Yes, that's us," said Jill. "So he's *King* Rilian now, is he? Oh, of course he would be. I forgot—"

"Nay," said Tirian, "I am the seventh in descent from him. He has been dead over two hundred years."

Jill made a face. "Ugh!" she said. "That's the horrid part about coming back to Narnia." But Eustace went on.

"Well, now you know who we are, Sire," he said. "And it was like this. The Professor and Aunt Polly had got all us friends of Narnia together—"

"I know not these names, Eustace," said Tirian.

"They're the two who came into Narnia at the very beginning, the day all the animals learned to talk."

"By the Lion's Mane," cried Tirian. "Those two! The Lord Digory and the Lady Polly! From the dawn of the world! And still alive in your place? The wonder and the glory of it! But tell me, tell me."

"She isn't really our aunt, you know," said Eustace. "She's Miss Plummer, but we call her Aunt Polly. Well, those two got us all together, partly just for fun, so that we could all have a good jaw about Narnia (for of course there's no one else we can ever talk to about things like that) but partly because the Professor had a feeling that we were somehow wanted over here.

"Well, then you came in like a ghost or goodness-knows-what and nearly frightened the lives out of us and vanished without saying a word. After that, we knew for certain there was something up. The next question was how to get here. You can't go just by wanting to. So we talked and talked and at last the Professor said the only way would be by the Magic Rings. It was by those Rings that he and Aunt Polly got here long, long ago when they were only kids, years before we younger ones were born.

"But the Rings had all been buried in the garden of a house in London (that's our big town, Sire) and the house had been sold. So then the problem was how to get at them. You'll never guess what we did in the end! Peter and Edmund – that's the High King Peter, the one who spoke to you – went up to London to get into the garden from the back, early in the morning before people were up. They were dressed like workmen so that if anyone did see them it would look as if they'd come to do something about the drains. I wish I'd been with them, it must have been glorious fun. And they must have succeeded for the next day, Peter sent us a wire –

that's a sort of message, Sire, I'll explain about it some other time – to say he'd got the Rings. And the day after that was the day Jill and I had to go back to school – we're the only two who are still at school and we're at the same one. So Peter and Edmund were to meet us at a place on the way down to school and hand over the Rings. It had to be us two who were to go to Narnia, you see, because the older ones couldn't come again.

"So we got into the train – that's a kind of thing people travel in in our world; a lot of wagons chained together – and the Professor and Aunt Polly and Lucy came with us. We wanted to keep together as long as we could. Well, there we were in the train. And we were just getting to the station where the others were to meet us, and I was looking out of the window to see if I could see them when suddenly there came a most frightful jerk and a noise: and there we were in Narnia and there was your Majesty tied up to the tree."

"So you never used the Rings?" said Tirian.

"No," said Eustace. "Never even saw them. Aslan did it all for us in his own way without any Rings."

"But the High King Peter has them," said Tirian.

"Yes," said Jill. "But we don't think he can use them. When the two other Pevensies – King Edmund and Queen Lucy – were last here, Aslan said they would never come to Narnia again. And he said something of the same sort to the High King, only longer ago. You may be sure he'll come like a shot if he's allowed."

"Gosh!" said Eustace. "It's getting hot in this sun. Are we nearly there, Sire?"

"Look," said Tirian and pointed. Not many yards away grey battlements rose above the tree-tops, and after a minute's more walking they came out in an open grassy space. A stream ran across it and on the far side of the stream stood a squat, square tower with very few and narrow windows and one heavy-looking door in the wall that faced them.

Tirian looked sharply this way and that to make sure that no enemies were in sight. Then he walked up to the tower and stood still for a moment fishing up his bunch of keys which he wore inside his hunting-dress on a narrow silver chain that went round his neck. It was a nice bunch of keys that he brought out, for two were golden and many were richly ornamented: you could see at once that they were keys made for opening solemn and secret rooms in palaces, or chests and caskets of sweet-smelling wood that contained royal treasures. But the key which he now put into the lock of the door was big and plain and more rudely made. The lock was stiff and for a moment Tirian began to be afraid that he would not be able to turn it: but at last he did and the door swung open with a sullen creak.

"Welcome, friends," said Tirian. "I fear this is the best palace that the King of Narnia can now offer to his guests."

Tirian was pleased to see that the two strangers had been well brought up. They both said not to mention it and that they were sure it would be very nice.

As a matter of fact it was not particularly nice. It was rather dark and smelled very damp. There was only one room in it and this room went right up to the stone roof: a wooden staircase in one corner led up to a trap door by which you could get out on the battlements. There were a few rude bunks to sleep in, and a great many lockers and bundles. There was also a hearth which looked as if nobody had lit a fire in it for a great many years.

"We'd better go out and gather some firewood first thing, hadn't we?" said Jill.

"Not yet, comrade," said Tirian. He was determined that they should not be caught unarmed, and began searching the lockers, thankfully remembering that he had always been careful to have these garrison towers inspected once a year and to make sure that they were stocked with all things needful. The bow strings were there in their coverings of oiled silk, the swords and spears were greased against rust, and the armour was kept bright in its wrappings. But there was something even better. "Look you!" said Tirian as he drew out a long mail shirt of a curious pattern and flashed it before the children's eyes.

"That's funny-looking mail, Sire," said Eustace.

"Aye, lad," said Tirian. "No Narnian dwarf smithied that. 'Tis mail of Calormen, outlandish gear. I have ever kept a few suits of it in readiness, for I never knew when I or my friends might have reason to walk unseen in the Tisroc's land. And look on this stone bottle. In this there is a juice which, when we have rubbed it on our hands and faces, will make us brown as Calormenes."

"Oh, hurray!" said Jill. "Disguise! I love disguises."

Tirian showed them how to pour out a little of the juice into the palms of their hands and then rub it well over their faces and necks, right down to the shoulders, and then on their hands, right up to the elbows. He did the same himself.

"After this has hardened on us," he said, "we may wash in water and it will not change. Nothing but oil and ashes will make us white Narnians again. And now, sweet Jill, let us go see how this mail shirt becomes you. 'Tis something too long, yet not so much as I feared. Doubtless it belonged to a page in the train of one of their Tarkaans."

After the mail shirts they put on Calormene helmets, which are little round ones fitting tight to the head and having a spike on top. Then Tirian took long rolls of some white stuff out of the locker and wound them over the helmets till they became turbans: but the little steel spike still stuck up in the middle. He and Eustace took curved Calormene swords and little round shields. There was no sword light enough for Jill, but he gave her a long, straight hunting knife which might do for a sword at a pinch.

"Hast any skill with the bow, maiden?" said Tirian.

"Nothing worth talking of," said Jill, blushing. "Scrubb's not bad."

"Don't you believe her, Sire," said Eustace. "We've both been practising archery ever since we got back from Narnia last time, and she's about as good as me now. Not that either of us is much."

Then Tirian gave Jill a bow and a quiver full of arrows. The next business was to light a fire, for inside that tower it still felt more like a cave than like anything indoors and set one shivering. But they got warm gathering wood – the sun was now at its highest – and once the blaze was roaring up the chimney the place began to look cheerful.

Dinner was, however, a dull meal, for the best they could do was to pound up some of the hard biscuit which they found in a locker and pour it into boiling water, with salt, so as to make a kind of porridge. And of course there was nothing to drink but water.

"I wish we'd brought a packet of tea," said Jill.

"Or a tin of cocoa," said Eustace.

"A firkin or so of good wine in each of these towers would not have been amiss," said Tirian.

CHAPTER SIX

A GOOD NIGHT'S WORK

About four hours later Tirian flung himself into one of the bunks to snatch a little sleep. The two children were already snoring: he had made them go to bed before he did because they would have to be up most of the night and he knew that at their age they couldn't do without sleep. Also, he had tired them out. First he had given Jill some practice in archery and found that, though not up to Narnian standards, she was really not too bad. Indeed she had succeeded in shooting a rabbit (not a *Talking* rabbit, of course: there are lots of the ordinary kind about in Western Narnia) and it was already skinned, cleaned, and hanging up. He had found that both the children knew all about this chilly and smelly job; they had learned that kind of thing on their great journey though Giant-Land in the days of Prince Rilian.

Then he had tried to teach Eustace how to use his sword and shield. Eustace had learned quite a lot about sword fighting on his earlier adventures but that had been all with a straight Narnian sword. He had never handled a curved Calormene scimitar and that made it hard, for many of the strokes are quite different and some of the habits he had learned with the long sword had now to be unlearned again. But Tirian found that he had a good eye and was very quick on his feet. He was surprised at the strength of both the children: in fact they both seemed to be already much stronger and bigger and more grown-up than they had been when he first met them a few hours before. It is one of the effects which Narnian air often has on visitors from our world.

All three of them agreed that the very first thing they must do was to go back to Stable Hill and try to rescue Jewel the Unicorn. After that, if they succeeded, they would try to get away Eastward and meet the little army which Roonwit the Centaur would be bringing from Cair Paravel.

An experienced warrior and huntsman like Tirian can always wake up at the time he wants. So he gave himself till nine o'clock that night and then put all worries out of his head and fell asleep at once. It seemed only a moment later when he woke but he knew by the light and the very feel of things that he had timed his sleep exactly. He got up, put on his helmet-and-turban (he had slept in his mail shirt), and then shook the other two till they woke up. They looked, to tell the truth, very grey and dismal as they climbed out of their bunks and there was a good deal of yawning.

"Now," said Tirian, "we go due North from here – by good fortune 'tis a starry night – and it will be much shorter than our journey this morning, for then we went round-about but now we shall go straight. If we are challenged, then do you two hold your peace and I will do my best to talk like a curst, cruel, proud lord of Calormen. If I draw my sword then thou, Eustace, must do likewise and let Jill leap behind us and stand with an arrow on the string. But if I cry 'Home', then fly for the Tower, both of you. And let none try to fight on – not even one stroke – after I have given the retreat: such false valour has spoiled many notable plans in the wars. And now, friends, in the name of Aslan let us go forward."

Out they went into the cold night. All the great Northern stars were burning above the tree-tops. The North-Star of that world is called the Spear-Head: it is brighter than our Pole Star.

For a time they could go straight towards the Spear-Head but presently they came to a dense thicket so that they had to go out of their course to get round it. And after that – for they were still overshadowed by branches – it was hard to pick up their bearings. It was Jill who set them right again: she had been an excellent Guide in England. And of course she knew her Narnian stars perfectly, having travelled so much in the wild Northern Lands, and could work out the direction from other stars even when the Spear-Head was hidden.

As soon as Tirian saw that she was the best pathfinder of the three of them he put her in front. And then he was astonished to find how silently and almost invisibly she glided on before them.

"By the Mane!" he whispered to Eustace. "This girl is a wondrous wood-maid. If she had Dryad's blood in her she could scarce do it better."

"She's so small, that's what helps," whispered Eustace. But Jill from in front said: "S-s-s-h, less noise."

All round them the wood was very quiet. Indeed it was far too quiet. On an ordinary Narnia night there ought to have been noises – an occasional cheery "Goodnight" from a hedgehog, the cry of an owl overhead, perhaps a flute in the distance to tell of Fauns dancing, or some throbbing, hammering noises from Dwarfs underground. All that was silenced: gloom and fear reigned over Narnia.

After a time they began to go steeply uphill and the trees grew further apart. Tirian could dimly make out the well-known hill-top and the stable. Jill was now going with more and more caution: she kept on making signs to the others with her hand to do the same. Then she stopped dead still and Tirian saw her gradually sink down into the grass and disappear without a sound. A moment later she rose again, put her mouth close to Tirian's ear, and said in the lowest possible whisper, "Get down. *Thee* better." She said *thee* for *see* not because she had a lisp but because she knew the hissing letter S is the part of a whisper most likely to be overheard.

Tirian at once lay down, almost as silently as Jill, but not quite, for he was heavier and older. And once they were down, he saw how from that position you could see the edge of the hill sharp against the star-strewn sky. Two black shapes rose against it: one was the stable, and the other, a few feet in front of it, was a Calormene sentry. He was keeping very ill watch; not walking or even standing but sitting with his spear over his shoulder and his chin on his chest.

"Well done," said Tirian to Jill. She had shown him exactly what he needed to know.

They got up and Tirian now took the lead. Very slowly, hardly daring to breathe, they made their way up to a little clump of trees which was not more than forty feet away from the sentinel.

"Wait here till I come again," he whispered to the other two. "If I miscarry, fly." Then he sauntered out boldly in full view of the enemy. The man started when he saw him and was just going to jump to his feet: he was afraid Tirian might be one of his own officers and that he would get into trouble for sitting down. But before he could get up Tirian had dropped on one knee beside him, saying:

"Art thou a warrior of the Tisroc's, may he live for ever? It cheers my heart to meet thee among all these beasts and devils of Narnians. Give me thy hand, friend."

Before he well knew what was happening the Calormene sentry found his right hand seized in a mighty grip. Next instant someone was kneeling on his legs and a dagger was pressed against his neck.

"One noise and thou art dead," said Tirian in his ear. "Tell me where the Unicorn is and thou shalt live."

"B – behind the stable, O My Master," stammered the unfortunate man.

"Good. Rise up and lead me to him."

As the man got up the point of the dagger never left his neck. It only travelled round (cold and rather ticklish) as Tirian got behind him and settled it at a convenient place under his ear. Trembling, he went round to the back of the stable.

Though it was dark Tirian could see the white shape of Jewel at once.

"Hush!" he said. "No, do not neigh. Yes, Jewel, it is I. How have they tied thee?"

"Hobbled by all four legs and tied with a bridle to a ring in the stable wall," came Jewel's voice.

"Stand here, sentry, with your back to the wall. So. Now, Jewel, set the point of your horn against this Calormene's breast."

"With a good will, Sire," said Jewel.

"If he moves, rive him to the heart." Then in a few seconds Tirian cut the ropes. With the remains of them he bound the sentry hand and foot. Finally he made him open his mouth, stuffed it full of grass and tied him up from scalp to chin so that he could make no noise, lowered the man into a sitting position and set him against the wall.

"I have done thee some discourtesy, soldier," said Tirian. "But such was my need. If we meet again I may happen to do thee a better turn. Now, Jewel, let us go softly."

He put his left arm round the beast's neck and bent and kissed its nose and both had great joy. They went back as quietly as possible to the place where he had left the children. It was darker in there under the trees and he nearly ran into Eustace before he saw him.

"All's well," whispered Tirian. "A good night's work. Now for home."

They turned and had gone a few paces when Eustace said, "Where are you, Pole?" There was no answer. "Is Jill on the other side of you, Sire?" he asked.

"What?" said Tirian. "Is she not on the other side of *you*?"

It was a terrible moment. They dared not shout but they whispered her name in the loudest whispers they could manage. There was no reply.

"Did she go from you while I was away?" asked Tirian.

"I didn't see or hear her ɡo," said Eustace. "But she could have gone without my knowing. She can be as quiet as a cat; you've seen for yourself."

At that moment a far off drumbeat was heard. Jewel moved his ears forward. "Dwarfs," he said.

"And treacherous Dwarfs, enemies, as likely as not," muttered Tirian.

"And here comes something on hoofs, much nearer," said Jewel.

The two humans and the Unicorn stood dead still. There were now so many different things to worry about that they didn't know what to do. The noise of hoofs came steadily nearer.

And then, quite close to them, a voice whispered: "Hallo! Are you all there?"

Thank heaven, it was Jill's.

"Where the *devil* have you been to?" said Eustace in a furious whisper, for he had been very frightened.

"In the Stable," gasped Jill, but it was the sort of gasp you give when you're struggling with suppressed laughter.

"Oh," growled Eustace, "you think it funny, do you? Well, all I can say is—"

"Have you got Jewel, Sire?" asked Jill.

"Yes. Here he is. What is that beast with you?"

"That's *him*," said Jill. "But let's be off home before anyone wakes up." And again there came little explosions of laughter.

The others obeyed at once for they had already lingered long enough in that dangerous place and the dwarf drums seemed to have come a little nearer.

It was only after they had been walking southward for several minutes that Eustace said:

"Got *him*? What do you mean?"

"The false Aslan," said Jill.

"What?" said Tirian. "Where have you been? What have you done?"

"Well, Sire," said Jill. "As soon as I saw that you'd got the sentry out of the way I thought hadn't I better have a look inside the Stable and see what really *is* there? So I crawled along. It was as easy as anything to draw the bolt. Of course it was pitch black inside and smelled like any other stable. Then I struck a light and – would you believe it? – there was nothing at all there but this old donkey with a bundle of lion-skin tied on to his back. So I drew my knife and told him he'd have to come along with me. As a matter of fact I needn't have threatened him with the knife at all. He was very fed up with the stable and quite ready to come – weren't you, Puzzle, dear?"

"Great Scott!" said Eustace. "Well I'm – I'm jiggered. I was jolly angry with you a moment ago, and I still think it was mean of you to sneak off without the rest of us. But I must admit – well, I mean to say – well, it was a perfectly gorgeous thing to do. If she was a boy she'd have to be knighted, wouldn't she, Sire?"

"If she was a boy," said Tirian, "she'd be whipped for disobeying orders." And in the dark no one could see whether he said this with a frown or a smile. Next minute there was a sound of rasping metal.

"What are you doing, Sire?" asked Jewel sharply.

"Drawing my sword to smite off the head of the accursed Ass," said Tirian in a terrible voice. "Stand clear, girl."

"Oh, don't, please don't," said Jill. "Really, you mustn't. It wasn't his fault. It was all the Ape. He didn't know any better. And he's very sorry.

And he's a nice donkey. His name's Puzzle. And I've got my arms round his neck."

"Jill," said Tirian, "you are the bravest and most wood-wise of all my subjects, but also the most malapert and disobedient. Well: let the Ass live. What have you to say for yourself, Ass?"

"Me, Sire?" came the donkey's voice. "I'm sure I'm very sorry if I've done wrong. The Ape said Aslan *wanted* me to dress up like that. And I thought he'd know. I'm not clever like him. I only did what I was told. It wasn't any fun for me living in that stable. I don't even know what's been going on outside. He never let me out except for a minute or two at night. Some days they forgot to give me any water too."

"Sire," said Jewel. "Those Dwarfs are coming nearer and nearer. Do we want to meet them?"

Tirian thought for a moment and then suddenly gave a great laugh out loud. Then he spoke, not this time in a whisper.

"By the Lion," he said, "I am growing slow-witted! Meet them? Certainly we will meet them. We will meet anyone now. We have this Ass to show them. Let them see the thing they have feared and bowed to. We can show them the truth of the Ape's vile plot. His secret's out. The tide's turned. Tomorrow we shall hang that Ape on the highest tree in Narnia. No more whispering and skulking and disguises. Where are these honest Dwarfs? We have good news for them."

When you have been whispering for hours the mere sound of anyone talking out loud has a wonderfully stirring effect. The whole party began talking and laughing: even Puzzle lifted up his head and gave a grand *Haw-hee-haw-hee-hee*; a thing the Ape hadn't allowed him to do for days.

Then they set off in the direction of the drumming. It grew steadily louder and soon they could see torchlight as well. They came out on one of those rough roads (we should hardly call them roads at all in England) which ran through Lantern Waste. And there, marching sturdily along, were about thirty Dwarfs, all with their little spades and mattocks over their shoulders. Two armed Calormenes led the column and two more brought up the rear.

"Stay!" thundered Tirian as he stepped out on the road. "Stay, soldiers. Whither do you lead these Narnian Dwarfs and by whose orders?"

Chapter Seven

Mainly About Dwarfs

The two Calormene soldiers at the head of the column, seeing what they took for a Tarkaan or great lord with two armed pages, came to a halt and raised their spears in salute.

"O My Master," said one of them, "we lead these manikins to Calormen to work in the mines of the Tisroc, may-he-live-forever."

"By the great god Tash, they are very obedient," said Tirian. Then suddenly he turned to the Dwarfs themselves. About one in six of them carried a torch and by that flickering light he could see their bearded faces all looking at him with grim and dogged expressions.

"Has the Tisroc fought a great battle, Dwarfs, and conquered your land?" he asked, "that thus you go patiently to die in the salt-pits of Pugrahan?"

The two soldiers glared at him in surprise but the Dwarfs all answered, "Aslan's orders, Aslan's orders. He's sold us. What can we do against *him*?"

"Tisroc indeed!" added one and spat. "I'd like to see him try it!"

"Silence, dog!" said the chief soldier.

"Look!" said Tirian, pulling Puzzle forward into the light. "It has all been a lie. Aslan has not come to Narnia at all. You have been cheated by the Ape. This is the thing he brought out of the stable to show you. Look at it."

What the Dwarfs saw, now that they could see it close, was certainly enough to make them wonder how they had ever been taken in. The lion-skin had got pretty untidy already during Puzzle's long imprisonment in the stable and it had been knocked crooked during his journey through the dark wood. Most of it was in a big lump on one shoulder. The head, besides being pushed sideways, had somehow got very far back so that anyone could now see his silly, gentle, donkeyish face gazing out of it. Some grass stuck out of one corner of his mouth, for he'd been doing a little quiet nibbling as they brought him along. And he was muttering, "It wasn't my fault, I'm not clever. I never said I *was*."

For one second all the Dwarfs were staring at Puzzle with wide open mouths and then one of the soldiers said sharply, "Are you mad, my Master? What are you doing to the slaves?" and the other said, "And who are you?" Neither of their spears was at the salute now – both were down and ready for action.

"Give the password," said the chief soldier.

"This is my password," said the King as he drew his sword. "*The light is dawning, the lie broken*. Now guard thee, miscreant, for I am Tirian of Narnia."

He flew upon the chief soldier like lightning. Eustace, who had drawn his sword when he saw the King draw his, rushed at the other one: his face was deadly pale, but I wouldn't blame him for that. And he had the luck that beginners sometimes do have. He forgot all that Tirian had tried to teach him that afternoon, slashed wildly (indeed I'm not sure his eyes weren't shut) and suddenly found, to his own great surprise, that the Calormene lay dead at his feet. And though that was a great relief, it was, at the moment, rather frightening. The King's fight lasted a second or two longer: then he too had killed his man and shouted to Eustace, "'Ware the other two."

But the Dwarfs had settled the two remaining Calormenes. There was no enemy left.

"Well struck, Eustace!" cried Tirian, clapping him on the back. "Now, Dwarfs, you are free. Tomorrow I will lead you to free all Narnia. Three cheers for Aslan!"

But the result which followed was simply wretched. There was a feeble attempt from a few Dwarfs (about five) which died away all at once: from several others there were sulky growls. Many said nothing at all.

"Don't they understand?" said Jill impatiently. "What's wrong with all you Dwarfs? Don't you hear what the King says? It's all over. The Ape isn't going to rule Narnia any longer. Everyone can go back to ordinary life. You can have fun again. Aren't you glad?"

After a pause of nearly a minute, a not-very-nice-looking Dwarf with hair and beard as black as soot said: "And who might you be, Missie?"

"I'm Jill," she said. "The same Jill who rescued King Rilian from the enchantment – and this is Eustace who did it too – and we've come back from another world after hundreds of years. Aslan sent us."

The Dwarfs all looked at one another with grins; sneering grins, not merry ones.

"Well," said the Black Dwarf (whose name was Griffle), "I don't know how all you chaps feel, but I feel I've heard as much about Aslan as I want to for the rest of my life."

"That's right, that's right," growled the other Dwarfs. "It's all a plant, all a blooming plant."

"What do you mean?" said Tirian. He had not been pale when he was fighting but he was pale now. He had thought this was going to be a beautiful moment, but it was turning out more like a bad dream.

"You must think we're blooming soft in the head, that you must," said Griffle. "We've been taken in once and now you expect us to be taken in again the next minute. We've no more use for stories about Aslan, see! Look at him! An old moke with long ears!"

"By heaven, you make me mad," said Tirian. "Which of us said *that* was Aslan? That is the Ape's imitation of the real Aslan. Can't you understand?"

"And you've got a better imitation, I suppose!" said Griffle. "No thanks. We've been fooled once and we're not going to be fooled again."

"I have not," said Tirian angrily, "I serve the real Aslan."

"Where's he? Who's he? Show him to us!" said several Dwarfs.

"Do you think I keep him in my wallet, fools?" said Tirian. "Who am I that I could make Aslan appear at my bidding? He's not a tame lion."

The moment those words were out of his mouth he realized that he had made a false move. The Dwarfs at once began repeating "not a tame lion, not a tame lion," in a jeering sing-song. "That's what the other lot kept on telling us," said one.

"Do you mean you don't believe in the real Aslan?" said Jill. "But I've seen him. And he has sent us two here out of a different world."

"Ah," said Griffle with a broad smile. "So *you* say. They've taught you your stuff all right. Saying your lessons, ain't you?"

"Churl," cried Tirian, "will you give a lady the lie to her very face?"

"You keep a civil tongue in your head, Mister," replied the Dwarf. "I don't think we want any more Kings — if you *are* Tirian, which you don't look like him — no more than we want any Aslans. We're going to look after ourselves from now on and touch our caps to nobody. See?"

"That's right," said the other Dwarfs. "We're on our own now. No more Aslan, no more Kings, no more silly stories about other worlds. The Dwarfs are for the Dwarfs." And they began to fall into their places and to get ready for marching back to wherever they had come from.

"Little beasts!" said Eustace. "Aren't you even going to say *thank you* for being saved from the salt-mines?"

"Oh, we know all about that," said Griffle over his shoulder. "You wanted to make use of us, that's why you rescued us. You're playing some game of your own. Come on, you chaps."

And the Dwarfs struck up the queer little marching song which goes with the drumbeat, and off they tramped into the darkness.

Tirian and his friends stared after them. Then he said the single word "Come," and they continued their journey.

They were a silent party. Puzzle felt himself to be still in disgrace, and also he didn't really quite understand what had happened. Jill, besides being disgusted with the Dwarfs, was very impressed with Eustace's victory over the Calormene and felt almost shy. As for Eustace, his heart was still beating rather quickly.

Tirian and Jewel walked sadly together in the rear. The King had his arm on the Unicorn's shoulder and sometimes the Unicorn nuzzled the King's cheek with his soft nose. They did not try to comfort one another with words. It wasn't very easy to think of anything to say that would be comforting. Tirian had never dreamed that one of the results of an Ape's setting up a false Aslan would be to stop people from believing in the real one. He had felt quite sure that the Dwarfs would rally to his side the moment he showed them how they had been deceived. And then the next night he would have led them to Stable Hill and shown Puzzle to all the creatures and everyone would have turned against the Ape and, perhaps after a scuffle with the Calormenes, the whole thing would have been over. But now, it seemed, he could count on nothing. How many other Narnians might turn the same way as the Dwarfs?

"Somebody's coming after us, I think," said Puzzle suddenly.

They stopped and listened. Sure enough, there was a thump-thump of small feet behind them.

"Who goes there?" shouted the King.

"Only me, Sire," came a voice. "Me, Poggin the Dwarf. I've only just managed to get away from the others. I'm on your side, Sire; and on Aslan's. If you can put a Dwarfish sword in my fist, I'd gladly strike a blow on the right side before all's done."

Everyone crowded round him and welcomed him and praised him and slapped him on the back. Of course one single Dwarf could not make a very great difference, but it was somehow very cheering to have even one. The whole party brightened up. But Jill and Eustace didn't stay bright for very long, for they were now yawning their heads off and too tired to think about anything but bed.

It was at the coldest hour of the night, just before dawn, that they got back to the Tower. If there had been a meal ready for them they would have been glad enough to eat, but the bother and delay of getting one was not to be thought of. They drank from a stream, splashed their faces with water, and tumbled into their bunks, except for Puzzle and Jewel who said they'd be more comfortable outside. This perhaps was just as well, for a Unicorn and a fat, full-grown donkey indoors always make a room feel rather crowded.

Narnian Dwarfs, though less than four feet high, are for their size about the toughest and strongest creatures there are, so that Poggin, in spite of a heavy day and a late night, woke fully refreshed before any of the others. He at once took Jill's bow, went out and shot a couple of wood pigeons. Then he sat plucking them on the doorstep and chatting to Jewel and Puzzle.

Puzzle looked and felt a good deal better that morning. Jewel, being a Unicorn and therefore one of the noblest and delicatest of beasts, had been very kind to him, talking to him about things of the sort they could both understand like grass and sugar and the care of one's hoofs.

When Jill and Eustace came out of the Tower yawning and rubbing their eyes at almost half past ten, the Dwarf showed them where they could gather plenty of a Narnian weed called Wild Fresney, which looks rather like our wood-sorrel but tastes a good deal nicer when cooked. (It needs a little butter and pepper to make it perfect, but they hadn't got these.) So that what with one thing and another, they had the makings of a capital stew for their breakfast or dinner, whichever you choose to call it. Tirian went a little further off into the wood with an axe and brought back some branches for fuel.

While the meal was cooking – which seemed a very long time, especially as it smelled nicer and nicer the nearer it came to being done – the King found a complete Dwarfish outfit for Poggin: mail shirt, helmet, shield, sword, belt and dagger. Then he inspected Eustace's sword and found that Eustace had put it back in the sheath all messy from killing the Calormene. He was scolded for that and made to clean and polish it.

All this while Jill went to and fro, sometimes stirring the pot and sometimes looking out enviously at the Donkey and the Unicorn who were contentedly grazing. How many times that morning she wished she could eat grass!

But when the meal came everyone felt it had been worth waiting for, and there were second helpings all round.

When everyone had eaten as much as he could, the three humans and the Dwarf came and sat on the doorstep, the four-footed ones lay down facing them, the Dwarf (with permission both from Jill and from Tirian) lit his pipe, and the King said: "Now, friend Poggin, you have more news of the enemy, belike, than we. Tell us all you know. And first, what tale do they tell of my escape?"

"As cunning a tale, Sire, as ever was devised," said Poggin. "It was the Cat, Ginger, who told it, and most likely made it up too. This Ginger, Sire – oh, he's a slyboots if ever a cat was – said he was walking past the tree to which those villains bound your Majesty. And he said (saving your reverence) that you were howling and swearing and cursing Aslan: 'language I wouldn't like to repeat' were the words he used, looking ever so prim and proper – you know the way a Cat can when it pleases. And then, says Ginger, Aslan himself suddenly appeared in a flash of lightning and swallowed your Majesty up at one mouthful.

"All the Beasts trembled at this story and some fainted right away. And of course the Ape followed it up. There, he says, see what Aslan does to those who don't respect him. Let that be a warning to you all. And the poor creatures wailed and whined and said, it will, it will. So that in the upshot your Majesty's escape has not set them thinking whether you still have loyal friends to aid you, but only made them more afraid and more obedient to the Ape."

"What devilish policy!" said Tirian. "This Ginger, then, is close in the Ape's counsels."

"It's more a question by now, Sire, if the Ape is in his counsels," replied the Dwarf. "The Ape has taken to drinking, you see. My belief is that the plot is now mostly carried on by Ginger or Rishda – that's the Calormene captain. And I think some words that Ginger has scattered among the Dwarfs are chiefly to blame for the scurvy return they made you. And I'll tell you why.

"One of those dreadful midnight meetings had just broken up the night before last and I'd gone a bit of the way home when I found I'd left my pipe behind. It was a real good 'un, an old favourite, so I went back to look for it. But before I got to the place where I'd been sitting (it was black as pitch there) I heard a cat's voice say *Mew* and a Calormene voice say 'here… speak softly,' so I just stood as still as if I was frozen. And these two were Ginger and Rishda Tarkaan as they call him.

"'Noble Tarkaan,' said the Cat in that silky voice of his, 'I just wanted to know exactly what we both meant today about Aslan meaning *no more* than Tash.'

"'Doubtless, most sagacious of cats,' says the other, 'you have perceived my meaning.'

"'You mean,' says Ginger, 'that there's no such person as either.'

"'All who are enlightened know that,' said the Tarkaan.

"'Then we can understand one another,' purrs the Cat.

"'Do you, like me, grow a little weary of the Ape?'

"'A stupid, greedy brute,' says the other, 'but we must use him for the present. Thou and I must provide for all things in secret and make the Ape do our will.'

"'And it would be better, wouldn't it,' said Ginger, 'to let some of the more enlightened Narnians into our counsels, one by one as we find them apt. For the Beasts who really believe in Aslan may turn at any moment – and will, if the Ape's folly betrays his secret. But those who care neither for Tash nor Aslan but have only an eye to their own profit and such reward as the Tisroc may give them when Narnia is a Calormene province, will be firm.'

"'Excellent, Cat,' said the Captain. 'But choose which ones carefully.'"

While the Dwarf had been speaking the day seemed to have changed. It had been sunny when they sat down. Now Puzzle shivered. Jewel shifted his head uneasily. Jill looked up.

"It's clouding over," she said.

"And it's so cold," said Puzzle.

"Cold enough, by the Lion!" said Tirian, blowing on his hands. "And faugh! What foul smell is this?"

"Phew!" gasped Eustace. "It's like something dead. Is there a dead bird somewhere about? And why didn't we notice it before?"

With a great upheaval Jewel scrambled to his feet and pointed with his horn.

"Look!" he cried. "Look at it! Look, look!"

Then all six of them saw; and over all their faces there came an expression of uttermost dismay.

Chapter Eight

What News the Eagle Brought

In the shadow of the trees on the far side of the clearing something was moving. It was gliding very slowly Northward. At a first glance you might have mistaken it for smoke, for it was grey and you could see things through it. But the deathly smell was not the smell of smoke. Also, this thing kept its shape instead of billowing and curling as smoke would have done. It was roughly the shape of a man but it had the head of a bird; some bird of prey with a cruel, curved beak. It had four arms which it held high above its head, stretching them out Northward as if it wanted to snatch all Narnia in its grip; and its fingers – all twenty of them – were curved like its beak and had long, pointed, bird-like claws instead of nails. It floated on the grass instead of walking, and the grass seemed to wither beneath it.

After one look at it, Puzzle gave a screaming bray and darted into the Tower. And Jill (who was no coward, as you know) hid her face in her hands to shut out the sight of it. The others watched it for perhaps a minute, until it streamed away into the thicker trees on their right and disappeared. Then the sun came out again, and the birds once more began to sing.

Everyone started breathing properly again and moved. They had all been still as statues while it was in sight.

"What was it?" said Eustace in a whisper.

"I have seen it once before," said Tirian. "But that time it was carved in stone and overlaid with gold and had solid diamonds for eyes. It was when I was no older than thou, and had gone as a guest to the Tisroc's court in Tashbaan. He took me into the great temple of Tash. There I saw it, carved above the altar."

"Then that – that thing – was Tash?" said Eustace.

But instead of answering him, Tirian slipped his arm behind Jill's shoulders and said, "How is it with you, Lady?"

"A-all right," said Jill, taking her hands away from her pale face and trying to smile. "I'm all right. It only made me feel a little sick for a moment."

"It seems, then," said the Unicorn, "that there is a real Tash, after all."

"Yes," said the Dwarf. "And this fool of an Ape, who didn't believe in Tash, will get more than he bargained for! He called for Tash; Tash has come."

"Where has it – he – the Thing – gone to?" said Jill.

"North into the heart of Narnia," said Tirian. "It has come to dwell among us. They have called it and it has come."

"Ho, ho, ho!" chuckled the Dwarf, rubbing his hairy hands together. "It will be a surprise for the Ape. People shouldn't call for demons unless they really mean what they say."

"Who knows if Tash will be visible to the Ape?" said Jewel.

"Where has Puzzle got to?" said Eustace.

They all shouted out Puzzle's name and Jill went round to the other side of the Tower to see if he had gone there.

They were quite tired of looking for him when at last his large grey head peered cautiously out of the doorway and he said, "Has it gone away?" And when at last they got him to come out, he was shivering the way a dog shivers before a thunderstorm.

"I see now," said Puzzle, "that I really have been a very bad donkey. I ought never to have listened to Shift. I never thought things like this would begin to happen."

"If you'd spent less time saying you weren't clever and more time trying to be as clever as you could—" began Eustace but Jill interrupted him.

"Oh, leave poor old Puzzle alone," she said. "It was all a mistake; wasn't it, Puzzle dear?" And she kissed him on the nose.

Though rather shaken by what they had seen, the whole party now sat down again and went on with their talk.

Jewel had little to tell them. While he was a prisoner he had spent nearly all his time tied up at the back of the stable, and had of course heard none of the enemies' plans. He had been kicked (he'd done some kicking back too) and beaten and threatened with death unless he would say that he believed it was Aslan who was brought out and shown to them by firelight every night. In fact he was going to be executed that very morning if he had not been rescued. He didn't know what had happened to the Lamb.

The question they had to decide was whether they would go to Stable Hill again that night, show Puzzle to the Narnians and try to make them see how they had been tricked, or whether they should steal away eastward to meet the help which Roonwit the Centaur was bringing up from Cair Paravel and return against the Ape and his Calormenes in force.

Tirian would very much like to have followed the first plan: he hated the idea of leaving the Ape to bully his people one moment longer than need be. On the other hand, the way the Dwarfs had behaved the previous night was a warning. Apparently one couldn't be sure how people would take it even if he showed them Puzzle. And there were the Calormene soldiers to be reckoned with. Poggin thought there were about thirty of them. Tirian felt sure that if the Narnians all rallied to his side, he and Jewel and the children and Poggin (Puzzle didn't count for much) would have a good chance of beating them. But how if half the Narnians – including all the Dwarfs – just sat and looked on? or even fought against him? The risk was too great. And there was, too, the cloudy shape of Tash. What might it do?

And then, as Poggin pointed out, there was no harm in leaving the Ape to deal with his own difficulties for a day or two. He would have no Puzzle to bring out and show now. It wasn't easy to see what story he – or Ginger – could make up to explain that. If the Beasts asked night after night to see Aslan, and no Aslan was brought out, surely even the simplest of them would get suspicious.

In the end they all agreed that the best thing was to go off and try to meet Roonwit.

As soon as they had decided this, it was wonderful how much more cheerful everyone became. I don't honestly think that this was because any of them was afraid of a fight (except perhaps Jill and Eustace). But I daresay that each of them, deep down inside, was very glad not to go any nearer – or not yet – to that horrible bird-headed thing which, visible or invisible, was now probably haunting Stable Hill. Anyway, one always feels better when one has made up one's mind.

Tirian said they had better remove their disguises, as they didn't want to be mistaken for Calormenes and perhaps attacked by any loyal Narnians they might meet. The Dwarf made up a horrid-looking mess of ashes from the hearth and grease out of the jar of grease which was kept for rubbing on swords and spear-heads. Then they took off their Calormene armour and went down to the stream.

The nasty mixture made a lather just like soft soap: it was a pleasant, homely sight to see Tirian and the two children kneeling beside the water and scrubbing the backs of their necks or puffing and blowing as they splashed the lather off. Then they went back to the Tower with red, shiny faces, looking like people who have been given an extra special good wash before a party. They re-armed themselves in true Narnian style, with straight swords and three-cornered shields. "Body of me," said Tirian. "That is better. I feel a true man again."

Puzzle begged very hard to have the lion-skin taken off him. He said it was too hot and the way it was rucked up on his back was uncomfortable: also, it made him look so silly. But they told him he would have to wear it a bit longer, for they still wanted to show him in that get-up to the other Beasts, even though they were now going to meet Roonwit first.

What was left of the pigeon-meat and rabbit-meat was not worth bringing away but they took some biscuits. Then Tirian locked the door of the Tower and that was the end of their stay there.

It was a little after two in the afternoon when they set out, and it was the first really warm day of that spring. The young leaves seemed to be much further out than yesterday: the snow-drops were over, but they saw several primroses. The sunlight slanted through the trees, birds sang, and always (though usually out of sight) there was the noise of running water. It was hard to think of horrible things like Tash. The children felt, "This is really Narnia at last." Even Tirian's heart grew lighter as he walked ahead of them, humming an old Narnian marching song which had the refrain:

> Ho, rumble, rumble, rumble, rumble
> Rumble drum belaboured.

After the King came Eustace and Poggin the Dwarf. Poggin was telling Eustace the names of all the Narnian trees, birds, and plants which he didn't know already. Sometimes Eustace would tell him about English ones.

After them came Puzzle, and after him Jill and Jewel walking very close together. Jill had, as you might say, quite fallen in love with the Unicorn. She thought – and she wasn't far wrong – that he was the shiningest, delicatest, most graceful animal she had ever met: and he was so gentle and soft of speech that, if you hadn't known, you would hardly have believed how fierce and terrible he could be in battle.

"Oh, this is nice!" said Jill. "Just walking along like this. I wish there could be more of *this* sort of adventure. It's a pity there's always so much happening in Narnia."

But the Unicorn explained to her that she was quite mistaken. He said that the Sons and Daughters of Adam and Eve were brought out of their own strange world into Narnia only at times when Narnia was stirred and upset, but she mustn't think it was always like that. In between their visits there were hundreds and thousands of years when peaceful King followed peaceful King till you could hardly remember their names or count their numbers, and there was really hardly anything to put into the History

Books. And he went on to talk of old Queens and heroes whom she had never heard of. He spoke of Swanwhite the Queen who had lived before the days of the White Witch and the Great Winter, who was so beautiful that when she looked into any forest pool the reflection of her face shone out of the water like a star by night for a year and a day afterwards. He spoke of Moonwood the Hare who had such ears that he could sit by Caldron Pool under the thunder of the great waterfall and hear what men spoke in whispers at Cair Paravel. He told how King Gale, who was ninth in descent from Frank the first of all Kings, had sailed far away into the Eastern seas and delivered the Lone Islanders from a dragon and how, in return, they had given him the Lone Islands to be part of the royal lands of Narnia for ever. He talked of whole centuries in which all Narnia was so happy that notable dances and feasts, or at most tournaments, were the only things that could be remembered, and every day and week had been better than the last. And as he went on, the picture of all those happy years, all the thousands of them, piled up in Jill's mind till it was rather like looking down from a high hill on to a rich, lovely plain full of woods and waters and cornfields, which spread away and away till it got thin and misty from distance. And she said:

"Oh, I do hope we can soon settle the Ape and get back to those good, ordinary times. And then I hope they'll go on for ever and ever and ever. *Our* world is going to have an end some day. Perhaps this one won't. Oh, Jewel – wouldn't it be lovely if Narnia just went on and on – like what you said it has been?"

"Nay, sister," answered Jewel, "all worlds draw to an end, except Aslan's own country."

"Well, at least," said Jill, "I hope the end of this one is millions of millions of millions of years away – hullo! What are we stopping for?"

The King and Eustace and the Dwarf were all staring up at the sky. Jill shuddered, remembering what horrors they had seen already. But it was nothing of that sort this time. It was small, and looked black against the blue.

"I dare swear," said the Unicorn, "from its flight, that it is a Talking bird."

"So think I," said the King. "But is it a friend, or a spy of the Ape's?"

"To me, Sire," said the Dwarf, "it has a look of Farsight the Eagle."

"Ought we to hide under the trees?" said Eustace.

"Nay," said Tirian, "best stand still as rocks. He would see us for certain if we moved."

"Look! He wheels, he has seen us already," said Jewel. "He is coming down in wide circles."

"Arrow on string, Lady," said Tirian to Jill. "But by no means shoot till I bid you. He may be a friend."

If one had known what was going to happen next it would have been a treat to watch the grace and ease with which the huge bird glided down. He alighted on a rocky crag a few feet from Tirian, bowed his crested head, and said in his strange eagle's voice, "Hail, King."

"Hail, Farsight," said Tirian. "And since you call me King, I may well believe you are not a follower of the Ape and his false Aslan. I am right glad of your coming."

"Sire," said the Eagle, "when you have heard my news you will be sorrier of my coming than of the greatest woe that ever befell you."

Tirian's heart seemed to stop beating at these words, but he set his teeth and said, "Tell on."

"Two sights have I seen," said Farsight. "One was Cair Paravel filled with dead Narnians and living Calormenes: the Tisroc's banner advanced upon your royal battlements: and your subjects flying from the city — this way and that, into the woods. Cair Paravel was taken from the sea. Twenty great ships of Calormen put in there in the dark of the night before last night."

No one could speak.

"And the other sight, five leagues nearer than Cair Paravel, was Roonwit the Centaur lying dead with a Calormene arrow in his side. I was with him in his last hour and he gave me this message to your Majesty: to remember that all worlds draw to an end and that noble death is a treasure which no one is too poor to buy."

"So," said the King, after a long silence, "Narnia is no more."

CHAPTER NINE

THE GREAT MEETING ON STABLE HILL

For a long time they could not speak nor even shed a tear. Then the Unicorn stamped the ground with his hoof, and shook his mane, and spoke.

"Sire," he said, "there is now no need of counsel. We see that the Ape's plans were laid deeper than we dreamed of. Doubtless he has been long in secret traffic with the Tisroc, and as soon as he had found the lion-skin he sent him word to make ready his navy for the taking of Cair Paravel and all Narnia. Nothing now remains for us seven but to go back to Stable Hill, proclaim the truth, and take the adventure that Aslan sends us. And if, by a great marvel, we defeat those thirty Calormenes who are with the Ape, then to turn again and die in battle with the far greater host of them that will soon march from Cair Paravel."

Tirian nodded. But he turned to the children and said: "Now, friends, it is time for you to go hence into your own world. Doubtless you have done all that you were sent to do."

"B – but we've done nothing," said Jill, who was shivering, not with fear exactly but because everything was so horrible.

"Nay," said the King, "you loosed me from the tree: you glided before me like a snake last night in the wood and took Puzzle: and you, Eustace, killed your man. But you are too young to share in such a bloody end as we others must meet tonight or, it may be, three days hence. I entreat you – nay, I command you – to return to your own place. I should be put to shame if I let such young warriors fall in battle on my side."

"No, no, no," said Jill (very white when she began speaking and then suddenly very red and then white again.) "We won't, I don't care what you say. We're going to stick to you whatever happens, aren't we, Eustace?"

"Yes, but there's no need to get so worked up about it," said Eustace, who had stuck his hands in his pockets (forgetting how very odd that looks when you are wearing a mail shirt). "Because, you see, we haven't any choice. What's the good of talking about our going back? How? We've got no magic for doing it!"

This was very good sense but, at the moment, Jill hated Eustace for saying it. He was fond of being dreadfully matter-of-fact when other people got excited.

When Tirian realized that the two strangers could not get home (unless Aslan suddenly whisked them away), he next wanted them to go across the Southern Mountains into Archenland where they might possibly be safe. But they didn't know their way and there was no one to send with them. Also, as Poggin said, once the Calormenes had Narnia they would certainly take Archenland in the next week or so: the Tisroc had always wanted to have these Northern countries for his own. In the end Eustace and Jill begged so hard that Tirian said they could come with him and take their chance – or, as he much more sensibly called it, "the adventure that Aslan would send them".

The King's first idea was that they should not go back to Stable Hill – they were sick of the very name of it by now – till after dark. But the Dwarf told them that if they arrived there by daylight they would probably find the place deserted, except perhaps for a Calormene sentry. The Beasts were far too frightened by what the Ape (and Ginger) had told them about this new angry Aslan – or Tashlan – to go near it except when they were called together for these horrible midnight meetings. And Calormenes are never good woodsmen. Poggin thought that even by daylight they could easily get round to somewhere behind the stable without being seen. This would be much harder to do when the night had come and the Ape might be calling the Beasts together and all the Calormenes were on duty. And when the meeting did begin they could leave Puzzle at the back of the stable, completely out of sight, till the moment at which they wanted to produce him. This was obviously a good thing: for their only chance was to give the Narnians a sudden surprise.

Everyone agreed and the whole party set off on a new line – north-west – towards the hated Hill. The Eagle sometimes flew to and fro above them, sometimes he sat perched on Puzzle's back. No one – not even the King himself except in some great need – would dream of *riding* on a Unicorn.

This time Jill and Eustace walked together. They had been feeling very brave when they were begging to be allowed to come with the others, but now they didn't feel brave at all.

"Pole," said Eustace in a whisper. "I may as well tell you I've got the wind up."

"Oh, *you're* all right, Scrubb," said Jill. "You can fight. But I — I'm just shaking, if you want to know the truth."

"Oh, shaking's nothing," said Eustace. "I'm feeling I'm going to be sick."

"Don't talk about *that*, for goodness' sake," said Jill.

They went on in silence for a minute or two.

"Pole," said Eustace presently.

"What?" said she.

"What'll happen if we get killed here?"

"Well, we'll be dead, I suppose."

"But I mean, what will happen in our own world? Shall we wake up and find ourselves back in that train? Or shall we just vanish and never be heard of any more? Or shall we be dead in England?"

"Gosh. I never thought of that."

"It'll be rum for Peter and the others if they saw me waving out of the window and then when the train comes in we're nowhere to be found! Or if they found two — I mean, if we're dead over there in England."

"Ugh!" said Jill. "What a horrid idea."

"It wouldn't be horrid for *us*," said Eustace. "*We* shouldn't be there."

"I almost wish — no I don't, though," said Jill.

"What were you going to say?"

"I *was* going to say I wished we'd never come. But I don't, I don't, I don't. Even if we *are* killed. I'd rather be killed fighting for Narnia than grow old and stupid at home and perhaps go about in a Bath chair and then die in the end just the same."

"Or be smashed up by British Railways!"

"Why d'you say that?"

"Well, when that awful jerk came — the one that seemed to throw us into Narnia — I thought it *was* the beginning of a railway accident. So I was jolly glad to find ourselves here instead."

While Jill and Eustace were talking about this, the others were discussing their plans and becoming less miserable. That was because they were now thinking of what was to be done this very night and the thought of what had happened to Narnia — the thought that all her glories and joys were over — was pushed away into the back part of their minds. The moment they stopped talking it would come out and make them wretched again: but they kept on talking. Poggin was really quite cheerful about the night's work they had to do. He was sure that the Boar and the Bear, and probably all the Dogs would come over to their side at once. And he couldn't believe that all the other Dwarfs would stick to Griffle. And fighting by firelight and in and out among trees would be an advantage to the weaker side. And then, if they could win tonight, need they really throw their lives away by meeting the main Calormene army a few days later?

Why not hide in the woods, or even up in the Western Waste beyond the great waterfall and live like outlaws? And then they might gradually get stronger and stronger, for Talking Beasts and Archenlanders would be joining them every day. And at last they'd come out of hiding and sweep the Calormenes (who would have got careless by then) out of the country and Narnia would be revived. After all, something very like that had happened in the time of King Miraz!

And Tirian heard all this and thought, "But what about Tash?" and felt in his bones that none of it was going to happen. But he didn't say so.

When they got nearer to Stable Hill of course everyone became quiet. Then the real wood-work began. From the moment at which they first saw the Hill to the moment at which they all arrived at the back of the Stable, it took them over two hours. It's the sort of thing one couldn't describe properly unless one wrote pages and pages about it. The journey from each bit of cover to the next was a separate adventure, and there were very long waits in between, and several false alarms. If you are a good Scout or a good Guide you will know already what it must have been like. By about sunset they were all safe in a clump of holly trees about fifteen yards behind the stable. They all munched some biscuit and lay down.

Then came the worst part, the waiting. Luckily for the children they slept for a couple of hours, but of course they woke up when the night grew cold, and what's worse, woke up very thirsty and with no chance of getting a drink. Puzzle just stood, shivering a little with nervousness, and said nothing. But Tirian, with his head against Jewel's flank, slept as soundly as if he were in his royal bed at Cair Paravel, till the sound of a gong beating awoke him and he sat up and saw that there was firelight on the far side of the stable and knew that the hour had come.

"Kiss me, Jewel," he said. "For certainly this is our last night on earth. And if ever I offended against you in any matter great or small, forgive me now."

"Dear King," said the Unicorn, "I could almost wish you had, so that I might forgive it. Farewell. We have known great joys together. If Aslan gave me my choice I would choose no other life than the life I have had and no other death than the one we go to."

Then they woke up Farsight, who was asleep with his head under his wing (it made him look as if he had no head at all), and crept forward to the stable. They left Puzzle (not without a kind word, for no one was angry with him now) just behind it, telling him not to move till someone came to fetch him, and took up their position at one end of the stable.

The bonfire had not been lit for long and was just beginning to blaze up. It was only a few feet away from them, and the great crowd of Narnian creatures were on the other side of it, so that Tirian could not at first see them very well, though of course he saw dozens of eyes shining with the reflection of the fire, as you've seen a rabbit's or cat's eyes in the headlights of a car. And just as Tirian took his place, the gong stopped beating and from somewhere on his left three figures appeared. One was Rishda Tarkaan the Calormene Captain. The second was the Ape. He was holding on to the Tarkaan's hand with one paw and kept whimpering and muttering, "Not so fast, don't go so fast, I'm not *at all* well. Oh, my poor head! These midnight meetings are getting too much for me. Apes aren't meant to be up at night: it's not as if I was a rat or a bat – oh, my poor head."

On the other side of the Ape, walking very soft and stately, with his tail straight up in the air, came Ginger the Cat. They were heading for the bonfire and were so close to Tirian that they would have seen him at once if they had looked in the right direction. Fortunately they did not. But Tirian heard Rishda say to Ginger in a low voice:

"Now, Cat, to thy post. See thou play the part well."

"Miaow, miaow. Count on me!" said Ginger. Then he stepped away beyond the bonfire and sat down in the front row of the assembled Beasts: in the audience, as you might say.

For really, as it happened, the whole thing was rather like a theatre. The crowd of Narnians were like the people in the seats; the little grassy place just in front of the stable, where the bonfire burned and the Ape and the Captain stood to talk to the crowd, was like the stage; the stable itself was like the scenery at the back of the stage; and Tirian and his friends were like people peering round from behind the scenery. It was a splendid position. If any of them stepped forward into the full firelight, all eyes would be fixed on him at once: on the other hand, so long as they stood still in the shadow of the end wall of the stable, it was a hundred to one against their being noticed.

Rishda Tarkaan dragged the Ape up close to the fire. The pair of them turned to face the crowd, and this of course meant that their backs were towards Tirian and his friends.

"Now, Monkey," said Rishda Tarkaan in a low voice. "Say the words that wiser heads have put into thy mouth. And hold up thy head." As he spoke he gave the Ape a little prod or kick from behind with the point of his toe.

"Do leave me alone," muttered Shift. But he sat up straighter and began, in a louder voice – "Now listen, all of you. A terrible thing has happened. A wicked thing. The wickedest thing that ever was done in Narnia. And Aslan—"

"Tashlan, fool," whispered Rishda Tarkaan.

"Tashlan, I mean, of course," said the Ape, "is very angry about it."

There was a terrible silence while the Beasts waited to hear what new trouble was in store for them. The little party by the end wall of the stable also held their breath. What on earth was coming now?

"Yes," said the Ape. "At this very moment, when the Terrible One himself is among us — there in the stable just behind me — one wicked Beast has chosen to do what you'd think no one would dare to do even if he were a thousand miles away. It has dressed itself up in a lion-skin and is wandering about in these very woods pretending to be Aslan."

Jill wondered for a moment if the Ape had gone mad. Was he going to tell the whole truth? A roar of horror and rage went up from the Beasts. "Grrr!" came the growls. "Who is he? Where is he? Just let me get my teeth into him!"

"It was seen last night," screamed the Ape, "but it got away. It's a donkey! A common, miserable Ass! If any of you see that Ass——"

"Grrr!" growled the Beasts. "We will, we will. He'd better keep out of *our* way."

Jill looked at the King: his mouth was open and his face was full of horror. And then she understood the devilish cunning of the enemies' plan. By mixing a little truth with it they had made their lie far stronger. What was the good, now, of telling the Beasts that an ass had been dressed up as a lion to deceive them? The Ape would only say, "That's just what I've said." What was the good of showing them Puzzle in his lion-skin? They would only tear him in pieces.

"That's taken the wind out of our sails," whispered Eustace.

"The ground is taken from under our feet," said Tirian.

"Cursed, cursed cleverness!" said Poggin. "I'll be sworn that this new lie is of Ginger's making."

CHAPTER TEN

WHO WILL GO INTO THE STABLE?

Jill felt something tickling her ear. It was Jewel the Unicorn, whispering to her with the wide whisper of a horse's mouth. As soon as she heard what he was saying she nodded and tiptoed back to where Puzzle was standing. Quickly and quietly she cut the last cords that bound the lion-skin to him. It wouldn't do for him to be caught with *that* on, after what the Ape had said! She would like to have hidden the skin somewhere very far away, but it was too heavy. The best she could do was to kick it in among the thickest bushes. Then she made signs to Puzzle to follow her and they both joined the others.

The Ape was speaking again.

"And after a horrid thing like that, Aslan – Tashlan – is angrier than ever. He says he's been a great deal too good to you, coming out every night to be looked at, see! Well, he's not coming out any more."

Howls and mewings and squeals and grunts were the Animals' answer to this, but suddenly a quite different voice broke in with a loud laugh.

"Hark what the monkey says," it shouted. "We know why he isn't going to bring his precious Aslan out. I'll tell you why: because he hasn't got him. He never had anything except an old donkey with a lion-skin on its back. Now he's lost *that* and he doesn't know what to do."

Tirian could not see the faces on the other side of the fire very well but he guessed this was Griffle the Chief Dwarf. And he was quite certain of it when, a second later, all the Dwarfs' voices joined in, singing: "Don't know what to do! Don't know what to do! Don't know what to do-o-o!"

"Silence!" thundered Rishda Tarkaan. "Silence, children of mud! Listen to me, you other Narnians, lest I give command to my warriors to fall upon you with the edge of the sword. The Lord Shift has already told you of that wicked ass. Do you think, because of him that there is no *real* Tashlan in the Stable? Do you? Beware, beware!"

"No, no," shouted most of the crowd. But the Dwarfs said, "That's right, Darkie, you've got it. Come on, Monkey, show us what's in the Stable, seeing is believing."

When next there was a moment's quiet the Ape said: "You Dwarfs think you're very clever, don't you? But not so fast. I never said you couldn't see Tashlan. Anyone who likes can see him."

The whole assembly became silent. Then, after nearly a minute, the Bear began in a slow, puzzled voice:

"I don't quite understand all this," it grumbled, "I thought you said—"

"*You* thought!" repeated the Ape. "As if anyone could call what goes on in your head *thinking*. Listen, you others. Anyone can see Tashlan. But he's not coming out. You have to go in and see *him*."

"Oh, thank you, thank you, thank you," said dozens of voices. "That's what we wanted! We can go in and see him face to face. And now he'll be kind and it will all be as it used to be." And the Birds chattered, and the dogs barked excitedly. Then suddenly, there was a great stirring and a noise of creatures rising to their feet, and in a second the whole lot of them would have been rushing forward and trying to crowd into the Stable door all together.

But the Ape shouted: "Get back! Quiet! Not so fast."

The Beasts stopped, many of them with one paw in the air, many with tails wagging, and all of them with heads on one side.

"I thought you said," began the Bear, but Shift interrupted.

"Anyone can go in," he said. "But one at a time. Who'll go first? He didn't *say* he was feeling very kind. He's been licking his lips a lot since he swallowed up the wicked King the other night. He's been growling a good deal this morning. I wouldn't much like to go into that Stable myself tonight. But just as you please. Who'd like to go in first? Don't blame me if he swallows you whole or blasts you into a cinder with the mere terror of his eyes. That's your affair. Now then! Who's first? What about one of you Dwarfs?"

"Dilly, dilly, come and be killed!" sneered Griffle. "How do we know what you've got in there?"

"Ho-ho!" cried the Ape. "So you're beginning to think there's *something* there, eh? Well, all you Beasts were making noise enough a minute ago. What's struck you all dumb? Who's going in first?"

But the Beasts all stood looking at one another and began backing away from the Stable. Very few tails were wagging now. The Ape waddled to and fro jeering at them. "Ho-ho-ho!" he chuckled. "I thought you were all so eager to see Tashlan face to face! Changed your mind, eh?"

Tirian bent his head to hear something that Jill was trying to whisper in his ear.

"What do you think is really inside the Stable?" she said.

"Who knows?" said Tirian. "Two Calormenes with drawn swords, as likely as not, one on each side of the door."

"You don't think," said Jill, "it might be... you know... that horrid thing we saw?"

"Tash himself?" whispered Tirian. "There's no knowing. But courage, child: we are all between the paws of the true Aslan."

Then a most surprising thing happened. Ginger the Cat said in a cool, clear voice, not at all as if he was excited, "I'll go in, if you like."

Every creature turned and fixed its eyes on the Cat. "Mark their subtleties, sire," said Poggin to the King. "This cursed cat is in the plot, in the very centre of it. Whatever is in the Stable will not hurt him, I'll be bound. Then Ginger will come out again and say that he has seen some wonder."

But Tirian had no time to answer him. The Ape was calling the Cat to come forward.

"Ho-ho!" said the Ape. "So you, a pert Puss, would look upon Him face to face. Come on, then! I'll open the door for you. Don't blame me if He scares the whiskers off your face. That's your affair."

And the Cat got up and came out of its place in the crowd, walking primly and daintily, with its tail in the air, not one hair on its sleek coat out of place. It came on till it had passed the fire and was so close that Tirian, from where he stood with his shoulder against the end-wall of the stable, could look right into its face. Its big green eyes never blinked. ("Cool as a cucumber," muttered Eustace. "*It* knows it has nothing to fear.")

The Ape, chuckling and making faces, shuffled across beside the Cat: put up his paw: drew the bolt and opened the door. Tirian thought he could hear the Cat purring as it walked into the dark doorway.

"Aii-aii-aouwee!—" The most horrible caterwaul you ever heard made everyone jump. You have been wakened yourself by cats quarrelling or making love on the roof in the middle of the night: you know the sound.

This was worse. The Ape was knocked head over heels by Ginger coming back out of the Stable at top speed. If you had not known he was a cat, you might have thought he was a ginger-coloured streak of lightning. He shot across the open grass, back into the crowd. No one wants to meet a cat in that state. You could see animals getting out of his way to left and right. He dashed up a tree, whisked around, and hung head downwards. His tail was bristled out till it was nearly as thick as his whole body: his eyes were like saucers of green fire: along his back every single hair stood on end.

"I'd give my beard," whispered Poggin, "to know whether that brute is only acting or whether it has really found something in there that frightened it!"

"Peace, friend," said Tirian, for the Captain and the Ape were also whispering and he wanted to hear what they said. He did not succeed, except that he heard the Ape once more whimpering "My head, my head," but he got the idea that those two were almost as puzzled by the cat's behaviour as himself.

"Now, Ginger," said the Captain. "Enough of that noise. Tell them what thou hast seen."

"Aii — Aii — Aaow — Awah," screamed the Cat.

"Art thou not called a *Talking* Beast?" said the Captain. "Then hold thy devilish noise and talk."

What followed was rather horrible. Tirian felt quite certain (and so did the others) that the Cat was trying to say something: but nothing came out of its mouth except the ordinary, ugly cat-noises you might hear from any angry or frightened old Tom in a backyard in England. And the longer he caterwauled the less like a Talking Beast he looked. Uneasy whimperings and little sharp squeals broke out from among the other Animals.

"Look, look!" said the voice of the Bear. "It can't talk. It has forgotten how to talk! It has gone back to being a dumb beast. Look at its face."

Everyone saw that it was true. And then the greatest terror of all fell upon those Narnians. For every one of them had been taught — when it was only a chick or a puppy or a cub — how Aslan at the beginning of the world had turned the beasts of Narnia into Talking Beasts and warned them that if they weren't good they might one day be turned back again and be like the poor witless animals one meets in other countries. "And now it is coming upon us," they moaned.

"Mercy! Mercy!" wailed the Beasts. "Spare us, Lord Shift, stand between us and Aslan, you must always go in and speak to him for us. We daren't, we daren't."

Ginger disappeared further up into the tree. No one ever saw him again.

Tirian stood with his hand on his sword-hilt and his head bowed. He was dazed with the horrors of that night. Sometimes he thought it would be best to draw his sword at once and rush upon the Calormenes: then the next moment he thought it would be better to wait and see what new turn affairs might take. And now a new turn came.

"My Father," came a clear, ringing voice from the left of the crowd. Tirian knew at once that it was one of the Calormenes speaking, for in the Tisroc's army the common soldiers call the officers "My Master" but the officers call their senior officers "My Father". Jill and Eustace didn't know this but, after looking this way and that, they saw the speaker, for of course people at the sides of the crowd were easier to see than people in the middle where the glare of the fire made all beyond it look rather black. He was young and tall and slender, and even rather beautiful in the dark, haughty, Calormene way.

"My Father," he said to the Captain, "I also desire to go in."

"Peace, Emeth," said the Captain. "Who called thee to counsel? Does it become a boy to speak?"

"My Father," said Emeth. "Truly I am younger than thou, yet I also am of the blood of the Tarkaans even as thou art, and I also am the servant of Tash. Therefore… "

"Silence," said Rishda Tarkaan. "Am not I thy Captain? Thou hast nothing to do with this Stable. It is for the Narnians."

"Nay, my Father," answered Emeth. "Thou hast said that their Aslan and our Tash are all one. And if that is the truth, then Tash himself is in yonder. And how then sayest thou that I have nothing to do with Him? For gladly would I die a thousand deaths if I might look once on the face of Tash."

"Thou art a fool and understandest nothing," said Rishda Tarkaan. "These be high matters."

Emeth's face grew sterner. "Is it then not true that Tash and Aslan are all one?" he asked. "Has the Ape lied to us?"

"Of course they're all one," said the Ape.

"Swear it, Ape," said Emeth.

"Oh dear!" whimpered Shift, "I wish you'd all stop bothering me. My head does ache. Yes, yes, I swear it."

"Then, my Father," said Emeth, "I am utterly determined to go in."

"Fool," began Rishda Tarkaan, but at once the Dwarfs began shouting: "Come along, Darkie. Why don't you let him in? Why do you let Narnians in and keep your own people out? What have you got in there that you don't want your own men to meet?"

Tirian and his friends could only see the back of Rishda Tarkaan, so they never knew what his face looked like as he shrugged his shoulders and said, "Bear witness all that I am guiltless of this young fool's blood. Get thee in, rash boy, and make haste."

Then, just as Ginger had done, Emeth came walking forward into the open strip of grass between the bonfire and the Stable. His eyes were shining, his face very solemn, his hand was on his sword-hilt, and he carried his head high. Jill felt like crying when she looked at his face. And Jewel whispered in the King's ear, "By the Lion's Mane, I almost love this young warrior, Calormene though he be. He is worthy of a better god than Tash."

"I do wish we knew what is really inside there," said Eustace.

Emeth opened the door and went in, into the black mouth of the Stable. He closed the door behind him. Only a few moments passed — but it seemed longer — before the door opened again. A figure in Calormene armour reeled out, fell on its back, and lay still: the door closed behind it. The Captain leapt towards it and bent down to stare at its face. He gave a start of surprise. Then he recovered himself and turned to the crowd, crying out:

"The rash boy has had his will. He has looked on Tash and is dead. Take warning, all of you."

"We will, we will," said the poor Beasts. But Tirian and his friends stared first at the dead Calormene and then at one another. For they, being so close, could see what the crowd, being further off and beyond the fire, could not see: this dead man was not Emeth. He was quite different, an older man, thicker and not so tall, with a big beard.

"Ho-ho-ho," chuckled the Ape. "Any more? Anyone else want to go in? Well, as you're all shy, I'll choose the next. You, you Boar! On you come. Drive him up, Calormenes. He *shall* see Tashlan face to face."

"O-o-omph," grunted the Boar, rising heavily to its feet. "Come on, then. Try my tusks."

When Tirian saw that brave Beast getting ready to fight for its life — and Calormene soldiers beginning to close in on it with their drawn scimitars — and no one going to its help — something seemed to burst inside him. He no longer cared if this was the best moment to interfere or not.

"Swords out," he whispered to the others. "Arrow on string. Follow."

Next moment the astonished Narnians saw seven figures leap forth in front of the Stable, four of them in shining mail. The King's sword flashed in the firelight as he waved it above his head and cried in a great voice:

"Here stand I, Tirian of Narnia, in Aslan's name, to prove with my body that Tash is a foul fiend, the Ape a manifold traitor, and these Calormenes worthy of death. To my side, all true Narnians. Would you wait till your new masters have killed you all one by one?"

CHAPTER ELEVEN

THE PACE QUICKENS

Quick as lightning, Rishda Tarkaan leapt back out of reach of the King's sword. He was no coward, and would have fought single-handed against Tirian and the Dwarf if need be. But he could not take on the Eagle and the Unicorn as well. He knew how Eagles can fly into your face and peck at your eyes and blind you with their wings. And he had heard from his father (who had met Narnians in battle) that no man, except with arrows, or a long spear, can match a Unicorn, for it rears on its hind legs as it falls upon you and then you have its hoofs and its horn and its teeth to deal with all at once. So he rushed into the crowd and stood calling out:

"To me, to me, warriors of the Tisroc, may-he-live-forever. To me, all loyal Narnians, lest the wrath of Tashlan fall upon you!"

While this was happening two other things happened as well. The Ape had not realized his danger as quickly as the Tarkaan. For a second or so he remained squatting beside the fire staring at the newcomers. Then Tirian rushed upon the wretched creature, picked it up by the scruff of the neck, and dashed back to the Stable shouting, "Open the door!" Poggin opened it. "Go and drink your own medicine, Shift!" said Tirian and hurled the Ape through into the darkness. But as the Dwarf banged the door shut again, a blinding greenish-blue light shone out from the inside of the Stable, the earth shook, and there was a strange noise – a clucking and screaming as if it was the hoarse voice of some monstrous bird.

The Beasts moaned and howled and called out "Tashlan! Hide us from him!" and many fell down, and many hid their faces in their wings or paws. No one except Farsight the Eagle, who has the best eyes of all living things, noticed the face of Rishda Tarkaan at that moment. And from what Farsight saw there he knew at once that Rishda was just as surprised, and nearly as frightened, as everyone else.

"There goes one," thought Farsight, "who has called on gods he does not believe in. How will it be with him if they have really come?"

The third thing – which also happened at the same moment – was the only really beautiful thing that night. Every single Talking Dog in the whole meeting (there were fifteen of them) came bounding and barking joyously to the King's side. They were mostly great big dogs with thick shoulders and heavy jaws. Their coming was like the breaking of a great wave on the sea-beach: it nearly knocked you down. For though they were Talking Dogs they were just as doggy as they could be: and they all stood up and put their front paws on the shoulders of the humans and licked their faces, all saying at once: "Welcome! Welcome! We'll help, we'll help, help, help. Show us how to help, show us how, how. How-how-how?"

It was so lovely that it made you want to cry. This, at last, was the sort of thing they had been hoping for. And when, a moment later, several little animals (mice and moles and a squirrel or so) came pattering up, squealing with joy, and saying "See, see. We're here," and when, after that, the Bear and the Boar came too, Eustace began to feel that perhaps, after all, everything might be going to come right. But Tirian gazed round and saw how very few of the animals had moved.

"To me! To me!" he called. "Have you all turned cowards since I was your King?"

"We daren't," whimpered dozens of voices. "Tashlan would be angry. Shield us from Tashlan."

"Where are all the Talking Horses?" said Tirian to the Boar.

"We've seen, we've seen," squealed the Mice. "The Ape has made them work. They're all tied – down at the bottom of the hill."

"Then all you little ones," said Tirian, "you nibblers and gnawers and nutcrackers, away with you as fast as you can scamper and see if the Horses are on our side. And if they are, get your teeth into the ropes and gnaw till the Horses are free and bring them hither."

"With a good will, Sire," came the small voices, and with a whisk of tails those sharp-eyed and sharp-toothed folk were off. Tirian smiled for mere love as he saw them go. But it was already time to be thinking of other things. Rishda Tarkaan was giving his orders.

"Forward," he said. "Take all of them alive if you can and hurl them into the Stable, or drive them into it. When they are all in we will put fire to it and make them an offering to the great god Tash."

"Ha!" said Farsight to himself. "So that is how he hopes to win Tash's pardon for his unbelief."

The enemy line – about half of Rishda's force – was now moving forward, and Tirian had barely time to give his orders.

"Out on the left, Jill, and try to shoot all you may before they reach us. Boar and Bear next to her. Poggin on my left, Eustace on my right. Hold the right wing, Jewel. Stand by him, Puzzle, and use your hoofs. Hover and strike, Farsight. You Dogs, just behind us. Go in among them after the sword-play has begun. Aslan to our aid!"

Eustace stood with his heart beating terribly, hoping and hoping that he would be brave. He had never seen anything (though he had seen both a dragon and a sea-serpent) that made his blood run so cold as that line of dark-faced bright-eyed men. There were fifteen Calormenes, a Talking Bull of Narnia, Slinkey the Fox, and Wraggle the Satyr. Then he heard twang-and-zipp on his left, and one Calormene fell: then twang-and-zipp again and the Satyr was down. "Oh, well done, daughter!" came Tirian's voice; and then the enemy were upon them.

Eustace could never remember what happened in the next two minutes. It was all like a dream (the sort you have when your temperature is over 100°) until he heard Rishda Tarkaan's voice calling out from the distance:

"Retire. Back hither and re-form."

Then Eustace came to his senses and saw the Calormenes scampering back to their friends. But not all of them. Two lay dead, pierced by Jewel's horn, one by Tirian's sword. The Fox lay dead at his own feet, and he wondered if it was he who had killed it. The Bull also was down, shot through the eye by an arrow from Jill and gashed in his side by the Boar's tusk. But the Narnian side had its losses too. Three dogs were killed and a fourth was hobbling behind the line on three legs and whimpering. The Bear lay on the ground, moving feebly. Then it mumbled in its throaty voice, bewildered to the last, "I – I don't – understand," laid its big head down on the grass as quietly as a child going to sleep, and never moved again.

In fact, the first attack had failed. Eustace didn't seem able to be glad about it: he was so terribly thirsty and his arm ached so.

As the defeated Calormenes went back to their commander, the Dwarfs began jeering at them.

"Had enough, Darkies?" they yelled. "Don't you like it? Why doesn't your great Tarkaan go and fight himself instead of sending you to be killed? Poor Darkies!"

"Dwarfs," cried Tirian. "Come here and use your swords, not your tongues. There is still time. Dwarfs of Narnia! You can fight well, I know. Come back to your allegiance."

"Yah!" sneered the Dwarfs. "Not likely. You're just as big humbugs as the other lot. We don't want any Kings. The Dwarfs are for the Dwarfs. Boo!"

Then the Drum began: not a Dwarf drum this time, but a big bull's hide Calormene drum. The children from the very first hated the sound. *Boom — boom — ba-ba-boom* it went. But they would have hated it far worse if they had known what it meant. Tirian did. It meant that there were other Calormene troops somewhere near and that Rishda Tarkaan was calling them to his aid. Tirian and Jewel looked at one another sadly. They had just begun to hope that they might win that night: but it would be all over with them if new enemies appeared.

Tirian gazed despairingly round. Several Narnians were standing with the Calormenes, whether through treachery or in honest fear of "Tashlan". Others were sitting still, staring, not likely to join either side. But there were fewer animals now: the crowd was much smaller. Clearly, several of them had just crept quietly away during the fighting.

Boom — boom — ba-ba-boom went the horrible drum. Then another sound began to mix with it. "Listen!" said Jewel: and then, "Look!" said Farsight. A moment later there was no doubt what it was. With a thunder of hoofs, with tossing heads, widened nostrils, and waving manes, over a score of Talking Horses of Narnia came charging up the hill. The gnawers and nibblers had done their work.

Poggin the Dwarf and the children opened their mouths to cheer but that cheer never came. Suddenly the air was full of the sound of twanging bow-strings and hissing arrows. It was the Dwarfs who were shooting and — for a moment Jill could hardly believe her eyes — they were shooting the Horses. Dwarfs are deadly archers. Horse after horse rolled over. Not one of those noble Beasts ever reached the King.

"Little *swine*," shrieked Eustace, dancing in his rage. "Dirty, filthy, treacherous little brutes."

Even Jewel said, "Shall I run after those Dwarfs, Sire, and spit ten of them on my horn at each plunge?"

But Tirian with his face as stern as stone, said, "Stand fast, Jewel. If you must weep, sweetheart," (this was to Jill), "turn your face aside and see you wet not your bow-string. And peace, Eustace. Do not scold, like a kitchen-girl. No warrior scolds. Courteous words or else hard knocks are his only language."

But the Dwarfs jeered back at Eustace. "That was a surprise for you, little boy, eh? Thought we were on your side, did you? No fear. We don't want any Talking Horses. We don't want you to win any more than the other gang. You can't take *us* in. The Dwarfs are for the Dwarfs."

Rishda Tarkaan was still talking to his men, doubtless making arrangements for the next attack and probably wishing he had sent his whole force into the first. The drum boomed on. Then, to their horror, Tirian and his friends heard, far fainter as if from a long way off, an answering drum. Another body of Calormenes had heard Rishda's signal and were coming to support him. You would not have known from Tirian's face that he had now given up all hope.

"Listen," he whispered in a matter-of-fact voice, "we must attack now, before yonder miscreants are strengthened by their friends."

"Bethink you, Sire," said Poggin, "that here we have the good wooden wall of the Stable at our backs. If we advance, shall we not be encircled and get sword-points between our shoulders?"

"I would say as you do, Dwarf," said Tirian, "were it not their very plan to force us into the Stable. The further we are from its deadly door, the better."

"The King is right," said Farsight. "Away from this accursed Stable, and whatever goblin lives inside it, at all costs."

"Yes, do let's," said Eustace. "I'm coming to hate the very sight of it."

"Good," said Tirian. "Now look yonder to our left. You see a great rock that gleams white like marble in the firelight. First we will fall upon those Calormenes. You, maiden, shall move out on our left and shoot as fast as ever you may into their ranks; and you, Eagle, fly at their faces from the right. Meanwhile we others will be charging them. When we are so close, Jill, that you can no longer shoot at them for fear of striking us, go back to the white rock and wait. You others, keep your ears wide even in the fighting. We must put them to flight in a few minutes or else not at all, for we are fewer than they. As soon as I call *Back*, then rush to join Jill at the white rock, where we shall have protection behind us and can breathe awhile. Now, be off, Jill."

Feeling terribly alone, Jill ran out about twenty feet, put her right leg back and her left leg forward, and set an arrow to her string. She wished her hands were not shaking so.

"That's a rotten shot!" she said as her first arrow sped towards the enemy and flew over their heads. But she had another on the string next moment: she knew that speed was what mattered. She saw something big and black darting into the faces of the Calormenes. That was Farsight. First one man, and then another, dropped his sword and put up both his hands to defend his eyes. Then one of her own arrows hit a man, and another hit a Narnian wolf, who had, it seemed, joined the enemy.

But she had been shooting only for a few seconds when she had to stop. With a flash of swords and of the Boar's tusks and Jewel's horn, and with deep baying from the dogs, Tirian and his party were rushing on their enemies, like men in a hundred yards' race. Jill was astonished to see how unprepared the Calormenes seemed to be. She did not realize that this was the result of her work and the Eagle's. Very few troops can keep on looking steadily to the front if they are getting arrows in their faces from one side and being pecked by an eagle on the other.

"Oh, well done. *Well* done!" shouted Jill. The King's party were cutting their way right into the enemy. The Unicorn was tossing men as you'd toss hay on a fork. Even Eustace seemed to Jill (who after all didn't know very much about swordsmanship) to be fighting brilliantly. The Dogs were at the Calormenes' throats. It was going to work! It was victory at last—

With a horrible, cold shock, Jill noticed a strange thing. Though Calormenes were falling at each Narnian sword-stroke, they never seemed to get any fewer. In fact, there were actually more of them now than when the fight began. There were more every second. They were running up from every side. They were new Calormenes. These new ones had spears. There was such a crowd of them that she could hardly see her own friends.

Then she heard Tirian's voice crying:

"Back! To the rock!"

The enemy had been reinforced. The drum had done its work.

CHAPTER TWELVE

THROUGH THE STABLE DOOR

Jill ought to have been back at the white rock already but she had quite forgotten that part of her orders in the excitement of watching the fight. Now she remembered. She turned at once and ran to it, and arrived there barely a second before the others. It thus happened that all of them, for a moment, had their backs to the enemy. They all wheeled round the moment they had reached it. A terrible sight met their eyes.

A Calormene was running towards the Stable door carrying something that kicked and struggled. As he came between them and the fire they could see clearly both the shape of the man and the shape of what he carried. It was Eustace.

Tirian and the Unicorn rushed out to rescue him. But the Calormene was now far nearer to the door then they. Before they had covered half the distance he had flung Eustace in and shut the door on him. Half a dozen more Calormenes had run up behind him. They formed a line on the open space before the Stable. There was no getting at it now.

Even then Jill remembered to keep her face turned aside, well away from her bow. "Even if I can't stop blubbing, I *won't* get my string wet," she said.

"'Ware arrows," said Poggin suddenly.

Everyone ducked and pulled his helmet well over his nose. The Dogs crouched behind. But though a few arrows came their way it soon became clear that they were not being shot at. Griffle and his Dwarfs were at their archery again. This time they were coolly shooting at the Calormenes.

"Keep it up, boys!" came Griffle's voice. "All together. Carefully. We don't want Darkies any more than we want Monkeys – or Lions – or Kings. The Dwarfs are for the Dwarfs."

Whatever else you may say about Dwarfs, no one can say they aren't brave. They could easily have got away to some safe place. They preferred to stay and kill as many of both sides as they could, except when both sides were kind enough to save them trouble by killing one another. They wanted Narnia for their own.

What perhaps they had not taken into account was that the Calormenes were mail-clad and the Horses had had no protection. Also the Calormenes had a leader. Rishda Tarkaan's voice cried out:

"Thirty of you keep watch on those fools by the white rock. The rest, after me, that we may teach these Sons of Earth a lesson."

Tirian and his friends, still panting from their fight and thankful for a few minutes' rest, stood and looked on while the Tarkaan led his men against the Dwarfs. It was a strange scene by now. The fire had sunk lower: the light it gave was now less and of a darker red. As far as one could see, the whole place of assembly was now empty except for the Dwarfs and the Calormenes. In that light one couldn't make out much of what was happening. It sounded as if the Dwarfs were putting up a good fight. Tirian could hear Griffle using dreadful language, and every now and then the Tarkaan calling, "Take all you can alive! Take them alive!"

Whatever that fight may have been like, it did not last long. The noise of it died away. Then Jill saw the Tarkaan coming back to the stable: eleven men followed him, dragging eleven bound Dwarfs. (Whether the others had all been killed, or whether some of them had got away, was never known.)

"Throw them into the shrine of Tash," said Rishda Tarkaan.

And when the eleven Dwarfs, one after the other, had been flung or kicked into that dark doorway and the door had been shut again, he bowed low to the Stable and said:

"These also are for thy burnt offering, Lord Tash."

And all the Calormenes banged the flats of their swords on their shields and shouted, "Tash! Tash! The great god Tash! Inexorable Tash!" (There was no nonsense about "Tashlan" now.)

The little party by the white rock watched these doings and whispered to one another. They had found a trickle of water coming down the rock and all had drunk eagerly — Jill and Poggin and the King in their hands, while the four-footed ones lapped from the little pool which it had made at the foot of the stone. Such was their thirst that it seemed the most delicious drink they had ever had in their lives, and while they were drinking they were perfectly happy and could not think of anything else.

"I feel in my bones," said Poggin, "that we shall all, one by one, pass through that dark door before morning. I can think of a hundred deaths I would rather have died."

"It is indeed a grim door," said Tirian. "It is more like a mouth."

"Oh, can't we do *anything* to stop it?" said Jill in a shaken voice.

"Nay, fair friend," said Jewel, nosing her gently. "It may be for us the door to Aslan's country and we shall sup at his table tonight."

Rishda Tarkaan turned his back on the Stable and walked slowly to a place in front of the white rock.

"Hearken," he said. "If the Boar and the Dogs and the Unicorn will come over to me and put themselves in my mercy, their lives shall be spared. The Boar shall go to a cage in the Tisroc's garden, the Dogs to the Tisroc's kennels, and the Unicorn, when I have sawn his horn off, shall draw a cart. But the Eagle, the children, and he who was the King shall be offered to Tash this night."

The only answer was growls.

"Get on, warriors," said the Tarkaan. "Kill the beasts, but take the two-legged ones alive."

And then the last battle of the last King of Narnia began.

What made it hopeless, even apart from the numbers of the enemy, was the spears. The Calormenes who had been with the Ape almost from the beginning had had no spears: that was because they had come into Narnia by ones and twos, pretending to be peaceful merchants, and of course they had carried no spears for a spear is not a thing you can hide. The new ones must have come in later, after the Ape was already strong and they could march openly. The spears made all the difference. With a long spear you can kill a boar before you are in reach of his tusks and a unicorn before you are in reach of his horn; if you are very quick and keep your head. And now the levelled spears were closing in on Tirian and his last friends. Next minute they were all fighting for their lives.

In a way it wasn't quite so bad as you might think. When you are using every muscle to the full – ducking under a spear-point here, leaping over it there, lunging forward, drawing back, wheeling round – you haven't much time to feel either frightened or sad.

Tirian knew he could do nothing for the others now; they were all doomed together. He vaguely saw the Boar go down on one side of him, and Jewel fighting furiously on the other. Out of the corner of one eye he saw, but only just saw, a big Calormene pulling Jill away somewhere by her hair. But he hardly thought about any of these things. His only thought now was to sell his life as dearly as he could. The worst of it was that he couldn't keep to the position in which he had started, under the white rock. A man who is fighting a dozen enemies at once must take his chances wherever he can; must dart in wherever he sees an enemy's breast or neck unguarded. In a very few strokes this may get you quite a distance from the spot where you began. Tirian soon found that he was getting further and further to the right, nearer to the Stable. He had a vague idea in his mind that there was some good reason for keeping away from it. But he couldn't now remember what the reason was. And anyway, he couldn't help it.

All at once everything came quite clear. He found he was fighting the Tarkaan himself. The bonfire (what was left of it) was straight in front. He was in fact fighting in the very doorway of the Stable, for it had been opened and two Calormenes were holding the door, ready to slam it shut the moment he was inside. He remembered everything now, and he realized that the enemy had been edging him to the Stable on purpose ever since the fight began. And while he was thinking this he was still fighting the Tarkaan as hard as he could.

A new idea came into Tirian's head. He dropped his sword, darted forward, in under the sweep of the Tarkaan's scimitar, seized his enemy by the belt with both hands, and jumped back into the Stable, shouting:

"Come in and meet Tash yourself!"

There was a deafening noise. As when the Ape had been flung in, the earth shook and there was a blinding light.

The Calormene soldiers outside screamed, "Tash, Tash!" and banged the door. If Tash wanted their own Captain, Tash must have him. They, at any rate, did not want to meet Tash.

For a moment or two Tirian did not know where he was or even who he was. Then he steadied himself, blinked, and looked around. It was not dark inside the Stable, as he had expected. He was in strong light: that was why he was blinking.

He turned to look at Rishda Tarkaan, but Rishda was not looking at him. Rishda gave a great wail and pointed; then he put his hands before his face and fell flat, face downwards, on the ground. Tirian looked in the direction where the Tarkaan had pointed. And then he understood.

A terrible figure was coming towards them. It was far smaller than the shape they had seen from the Tower, though still much bigger than a man, and it was the same. It had a vulture's head and four arms. Its beak was open and its eyes blazed. A croaking voice came from its beak.

"Thou hast called me into Narnia, Rishda Tarkaan. Here I am. What hast thou to say?"

But the Tarkaan neither lifted his face from the ground nor said a word. He was shaking like a man with a bad hiccup. He was brave enough in battle: but half his courage had left him earlier that night when he first began to suspect that there might be a real Tash. The rest of it had left him now.

With a sudden jerk − like a hen stooping to pick up a worm − Tash pounced on the miserable Rishda and tucked him under the upper of his two right arms. Then Tash turned his head sidewise to fix Tirian with one of his terrible eyes: for of course, having a bird's head, he couldn't look at you straight.

But immediately, from behind Tash, strong and calm as the summer sea, a voice said:

"Begone, Monster, and take your lawful prey to your own place: in the name of Aslan and Aslan's great Father, the Emperor-over-Sea."

The hideous creature vanished, with the Tarkaan still under its arm. And Tirian turned to see who had spoken. And what he saw then set his heart beating as it had never beaten in any fight.

Seven Kings and Queens stood before him, all with crowns on their heads and all in glittering clothes, but the Kings wore fine mail as well and had their swords drawn in their hands.

Tirian bowed courteously and was about to speak when the youngest of the Queens laughed. He stared hard at her face, and then gasped with amazement, for he knew her. It was Jill: but not Jill as he had last seen her, with her face all dirt and tears and an old drill dress half slipping off one shoulder. Now she looked cool and fresh, as fresh as if she had just come from bathing. And at first he thought she looked older, but then didn't, and he could never make up his mind on that point. And then he saw that the youngest of the Kings was Eustace: but he also was changed as Jill was changed.

Tirian suddenly felt awkward about coming among these people with the blood and dust and sweat of a battle still on him. Next moment he realized that he was not in that state at all. He was fresh and cool and clean, and dressed in such clothes as he would have worn for a great feast at Cair Paravel. (But in Narnia your good clothes were never your uncomfortable ones. They knew how to make things that felt beautiful as well as looking beautiful in Narnia: and there was no such thing as starch or flannel or elastic to be found from one end of the country to the other.)

"Sire," said Jill, coming forward and making a beautiful curtsey, "let me make you known to Peter, the High King over all Kings in Narnia."

Tirian had no need to ask which was the High King, for he remembered his face (though here it was far nobler) from his dream. He stepped forward, sank on one knee and kissed Peter's hand.

"High King," he said. "You are welcome to me."

And the High King raised him and kissed him on both cheeks as a High King should. Then he led him to the eldest of the Queens — but even she was not old, and there were no grey hairs on her head and no wrinkles on her cheek — and said, "Sir, this is that Lady Polly who came into Narnia on the First Day, when Aslan made the trees grow and the Beasts talk."

He brought him next to a man whose golden beard flowed over his breast and whose face was full of wisdom. "And this," he said, "is the Lord

Digory who was with her on that day. And this is my brother, King Edmund: and this my sister, Queen Lucy."

"Sire," said Tirian, when he had greeted all these, "if I have read the chronicles aright, there should be another. Has not your Majesty two sisters? Where is Queen Susan?"

"My sister Susan," answered Peter shortly and gravely, "is no longer a friend of Narnia."

"Yes," said Eustace, "and whenever you've tried to get her to come and talk about Narnia or do anything about Narnia, she says 'What wonderful memories you have! Fancy your still thinking about all those funny games we used to play when we were children.'"

"Oh, Susan!" said Jill. "She's interested in nothing nowadays except nylons and lipstick and invitations. She always was a jolly sight too keen on being grown-up."

"Grown-up, indeed," said the Lady Polly. "I wish she *would* grow up. She wasted all her school time wanting to be the age she is now, and she'll waste all the rest of her life trying to stay that age. Her whole idea is to race on to the silliest time of one's life as quick as she can and then stop there as long as she can."

"Well, don't let's talk about that now," said Peter. "Look! Here are lovely fruit trees. Let us taste them."

And then, for the first time, Tirian looked about him and realized how very queer this adventure was.

CHAPTER THIRTEEN

HOW THE DWARFS REFUSED TO BE TAKEN IN

Tirian had thought – or he would have thought if he had had time to think at all – that they were inside a little thatched stable, about twelve feet long and six feet wide. In reality they stood on grass, the deep blue sky was overhead, and the air which blew gently on their faces was that of a day in early summer.

Not far away from them rose a grove of trees, thickly leaved, but under every leaf there peeped out the gold or faint yellow or purple or glowing red of fruits such as no one has seen in our world. The fruit made Tirian feel that it must be autumn, but there was something in the feel of the air that told him it could not be later than June. They all moved towards the trees.

Everyone raised his hand to pick the fruit he best liked the look of, and then everyone paused for a second. This fruit was so beautiful that each felt, "It can't be meant for me... surely we're not allowed to pluck it."

"It's all right," said Peter. "I know what we're all thinking. But I'm sure, quite sure, we needn't. I've a feeling we've got to the country where everything is allowed."

"Here goes, then!" said Eustace. And they all began to eat.

What was the fruit like? Unfortunately no one can describe a taste. All I can say is that, compared with those fruits, the freshest grapefruit you've ever eaten was dull, and the juiciest orange was dry, and the most melting pear was hard and woody, and the sweetest wild strawberry was sour. And there were no seeds or stones, and no wasps. If you had once eaten that fruit, all the nicest things in this world would taste like medicines after it. But I can't describe it. You can't find out what it is like unless you can get to that country and taste it for yourself.

When they had eaten enough, Eustace said to King Peter, "You haven't yet told us how you got here. You were just going to, when King Tirian turned up."

"There's not much to tell," said Peter. "Edmund and I were standing on the platform and we saw your train coming in. I remember thinking it was taking the bend far too fast. And I remember thinking how funny it was that our people were probably in the same train though Lucy didn't know about it—"

"Your people, High King?" said Tirian.

"I mean my father and mother – Edmund's and Lucy's and mine."

"Why were they?" asked Jill. "You don't mean to say *they* know about Narnia?"

"Oh no, it had nothing to do with Narnia. They were on their way to Bristol. I'd only heard they were going that morning. But Edmund said they'd be bound to be going by that train." (Edmund was the sort of person who knows about railways.)

"And what happened then?" said Jill.

"Well, it's not very easy to describe, is it, Edmund?" said the High King.

"Not very," said Edmund. "It wasn't at all like that other time when we were pulled out of our own world by Magic. There was a frightful roar and something hit me with a bang, but it didn't hurt. And I felt not so much scared as – well, excited. Oh – and this is one queer thing. I'd had a rather sore knee, from a hack at rugger. I noticed it had suddenly gone. And I felt very light. And then – here we were."

"It was much the same for us in the railway carriage," said the Lord Digory, wiping the last traces of the fruit from his golden beard. "Only I think you and I, Polly, chiefly felt that we'd been unstiffened. You youngsters won't understand. But we stopped feeling old."

"Youngsters, indeed!" said Jill. "I don't believe you two really are much older than we are here."

"Well, if we aren't, we have been," said the Lady Polly.

"And what has been happening since you got here?" asked Eustace.

"Well," said Peter, "for a long time (at least I suppose it was a long time) nothing happened. Then the door opened—"

"The door?" said Tirian.

"Yes," said Peter. "The door you came in – or came out – by. Have you forgotten?"

"But where is it?"

"Look," said Peter and pointed.

Tirian looked and saw the queerest and most ridiculous thing you can imagine. Only a few yards away, clear to be seen in the sunlight, there stood up a rough wooden door and, round it, the framework of the doorway: nothing else, no walls, no roof. He walked towards it, bewildered, and the others followed, watching to see what he would do. He walked round to the other side of the door. But it looked just the same from the other side: he was still in the open air, on a summer morning. The door was simply standing up by itself as if it had grown there like a tree.

"Fair Sir," said Tirian to the High King, "this is a great marvel."

"It is the door you came through with that Calormene five minutes ago," said Peter, smiling.

"But did I not come in out of the wood into the Stable? Whereas this seems to be a door leading from nowhere to nowhere."

"It looks like that if you walk *round* it," said Peter. "But put your eye to that place where there is a crack between two of the planks and look *through*."

Tirian put his eye to the hole. At first he could see nothing but blackness. Then, as his eyes grew used to it, he saw the dull red glow of a bonfire that was nearly going out, and above that, in a black sky, stars. Then he could see dark figures moving about or standing between him and the fire: he could hear them talking and their voices were like those of Calormenes. So he knew that he was looking out through the Stable door into the darkness of Lantern Waste where he had fought his last battle. The men were discussing whether to go in and look for Rishda Tarkaan (but none of them wanted to do that) or to set fire to the Stable.

He looked round again and could hardly believe his eyes. There was the blue sky overhead, and grassy country spreading as far as he could see in every direction, and his new friends all round him, laughing.

"It seems, then," said Tirian, smiling himself, "that the Stable seen from within and the Stable seen from without are two different places."

"Yes," said the Lord Digory. "Its inside is bigger than its outside."

"Yes," said Queen Lucy. "In our world too, a Stable once had something inside it that was bigger than our whole world."

It was the first time she had spoken, and from the thrill in her voice, Tirian now knew why. She was drinking everything in even more deeply than the others. She had been too happy to speak. He wanted to hear her speak again, so he said:

"Of your courtesy, Madam, tell on. Tell me your whole adventure."

"After the shock and the noise," said Lucy, "we found ourselves here. And we wondered at the door, as you did. Then the door opened for the first time (we saw darkness through the doorway when it did) and there came through a big man with a naked sword. We saw by his arms that he was a Calormene.

"He took his stand beside the door with his sword raised, resting on his shoulder, ready to cut down anyone who came through. We went to him and spoke to him, but we thought he could neither see nor hear us. And he never looked round on the sky and the sunlight and the grass: I think he couldn't see them either. So then we waited a long time. Then we heard the bolt being drawn on the other side of the door. But the man didn't get ready to strike with his sword till he could see who was coming in. So we supposed he had been told to strike some and spare others. But at the very moment when the door opened, all of a sudden Tash was there, on this side of the door; None of us saw where he came from. And through the door there came a big Cat. It gave one look at Tash and ran for its life: just in time, for he pounced at it and the door hit his beak as it was shut. The man could see Tash. He turned very pale and bowed down before the Monster: but it vanished away.

"Then we waited a long time again. At last the door opened for the third time and there came in a young Calormene. I liked him. The sentinel at the door started, and looked very surprised, when he saw him. I think he'd been expecting someone quite different—"

"I see it all now," said Eustace (he had the bad habit of interrupting stories). "The Cat was to go in first and the sentry had orders to do him no harm. Then the Cat was to come out and say he'd seen their beastly Tashlan and *pretend* to be frightened so as to scare the other Animals. But what Shift never guessed was that the real Tash would turn up; so Ginger came out really frightened. And after that, Shift would send in anyone he wanted to get rid of and the sentry would kill them. And—"

"Friend," said Tirian softly, "you hinder the lady in her tale."

"Well," said Lucy, "the sentry was surprised. That gave the other man just time to get on guard. They had a fight. He killed the sentry and flung him outside the door. Then he came walking slowly forward to where we were. He could see us, and everything else. We tried to talk to him but he was rather like a man in a trance. He kept on saying, *Tash, Tash, where is Tash? I go to Tash.* So we gave it up and he went away somewhere – over there. I liked him. And after that... ugh!" Lucy made a face.

"After that," said Edmund, "someone flung a monkey through the door. And Tash was there again. My sister is so tender-hearted she doesn't like to tell you that Tash made one peck and the Monkey was gone!"

"Serve him right!" said Eustace. "All the same, I hope he'll disagree with Tash, too."

"And after that," said Edmund, "came about a dozen Dwarfs: and then Jill, and Eustace, and last of all yourself."

"I hope Tash ate the Dwarfs too," said Eustace. "Little swine."

"No, he didn't," said Lucy. "And don't be horrid. They're still here. In fact you can see them from here. And I've tried and tried to make friends with them but it's no use."

"*Friends* with them!" cried Eustace. "If you knew how those Dwarfs have been behaving!"

"Oh, stop it, Eustace," said Lucy. "Do come and see them. King Tirian, perhaps *you* could do something with them."

"I can feel no great love for Dwarfs today," said Tirian. "Yet at your asking, Lady, I would do a greater thing than this."

Lucy led the way and soon they could all see the Dwarfs. They had a very odd look. They weren't strolling about or enjoying themselves (although the cords with which they had been tied seemed to have vanished) nor were they lying down and having a rest. They were sitting very close together in a little circle facing one another. They never looked round or took any notice of the humans till Lucy and Tirian were almost near enough to touch them. Then the Dwarfs all cocked their heads as if they couldn't see anyone but were listening hard and trying to guess by the sound what was happening.

"Look out!" said one of them in a surly voice. "Mind where you're going. Don't walk into our faces!"

"All right!" said Eustace indignantly. "We're not blind. We've got eyes in our heads."

"They must be darn good ones if you can see in here," said the same Dwarf whose name was Diggle.

"In where?" asked Edmund.

"Why, you bonehead, in *here* of course," said Diggle. "In this pitch-black, poky, smelly little hole of a stable."

"Are you blind?" said Tirian.

"Ain't we all blind in the dark?" said Diggle.

"But it isn't dark, you poor stupid Dwarfs," said Lucy. "Can't you see? Look up! Look round! Can't you see the sky and the trees and the flowers? Can't you see *me*?"

"How in the name of all Humbug can I see what ain't there? And how can I see you any more than you can see me in this pitch darkness?"

"But I *can* see you," said Lucy. "I'll prove I can see you. You've got a pipe in your mouth."

"Anyone that knows the smell of baccy could tell that," said Diggle.

"Oh, the poor things! This is dreadful," said Lucy. Then she had an idea. She stopped and picked some wild violets. "Listen, Dwarf," she said. "Even if your eyes are wrong, perhaps your nose is all right: can you smell *that*?" She leant across and held the fresh, damp flowers to Diggle's ugly nose. But she had to jump back quickly in order to avoid a blow from his hard little fist.

"None of that!" he shouted. "How dare you! What do you mean by shoving a lot of filthy stable-litter in my face? There was a thistle in it too. It's like your sauce! And who are you anyway?"

"Earth-man," said Tirian, "she is the Queen Lucy, sent hither by Aslan out of the deep past. And it is for her sake alone that I, Tirian your lawful King, do not cut all your heads from your shoulders, proved and twice-proved traitors that you are."

"Well, if that doesn't beat everything!" exclaimed Diggle. "How *can* you go on talking all that rot? Your wonderful Lion didn't come and help you, did he? Thought not. And now – even now – when you've been beaten and shoved into this black hole, just the same as the rest of us, you're still at your old game. Starting a new lie! Trying to make us believe we're none of us shut up, and it ain't dark, and heaven knows what."

"There *is* no black hole, save in your own fancy, fool," cried Tirian. "Come *out of* it." And, leaning forward, he caught Diggle by the belt and the hood and swung him right out of the circle of Dwarfs. But the moment Tirian put him down, Diggle darted back to his place among the others, rubbing his nose and howling:

"Ow! Ow! What d'you do that for! Banging my face against the wall. You've nearly broken my nose."

"Oh dear!" said Lucy, "What *are* we to do for them?"

"Let 'em alone," said Eustace: but as he spoke the earth trembled. The sweet air grew suddenly sweeter. A brightness flashed behind them. All turned. Tirian turned last because he was afraid. There stood his heart's desire, huge and real, the golden Lion, Aslan himself, and already the others were kneeling in a circle round his forepaws and burying their hands and faces in his mane as he stooped his great head to touch them with his tongue. Then he fixed his eyes upon Tirian, and Tirian came near, trembling, and flung himself at the Lion's feet, and the Lion kissed him and said, "Well done, last of the Kings of Narnia who stood firm at the darkest hour."

"Aslan," said Lucy through her tears, "could you – will you – do something for these poor Dwarfs?"

"Dearest," said Aslan, "I will show you both what I can, and what I cannot do." He came close to the Dwarfs and gave a low growl: low, but it set all the air shaking. But the Dwarfs said to one another, "Hear that? That's the gang at the other end of the Stable. Trying to frighten us. They do it with a machine of some kind. Don't take any notice. They won't take *us* in again!"

Aslan raised his head and shook his mane. Instantly a glorious feast appeared on the Dwarfs' knees: pies and tongues and pigeons and trifles and ices, and each Dwarf had a goblet of good wine in his right hand. But it wasn't much use. They began eating and drinking greedily enough, but it was clear that they couldn't taste it properly. They thought they were eating and drinking only the sort of things you might find in a Stable. One said he was trying to eat hay and another said he had got a bit of an old turnip and a third said he'd found a raw cabbage leaf. And they raised golden goblets of rich red wine to their lips and said "Ugh! Fancy drinking dirty water out of a trough that a donkey's been at! Never thought we'd come to this."

But very soon every Dwarf began suspecting that every other Dwarf had found something nicer than he had, and they started grabbing and snatching, and went on to quarrelling, till in a few minutes there was a free fight and all the good food was smeared on their faces and clothes or trodden under foot.

But when at last they sat down to nurse their black eyes and their bleeding noses, they all said: "Well, at any rate there's no Humbug here. We haven't let anyone take us in. The Dwarfs are for the Dwarfs."

"You see," said Aslan. "They will not let us help them. They have chosen cunning instead of belief. Their prison is only in their own minds, yet they are in that prison; and so afraid of being taken in that they cannot be taken out. But come, children. I have other work to do."

He went to the door and they all followed him. He raised his head and roared, "Now it is time!" then louder, "Time!"; then so loud that it could have shaken the stars, "TIME". The Door flew open.

CHAPTER FOURTEEN

NIGHT FALLS ON NARNIA

They all stood beside Aslan, on his right side, and looked through the open doorway.

The bonfire had gone out. On the earth all was blackness: in fact you could not have told that you were looking into a wood if you had not seen where the dark shapes of the trees ended and the stars began. But when Aslan had roared yet again, out on their left they saw another black shape. That is, they saw another patch where there were no stars: and the patch rose up higher and higher and became the shape of a man, the hugest of all giants. They all knew Narnia well enough to work out where he must be standing. He must be on the high moorlands that stretch away to the north beyond the River Shribble.

Then Jill and Eustace remembered how once long ago, in the deep caves beneath those moors, they had seen a great giant asleep and been told that his name was Father Time, and that he would wake on the day the world ended.

"Yes," said Aslan, though they had not spoken. "While he lay dreaming his name was Time. Now that he is awake he will have a new one."

Then the great giant raised a horn to his mouth. They could see this by the change of the black shape he made against the stars. After that — quite a bit later, because sound travels so slowly — they heard the sound of the horn: high and terrible, yet of a strange, deadly beauty.

Immediately the sky became full of shooting stars. Even one shooting star is a fine thing to see, but these were dozens, and then scores, and then hundreds, till it was like silver rain: and it went on and on. And when it had gone on for some while, one or two of them began to think that there was another dark shape against the sky as well as the giant's. It was in a different place, right overhead, up in the very roof of the sky as you might call it. "Perhaps it is a cloud," thought Edmund. At any rate, there were no stars there: just blackness. But all around, the downpour of stars went on. And then the starless patch began to grow, spreading further and further out from the centre of the sky. And presently a quarter of the whole sky was black, and then a half, and at last the rain of shooting stars was going on only low down near the horizon.

With a thrill of wonder (and there was some terror in it too) they all suddenly realized what was happening. The spreading blackness was not a cloud at all: it was simply emptiness. The black part of the sky was the part in which there were no stars left. All the stars were falling: Aslan had called them home.

The last few seconds before the rain of stars had quite ended were very exciting. Stars began falling all round them. But stars in that world are not the great flaming globes they are in ours. They are people (Edmund and Lucy had once met one). So now they found showers of glittering people, all with long hair like burning silver and spears like white-hot metal, rushing down to them out of the black air, swifter than falling stones. They made a hissing noise as they landed and burnt the grass. And all these stars glided past them and stood somewhere behind, a little to the right.

This was a great advantage, because otherwise, now that there were no stars in the sky, everything would have been completely dark and you could have seen nothing. As it was, the crowd of stars behind them cast a fierce, white light over their shoulders. They could see mile upon mile of Narnian woods spread out before them, looking as if they were floodlit. Every bush and almost every blade of grass had its black shadow behind it. The edge of every leaf stood out so sharp that you'd think you could cut your finger on it.

On the grass before them lay their own shadows. But the great thing was Aslan's shadow. It streamed away to their left, enormous and very terrible. And all this was under a sky that would now be starless for ever.

The light from behind them (and a little to their right) was so strong that it lit up even the slopes of the Northern Moors. Something was moving there. Enormous animals were crawling and sliding down into Narnia: great dragons and giant lizards and featherless birds with wings like bats' wings. They disappeared into the woods and for a few minutes there was a silence.

Then there came – at first from very far off – sounds of wailing and then, from every direction, a rustling and a pattering and a sound of wings. It came nearer and nearer. Soon one could distinguish the scamper of little feet from the padding of big paws, and the clack-clack of light little hoofs from the thunder of great ones. And then one could see thousands of pairs of eyes gleaming. And at last, out of the shadow of the trees, racing up the hill for dear life, by thousands and by millions, came all kinds of creatures — Talking Beasts, Dwarfs, Satyrs, Fauns, Giants, Calormenes, men from Archenland, Monopods, and strange unearthly things from the remote islands or the unknown Western lands. And all these ran up to the doorway where Aslan stood.

This part of the adventure was the only one which seemed rather like a dream at the time and rather hard to remember properly afterwards. Especially, one couldn't say how long it had taken. Sometimes it seemed to have lasted only a few minutes, but at others it felt as if it might have gone on for years. Obviously, unless either the Door had grown very much larger or the creatures had suddenly grown as small as gnats, a crowd like that couldn't ever have tried to get through it. But no one thought about that sort of thing at the time.

The creatures came rushing on, their eyes brighter and brighter as they drew nearer and nearer to the standing Stars. But as they came right up to Aslan one or other of two things happened to each of them. They all looked straight in his face, I don't think they had any choice about that. And when some looked, the expression of their faces changed terribly — it was fear and hatred: except that, on the faces of Talking Beasts, the fear and hatred lasted only for a fraction of a second. You could see that they suddenly ceased to be *Talking* Beasts. They were just ordinary animals. And all the creatures who looked at Aslan in that way swerved to their right, his left, and disappeared into his huge black shadow, which (as you have heard) streamed away to the left of the doorway. The children never saw them again. I don't know what became of them. But the others looked in the face of Aslan and loved him, though some of them were very frightened at the same time. And all these came in at the Door, in on Aslan's right. There were some queer specimens among them. Eustace even recognized one of those very Dwarfs who had helped to shoot the Horses. But he had not time to wonder about that sort of thing (and anyway it was no business of his) for a great joy put everything else out of his head. Among the happy creatures who now came crowding round Tirian and his friends were all those whom they had thought dead. There was Roonwit the Centaur and Jewel the Unicorn, and the good Boar and the good Bear, and Farsight the Eagle, and the dear Dogs and the Horses, and Poggin the Dwarf.

"Further in and higher up!" cried Roonwit and thundered away in a gallop to the West. And though they did not understand him, the words somehow set them tingling all over. The Boar grunted at them cheerfully. The Bear was just going to mutter that he still didn't understand, when he caught sight of the fruit trees behind them. He waddled to those trees as fast as he could and there, no doubt, found something he understood very well. But the Dogs remained, wagging their tails, and Poggin remained, shaking hands with everyone and grinning all over his honest face. And Jewel leaned his snowy white head over the King's shoulder and the King whispered in Jewel's ear. Then everyone turned his attention again to what could be seen through the Doorway.

The Dragons and Giant Lizards now had Narnia to themselves. They went to and fro tearing up the trees by the roots and crunching them up as if they were sticks of rhubarb. Minute by minute the forests disappeared. The whole country became bare and you could see all sorts of things about its shape – all the little humps and hollows – which you had never noticed before. The grass died. Soon Tirian found that he was looking at a world of bare rock and earth. You could hardly believe that anything had ever lived there. The monsters themselves grew old and lay down and died. Their flesh shrivelled up and the bones appeared: soon they were only huge skeletons that lay here and there on the dead rock, looking as if they had died thousands of years ago. For a long time everything was still.

At last something white – a long, level line of whiteness that gleamed in the light of the standing stars – came moving towards them from the eastern end of the world. A widespread noise broke the silence: first a murmur, then a rumble, then a roar. And now they could see what it was that was coming, and how fast it came. It was a foaming wall of water. The sea was rising. In that treeless world you could see it very well. You could see all the rivers getting wider and the lakes getting larger, and separate lakes joining into one, and valleys turning into new lakes, and hills turning into islands, and then those islands vanishing. And the high moors to their left and the higher mountains to their right crumbled and slipped down with a roar and a splash into the mounting water; and the water came swirling up to the very threshold of the Doorway (but never passed it) so that the foam splashed about Aslan's forefeet. All now was level water from where they stood to where the water met the sky.

And out there it began to grow light. A streak of dreary and disastrous dawn spread along the horizon, and widened and grew brighter, till in the end they hardly noticed the light of the stars who stood behind them. At last the sun came up. When it did, the Lord Digory and the Lady Polly looked at one another and gave a little nod: those two, in a different world, had once seen a dying sun, and so they knew at once that this sun was also dying. It was three times – twenty times – as big as it ought to be, and very dark red. As its rays fell upon the great Time-giant, he turned red too: and in the reflection of that sun the whole waste of shoreless waters looked like blood.

Then the Moon came up, quite in her wrong position, very close to the sun, and she also looked red. And at the sight of her the sun began shooting out great flames, like whiskers or snakes of crimson fire, towards her. It is as if he were an octopus trying to draw her to himself in his tentacles. And perhaps he did draw her. At any rate she came to him, slowly at first, but then more and more quickly, till at last his long flames licked round her and the two ran together and became one huge ball like a burning coal. Great lumps of fire came dropping out of it into the sea and clouds of steam rose up.

Then Aslan said, "Now make an end."

The giant threw his horn into the sea. Then he stretched out one arm – very black it looked, and thousands of miles long – across the sky till his hand reached the sun. He took the sun and squeezed it in his hand as you would squeeze an orange. And instantly there was total darkness.

Everyone except Aslan jumped back from the ice-cold air which now blew through the Doorway. Its edges were already covered with icicles.

"Peter, High King of Narnia," said Aslan. "Shut the Door."

Peter, shivering with cold, leant out into the darkness and pulled the Door to. It scraped over ice as he pulled it. Then, rather clumsily (for even in that moment his hands had gone numb and blue) he took out a golden key and locked it.

They had seen strange things enough through that Doorway. But it was stranger than any of them to look round and find themselves in warm daylight, the blue sky above them, flowers at their feet, and laughter in Aslan's eyes.

He turned swiftly round, crouched lower, lashed himself with his tail and shot away like a golden arrow.

"Come further in! Come further up!" he shouted over his shoulder. But who could keep up with him at that pace? They set out walking westward to follow him.

"So," said Peter, "night falls on Narnia. What, Lucy! You're not *crying*? With Aslan ahead, and all of us here?"

"Don't try to stop me, Peter," said Lucy, "I am sure Aslan would not. I am sure it is not wrong to mourn for Narnia. Think of all that lies dead and frozen behind that door."

"Yes and I *did* hope," said Jill, "that it might go on for ever. I knew *our* world couldn't. I did think Narnia might."

"I saw it begin," said the Lord Digory. "I did not think I would live to see it die."

"Sirs," said Tirian. "The ladies do well to weep. See, I do so myself. I have seen my mother's death. What world but Narnia have I ever known? It were no virtue, but great discourtesy, if we did not mourn."

They walked away from the Door and away from the Dwarfs who still sat crowded together in their imaginary Stable. And as they went they talked to one another about old wars and old peace and ancient Kings and all the glories of Narnia.

The Dogs were still with them. They joined in the conversation but not much because they were too busy racing on ahead and racing back and rushing off to sniff at smells in the grass till they made themselves sneeze. Suddenly they picked up a scent which seemed to excite them very much. They all started arguing about it – "Yes, it is – No, it isn't – That's just what I said – Anyone can smell what *that* is – Take your great nose out of the way and let someone else smell."

"What is it, cousins?" said Peter.

"A Calormene, Sire," said several Dogs at once.

"Lead on to him, then," said Peter. "Whether he meets us in peace or war, he shall be welcome."

The Dogs darted on ahead and came back a moment later, running as if their lives depended on it, and barking loudly to say that it really was a Calormene. (Talking Dogs, just like the common ones, behave as if they thought whatever they are doing at the moment immensely important.)

The others followed where the Dogs led them and found a young Calormene sitting under a chestnut tree beside a clear stream of water. It was Emeth. He rose at once and bowed gravely.

"Sir," he said to Peter, "I know not whether you are my friend or my foe, but I should count it my honour to have you for either. Has not one of the poets said that a noble friend is the best gift and a noble enemy the next best?"

"Sir," said Peter, "I do not know that there need be any war between you and us."

"Do tell us who you are and what's happened to you," said Jill.

"If there's going to be a story, let's all have a drink and sit down," barked the Dogs. "We're quite blown."

"Well, of course you will be if you keep tearing about the way you have done," said Eustace.

So the humans sat down on the grass. And when the Dogs had all had a very noisy drink out of the stream they all sat down, bolt upright, panting, with their tongues hanging out of their heads a little on one side to hear the story. But Jewel remained standing, polishing his horn against his side.

CHAPTER FIFTEEN

FURTHER UP AND FURTHER IN

"Know, O Warlike Kings," said Emeth, "and you, O Ladies whose beauty illuminates the universe, that I am Emeth the seventh son of Harpha Tarkaan of the city of Tehishbaan, Westward beyond the desert. I came lately into Narnia with nine and twenty others under the command of Rishda Tarkaan. Now when I first heard that we should march upon Narnia I rejoiced, for I had heard many things of your Land and desired greatly to meet you in battle. But when I found that we were to go in disguised as merchants (which is a shameful dress for a warrior and the son of a Tarkaan) and to work by lies and trickery, then my joy departed from me. And most of all when I found we must wait upon a monkey, and when it began to be said that Tash and Aslan were one, then the world became dark in my eyes. For always since I was a boy I have served Tash and my great desire was to know more of him and, if it might be, to look upon his face. But the name of Aslan was hateful to me.

"And, as you have seen, we were called together outside the straw-roofed hovel, night after night, and the fire was kindled, and the Ape brought forth out of the hovel something upon four legs that I could not well see. And the people and the Beasts bowed down and did honour to it. But I thought, the Tarkaan is deceived by the Ape: for this thing that comes out of the stable is neither Tash nor any other god. But when I watched the Tarkaan's face, and marked every word that he said to the Monkey, then I changed my mind: for I saw that the Tarkaan did not believe in it himself. And then I understood that he did not believe in Tash at all: for if he had, how could he dare to mock him?

"When I understood this, a great rage fell upon me and I wondered that the true Tash did not strike down both the Monkey and the Tarkaan with fire from heaven. Nevertheless I hid my anger and held my tongue and waited to see how it would end. But last night, as some of you know, the Monkey brought not forth the yellow thing but said that all who desired to look upon Tashlan – for so they mixed the two words to pretend that they were all one – must pass one by one into the hovel. And I said to myself, Doubtless this is some other deception. But when the Cat had gone in and had come out again in a madness of terror, then I said to myself, Surely the true Tash, whom they called on without knowledge or belief, has now come among us, and will avenge himself. And though my heart was turned into water inside me because of the greatness and terror of Tash, yet my desire was stronger than my fear, and I put force upon my knees to stay them from trembling, and on my teeth that they should not chatter, and resolved to look upon the face of Tash though he should slay me. So I offered myself to go into the hovel; and the Tarkaan, though unwillingly, let me go.

"As soon as I had gone in at the door, the first wonder was that I found myself in this great sunlight (as we all are now) though the inside of the hovel had looked dark from outside. But I had not time to marvel at this, for immediately I was forced to fight for my head against one of our own men. As soon as I saw him I understood that the Monkey and the Tarkaan had set him there to slay any who came in if he were not in their secrets: so that this man also was a liar and a mocker and no true servant of Tash. I had the better will to fight him; and having slain the villain, I cast him out behind me through the door.

"Then I looked about me and saw the sky and the wide lands, and smelled the sweetness. And I said, By the Gods, this is a pleasant place: it may be that I am come into the country of Tash. And I began to journey into the strange country and to seek him.

"So I went over much grass and many flowers and among all kinds of wholesome and delectable trees till lo! in a narrow place between two rocks there came to meet me a great Lion. The speed of him was like the ostrich, and his size was an elephant's; his hair was like pure gold and the brightness of his eyes like gold that is liquid in the furnace. He was more terrible than the Flaming Mountain of Lagour, and in beauty he surpassed all that is in the world even as the rose in bloom surpasses the dust of the desert.

"Then I fell at his feet and thought, Surely this is the hour of death, for the Lion (who is worthy of all honour) will know that I have served Tash all my days and not him. Nevertheless, it is better to see the Lion and die than to be Tisroc of the world and live and not to have seen him. But the Glorious One bent down his golden head and touched my forehead with his tongue and said, 'Son, thou art welcome.' But I said, 'Alas, Lord, I am no son of thine but the servant of Tash.' He answered, 'Child, all the service thou hast done to Tash, I account as service done to me.' Then by reason of my great desire for wisdom and understanding, I overcame my fear and questioned the Glorious One and said, 'Lord, is it then true, as the Ape said, that thou and Tash are one?' The Lion growled so that the earth shook (but his wrath was not against me) and said, 'It is false. Not because he and I are one, but because we are opposites – I take to me the services which thou hast done to him. For I and he are of such different kinds that no service which is vile can be done to me, and none which is not vile can be done to him. Therefore, if any man swear by Tash and keep his oath for the oath's sake, it is by me that he has truly sworn, though he know it not, and it is I who reward him. And if any man do a cruelty in my name, then, though he says the name Aslan, it is Tash whom he serves and by Tash his deed is accepted. Dost thou understand, Child?' I said, 'Lord, thou knowest how much I understand.' But I said also (for the truth constrained me), 'Yet I have been seeking Tash all my days.' 'Beloved,' said the Glorious One, 'unless thy desire had been for me thou wouldst not have sought so long and so truly. For all find what they truly seek.'

"Then he breathed upon me and took away the trembling from my limbs and caused me to stand upon my feet. And after that, he said not much, but that we should meet again, and I must go further up and further in. Then he turned him about in a storm and flurry of gold and was gone suddenly.

"And since then, O Kings and Ladies, I have been wandering to find him and my happiness is so great that it even weakens me like a wound. And this is the marvel of marvels, that he called me Beloved, me who am but as a dog—"

"Eh? What's that?" said one of the Dogs.

"Sir," said Emeth. "It is but a fashion of speech which we have in Calormen."

"Well, I can't say it's one I like very much," said the Dog.

"He doesn't mean any harm," said an older Dog. "After all, *we* call our puppies *Boys* when they don't behave properly."

"So we do," said the first Dog. "Or *girls*."

"S-s-sh!" said the Old Dog. "That's not a nice word to use. Remember where you are."

"Look!" said Jill suddenly. Someone was coming, rather timidly, to meet them: a graceful creature on four feet, all silvery-grey. And they stared at him for a whole ten seconds before five or six voices said all at once, "Why, it's old Puzzle!" They had never seen him by daylight with the lion-skin off, and it made an extraordinary difference. He was himself now: a beautiful donkey with such a soft, grey coat and such a gentle, honest face that if you had seen him you would have done just what Jill and Lucy did – rushed forward and put your arms round his neck and kissed his nose and stroked his ears.

When they asked him where he had been he said he had come in at the door along with all the other creatures but he had – well, to tell the truth, he had been keeping out of their way as much as he could; and out of Aslan's way. For the sight of the real Lion had made him so ashamed of all that nonsense about dressing up in a lion-skin that he did not know

how to look anyone in the face. But when he saw that all his friends were going away westward, and after he had had a mouthful or so of grass ("And I've never tasted such good grass in my life," said Puzzle), he plucked up his courage and followed. "But what I'll do if I really have to meet Aslan, I'm sure I don't know," he added.

"You'll find it will be all right when you really do," said Queen Lucy.

Then they went forward together, always westward, for that seemed to be the direction Aslan had meant when he cried out, "Further up and further in." Many other creatures were slowly moving the same way, but that grassy country was very wide and there was no crowding.

It still seemed to be early, and the morning freshness was in the air. They kept on stopping to look round and to look behind them, partly because it was so beautiful but partly also because there was something about it which they could not understand.

"Peter," said Lucy, "where is this, do you suppose?"

"I don't know," said the High King. "It reminds me of somewhere but I can't give it a name. Could it be somewhere we once stayed for a holiday when we were very, very small?"

"It would have to have been a jolly good holiday," said Eustace. "I bet there isn't a country like this anywhere in our world. Look at the colours! You couldn't get a blue like the blue on those mountains in our world."

"Is it not Aslan's country?" said Tirian.

"Not like Aslan's country on top of that mountain beyond the eastern end of the world," said Jill. "I've been there."

"If you ask me," said Edmund, "it's like somewhere in the Narnian world. Look at those mountains ahead – and the big ice-mountains beyond them. Surely they're rather like the mountains we used to see from Narnia, the ones up Westward beyond the Waterfall?"

"Yes, so they are," said Peter. "Only these are bigger."

"I don't think *those* ones are so very like anything in Narnia," said Lucy. "But look there." She pointed southward to their left, and everyone stopped and turned to look. "Those hills," said Lucy, "the nice woody ones and the blue ones behind — aren't they very like the southern border of Narnia?"

"Like!" cried Edmund after a moment's silence. "Why, they're exactly like. Look, there's Mount Pire with his forked head, and there's the pass into Archenland and everything!"

"And yet they're not like," said Lucy. "They're different. They have more colours on them and they look further away than I remembered and they're more... more... oh, I don't know..."

"More like the real thing," said the Lord Digory softly.

Suddenly Farsight the Eagle spread his wings, soared thirty or forty feet up into the air, circled round and then alighted on the ground.

"Kings and Queens," he cried, "we have all been blind. We are only beginning to see where we are. From up there I have seen it all — Ettinsmuir, Beaversdam, the Great River, and Cair Paravel still shining on the edge of the Eastern Sea. Narnia is not dead. This is Narnia."

"But how can it be?" said Peter. "For Aslan told us older ones that we should never return to Narnia, and here we are."

"Yes," said Eustace. "And we saw it all destroyed and the sun put out."

"And it's all so different," said Lucy.

"The Eagle is right," said the Lord Digory. "Listen, Peter. When Aslan said you could never go back to Narnia, he meant the Narnia you were thinking of. But that was not the real Narnia. That had a beginning and an end. It was only a shadow or a copy of the real Narnia which has always been here and always will be here: just as our own world, England and all, is only a shadow or copy of something in Aslan's real world. You need not mourn over Narnia, Lucy. All of the old Narnia that mattered, all the dear creatures, have been drawn into the real Narnia through the Door. And of course it is different; as different as a real thing is from a shadow or as waking life is from a dream."

His voice stirred everyone like a trumpet as he spoke these words: but when he added under his breath, "It's all in Plato, all in Plato, bless me, what *do* they teach them at these schools?" the older ones laughed. It was so exactly like the sort of thing they had heard him say long ago in that other world where his beard was grey instead of golden. He knew why they were laughing and joined in the laugh himself. But very quickly they all became grave again: for, as you know, there is a kind of happiness and wonder that makes you serious. It is too good to waste on jokes.

It is as hard to explain how this sunlit land was different from the old Narnia as it would be to tell you how the fruits of that country taste. Perhaps you will get some idea of it if you think like this. You may have been in a room in which there was a window that looked out on a lovely bay of the sea or a green valley that wound away among mountains. And in the wall of that room opposite to the window there may have been a looking-glass. And as you turned away from the window you suddenly caught sight of that sea or that valley, all over again, in the looking glass. And the sea in the mirror, or the valley in the mirror, were in one sense just the same as the real ones: yet at the same time they were somehow different – deeper, more wonderful, more like places in a story: in a story you have never heard but very much want to know.

The difference between the old Narnia and the new Narnia was like that. The new one was a deeper country: every rock and flower and blade of grass looked as if it meant more. I can't describe it any better than that: if ever you get there you will know what I mean.

It was the Unicorn who summed up what everyone was feeling. He stamped his right fore-hoof on the ground and neighed, and then cried:

"I have come home at last! This is my real country! I belong here. This is the land I have been looking for all my life, though I never knew it till now. The reason why we loved the old Narnia is that it sometimes looked a little like this. Bree-hee-hee! Come further up, come further in!"

He shook his mane and sprang forward into a great gallop – a Unicorn's gallop which, in our world, would have carried him out of sight in a few moments. But now a most strange thing happened. Everyone else began to run, and they found, to their astonishment, that they could keep up with him: not only the dogs and the humans but even fat little Puzzle and short-legged Poggin the Dwarf. The air flew in their faces as if they were driving fast in a car without a windscreen. The country flew past as if they were seeing it from the windows of an express train. Faster and faster they raced, but no one got hot or tired or out of breath.

CHAPTER SIXTEEN

FAREWELL TO SHADOWLANDS

If one could run without getting tired, I don't think one would often want to do anything else. But there might be special reasons for stopping, and it was a special reason which made Eustace presently shout:

"I say! Steady! Look what we're coming to!"

And well he might. For now they saw before them Caldron Pool and beyond the Pool the high unclimbable cliffs and, pouring down the cliffs, thousands of tons of water every second, flashing like diamonds in some places and dark, glassy green in others, the Great Waterfall; and already the thunder of it was in their ears.

"Don't stop! Further up and further in," called Farsight, tilting his flight a little upwards.

"It's all very well for *him*," said Eustace, but Jewel also cried out:

"Don't stop. Further up and further in! Take it in your stride."

His voice could only just be heard above the roar of the water but next moment everyone saw that he had plunged into the Pool and helter-skelter behind him, with splash after splash, all the others did the same. The water was not bitingly cold as all of them (and especially Puzzle) expected, but of a delicious foamy coolness. They all found they were swimming straight for the Waterfall itself.

"This is absolutely crazy," said Eustace to Edmund.

"I know. And yet——" said Edmund.

"Isn't it wonderful?" said Lucy. "Have you noticed one can't feel afraid, even if one wants to? Try it."

"By Jove, neither one can," said Eustace after he had tried.

Jewel reached the foot of the waterfall first, but Tirian was only just behind him. Jill was last, so she could see the whole thing better than the others. She saw something white moving steadily up the face of the waterfall. That white thing was the Unicorn. You couldn't tell whether he was swimming or climbing, but he moved on, higher and higher. The point of his horn divided the water just above his head, and it cascaded out in two rainbow-coloured streams all round his shoulders. Just behind him came King Tirian. He moved his legs and arms as if he were swimming but he moved straight upwards: as if one could swim up the wall of a house.

What looked funniest was the Dogs. During the gallop they had not been at all out of breath, but now, as they swarmed and wriggled upwards, there was plenty of spluttering and sneezing among them: that was because they would keep on barking, and every time they barked they got their mouths and noses full of water. But before Jill had time to notice all these things fully, she was going up the waterfall herself. It was the sort of thing that would have been quite impossible in our world. Even if you hadn't been drowned, you would have been smashed to pieces by the terrible weight of water against the countless jags of rock. But in that world you could do it. You went on, up and up, with all kinds of reflected lights flashing at you from the water and all manner of coloured stones flashing through it, till it seemed as if you were climbing up light itself – and always higher and higher till the sense of height would have terrified you if you could be terrified, but here it was only gloriously exciting. And then at last one came to the lovely, smooth green curve in which the water poured over the top and found that one was out on the level river above the waterfall. The current was racing away behind you, but you were such a wonderful swimmer that you could make headway against it. Soon they were all on the bank, dripping but happy.

A long valley opened ahead and great snow-mountains, now much nearer, stood up against the sky.

"Further up and further in," cried Jewel and instantly they were off again.

They were out of Narnia now and up into the Western Wild which neither Tirian nor Peter nor even the Eagle had ever seen before. But the Lord Digory and the Lady Polly had. "Do you remember? Do you remember?" they said – and said it in steady voices too, without panting, though the whole party was now running faster than an arrow flies.

"What, Lord?" said Tirian. "Is it then true, as stories tell, that you two journeyed here on the very day the world was made?"

"Yes," said Digory, "and it seems to me as if it were only yesterday."

"And on a flying horse?" asked Tirian. "Is that part true?"

"Certainly," said Digory.

But the Dogs barked, "Faster, faster!"

So they ran faster and faster till it was more like flying than running, and even the Eagle overhead was going no faster than they. And they went through winding valley after winding valley and up the steep sides of hills and, faster than ever, down the other sides, following the river and sometimes crossing it and skimming across mountain lakes as if they were living speed-boats, till at last at the far end of one long lake which looked as blue as a turquoise, they saw a smooth green hill. Its sides were as steep as the sides of a pyramid and round the very top of it ran a green wall: but above the wall rose the branches of trees whose leaves looked like silver and their fruit like gold.

"Further up and further in!" roared the Unicorn, and no one held back. They charged straight at the foot of the hill and then found themselves running up it almost as water from a broken wave runs up a rock out at the point of some bay. Though the slope was nearly as steep as the roof of a house and the grass was smooth as a bowling green, no one slipped.

Only when they had reached the very top did they slow up; that was because they found themselves facing great golden gates. And for a moment none of them was bold enough to try if the gates would open. They all felt just as they had felt about the fruit – "Dare we? Is it right? Can it be meant for *us*?"

But while they were standing thus a great horn, wonderfully loud and sweet, blew from somewhere inside that walled garden and the gates swung open.

Tirian stood holding his breath and wondering who would come out. And what came out was the last thing he had expected: a little, sleek, bright-eyed Talking Mouse with a red feather stuck in a circlet on its head and its left paw resting on a long sword. It bowed, a most beautiful bow, and said in its shrill voice:

"Welcome, in the Lion's name. Come further up and further in."

Then Tirian saw King Peter and King Edmund and Queen Lucy rush forward to kneel down and greet the Mouse and they all cried out, "Reepicheep!" And Tirian breathed fast with the sheer wonder of it, for now he knew that he was looking at one of the great heroes of Narnia, Reepicheep the Mouse who had fought at the great Battle of Beruna and afterwards sailed to the World's End with King Caspian the Seafarer. But before he had had much time to think of this he felt two strong arms thrown about him and felt a bearded kiss on his cheeks and heard a well-remembered voice saying:

"What, lad? Art thicker and taller since I last touched thee!"

It was his own father, the good King Erlian: but not as Tirian had seen him last when they brought him home pale and wounded from his fight with the giant, nor even as Tirian remembered him in his later years when he was a grey-headed warrior. This was his father, young and merry, as he could just remember him from very early days when he himself had been a little boy playing games with his father in the castle garden at Cair Paravel, just before bedtime on summer evenings. The very smell of the bread and milk he used to have for supper came back to him.

Jewel thought to himself, "I will leave them to talk for a little and then I will go and greet the good King Erlian. Many a bright apple has he given me when I was but a colt." But next moment he had something else to think of, for out of the gateway there came a horse so mighty and noble that even a Unicorn might feel shy in its presence: a great winged horse. It looked a moment at the Lord Digory and the Lady Polly and neighed out, "What, cousins!" and they both shouted "Fledge! Good old Fledge!" and rushed to kiss it.

But by now the Mouse was again urging them to come in. So all of them passed in through the golden gates, into the delicious smell that blew towards them out of that garden and into the cool mixture of sunlight and shadow under the trees, walking on springy turf that was all dotted with white flowers. The very first thing which struck everyone was that the place was far larger than it had seemed from outside. But no one had time to think about that for people were coming up to meet the newcomers from every direction.

Everyone you had ever heard of (if you knew the history of these countries) seemed to be there. There was Glimfeather the Owl and Puddleglum the Marsh-wiggle, and King Rilian the Disenchanted, and his mother, the Star's daughter and his great father Caspian himself. And close beside him were the Lord Drinian and the Lord Berne and Trumpkin the Dwarf and Trufflehunter the good Badger with Glenstorm the Centaur and a hundred other heroes of the great War of Deliverance. And then from another side came Cor the King of Archenland with King Lune his father and his wife Queen Aravis and the brave prince Corin Thunder-Fist, his brother, and Bree the Horse and Hwin the Mare. And then — which was a wonder beyond all wonders to Tirian — there came from further away in the past, the two good Beavers and Tumnus the Faun. And there was greeting and kissing and handshaking and old jokes revived, (you've no idea how good an old joke sounds when you take it out again after a rest of five or six hundred years) and the whole company moved forward to the centre of the orchard where the Phoenix sat in a tree and looked down upon them all, and at the foot of that tree were two thrones and in those two thrones a King and Queen so great and beautiful that everyone bowed down before them. And well they might, for these two were King Frank and Queen Helen from whom all the most ancient Kings of Narnia and Archenland are descended. And Tirian felt as you would feel if you were brought before Adam and Eve in all their glory.

About half an hour later – or it might have been half a hundred years later, for time there is not like time here – Lucy stood with her dear friend, her oldest Narnian friend, the Faun Tumnus, looking down over the wall of that garden, and seeing all Narnia spread out below. But when you looked down you found that this hill was much higher than you had thought: it sank down with shining cliffs, thousands of feet below them and trees in that lower world looked no bigger than grains of green salt. Then she turned inward again and stood with her back to the wall and looked at the garden.

"I see," she said at last, thoughtfully. "I see now. This garden is like the Stable. It is far bigger inside than it was outside."

"Of course, Daughter of Eve," said the Faun. "The further up and the further in you go, the bigger everything gets. The inside is larger than the outside."

Lucy looked hard at the garden and saw that it was not really a garden at all, but a whole world, with its own rivers and woods and sea and mountains. But they were not strange: she knew them all.

"I see," she said. "This is still Narnia, and more real and more beautiful than the Narnia down below, just as *it* was more real and more beautiful than the Narnia outside the Stable door! I see... world within world, Narnia within Narnia..."

"Yes," said Mr Tumnus, "like an onion: except that as you go in and in, each circle is larger than the last."

And Lucy looked this way and that and soon found that a new and beautiful thing had happened to her. Whatever she looked at, however far away it might be, once she had fixed her eyes steadily on it, became quite clear and close as if she were looking through a telescope. She could see the whole Southern desert and beyond it the great city of Tashbaan: to Eastward she could see Cair Paravel on the edge of the sea and the very window of the room that had once been her own.

And far out to sea she could discover the islands, island after island to the End of the World, and, beyond the end, the huge mountain which they had called Aslan's country. But now she saw that it was part of a great chain of mountains which ringed round the whole world. In front of her it seemed to come quite close.

Then she looked to her left and saw what she took to be a great bank of brightly-coloured cloud, cut off from them by a gap. But she looked harder and saw that it was not a cloud at all but a real land. And when she had fixed her eyes on one particular spot of it, she at once cried out, "Peter! Edmund! Come and look! Come quickly." And they came and looked, for their eyes also had become like hers.

"Why!" exclaimed Peter. "It's England. And that's the house itself — Professor Kirke's old home in the country where all our adventures began!"

"I thought that house had been destroyed," said Edmund.

"So it was," said the Faun. "But you are now looking at the England within England, the real England just as this is the real Narnia. And in that inner England no good thing is destroyed."

Suddenly they shifted their eyes to another spot, and then Peter and Edmund and Lucy gasped with amazement and shouted out and began waving: for there they saw their own father and mother, waving back at them across the great, deep valley. It was like when you see people waving at you from the deck of a big ship when you are waiting on the quay to meet them.

"How can we get at them?" said Lucy.

"That is easy," said Mr Tumnus. "That country and this country — all the *real* countries — are only spurs jutting out from the great mountains of Aslan. We have only to walk along the ridge, upward and inward, till it joins on. And listen! There is King Frank's horn: we must all go up."

And soon they found themselves all walking together — and a great, bright procession it was — up towards mountains higher than you could see in this world even if they were there to be seen. But there was no snow on those mountains: there were forests and green slopes and sweet orchards and flashing waterfalls, one above the other, going up for ever. And the land they were walking on grew narrower all the time, with a deep valley on each side: and across that valley the land which was the real England grew nearer and nearer.

The light ahead was growing stronger. Lucy saw that a great series of many-coloured cliffs led up in front of them like a giant's staircase. And then she forgot everything else, because Aslan himself was coming, leaping down from cliff to cliff like a living cataract of power and beauty.

And the very first person whom Aslan called to him was Puzzle the Donkey. You never saw a donkey look feebler and sillier than Puzzle did as he walked up to Aslan, and he looked, beside Aslan, as small as a kitten looks beside a St Bernard. The Lion bowed down his head and whispered something to Puzzle at which his long ears went down, but then he said something else at which the ears perked up again. The humans couldn't hear what he had said either time.

Then Aslan turned to them and said: "You do not yet look so happy as I mean you to be."

Lucy said, "We're so afraid of being sent away, Aslan. And you have sent us back into our own world so often."

"No fear of that," said Aslan. "Have you not guessed?"

Their hearts leapt, and a wild hope rose within them.

"There *was* a real railway accident," said Aslan softly. "Your father and mother and all of you are — as you used to call it in the Shadowlands — dead. The term is over: the holidays have begun. The dream is ended: this is the morning."

And as He spoke, He no longer looked to them like a lion; but the things that began to happen after that were so great and beautiful that I cannot write them. And for us this is the end of all the stories, and we can most truly say that they all lived happily ever after. But for them it was only the beginning of the real story. All their life in this world and all their adventures in Narnia had only been the cover and the title page: now at last they were beginning Chapter One of the Great Story which no one on earth has read: which goes on for ever: in which every chapter is better than the one before.